Advanced Vibro-Acoustic Technology: Intelligent Algorithms, Smart Materials and Dynamics

Advanced Vibro-Acoustic Technology: Intelligent Algorithms, Smart Materials and Dynamics

Guest Editors

Kai Yang
Junlei Wang

MDPI

Basel • Beijing • Wuhan • Barcelona • Belgrade • Novi Sad • Cluj • Manchester

Guest Editors

Kai Yang
School of Aerospace Engineering
Huazhong University of Science and Technology
Wuhan
China

Junlei Wang
School of Mechanical and Power Engineering
Zhengzhou University
Zhengzhou
China

Editorial Office
MDPI AG
Grosspeteranlage 5
4052 Basel, Switzerland

This is a reprint of the Special Issue, published open access by the journal *Applied Sciences* (ISSN 2076-3417), freely accessible at: https://www.mdpi.com/journal/applsci/special_issues/VAEHC.

For citation purposes, cite each article independently as indicated on the article page online and as indicated below:

Lastname, A.A.; Lastname, B.B. Article Title. *Journal Name* **Year**, *Volume Number*, Page Range.

ISBN 978-3-7258-7094-3 (Hbk)
ISBN 978-3-7258-7095-0 (PDF)
https://doi.org/10.3390/books978-3-7258-7095-0

Contents

About the Editors

Kai Yang

Kai Yang, an Associate Professor at the School of Aerospace, Huazhong University of Science and Technology, and specializes in active vibration and noise control, nonlinear vibrations, and intelligent monitoring integrated with artificial intelligence. He earned his bachelor's degree in Aircraft Design and Engineering from Beihang University in 2008 and completed his Ph.D. in Aircraft Design in 2015. He worked at the University of Michigan and the China Shipbuilding Industry Corporation before joining Huazhong University in 2018. Professor Yang has led over 10 major research projects, including those funded by the National Natural Science Foundation, and published over 30 papers in top-tier SCI journals. He has garnered recognition as a highly cited researcher and earned multiple patents, including for bistable nonlinear energy harvesting devices. He is also involved in developing a multi-channel adaptive active vibration reduction system with applications in aerospace, maritime, and precision instrumentation.

Junlei Wang

Junlei Wang, born in August 1988 in Gushi, Henan, is currently a Vice Dean, Professor, and Doctoral Supervisor at the School of Mechanical and Power Engineering at Zhengzhou University. He obtained his Ph.D. in Energy and Power Engineering from Chongqing University in 2014, under the mentorship of Professor Jingyu Ran. Since 2015, he has been engaged in teaching and research at Zhengzhou University, with a focus on micro-energy harvesting and self-powered sensing theories and devices for air–ground–sea environments, as well as mechanisms and theoretical methods for flow-induced vibration suppression and high-efficiency energy harvesting. Professor Wang has also participated in academic exchanges at institutions such as the Beijing Institute of Technology, Hong Kong University of Science and Technology, and the University of Auckland. His research interests include flow-induced vibration suppression and efficient energy harvesting mechanisms, and he has led several key projects, including three National Natural Science Foundation projects. His work has earned numerous awards, including the Henan Province Natural Science Second Prize and the China Vibration Engineering Society Science and Technology First Prize. Professor Wang has published more than 60 papers as first or corresponding author in leading international and domestic journals. He has also been recognized as one of China's Highly Cited Scholars by Elsevier. In addition to his research, Professor Wang is actively involved in academic service, serving as a youth editorial board member for several journals, including *Journal of Mechanical Engineering* and *Journal of Dynamics and Control*. He also plays a key role in organizing conferences such as VEH 2024 and VEH 2026 and is a committee member of the China Vibration Engineering Society's Vibration Utilization Engineering Committee.

applied sciences

MDPI

rticle

/ibration Isolation and Launch Performance Enhancement of the ;pacecraft In-Orbit Launch Design Using the Nonlinear)ynamic Feature

u Zhou [1], Weihao Tong [2], Lu Dai [3,*] and Boyuan Wei [2,*]

1 Space Star Technology Co., Ltd., Beijing 100089, China
2 School of Aerospace Engineering, Huazhong University of Science and Technology, Wuhan 430074, China
3 Science and Technology on Thermal Energy and Power Laboratory, Wuhan 2nd Ship Design and Research Institute, Wuhan 430205, China
* Correspondence: sys2017@126.com (L.D.); m202372018@hust.edu.cn (B.W.)

Abstract: This paper proposes a new spacecraft in-orbit launch design using a nonlinear configuration to utilize nonlinear dynamics for the enhancement of vibration isolation and launch performance. The in-orbit launch device has four springs, where the stroke directions of two springs are perpendicular to the launch direction so as to produce nonlinearity with negative stiffness for enhancing the launch velocity. The other two springs are designed to counterbalance the above negative stiffness when the launch outlet is shut down, leading to quasi-zero dynamic stiffness for vibration isolation enhancement. The dynamic equations of the in-orbit launch device for both the on- and off-launch are presented. Then the performance enhancement of both the vibration isolation and launch performance is thoroughly investigated via comparative study and parametric study. The resonance peak is reduced by 4.16 dB, the effective vibration isolation bandwidth is increased by 57%, and the launch speed is increased 1.64 times. This validates the performance improvement of the new launch device design and presents a useful guideline for application.

Keywords: launch device; nonlinear dynamics; vibration isolation; quasi-zero dynamic stiffness

1. Introduction

With the rapid development of space technology, there is a growing demand for more efficient and reliable in-orbit launch systems [1,2]. In-orbit launch systems allow spacecraft to be launched directly in earth orbit or deep space, and they offer advantages over traditional ground-based launch methods, such as high cost effectiveness, low environmental impact, and short launch preparation time [3,4]. However, how to improve the launch speed while ensuring effective vibration isolation to protect sensitive payloads from damage remains a key challenge in the design of in-orbit launch systems.

Traditional vibration isolation systems are designed mostly based on linear dynamics design and face problems of low efficiency when dealing with large-amplitude vibrations and dynamic payload changes [5,6]. These systems often fail to provide ideal vibration isolation performance across a wide frequency range, especially in terms of low-frequency vibration. The limitations of this linear design approach have prompted researchers to explore the characteristics of nonlinear dynamics, especially the applications of nonlinear vibration isolation systems in the hope of achieving better vibration isolation performance.

Nonlinear vibration isolation technology in the form of quasi-zero stiffness (QZS) isolators has been proven to effectively reduce the system's natural frequency and isolate vibrations across a wider frequency range [7,8]. This particularly applies to the low frequency vibrations commonly encountered in in-orbit launch systems. For example, Ye et al. [9] proposed an optimized QZS vibration isolation system with a multi-cam-roller mechanism, which demonstrated superior low-frequency vibration isolation performance.

Zhao et al. [10] designed an advanced QZS isolator with three pairs of oblique springs, which offered enhanced design flexibility and superior performance over conventional one-pair and linear isolators. Wen et al. [11] presented a QZS system with an oblique linear spring structure, which showed enhanced low-frequency vibration isolation ability by expanding the zero stiffness range. Gatti et al. [12,13] designed an X-shaped-spring suspension nonlinear isolator, which could achieve QZS and a broader isolation frequency band through a quintic characteristic. Liu et al. [14] proposed a bi-directional horizontal QZS isolation system utilizing pre-compressed oblique spring mechanisms, showing superior low-frequency vibration isolation performance. Yu et al. [15] designed a five-spring QZS vibration isolator, in which four oblique springs provided negative stiffness and one vertical spring provided positive stiffness. The results show that the initial frequency of isolation could be reduced to 2.82 Hz. Yan et al. [16] proposed a new QZS vibration isolator composed of a link-oblique spring negative stiffness mechanism and a linear spring, which had a significantly better low-frequency isolation effect while maintaining high-frequency isolation ability compared with linear isolators. Chai et al. [17] designed a new "X" type QZS isolator using a spring arrangement method of tunable contact mechanism based on an X-shaped anti-vibration structure. This isolator was better than a linear isolator in the ultra-low frequency range with lower resonance frequency and wider isolation band. Han et al. [18] combined the Miura origami unit to propose a QZS vibration isolator composed of four rods and two springs. The structure could effectively reduce the formant and expand the effective vibration isolation band due to its nonlinear stiffness and nonlinear vertical damping. Zhou et al. [19] proposed a new type of passive asymmetric QZS isolator consisting of two linear springs in parallel with a negative stiffness element. Experimental results showed that the isolator had a smaller initial frequency and lower displacement transmissibility than the linear model. Yan et al. [20] proposed a lever-type QZS vibration isolator, using magnetic springs to achieve QZS characteristics. It was found that reasonable configuration of structural parameters could greatly improve vibration isolation performance.

The aforementioned studies indicate that the design of QZS isolators utilizes the nonlinear force-displacement relationship, which can significantly reduce the amplitude of vibrations transmitted to the payload, thereby protecting sensitive equipment from vibrational damage during the in-orbit and launch process. Furthermore, nonlinear characteristics can provide new ideas for in-orbit launch design.

Traditional linear launch system designs are often limited by their dynamic performance and cannot achieve significant launch speed improvement without sacrificing system stability and safety. In previous studies, nonlinear characteristics (especially the negative stiffness phenomenon) have been shown to significantly enhance the dynamic response of the system. The relationship of the enhancement mechanism of the negative stiffness mechanism, consisting of mechanical spring [21,22], buckled beam [23,24], magnetic structure [25,26] and bionic structure [27,28], to the dynamic response of nonlinear system has been widely studied. For example, Andrea et al. [29] replaced the traditional negative stiffness spring pair with super-elastic springs and found that the negative stiffness mechanism presented a dynamic amplification effect. Zhang et al. [30] constructed a negative stiffness mechanism based on magnetic springs, which was sensitive to micro-displacement and could amplify the response in the resonance region. Dai et al. [31] proposed a completely symmetrical cross-type structure with equal rod length to achieve negative stiffness characteristics. Results showed that the subharmonic response could be enhanced by adjusting the structural parameters of the cross-type structure. Therefore, compared with the traditional linear design, a nonlinear configuration can achieve higher system flexibility and adaptability under certain conditions, thereby improving the overall launch performance.

To address the evident limitations of traditional linear launch system designs in terms of vibration isolation and launch performance, this paper presents a novel aircraft in-orbit launch design utilizing nonlinear dynamic characteristics to enhance vibration isolation and launch performance. The design configures four springs, two of which are oriented perpendicularly to the launch direction to produce negative stiffness, thereby providing additional kinetic energy at critical moments to increase launch speed. The other two springs are designed to balance the aforementioned negative stiffness when the launch outlet is closed, achieving quasi-zero dynamic stiffness to enhance vibration isolation performance. By integrating quasi-zero stiffness isolation technology with nonlinear dynamics in the in-orbit launch system, this research not only overcomes the limitations of traditional linear design methods but also demonstrates how sophisticated nonlinear design can enhance launch speed and achieve efficient vibration isolation. These findings provide valuable insights for the further development of in-orbit launch technology and offer new ideas for future system design and optimization.

This paper is organized as follows. Section 2 presents the research model of the proposed aircraft in-orbit launch design. The governing equations for vibration isolation and in-orbit launch are derived in Section 3. Section 4 performs the performance comparison with linear design. Parametric study is conducted in Section 5. The influences on the vibration isolation and launch speed performance of the structure parameters are discussed in detail. All the findings are summarized in Section 6.

2. Design Concept

Figure 1a presents the spacecraft's in-orbit launch design for in-orbit vibration isolation. The base frame is fixedly connected within the in-orbit launch system. When the launch outlet is closed, the spacecraft m is supported by four springs. Two vertical springs, k_1 and k_3, provide negative stiffness, and, together with the other two transverse springs, k_2 and k_4, form quasi-zero stiffness characteristics. Therefore, these four springs constitute a quasi-zero stiffness (QZS) vibration isolation system to isolate the vibration $\ddot{y}$ generated by the base framework.

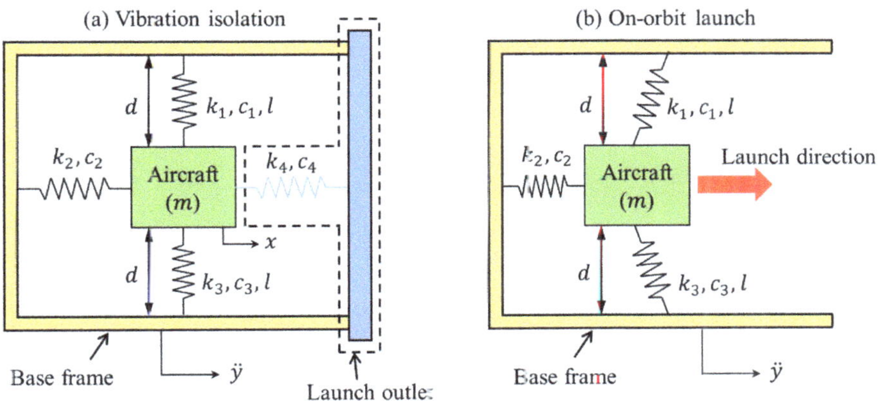

Figure 1. Schematic of the spacecraft in-orbit launch design: (**a**) vibration isolation and (**b**) in-orbit launch.

Figure 1b shows the spacecraft's in-orbit launch design for in-orbit launch. When the launch outlet is open, the spacecraft m is supported by the two pre-stretched vertical springs k_1 and k_3 and the pre-compressed transverse spring k_2. The vertical springs k_1 and k_3 produce negative stiffness to enhance launch speed. As shown in Figure 2, first, in the initial state (State 1), the spacecraft m is prepared for release and then disconnects from these three springs when it moves to the position of State 2. Finally, the spacecraft m leaves the base frame (the in-orbit launch system) with an initial velocity v_0.

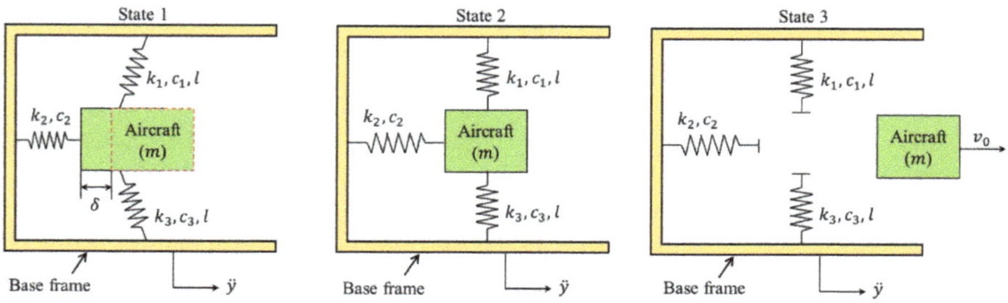

Figure 2. Schematic of the in-orbit launch process.

3. Mathematical Modeling

In this section, to understand the dynamic insight of the spacecraft in-orbit launch design, the governing equations for vibration isolation and in-orbit launch subjected to fundamental harmonic excitation are formulated.

3.1. Dynamic Equations When the Launch Is Off

As shown in Figure 1a, in the vibration isolation design, the distances between the top and bottom of the base frame and the spacecraft m are both d, and the original lengths of the vertical springs k_1 and k_3 are both l. When the spacecraft m is in its initial position, the two transverse springs k_2 and k_4 are at their original lengths, and the two vertical springs are perpendicular to the direction of the transverse springs. The damping coefficients of the four springs are c_1, c_2, c_3, c_4, respectively. x is the distance by which the spacecraft m deviates from its initial position. The kinetic energy K, potential energy V, and dissipation function D of the system are expressed as follows:

$$K = \frac{1}{2}m(\dot{x} + \dot{y})^2 \tag{1}$$

$$V = \frac{1}{2}k_1\left(\sqrt{d^2 + x^2} - l\right)^2 + \frac{1}{2}k_2x^2 + \frac{1}{2}k_3\left(\sqrt{d^2 + x^2} - l\right)^2 + \frac{1}{2}k_4x^2 \tag{2}$$

$$D = \frac{1}{2}c_1\left(\frac{x\dot{x}}{\sqrt{d^2 + x^2}}\right)^2 + \frac{1}{2}c_2\dot{x}^2 + \frac{1}{2}c_3\left(\frac{x\dot{x}}{\sqrt{d^2 + x^2}}\right)^2 + \frac{1}{2}c_4\dot{x}^2 \tag{3}$$

The governing equation for vibration isolation obtained from the Lagrange equation is:

$$m\ddot{x} + \left[(c_2 + c_4) + (c_1 + c_3)\frac{x^2}{x^2 + d^2}\right]\dot{x} + \left[(k_2 + k_4) + (k_1 + k_3)\left(1 - \frac{l}{\sqrt{d^2 + x^2}}\right)\right]x = -m\ddot{y}$$

Based on the above equation, it can be seen that the two vertical springs k_1 and k_3 have the same effect on the vibration isolation system, and the two transverse springs k_2 and k_4 also have the same effect on the vibration isolation system. For the convenience of subsequent analysis, let:

$$\begin{cases} k_1 = k_3 = k_v, \ c_1 = c_3 = c_v \\ k_2 = k_4 = k_h, \ c_2 = c_4 = c_h \end{cases} \tag{5}$$

Then, Equation (2) can be simplified as:

$$m\ddot{x} + \left(2c_h + 2c_v\frac{x^2}{x^2 + d^2}\right)\dot{x} + \left[2k_h + 2k_v\left(1 - \frac{l}{\sqrt{d^2 + x^2}}\right)\right]x = -m\ddot{y} \tag{6}$$

According to reference [32], the parameter condition for achieving quasi-zero stiffness is $k_v/k_h = d/(l-d)$. Define the stiffness ratio $\alpha = k_v/k_h$, and length ratio $\lambda = l/d$; then the condition for quasi-zero stiffness is:

$$\alpha = \frac{1}{\lambda - 1} \tag{7}$$

For a general quasi-zero stiffness vibration isolation system, $\lambda > 1$. Define the vibration transmissibility T thusly:

$$T = \frac{|\ddot{x} + \ddot{y}|}{|\ddot{y}|} \tag{8}$$

Vibration isolation performance is evaluated by the vibration transmissibility T: the smaller T is, the better the vibration isolation performance. In the subsequent study of vibration isolation performance, it is assumed that the base excitation is a simple harmonic excitation $\ddot{y} = Acos(2\pi ft)$, where A is the excitation amplitude and f is the excitation frequency.

3.2. Dynamic Equations When the Launch Is On

As shown in Figure 2, in the in-orbit launch design, the initial state (State 1) involves the transverse spring k_2 being pre-compressed by δ. Thus, the total elastic potential energy of the system at initial state is:

$$V_0 = \frac{1}{2}k_1\left(\sqrt{d^2+\delta^2} - l\right)^2 + \frac{1}{2}k_2\delta^2 + \frac{1}{2}k_3\left(\sqrt{d^2+\delta^2} - l\right)^2 \tag{9}$$

When Equation (5) is substituted with Equation (9), the following occurs:

$$V_0 = k_v\left(\sqrt{d^2+\delta^2} - l\right)^2 + \frac{1}{2}k_h\delta^2 \tag{10}$$

The spacecraft m is released when it moves to State 2. According to the law of energy conservation, the elastic potential energy is completely converted into kinetic energy at State 2:

$$T_0 = \frac{1}{2}mv_0^2 = V_0 \tag{11}$$

Therefore, the launch velocity v_0 is:

$$v_0 = \sqrt{\frac{2k_v\left(\sqrt{d^2+\delta^2} - l\right)^2 + k_h\delta^2}{m}} \tag{12}$$

It is noteworthy from the above equation that when the pre-compression length δ of the transverse spring k_2 is zero, since $\lambda = l/d > 1 (l > d)$, the two vertical springs have a pre-compression length. Hence the system still possesses unreleased elastic potential energy, which can also provide kinetic energy for launch. As δ increases, the pre-compression length of the vertical springs is actually reduced, and the reduced potential energy is not enough to balance the increased potential energy from the compression of the transverse spring, resulting in a decrease in the system's total potential energy and launch velocity. During this process, there exists a minimum point $\delta_e = \frac{\sqrt{(2k_vl-dk_h-2dk_v)(2k_vl+dk_h+2dk_v)}}{k_h+2k_v}$. When $\delta > \delta_e$, the launch velocity increases with δ. When the pre-compression length reaches the critical value δ_c (satisfying $2k_v\left(\sqrt{d^2+\delta^2} - l\right)^2 + k_h\delta^2 = 2k_v(d-l)^2$), the system's elastic potential energy is exactly equal to that when $\delta = 0$. Thereafter, the launch velocity increases approximately in direct proportion to δ. Moreover, it is obvious that the stiffness ratio $\alpha = k_v/k_h$ determines the value δ_e and δ_c.

4. Performance Comparison

To further investigate the vibration isolation and launch velocity performance of the proposed spacecraft in-orbit launch design, this section will compare the proposed design with traditional linear design to demonstrate the advantages of the proposed design in enhancing performance. The mathematical model is validated through MSC Adams 2020 software in Appendix A. In the subsequent simulation calculations, the numerical solutions are solved through the 4th Runge–Kutta method subjected to the frequency-sweeping base excitations from 0.1 Hz to 5 Hz with a rate of 0.001 Hz/s.

4.1. Vibration Isolation Performance Comparison

Figure 3 shows the vibration transmissibility T of linear design and the proposed design subjected to different fundamental excitations where amplitude $A = [0.05, 0.1, 0.3]$ m/s^2. Table 1 lists the structure parameters. The selection of parameters considers the realization condition of quasi-zero stiffness (Equation (7)). It can be seen that the peak frequency of the proposed design increases with the increase of the base excitation amplitude, and the peak value of the vibration transmissibility corresponding to the peak frequency also gradually increases. However, the high-frequency low-orbit curves under these three excitations completely overlap and are much lower than those resulting from the linear design, exceeding 30 dB. With the linear design, once the structural parameters are determined, the vibration transmissibility is uniquely determined and unaffected by the base excitation. The peak frequency of the linear design is 2.25 Hz, with a corresponding peak amplitude of 36.43 dB. When the base excitation amplitude $A = 0.05$ m/s^2, the peak frequency of the proposed design is 0.96 Hz, with a peak amplitude of 32.27 dB. Compared to the linear design, the peak is reduced by 4.16 dB, and the effective vibration isolation bandwidth is increased by 57%. However, when the base excitation amplitude $A = 0.3$ m/s^2, the peak amplitude of the proposed design is slightly larger than that of the linear design, and the peak frequency is only slightly reduced compared to the linear design. This indicates that the vibration isolation performance of the proposed design under small amplitude excitation is significantly better than that of traditional linear vibration isolator. Therefore, in view of the common micro-vibration disturbance of spacecraft, the proposed design can effectively isolate the wide-band vibration to ensure the safety of spacecraft on orbit.

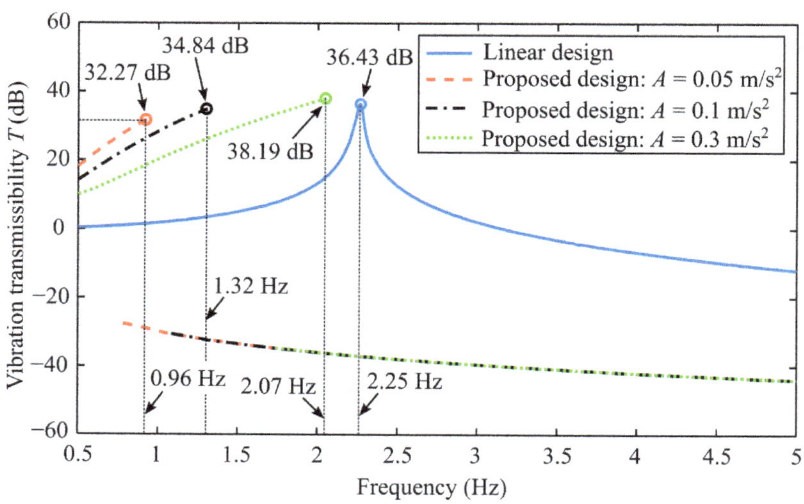

Figure 3. The vibration transmissibility T of the linear design and the proposed design with different excitation amplitudes $A = [0.05, 0.1, 0.3]$ m/s^2.

Table 1. The structure parameters for vibration isolation performance comparison.

Properties	Proposed Design	Linear Design
m	10 kg	10 kg
k_h	1000 N/m	2000 N/m (Equivalent stiffness)
c_h	1 Ns/m	2 Ns/m (Equivalent damping)
k_v	2000 N/m	None
c_v	0.1 Ns/m	
l	0.15 m	
d	0.1 m	

4.2. Launch Velocity Comparison

Considering the realization condition of quasi-zero stiffness (Equation (7)), two sets of different parameter values shown in Table 2 are selected for comparative analysis of the launch velocity v_0. Figure 4 shows the launch velocity v_0 curve versus pre-compression length δ under the two parameter sets. The comparison of parameter Set 1 shows that for linear design, the launch velocity is strictly proportional to the pre-compression length, with a slope of 10. Since the original length l of the two vertical springs is greater than the vertical distance d, there is pre-compression in the two vertical springs at the initial state. Thus, there is elastic potential energy at $\delta = 0$ for the proposed design, which can be converted into launch kinetic energy. At the beginning ($\delta < 0.098$ m), the compression amount of the two vertical springs decreases with the increase of the transverse spring pre-compression length δ, and the reduced elastic potential energy is greater than that increased by the transverse spring compressing. Therefore, the total elastic potential energy of the system is lower than that of the initial state, and the launch velocity is also lower than the initial launch velocity. In this process, when $\delta < 0.0663$ m, the launch velocity decreases with the increase of δ; when 0.0663 m $< \delta <$ 0.098 m, the launch velocity increases with the increase of δ. After $\delta >$ 0.098 m, the launch velocity approximately shows a linear increasing relationship with δ, with a slope of 21.55, which means that the launch velocity of the proposed design is increased 1.16-fold compared to the linear design. Since the stiffness ratio $\alpha = k_v/k_h$ of the two parameter sets is the same, the results of parameter Set 2 also show the same trend as the launch velocity curve of parameter Set 1. The slope of launch velocity relative to δ is approximately 26.38, which is 1.64 times higher than that of linear design.

Table 2. The structure parameters for launch velocity comparison.

Properties	Set 1		Set 2	
	Proposed Design	Linear Design	Proposed Design	Linear Design
m	10 kg	10 kg	10 kg	10 kg
k_h	1000 N/m	1000 N/m	1500 N/m	1500 N/m
c_h	1 Ns/m	1 Ns/m	1 Ns/m	1 Ns/m
k_v	2000 N/m	None	3000 N/m	None
c_v	0.1 Ns/m		0.1 Ns/m	
l	0.15 m		0.15 m	
d	0.1 m		0.1 m	

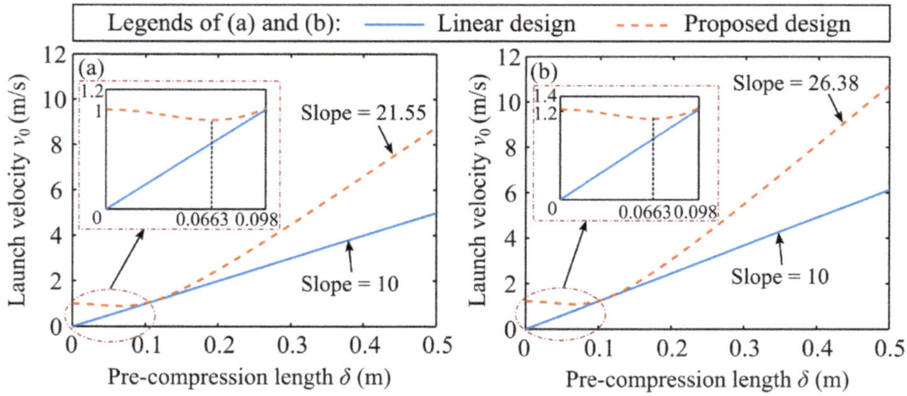

Figure 4. The launch velocity v_0 curve versus pre-compression length δ of the linear design and the proposed design with (**a**) parameter set 1 and (**b**) parameter set 2.

5. Parametric Study

In this section, parametric study will be conducted to further investigate the impact of structural parameters on vibration isolation and launch velocity performance.

5.1. Comprehensive Study of Vibration Isolation

In the analysis of vibration isolation performance, the influence of vertical spring stiffness k_v and damping c_v on vibration isolation performance is mainly studied. Initially the conditions for achieving quasi-zero stiffness are disregarded, and only the vertical spring stiffness k_v is changed, allowing for exploration of the variation of the vibration transmissibility in relation to k_v. Figure 5a shows the vibration transmissibility curve under different k_v, and the values of other parameters are the same as those shown in Table 1. The base excitation amplitude is $A = 0.05\ \mathrm{m/s^2}$. It can be seen that when k_v changes from 1000 N/m to 2000 N/m, the peak of the vibration transmissibility curve gradually shifts to the left and the low orbit gradually decreases, indicating an improvement in vibration isolation performance. However, when k_v continues to increase, the peak of the vibration transmissibility curve moves to the right and the low orbit increases, indicating a deterioration in vibration isolation performance.

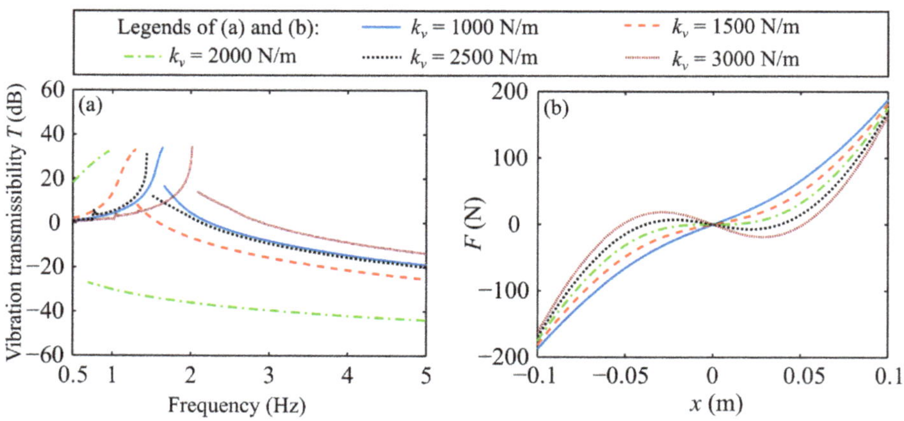

Figure 5. (**a**) The vibration transmissibility T and (**b**) the nonlinear restoring force with different k_v of the proposed design.

To understand the essence of this changing pattern, the relation curve between nonlinear restoring force F and displacement x is drawn in Figure 5b. It can be seen that when $k_v = 1000,\ 1500$ N/m, the negative stiffness provided by the two vertical springs is insufficient to offset the positive stiffness of the transverse springs, thus exhibiting positive stiffness characteristics near $x = 0$. The smaller k_v is, the greater the positive stiffness, making the system tend towards a linear vibration isolation system. When $k_v = 2000$ N/m, according to Equation (7), the condition for quasi-zero stiffness is exactly met, showing zero stiffness characteristics near $x = 0$. Figure 5a indicates that under this condition, the peak is the smallest, the low-frequency range is the lowest, and the vibration isolation performance is the best. When $k_v = 2500,\ 3000$ N/m, the negative stiffness is too large, and the system exhibits negative stiffness near $x = 0$. The vibration transmissibility curve displays abnormal distortion, and the vibration isolation performance becomes worse. From the above analysis, it is clear that the best vibration isolation performance is achieved when the structural parameters satisfy the condition for quasi-zero stiffness.

When considering quasi-zero stiffness characteristics, the stiffness ratio α and the length ratio λ have a definite relationship: $\alpha = 1/\lambda - 1$; thus, it can be said that the stiffness ratio and the length ratio have the same influence on the vibration isolation performance. Then, the influence of stiffness ratio α on vibration isolation performance is studied by changing the parameter k_v while keeping k_h and d unchanged. Based on the deterministic relation $\alpha = 1/\lambda - 1$, the length ratio λ changes with the stiffness ratio α, meaning that l changes with k_v. Figure 6 shows the vibration transmissibility curve under different stiffness ratio α. The values of other parameters are the same as those shown in Table 1. The base excitation amplitude is $A = 0.05\ \text{m/s}^2$. It can be seen that with the increase of stiffness ratio α, the peak frequency gradually increases, and the peak amplitude also gradually increases. However, the stiffness ratio α has no effect on the low-orbit region. This indicates that a smaller stiffness ratio provides better vibration isolation performance. However, as the transverse spring stiffness k_h and vertical distance d remain unchanged, a smaller stiffness ratio means a smaller vertical spring stiffness k_v and a larger vertical spring original length l, implying that the vertical springs are very soft, which does not meet the requirements of practical installation conditions. Therefore, it is necessary to consider the structural design requirements of vertical spring while reducing the stiffness ratio α to obtain better vibration isolation performance.

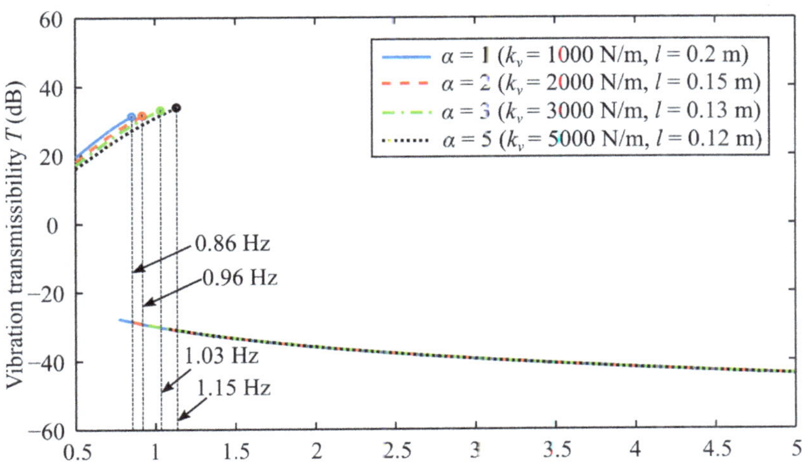

Figure 6. The vibration transmissibility T with different α (configurations of k_v and l) of the proposed design.

Finally, the effect of vertical spring damping c_v on vibration isolation performance is discussed. Figure 7 shows the vibration transmissibility curve under a different c_v, and the values of other parameters are the same as those shown in Table 1. The base excitation amplitude is $A = 0.05\ \mathrm{m/s^2}$. Results show that the damping coefficient c_v has little influence on vibration isolation performance. With the increase of damping c_v, the peak frequency only decreases slightly, and the peak amplitude also decreases slightly. Compared with the influence of stiffness k_v, the influence of damping c_v can be ignored.

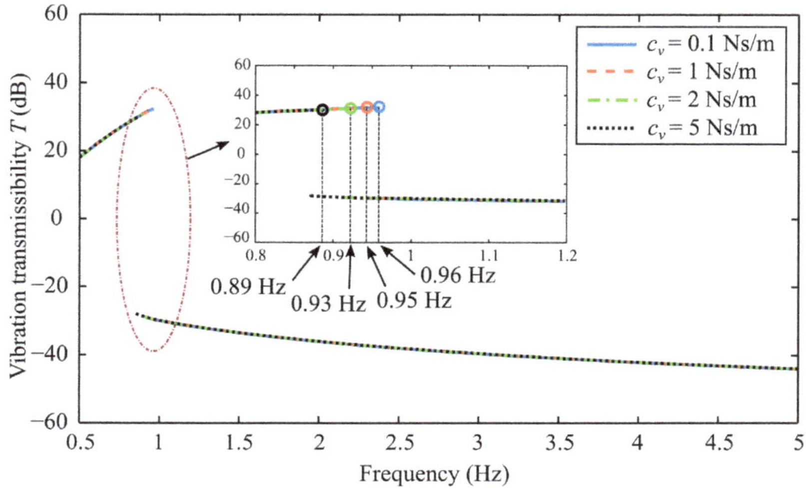

Figure 7. The vibration transmissibility T with different c_v of the proposed design.

5.2. Comprehensive Study of Launch Velocity

In the previous section on vibration isolation performance parameter study, it was found that the vibration isolation performance is best when the structural parameters satisfy the quasi-zero stiffness condition. Based on the quasi-zero stiffness characteristics, this section will delve into the impact of structural parameters on launch velocity in detail. According to Equation (12), the structural parameters affecting the launch velocity include vertical spring stiffness k_v, vertical spring original length l, transverse spring stiffness k_h, and vertical distance d. Under the consideration of quasi-zero stiffness characteristics, the stiffness ratio $\alpha = k_v/k_h$ and the length ratio $\lambda = l/d$ satisfy a definite relationship $\alpha = 1/(\lambda - 1)$. Thus, these four parameters are interdependently determined. Then, by keeping k_h and d unchanged, the effect of stiffness ratio α on the launch velocity is studied by changing the parameter k_v (with l changing correspondingly with k_v). Figure 8 shows the launch velocity v_0 curve versus pre-compression length δ with a different α. It is seen that when δ is less than 0.1 m, the launch velocity v_0 does not change much with the pre-compression length δ. In this range, the larger α is, the smaller the launch velocity v_0 is. When δ is greater than 0.15, the slope of the second half of the launch velocity curve gradually increases with the increase of α, which means that a small pre-compression δ can bring a higher launch velocity v_0.

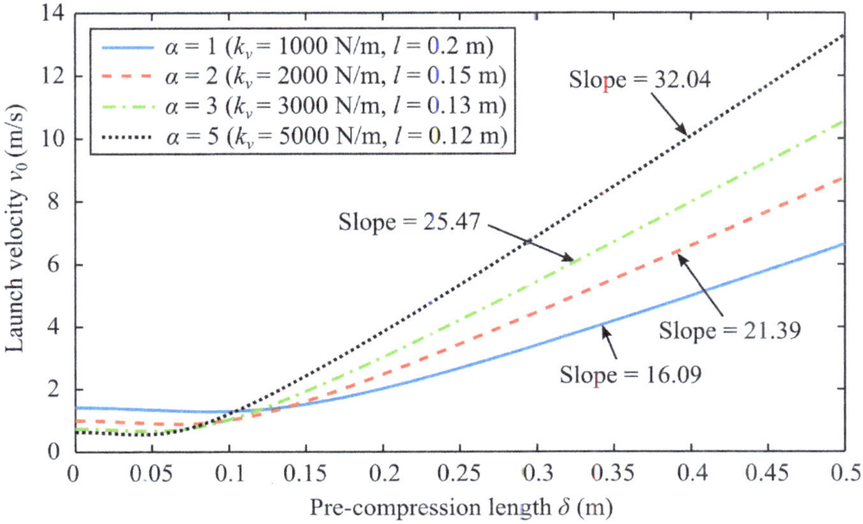

Figure 8. The launch velocity v_0 curve versus pre-compression length δ with different α (configurations of k_v and l) of the proposed design.

Therefore, it can be concluded that when the pre-compression δ of the transverse spring is small, a smaller stiffness ratio α can obtain a higher launch velocity v_0. When the pre-compression δ of transverse spring is large, the higher stiffness ratio α can produce the higher launch velocity v_0. Moreover, the critical value of stiffness ratio should be determined according to different structural parameters.

6. Conclusions

This paper proposed a new in-orbit launch design utilizing nonlinear dynamics to enhance vibration isolation and in-orbit launch performance. The design consists of four springs, of which two vertical springs have a travel direction perpendicular to the launch direction to produce negative stiffness and increase launch speed. Two additional transverse springs are used to balance the negative stiffness when the launch outlet is closed, thus achieving quasi-zero stiffness to enhance vibration isolation performance. Based on the governing equation of vibration isolation and in-orbit launch validated by Adams, this paper comprehensively analyzes the enhancement effect of vibration isolation and launch performance by comparing with traditional linear design. The resonance peak is reduced by 4.16 dB, the effective vibration isolation bandwidth is increased by 57%, and the launch speed is increased 1.64-fold. The subsequent parametric study shows that reducing the stiffness ratio can obtain better vibration isolation performance while considering the structural design requirements of the vertical spring and quasi-zero stiffness conditions. In addition, when the pre-compression of the transverse spring is small, a smaller stiffness ratio can produce a higher launching speed. When the transverse spring pre-compression is large, the higher launch speed requires a larger stiffness ratio. These results validate the effect of the proposed in-orbit launch design on vibration isolation and launch speed performance, and provide useful guidance for subsequent applications.

Author Contributions: Conceptualization, B.W.; Methodology, X.Z. and W.T.; Software, W.T.; Validation, L.D.; Formal analysis, X.Z.; Data curation, W.T. and L.D.; Writing—original draft, X.Z.; Writing—review & editing, W.T. and B.W.; Supervision, B.W.; Funding acquisition, X.Z. All authors have read and agreed to the published version of the manuscript.

Funding: This work was supported by the Open Fund of the State Key Laboratory of Robotics and the Innovation Fund of the Maritime Defense Technology Innovation Center (Grant No. JJ2021-719-01).

Institutional Review Board Statement: Not applicable.

Informed Consent Statement: Not applicable.

Data Availability Statement: The raw data supporting the conclusions of this article will be made available by the authors on request.

Conflicts of Interest: Author Xu Zhou was employed by the company Space Star Technology Co., Ltd. The remaining authors declare that the re-search was conducted in the absence of any commercial or financial relationships that could be construed as a potential conflict of interest.

Appendix A. Model Validation Using the MSC Adams Software

The software program MSC Adams 2020 is used to validate the mathematical model of the spacecraft in-orbit launch design. Since the governing equation of launch velocity is a definite expression that can be calculated directly with parameter values, it does not require validation. Only the governing equation of vibration isolation is validated in this appendix. Figure A1 shows the dynamic model of the proposed spacecraft in-orbit launch design established in MSC Adams. The structure parameters are selected from Table 1. Figure A2 shows the displacement x, velocity $\dot{x}$, and acceleration $\ddot{x}$ time-domain responses obtained by Adams and numerical results solved by the 4th Runge–Kutta method under forward swept harmonic base excitation from 0.1 Hz to 5 Hz with amplitude $A = 0.3\ \text{m/s}^2$. The sweeping rate is 0.05 Hz/s. It can be seen that the numerical results are in good agreement with the Adams results for displacement x, velocity $\dot{x}$, and acceleration $\ddot{x}$.

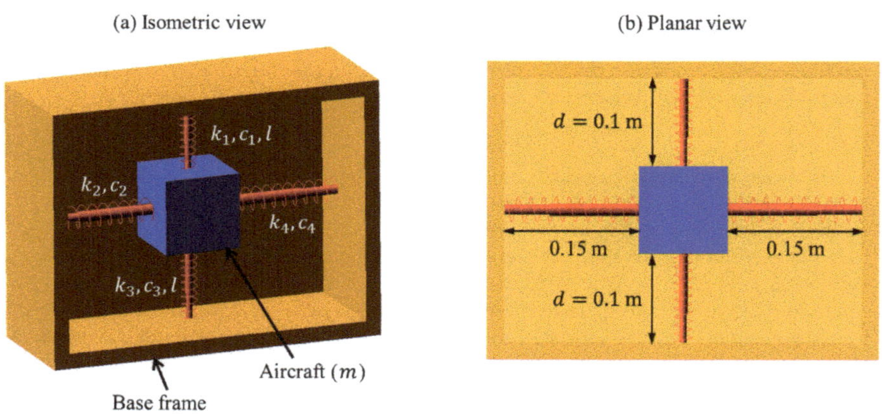

Figure A1. The (**a**) isometric view and (**b**) planar view of the proposed spacecraft in-orbit launch design for vibration isolation in Adams software.

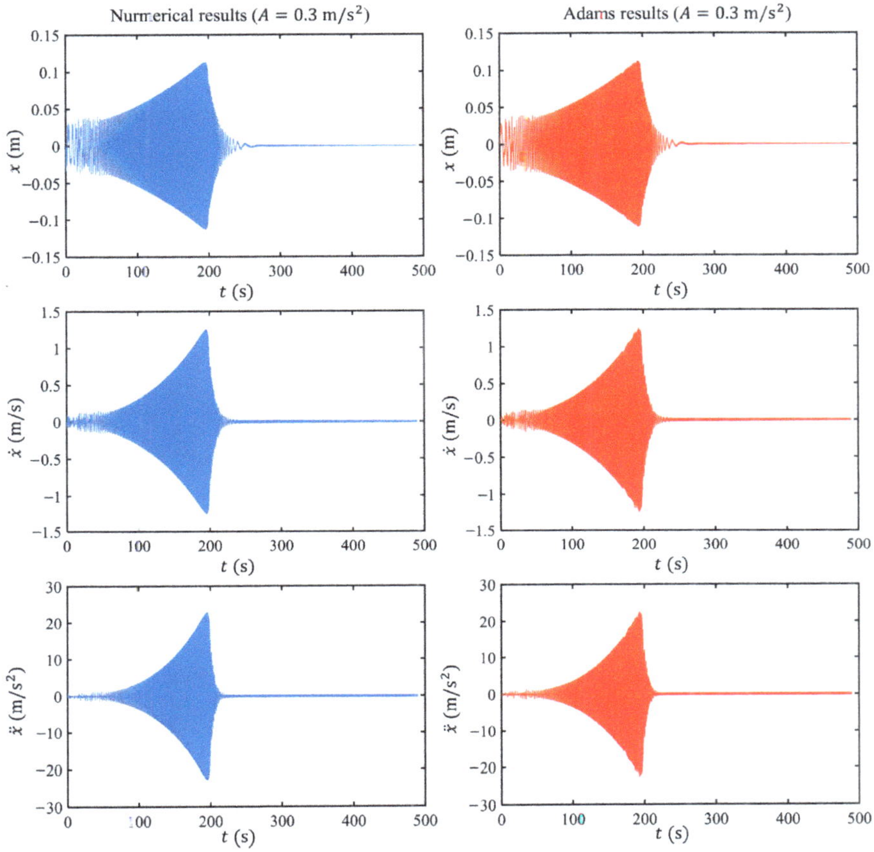

Figure A2. The displacement x, velocity $\dot{x}$, and acceleration $\ddot{x}$ time-domain responses obtained by Adams and numerical results solved by the 4th Runge–Kutta method under forward swept harmonic base excitation from 0.1 Hz to 5 Hz with the amplitude $A = 0.3\ \mathrm{m/s^2}$.

References

1. Li, W.-J.; Cheng, D.-Y.; Liu, X.-G.; Wang, Y.-B.; Shi, W.-H.; Tang, Z.-X.; Gao, F.; Zeng, F.-M.; Chai, H.-Y.; Luo, W.-B.; et al. On-orbit service (OOS) of spacecraft: A review of engineering developments. *Prog. Aerosp. Sci.* **2019**, *108*, 32–120. [CrossRef]
2. Chiarelli, M.R.; Borrometi, F.B.; Cipolla, V.; Binante, V.; Abu Salem, K.; Palaia, G. Design and Feasibility Study of Novel Flying Wing Carrier for Launching Small Satellites in Low Earth Orbit. *Appl. Sci.* **2023**, *13*, 4712. [CrossRef]
3. Liu, J.; Zhao, P.; Wu, C.; Chen, K.; Ren, W.; Liu, L.; Tang, Y.; Ji, C.; Sang, X. SIASAIL-I solar sail: From system design to on-orbit demonstration mission. *Acta Astronaut.* **2022**, *192*, 133–142. [CrossRef]
4. Zhao, X.; Zhao, C.; Li, J.; Guan, Y.; Chen, S.; Zhang, L. Research on Design, Simulation, and Experiment of Separation Mechanism for Micro-Nano Satellites. *Appl. Sci.* **2022**, *12*, 5997. [CrossRef]
5. Yan, B.; Yu, N.; Wu, C. A state-of-the-art review on low-frequency nonlinear vibration isolation with electromagnetic mechanisms. *Appl. Math. Mech.* **2022**, *43*, 1045–1062. [CrossRef]
6. Tong, W.; Wei, B.; Moshrefi-Torbati, M.; Zhou, X.; Yurchenko, D.; Yang, K. Investigation of a monostable nonlinear vibration isolator with the inertia-elastic boundary. *Commun. Nonlinear Sci. Numer. Simul.* **2024**, *132*, 107887. [CrossRef]
7. Li, H.; Li, Y.; Li, J. Negative stiffness devices for vibration isolation applications: A review. *Adv. Struct. Eng.* **2020**, *23*, 1739–1755. [CrossRef]
8. Wang, S.; Xin, W.; Ning, Y.; Li, B.; Hu, Y. Design, experiment, and improvement of a quasi-zero-stiffness vibration isolation system. *Appl. Sci.* **2020**, *10*, 2273. [CrossRef]
9. Ye, K.; Ji, J.; Brown, T. Design of a quasi-zero stiffness isolation system for supporting different loads. *J. Sound Vib.* **2020**, *471*, 115198. [CrossRef]

10. Zhao, F.; Ji, J.; Ye, K.; Luo, Q. An innovative quasi-zero stiffness isolator with three pairs of oblique springs. *Int. J. Mech. Sci.* **202** *192*, 106093. [CrossRef]
11. Wen, G.; He, J.; Liu, J.; Lin, Y. Design, analysis and semi-active control of a quasi-zero stiffness vibration isolation system with si oblique springs. *Nonlinear Dyn.* **2021**, *106*, 309–321. [CrossRef]
12. Gatti, G. A nonlinear quasi-zero stiffness vibration isolator with quintic restoring force characteristic: A fundamental analytic insight. *J. Vib. Control* **2023**, 1–14. [CrossRef]
13. Gatti, G.; Svelto, C. Exploiting nonlinearity for the design of linear oscillators: Application to an inherently strong nonlinea X-shaped-spring suspension. *Mech. Syst. Signal Process.* **2023**, *197*, 110362. [CrossRef]
14. Liu, T.; Li, A.; Zhang, H. Quasi-zero stiffness interval optimization design and dynamics analysis of a new bi-directional horizont isolation system. *Mech. Syst. Signal Process.* **2024**, *206*, 110852. [CrossRef]
15. Liu, C.; Yu, K. Design and experimental study of a quasi-zero-stiffness vibration isolator incorporating transverse groove spring *Arch. Civ. Mech. Eng.* **2020**, *20*, 67. [CrossRef]
16. Yan, G.; Zou, H.-X.; Wang, S.; Zhao, L.-C.; Gao, Q.-H.; Tan, T.; Zhang, W.-M. Large stroke quasi-zero stiffness vibration isolatc using three-link mechanism. *J. Sound Vib.* **2020**, *478*, 115344. [CrossRef]
17. Chai, Y.; Jing, X.; Chao, X. X-shaped mechanism based enhanced tunable QZS property for passive vibration isolation. *Int. Mech. Sci.* **2022**, *218*, 107077. [CrossRef]
18. Han, H.; Sorokin, V.; Tang, L.; Cao, D. A nonlinear vibration isolator with quasi-zero-stiffness inspired by Miura-origami tub *Nonlinear Dyn.* **2021**, *105*, 1313–1325. [CrossRef]
19. Zhou, X.; Zhao, D.; Sun, X.; Yang, X.; Zhang, J.; Ni, T.; Tang, K. An asymmetric quasi-zero stiffness vibration isolator with lon stroke and large bearing capacity. *Nonlinear Dyn.* **2022**, *108*, 1903–1930. [CrossRef]
20. Yan, B.; Yu, N.; Wang, Z.; Wu, C.; Wang, S.; Zhang, W. Lever-type quasi-zero stiffness vibration isolator with magnetic spring. *Sound Vib.* **2022**, *527*, 116865. [CrossRef]
21. Liu, Y.; Ji, W.; Gu, H.; Deng, E.; Wang, X.; Song, C. Force transmissibility of a 6-DOF passive quasi-zero stiffness vibration isolatio platform. *J. Mech. Sci. Technol.* **2021**, *35*, 2313–2324. [CrossRef]
22. Lan, C.-C.; Yang, S.-A.; Wu, Y.-S. Design and experiment of a compact quasi-zero-stiffness isolator capable of a wide range c loads. *J. Sound Vib.* **2014**, *333*, 4843–4858. [CrossRef]
23. Fulcher, B.A.; Shahan, D.W.; Haberman, M.R.; Seepersad, C.; Wilson, P.S. Analytical and Experimental Investigation of Buckle Beams as Negative Stiffness Elements for Passive Vibration and Shock Isolation Systems. *J. Vib. Acoust.* **2014**, *136*, 03100 [CrossRef]
24. Liu, X.; Zhao, Q.; Zhang, Z.; Zhou, X. An experiment investigation on the effect of Coulomb friction on the displacemen transmissibility of a quasi-zero stiffness isolator. *J. Mech. Sci. Technol.* **2019**, *33*, 121–127. [CrossRef]
25. Zheng, Y.; Zhang, X.; Luo, Y.; Zhang, Y.; Xie, S. Analytical study of a quasi-zero stiffness coupling using a torsion magnetic sprin with negative stiffness. *Mech. Syst. Signal Process.* **2018**, *100*, 135–151. [CrossRef]
26. Yan, B.; Ma, H.; Zhao, C.; Wu, C.; Wang, K.; Wang, P. A vari-stiffness nonlinear isolator with magnetic effects: Theoretica modeling and experimental verification. *Int. J. Mech. Sci.* **2018**, *148*, 745–755. [CrossRef]
27. Wang, Y.; Jing, X.; Dai, H.; Li, F.-M. Subharmonics and ultra-subharmonics of a bio-inspired nonlinear isolation system. *Int. Mech. Sci.* **2019**, *152*, 167–184. [CrossRef]
28. Wang, Y.; Jing, X.; Guo, Y. Nonlinear analysis of a bio-inspired vertically asymmetric isolation system under different structura constraints. *Nonlinear Dyn.* **2019**, *95*, 445–464. [CrossRef]
29. Salvatore, A.; Carboni, B.; Lacarbonara, W. Nonlinear dynamic response of an isolation system with superelastic hysteresis an negative stiffness. *Nonlinear Dyn.* **2022**, *107*, 1765–1790. [CrossRef]
30. Zhang, F.; Xu, M.; Shao, S.; Xie, S. A new high-static-low-dynamic stiffness vibration isolator based on magnetic negative stiffnes mechanism employing variable reluctance stress. *J. Sound Vib.* **2020**, *476*, 115322. [CrossRef]
31. Dai, H.; Cao, X.; Jing, X.; Wang, X.; Yue, X. Bio-inspired anti-impact manipulator for capturing non-cooperative spacecraft: Theor and experiment. *Mech. Syst. Signal Process.* **2020**, *142*, 106785. [CrossRef]
32. Carrella, A.; Brennan, M.J.; Waters, T.P. Static analysis of a passive vibration isolator with quasi-zero-stiffness characteristic. *Sound Vib.* **2007**, *301*, 678–689. [CrossRef]

applied sciences

MDPI

ticle

erformance and Optimization of a Dual-Stage Vibration solation System Using Bio-Inspired Vibration Isolators

ou Huang [1], Xianjie Shi [1,*], Dong Mu [1], Xin Huang [1] and Weihao Tong [2,*]

[1] Institute of Systems Engineering, China Academy of Engineering Physics, Mianyang 621900, China
[2] School of Aerospace Engineering, Huazhong University of Science and Technology, Wuhan 430074, China
* Correspondence: 411shixj@caep.cn (X.S.); wehotung@hust.edu.cn (W.T.)

Abstract: This paper thoroughly investigates the performance and multi-parameter optimization of a dual-stage vibration isolation system with bio-inspired isolators (BI-DSVI) under different base excitations. The dynamic equations of the BI-DSVI are derived. Then, the optimization problem is defined, where three types of base excitation (translation and rotations around the two horizontal axes) are studied. The optimization results show that the vibration transmissibility can be greatly reduced (more than 30 dB) by multi-parameter optimization and an optimal configuration of structural parameters exists for the bio-inspired isolators. The effective vibration isolation bandwidth is significantly widened. Finally, the paper thoroughly discusses the influence of the structural parameters of the bio-inspired isolators and the base excitation types on the vibration isolation performance. The parameter studies provide useful guidelines for the application of the bio-inspired isolator in dual-stage vibration isolation.

Keywords: dual-stage; bio-inspired isolator; vibration isolation; multi-parameter optimization

1. Introduction

Vibration isolation is an essential part of most engineering designs. Harmful vibration will affect the mechanical properties of materials and cause fatigue and wear, leading to the destruction of structures [1,2]. The traditional linear vibration isolation system requires a lower natural frequency to achieve higher efficiency of vibration attenuation, which may degrade the isolation system's capability of supporting the payload [3–5]. Thus, there is a conflict between the wider effective frequency band and larger loading capacity.

In nature, many animals have evolved simple limb trunk structures to isolate low-frequency vibrations, which can not only carry their large weight but still maintain good stability in high-speed motion. In recent years, the design of bio-inspired vibration isolators based on animal limb structures has been widely studied [6–18]. Jing and his coworkers presented a series of bio-inspired isolators composed of X-shaped structures and studied the dynamic characteristics of various vibration isolation systems [6–14]. For instance, inspired by the kangaroo's limbs, Dai et al. [6] proposed a bio-inspired quadrilateral shape (BIQS) structure to suppress the vibration from the acquisition target to the satellite platform. They used the harmonic balance method to analyze the dynamic response of the vibration isolation system and studied the influence of BIQS' structural parameters on the vibration isolation performance. The results show that the vibration isolator has better performance than the ordinary spring-mass-damper vibration isolator. Considering leg posture adjustment, Yan et al. [15] designed a bio-inspired polygon skeleton structure, in which the load capacity and working bandwidth can be adjusted by the initial parameters of the structure. The proposed structure can effectively suppress the vibration under various excitation conditions.

According to the above studies, bio-inspired isolators composed of X-shaped structures present excellent vibration isolation performance. However, the studies of bio-inspired isolators are currently limited to simple single-stage vibration isolation systems and the corresponding structural parameters' analysis. In power units (gas turbines, gear pumps, etc.) or precision instruments (optical interferometers, space telescopes, etc.) with complex vibration isolation systems [19–25], a single-stage vibration isolation system often leads to resonant peaks and standing wave effects at high frequencies [26–29], which cannot meet the vibration isolation requirements. A dual-stage vibration isolation system draws great interest owing to its better high-frequency effect and higher stability [30–36].

In the dual-stage vibration isolation system, two layers of vibration isolators are installed between the control object and the base, and an intermediate mass is inserted between the two layers of vibration isolators. The inertia of the intermediate mass is used to offset part of the base excitation, to attenuate the vibration transmission rate from the base to the control object [30]. Linear isolators are usually used in the ordinary dual-stage vibration isolation system. Due to the large intermediate mass required in the dual-stage isolation system, the linear isolators will undergo excessive static deformation, resulting in instability. The bio-inspired isolators may solve this problem and further improve the effect of dual-stage vibration isolation. However, limited studies have been conducted on dual-stage vibration isolation systems using bio-inspired isolators. The influence mechanism of bio-inspired isolators on the dual-stage vibration isolation performance is still unclear. Moreover, in the real application environment of dual-stage vibration isolation systems, there are various complex excitation types, including translation and rotations. Under different excitation types, the structural parameters and placement positions of the bio-inspired isolators will exert a significant impact on the dual-stage vibration isolation performance. Thus, it is necessary to appropriately design the structural parameters and carefully determine the positions of the isolators to realize better vibration isolation performance under different excitation types.

This paper will investigate the performance of bio-inspired isolators in the dual-stage vibration isolation system. The multi-parameter optimization study of the vibration isolator's structural parameters and placement positions will be carried out to obtain the optimal parameter configuration for the best vibration isolation performance under different excitation types.

The rest of the paper is organized as follows: Section 2 presents the dynamic model of the dual-stage vibration isolation system with bio-inspired isolators. Section 3 proposes the optimization problem and analyzes the optimization results. Section 4 performs the parameter study. The influences on the vibration isolation performance of the structural parameters of the bio-inspired isolator and the base excitations are discussed in detail. All the findings are summarized in Section 5.

2. Dynamic Model

2.1. Model Description

The dual-stage vibration isolation system with the bio-inspired vibration isolator (BI-DSVI) is illustrated in Figure 1. The control object m_u (which needs vibration isolation from the base excitation z_{01}, z_{02}, z_{03}, z_{04}) is connected to the intermediate mass m_d with four linear isolators (each with linear spring k_u and linear damping c_u). The intermediate mass is supported on the base by four bio-inspired vibration isolators, each containing a linear damping c_d and a bio-inspired structure [6,7], as shown in Figure 1a. l_d is the length of the connecting rods, k_d is the stiffness of the transverse spring between the connecting joints, and the initial assembly angle is φ_{d0}. The absolute displacements of the control object and the intermediate mass are z_u and z_d, respectively. The rotation angles of the control object around its horizontal inertia principal axes paralleling the x, y axes are α and β, and the rotation angles of the intermediate mass around its horizontal inertia principal axes paralleling the x, y axes are ψ and θ. To simplify the problem, only the translational motion along the height direction of the isolator (i.e., the direction of the coordinate axis z) and the rotational motion around the horizontal coordinate axes are considered. Thus, there are six generalized coordinates in the dynamic model: $z_u, \psi, \theta, z_d, \alpha, \beta$.

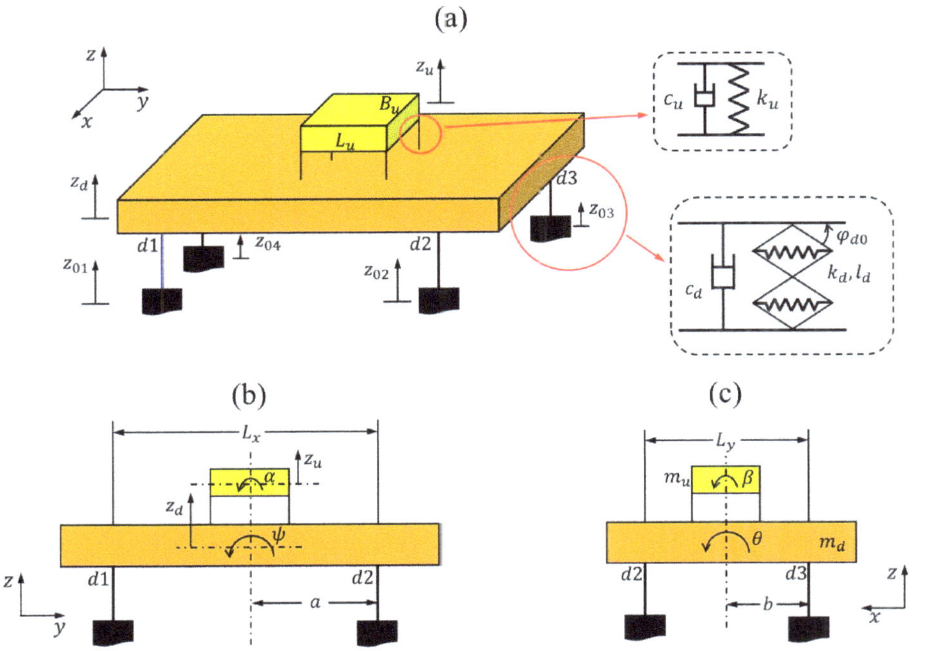

Figure 1. The dynamic model of the BI-DSVI (**a**) axonometric view (**b**) front view (**c**) right view.

2.2. Governing Equations

The dynamic equations of the BI-DSVI can be described as

$$\begin{aligned} & m_d\ddot{z}_d + c_d\left[4\dot{z}_d + (4a - L_y)\dot{\psi} + (4b - L_x)\dot{\theta} - \dot{z}_{01} - \dot{z}_{02} - \dot{z}_{03} - \dot{z}_{04}\right] + 4c_u(\dot{z}_d - \dot{z}_u) \\ & +2k_d[B_1(z_d,\psi,\theta) + B_2(z_d,\psi,\theta) + B_3(z_d,\psi,\theta) + B_4(z_d,\psi,\theta)] + 4k_u(z_d - z_u) = 0 \end{aligned} \tag{1}$$

$$\begin{aligned} J_{dx}\ddot{\psi} + c_d[(4a- \; & 2L_y)\dot{z}_d + \left(4a^2 - L_y a + 2L_y^2 - 2L_y a\right)\dot{\psi} + (4ab - L_x a + L_y L_x - 2L_y b)\dot{\theta} - (a - L_y)\dot{z}_{01} \\ & -a\dot{z}_{02} - a\dot{z}_{03} - (a - L_y)\dot{z}_{04}] + c_u L_u^2\left(\dot{\psi} - \dot{\alpha}\right) \\ & +2k_d[(a - L_y)B_1(z_d,\psi,\theta) + aB_2(z_d,\psi,\theta) + aB_3(z_d,\psi,\theta) + (a - L_y)B_4(z_d,\psi,\theta)] \\ & +k_u L_u^2(\psi - \alpha) = 0 \end{aligned} \tag{2}$$

$$\begin{aligned} J_{dy}\ddot{\theta} + c_d[(4b- \; & 2L_x)\dot{z}_d + (4ab - L_y b + L_x L_y - 2L_x a)\dot{\psi} + \left(4b^2 - L_x b + 2L_x^2 - 2L_x b\right)\dot{\theta} - (b - L_x)\dot{z}_{01} \\ & -(b - L_x)\dot{z}_{02} - b\dot{z}_{03} - b\dot{z}_{04}] + c_u B_u^2\left(\dot{\theta} - \dot{\beta}\right) \\ & +2k_d[(b - L_x)B_1(z_d,\psi,\theta) + (b - L_x)B_2(z_d,\psi,\theta) + bB_3(z_d,\psi,\theta) + bB_4(z_d,\psi,\theta)] \\ & +k_u B_u^2(\theta - \beta) = 0 \end{aligned} \tag{3}$$

$$m_u\ddot{z}_u + 4c_u(\dot{z}_d - \dot{z}_u) + 4k_u(z_d - z_u) = 0 \tag{4}$$

$$J_{ux}\ddot{\alpha} + c_u L_u^2\left(\dot{\alpha} - \dot{\psi}\right) + k_u L_u^2(\alpha - \psi) = 0 \tag{5}$$

$$J_{uy}\ddot{\beta} + c_u B_u^2\left(\dot{\beta} - \dot{\theta}\right) + k_u B_u^2(\beta - \theta) = 0 \tag{6}$$

$B_1(z_d,\psi,\theta)$, $B_2(z_d,\psi,\theta)$, $B_3(z_d,\psi,\theta)$, $B_4(z_d,\psi,\theta)$ are functions of the three generalized coordinates z_d,ψ,θ:

$$B_1(z_d,\psi,\theta) = \frac{l_d \cos\varphi_{d0}}{\sqrt{l_d^2 - h_1^2}} - h_1 \tag{7}$$

$$B_2(z_d, \psi, \theta) = \frac{l_d cos\varphi_{d0}}{\sqrt{l_d^2 - h_2^2}} - h_2 \tag{8}$$

$$B_3(z_d, \psi, \theta) = \frac{l_d cos\varphi_{d0}}{\sqrt{l_d^2 - h_3^2}} - h_3 \tag{9}$$

$$B_4(z_d, \psi, \theta) = \frac{l_d cos\varphi_{d0}}{\sqrt{l_d^2 - h_4^2}} - h_4 \tag{10}$$

where

$$\begin{cases} h_1 = \left[z_d - \psi(L_y - a) - \theta(L_x - b) - z_{01}\right]/4, \\ h_2 = \left[z_d + \psi a - \theta(L_x - b) - z_{02}\right]/4, \\ h_3 = (z_d + \psi a + \theta b - z_{03})/4, \\ h_4 = \left[z_d - \psi(L_y - a) + \theta b - z_{04}\right]/4. \end{cases} \tag{11}$$

We assume that the base excitation is $\ddot{z}_{0i} = Acos(2\pi f t + \phi_{0i}), i = 1,2,3,4$, where A is the excitation amplitude, f is the excitation frequency, and ϕ_{0i} is the initial phase. We define the vibration transmissibility as

$$T = \frac{|\ddot{z}_u|}{A} \tag{12}$$

where $|\ |$ represents the amplitude. In other words, the smaller the vibration transmissibility T, the better the vibration isolation performance. By changing the initial phase values at the four base positions, different types of base excitation can be achieved. For instance, $\phi_{01} = \phi_{02} = 0$, $\phi_{03} = \phi_{04} = \pi$ means the rotation excitation of the base around the y axis, and $\phi_{01} = \phi_{04} = 0$, $\phi_{02} = \phi_{03} = \pi$ means the rotation excitation of the base around the x axis.

In the following study of this paper, a sweep signal with amplitude $A = 1\ \mathrm{m/s^2}$ will be used as the base excitation, in which excitation frequency f is linearly increased with the rate 0.01 Hz/s from 2 Hz to 12 Hz. The dynamic Equations (1)–(6) will be numerically solved by the 4th-order Runge–Kutta method with a 0.01 s time step and the initial conditions are $[0\ 0\ 0\ 0\ 0\ 0]$. The numerical solution is verified by Adams in the Appendix A.

3. Performance Optimization Using Genetic Algorithm

In practical applications, the base excitation is often a complex motion composed of translational and rotational motions. Thus, it is necessary to optimize the bio-inspired isolator parameters and placement positions under different base excitation values. This section will discuss the optimization problem of isolator parameters and placement positions considering three different base excitation types: translation along the z axis, rotation about the x axis, and rotation about the y axis.

3.1. Definition of the Optimization Problem

In vibration isolation, minimizing the total vibrational energy of the control object in a working frequency band is the optimization goal. By selecting optimal design parameters, the total vibrational energy will reach the minimum, and the optimal distribution of the vibration transmissibility T in a given frequency band can be realized. In this paper, the motion of the control object m_u is described by three generalized coordinates z_u, α, β. Thus, the total vibration energy from frequency f_s to f_e can be defined as

$$G = \int_{f_s}^{f_e} \left(|\ddot{z}_u|^2 + |\ddot{\alpha}|^2 + \left|\ddot{\beta}\right|^2 \right) df \tag{13}$$

where $f_s = 2$ Hz is the sweep start frequency and $f_e = 12$ Hz is the stop frequency; the envelopes are used as the amplitude of the vibration acceleration $\ddot{z}_u, \ddot{\alpha}, \ddot{\beta}$. A lower G

indicates better isolation performance. To simulate the actual complex base excitation, three typical basic excitation types are selected for the optimization research:

Excitation 1: $\phi_{01} = \phi_{02} = \phi_{03} = \phi_{04} = 0$ (translation excitation along the z axis);

Excitation 2: $\phi_{01} = \phi_{02} = 0$, $\phi_{03} = \phi_{04} = \pi$ (rotation excitation around the y axis);

Excitation 3: $\phi_{01} = \phi_{04} = 0$, $\phi_{02} = \phi_{03} = \pi$ (rotation excitation around the x axis).

The design parameters contain three structural parameters of the bio-inspired isolator: the connecting rod length l_d, the transverse spring stiffness k_d, the initial assembly angle φ_{d0}, and two placement position parameters a, b. Other structural parameters are shown in Table 1.

Table 1. Parameters for BI-DSVI.

Parameters	Description	Values
m_u	Control object mass	2 kg
J_{ux}	Moment of inertia about axis x of m_u	1 kg·m^2
J_{uy}	Moment of inertia about axis y of m_u	1 kg·m^2
L_u	Length of m_u	0.1
B_u	Width of m_u	0.1 m
k_u	Stiffness of the linear isolator	1000 N/m
c_u	Damping of the linear isolator	1 N·s/m
m_d	Intermediate mass	10 kg
J_{dx}	Moment of inertia about axis x of m_d	10 kg·m^2
J_{dy}	Moment of inertia about axis y of m_d	8 kg·m^2
L_x	Distance between bio − inspired isolators along axis y	0.5 m
L_y	Distance between bio − inspired isolators along axis x	0.4 m
c_d	Damping of the bio-inspired isolator	5 N·s/m

Based on the above description, consider the fitness function $F(\boldsymbol{p}) = 1/G(\boldsymbol{p})$, which represents the inverse of the total vibration energy generated by given parameter vector $\boldsymbol{p}$. The vector $\boldsymbol{p}$ contains all the design parameters, i.e., $\boldsymbol{p} = \begin{bmatrix} l_d & k_d & \varphi_{d0} & a & b \end{bmatrix}$. Thus, an objective function is defined as

$$\max F(\boldsymbol{p}) \text{ when } \boldsymbol{p}_l < \boldsymbol{p} < \boldsymbol{p}_u \tag{14}$$

where $\boldsymbol{p}_l$ and $\boldsymbol{p}_u$ are the upper and lower limits of the design parameter vector. The optimization goal is to find the maximum F subjected to $\boldsymbol{p}_l < \boldsymbol{p} < \boldsymbol{p}_u$ under the above three base excitations, respectively.

3.2. Optimization Procedure

In this paper, the genetic algorithm (GA) will be used to optimize the solution. Figure 2 presents the flowchart of the optimization algorithm, and the detailed steps are presented as follows:

Begin

Step1: Initialize GA parameters; the population size is set to 20, the cross probability is 0.8, the mutation probability is 0.2, the max iteration is 200, and the elitist preservation proportion is 0.1.

Step2: Define the optimization fitness function $F = 1/G$ and the range of the design parameters:

$$l_d \in [0.2,\ 0.4] \text{ m}, k_d \in [5000,\ 10{,}000] \text{ N/m}, \varphi_{d0} \in \left[\frac{\pi}{6}, \frac{\pi}{3}\right], a \in [0.1,\ 0.4] \text{ m}, b \in [0.1,\ 0.3] \text{ m}$$

Step3: Generate a random initial population and calculate the initial fitness of all individuals.

Step4: Initialize the count number $gen = 1$.

Step5: Perform selection, crossover, and mutation operations.

Step6: Update the count number $gen = gen + 1$.

Step7: Go back to step 4 until $gen = 200$. When $gen = 200$, go to *Step 8*.

Step8: Output the optimal fitness value $1/G$ and the corresponding design parameters $[l_d \quad k_d \quad \varphi_{d0} \quad a \quad b]$.

End

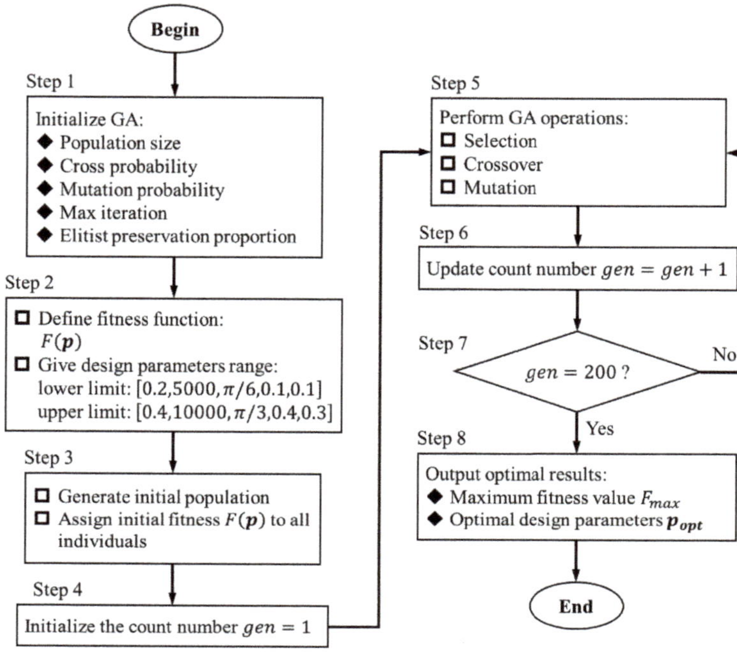

Figure 2. The flowchart of the GA optimization method.

3.3. Performance Comparison

This section describes a comparison between the optimal solutions under the above three different base excitations, which would prove the effectiveness of the performance optimization of the BI-DSVI. The iteration curves and the vibration transmissibility comparison before and after optimization for the three optimization cases are presented in Figures 3–5. The design parameters before optimization are taken as $l_d = 0.2$ m, $k_d = 6000$ N/m, $\varphi_{d0} = \pi/4$, $a = 0.25$ m, $b = 0.2$ m.

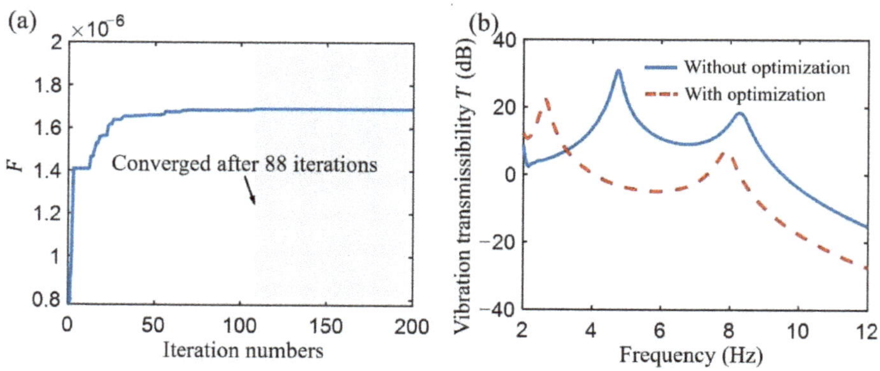

Figure 3. (**a**) The iteration curve and (**b**) the vibration transmissibility under optimal design parameters and basic design parameters, when $\phi_{01} = \phi_{02} = \phi_{03} = \phi_{04} = 0$.

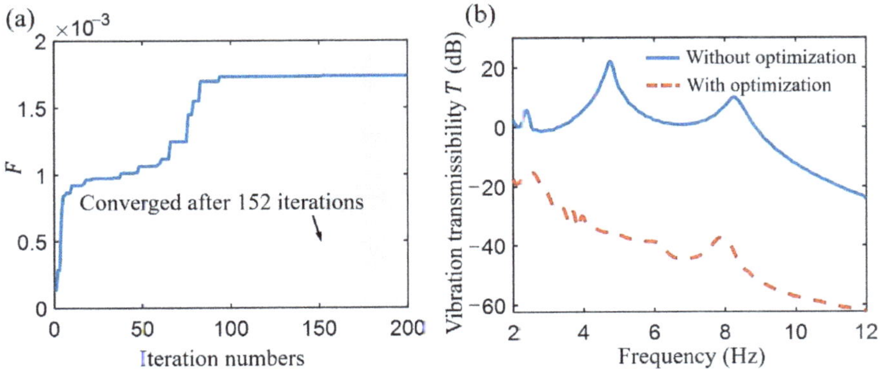

Figure 4. (**a**) The iteration curve and (**b**) the vibration transmissibility under optimal design parameters and basic design parameters, when $\phi_{01} = \phi_{02} = 0$, $\phi_{03} = \phi_{04} = \pi$.

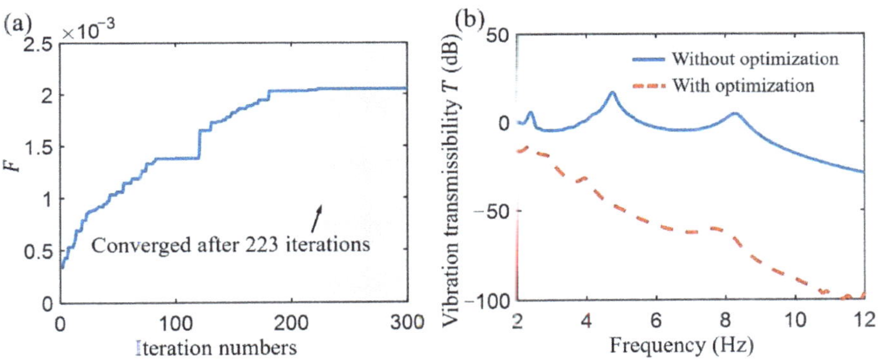

Figure 5. (**a**) The iteration curve and (**b**) the vibration transmissibility under optimal design parameters and basic design parameters, when $\phi_{01} = \phi_{04} = 0$, $\phi_{02} = \phi_{03} = \pi$.

As shown in Figure 3b, the BI-DSVI system exhibits two resonance peaks in the frequency range of 2–12 Hz. Through the optimized design, the resonance peaks are significantly reduced and the resonance frequencies are shifted to the left, which greatly broadens the vibration isolation bandwidth. The other two cases show consistent patterns. However, Figures 4b and 5b present another resonance peak between 2 and 4 Hz without optimization, which is probably due to the rotational motion of the base. Through parameter optimization, the extra resonance peak is suppressed below 0 dB, which means that complete vibration isolation is realized. In the three cases, the maximum transmissibility T without optimization is 30.97 dB, 22.10 dB, and 16.50 dB. At the same frequency locations, the transmissibility with optimization is −3.16 dB, −36.16 dB, and −46.96 dB. In other words, the vibrations are attenuated by 34.13 dB, 58.26 dB, 63.46 dB, respectively. Thus, the vibration isolation performance of the BI-DSVI can be greatly improved by multi-parameter optimization.

Table 2 presents the optimal design parameter values of the three different base excitations. For the three cases, the optimal structural parameters of the bio-inspired isolators are the same, and only the placement position parameters are different. Hence, there are optimal structural parameters of the bio-inspired isolator in a reasonable range (for instance, the stiffness k_d has a lower bound to ensure the basic loading capacity), which achieves the best vibration isolation performance. In other words, for different base excitations, it is only necessary to optimize the placement positions of the isolators to obtain the optimal vibration transmissibility distribution in a frequency band.

Table 2. The optimal design parameters of the three different base excitations.

Initial Phase of the Base Excitation	l_d	k_d	φ_{d0}	a	b
$\phi_{01} = \phi_{02} = \phi_{03} = \phi_{04} = 0$	0.4	5000	$\pi/6$	0.10	0.10
$\phi_{01} = \phi_{02} = 0,\ \phi_{03} = \phi_{04} = \pi$	0.4	5000	$\pi/6$	0.20	0.10
$\phi_{01} = \phi_{04} = 0,\ \phi_{02} = \phi_{03} = \pi$	0.4	5000	$\pi/6$	0.21	0.21

4. Parameter Study

4.1. Influence of the Isolator Parameters k_d, l_d, φ_{d0} on Vibration Isolation Performance

To further reveal the influence of the design parameters on the vibration isolation performance, the effects of the structural parameters k_d, l_d, φ_{d0} on the vibration transmissibility T of the BI-DSVI are investigated in this section. In the following analysis, the value of a is set to 0.25 m, and b is 0.2 m. The other parameter values are taken from Table 1 and the initial phase of the base excitation is $\phi_{01} = \phi_{02} = \phi_{03} = \phi_{04} = 0$.

Figure 6a shows the vibration transmissibility curves of the BI-DSVI with different transverse spring stiffness k_d. The values of l_d and φ_{d0} are set to 0.4 m and $\pi/4$, respectively. It is obvious that with the increase in k_d, both the first and second peaks of the vibration transmissibility curves increase. In the given frequency band (2–12 Hz), as k_d increases, the overall vibration transmissibility curve shifts to the right, which indicates that the effective vibration isolation bandwidth becomes narrower.

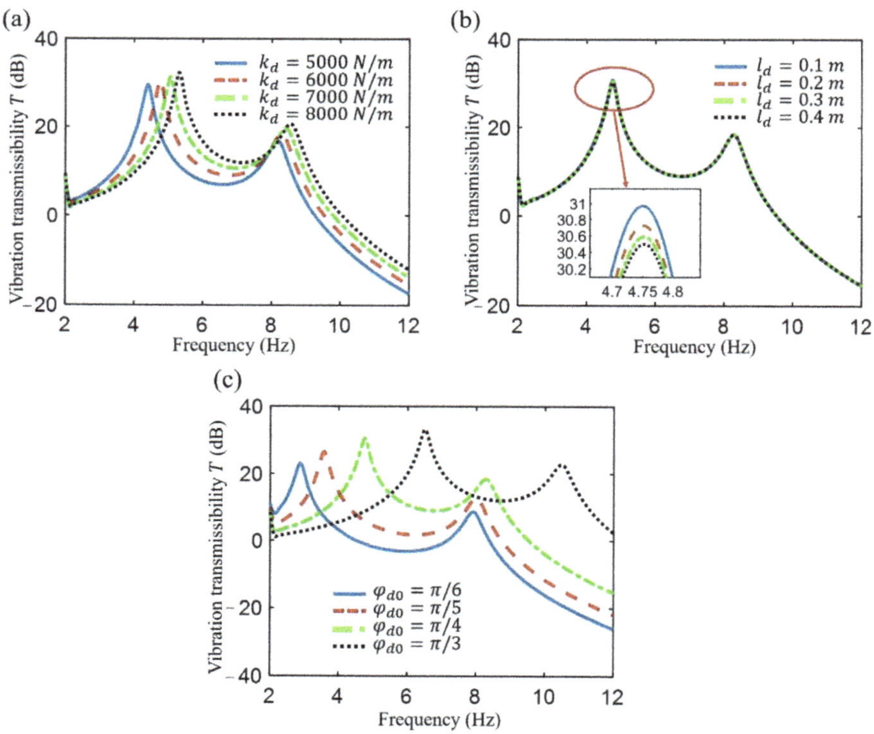

Figure 6. Vibration transmissibility T of the BI-DSVI with different structural parameters of the bio-inspired isolator: (**a**) the transverse spring stiffness k_d, (**b**) the connecting rod length l_d, (**c**) the initial assembly angle φ_{d0}.

Figure 6b shows the vibration transmissibility curves of the BI-DSVI with different connecting rod lengths l_d. The values of k_d and φ_{d0} are set to 6000 N/m and $\pi/4$, respectively. Near the first resonant frequency, the vibration transmissibility slightly decreases with the increase in l_d, which is suitable for vibration isolation. However, in the other frequency regions, l_d has no effect on the vibration transmissibility.

Figure 6c shows the vibration transmissibility curves of the BI-DSVI with different initial assembly angles φ_{d0}. The values of l_d and k_c are set to 0.4 m and 6000 N/m, respectively. With the angle φ_{d0} varying from $\pi/6$ to $\pi/3$, both the first and the second resonant frequencies increase significantly. Moreover, the peak values of the first and second resonant frequencies also increase significantly. The results indicate that a small initial assembly angle φ_{d0} may lead to better vibration isolation performance, including a wider effective vibration isolation bandwidth and lower resonance peak.

Through the above parameter analysis, it can be seen that the vibration isolation performance is significantly influenced by the following structural parameters: the transverse spring stiffness k_d and the initial assembly angle φ_{d0}. The connecting rod length l_d also has a slight effect on the vibration isolation performance. The vibration isolation performance is better when using a smaller k_d, φ_{d0} and longer l_d. This conclusion validates the optimization results in Section 3.

4.2. Influence of the Base Excitation on System Response

Considering the effect of the base rotation excitation on the control object m_u, we define the vibration transmissibility T_v as

$$T_v = \frac{|\ddot{z}_v|}{A} \tag{15}$$

where $\ddot{z}_v = \ddot{z}_u - \frac{L_u}{2}\alpha - \frac{B_u}{2}\beta$ represents the acceleration along the z axis of a vertex of the control object m_u. Figure 7a shows the vibration transmissibility T under the three different base excitations investigated in Section 3. The structural parameters of the bio-inspired isolators are taken from the optimal values obtained in Table 2 and the other parameters are the same as in Table 1. When the base excitation phase is 0, the whole system displays upward base acceleration, and the vibration transmissibility T is relatively large. When inverse-phase base excitation is applied, the vibration transmissibility T is greatly reduced. To clearly describe the influence of the base rotation excitation on the control object, the comparison curves of T and T_v are shown in Figure 7b. It can be seen that T and T_v coincide completely, which means that the motion of the vertex of the control object in the z direction is consistent with z_u. This indicates that the bio-inspired isolator used in the BI-DSVI can well isolate the disturbance due to the base rotational motion.

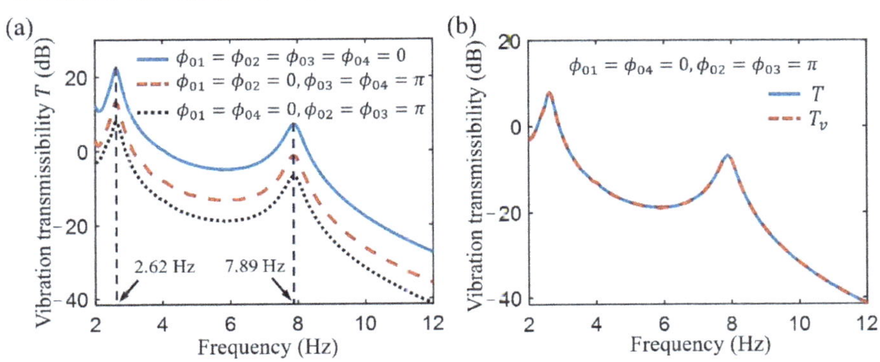

Figure 7. (**a**) The vibration transmissibility T under three different base excitations; (**b**) the vibration transmissibility comparison of T and T_v when $\phi_{01} = \phi_{04} = 0$, $\phi_{02} = \phi_{03} = \pi$.

To develop insight into the dynamic behaviors of the BI-DSVI in vibration isolation under different base excitations, the responses at frequency 2.62 Hz (the first resonance frequency of the BI-DSVI system) are investigated. As shown in Figure 8a,b, under the excitation of the base rolling motion, the vibration acceleration amplitude of the control object along the z direction is reduced significantly, which results in the lower vibration transmissibility T at frequency 2.62 Hz shown in Figure 7a. Figure 8c plots the phase trajectory of the BI-DSVI under two different base excitations. After reaching the steady state, the first excitation condition ($\phi_{01} = \phi_{02} = \phi_{03} = \phi_{04} = 0$) exhibits periodic motion, while the second excitation condition ($\phi_{01} = \phi_{04} = 0,\ \phi_{02} = \phi_{03} = \pi$) exhibits periodic motion in which the vibration amplitude varies in a small range. It can be obtained from the above results that the base rotational motion has little influence on the translational motion along the z direction of the control object. In other words, the bio-inspired isolator can effectively isolate the vibration caused by the base rotation excitation.

The dual-stage vibration isolation system is usually sensitive to base excitation with the natural frequency of the bottom vibration isolators. On this account, a simulation for a single bio-inspired isolator with an oscillator mass is conducted to find the natural frequency of the bio-inspired isolators. In the above studies, the intermediate mass and the control object mass are 12 kg in total—that is, the oscillator mass should be 3 kg. According to the optimal structural parameters and the oscillator mass, the vibration transmissibility of the single bio-inspired isolation system is calculated and is shown in Figure 9a. It can be seen that the natural frequency of the bio-inspired isolator is 1.72 Hz. Figure 9b–d show the time history results, FFT results, and phase plots of the BI-DSVI under two different base excitations $\phi_{01} = \phi_{02} = \phi_{03} = \phi_{04} = 0$ and $\phi_{01} = \phi_{04} = 0,\ \phi_{02} = \phi_{03} = \pi$ at frequency 1.72 Hz. The results present similar dynamic behaviors to the base excitations with 2.62 Hz. Moreover, the amplitude of $\ddot{z}_u$ is much smaller than the case of 2.62 Hz, which means that the BI-DSVI is insensitive to the resonance of the bio-inspired isolators. However, as shown in Figure 9d, under the base rotation excitation, the control object exhibits asymmetric periodic motion, probably affected by the resonance of the bio-inspired isolators. In a nutshell, the isolation performance of the BI-DSVI is not much affected by the base excitation with the natural frequency of the base bio-inspired isolators.

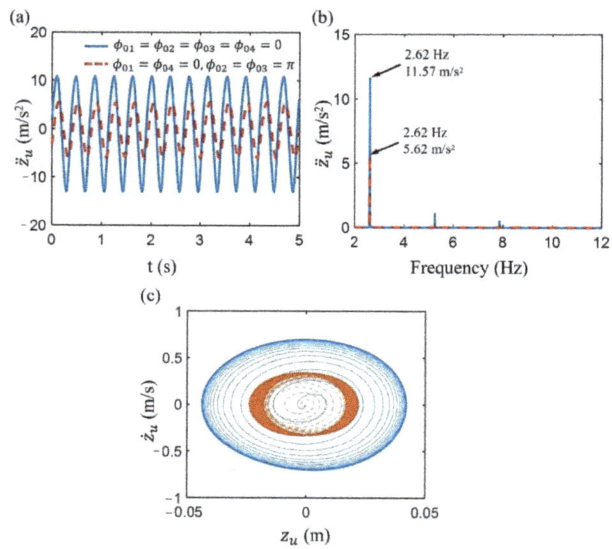

Figure 8. (**a**) The time history results, (**b**) the FFT results, and (**c**) the phase plots of the BI-DSVI under two different base excitations: $\phi_{01} = \phi_{02} = \phi_{03} = \phi_{04} = 0$ and $\phi_{01} = \phi_{04} = 0,\ \phi_{02} = \phi_{03} = \pi$.

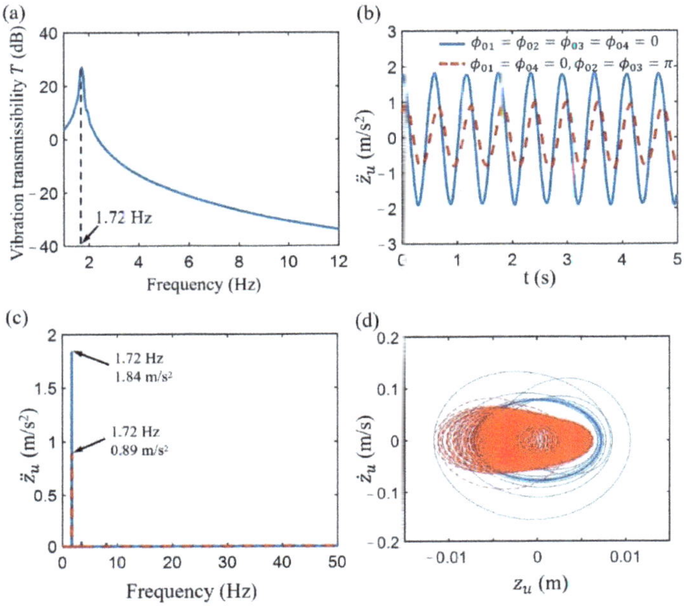

Figure 9. (**a**) The vibration transmissibility of the single bio-inspired isolation system; (**b**) the time history results, (**c**) the FFT results, and (**d**) the phase plots of the BI-DSVI under two different base excitations: $\phi_{01} = \phi_{02} = \phi_{03} = \phi_{04} = 0$ and $\phi_{01} = \phi_{04} = 0$, $\phi_{02} = \phi_{03} = \pi$, where the excitation frequency is 1.72 Hz.

5. Conclusions

This paper investigates the performance and multi-parameter optimization of a dual-stage vibration isolation system with bio-inspired isolators (BI-DSVI) under three different base excitations: translation along the z axis, rotation about the x axis, and rotation about the y axis. The dynamic equations of the BI-DSVI are derived first. The optimization problem consists of five design parameters, including three structural parameters of the bio-inspired isolator and two placement position parameters. Results under three different base excitations show that there is an optimal configuration of vibration isolator parameters in a reasonable range, and the vibration transmissibility is the lowest. The vibration transmissibility can be reduced by more than 30 dB by multi-parameter optimization, and the effective vibration isolation bandwidth is significantly widened. Finally, the influence of the isolator parameters and base excitation types on the vibration isolation performance is investigated. A smaller transverse spring stiffness and initial assembly angle and longer connecting rod length lead to lower vibration transmissibility. Compared to the translation excitation along the z axis, the bio-inspired isolator exhibits better vibration isolation performance under the base rotation excitation. Moreover, the BI-DSVI is insensitive to base excitation with the natural frequency of the base bio-inspired isolators.

Author Contributions: Conceptualization, Z.H. and W.T.; methodology, W.T.; software, W.T. and X.H.; validation, X.S.; formal analysis, Z.H. and W.T.; investigation, D.M.; resources, Z.H.; data curation, X.H., X.S. and D.M.; writing—original draft preparation, W.T.; writ-ing—review and editing, Z.H.; visualization, W.T.; supervision, Z.H.; project administration, Z.H.; funding acquisition, Z.H. All authors have read and agreed to the published version of the manuscript.

Funding: This research was funded by the National Natural Science Foundation of China (No. 51975547).

Conflicts of Interest: The authors declare no conflict of interest.

Appendix A

Figure A1 shows the dynamic model of the BI-DSVI established in Adams. The design parameters are set as $l_d = 0.2$ m, $\varphi_{d0} = \pi/4, a = 0.25$ m, $b = 0.2$ m and the other structural parameters are the same as in Table 1.

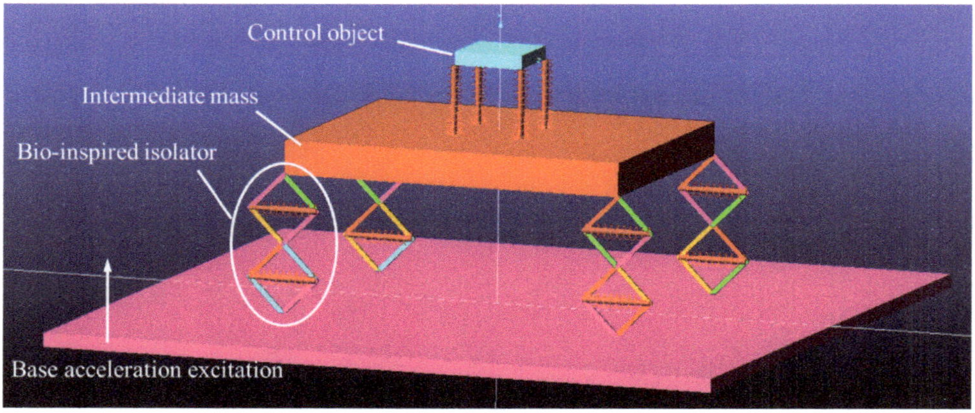

Figure A1. The dynamic model of the BI-DSVI established in Adams.

Figure A2 shows the Matlab and Adams simulation results (the acceleration amplitude of the control object) with different transverse spring stiffness k_d under the same base acceleration excitation: $\ddot{z}_0 = 1$ m/s^2. It can be seen that the results of the two methods are in good agreement on the whole, with only a minor difference in several frequencies. The results verify the validity of the BI-DSVI mathematical model derived in Section 2.

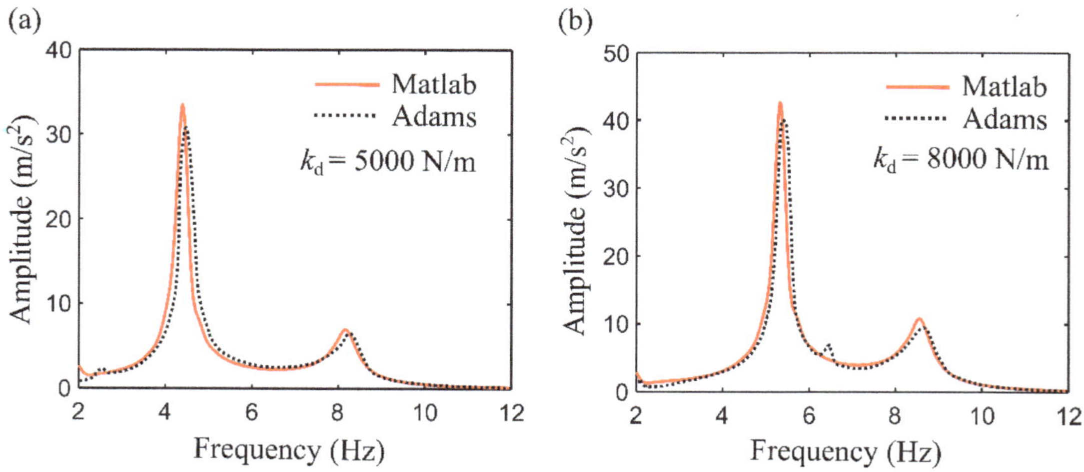

Figure A2. Comparison of the Matlab and Adams simulation results (the acceleration amplitude of the control object): (**a**) $k_d = 5000$ N/m; (**b**) $k_d = 8000$ N/m.

ferences

Hou, R.; Xia, Y. Review on the new development of vibration-based damage identification for civil engineering structures: 2010–2019. *J. Sound Vib.* **2021**, *491*, 115741. [CrossRef]

Feng, K.; Ji, J.C.; Ni, Q.; Beer, M. A review of vibration-based gear wear monitoring and prediction techniques. *Mech. Syst. Signal Process.* **2023**, *182*, 109605. [CrossRef]

Deng, T.; Wen, G.; Ding, H.; Lu, Z.Q.; Chen, L.Q. A bio-inspired isolator based on characteristics of quasi-zero stiffness and bird multi-layer neck. *Mech. Syst. Signal Process.* **2020**, *145*, 106967. [CrossRef]

Yan, B.; Wang, Z.; Ma, H.; Bao, H.; Wang, K.; Wu, C. A novel lever-type vibration isolator with eddy current damping. *J. Sound Vib.* **2021**, *494*, 115862. [CrossRef]

Hur, D.-J.; Hong, S.-C. Analysis of an Isolation System with Vertical Spring-viscous Dampers in Horizontal and Vertical Ground Motion. *Appl. Sci.* **2020**, *10*, 1411. [CrossRef]

Dai, H.; Jing, X.; Wang, Y.; Yue, X.; Yuan, J. Post-capture vibration suppression of spacecraft via a bio-inspired isolation system. *Mech. Syst. Signal Process.* **2018**, *105*, 214–240. [CrossRef]

Jing, X.; Zhang, L.; Feng, X.; Sun, B.; Li, Q. A novel bio-inspired anti-vibration structure for operating hand-held jackhammers. *Mech. Syst. Signal Process.* **2019**, *118*, 317–339. [CrossRef]

Wang, Y.; Jing, X.; Guo, Y. Nonlinear analysis of a bio-inspired vertically asymmetric isolation system under different structural constraints. *Nonlinear Dyn.* **2019**, *95*, 445–464. [CrossRef]

Bian, J.; Jing, X. Superior nonlinear passive damping characteristics of the bio-inspired limb-like or X-shaped structure. *Mech. Syst. Signal Process.* **2019**, *125*, 21–51. [CrossRef]

Dai, H.; Jing, X.; Sun, C.; Wang, Y.; Yue, X. Accurate modeling and analysis of a bio-inspired isolation system: With application to on-orbit capture. *Mech. Syst. Signal Process.* **2018**, *109*, 111–133. [CrossRef]

Dai, H.; Cao, X.; Jing, X.; Wang, X.; Yue, X. Bio-inspired anti-impact manipulator for capturing non-cooperative spacecraft: Theory and experiment. *Mech. Syst. Signal Process.* **2020**, *142*, 106785. [CrossRef]

Wang, Y.; Jing, X. Nonlinear stiffness and dynamical response characteristics of an asymmetric X-shaped structure. *Mech. Syst. Signal Process.* **2019**, *125*, 142–169. [CrossRef]

Zhang, Z.; Zhang, J.; Yin, H.; Zhang, B.; Jing, X. Bio-inspired structure reference model oriented robust full vehicle active suspension system control via constraint-following. *Mech. Syst. Signal Process.* **2022**, *179*, 109368. [CrossRef]

Chai, Y.; Jing, X. Low-frequency multi-direction vibration isolation via a new arrangement of the X-shaped linkage mechanism. *Nonlinear Dyn.* **2022**, *109*, 2383–2421. [CrossRef]

Yan, G.; Wang, S.; Zou, H.; Zhao, L.; Gao, Q.; Zhang, W. Bio-inspired polygonal skeleton structure for vibration isolation: Design, modelling, and experiment. *Sci. China Technol. Sci.* **2020**, *63*, 2617–2630. [CrossRef]

Gatti, G. A K-shaped spring configuration to boost elastic potential energy. *Smart Mater. Struct.* **2019**, *28*, 077002. [CrossRef]

Zhao, Y.; Meng, G. A bio-inspired semi-active vibration isolator with variable-stiffness dielectric elastomer: Design and modeling. *J. Sound Vib.* **2020**, *485*, 115592. [CrossRef]

Shi, X.; Chen, T.; Zhang, J.; Su, B.; Cong, Q.; Tian, W. A Review of Bioinspired Vibration Control Technology. *Appl. Sci.* **2021**, *11*, 10584. [CrossRef]

Chen, S.; Xuan, M.; Xin, J.; Liu, Y.; Gu, S.; Li, J.; Zhang, L. Design and experiment of dual micro-vibration isolation system for optical satellite flywheel. *Int. J. Mech. Sci.* **2020**, *179*, 105592. [CrossRef]

Yang, T.; Cao, Q. Modeling and analysis of a novel multi-directional micro-vibration isolator with spring suspension struts. *Arch. Appl. Mech.* **2022**, *92*, 801–819. [CrossRef]

Li, L.; Tan, L.; Kong, L.; Wang, D.; Yang, H. The influence of flywheel micro vibration on space camera and vibration suppression. *Mech. Syst. Signal Process.* **2018**, *100*, 360–370. [CrossRef]

Wang, X.; Wu, H.; Yang, B. Micro-vibration suppressing using electromagnetic absorber and magnetostrictive isolator combined platform. *Mech. Syst. Signal Process.* **2020**, *139*, 106606. [CrossRef]

Hadroug, N.; Hafaifa, A.; Alili, B.; Iratni, A.; Chen, X. Fuzzy Diagnostic Strategy Implementation for Gas Turbine Vibrations Faults Detection: Towards a Characterization of Symptom–fault Correlations. *J. Vib. Eng. Technol.* **2022**, *10*, 225–251. [CrossRef]

Qian, Y.; Xie, Y.; Jia, J.; Zhang, L. Development of Active Microvibration Isolation System for Precision Space Payload. *Appl. Sci.* **2022**, *12*, 4548. [CrossRef]

Lei, Y.J.; Li, R.J.; Zhang, L.S.; Hu, P.H.; Huang, Q.X. Optical Accelerometers for Detecting Low-Frequency Micro-Vibrations. *Appl. Sci.* **2022**, *12*, 3994. [CrossRef]

Wang, Y.; Li, H.X.; Cheng, C.; Ding, H.; Chen, L.Q. A nonlinear stiffness and nonlinear inertial vibration isolator. *J. Vib. Control* **2020**, *27*, 1336–1352. [CrossRef]

Yan, B.; Yu, N.; Wu, C. A state-of-the-art review on low-frequency nonlinear vibration isolation with electromagnetic mechanisms. *Appl. Math. Mech.* **2022**, *43*, 1045–1062. [CrossRef]

Zhang, F.; Xu, M.; Shao, S.; Xie, S. A new high-static-low-dynamic stiffness vibration isolator based on magnetic negative stiffness mechanism employing variable reluctance stress. *J. Sound Vib.* **2020**, *476*, 115322. [CrossRef]

Mofidian, S.M.M.; Bardaweel, H. A dual-purpose vibration isolator energy harvester: Experiment and model. *Mech. Syst. Signal Process.* **2019**, *118*, 360–376. [CrossRef]

30. Yun, H.; Liu, L.; Li, Q.; Yang, H. Investigation on two-stage vibration suppression and precision pointing for space opti payloads. *Aerosp. Sci. Technol.* **2020**, *96*, 105543. [CrossRef]
31. Lu, Z.; Brennan, M.; Ding, H.; Chen, L. High-static-low-dynamic-stiffness vibration isolation enhanced by damping nonlinear *Sci. China Technol. Sci.* **2019**, *62*, 1103–1110. [CrossRef]
32. Yang, T.; Wu, L.; Li, X.; Zhu, M.; Brennan, M.J.; Liu, Z. Active Vibration Isolation of a Diesel Generator in a Small Marine Ves An Experimental Study. *Appl. Sci.* **2020**, *10*, 3025. [CrossRef]
33. Qin, C.; Xu, Z.; Xia, M.; He, S.; Zhang, J. Design and optimization of the micro-vibration isolation system for large space telesco *J. Sound Vib.* **2020**, *482*, 115461. [CrossRef]
34. Wang, Z.; Tian, D.; Shi, L.; Liu, J. Multi-Body Dynamics Modeling and Control for Strapdown Inertially Stabilized Platfor Considering Light Base Support Characteristics. *Appl. Sci.* **2020**, *10*, 7175. [CrossRef]
35. Lei, X.; Wu, C.; Wu, H. A novel composite vibration control method using double-decked floating raft isolation system a particle damper. *J. Vib. Control* **2018**, *24*, 4407–4418. [CrossRef]
36. Feng, X.; Chen, H.; Wu, G.; Zhang, A.; Zhao, Z. A New Vibration Controller Design Method Using Reinforcement Learning a FIR Filters: A Numerical and Experimental Study. *Appl. Sci.* **2022**, *12*, 9869. [CrossRef]

applied sciences

MDPI

Article

Vibration Control with Reinforcement Learning Based on Multi-Reward Lightweight Networks

Yucheng Shu *, Chaogang He, Lihong Qiao *, Bin Xiao and Weisheng Li

Chongqing Key Laboratory of Image Cognition, School of Computer Science and Technology, Chongqing University of Posts and Telecommunications, Chongqing 400065, China; s210201035@stu.cqupt.edu.cn (C.H.); xiaobin@cqupt.edu.cn (B.X.); liws@cqupt.edu.cn (W.L.)
* Correspondence: shuyc@cqupt.edu.cn (Y.S.); qiaolh@cqupt.edu.cn (L.Q.)

Abstract: This paper proposes a reinforcement learning method using a deep residual shrinkage network based on multi-reward priority experience playback for high-frequency and high-dimensional continuous vibration control. Firstly, we keep the underlying equipment unchanged and construct a vibration system simulator using FIR filters to ensure the complete fidelity of the physical model. Then, by interacting with the simulator using our proposed algorithm, we identify the optimal control strategy, which is directly applied to real-world scenarios in the form of a neural network. A multi-reward mechanism is proposed to assist the lightweight network to find a near-optimal control strategy, and a priority experience playback mechanism is used to prioritize the data to accelerate the convergence speed of the neural network and improve the data utilization efficiency. At the same time, the deep residual shrinkage network is introduced to realize adaptive denoising and lightweightness of the neural network. The experimental results indicate that under narrowband white-noise excitation ranging from 0 to 100 Hz, the DDPG algorithm achieved a vibration reduction effect of 12.728 dB, while our algorithm achieved a vibration reduction effect of 20.240 dB. Meanwhile, the network parameters were reduced by more than 7.5 times.

Keywords: active vibration control; reinforcement learning; lightweight; neural network; prioritized experience replaying; reward function

1. Introduction

When it comes to active vibration control, we face a high-dimensional, high-frequency, continuous, and complex dynamic problem. In order to cope with this challenge, a variety of traditional methods have been proposed. For example, PID controllers [1–4] are used to control complex objects, especially those with large time delays, rapid parameter changes, significant uncertainties, and severe nonlinearity. However, the PID controller has poor control quality in these cases, and a large number of parameters need to be designed in advance. Another common method employs the LQR controller [5–7], which uses a quadratic performance index. However, in practical applications, not every scenario is suitable for such an indicator, and it can only be applied to systems that can be represented by state-space equations. Another method involves the FxLMS controller [8–10], which not only needs to construct the reference signal, but also needs to identify the auxiliary path. However, studies have shown that although these traditional methods can play a role in control, they all require a lot of design work and manual intervention.

In recent years, the use of reinforcement learning (RL) technology to improve the efficiency of vibration controller designs has become a method of great concern. This method uses the reinforcement learning algorithm to automatically obtain the parameters of the controller, which brings new possibilities for vibration control. Compared with traditional methods, the reinforcement learning method is a data-driven approach, which does not require physical information on vibration control, such as the mass matrix, damping matrix, and stiffness matrix, thus reducing the required engineering and design investment. In fact, the use of reinforcement learning methods to construct agents to learn vibration control in complex environments has achieved remarkable results [11–15]. This method has been applied in many fields, such as for suspension vibration control [16,17], manipulator vibration control [18–20], magnetorheological damper vibration control [21,22], and other vibration control applications [23–25], and has made remarkable progress.

In the field of suspension vibration control [16,17], Li et al. [16] integrated model-free learning with model-based safety supervision. They used the underlying system dynamics and security-related constraints, used recursive feasibility techniques to construct security sets, and integrated them into the detection system constraints of reinforcement learning. This secure reinforcement learning framework was applied to the active suspension control system. Their experiments show that this secure reinforcement learning system can learn the control strategy safely and has better performance than the standard controller. Zhao et al. [17] discussed the set value tracking problem for the suspension system of a medium-speed maglev train, aiming at maintaining a fixed distance between the train and the track. They describe the set point tracking problem as a continuous-state and continuous-action Markov decision process under unknown transition probabilities, and obtain the state feedback controller from the sampled data of the suspension system through a Deterministic Policy Gradient and neural network approximation reinforcement learning algorithm. Their simulation results demonstrate the high performance of this model-free method, especially given that the response speed of their controller is 50 times faster than that of PID and no additional modeling work is required.

In the field of robotic arm control [18–20], Ding et al. [18] proposed an innovative human–computer interaction system and applied it to the cooperative operation control task of a robotic arm. Their human–computer interaction system includes an impedance model controller and a manipulator controller. The model-based reinforcement learning method is applied to the impedance mode for operator adaptation. The newly designed adaptive manipulator controller realizes a speed-free filter. Their simulation results verify the effectiveness of the human–computer interaction system based on the real manipulator parameters. On the other hand, Adel et al. [19] proposed a learning framework for robot manipulators based on nonlinear model predictive control, which aims to solve the motion planning problem of robot manipulators in the presence of obstacles. The cost function, system constraints, and manipulator model were parameterized by using the value function of the reinforcement learning framework and the myopic value of the action-value function. The controller was applied to the robot manipulator of a 6-DOF model. Their numerical simulation results show that this controller can effectively control the attitude of the end effector, avoid the collision between the manipulator and the obstacle, and improve the efficiency of the control loop by 21%. Additionally, Vighnesh et al. [20] designed a two-wheeled inverted pendulum mobile manipulator for retail shelf inspections. In comparison to PID control, in simulation tests, the controller based on reinforcement learning exhibited stronger robustness against variations in initial conditions, changes in inertia parameters, and disturbances applied to the robot.

In the field of magnetorheological damper vibration control [21,22], Park et al. [21] proposed a reinforcement learning method for magnetorheological elastomer vibration control based on Q-learning. Their research shows that it is feasible to use a model-free reinforcement learning model to realize an adaptive controller based on the application of highly nonlinear magnetorheological elastomers. When compared with a model without the controller, this method suppressed the vibration level by up to 57%. In addition, Yuan et al. [22] proposed a magnetorheological damping semi-active control strategy based on a reinforcement learning Q-learning algorithm. Their simulation results show that this method is simpler, easier to implement, and more robust. They used the reinforcement learning semi-active control strategy to study the vibration reduction of a two-story frame structure. The results show that the strategy is superior to the simple bang–bang control method.

At present, some progress has been made in the combination of reinforcement learning and finite-impulse response filters. Feng et al. [26] successfully solved the multi-input/multi-output actual vibration control problem in a frequency range by using RL and FIR filters, which marks the first time that reinforcement learning has been used to solve high-dimensional high-frequency vibration control problems. In order to meet the lightweight requirements of the underlying equipment, they designed the simplest fully connected neural network. However, this method may face the challenge of overfitting or underfitting when solving more complex and variable dynamic problems. In order to solve this problem, we try to find a way to both maintain lightweightness and solve complex problems.

In the field of deep learning, the way to achieve lightweightness is to reduce resource consumption and model complexity. In this regard, some achievements have been made [27–30]. Among the research on lightweightness, He et al. [27] proposed a residual network framework to reduce the burden of network training. They explicitly redefined each layer as the input of the reference layer and learned the residual function instead of learning an unknown function. Through comprehensive experimental data, they clarified that their residual network is easier to optimize, and that increasing the network depth can achieve higher accuracy. This method improved the results in the COCO target detection dataset by 28%, and won the first place in the COCO target detection and image segmentation tasks. On the other hand, Howard et al. [28] proposed an efficient model called MobileNets, which uses deep separable convolution to construct a lightweight deep neural network. Through extensive resource and accuracy experiments, MobileNets showed strong performance compared with other popular ImageNet classification models. They also demonstrate the effectiveness of this method in object detection, fine-grained classification, face attributes, and large-scale geolocation. Zhang et al. [29] proposed a computationally efficient CNN architecture called ShuffleNet. This method uses two new operations, point group convolution, and channel rearrangement, which greatly reduces the computational cost while maintaining accuracy. Their experiments on ImageNet classification and MS COCO target detection show that ShuffleNet is superior to other structures. On ARM-based mobile devices, the speedup of ShuffleNet is about 13 times higher than that of AlexNet, and it maintains considerable accuracy. In addition, Zhao et al. [30] proposed a deep residual shrinkage network to improve the feature learning ability of high-noise vibration signals. They inserted the adaptive soft threshold as a nonlinear transformation layer into the deep architecture to eliminate unimportant features. The effectiveness of their developed method was verified through various types of noise experiments.

At present, reinforcement learning forms a very mature system. It is mainly divided into two categories: value-based learning and probability-based learning, and has algorithms that combine these two methods. Probability-based reinforcement learning is one of the most direct methods and makes decisions by directly outputting the probability of the next possible action. In this method, each action has the opportunity to be selected, but the size of these opportunities is different. For example, the Policy Gradients approach [31] is a probability-based approach. In contrast, the value-based approach involves outputting the value of all actions and selecting the action with the highest value in the decision-making process. For example, algorithms such as Q-learning [32] are value-based methods. Combining the advantages of these two methods, some more optimized algorithms have been derived, such as Actor–Critic [33]. In this structure, the Actor makes an action based on probability, while the Critic assesses the value of the action. This combination optimizes the original Policy Gradients approach and accelerates the learning process. At present, the AC method has many extensions, including the Deep Deterministic Policy Gradient (DDPG) [34], Soft Actor–Critic (SAC) [35], and Twin Delayed Deep Deterministic Policy Gradient (TD3) [36] techniques.

Regarding the Actor–Critic method of reinforcement learning, Lillicrap et al. [34] proposed an Actor–Critic model-free algorithm based on Deterministic Policy Gradients, which can operate in a continuous-action space. They successfully solved the challenges of more than 20 simulated physical tasks by using the same learning algorithm, network architecture, and hyperparameters. Haarnoja et al. [35] described the Soft Actor–Critic approach, which is an offline strategy Actor–Critic algorithm based on a reinforcement learning framework. Its goal is to maximize both the expected return and entropy. This method is superior to the previous online strategy and offline strategy methods in terms of the sample utilization efficiency and progressive performance. In addition, Fujimoto et al. [36] found that in value-based reinforcement learning methods, known function approximation errors may lead to overestimation and suboptimal strategies for value estimation. Based on this, they propose a new mechanism called Twin Delayed Deep Deterministic Policy Gradient to mitigate the overestimation issues of Actor–Critic algorithms. They suggest constraining overestimation by taking the minimum of a pair of critics based on the foundation of double Q-learning. When evaluating their approach, it consistently outperformed current state-of-the-art methods across various testing environments.

However, due to the large number of parameters required in stacking neural networks to solve complex problems, previous algorithms have limitations such as algorithmic simplicity or a larger parameter count, impacting the timely control of controllers. To address this issue, this paper proposes vibration control with reinforcement learning based on a multi-reward lightweight network. Specifically, it is a deep residual shrinkage lightweight method based on deep reinforcement learning with multi-reward prioritized experience replay (DRSL-MPER). We introduce a multi-reward mechanism to assist the TD3 algorithm in finding control policies close to optimal. At the same time, we also introduce a priority experience playback mechanism to assign priority to the data, thereby accelerating the convergence speed of the neural network and improving the data utilization efficiency. In addition, we also introduce a deep residual shrinkage network to achieve adaptive denoising and lightweightness of the neural network. The algorithm proposed in this paper has two significant and practical advantages. Firstly, it employs a lightweight network, which not only enhances the computational efficiency and reduces the energy consumption but also facilitates deployment and maintenance in real-world scenarios, while supporting rapid iterative updates of the system. Secondly, the algorithm demonstrates excellent control performance and good generalization capabilities, which can significantly improve the performance and lifespan of equipment, enhance the reliability and safety of the system, and increase its adaptability and flexibility.

The rest of this paper is organized as follows: Firstly, the vibration control problem is described. Secondly, our lightweight method of multi-reward priority experience playback based on deep reinforcement learning is proposed. Then, the vibration controller designed using this method is verified through experiments. Finally, we draw our conclusions.

2. Problem Formulation

2.1. Dynamic Model

Figure 1 shows the dynamic model of the high-dimensional high-frequency vibration control system considered in this paper. The vibration exciter m is installed on the equipment platform M, which is supported on the foundation by four rubber dampers. The rubber dampers can be regarded as a spring damping system composed of linear spring k and linear damping c. Four electromagnetic actuators are mounted on the equipment platform, which generate counteracting control forces to reduce the vibration of the equipment platform caused by the vibration exciter. The rotation angles of the equipment platform around its horizontal inertia principal axes paralleling to the x-axis and y-axis are ψ and θ. The vibration exciter generates excitation forces in three directions, denoted as F_{ex}, F_{ey}, F_{ez}. However, since the actuators can only generate control forces in the z-direction $(F_{c1}, F_{c2}, F_{c3}, F_{c4})$, only the translational motion along the z-axis and the rotational motion around the horizontal axis are considered. Thus, there are three generalized coordinates in the dynamic model: z, ψ, θ.

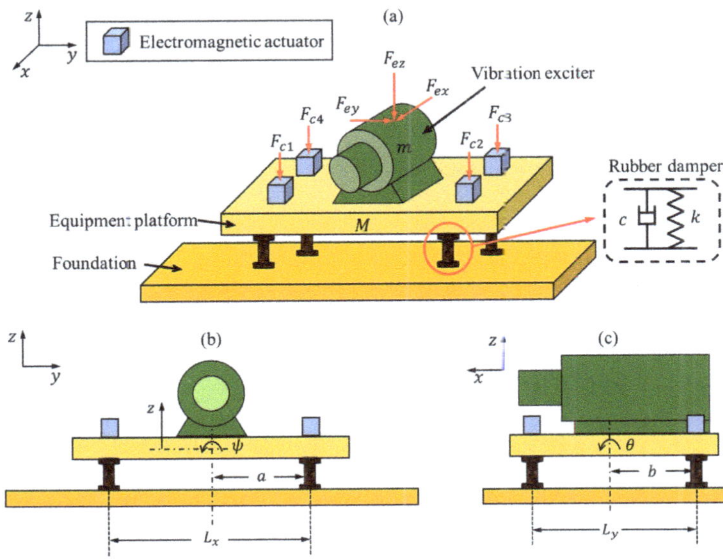

Figure 1. Schematic of the vibration control system: (**a**) axonometric view; (**b**) front view; (**c**) right view.

Using the Lagrange equation, the dynamic equations of the vibration control system can be described as follows:

$$\begin{aligned}(M+m)\ddot{z} &+ c\left[4\dot{z} + (4a - L_y)\dot{\psi} + (4b - L_x)\dot{\theta}\right] \\ &+ k\left[4z + (4a - L_y)\psi + (4b - L_x)\theta\right] \\ &= -F_{ez} - F_{c1} - F_{c2} - F_{c3} - F_{c4}\end{aligned} \tag{1}$$

$$\begin{aligned}J_x\ddot{\psi} + c\big[(4a - 2L_y)\dot{z} &+ \left(4a^2 - L_y a + 2L_y^2 - 2L_y a\right)\dot{\psi} \\ &+ (4ab - L_x a + L_y L_x - 2L_y b)\dot{\theta}\big] \\ &+ k\left[(4a - 2L_y)z + \left(4a^2 - L_y a + 2L_y^2 - 2L_y a\right)\psi\right. \\ &\left.+ (4ab - L_x a + L_y L_x - 2L_y b)\theta\right] \\ &= F_{c1}(L_x - a) - F_{c2}a - F_{c3}a + F_{c4}(L_x - a)\end{aligned} \tag{2}$$

$$\begin{aligned}J_y\ddot{\theta} + c\big[(4b - 2L_x)\dot{z} &+ (4ab - L_y b + L_x L_y - 2L_x a)\dot{\psi} \\ &+ \left(4b^2 - L_x b + 2L_x^2 - 2L_x b\right)\dot{\theta}\big] \\ &+ k\left[(4b - 2L_x)z + (4ab - L_y b + L_x L_y - 2L_x a)\psi\right. \\ &\left.+ \left(4b^2 - L_x b + 2L_x^2 - 2L_x b\right)\theta\right] \\ &= F_{c1}(L_y - b) + F_{c2}(L_y - b) - F_{c3}b - F_{c4}b\end{aligned} \tag{3}$$

where J_x and J_y represent the moment of inertia of the system with respect to the x-axis and y-axis, m = 100 kg, M = 913 kg, L_x = 1.6 m, L_y = 1.2 m, a = 0.8 m, b = 0.6 m, J_x = 76 kg*m^2, J_y = 58 kg*m^2, k = 600,000 N/m, and c = 100 Ns/m.

The equipment platform generates vibrations in the z-direction subjected to the excitation force F_{ez}. It is evident from Equations (1)–(3) that by adjusting the value of the control forces $F_{c1}, F_{c2}, F_{c3}, F_{c4}$, the vibrations of the equipment platform can be reduced, achieving active vibration control. In this paper, the vibration exciter is supposed to generate random multi-frequency excitations, making this vibration system a typical high-dimensional high-frequency vibration control problem.

2.2. Active Control Implementation

In active vibration control, the control algorithm needs to calculate the control signal based on the system's response. This section presents the implementation of the high-dimensional high-frequency vibration control problem, as shown in Figure 2. An acceleration sensor is installed near each of the four electromagnetic actuators to collect the acceleration signals at the respective positions. The four control signals are computed in real time by the controller running a trained reinforcement learning neural network, based on signals from the four acceleration sensors located near the actuators. The signal conditioner is used to filter and amplify the signals from the four acceleration sensors, which are then converted into digital signals via an AD module and fed into the controller for processing. The control signals are amplified by a driver into control current signals after being processed via a DA module to drive the actuators. The electromagnetic actuator consists of a permanent magnet armature and a coil, with the permanent magnet armature positioned in the middle of the coil. When current flows through the coil, the permanent magnet armature moves up and down under the influence of the coil's magnetic field, generating actuating force. The driver is a power amplifier that amplifies the control signal calculated by the controller into current to drive the electromagnetic actuator to operate.

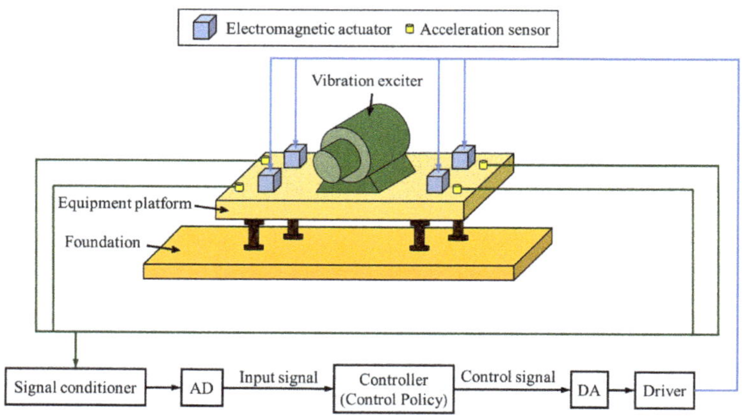

Figure 2. The active vibration control process of the vibration control system.

Since the vibration control system is often applied in complex vibration environments, where theoretical models cannot accurately describe the input–output response of the system, real experimental data are used for the research in this paper. In the following sections, the vibration control system is modeled as a simulator constructed from these experimental data. Based on the simulator, a neural network vibration controller is designed using reinforcement learning methods to solve the high-dimensional high-frequency vibration control problem.

3. Method

3.1. Vibration System Simulator

Figure 3 shows the vibration control simulator built using the finite-impulse response (FIR) filter. This simulator is used to describe the real vibration control system shown in

Figure 1, involving five inputs and four outputs. Among them, the five inputs represent the force of the exciter and four electromagnetic actuators; the four outputs correspond to four acceleration signals. Before establishing the simulator, narrowband Gaussian white-noise force signals ranging from 0 to 100 Hz are separately inputted into the exciter and the four actuators, and experimental data from the four acceleration sensors are pre-collected. Subsequently, the input force signals and the collected acceleration data are used for the identification process of the FIR filters. These filters make up the simulator, which is capable of simulating the responses of the four acceleration sensors in the real vibration system by applying specified force signals to the exciter and electromagnetic actuator.

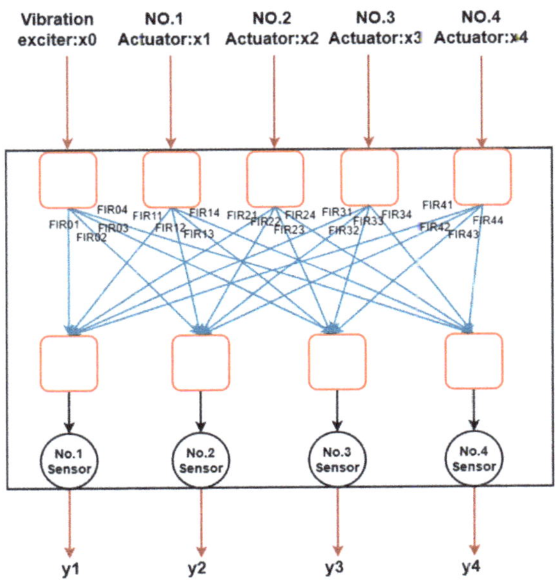

Figure 3. Description of the vibration system simulator. The FIR filter-identified signal is shown in blue, while the input–output vibration signal is shown in red.

3.1.1. FIR Filter

Adaptive FIR filters are used to construct the simulator. As shown in Figure 4, in order to realize the FIR filter, we need to obtain the input signal $x(n)$ and the desired input and output signals $d(n)$, $x(n)$ and $d(n)$ as vectors:

$$x(n) = [x(n)x(n-1)\cdots x(n-N+1)]^T \tag{4}$$

$$d(n) = [d(n)d(n-1)\cdots d(n-N+1)]^T \tag{5}$$

where N is the length of the filter. The input signal $x(n)$ of a given filter is known, and the output signal $y(n)$ of the filter is expressed as follows:

$$y(n) = \omega^T(n)x(n) \tag{6}$$

where n indicates the serial number of the discrete-time data, and $\omega(n)$ is the vector of the filter value.

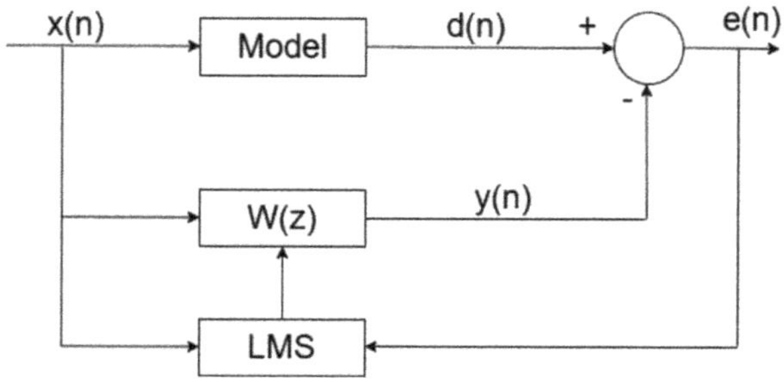

Figure 4. Schematic diagram of an FIR filter.

The output signal $y(n)$ is the estimation of the desired signal $d(n)$. The error $e(n)$ between the output signal $y(n)$ and the desired signal $d(n)$ is defined as follows:

$$e(n) = d(n) - y(n) \tag{7}$$

By using the least-mean-square (LMS) algorithm [37], we estimate the filter weight $\omega(n)$ to minimize the error $e(n)$:

$$\omega(n+1) = \omega(n) - 2\mu e(n)x(n) \tag{8}$$

where μ is the step size.

If the appropriate input signal $x(n)$ and the desired output signal $d(n)$ are given, it is easy to estimate the filter weight $\omega(n)$. In this paper, both the input signal and the expected output signal are experimental data.

3.1.2. Using FIR Filters to the Build Simulator

The simulator can be viewed as a five-input/four-output filter. The input signals are denoted as $x_0(n)$, $x_1(n)$, $x_2(n)$, $x_3(n)$, and $x_4(n)$, where $x_0(n)$ represents the force signal of the exciter, and $x_1(n)$, $x_2(n)$, $x_3(n)$, and $x_4(n)$ represent the force signals of the four electromagnetic actuators. The required output signals are recorded as $d_1(n)$, $d_2(n)$, $d_3(n)$, and $d_4(n)$, which represent the acceleration signals, respectively. $y_j(n)$ is the estimated value of the expected output ($d_j(n)$, j = 1, 2, 3, 4).

Obviously, there are 5 × 4 = 20 channels between the input and output, each of which can be represented by an FIR filter. We can suppose that C_{ij} represents a filter between $x_i(n)$ and $d_j(n)$, where i = 0, 1, 2, 3, 4 and j = 1, 2, 3, 4.

Note that $d_1(n)$ is the open-loop response under $x_0(n)$, $x_1(n)$, $x_2(n)$, $x_3(n)$, and $x_4(n)$ excitation. Therefore, the estimation of $d_1(n)$ can be expressed as follows:

$$\begin{aligned} y_1 &= \omega_{01}^T(n)x_0(n) + \omega_{11}^T(n)x_1(n) + \omega_{21}^T(n)x_2(n) + \omega_{31}^T(n)x_3(n) \\ &+ \omega_{41}^T(n)x_4(n) \end{aligned} \tag{9}$$

where $y_1(n)$ is the estimated value of d_1, and $\omega_{i1}(n)$ is the filter weight of the filter C_{i1}. It can be found that $y_1(n)$ is the superposition of the outputs of five FIR filters. Similarly, the estimated values of $d_2(n)$, $d_3(n)$, and $d_4(n)$ are expressed as follows:

$$\begin{aligned} y_2 &= \omega_{02}^T(n)x_0(n) + \omega_{12}^T(n)x_1(n) + \omega_{22}^T(n)x_2(n) + \omega_{32}^T(n)x_3(n) \\ &+ \omega_{42}^T(n)x_4(n) \end{aligned} \tag{10}$$

$$\begin{aligned} y_3 &= \omega_{03}^T(n)x_0(n) + \omega_{13}^T(n)x_1(n) + \omega_{23}^T(n)x_2(n) + \omega_{33}^T(n)x_3(n) \\ &+ \omega_{43}^T(n)x_4(n) \end{aligned} \tag{11}$$

$$\begin{aligned} y_4 &= \omega_{04}^T(n)x_0(n) + \omega_{14}^T(n)x_1(n) + \omega_{24}^T(n)x_2(n) + \omega_{34}^T(n)x_3(n) \\ &+ \omega_{44}^T(n)x_4(n) \end{aligned} \tag{12}$$

Formulas (10)–(12) can be written as a reduced version of Formula (13), which is the simulator of the vibration system.

$$Y(n) = W(n)X(n) \tag{13}$$

$$Y(n) = [y_1(n)y_2(n)y_3(n)y_4(n)]^T \tag{14}$$

$$X(n) = \left[x_0^T(n)x_1^T(n)x_2^T(n)x_3^T(n)x_4^T(n)\right]^T \tag{15}$$

$$W(n) = \begin{bmatrix} \omega_{01}^T(n) & \cdots & \omega_{41}^T(n) \\ \vdots & \ddots & \vdots \\ \omega_{04}^T(n) & \cdots & \omega_{44}^T(n) \end{bmatrix} \tag{16}$$

The simulator consists of 20 single-input/single-output filters. The matrix $W(n)$ contains the weights of 20 filters, where $W_{ij}(n)$ is the weight vector of the filter C_{ij}: i = 0, 1, 2, 3, 4 and j = 1, 2, 3, 4.

3.2. Algorithm Framework

We consider a standard reinforcement learning setting consisting of an agent interacting with a discrete-time step-size environment E. At each time step t, the agent can receive the observed value s_t, take an action a_t, and receive a scalar reward r_t. The behavior of the agent is defined according to the strategy π, which maps the state to the probability distribution of the action $\pi: S \to P(A)$. The environment E may also be random. We model it as a state-space S, action-space $A = R^N$, initial-state distribution $P(s_t)$, transition dynamics $P(s_{t+1}|s_t, a_t)$ reward function $r(s_t, a_t)$. The reward is defined as the sum of future reward discounts: $R_t = \sum_{i=t}^{r} \gamma^{i-t} r(s_i, a_i)$. The discount factor is $\gamma \in [0,1]$. The payoff depends on the chosen behavior, and therefore depends on the strategy π, and may be random. The goal of reinforcement learning is to learn a strategy that maximizes the expected revenue of the initial distribution: $J = E_{r,s_i \in E, a_i \in \pi}[R_1]$. When t = i, we use the minimum value of the output of the two critic networks, i.e., the output of $Q_{1t}(s_t, a_t)$ and $Q_{2t}(s_t, a_t)$ critic networks.

$$Q_t(s_t, a_t) = min(Q_{1t}(s_t, a_t), Q_{2t}(s_t, a_t)) \tag{17}$$

Many of the methods in reinforcement learning utilize the recursive relationship of the Bellman equation:

$$Q^\pi(s_t, a_t) = E_{r_i, s_{i+1} \in E}\left[r(s_t, a_t) + \gamma \cdot E_{a_{i+1} \in E}[Q^\pi(s_{t+1}, a_{t+1})]\right] \tag{18}$$

If the target policy is deterministic, we can describe it as a function $\mu : S \leftarrow A$, thus avoiding internal expectations.

$$Q^\pi(s_t, a_t) = E_{r_i, s_{i+1} \in E}[r(s_t, a_t) + \gamma \cdot Q^\mu(s_{t+1}, \mu(s_{t+1}))] \tag{19}$$

Expectations depend only on the environment. This means that the transfer generated by different random behavior strategies β can be used to learn the Q^μ offline strategy. We consider a function approximator with θ^Q as a parameter and optimize it by minimizing the loss:

$$L(\theta^Q) = E_{s_t \in E, a_t \in \pi, r_t \in E}\left[Q^\mu(s_{t-1}, a_t|\theta^Q) - y_t\right]^2 \tag{20}$$

$$y_t = r_t + \gamma \cdot min(Q_{1_{t+1}}(s_{t+1}, a_{t+1}), Q_{2_{t+1}}(s_{t+1}, a_{t+1})) \tag{21}$$

Here, r_t is the environmental reward, γ is the discount factor, and $t+1$ is the index of the next state.

As shown in Figure 5, the algorithm used in this paper is mainly divided into two parts: the yellow part represents the environment (simulator) and experience playback, and the virtual part is the Actor–Critic (AC) network. Specifically, first, the environment interacts with the AC network and stores multiple data (s_t, a_t, s_{t+1}) into the experience pool. Here, s_t denotes the state at time t, a_t denotes the action at time t, and s_{t+1} denotes the state at time $t+1$. Each data point in the experience pool is given an initial priority. When the data reach a certain amount, priority data sampling B is performed for the data in the experience pool. s_t is passed to the Actor network, and the Actor network is passed to the Critic a network and the Critic b network together with s_t, based on s_t's a_t. At the same time, s_{t+1} is transmitted to the Actor Target network, and the a_{t+1} obtained by the Actor Target network based on s_{t+1} is transmitted to the Critic Target c network and the Critic Target d network together with s_{t+1}. The task of the Critic networks is to score the actions obtained from the Actor network. Here, we use four Critic networks, where the Critic a network and the Critic b network take the minimum value, and the Critic Target c network and the Critic Target d network also take the minimum value. Finally, the error is calculated using the Formulas (20) and (21). The dotted arrow represents the feedback neural network, and the Actor network and Critic network are updated in this way. The Actor Target network and Critic Target network adjust the neural network parameters through weight transfer. The final error is calculated using the priority formula and then used to update the priority of the data in the experience pool. When the amount of experience pool data is large enough, older data can be removed to free up space.

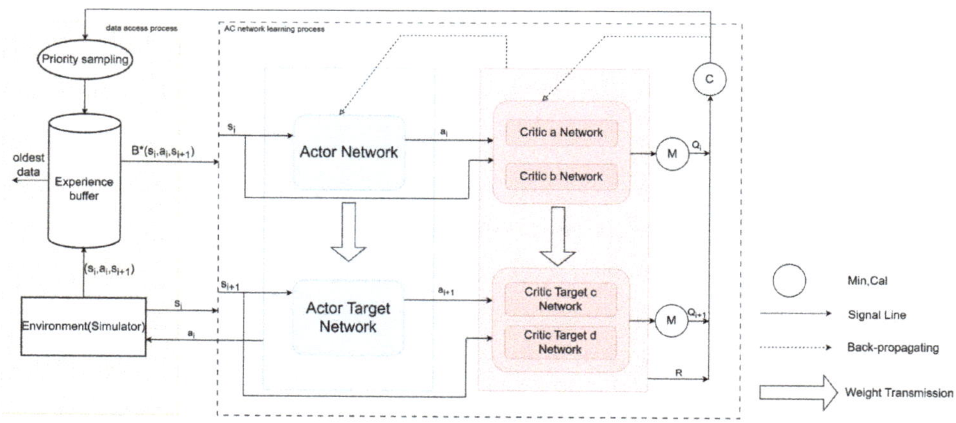

Figure 5. Algorithm framework. Specifically, the algorithm is mainly divided into two parts: the yellow part represents the environment (simulator) and experience replaying, and the dotted line part represents the AC network.

In terms of updating the parameters, the critic network parameter update is as follows:

$$\nabla_{\theta_1} J = \frac{1}{N}\sum_{i=1}^{M} (y_i - Q_{1i}(s_i, a_i)) \cdot \nabla_{\theta_1} Q_{1i}(s_i, a_i) \tag{22}$$

$$\nabla_{\theta_2} J = \frac{1}{N}\sum_{i=1}^{N} (y_i - Q_{2i}(s_i, a_i)) \cdot \nabla_{\theta_2} Q_{2i}(s_i, a_i) \tag{23}$$

The Actor network updates the strategy according to the feedback of the critic network, that is, the gradient of the Q-value function:

$$\nabla_{\theta_\mu} J = -\frac{1}{N}\sum_{i=1}^{N} Q_{1i}\left(s_i, \mu_{\theta_\mu}(s_i)\right)\cdot\nabla_{\theta_\mu}\mu_{\theta_\mu}(s_i) \quad (24)$$

where $\mu_{\theta_\mu}(s_i)$ represents the output action of the Actor network to the state s_i.

In addition, the Actor Target network and Target network update is as follows:

$$\theta_i' \leftarrow \tau\theta_i + (1-\tau)\theta_i' \quad (25)$$

$$\mu' \leftarrow \tau\mu + (1-\tau)\mu' \quad (26)$$

where i is the index of the Critic Target network and τ is the hyperparameter representing the weight of the update.

3.3. Actor–Critic (AC) Network

In this section, we focus on the AC network, where the Actor and Critic structures are the same, so we only need to explain one network structure. In order to make the network lighter and have a stronger generalization ability, we initially considered the application of convolution. However, in general, convolution requires multi-layer stacking, and too many neural network layers can easily lead to performance degradation, which may lead to gradient disappearance or gradient explosion. In order to solve this challenge, we considered and adopted the ResNet method [27]. Since we are dealing with vibration control problems, we further considered the variant deep residual shrinkage network (DRSN) [30] using ResNets.

3.3.1. Classic ResNet Architecture

The ResNet approach an emerging deep learning method that has attracted much attention in recent years [27]. Remaining building units (RBUs) are the basic components. As shown in Figure 6a, an RBU consists of two BNs, two ReLUs, two convolutional layers, and a unit shortcut. The identity shortcut is the part that makes ResNets superior to convnets in general. In general, in convolutional neural networks, the cross-entropy error gradient is propagated backward layer by layer. Using the identity shortcut, the gradient can effectively flow to the earlier layer near the input layer, so that the parameters can be updated more effectively. Figure 6b,c shows the RBUs that produce output eigenmaps of different sizes. The aim of reducing the width of the output feature map is to reduce the amount of calculation for the next layer, and the aim of increasing the number of channels of the output feature map is to facilitate the integration of different features into discriminant features. Figure 6d shows the overall architecture of a ResNet, which consists of an input layer, a convolution layer, multiple RBUs, a BN, a ReLU, a GAP, and an output full-connection (FC) layer.

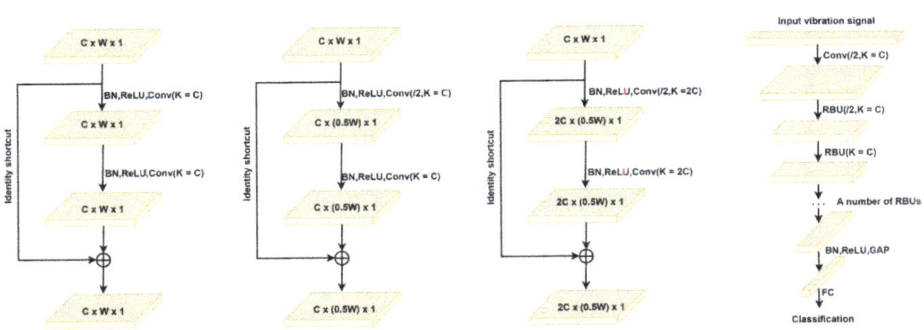

Figure 6. Three kinds of remaining building units (RBUs), including (**a**) an RBU in which the output feature map is the same size as the input feature map; (**b**) an RBU with a stride of 2, in which the

width of the output feature map is reduced to half of that of the input feature map; and (**c**) an RBU with a stride of 2 and a doubled number of convolutional kernels, in which the number of channels of the output feature map is doubled. (**d**) The overall architecture of a ResNet. In this figure, "/2" means to move the convolutional kernel with a stride of 2 to reduce the width of the output feature map; C, W, and 1 are the indicators of the number of channels, width, and height of the feature map, respectively; K is the number of convolutional kernels in the convolutional layer.

3.3.2. The Basic Architecture Design of DRSNs

In this section, the motivation for developing DRSNs is introduced, and the architecture of two developed DRSNs is described in detail, including a deep residual shrinkage network with channel-shared thresholds (DRSN-CS) and a deep residual shrinkage network with channel-wise thresholds (DRSN-CW).

(1) Theoretical background

In the past 20 years, soft threshold segmentation has often been used as a key step in many signal denoising methods [37,38]. The advantage of this method is that it transforms the original signal into a domain where the number of near-zeros is not important, and then applies the soft threshold to convert the near-zero feature to zero. In order to ensure the good performance of signal denoising, a key task of the wavelet threshold method is to design a filter to transform useful information into very positive or negative features, and transform noise information into near-zero features. However, designing such filters requires a lot of signal processing expertise and has always been a challenging problem. Deep learning provides a new way to solve this problem. Deep learning is not designed by experts, but uses the gradient descent algorithm to automatically learn the filter. The formula for the soft threshold can be expressed as follows:

$$y = \begin{cases} x + \xi & x > \xi \\ 0 & -\xi \leq x \leq \xi \\ x + \xi & x < -\xi \end{cases} \tag{27}$$

Within this formula is the input feature, the output feature, and the threshold, that is, the positive parameter. The soft threshold method does not set the negative features in the ReLU activation function to zero, but sets the features close to zero to zero, thereby retaining useful negative features.

It can be seen that the derivative of the output to the input is either 1 or 0, which can effectively prevent gradient disappearance and explosion problems. The derivative can be expressed as follows:

$$\frac{\partial_y}{\partial_x} = \begin{cases} 1 & x > \xi \\ 0 & -\xi \leq x \leq \xi \\ 1 & x < -\xi \end{cases} \tag{28}$$

In a classical signal denoising algorithm, it is usually difficult to set an appropriate value for the threshold. In addition, the optimal value varies from case to case. To solve this problem, the threshold used in the developed DRSNs is automatically determined in the deep architecture, avoiding the trouble of manual operation. In the following chapters, the method of determining the threshold in the developed DRSNs will be introduced.

(2) Developed DRSN-CS framework

The developed DRSN-CS is a variant of the ResNet, which uses soft thresholds to remove noise-related features. The soft threshold is inserted into the building unit as a nonlinear transformation layer. In addition, the value of the threshold can be learned in the building unit, as described below.

As shown in Figure 7a, unlike the RBU in Figure 6a, RSBU-CS has a dedicated module for soft threshold estimation. In this special module, Global Average Pooling (GAP) is performed on the absolute values of the feature map to obtain a one-dimensional vector.

Then, the one-dimensional vector is propagated into a two-layer FC network to obtain a scaling parameter, similar to [39].

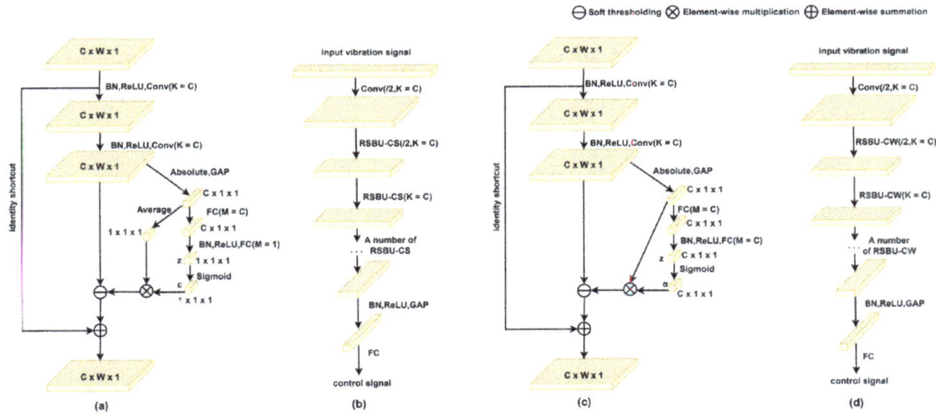

Figure 7. (**a**) A residual shrinkage building unit with channel-shared thresholds (RSBU-CS). (**b**) DRSN-CS overall architecture. (**c**) A residual shrinkage building unit with channel-shared thresholds (RSBU-CW). (**d**) DRSN-CW overall architecture, where K is the number of convolution kernels in the convolutional layer; m is the number of neurons in the FC network; and the C, W, and 1 in C × W× 1 represent the number of channels, width, and height of the feature map, respectively. When determining the threshold, the index of the feature map to be used is α.

The sigmoid function is applied at the end of the two-layer FC network so that the scaling parameters are scaled to the range of (0, 1), which can be expressed as follows:

$$\alpha = \frac{1}{1+e^{-z}} \quad (29)$$

From this equation, we can find the output of the two-layer FC network in the RSBU-CS, and the delay parameter is the corresponding scaling parameter. After that, the scaling parameter delay is multiplied by the average value of the $|x|$ score to obtain the threshold. The reason for this arrangement is that the threshold of the soft threshold should not only be positive, but also not too large. If the threshold is greater than the maximum absolute value of the feature map, the output of the soft threshold is zero. In summary, the thresholds used in the RSBU-CS are expressed as follows:

$$\xi = \alpha \cdot \underset{i,j,c}{average} \left| x_{i,j,c} \right| \quad (30)$$

Here, α is the threshold, and i, j, and c are the width, height, and channel index of the feature map, respectively. The threshold can be kept within a reasonable range so that the output of the soft threshold will not be all zeroes. The two-step RSBU-CS with a doubled number of channels can be constructed similar to the RBUs in Figure 6b,c.

The brief architecture of the developed DRSN-CS is shown in Figure 7b, which is similar to the classic ResNet in Figure 6d. The only difference is that the RSBU-CS is used as a building block instead of RBUs. Multiple RSBU-CSs are stacked in the DRSN-CS to gradually reduce noise-related features. Another advantage of the DRSN-CS is that the thresholds are automatically learned in the deep architecture, rather than being manually set by experts. Therefore, professional signal processing knowledge is not required to implement the developed DRSN-CS.

(3) *Developed DRSN-CW framework*

The developed DRSN-CW is another variant of a ResNet. Unlike the DRSN-CS, it applies a separate threshold to each channel of the feature map, which will be introduced below. Figure 7c shows the RSBU-CW. Through absolute operation and the GAP layer, the upper and lower lines of the feature map x are reduced to one-dimensional vectors, and they are propagated to the two-layer FC network.

$$\alpha_c = \frac{1}{1+e^{-z_c}} \tag{31}$$

Here, z_c is the feature at the cth neuron, and α_c is the cth scaling parameter. After that, the threshold can be calculated:

$$\xi_c = \alpha_c \cdot \underset{i,j}{average}\left|x_{i,j,c}\right| \tag{32}$$

where i, j, and c denote the width, height, and channel index of the feature map x, respectively. Similar to the DRSN-CS, the threshold can be positive and maintained within a reasonable range to prevent the output feature from being all zeros.

The overall architecture of the developed DRSN-CW is shown in Figure 7d. By superimposing multiple RSBU-CWs, through various nonlinear transformations, the soft threshold is used as the shrinkage function to learn the discriminant features and eliminate the noise-related information.

(4) *Detailed Network Architecture of the Actor*

In Figure 8, there are dashed- and solid-line skips. When the input and output dimensions are the same (solid-line skips), residual learning is directly applied, i.e., $x + f(x)$, where $f(x)$ represents the output result of the construction unit. In cases where the dimensions increase (dashed-line skips), matching dimensions occur (achieved by 1×1 convolution) with a stride of 2. Finally, through Avgpooling and flattening, we obtain [B, 32], which, via FC, leads to [B, 4] dimensions, representing the action signals from four sensors. The structure of the Critic's four networks resembles that of the Actor network, differing only in the input and output. The input is $\{s_t, a_t\}$[= {[B, 1, 4, 100], [B, 4]}, and the output is [B, 1]. Here, the input data are preprocessed as [B, 1, 4, 101], signifying 100 dimensions for each sensor's data and the action's value.

3.4. Multi-Reward Mechanism

The multi-reward mechanism is a technology in reinforcement learning that is used to introduce and process multiple reward signals more effectively to enhance the learning and decision-making ability of agents. In some complex environments, a single reward signal may not fully express the diversity and complexity of the environment. Therefore, the introduction of multiple reward signals helps to provide more comprehensive and accurate training signals to improve the learning process and strategies. Compared with the previous method [26], the reward function is as follows:

$$r_{OM} = -\left(x_1^2 + x_2^2 + x_3^2 + x_4^2\right) \tag{33}$$

We propose three other reward functions, as follows (34)–(36):

$$r_{MSV} = -\frac{1}{N} \cdot \sum_{i=1}^{N} \left(x_{1i}^2 + x_{2i}^2 + x_{3i}^2 + x_{4i}^2\right) \tag{34}$$

As shown in Formula (34), considering the mean square of four sensors over a period of time as the reward signal helps to reduce noise and fluctuations, making it smoother. This aids the agent to better understand the long-term trends of the environment, avoiding excessive interference from individual time-step rewards, and improving the stability and reliability of training. This approach also helps the agent to better consider long-term gains, reinforcing awareness of long-term planning and decision making rather than just focusing on immediate rewards. Averaging the reward signal also reduces the impact of environmental noise and randomness, enhancing the agent's ability to handle complex situations. Overall, adopting the average value over a period of time as the reward function can improve training stability, smooth the reward signal, better consider long-term gains, and enhance the agent's resistance to interference, effectively improving the training effectiveness of reinforcement learning models.

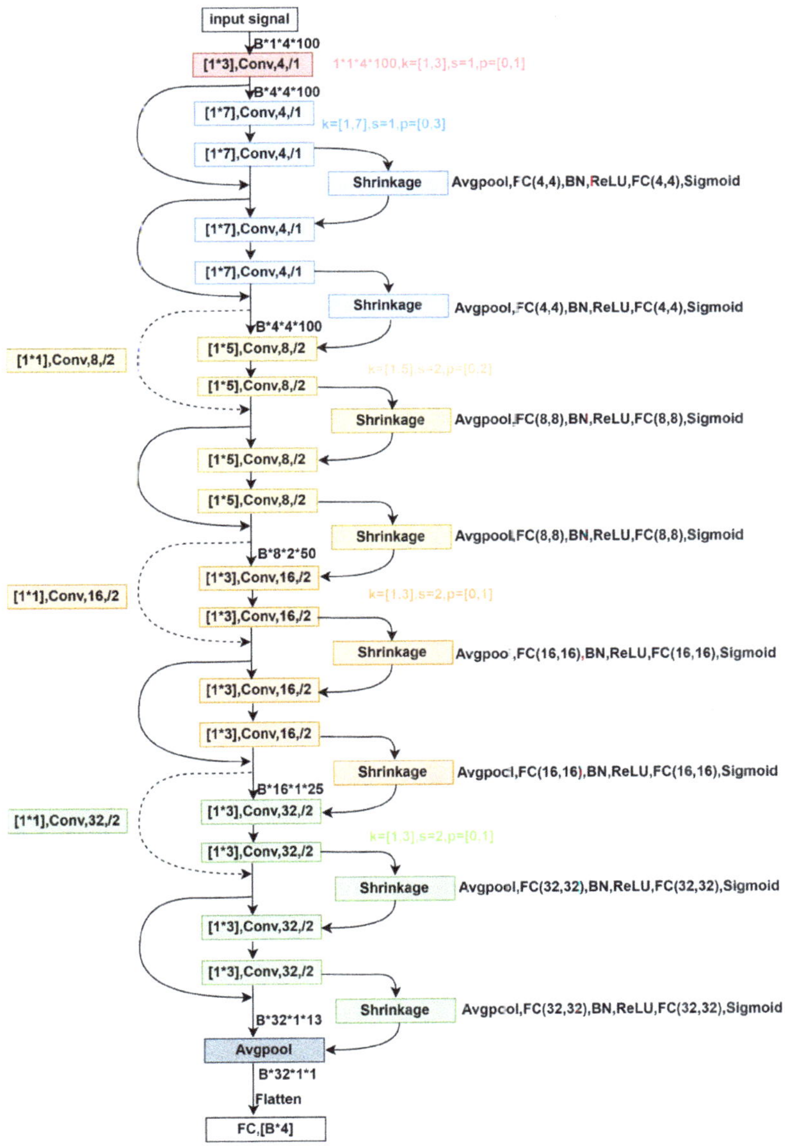

Figure 8. The DRSN_CW with 18 layers. Our Actor network is influenced by the ResNet architecture, with differences in each layer's convolutional kernels, stride, and channels, and an added shrinkage

component. Specifically, the input data dimensions are [B, 1, 4, 100], where B represents the batch size, 4 indicates the four sensors, 100 signifies 100 time dimensions, and 1 denotes a reserved specific feature dimension. The data pass through a red-colored convolutional layer with a kernel size of [1, 3], a stride of 1, an input channel of 1, and an output channel of 4, resulting in data dimensions of [B, 4, 4, 100]. The setting for convolutional layers within the same-colored modules remains consistent. Every two convolutional modules combined with the shrinkage component form an RSBU-CW construction unit, where units of the same color share the same network settings.

$$\begin{aligned} r_{RMSE} &= -\frac{1}{M}\cdot\sum_{j=1}^{M}\sqrt{\frac{\sum_{i=1}^{N}x_{ji}^2}{N}} \\ &= -\frac{1}{M}\cdot\left(\sqrt{\frac{\sum_{i=1}^{N}x_{1i}^2}{N}}+\sqrt{\frac{\sum_{i=1}^{N}x_{2i}^2}{N}}+\sqrt{\frac{\sum_{i=1}^{N}x_{3i}^2}{N}}+\sqrt{\frac{\sum_{i=1}^{N}x_{4i}^2}{N}}\right) \end{aligned} \tag{35}$$

As shown in Formula (35), adopting the average of the root mean square (RMSE) of four sensors as the reward function has several advantages. Firstly, compared to extreme values, it exhibits higher robustness and stability. This means that the RMSE has less impact on the reward function when dealing with outliers, more evenly considers the overall characteristics of the data, and is less affected by extreme values. Additionally, the RMSE, being the square root of the mean square error, provides a more intuitive and understandable measurement. Compared to the mean square error, RMSE offers a more intuitive description of the error magnitude, emphasizing the size of the average error rather than the square of errors. It is noteworthy that the RMSE is less influenced by noise because it takes the square root of the mean error, resulting in a smoother signal. In certain situations, the RMSE better reflects real-world error scenarios, aligning more closely with the background and requirements of actual tasks. Lastly, due to its wide applicability, the RMSE as a reward function is suitable for various problems and scenarios and is commonly used in performance evaluation. In conclusion, selecting the RMSE as the reward function can provide a more robust, smooth, and understandable reward signal for training, helping the agent learn and adapt to the environment more effectively.

$$r_v = -\sum_{j=1}^{M}\frac{\sum_{i=1}^{N}\left(x_{ji}-\overline{x}_j\right)^2}{N} \tag{36}$$

As shown in Formula (36), adopting the average of the variance of the four sensors as the reward function has unique advantages. It is a statistical measure of data dispersion, providing a metric for the diversity of behaviors exhibited by the agent in reinforcement learning. By evaluating the degree of behavioral variation, variance helps us to understand the consistency and diversity of the agent's actions across different states. Additionally, variance also reflects the stability of the agent's policy execution. A smaller variance may indicate more consistent and predictable behavioral patterns, while a larger variance implies more diversified actions taken across different states. Variance also indicates the agent's sensitivity to environmental changes, and its adaptability to environmental changes can also be measured through variance. Overall, variance as a reward function provides a quantitative measure of the diversity, stability, and adaptability of the agent's behavior in reinforcement learning. By assessing behavioral changes, variance helps us to gain insight into the agent's learning process and strategy adjustments, guiding its optimization in complex environments.

We combine the influence of four different reward functions on the control strategy. Through comparative experiments, the optimal reward method is obtained, which can be seen in the subsequent analyses.

3.5. Priority Experience Replaying

The motivation of introducing priority experience replaying is to optimize the training process and solve the problems in traditional experience replaying. The traditional replaying method treats all empirical samples equally, but in fact, some experience is more important for model learning. Priority experience replaying introduces a mechanism that can focus more frequently on learning those experiences that have a greater impact on the model, thereby improving the efficiency of training and the performance of the model. In order to overcome these problems, we introduce a random sampling method [40] between pure greedy priority and uniform random sampling. We ensure that the probability of being sampled in the priority of a transition is monotonic, and that the probability is non-zero even for the transition of the lowest priority. Specifically, we define the probability i of the sampling transition as follows:

$$P(i) = \frac{p_i^{\alpha}}{\sum_k p_k^{\alpha}} \tag{37}$$

where $P_i > 0$ is the priority of conversion i. The index α determines how much priority is used, and $\alpha = 0$ corresponds to the uniform case.

The first variant we consider is a direct, proportional priority, where $P_i = |\delta_i| + \varepsilon$, and ε is a small positive constant that prevents the transition edge from not being revisited once the error is zero. The second variant is an indirect, rank-based priority, where $P_i = \frac{1}{rank(i)}$, and $rank(i)$ is the level of data i sorted by $|\delta_i$ in the experience pool. In this case, P becomes a power-law distribution with exponent α. In error, both distributions are monotonic, but the latter is more robust because it is not sensitive to outliers.

In order to effectively sample from the distribution in Equation (37), the complexity cannot depend on the capacity N of the empirical pool. For rank-based variants, we can approximate the cumulative density function using a piecewise linear function with k equal probability segments. The segment boundaries can be calculated in advance (they only change when N or α changes). At runtime, we sample a fragment and then uniformly sample it in the transformation. This is especially effective when combined with minibatch-based learning algorithms: selecting k as the size of the minibatch and sampling a transition from each segment precisely is a form of stratified sampling that has the additional advantage of balancing the minibatch. The proportional variables are different, and also allow effective implementation based on the "sum-tree" data structure (where each node is the sum of its child nodes, and the priority is the leaf node), which can be effectively updated and sampled.

4. Experimental Results and Discussion

This chapter mainly introduces some comparative experiments and ablation experiments, including lightweight comparative experiments, priority experience replaying comparative experiments, optimal reward function combination, demonstrating the feasibility of this lightweight method, alleviating overestimation experiments, and relevant comparative experiments.

4.1. Lightweight Comparative Experiment

Under narrowband white-noise excitation ranging from 0 to 100 Hz, with 0.3 s of data for root mean square calculation, Table 1 illustrates the setup of platform simulators for vibration control using our DRSL-MPER algorithm and under the DDPG framework using fully connected (FC), CNN, GoogleNet, and LSTM methods. The first column indicates various algorithms; the second column shows the values of the vibration signal before being controlled, measured in volts (V); the third column displays the values of the vibration signal after being controlled, also measured in volts (V); the fourth column indicates the parameter quantity, measured as a number (N), representing the total number of weight parameters and bias parameters in the neural network; and the fifth column represents the degree of vibration signal reduction, measured in decibels (dB).

Reference [26] proposed the fully connected network and DDPG framework as the primary points of comparison, detailing their parameters and vibration reduction levels. Considering the prevalent use of fully connected network methods in the current domain, we introduced methods such as convolutional neural networks (CNNs), GoogLeNet, and Long Short-Term Memory networks (LSTMs) to expand the experimental scope; relevant parameters and vibration reduction levels are listed in the table above. Under narrowband white-noise excitation ranging from 0 to 100 Hz, our DRSL-MPER method achieved a vibration reduction of up to 20.240 dB with a reduction in parameters by more than 7.5 times. A greater reduction indicates better vibration control effectiveness.

Table 1. Lightweight comparison experiment. Under the same experimental conditions, the method proposed in this paper achieves better control effectiveness with fewer parameters. The first row represents the algorithm, the second row displays the vibration signal values before being controlled, the third row shows the vibration signal values after being controlled, the fourth row indicates the parameter quantity, and the fifth row represents the reduction in vibration control, measured in dB.

Algorithm	Uncontrolled (V)	Controlled (V)	Parameter (N)	Reduction (dB)
FC	0.3311	0.0762	507398	12.750
CNN	0.3311	0.0870	3102254	11.604
GoogleNet	0.3311	0.0812	15774938	11.894
LSTM	0.3311	0.0875	375326	11.516
DRSL-MPER	0.3311	0.0328	67554	20.240

4.2. Comparison between Prioritized Experience Replaying and Non-Prioritized Experience Replaying

To clearly present the experimental results, we visualized the time-domain signals before and after the control, the frequency-domain signals obtained through Fourier transformation, the action-value signals, and the reward values. Similar experimental results are also summarized here for subsequent experiments. As shown in Figure 9, the first row (a)–(d) displays the time-domain control signals, where the x-axis represents time and the y-axis represents the control signal in volts (V); the second row (e)–(f) illustrates the frequency-domain control signals, with the x-axis representing the frequency range in Hz and the y-axis indicating the values after Fourier transformation (FFT); the third row (i)–(l) represents the action values of the agent; and the fourth row (m) represents the reward values. In the latter two rows, the x-axis represents time and the y-axis represents the magnitude of the action values or the number of rounds for the reward values. Although reward values may be negative, higher values indicate better control effectiveness, albeit not absolutely. These visualizations help demonstrate the performance of the algorithm during the control process and the variations in signals.

Figure 10 illustrates how the utilization of prioritized experience replay enhances the convergence speed and control effectiveness under both DRSN and TD3 reinforcement learning frameworks. Under narrowband white-noise excitation ranging from 0 to 100 Hz, Figure 10a shows that optimal performance is reached after approximately 2500 iterations, while Figure 10b shows that the same is achieved after only 1300 iterations, showcasing a convergence speed close to twice that of non-experience replay. To validate the effectiveness of prioritized experience replay, we conducted training with and without prioritized experience replay for 1000 episodes, as shown in Figure 10c,d, respectively. Through calculations, Figure 10c demonstrates a vibration reduction of 7.9 dB without prioritized experience replay, while Figure 10d indicates a reduction of up to 12.5 dB with prioritized experience replay. These contrasting experiments reveal that training with prioritized experience replay is more stable and exhibits higher data efficiency.

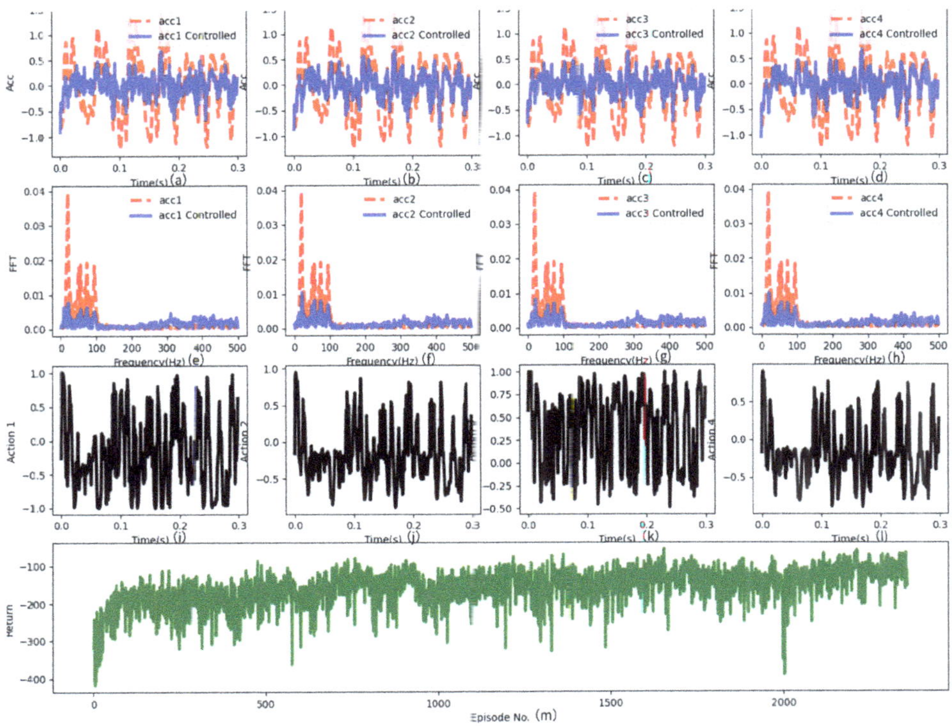

Figure 9. The control signal, Fourier transform signal, action signal, and reward value obtained through experimentation. The first row (**a–d**) exhibits the time-domain signals from four sensors, where the x-axis denotes time steps (300 time points were captured in the experiment, scaled to the range [0.0, 0.3] by dividing by 1000), while the y-axis represents the original signal in red and the controlled signal in blue. Clearly, through effective algorithmic control, the blue signals gradually shift towards zero. The second row (**e–h**) displays the frequency-domain signals obtained by performing Fourier transforms on the data from the first row for each sensor. It is noticeable that the red non-controlled signals primarily concentrate within the range of [0–100] Hz, with fewer signals in other frequency domains. However, the controlled blue signals exhibit a significant reduction in the frequency domain. The third row (**i–l**) illustrates the control signals emitted by the controller. The x-axis corresponds to the same time steps as in the first row, while the y-axis represents control signal values within the range of [−1.0, 1.0], due to the final network layer of the controller utilizing the tanh activation function. The final row (m) represents the reward values, where the x-axis indicates the episode, and the y-axis depicts the reward value for each episode.

4.3. Optimal Reward Function Combination

To explore the most suitable combination of reward functions, we synthesized the original reward function, variance, root mean square, and mean from [26], as detailed in Table 2. Under the conditions of employing both DRSN methods in the Actor and Critic networks, along with the application of prioritized experience replay, we experimented with various combinations of reward functions and drew conclusions. When used individually, the original reward function performed the poorest compared to variance, root mean square, and mean. Among the combined functions, as highlighted in red, the combination with the root mean square exhibited the most favorable effects. However, the data highlighted in blue indicated that the original reward function might have a detrimental impact on the combination, often leading to decreased performance. Therefore, we recommend using the combination of root mean square and mean values, which performs better in most cases, resulting in the maximum reduction of up to 20.240 dB.

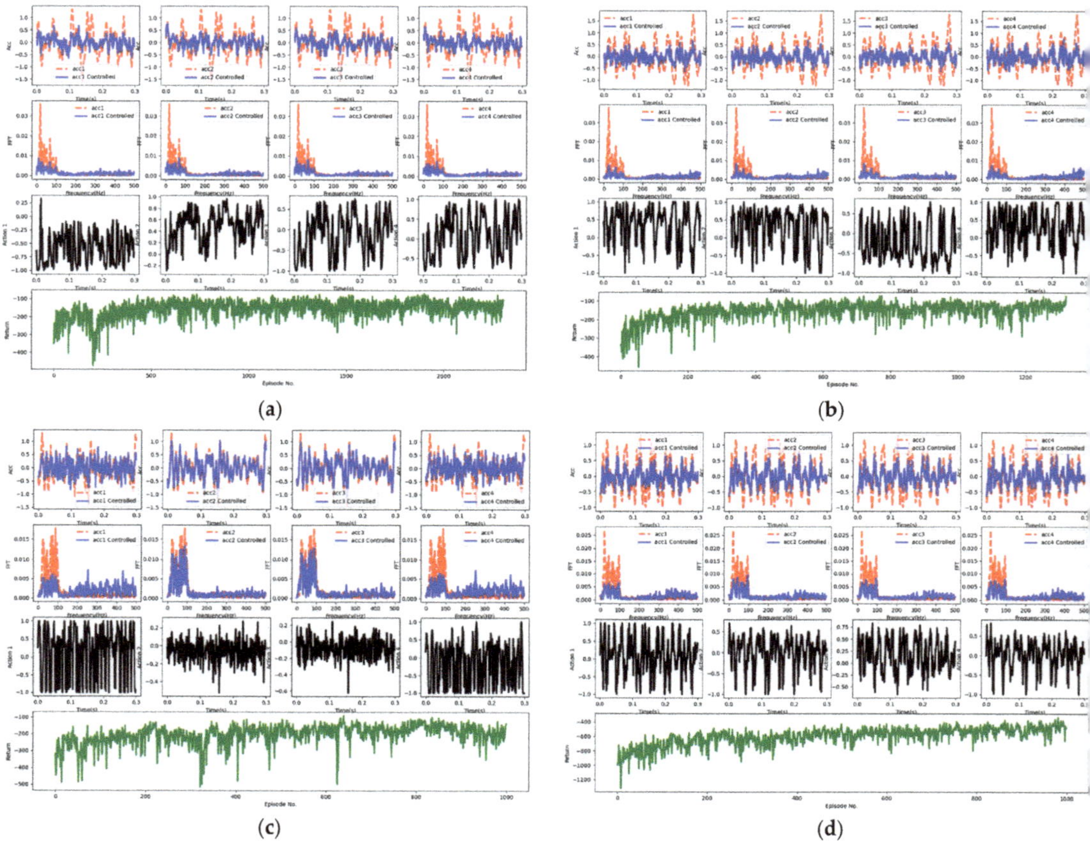

(**a**) (**b**) (**c**) (**d**)

Figure 10. In this figure, (**a**) depicts the network with DRSN and TD3 framework without prioritized experience replay, while (**b**) shows the network with DRSN and TD3 framework with prioritized experience replay; (**c**) represents training without prioritized experience replay for 1000 episodes, and (**d**) illustrates training with prioritized experience replay for 1000 episodes.

Table 2. In the cases of TD3 and DRSN, with combinations of multiple reward functions, we denote the variance, mean square value, root mean square, and original method as V, MSV, RMS, and OM, respectively. In the same experimental setting, the OM reward function exhibits negative effects, while the root mean square generates positive impacts.

V, MSV, RMS, OM	Reduction (dB)
V	15.988
MSV	16.032
RMS	16.284
OM	13.722
V, MSV	3.496
V, RMS	16.094
V, OM	12.062
MSV, RMS	20.240
MSV, OM	3.518

Table 2. *Cont.*

V, MSV, RMS, OM	Reduction (dB)
RMS, OM	9.238
V, MSV, RMS	16.402
V, MSV, OM	15.598
V, RMS, OM	2.234
MSV, RMS, OM	15.074
V, MSV, RMS, OM	13.858

4.4. Demonstrating the Feasibility of This Lightweight Method

To verify the feasibility of the lightweight method, we compared the performance of the fully connected networks under different settings. In this experiment, the Actor network structure was [400, x, x, 4], and the Critic network structure was [400, x, x, 1], where x is an integer. For both Figure 11a,b we gradually increased the size of the neural network's intermediate layers from 8 to 16, to 32, to 64, to 128, doubling each layer. In Figure 11a, the different colors represent different numbers of intermediate layers in the Critic network. As the number of intermediate layers in the Actor network increased, the effectiveness of vibration control gradually improved. In Figure 11b, the different colors represent different numbers of intermediate layers in the Actor network. As the number of intermediate layers in the Critic network increased, the effectiveness of vibration control also increased. In our DRSL-MPER method, the Actor and Critic networks used the same network structure, with parameter counts of 22,584 and 44,970, respectively, achieving a control effect of 20.24 dB. In contrast, when the intermediate layer size was 64, the Actor had 30,084 parameters, the Critic had 59,906 parameters, and the control effect reached 5.358 dB, which is close to our method in terms of the parameter count. This indicates that DRSL-MPER increased the damping effect by 14.882 dB with fewer parameters. In comparison, the best control effect occurred when the intermediate layers of both the Actor and Critic were 256, achieving a control effect of 15.57 dB. The Actor had 169,476 parameters, the Critic had 337,922 parameters, and DRSL-MPER improved the control effect by 4.67 dB with only 13% of the parameters of the 256-layer network. These results clearly demonstrate the significant advantages of our lightweight network in relation to both its effectiveness and its parameter count.

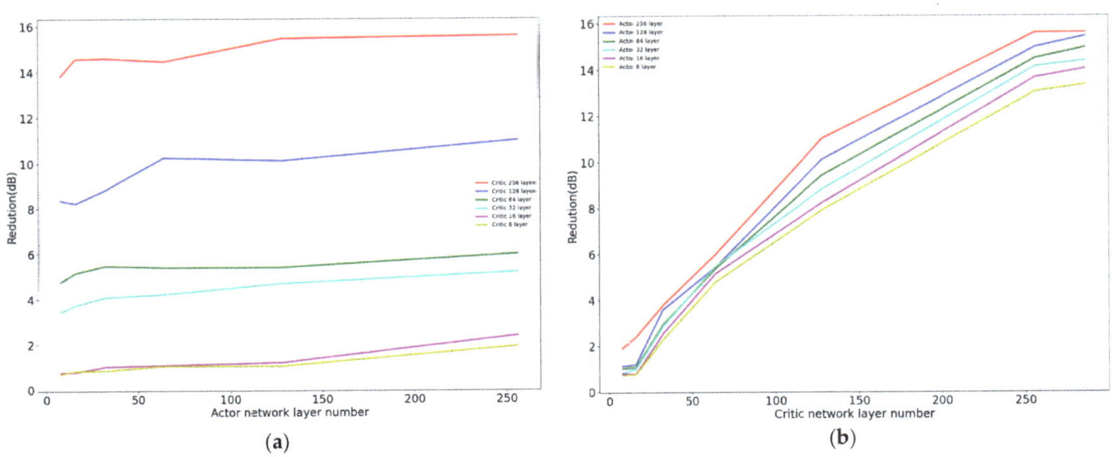

Figure 11. Impact diagrams of different Actor/Critic parameters on vibration control. Through experiments with varying numbers of FC layers in the Actor/Critic networks, this study demonstrates

the superiority of the proposed method in terms of both the parameter efficiency and control effectiveness. (**a**) With fixed Critic parameters, the effect of Actor parameter variation on vibration control. Here, the Actor network structure is [400, x, x, 4], where the horizontal x-axis represents a reduction in Actor network layers, and the vertical axis denotes the control rate (percentage), the ratio of controlled to uncontrolled states before and after the control process. (**b**) With fixed Actor parameters, the effect of Critic parameter variation on vibration control. The Critic network structure is [400, x, x, 1], where the horizontal x-axis represents a reduction in Critic network layers, and the vertical axis denotes the control rate (percentage), the ratio of controlled to uncontrolled states before and after the control process.

4.5. Alleviating Overestimation Experiments

This study adopts the TD3 algorithm, aiming to alleviate the common problem of value function overestimation in the Actor–Critic architecture. The Actor–Critic algorithm combines value function approximation (Critic) and policy approximation (Actor), where the Critic is responsible for estimating state-value or action-value functions, and the Actor updates the policy based on these estimates. However, due to errors in function approximation, nonlinear approximations, and limited sample sizes, the Critic network in the Actor–Critic algorithm often overestimates the true value, leading to suboptimal or even unstable policies. This experiment compared the DDPG framework with the TD3 framework. We recorded their Q-values and true values across 10,000 episodes. In Figure 12, the horizontal axis represents the episodes, and the vertical axis represents the magnitude of Q-values. Figure 12a shows the Q-values and true values of DDPG. It is observed that the Q-values are consistently higher than the true values, which also proves the existence of overestimation in the AC framework. Next, we introduced the TD3 framework, and in Figure 12b, it is shown that the Q-values of TD3 overlap significantly with the true values, indicating that the TD3 framework effectively alleviates the overestimation problem.

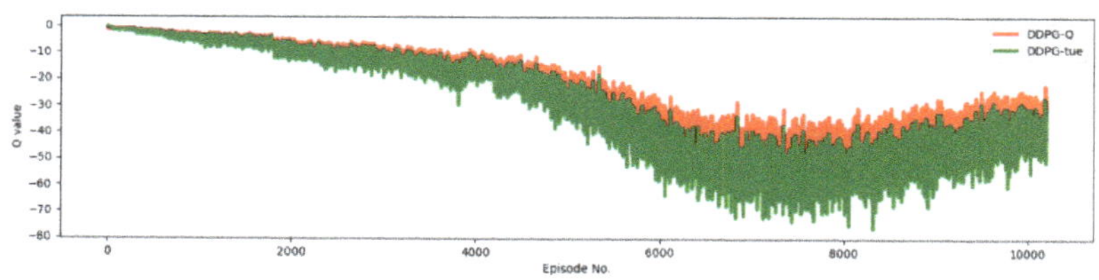

(**a**)

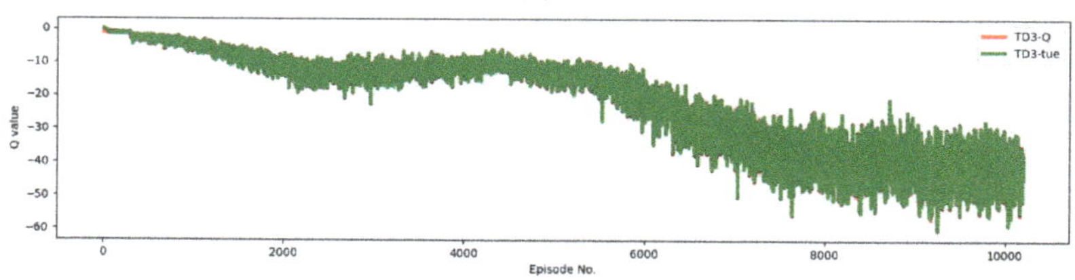

(**b**)

Figure 12. Comparison between the DDPG and TD3 frameworks, confirming the overestimation phenomenon in DDPG. The TD3 framework leverages the minimum value from two networks, mitigating the overestimation issue inherent in the DDPG framework. (**a**) The Q-values and ground-truth values for DDPG. (**b**) The Q-values and ground-truth values for TD3.

4.6. Relevant Comparative Experiments

4.6.1. Relevant Comparative Experiments for Lightweightness

In Section 4.1, we emphasized the feasibility and advantages of the lightweighting approach. To gain further insights into the impact of lightweighting experiments on different modules and parameter quantities, we conducted comparative experiments specifically focusing on the Actor, Critic, and reinforcement learning frameworks. The baseline model comprised Actor and Critic networks with fully connected layers of a 256 size (FC_{256}), utilizing the DDPG reinforcement learning framework. In Table 3, the first column represents the Actor network structure, the second column denotes the Critic network structure, the third column indicates the reinforcement learning framework, the fourth column details the total parameter count, and the fifth column presents the reduction, where smaller values are preferred. The experimental findings reveal that the DRSN performs better than FC_{256} in both the Actor and Critic networks. Additionally, despite the TD3 algorithm increasing the parameter count under the same network structure, there is a significant enhancement in the control effectiveness, and the increased parameter count remains within an acceptable range. Furthermore, we observed that improvements in the Critic network have a more pronounced impact on control effectiveness compared to improvements in the Actor network. The best vibration reduction can reach up to 20.240 dB.

Table 3. The impact of Actor and Critic networks as well as the reinforcement learning framework in the lightweighting comparative experiments. By controlling the Actor network, Critic network, RL framework, and parameter count, it was observed that in both the DDPG and TD3 frameworks, the influence of the Critic network on control effectiveness outweighs that of the Actor network.

Actor	Critic	RL	Parameter (N)	Reduction (dB)
FC_{256}	FC_{256}	DDPG	338437	12.722
DRSN	FC_{256}	DDPG	191545	13.102
FC_{256}	DRSN	DDPG	191961	14.727
DRSN	DRSN	DDPG	45069	12.966
FC_{256}	FC_{256}	TD3	507398	14.276
DRSN	FC_{256}	TD3	350506	16.196
FC_{256}	DRSN	TD3	214446	13.014
DRSN	DRSN	TD3	67554	20.240

4.6.2. Relevant Comparative Experiments for Prioritized Experience Replay

In Section 4.2, we emphasized the superiority of prioritized experience replay under the DRSN and TD3 reinforcement learning frameworks. To further demonstrate its generalizability, we conducted multiple experiments. Figure 13a–f demonstrate the enhanced data utilization efficiency by prioritized experience replay under both fully connected and DRSN conditions. Both (a) and (b) adopt the DDPG framework under the DRSN. In (a), the number of rounds taken to reach convergence under prioritized experience replay is around 350, while in (b), convergence is achieved at approximately 700 rounds. Both (c) and (d) utilize the TD3 framework under the fully connected network. In (c), the number of rounds taken to achieve convergence under prioritized experience replay is approximately 350, while in (f), convergence is not reached even after 1750 rounds. Both (e) and (f) adopt the DDPG framework under the fully connected network. In (e), the number of rounds taken to reach convergence under prioritized experience replay is approximately 400, with a vibration reduction of 9.25 dB, while in (f), convergence is achieved at approximately 600 rounds, with a vibration reduction of 3.53 dB. Both the DDPG and TD3 reinforcement learning algorithms exhibit effectiveness, highlighting that prioritized experience replay is not constrained by specific neural network architectures or reinforcement learning frameworks. It fundamentally enhances data utilization efficiency, proving its generalizability. While Figure 13a–f differ in the network structures, Figure 13 showcases more pronounced control effects, indirectly validating the feasibility of the DRSN method.

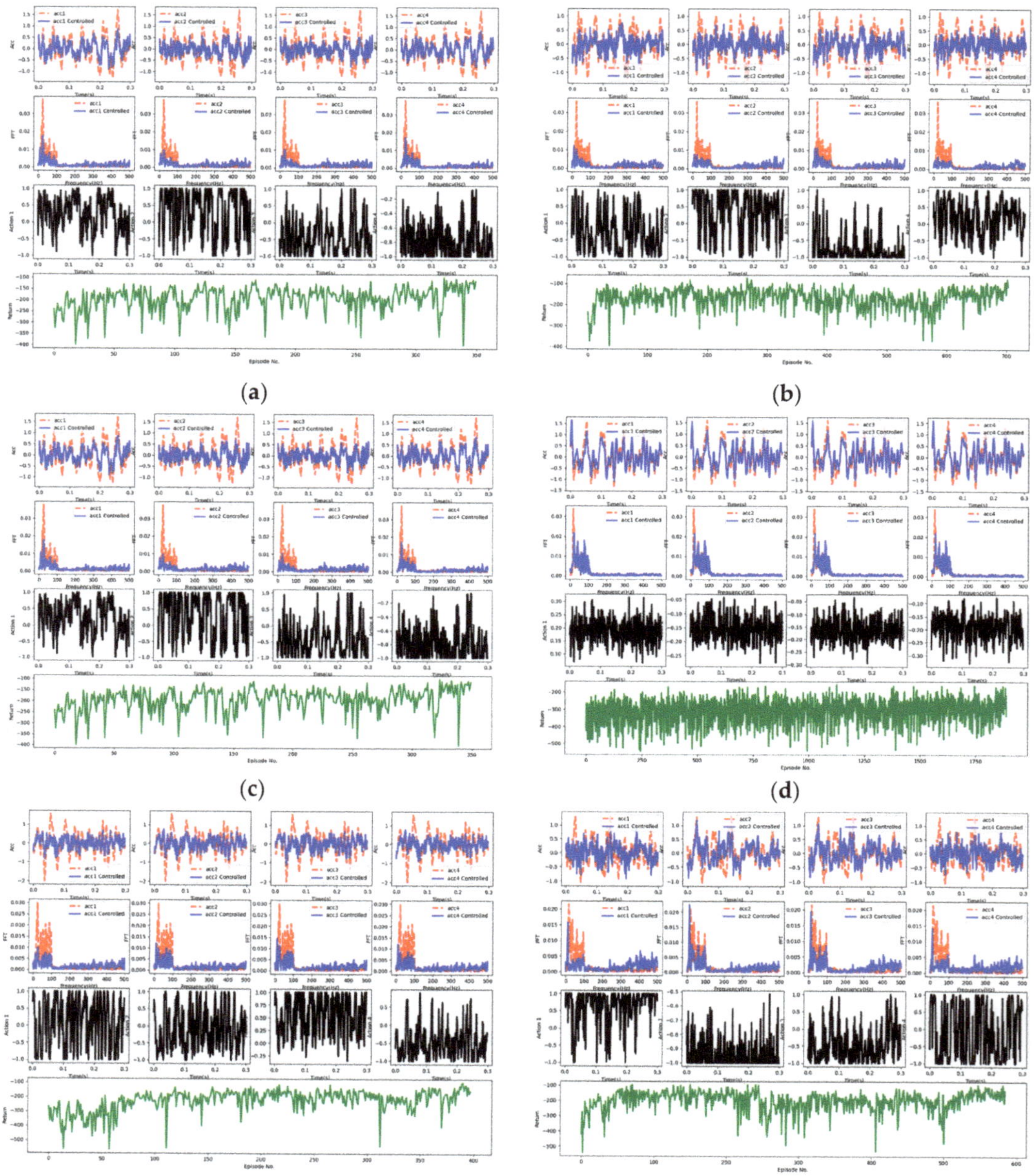

Figure 13. (**a**) Prioritized experience replay with the DRSN under the DDPG framework. (**b**) Non-prioritized experience replay with the DRSN under the DDPG framework. (**c**) Prioritized experience replay with the fully connected network under the TD3 framework. (**d**) Non-prioritized experience replay with fully connected network under the TD3 framework. (**e**) Prioritized experience replay with the fully connected network under the DDPG framework. (**f**) Non-prioritized experience replay with the fully connected network under the DDPG framework.

4.6.3. Relevant Comparative Experiments for the Optimal Reward Functions

In Section 4.3, we discussed the optimal reward function combinations within the DRSN and TD3 frameworks. To further investigate the applicability of these reward functions, we conducted additional studies under baseline experimental conditions, namely within the FC_{256} and DDPG frameworks. In Tables 2 and 4, similar trends can be observed. The data points highlighted in red indicate the superior effectiveness of combining the root mean square function. Conversely, the data points highlighted in blue suggest that the original reward function may adversely impact the combined performance, often resulting in inferior outcomes. Therefore, we recommend employing a combination of the root mean square and mean square value functions.

Table 4. In the cases of DDPG and FC_{256}, with combinations of multiple reward functions, we denote the variance, mean square value, root mean square, and original method as V, MSV, RMS, and OM, respectively. We assign a rating to the reward functions, utilizing measurements before and after the control process.

V, MSV, RMS, OM	Reduction (dB)
V	10.458
MSV	11.990
RMS	13.506
OM	9.156
V, MSV	1.938
V, RMS	13.386
V, OM	6.504
MSV, RMS	13.524
MSV, OM	2.256
RMS, OM	5.43
V, MSV, RMS	13.096
V, MSV, OM	11.508
V, RMS, OM	1.284
MSV, RMS, OM	10.526
V, MSV, RMS, OM	9.318

4.6.4. Ablation Experiments

In this section, ablation experiments were conducted on a narrowband white-noise excitation dataset ranging from 0 to 100 Hz to verify the effectiveness of the proposed modules. Table 5 illustrates the various methods studied alongside average convergence episodes, parameters, and reduction levels. We noticed that compared to the baseline, the introduction of the DRSN not only reduced the parameters by approximately 6.5 times but also increased the damping effect by 2.6 dB. Furthermore, the inclusion of the $R_{MSV+RMS}$ reward function resulted in an additional damping improvement of 0.882 dB. Subsequently, the introduction of prioritized experience replay reduced the average convergence rounds to 634 times. Lastly, the integration of the TD3 framework, although it increased the parameters and rounds slightly, did not affect the overall performance, yet achieved the peak control effectiveness of 20.240 dB.

Table 5. In the ablation experiments, OM, MSV, RMS, and PER, respectively, represent the original method, mean square value, root mean square, and prioritized experience replay. The ablation experiments demonstrated the efficiency of DRSN lightweighting and the MSV + RMS combination function, with a faster convergence speed for PER.

Algorithm	Average Convergence Episodes	Parameter	Reduction (dB)
Baseline DDPG (FC + R_{OM})	2031	338437	12.728
DDPG (DRSN + R_{OM})	1562	45069	15.328

Table 5. *Cont.*

Algorithm	Average Convergence Episodes	Parameter	Reduction (dB)
DDPG (DRSN + $R_{MSV+RMS}$)	1468	45069	16.210
DDPG (DRSN + $R_{MSV+RMS}$ + PER)	634	45069	18.108
DRSL-MPER (TD3 + DRSN + $R_{MSV+RMS}$ + PER)	652	67554	20.240

5. Conclusions

This work introduces a multi-reward mechanism to assist lightweight networks in finding nearly optimal control strategies. Additionally, a prioritized experience replay mechanism is introduced to assign priority to data, accelerating the convergence speed of neural networks and enhancing data utilization efficiency. The incorporation of a deep residual contraction network achieves adaptive denoising and lightweighting of the neural networks, making it currently one of the most preferable methods under real-world conditions. In these experiments, we utilized a continuous length of 100 time points from each sensor as the state, and our plans for future research involve further exploration of appropriate time point lengths for the sensors. Furthermore, the consideration of convolutional hyperparameters is also deemed worthwhile. Future research directions should encompass migrating this method to force control and magnetic control, as well as registration and classification tasks in medical imaging. Through these efforts, we aim to continuously optimize and advance the application of this method in various domains.

Author Contributions: Conceptualization, Y.S. and C.H.; methodology, Y.S.; software, C.H.; validation, L.Q., B.X. and W.L.; formal analysis, L.Q.; investigation, B.X.; resources, W.L.; data curation, Y.S.; writing—original draft preparation, C.H.; writing—review and editing, Y.S.; visualization, C.H.; supervision, L.Q.; project administration, W.L.; funding acquisition, B.X. All authors have read and agreed to the published version of the manuscript.

Funding: This research was funded in part by the National Natural Science Foundation of China 62276040, 62331008, National Major Scientific Research Instrument Development Project of China 62027827, National Natural Science Foundation of Chongqing CSTB2022NSCQ-MSX0436.

Institutional Review Board Statement: Not applicable.

Informed Consent Statement: Not applicable.

Data Availability Statement: The original contributions presented in the study are included in the article, further inquiries can be directed to the corresponding authors.

Conflicts of Interest: The authors declare no conflicts of interest.

References

1. Ab Talib, M.H.; Mat Darus, I.Z.; Mohd Samin, P.; Mohd Yatim, H.; Ardani, M.I.; Shaharuddin, N.M.R.; Hadi, M.S. Vibration control of semi-active suspension system using PID controller with advanced firefly algorithm and particle swarm optimization. *J. Ambient. Intell. Humaniz. Comput.* **2021**, *12*, 1119–1137. [CrossRef]
2. Li, W.; Yang, Z.; Li, K.; Wang, W. Hybrid feedback PID-FxLMS algorithm for active vibration control of cantilever beam with piezoelectric stack actuator. *J. Sound Vib.* **2021**, *509*, 116243. [CrossRef]
3. Wang, L.; Liu, J.; Yang, C.; Wu, D. A novel interval dynamic reliability computation approach for the risk evaluation of vibration active control systems based on PID controllers. *Appl. Math. Model.* **2021**, *92*, 422–446. [CrossRef]
4. Zhang, Q.; Yang, Z.; Wang, C.; Yang, Y.; Zhang, R. Intelligent control of active shock absorber for high-speed elevator car. *Proc. Inst. Mech. Eng. Part C J. Mech. Eng. Sci.* **2019**, *233*, 3804–3815. [CrossRef]
5. Tian, J.; Guo, Q.; Shi, G. Laminated piezoelectric beam element for dynamic analysis of piezolaminated smart beams and GA-based LQR active vibration control. *Compos. Struct.* **2020**, *252*, 112480. [CrossRef]
6. Takeshita, A.; Yamashita, T.; Kawaguchi, N.; Kuroda, M. Fractional-order LQR and state observer for a fractional-order vibratory system. *Appl. Sci.* **2021**, *11*, 3252. [CrossRef]
7. Lu, X.; Liao, W.; Huang, W.; Xu, Y.; Chen, X. An improved linear quadratic regulator control method through convolutional neural network–based vibration identification. *J. Vib. Control.* **2021**, *27*, 839–853. [CrossRef]

Niu, W.; Zou, C.; Li, B.; Wang, W. Adaptive vibration suppression of time-varying structures with enhanced FxLMS algorithm. *Mech. Syst. Signal Process.* **2019**, *118*, 93–107. [CrossRef]

Puri, A.; Modak, S.V.; Gupta, K. Modal filtered-x LMS algorithm for global active noise control in a vibro-acoustic cavity. *Mech. Syst. Signal Process.* **2018**, *110*, 540–555. [CrossRef]

Seba, B.; Nedeljkovic, N.; Paschedag, J.; Lohmann, B. H∞ Feedback control and Fx-LMS feedforward control for car engine vibration attenuation. *Appl. Acoust.* **2005**, *66*, 277–296. [CrossRef]

Carlucho, I.; de Paula, M.; Wang, S.; Petillot, Y.; Acosta, G. Adaptive low-level control of autonomous underwater vehicles using deep reinforcement learning. *Robot. Auton. Syst.* **2018**, *107*, 71–86. [CrossRef]

Pane, Y.P.; Nageshrao, S.P.; Kober, J.; Babuška, R. Reinforcement learning based compensation methods for robot manipulators. *Eng. Appl. Artif. Intell.* **2019**, *78*, 236–247. [CrossRef]

Silver, D.; Hubert, T.; Schrittwieser, J.; Antonoglou, I.; Lai, M.; Guez, A.; Lanctot, M.; Sifre, L.; Kumaran, D.; Graepel, T.; et al. A general reinforcement learning algorithm that masters chess, shogi, and Go through self-play. *Science* **2018**, *362*, 1140–1144. [CrossRef]

Ye, D.; Liu, Z.; Sun, M.; Shi, B.; Zhao, P.; Wu, H.; Yu, H.; Yang, S.; Wu, X.; Guo, Q.; et al. Mastering complex control in MOBA games with deep reinforcement learning. *arXiv* **2020**, arXiv:1912.09729. [CrossRef]

Degrave, J.; Felici, F.; Buchli. J.; Neunert, M.; Tracey, B.; Carpanese, F.; Ewalds, T.; Hafner, R.; Abdolmaleki, A.; de las Casas, D.; et al. Magnetic control of tokamak plasmas through deep reinforcement learning. *Nature* **2022**, *602*, 414–419. [CrossRef] [PubMed]

Li, Z.; Chu, T.; Kalabić, U. Dynamics-enabled safe deep reinforcement learning: Case study on active suspension control. In Proceedings of the 2019 IEEE Conference on Control Technology and Applications (CCTA), Hong Kong, China, 19–21 August 2019; pp. 585–591.

Zhao, F.; You, K.; Song, S.; Zhang, W.; Tong, L. Suspension regulation of medium-low-speed maglev trains via deep reinforcement learning. *IEEE Trans. Artif. Intell.* **2021**, *2*, 341–351. [CrossRef]

Ding, Z.; Song, C.; Xu, J.; Dou, Y. Human-Robot Interaction System Design for Manipulator Control Using Reinforcement Learning. In Proceedings of the 2021 36th Youth Academic Annual Conference of Chinese Association of Automation (YAC), Nanchang, China, 28–30 May 2021; pp. 660–665.

Baselizadeh, A.; Khaksar, W.; Torresen, J. Motion Planning and Obstacle Avoidance for Robot Manipulators Using Model Predictive Control-based Reinforcement Learning. In Proceedings of the 2022 IEEE International Conference on Systems, Man, and Cybernetics (SMC), Prague, Czech Republic, 9–12 October 2022; pp. 1584–1591.

Vatsal, V.; Purushothaman, B. Reinforcement Learning of Whole-Body Control Strategies to Balance a Dynamically Stable Mobile Manipulator. In Proceedings of the 2021 Seventh Indian Control Conference (ICC), Virtually, 20–22 December 2021; pp. 335–340.

Park, J.-E.; Lee, J.; Kim, Y.-K. Design of model-free reinforcement learning control for tunable vibration absorber system based on magnetorheological elastomer. *Smart Mater. Struct.* **2021**, *30*, 055016. [CrossRef]

Yuan, R.; Yang, Y.; Su, C.; Hu, S.; Zhang, H.; Cao, E. Research on vibration reduction control based on reinforcement learning. *Adv. Civ. Eng.* **2021**, *2021*, 7619214. [CrossRef]

Qiu, Z.; Chen, G.; Zhang, X. Trajectory planning and vibration control of translation flexible hinged plate based on optimization and reinforcement learning algorithm. *Mech. Syst. Signal Process.* **2022**, *179*, 109362. [CrossRef]

Qiu, Z.; Chen, G.; Zhang, X. Reinforcement learning vibration control for a flexible hinged plate. *Aerosp. Sci. Technol.* **2021**, *118*, 107056. [CrossRef]

Qiu, Z.; Yang, Y.; Zhang, X. Reinforcement learning vibration control of a multi-flexible beam coupling system. *Aerosp. Sci. Technol.* **2022**, *129*, 107801. [CrossRef]

Feng, X.; Chen, H.; Wu, G.; Zhang, A.; Zhao, Z. A New Vibration Controller Design Method Using Reinforcement Learning and FIR Filters: A Numerical and Experimental Study. *Appl. Sci.* **2022**, *12*, 9869. [CrossRef]

He, K.; Zhang, X.; Ren, S.; Sun, J. Deep residual learning for image recognition. In Proceedings of the IEEE Conference on Computer Vision and Pattern Recognition, Las Vegas, NV, USA, 27–30 June 2016; pp. 770–778.

Howard, A.G.; Zhu, M.; Chen, B.; Kalenichenko, D.; Wang, W.; Weyand, T.; Andreetto, M.; Adam, H. Mobilenets: Efficient convolutional neural networks for mobile vision applications. *arXiv* **2017**, arXiv:1704.04861.

Zhang, X.; Zhou, X.; Lin, M.; Sun, J. Shufflenet: An extremely efficient convolutional neural network for mobile devices. In Proceedings of the IEEE Conference on Computer Vision and Pattern Recognition, Salt Lake City, UT, USA, 18–23 June 2018; pp. 6848–6856.

Zhao, M.; Zhong, S.; Fu, X.; Tang, B.; Pecht, M. Deep residual shrinkage networks for fault diagnosis. *IEEE Trans. Ind. Inform.* **2019**, *16*, 4681–4690. [CrossRef]

Sutton, R.S.; McAllester, D.; Singh, S.; Mansour, Y. Policy gradient methods for reinforcement learning with function approximation. *Adv. Neural Inf. Process. Syst.* **1999**, *12*, 1057–1063.

Watkins, C.J.; Dayan, P. Q-learning. *Mach. Learn.* **1992**, *8*, 279–292. [CrossRef]

Konda, V.; Tsitsiklis, J. Actor-critic algorithms. *Adv. Neural Inf. Process. Syst.* **1999**, *13*, 1008–1014.

Lillicrap, T.P.; Hunt, J.J.; Pritzel, A.; Heess, N.; Erez, T.; Tassa, Y.; Silver, D.; Wierstra, D. Continuous control with deep reinforcement learning. *arXiv* **2015**, arXiv:1509.02971.

Haarnoja, T.; Zhou, A.; Hartikainen, K.; Tucker, G.; Ha, S.; Tan, J.; Kumar, V.; Zhu, H.; Gupta, A.; Abbeel, P. Soft actor-critic algorithms and applications. *arXiv* **2018**, arXiv:1812.05905.

36. Fujimoto, S.; Hoof, H.; Meger, D. Addressing function approximation error in actor-critic methods. In Proceedings of International Conference on Machine Learning, Vienna, Austria, 10–15 July 2018; pp. 1587–1596.
37. Hayes, M.H. *Statistical Digital Signal Processing and Modeling*; John Wiley & Sons: Hoboken, NJ, USA, 1996.
38. Donoho, D.L. De-noising by soft-thresholding. *IEEE Trans. Inf. Theory* **1995**, *41*, 613–627. [CrossRef]
39. Isogawa, K.; Ida, T.; Shiodera, T.; Takeguchi, T. Deep shrinkage convolutional neural network for adaptive noise reduction. *IE Signal Process. Lett.* **2017**, *25*, 224–228. [CrossRef]
40. Schaul, T.; Quan, J.; Antonoglou, I.; Silver, D. Prioritized experience replay. *arXiv* **2015**, arXiv:1511.05952.

applied sciences

MDPI

rticle

Reconstruction Fidelity of Acoustic Holograms Across 0.75–4.0 MHz Excitation Frequencies: A Simulation Study

Haseeb Khan and Jinwook Kim *

School of Mechanical Engineering, Kyungpook National University, Daegu 41566, Republic of Korea
* Correspondence: jinwookkim@knu.ac.kr

Abstract: Accurate reconstruction of pressure fields using phase-only acoustic holograms is critical for applications requiring high spatial precision, such as targeted ultrasound therapies. In this study, we investigate the effect of excitation frequency on reconstruction accuracy by performing a controlled sweep from 0.75 to 4.0 MHz, while keeping all other parameters such as aperture size, simulation grid, target patterns, and optimization settings constant. To evaluate performance, we employ five quantitative metrics: Mean Squared Error (MSE), Peak Signal-to-Noise Ratio (PSNR), Cross-Correlation, Uniformity, and Efficiency. The results show that reconstruction fidelity improves as frequency increases, particularly in the low-to-mid range, where finer spatial features become resolvable due to the shorter wavelengths. However, beyond a certain point, the gains begin to taper, and in some cases, high frequencies introduce subtle artifacts such as edge ringing or increased variance. Moreover, higher frequencies are associated with increased acoustic attenuation and imposing stricter fabrication demands on holographic elements. These findings suggest that frequency selection in acoustic holography must be application-specific, as both low and high frequencies offer distinct advantages depending on the target characteristics and system constraints.

Keywords: acoustic holograms; phase-only holograms; excitation frequency; pressure field shaping; frequency-dependency

1. Introduction

Micro-resolution control of ultrasound fields in three-dimensional space is increasingly important in various engineering applications including ultrasound therapies [1,2], non-contact particle manipulation [3,4], bio-sample patterning/processing [5,6], cavitation control [7], and medical imaging [8]. Conventional ultrasonic beam control methods typically rely on either a single-focus lens or multi-foci beamforming with a phased array transducer [9]. A single-element transducer with a spherical curved lens offers simplicity but requires mechanical wobbling or scanning for flexible beam control. In contrast, multi-element phased arrays enable electronic beam steering and focusing; however, their performance comes at the cost of high system complexity and expensive multi-channel electronics. Moreover, phased-array systems still face technical challenges in accurately reconstructing complex or high-resolution multi-target fields, particularly when multiple focal spots or intricate spatial patterns must be generated simultaneously [10]. To address these limitations, acoustic holograms have emerged over the past decade as a versatile tool in ultrasonic engineering [11].

Acoustic holograms, which encode a desired wavefront through phase and/or amplitude modulation at a hologram plane, enable highly customizable reconstruction of

 https://doi.org/10.3390/app152010991

complex acoustic fields at a predefined target plane [11–13]. They consist of high-resolution, pixelized (<100 μm) two-dimensional height profiles that precisely control the time delay across the aperture [14]. With the advancement of 3D printing, phase plates with pixel counts orders of magnitude higher than those of phased arrays or 2D matrix arrays can now be fabricated, for example, a ~300 × ~300 pixel phase map for 1.5 MHz waves achieved via stereolithography (SLA) 3D printing to generate a pressure amplitude profile with a predefined complex shape with the line width of 0.88λ, where λ is the wavelength of the acoustic medium [15]. Consequently, acoustic holograms have been actively utilized across a wide range of ultrasonic applications with associated design methodologies and acoustic hologram lens fabrication techniques [15–17].

Direct time-reversal (TR) approaches can retrieve the hologram profile in a single back-propagation step, inherently compensating for medium-induced aberrations and making them particularly suitable for transcranial applications such as blood–brain barrier opening, neuromodulation, or tumor ablation [16,18]. In contrast, a standardized design method in free-field holography is the iterative angular spectrum approach (IASA), which typically requires more than 50 iterations to sufficiently converge [11]. Although less efficient in heterogeneous media, IASA remains attractive in homogeneous conditions (e.g., water or air) because of its flexibility in enforcing arbitrary pressure distributions. Recently, acoustic hologram reconstruction has further advanced through diverse strategies, ranging from conventional numerical methods to modern artificial intelligence-based frameworks, including differentiable optimization [3], deep learning models [19], and physics-informed neural networks [20]. Despite this progress, most prior research has concentrated on hologram design strategies and the accuracy of reconstructed pressure patterns at a single operating frequency, often chosen arbitrarily without systematic justification.

While the theoretical resolution limit is often taken as the diffraction limit (~λ/2) [21], the systematic influence of excitation frequency, or equivalently, acoustic wavelength, on reconstruction fidelity, spatial resolution, and energy efficiency remains little explored. Excitation frequency plays a critical role in determining spatial resolution, penetration depth, attenuation losses, and overall transmission efficiency, yet its influence on holographic reconstruction has not been comprehensively examined using consistent evaluation metrics, although a simple qualitative analysis was previously conducted by simulation [22]. This gap is critical for phase-only passive acoustic holograms, which with phase wrapping [0, 2π] are typically frequency-specific and non-reconfigurable; however, if the phase is fully unwrapped (continuous values) before height conversion, a single hologram can function across multiple frequencies, albeit with reduced fidelity. This frequency dependence introduces practical design constraints that directly influence the quality and robustness of pressure field reconstruction [22].

To address this issue, the present study performs a frequency-dependent fidelity analysis of phase-only holographic reconstruction, holding common design parameters constant (e.g., aperture size, focal distance, initial excitation pressure amplitude, etc.) while varying excitation frequency from 0.75 to 4 MHz. Reconstruction accuracy is then quantitatively assessed using standardized performance metrics to reveal how frequency fundamentally governs hologram fidelity. This study aims to provide a frequency-resolved understanding of how wavelength governs trade-offs between spatial fidelity, energy distribution, and feasibility in passive hologram design, while offering practical guidelines for frequency selection and supporting the development of application-specific acoustic holography systems.

2. Theoretical Background and Methods

2.1. Iterative Angular Spectrum Approach

We employed the IASA, a numerical method that has proven effective in our previous studies for accurately simulating wave propagation and experimentally validating acoustic hologram design accuracy [23]. Adapted from optical holography principles [24], IASA is widely recognized as a robust computational technique for designing phase-only acoustic holograms. It enables the generation of predefined complex-shape three-dimensional acoustic fields using monolithic transmission elements, offering considerably greater design flexibility compared to conventional phased array transducers [25].

The foundation of IASA lies in the angular spectrum method, which models wave propagation exactly without relying on paraxial approximations. Detailed derivations of IASA can be found in prior acoustic hologram studies, and in this work we follow the previously established theoretical framework [11,15]. Accordingly, the acoustic pressure field can be mathematically expressed as:

$$p(x,y,z) = \hat{p}(x,y,z) \cdot e^{j\Phi(x,y,z)} \tag{1}$$

where $\hat{p}(x,y,z)$ and $e^{j\Phi(x,y,z)}$ represent the amplitude and phase distributions, respectively [11]. This representation fully characterizes the acoustic wavefront by preserving both magnitude and phase. The angular spectrum method achieves this by decomposing the wavefront into a superposition of plane waves, obtained via a two-dimensional Fourier transform [26], as shown in Equation (2).

$$P(k_x,k_y,z) = \iint_{-\infty}^{+\infty} p(x,y,z)\, e^{-j(k_x x+k_y y)}\, dx\, dy \tag{2}$$

The spatial frequencies $(k_x x + k_y y)$ in the spectral domain represent the directional cosines of the constituent plane waves scaled by the wavenumber ($k_m = 2\pi/\lambda$), where λ is the wavelength [27]. For numerical implementation, we used the MATLAB R2024a (The MathWorks Inc., Natick, MS, USA) function 'fft2' with 8 nodes per wavelength, which has been shown to yield a converged hologram plane with sufficient accuracy [15]. Wavefield propagation between parallel planes is then computed by multiplying the angular spectrum with a spectral transfer function, as given in Equation (3), where the propagator function $H\ (k_x,k_y,z)$ accounts for phase accumulation of each spectral component over distance z, as defined by Equation (4).

$$P(k_x,k_y,z) = P(k_x,k_y,0) \cdot H(k_x,k_y,z) \tag{3}$$

$$H(k_x,k_y,z) = e^{\left(-jz\sqrt{k_m^2-k_x^2-k_y^2}\right)} \tag{4}$$

This transfer function expresses the fundamental dispersion relation for acoustic waves in a homogeneous medium, where $k_m = \omega/c$ is the wavenumber determined by the angular frequency omega, ω, and the speed of sound, c in the propagation medium. The angular spectrum method reduces wave propagation between parallel planes to a frequency-domain filtering process. Each spatial frequency component acquires a phase factor (exponential term). This phase factor is oscillatory for propagating waves and becomes decaying for evanescent waves, enabling precise modeling of both far- and near-field behavior [27,28].

The complete angular spectrum propagation procedure involves a forward Fourier transform, spectral multiplication, and inverse Fourier transform sequence given by Equation (5), where the inverse Fourier transform reconstructs the spatial domain field as shown as Equation (6).

$$U(x, y, z) = F^{-1}\{P(k_x, k_y, 0)\, H(k_x, k_y, z)\} \quad (5)$$

$$U(x, y, z) = \frac{1}{(2\pi)^2} \iint_{-\infty}^{+\infty} P(k_x, k_y, z)\, e^{j(k_x x + k_y y)}\, dk_x\, dk_y \quad (6)$$

The inverse Fourier transform reconstructs the propagated wavefront by coherently summing all plane wave components, each with its accumulated phase. This process precisely recovers both amplitude and phase distributions in the observation plane, including contributions from propagating and evanescent waves [28]. For this inverse transformation during numerical simulations, we used MATLAB function 'ifft2'.

Thus, the angular spectrum method's strength lies in reducing three-dimensional wave propagation to simple frequency-domain multiplications, followed by an inverse transformation to obtain the full spatial field. This approach enables efficient forward and backward propagation, making it ideal for tasks like hologram optimization and source reconstruction through iterations, as shown in Figure 1.

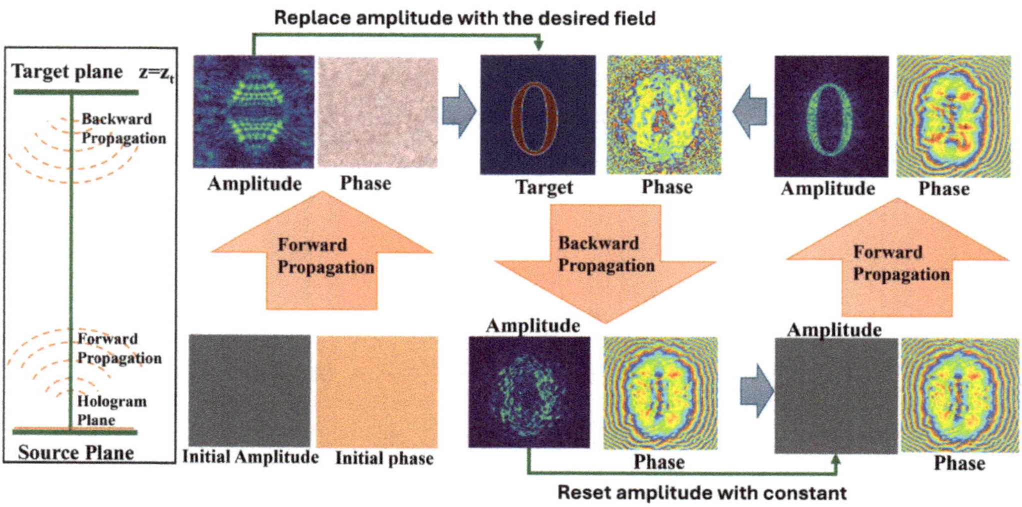

Figure 1. Acoustic hologram design workflow of the iterative angular spectrum approach.

Equations (1)–(6) provide an exact solution for acoustic field propagation in a homogeneous medium and form the foundation of the Iterative Angular Spectrum Approach. In practical applications, however an acoustic hologram lens is realized as a physical 3D-printed phase mask immersed in a coupling medium. To match the numerical design with experimental results, phase shifts caused by lens thickness and amplitude changes from transmission coefficients, addressed by Equations (7) and (8), must be considered, where t denotes propagation dimension (2.7), while subscripts m and h mean, propagation medium and hologram, respectively [11,12,15].

$$\Delta\phi(x, y) = (k_m - k_h)\Delta t(x, y) \quad (7)$$

$$t(x, y) = t_0 - \Delta t(x, y) \quad (8)$$

His thickness–phase-mapping bridges computational optimization with a fabricable 3D lens structure. In addition to phase modulation, the transmitted wave amplitude is influenced by impedance mismatches between different media, specifically the transducer, the hologram lens, and the surrounding medium (e.g., water or tissue). The effective transmission coefficient, given in Equation (9), accounts for these boundary effects, including multiple internal reflections within the lens, thereby aligning the modeled amplitude with experimental reality. The corrected pressure amplitude at the hologram plane is then expressed as Equation (10), where Z denote the acoustic impedance of each medium, and the subscript, t, denotes transducer (source) [11]. We explicitly incorporate Equations (7)–(10) into our simulations so that the numerical optimization reflects the same physical phenomena observed in experiments.

$$T(x,y) = \frac{4Z_t Z_h^2 Z_m}{Z_h^2 (Z_t + Z_m)^2 \cos^2(k_h t(x,y)) + (Z_h^2 + Z_t Z_m)^2 \sin^2(k_h t(x,y))} \tag{9}$$

$$\hat{p}(x,y,0) = T(x,y)\,\hat{p}_0(x,y) \tag{10}$$

2.2. Simulation and Frequency Depedency Evaluation

Building upon the theoretical foundation, we conducted a controlled frequency sweep to isolate the impact of wavelength on reconstruction quality. In this computational experiment, only the excitation frequency varied from 0.75 to 4.00 MHz, while all other parameters remained constant, including a 45 × 45 mm aperture [29]. The simulation parameters, stopping criterion, and target feature widths are summarized in Table 1, while the corresponding target fields are illustrated in Figure 2. A phase-only constraint was imposed throughout the simulations.

Table 1. Simulation parameters for acoustic pressure field modeling across multiple frequencies and target geometries.

Parameter	Value	Unit
Lateral size	45×10^{-3}	m
Frequencies	0.75, 1.0, 1.5, 2.0, 3.0, 4.0	MHz
Pressure (initialized)	0.1×10^{6}	Pa
Medium speed	1490	m/s
Density	1000	kg/m^3
Grid size (x, y)	1001 × 1001	Count
Iterations	50	Count
Target 1: Chessboard	Box size: 2.74 × 2.74	mm
Target 2: KNU Logo	Smallest feature: 0.745; Largest feature: 1.73	mm
Target 3: Dove	Smallest feature: 0.51	mm

For each frequency, the angular spectrum propagation kernel was updated accordingly, and the pressure field at the target plane was recomputed using the same optimization hyperparameters and normalization scheme. This protocol ensures that differences in spatial resolution, diffraction dynamics, and fidelity are attributable only to changes in wavelength, without interference from variations in aperture, sampling, or iterative design parameters. To mitigate edge effects and prevent FFT wrap-around [11,22], the target was rescaled to one-third of the simulation grid's linear size (approximately 334 × 334), and centrally embedded within the 1001 × 1001 grid. This "frequency-edge guard" technique keeps most spectral energy away from the boundaries, reduces aliasing and Gibbs ringing near sharp transitions, and enhances the stability and convergence of the IASA without altering the underlying target topology [26].

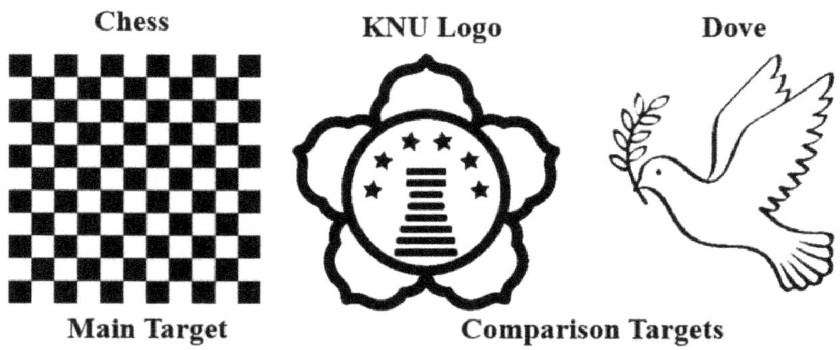

Figure 2. Target images for reconstruction accuracy evaluation and validation.

To evaluate performance on each frequency, we employ five quantitative metrics: Mean Squared Error (MSE), Peak Signal-to-Noise Ratio (PSNR), Cross-Correlation, Uniformity, and acoustic energy efficiency [19,30]. These metrics were selected because they directly capture both the accuracy of reconstruction and the practical needs of the intended applications. Mean squared error (MSE) was chosen because it provides a straightforward measure of how closely the reconstructed field matches the target pattern at that frequency, ensuring numerical fidelity [25]. Normalized cross-correlation was included to evaluate structural similarity, which is particularly important when higher frequencies are used to reproduce fine spatial details [19,25]. Field uniformity was selected to assess how evenly the acoustic energy is distributed within the target region, a property critical for biomedical treatments and particle manipulation, where consistent exposure across multiple foci is required [31]. Finally, acoustic energy efficiency was evaluated to determine how effectively the input acoustic power contributes to the desired field at each frequency, which is essential both for reducing energy waste and for ensuring safe operation in biomedical contexts [19]. By combining these five metrics, we ensured that hologram evaluation reflects not only mathematical accuracy but also frequency-dependent performance relevant to practical applications [19].

In addition, we characterized each target using three intrinsic descriptors that capture complementary aspects of their spatial structure. The bright-area fraction (BAF) quantifies the proportion of the aperture that is illuminated, providing a measure of overall area coverage. The edge density (ED) represents the total boundary length per unit area, reflecting how frequently transitions between bright and dark regions occur. The high-frequency energy ratio (HF50) denotes the fraction of spectral energy residing above half the Nyquist frequency, indicating the relative burden of fine spatial details. Together, these descriptors provide a concise summary of target geometry by distinguishing how much area is occupied, how complex the boundary structure is, and how strongly high-frequency components contribute. The measured values for BAF, ED, and HF50 for the chessboard, dove, and KNU logo are summarized in Table 2.

Table 2. Target descriptors: ED (edge density), BAF (bright-area fraction), and HF50 (high-frequency energy ratio), shown as percentages.

Target	ED (%)	BAF (%)	HF50 (%)
Chessboard	6.14	49.60	0.73
Dove	4.20	8.22	2.55
KNU logo	1.31	2.17	2.96

3. Results

As a result, Figure 3 illustrates the frequency-dependent evolution of the chessboard target's acoustic pressure field reconstructed via the acoustic hologram for each excitation frequency. Before quantitative evaluation, we qualitatively analyze the pressure amplitude reconstruction results. At the lower frequencies of 0.75 to 1.0 MHz, the lateral effective point-spread function (PSF) is broad, resulting in rounded edges and dominant halo artifacts around the squares. As the frequency increases to the 1.5 to 2.0 MHz range, the PSF narrows, allowing higher spatial harmonics near the edges to fall within the propagating band. This results in sharper square edges and flatter interiors, improving target fidelity. At even higher frequencies between 3 and 4 MHz, the smallest feature details become more sharply defined; however, faint ringing artifacts appear along high-contrast boundaries, which are characteristics of phase-only holographic synthesis under band-limited conditions. These results highlight how frequency governs spatial resolution and diffraction behavior in acoustic holography, balancing detail enhancement with artifact emergence typical of constrained phase-only reconstruction methods.

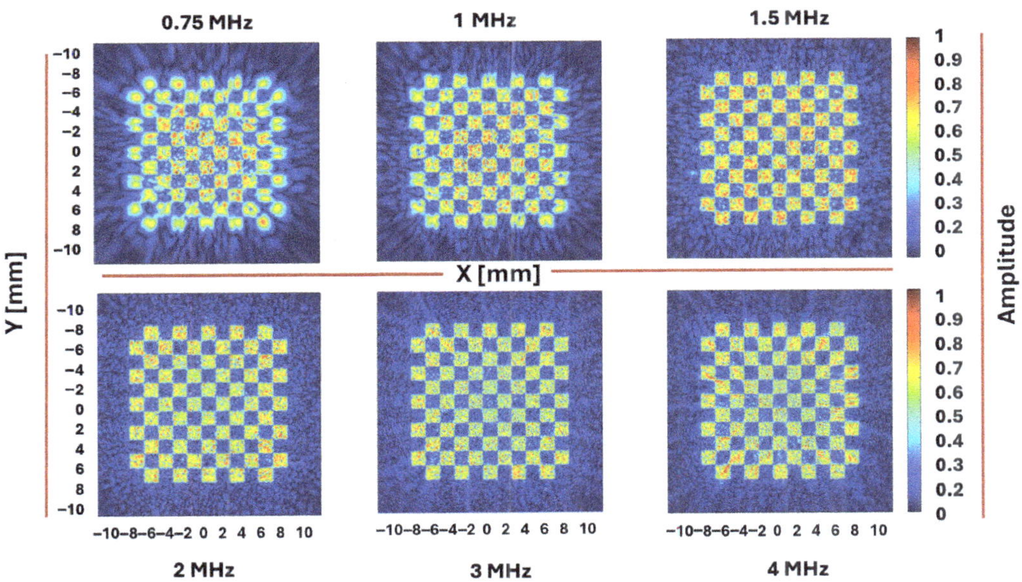

Figure 3. Normalized amplitude reconstruction results by the IASA process with the excitation frequencies, 0.75, 1.0, 1.5, 2.0, 3.0, and 4.0 MHz, respectively.

This frequency-dependent performance can be further understood by relating the chessboard's characteristic feature size to the wavelength-limited resolution of the aperture. The embedded chessboard pattern occupies about one-third of the 45 mm aperture, giving an overall tile size of approximately 15 mm across. Within this tile, the 11 × 11 division yields individual square widths of about 1.36 mm. This pitch defines the fundamental spatial frequency of the pattern at roughly 0.74 cycles/mm (1/p), while the sharp edges are encoded in higher harmonics such as $3/p \approx 2.2$ cycles/mm and $5/p \approx 3.7$ cycles/mm. The aperture's diffraction-limited lateral resolution can be estimated as $\delta \approx 1.22 \times \lambda \times z/D$, where $\lambda = c/f$ is the wavelength, D = 45 mm is the aperture width, and z = 25 mm is the distance. At 0.75 MHz ($\lambda \approx 1.99$ mm), the resolution is $\delta \approx 1.35$ mm, which is slightly worse than the 1.36 mm pitch, so adjacent squares are poorly resolved, and the reconstruction is dominated by blurred edges and halo artifacts. At 1.0 MHz ($\lambda \approx 1.49$ mm, $\delta \approx 1.01$ mm), the system begins to resolve the 1.36 mm squares, allowing the fundamental frequency to pass, but higher harmonics remain suppressed, and edges still appear soft. At 1.5 MHz ($\lambda \approx 0.99$ mm, $\delta \approx 0.67$ mm), the resolution limit drops below p/2, allowing the third harmonic to enter the passband. This results in sharper edges, flatter interiors, and peaks in PSNR, uniformity, and efficiency. At 2.0 MHz ($\lambda \approx 0.75$ mm, $\delta \approx 0.51$ mm), the resolution reaches about p/2–p/3, meaning nearly all structural content of the chessboard is captured, and cross-correlation and efficiency reach their maxima. At higher frequencies such as 3.0 MHz ($\lambda \approx 0.50$ mm, $\delta \approx 0.34$ mm), additional higher-order harmonics are admitted, which further sharpen edges but also increases ringing artifacts and local variance to the features that are already fully reconstructed by lower frequency.

This frequency–feature size relationship also aligns with the intrinsic target descriptors reported in Table 2, which capture differences in area coverage, edge density, and high-frequency across the three patterns. These qualitative trends are consistent with the target features summarized in Table 2. The chessboard, with large area coverage (BAF $\approx$ 49.6%) and very low high-frequency burden (HF50 $\approx$ 0.73%), reaches flat interiors and high efficiency once edges enter the passband, with only mild ringing thereafter. In contrast, the dove and KNU logo occupy much smaller areas but carry substantially more fine-detail energy (HF50 $\approx$ 2.6–3.0%), so their edges continue to sharpen with increasing frequency while becoming more susceptible to high-frequency ringing and local variance.

To quantitatively evaluate the frequency-dependent reconstruction results shown in Figure 3, five key metrics were computed for the main chessboard target and summarized in Table 3: MSE, PSNR, cross-correlation, uniformity, and efficiency. From 0.75 to 1.5 MHz, the accessible spatial frequency band broadens, and the lateral PSF significantly narrows. This results in a marked reduction in error energy, with MSE decreasing from 0.0145 to 0.0105. Correspondingly, PSNR increases, reaching its peak value of 19.7503 dB at 1.5 MHz, indicating improved overall reconstruction fidelity. As interference between adjacent tiles diminishes, the uniformity metric improves, also peaking at 1.5 MHz with a value of 0.9377. The global structure of the pressure field better matches the target design, leading cross-correlation to rise continuously and reach its maximum of 0.9297 at 2.0 MHz, even as PSNR begins to decline slightly. Moreover, the contracting PSF concentrates more acoustic energy within the chessboard region of interest, translating into enhanced efficiency, which increases steadily from 0.6759 at 0.75 MHz to its maximum of 0.7014 at 2.0 MHz. Together, these metrics capture the interplay between frequency, spatial resolution, and reconstruction accuracy, illustrating how increasing frequency sharpens feature rendition while balancing energy concentration and error reduction within the holographically generated acoustic field.

Table 3. Pressure reconstruction accuracy evaluation results using the chessboard pattern as a target amplitude profile.

Frequency (MHz)	MSE	PSNR (dB)	Cross-Correlation	Uniformity	Efficiency
0.75	0.0145	18.3801	0.8906	0.9123	0.6759
1	0.0128	18.9312	0.9104	0.9239	0.6933
1.5	0.0105	19.7503	0.9243	0.9377	0.6890
2	0.0115	19.3907	0.9297	0.9310	0.7014
3	0.0130	18.8511	0.9172	0.9257	0.6746
4	0.0126	18.9909	0.9165	0.9275	0.6829

However, beyond 2 MHz, the finite aperture causes the useful passband to saturate. As a result, further increases in frequency mainly sharpen already well-resolved edges but also introduce mild phase-only ringing artifacts. These artifacts slightly increase local variance and redistribute sidelobes within the reconstructed field. Consequently, MSE exhibits a gradual increase from 0.0115 to 0.0130 (MSE 0.1073 to 0.1142), while PSNR stabilizes around 19 dB (18.8511 to 18.9909 dB). Cross-correlation gently decreases to approximately 0.916–0.917, uniformity fluctuates near 0.926–0.928, and efficiency plateaus or slightly declines to roughly 0.675–0.683 at frequencies of 3–4 MHz. Together, these trends highlight a practical mid-band "knee" between 1.5 and 2.0 MHz: 1.5 MHz optimizes pixel-wise accuracy that is characterized by the lowest error, highest PSNR, and best uniformity, whereas 2.0 MHz maximizes structural similarity and energy concentration, reaching peak cross-correlation and efficiency. Beyond this range, visual sharpness continues to improve; however, global quantitative metrics show diminishing returns due to ringing and saturation effects in the passband. For completeness, we extended the identical frequency sweep to two additional target patterns (Figure 4), which similarly exhibited the same three-stage behavior observed in Target 1, and thus their detailed descriptions are omitted. At 0.75 to 1.0 MHz, fine details remain blurred, and background halos are significantly uniform interiors, and all metrics improve in concert PSNR rises, MSE decreases, cross-correlation climbs, uniformity approaches best values, and efficiency grows as more energy is confined within the region of interest. Above 3 to 4 MHz, the smallest features finally become distinguishable; however, global metrics saturate and show minor oscillations due to phase-only ringing edges that increase local variance despite enhanced edge sharpness.

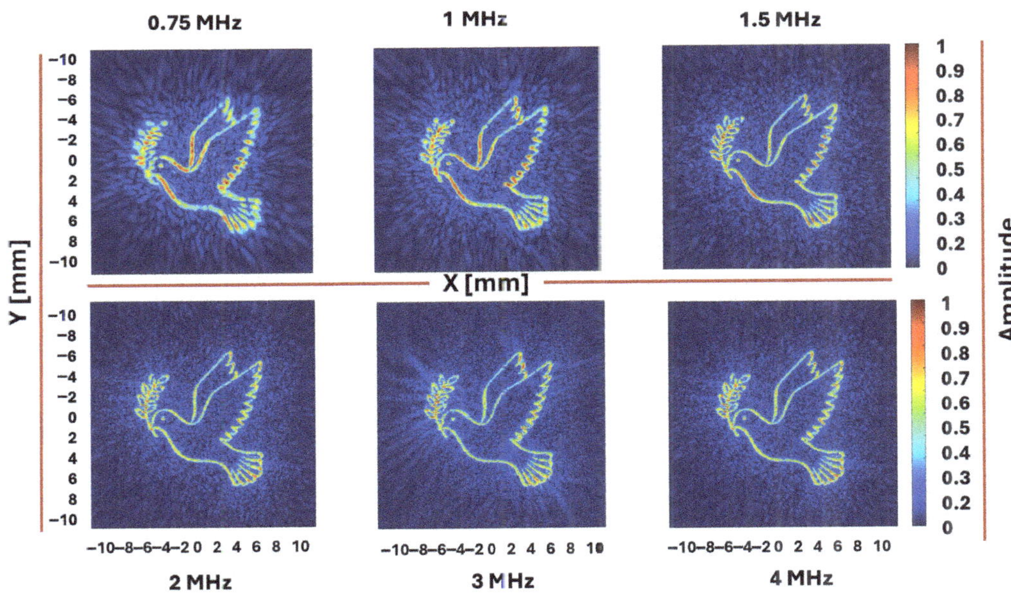

Figure 4. *Cont.*

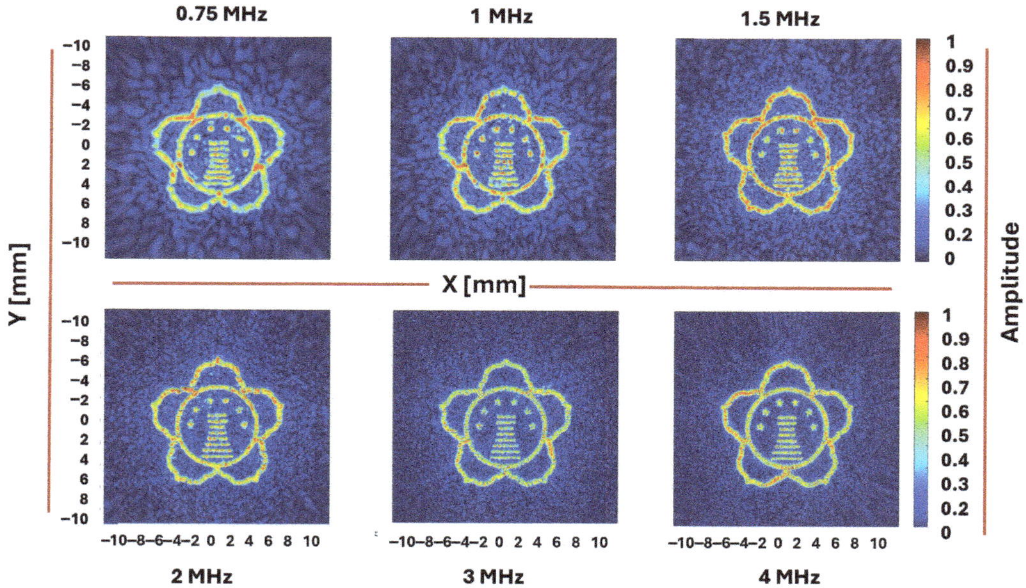

Figure 4. Normalized amplitude reconstructions of the KNU Logo and Dove target at the reconstruction plane for frequency of 0.75, 1.0, 1.5, 2.0, 3.0, 4.0 MHz using IASA.

These results collectively reveal that resolution is fundamentally constrained by the diffraction-limited lateral resolution, or the smallest feature spacing the system can resolve. Features narrower than this limit remains merged at low frequencies, became separable at the mid-band, and only the finest details emerge at the highest frequencies. This frequency-dependent behavior observed for Target 1 thus generalizes well to other target geometries. Comparing the three targets' metrics across frequency shows overall performance improvement with frequency, but the metric curves diverge at specific frequency bands due to differences in feature size and complexity among the targets. This analysis presents the trade-offs involved in acoustic hologram design, where increasing frequency enhances spatial resolution and feature clarity but introduces artifacts and performance limits imposed by system aperture and sampling.

In the primary target, all features share identical dimensions; thus, once the system's diffraction-limited lateral resolution fully resolves this characteristic feature size at a given frequency, further frequency increases yield minimal gains in resolution. This results in performance metrics improving consistently up to a mid-band, beyond which they saturate, as shown in Figure 5. The other two targets, featuring diverse lengths, widths, and curvatures, follow similar trends but exhibit approximately 5% deviation relative to the primary target. Notably, the uniformity metric varies non-monotonically because each target balances interior area and edge density differently within the ROI, causing uneven frequency response. For instance, the KNU logo has large homogeneous regions and few sharp edges, leading to early stabilization of interior uniformity and only minor mid-band fluctuations due to transient energy concentration at junctions. Conversely, the edge-dense chessboard, with sharp tile boundaries, shows an initial uniformity increase as cell interiors flatten, followed by slight decreases at higher frequencies due to phase-only ringing that raises local variance despite sharper edges. The dove target, dominated by thin strokes with little interior, exhibits persistent elevated local variance and a lower, flatter uniformity curve, with minor oscillations as various stroke widths become resolvable.

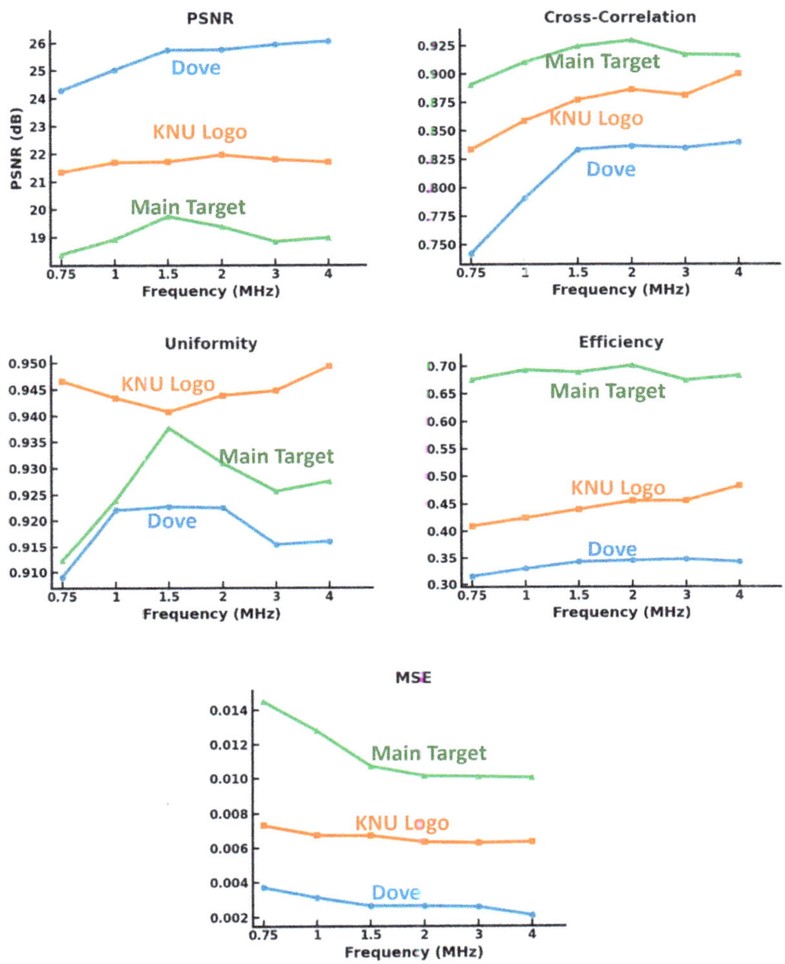

Figure 5. Comparison of metric variations for all three targets as a function of excitation frequency.

To further examine the role of feature distribution and spatial complexity on reconstruction performance, we performed a quantitative analysis of the three target patterns. Pixel counting revealed that the chessboard occupied approximately 49.6% of the pixels, while the dove and KNU logo occupied only approximately 8.3% and 2.1%, respectively. This difference in illuminated area directly affects efficiency but also interacts with boundary complexity: the chessboard, with relatively high edge density, experiences stronger mid-band uniformity gains as its many tile interiors flatten, whereas the dove and KNU logo, with far smaller brighter regions and lower edge density, exhibit distinct uniformity behavior. The KNU logo achieves the highest uniformity because its large homogeneous interiors dominate despite occupying only 2% of the aperture, while the dove remains lowest in uniformity since its energy is concentrated along thin strokes where ringing offsets interior smoothing.

This analysis indicates that the chessboard distributes acoustic energy across nearly half of the aperture, reducing effective focal gain, whereas the other two patterns concentrate energy into much smaller regions. Complementary frequency-domain analysis using 2D FFT confirmed these differences: the chessboard exhibited predominantly low-frequency components, consistent with its repetitive block structure, while the dove and KNU logo displayed broader spectra with stronger high-frequency contributions due to their sharper outlines and finer details. These quantitative measures explain the observed reconstruction results: the chessboard achieved higher efficiency because of its large, illuminated area but suffered reduced fidelity (lower PSNR and CC) as the energy was spread thinly across many pixels. In contrast, the dove and KNU logo, which occupy fewer pixels, produced reconstructions with higher focal gain and better pixelwise fidelity, but with increased edge-related ringing and nonuniformity arising from their higher spatial frequency content.

Beyond the above trends, it is important to note that frequency selection involves trade-offs, making 1.5–2.0 MHz the optimal range. While fidelity improves with increasing frequency, further gains are constrained by stronger acoustic attenuation and the fabrication complexity of high-resolution holograms [32]. This creates a balance between spatial resolution, attenuation losses, and practical feasibility. Accordingly, we selected 1.5–2.0 MHz as a practical operating band, since it provides the best compromise between reconstruction accuracy and experimental realizability for the present target geometries. We also emphasize that this choice is application-dependent: in medical contexts, where extremely fine resolution is critical, higher frequencies may still be preferred, while attenuation and fabrication challenges can be mitigated through additional techniques.

4. Discussion

The analysis demonstrates that spatial resolution in acoustic holography is fundamentally constrained by the diffraction-limited lateral resolution relative to feature size [33,34]. Features smaller than resolution limit remains unresolved, while finer features become distinguishable near a mid-band and only the finest details fully emerge at higher frequencies. This frequency-dependent reconstruction behavior generalizes across different target geometries due to inherent spatial scale differences, underscoring the importance of considering both global morphology and local spatial frequency content in evaluating reconstruction fidelity and optimizing hologram design [11].

Our findings align with and extend prior work showing that increasing frequency improves spatial resolution up to a saturation point. Melde et al. demonstrated that shorter wavelengths yield tighter focal spots and enhanced resolution but exacerbate diffraction-induced artifacts in phase-only systems [11]. It was also previously reported that performance plateaus emerge at high frequencies due to aperture-limited spectral support, a phenomenon that is quantitatively confirmed in our analysis [35].

As excitation frequency increased from 0.75 to 2.0 MHz, reconstruction improved considerably: MSE decreased steadily, PSNR peaked at 19.75 dB around 1.5 MHz, and cross-correlation reached a maximum of 0.9297 at 2.0 MHz, indicating optimal structural alignment. Beyond this range, gains diminished because the effective passband was saturated by system aperture and sampling, and additional high-frequency components only sharpened already resolved features while introducing mild phase-only ringing that slightly degraded quantitative metrics [36–38]. This frequency-dependent performance was consistent across all target types but varied with geometric complexity. The KNU logo's large homogeneous areas yielded high uniformity early and stable mid- to high-frequency performance. The edge-rich chessboard exhibited pronounced mid-band gains but saw high-frequency degradation from ringing-induced variance. The dove target, dominated by fine strokes, showed lower uniformity and less mid-band improvement, reflecting persistent variance despite resolution gains.

Comparisons with the literature on IASA-based and angular spectrum methods show our results fall within expected ranges. Prior studies report PSNR values of 18–20 dB and structure similarity up to 0.90 for IASA reconstructions [19], Consistent with our peak values, while higher frequencies improve spatial resolution, they also face practical limitations: increased attenuation in biomedical and fluid media reduces penetration depth, and fabrication of high-frequency phase-only holograms requires finer, more precise patterning. Importantly, as the wavelength becomes comparable to the resolution of the 3D printer, phase inaccuracies and surface roughness introduce artifacts that distort the target-plane reconstruction, further elevating sensitivity to defects [5].

Although simulations assume ideal propagation and neglect nonlinear and device-specific effects, they establish a foundation for frequency-aware hologram design. Future experimental validation and development of adaptive-frequency methods tailored to spatial complexity may enable higher-fidelity reconstructions in real applications. This work highlights a core design principle: optimal acoustic holography frequency must balance resolution gains against physical and practical system constraints to suit specific application requirements.

5. Conclusions

In this study, we evaluated the frequency-dependent reconstruction accuracy of phase-only acoustic holograms using line patterns (0.5–2.75 mm width) over a 30 × 30 mm target area with a 45 × 45 mm aperture. Our results show that spatial resolution improves with frequency up to a mid-band range of 1.5–2.0 MHz, beyond which performance saturates due to aperture fixed size, and phase-only ringing becomes prominent. These frequency-dependent trends are consistent across different geometries, with fidelity largely influenced by feature distribution and spatial complexity (e.g., chessboard bright-area fraction ≈ 49.6%, dove ≈ 8.2%, KNU logo ≈ 2.1%), while uniformity shows only a small variation of about ~2%. The findings confirm practical trade-offs among resolution, attenuation, fabrication precision, and hardware constraints. Importantly, the identified optimal frequency range provides a balance between accuracy, efficiency, and robustness, offering quantitative guidelines for frequency-aware hologram design and supporting future adaptive optimization for actual applications.

Author Contributions: Conceptualization, H.K. and J.K., methodology, H.K. and J.K.; software, H.K.; validation, H.K. and J.K.; formal analysis, H.K.; investigation, H.K.; resources, J.K.; data curation, H.K.; writing—original draft preparation, H.K.; writing—review and editing, H.K. and J.K.; visualization, H.K.; supervision, J.K.; project administration, J.K.; funding acquisition, J.K. All authors have read and agreed to the published version of the manuscript.

Funding: This work was supported by the National Research Foundation of Korea (NRF) through Korean Government [Ministry of Science and ICT (MSIT)] under Grant RS-2025-16072488.

Data Availability Statement: The data that support the findings of this study are available from the corresponding author upon reasonable request.

Acknowledgments: The authors thank Sandeep Kasoji of Triangle Biotechnology, Inc. for his support and valuable insights on acoustic hologram lens design technologies and potential applications.

Conflicts of Interest: Jinwook Kim is a co-inventor on patents related to the development and application of acoustic hologram lenses for biomedical treatments and has a financial interest in their commercialization.

References

1. Escoffre, J.-M.; Bouakaz, A. (Eds.) *Therapeutic Ultrasound*; Springer International Publishing: Cham, Switzerland, 2016; ISBN 978-3-319-22535-7.
2. Xu, Z.; Khokhlova, T.D.; Cho, C.S.; Khokhlova, V.A. Histotripsy: A Method for Mechanical Tissue Ablation with Ultrasound. *Annu. Rev. Biomed. Eng.* **2024**, *26*, 141–167. [CrossRef] [PubMed]

3. Fushimi, T.; Drinkwater, B.W.; Hill, T.L. What Is the Ultimate Capability of Acoustophoretic Volumetric Displays? *Appl. Phy Lett.* **2020**, *116*, 244101. [CrossRef]
4. Hirayama, R.; Martinez Plasencia, D.; Masuda, N.; Subramanian, S. A Volumetric Display for Visual, Tactile and Aud Presentation Using Acoustic Trapping. *Nature* **2019**, *575*, 320–323. [CrossRef]
5. Melde, K.; Kremer, H.; Shi, M.; Seneca, S.; Frey, C.; Platzman, I.; Degel, C.; Schmitt, D.; Schölkopf, B.; Fischer, P. Compa Holographic Sound Fields Enable Rapid One-Step Assembly of Matter in 3D. *Sci. Adv.* **2023**, *9*, eadf6182. [CrossRef]
6. Ma, Z.; Holle, A.W.; Melde, K.; Qiu, T.; Poeppel, K.; Kadiri, V.M.; Fischer, P. Acoustic Holographic Cell Patterning in Biocompatible Hydrogel. *Adv. Mater.* **2020**, *32*, 1904181. [CrossRef]
7. Kim, J.; Kasoji, S.; Durham, P.G.; Dayton, P.A. Acoustic Holograms for Directing Arbitrary Cavitation Patterns. *Appl. Phys. Le* **2021**, *118*, 051902. [CrossRef]
8. Schein, D.; Grutman, T.; Ilovitsh, T. Deep Learning-Based Ultrasound Beam Shaping for Spatiotemporal Acoustic Hologram Generation. *IEEE Trans. Ultrason. Ferroelectr. Freq. Control* **2023**, *70*, 551–561. [CrossRef]
9. Foster, F.S.; Hunt, J.W. The Design and Characterization of Short Pulse Ultrasound Transducers. *Ultrasonics* **1978**, *16*, 116–12 [CrossRef]
10. Hoskins, P.; Martin, K.; Thrush, A. *Diagnostic Ultrasound: Physics and Equipment*, 2nd ed.; Cambridge University Press: Cambridg UK, 2010.
11. Melde, K.; Mark, A.G.; Qiu, T.; Fischer, P. Holograms for Acoustics. *Nature* **2016**, *537*, 518–522. [CrossRef]
12. Xu, M.; Wang, J.; Harley, W.S.; Lee, P.V.S.; Collins, D.J. Programmable Acoustic Holography Using Medium-Sound-Spee Modulation. *Adv. Sci.* **2023**, *10*, 2301489. [CrossRef] [PubMed]
13. Brown, M.D. Phase and Amplitude Modulation with Acoustic Holograms. *Appl. Phys. Lett.* **2019**, *115*, 053701. [CrossRef]
14. Jiménez-Gambín, S.; Jiménez, N.; Benlloch, J.M.; Camarena, F. Generating Bessel Beams with Broad Depth-of-Field by Usin Phase-Only Acoustic Holograms. *Sci. Rep.* **2019**, *9*, 20104. [CrossRef]
15. Kim, J.; Kasoji, S.; Durham, P.G.; Dayton, P.A. Nanoparticle-Epoxy Composite Molding for Undeformed Acoustic Hologram with Tailored Acoustic Properties. *IEEE Trans. Ultrason. Ferroelectr. Freq. Control* **2023**, *70*, 1554–1562. [CrossRef]
16. Burstow, R.; Andrés, D.; Jiménez, N.; Camarena, F.; Thanou, M.; Pouliopoulos, A.N. Acoustic Holography in Biomedica Applications. *Phys. Med. Biol.* **2025**, *70*, 06TR01. [CrossRef] [PubMed]
17. Lin, Q.; Wang, J.; Cai, F.; Zhang, R.; Zhao, D.; Xia, X.; Wang, J.; Zheng, H. A Deep Learning Approach for the Fast Generation c Acoustic Holograms. *J. Acoust. Soc. Am.* **2021**, *149*, 2312–2322. [CrossRef] [PubMed]
18. Fink, M. Time Reversal of Ultrasonic Fields-Part I: Basic Principes. *IEEE Trans. Ultrason. Ferroelectr. Freq. Control* **1992**, *39*, 555–56 [CrossRef] [PubMed]
19. Lee, M.H.; Lew, H.M.; Youn, S.; Kim, T.; Hwang, J.Y. Deep Learning-Based Framework for Fast and Accurate Acoustic Hologra Generation. *IEEE Trans. Ultrason. Ferroelectr. Freq. Control* **2022**, *69*, 3353–3366. [CrossRef]
20. Li, B.; Lu, M.; Liu, C.; Liu, X.; Ta, D. Acoustic Hologram Reconstruction with Unsupervised Neural Network. *Front. Mater.* **202** *9*, 916527. [CrossRef]
21. Abdolali, A.; Barati Sedeh, H.; Fakheri, M.H.; Shen, C.; Sun, F. Breaking the Acoustic Diffraction Limit with an Arbitrary Shap Acoustic Magnifying Lens. *Sci. Rep.* **2021**, *11*, 12958. [CrossRef]
22. Bakhtiari-Nejad, M.; Elnahhas, A.; Hajj, M.R.; Shahab, S. Acoustic Holograms in Contactless Ultrasonic Power Transfer System Modeling and Experiment. *J. Appl. Phys.* **2018**, *124*, 244901. [CrossRef]
23. Kim, J.; Kasoji, S.; Dayton, P.A. Acoustic Metastructure-Lensed Multi-Focal Sonicator Designs for High-Throughput Therapeuti Ultrasound Testing In Vitro. In Proceedings of the 2024 IEEE Ultrasonics, Ferroelectrics, and Frequency Control Joint Symposiu (UFFC-JS), Taipei, Taiwan, 22–26 September 2024; pp. 1–4.
24. Mellin, S.D.; Nordin, G.P. Limits of Scalar Diffraction Theory and an Iterative Angular Spectrum Algorithm for Finite Apertur Diffractive Optical Element Design. *Opt. Express* **2001**, *8*, 705–722. [CrossRef]
25. Yao, X.; Piao, X.; Hong, S.; Ji, C.; Wang, M.; Wei, Y.; Xu, Z.; Pan, J.-J.; Pei, Y.; Cheng, B. Acoustic Hologram-Enabled Simultaneou Multi-Target Blood-Brain Barrier Opening (AH-SiMBO). *Commun. Eng.* **2025**, *4*, 99. [CrossRef]
26. Zeng, X.; McGough, R.J. Evaluation of the Angular Spectrum Approach for Simulations of Near-Field Pressures. *J. Acoust. So Am.* **2008**, *123*, 68–76. [CrossRef] [PubMed]
27. Liu, D.-L.; Waag, R.C. Propagation and Backpropagation for Ultrasonic Wavefront Design. *IEEE Trans. Ultrason. Ferroelectr. Fre Control* **1997**, *44*, 1–13. [CrossRef] [PubMed]
28. Treeby, B.E.; Cox, B.T. K-Wave: MATLAB Toolbox for the Simulation and Reconstruction of Photoacoustic Wave Fields. *J. Biome Opt.* **2010**, *15*, 21314. [CrossRef] [PubMed]
29. Sapozhnikov, O.A.; Tsysar, S.A.; Khokhlova, V.A.; Kreider, W. Acoustic Holography as a Metrological Tool for Characterizin Medical Ultrasound Sources and Fields. *J. Acoust. Soc. Am.* **2015**, *138*, 1515–1532. [CrossRef]
30. Weerasinghe, G.; Servais, B.; Heath, D.; Martin, S.T.; Collins, D.J. Improved Acoustic Holograms Using Simulated Annealing *Biomicrofluidics* **2025**, *19*, 24105. [CrossRef]

Wang, J.; Sarkar, D.; Suo, J.; Chortos, A. Harnessing Deep Learning of Point Clouds for Morphology Mimicking of Universal 3D Shape-Morphing Devices. *Adv. Intell. Syst.* **2024**, *7*, 2400550. [CrossRef]
Kim, J.; Kang, H.; Choi, S.; Kim, D. Additive Manufacturing Techniques for Acoustic Hologram Lens Microfabrication. *Micromachines* **2025**, *16*, 1119. [CrossRef]
Lu, Q.; Zhong, C.; Liu, Q.; Su, H.; Liu, S. Deep Learning-Based Super-Resolution Acoustic Holography for Phased Transducer Array. *J. Appl. Phys.* **2024**, *135*, 134902. [CrossRef]
Zhong, C.; Sun, Z.; Li, J.; Jiang, Y.; Su, H.; Liu, S. Accurate and Real-Time Acoustic Holography Using Super-Resolution and Physics Combined Deep Learning. *Appl. Phys. Lett.* **2025**, *126* 54103. [CrossRef]
Peralta, L.; Ramalli, A.; Reinwald, M.; Eckersley, R.J.; Hajnal, J.V. Impact of Aperture, Depth, and Acoustic Clutter on the Performance of Coherent Multi-Transducer Ultrasound Imaging. *Appl. Sci.* **2020**, *10*, 7655. [CrossRef]
Gholampour, A.; Cano, C.; de Hoop, H.; van Sambeek, M.R.H.M.; Lopata, R.G.P.; Wu, M.; Schwab, H.-M. SNR Analysis of Multi-Aperture Ultrasound and Photoacoustic Imaging Systems. *J. Acoust. Soc. Am.* **2025**, *157*, 1228–1240. [CrossRef] [PubMed]
Chardon, G.; Daudet, L.; Peillot, A.; Ollivier, F.; Bertin, N.; Gribonval, R. Near-Field Acoustic Holography Using Sparse Regularization and Compressive Sampling Principles. *J. Acoust. Soc. Am.* **2012**, *132*, 1521–1534. [CrossRef] [PubMed]
Harris, R.A.; Follett, D.H.; Halliwell, M.; Wells, P.N.T. Ultimate Limits in Ultrasonic Imaging Resolution. *Ultrasound Med. Biol.* **1991**, *17*, 547–558. [CrossRef] [PubMed]

applied sciences

MDPI

Article

Uncertainty Propagation for Vibrometry-Based Acoustic Predictions Using Gaussian Process Regression

Andreas Wurzinger † and Stefan Schoder *,†

Aeroacoustic and Vibroacoustic Group, Institute of Fundamentals and Theory in Electrical Engineering, Graz University of Technology, Inffeldgasse 16c, 8010 Graz, Austria; andreas.wurzinger@tugraz.at

* Correspondence: stefan.schoder@tugraz.at

† These authors contributed equally to this work.

Abstract: Shell-like housing structures for motors and compressors can be found in everyday products. Consumers significantly evaluate acoustic emissions during the first usage of products. Unpleasant sounds may raise concerns and cause complaints to be issued. A prevention strategy is a holistic acoustic design, which includes predicting the emitted sound power as part of end-of-line testing. The hybrid experimental-simulative sound power prediction based on laser scanning vibrometry (LSV) is ideal in acoustically harsh production environments. However, conducting vibroacoustic testing with laser scanning vibrometry is time-consuming, making it difficult to fit into the production cycle time. This contribution discusses how the time-consuming sampling process can be accelerated to estimate the radiated sound power, utilizing adaptive sampling. The goal is to predict the acoustic signature and its uncertainty from surface velocity data in seconds. Fulfilling this goal will enable integration into a product assembly unit and final acoustic quality control without the need for an acoustic chamber. The Gaussian process regression based on PyTorch 2.6.0 performed 60 times faster than the preliminary reference implementation, resulting in a regression estimation time of approximately one second for each frequency bin. In combination with the Equivalent Radiated Power prediction of the sound power, a statistical measure is available, indicating how the uncertainty of a limited number of surface velocity measurement points leads to predictions of the uncertainty inside the acoustical signal. An adaptive sampling algorithm reduces the prediction uncertainty in real-time during measurement. The method enables on-the-fly error analysis in production, assessing the risk of violating agreed-upon acoustic sound power thresholds, and thus provides valuable feedback to the product design units.

Keywords: Gaussian process regression; Vibro-Acoustics; production; measurements; laser scanning vibrometry; risk mitigation

1. Introduction

Quantifying the sound generation of highly integrated products is essential during design and production. The overall goal is to enhance product quality and meet contractual and legal requirements. For any device with direct user interaction, noise emissions can negatively affect both the user and the user's environment [1]. Therefore, tools [2] to predict and quantify sound emissions should be integrated early in the design process and aligned with production-ready methods for quality control and production-based design feedback [3]. A production-ready system for acoustic end-of-line testing to meet vibroacoustic requirements is presented in [4]. Ref. [4] requires an acoustically treated environment for accurate sound measures, whereas the used acoustic measurement method [5] does not rely on a specific treatment of the acoustics in the production facility.

We identify the following specifications of the system [4]: firstly (specification 1), the system should be ready to perform measurements at different locations, contactless, and without any additional assembly cost in a harsh acoustic environment such as a production facility. Secondly (specification 2), the system should select observation points based on the data prediction accuracy and uncertainty calculated by a self-learned data-driven method. Thirdly (specification 3), the technique should provide data that gives the maximum valuable insight into specific characteristics where the deviations occurred over time. Fourthly and finally (specification 4), the measurement time should align with the production cycle of a production line and the performance test of the end test before delivery.

The objective of the work is to establish an acoustic measurement technique for acoustic end-of-line testing that fulfills system specification 1 and 2, and establish the necessary pre-conditions for system specification 3 and 4. The development of experimental sound prediction methods with far-field prediction based on the boundary element method (BEM) was found to provide accurate results even in non-favorable acoustic environments [5] (realizing specification 1 through being contactless). This method is well-suited to fulfill specification two by utilizing data-driven mapping techniques, such as Gaussian process regression (GPR) [6], to minimize the overall uncertainty of the sound prediction method [7]. The benefit of using GPR is a direct estimate of the uncertainty quantification and risk estimation of exceeding limits is possible [8]. For instance, the next best training points are collected based on where the data is most likely to be the most informative. This Bayesian optimization strategy [9,10] is beneficial in situations where data acquisition is costly or slow, and can improve convergence. It is an iterative search (adaptive) of the next best sampling point based on previous samples. The sampling is updated to focus on areas of the input space that are expected to yield the most significant improvement of the model [11].

In the data acquisition process of surface motion data, GPR was used in various applications of robotics and biomechanics [12–14], including real-time [15,16]. In general, the main advantage of GPR over other existing interpolation methods is that it provides a maximum of information of the statistical description from the given data [11,17]. This maximum information gain is well-suited to the stated specifications in the introduction and can further benefit from the sequential design of experiments. However, specification 4 represents a significant obstacle in industrial integration for acoustic testing. Therefore, the contribution of this publication is that it presents the first application of GPR-based uncertainty predictions in vibroacoustics based on descriptive statistics and it discusses the potential speed-up of the Monte Carlo simulation method used in [7]. Firstly, the sampling will be discussed, starting with a minimum number of sampling points and then iteratively refining the number of sampling points. Secondly, the GPR routine of GPyTorch [18] will significantly improve the training and prediction speed of the GPR while continuously updating the model. Thirdly, the far-field prediction will be replaced by the low-fidelity and rapid Equivalent Radiated Power (ERP) method, which is known to be as accurate as the boundary element method (BEM) for high frequencies. Based on the uncertainty estimates from the GPR of the surface velocity, uncertainty in the resulting acoustic signal can be described by the ERP method presented in this work. The usage of BEM would require either the eigenvalues of the correlation matrix of the data points or a Monte Carlo Simulation [19].

In [20], the GPR was performed using scikit-learn 1.6.1 [21], considering 30 restarts to guarantee a robust minimum of the marginal log likelihood cost function. Therewith, at each frequency step (for 32 frequencies), an independent GPR was fitted separately to both the real and imaginary parts of the surface normal velocity frequency response. For each frequency step, 2 GPRs were trained, and restarted 30 times, for 128 sampling points. Subsequently, the two converged GPRs were evaluated using a Monte Carlo method 100 times to compute the mean of the radiated sound power at each vibration frequency. The computation of the radiated sound power was performed using three-dimensional conventional collocational BEM using the Burton–Miller method. The total sound power (BEM) estimation time of this computation was composed of 188.6 s for the GPR training (in total 2×32, 64 GPR were executed), 1072 s for drawing the Monte Carlo samples (in total $2 \times 32 \times 100$, 6400 samples were drawn) and 387.9 s to evaluate the BEM (in total 32 BEM systems were solved and 100×32 BEM result calculations were performed) on the reference machine (2× Intel Xeon G 5218-16 cores, Intel, Santa Clara, CA, USA). All three steps (GPR training, sample drawing, and the BEM simulations) consume a significant amount of time and consume a large fraction of the process time. In this article, statistical measures for the sound power uncertainty are derived, the speed-up potential of the workflow is discussed, and an adaptive refinement scheme to reduce the uncertainty in the predicted sound power is presented. To show the accuracy of the uncertainty propagation, the statistical sampling is compared to a Monte Carlo (BEM)-simulated reference acoustic prediction.

In summary, integrating GPR into the experimental sound field estimation provides a new perspective on assessing surface vibration measurements for acoustical quantification. In Section 2.1, the GPR details are discussed. Section 3 describes the experimental sound field estimation using laser scanning Doppler vibrometry (LSV). It is followed by the results Section 5, which reports the accuracy, performance, and adaptive refinement procedure of the proposed workflow. Concluding remarks are given in Section 6.

2. Methodology

Figure 1 depicts the proposed workflow schematically. It is based on the workflow presented in [5], where the boundary element method (BEM) was used to predict the radiated sound field based on the structural dynamic. At first, the surface velocity will be obtained from a region of interest (ROI) by data acquisition at a limited number of probing locations, by means of e.g., Laser Scanning Vibrometry (LSV) and Finite Element (FE) simulation. The data is then mapped by a standard interpolation technique [5] or Gaussian process regression (GPR) [20] onto the geometry and the evaluation points for the sound power prediction. Finally, the sound propagation is simulated. The radiated sound field can be predicted in various ways, such as using finite element method, BEM, or comparably fast low-fidelity methods. In this work, GPR is used on a dataset at given sample points to obtain a statistical description of the normal velocity field on the whole structure. Therewith, a statistical description of the sound emission based on the Equivalent Radiated Power (ERP) is computed based on either the Monte Carlo method or direct evaluation as proposed in Section 2.4. The statistical description of the ERP can then be used to assess the quality of the prediction and, finally, additional sample points can be defined in an adaptive refinement step based on an expected improvement function as described in Section 2.5.

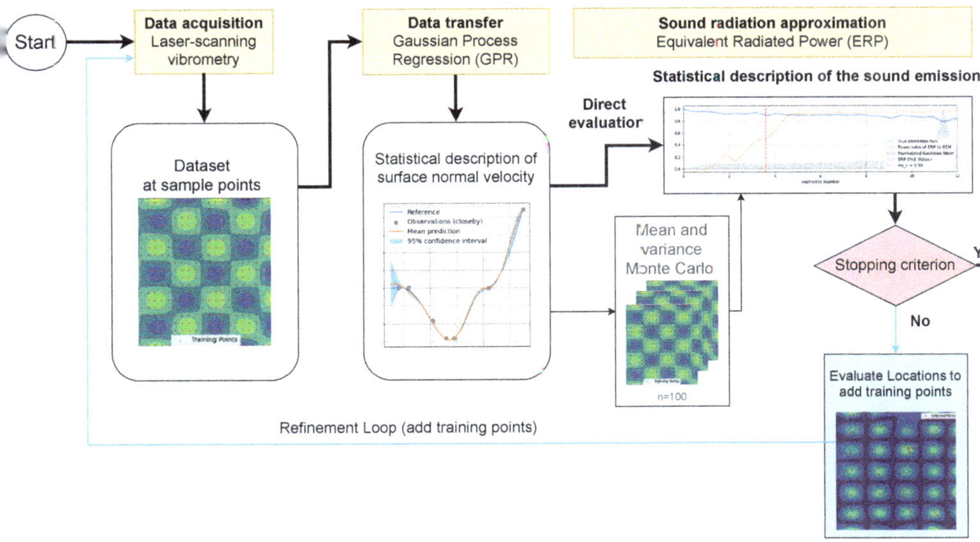

Figure 1. Schematic of the presented workflow predicting the radiated sound field based on surface velocity measurements, including an adaptive refinement procedure.

2.1. Interpolation Based on Gaussian Process Regression

In this article, the Gaussian process regression (GPR) is selected as an interpolation technique to provide both a mean and an uncertainty quantification [22] of the underlying physical process. If it cannot explain the data, the GPR has a noise level that increases, which may be used as an indication of such an event. It is known to reconstruct statistical distributions from noisy observations without overfitting [23], making it an ideal method for this experimental sound power estimate. The output is modeled at different input points with a mean and a covariance function. It has cubic complexity $O(n^3)$ in terms of the input data points n, which limits its application to large datasets. As a consequence, a variational Gaussian process is chosen to reduce the computational complexity [24,25] based on approximate inference [26]. The radial basis function (RBF) kernels are a valid choice for a spatially decreasing correlation and may improve the computational speed due to the sparsity of the correlation function. In [20], the complex-valued normal surface velocity $\boldsymbol{v}_\mathrm{s} \cdot \boldsymbol{n} := v_\mathrm{n}(\boldsymbol{x})$ was expressed as Gaussian processes (GP) $v_\mathrm{n} \sim \mathcal{GP}\{\mu, k\}$ for both real and imaginary part. Sampling this distribution of functions, this results in the Gaussian vector

$$v_\mathrm{n} \sim \mathcal{GP}\{\boldsymbol{\mu}, \boldsymbol{K}\} \tag{1}$$

where $\boldsymbol{\mu} := \mu(\boldsymbol{x})$ defines the GP's mean and $\boldsymbol{K} := \mathrm{cov}(\boldsymbol{x}, \boldsymbol{x}', \boldsymbol{\theta})$ the covariance matrix, with $\boldsymbol{\theta}$ denoting hyper-parameters. The radial basis kernel function used to evaluate the covariance matrix reads

$$\boldsymbol{K} = \sigma_x^2 \exp\left(-\frac{1}{2}\sum_{j=1}^{d} \frac{\|\boldsymbol{d}\|_2^2}{l^2}\right). \tag{2}$$

Here, $\boldsymbol{d} = \boldsymbol{x} - \boldsymbol{x}'$ is the distance vector, l length scale of the automatic relevance determination (ARD) for adjustable length scales for different input dimensions d [27], and σ_x^2 is a gain parameter. The hyperparameters $\boldsymbol{\theta}$ of the Gaussian process are adapted by optimization to minimize the negative log marginal likelihood objective function $L(\boldsymbol{y}, \boldsymbol{\theta})$ [28]

$$\underset{\boldsymbol{\theta}}{\operatorname{argmin}}\{-\log L(\boldsymbol{v}, \boldsymbol{\theta})\} \tag{3}$$

from an initial prior distribution (zero-mean Gaussian process $\sim \mathcal{N}(\boldsymbol{0}, \boldsymbol{K})$). Thereafter, the interpolation operation using GPR can be performed by making a prediction $\boldsymbol{v}_{\mathrm{n}}^*$ at location $\boldsymbol{x}^*$ based on the set of training data $\boldsymbol{v}_{\mathrm{n}}$ at $\boldsymbol{x}$ as described in [28]. The joint distribution reads

$$\begin{bmatrix} \boldsymbol{v}_{\mathrm{n}} \\ \boldsymbol{v}_{\mathrm{n}}^* \end{bmatrix} \sim \mathcal{N}\left(\begin{bmatrix} \boldsymbol{\mu}(\boldsymbol{x}) \\ \boldsymbol{\mu}(\boldsymbol{x}^*) \end{bmatrix}, \begin{bmatrix} \boldsymbol{K}(\boldsymbol{x},\boldsymbol{x}) + \sigma_*^2 \boldsymbol{I} & \boldsymbol{K}(\boldsymbol{x},\boldsymbol{x}^*) \\ \boldsymbol{K}(\boldsymbol{x}^*,\boldsymbol{x}) & \boldsymbol{K}(\boldsymbol{x}^*,\boldsymbol{x}^*) \end{bmatrix} \right) \tag{4}$$

with the predictive uncertainty σ_*^2 and leads to the predictive equation

$$\begin{aligned} \boldsymbol{v}_{\mathrm{n}}^* \sim \mathcal{N}\Big(&\boldsymbol{\mu}(\boldsymbol{x}^*) + \boldsymbol{K}(\boldsymbol{x}^*,\boldsymbol{x})\left[\boldsymbol{K}(\boldsymbol{x},\boldsymbol{x}) + \sigma_*^2 \boldsymbol{I}\right]^{-1} [\boldsymbol{v}_{\mathrm{n}} - \boldsymbol{\mu}(\boldsymbol{x})], \\ &\boldsymbol{K}(\boldsymbol{x}^*,\boldsymbol{x}^*) - \boldsymbol{K}(\boldsymbol{x}^*,\boldsymbol{x})\left[\boldsymbol{K}(\boldsymbol{x},\boldsymbol{x}) + \sigma_*^2 \boldsymbol{I}\right]^{-1} \boldsymbol{K}(\boldsymbol{x},\boldsymbol{x}^*)\Big). \end{aligned} \tag{5}$$

Typically, to improve the condition of the numerical optimization, the input and output data are normalized independently. The mean of the training data μ_{scaler} is subtracted and it is scaled to unit variance by $X = \frac{x-\mu_{\text{scaler}}}{\sigma_{\text{scaler}}}$. Consequently, due to $E\left(\frac{X-\mu_{\text{scaler}}}{\sigma_{\text{scaler}}}\right) = \frac{E(X)-\mu_{\text{scaler}}}{\sigma_{\text{scaler}}}$ and $COV\left(\frac{X-\mu_{\text{scaler}}}{\sigma_{\text{scaler}}}\right) = \frac{COV(X)}{\sigma_{\text{scaler}}^2}$ the fitted Gaussian process has to be rescaled as

$$\mathcal{GP}_x\{\boldsymbol{\mu}, \boldsymbol{K}\} = \mathcal{GP}_X\left\{\sigma_{\text{scaler}}\boldsymbol{\mu} + \mu_{\text{scaler}}\boldsymbol{e}, \sigma_{\text{scaler}}^2 \boldsymbol{K}\right\} \tag{6}$$

with $\boldsymbol{e}$ defining a vector of ones with the size of $\boldsymbol{\mu}$. In doing so, the predictive uncertainty of the GPR on the normalized dataset can be defined as the sum of the model variance and the noise variance.

2.2. Sound Power Estimates

As presented in [5], the sound propagation is solved using the open-source BEM library NiHu [29]. It solves the Helmholtz boundary integral equation for smooth boundaries [2]

$$p_{\mathrm{a}} = \frac{1}{2}\int_{\Gamma_{\mathrm{s}}} \left(p_{\mathrm{a}} \frac{\partial G}{\partial y_i} - G \frac{\partial p_{\mathrm{a}}}{\partial y_i} \right) \cdot \boldsymbol{n}\, \mathrm{d}\Gamma, \tag{7}$$

where p_{a} is the fluctuating acoustic pressure and $G(\boldsymbol{x}|\boldsymbol{y}, k)$ the three-dimensional free-field Green's function. The Neumann boundary condition for the acoustic pressure (7) can be expressed by Euler's equation of motion

$$\Gamma_{\mathrm{s}} : \frac{\partial p_{\mathrm{a}}}{\partial y_i} n_i = \rho_0\, j\omega\, v_{\mathrm{n}}, \tag{8}$$

with angular frequency $\omega = 2\pi f$ and mean density of air at ambient conditions $\rho_0 = 1.225\,\frac{\mathrm{kg}}{\mathrm{m}^3}$. The Burton–Miller method [30] was used to solve the Helmholtz boundary integral equation. The radiated sound power

$$P_{\mathrm{a}} = \frac{1}{2}\int_{\Gamma_{\mathrm{s}}} \Re\{p_{\mathrm{a}} v_{\mathrm{n}}^*\} \mathrm{d}\Gamma, \tag{9}$$

with the complex conjugate being denoted by the superscript * was computed as an integral metric of the acoustic far field. Whenever the radiation efficiency is one, typically encountered at higher frequency vibrations, the BEM simulation can be approximated by the ERP accurately as mentioned, e.g., in [31]. In contrast to the BEM, no system of equations has to be solved, which makes it computationally efficient. The ERP sound power estimate is defined as

$$P_{\mathrm{ERP}} = \frac{1}{2} c_0 \rho_0 \int_{\Gamma_{\mathrm{s}}} \|v_{\mathrm{n}}\|^2 \mathrm{d}\Gamma \approx \frac{1}{2} c_0 \rho_0 \sum_i A_i v_{\mathrm{n},i} v_{\mathrm{n},i}^* \tag{10}$$

with A_i denoting the area of element i. The major benefit of the ERP estimate is its fast computation. Assuming constant-valued elements on the boundary Γ_{s}, the surface integral simplifies to a summation of the corresponding element values.

The ERP gives a good approximation of the radiated sound power for convex rigid bodies and at high frequencies [32]. This is due to modeling all sources with a constant radiation efficiency of 1, which gives an upper bound for the structure-induced acoustical field in most cases [32]. A good indicator for the appropriate frequency range to use the ERP is the coincidence frequency, which is sometimes referred to as the critical frequency. The coincidence frequency indicates the frequency at which the phase speed of bending and acoustic waves is equal [33]. Below the frequency, the radiation efficiency is expected to be low, and cancellation effects must be considered for predicting the radiated sound power, as mentioned in, e.g., [34]. For frequencies larger than f_c, the radiation efficiency is high, and the ERP gives a good approximation of the radiated sound power.

2.3. Confidence of the Sound Power Prediction

For each frequency ω, the real and the imaginary parts of the Fourier transformed normal velocity are fit to a Gaussian process

$$\Re\{v_n(\boldsymbol{x},\omega)\} \sim \mathcal{GP}\{\boldsymbol{\mu}_{\omega,\Re}, \boldsymbol{K}_{\omega,\Re}\}, \tag{11}$$

$$\Im\{v_n(\boldsymbol{x},\omega)\} \sim \mathcal{GP}\{\boldsymbol{\mu}_{\omega,\Im}, \boldsymbol{K}_{\omega,\Im}\}, \tag{12}$$

The Gaussian process can be used with Monte Carlo simulation to estimate the ERP of the surface velocity for every frequency and evaluation point, and then estimate the variance $VAR[ERP]$ and the expected value $E[ERP]$ of the acoustic signal. This brute force technique can also be performed for the sound power estimate of the BEM. In each sampling location $\boldsymbol{X} \in \mathbb{R}^{2\times m} \rightarrow \Re\{V_n(\omega)\} \in \mathbb{R}^m$ and $\boldsymbol{X} \in \mathbb{R}^{2\times m} \rightarrow \Im\{V_n(\omega)\} \in \mathbb{R}^m$. The evaluation is that of a multivariate normal distribution $\boldsymbol{x} \sim \mathcal{N}(\boldsymbol{\mu}, \boldsymbol{K})$ with a symmetric, real-valued, and positive definite covariance matrix $\boldsymbol{K}$. A computationally efficient draw of samples can be performed by

$$\boldsymbol{x} = \boldsymbol{\mu} + \boldsymbol{L}\boldsymbol{z} \tag{13}$$

with the standard normal random vector $\boldsymbol{z} \sim \mathcal{N}(\boldsymbol{0}, \boldsymbol{I})$ and the lower triangular matrix $\boldsymbol{L}$ defined as $\boldsymbol{K} = \boldsymbol{L}\boldsymbol{L}^\top$. $\boldsymbol{L}$ can be computed efficiently by Cholesky decomposition.

This brute force technique is relatively inefficient, since a large number of GP realizations have to be computed.

Alternatively, the collective normal velocity can be described by the descriptive statistics of a multivariate normal distribution with a given mean and covariance $\Re\{V_n(\omega)\} \sim \mathcal{N}(\boldsymbol{\mu}_\Re, \boldsymbol{K}_\Re)$, $\Im\{V_n(\omega)\} \sim \mathcal{N}(\boldsymbol{\mu}_\Im, \boldsymbol{K}_\Im)$ connected to the Gaussian processes, respectively. The

$$ERP \sim (\Re\{V_n(\omega)\})^{\mathrm{T}}(\Re\{V_n(\omega)\}) + (\Im\{V_n(\omega)\})^{\mathrm{T}}(\Im\{V_n(\omega)\}) \sim \chi^2_{gen,\Re} + \chi^2_{gen,\Im} \tag{14}$$

which is proportional to the surface motion energy, being proportional to the square of the collective normal velocities. The individual distributions of the two terms are uncorrelated general chi-squared distributions. The collective expected value and variance are the sum of the individual expected value and variance

$$E[\chi^2_{gen,\Re} + \chi^2_{gen,\Im}] = E[\chi^2_{gen,\Re}] + E[\chi^2_{gen,\Im}] \tag{15}$$

$$VAR[\chi^2_{gen,\Re} + \chi^2_{gen,\Im}] = VAR[\chi^2_{gen,\Re}] + VAR[\chi^2_{gen,\Im}] \tag{16}$$

The individual terms are computed as follows [35]: given a column vector $\boldsymbol{x} \sim \mathcal{N}(\boldsymbol{\mu}, \boldsymbol{K})$, which could be the normal velocity, find the probability of the squared sum of the individual samples

$$q(\boldsymbol{x}) = \boldsymbol{x}^{\mathrm{T}}\mathbf{I}\boldsymbol{x} > 0. \tag{17}$$

With **I** being the identity matrix. This can be viewed as the multi-dimensional integral or sum of the energy of a multivariant normally distributed function, $\boldsymbol{x} = \sqrt{\mathbf{K}}\boldsymbol{z} + \boldsymbol{\mu}$. $\sqrt{\mathbf{K}} = \boldsymbol{V}^{\mathrm{T}}\sqrt{\mathbf{D}}\boldsymbol{V}$, where **D** is the diagonal of the eigenvalues and $\boldsymbol{V}$ the respective eigenvectors of the eigenvalues. Now, we can transform the expression to $\boldsymbol{z} \sim \mathcal{N}(\boldsymbol{0}, \boldsymbol{I})$ by the inverse $\boldsymbol{z} = \mathbf{K}^{-1/2}(\boldsymbol{x} - \boldsymbol{\mu})$. This decorrelates the variables $\boldsymbol{x}$, and transforms the integration domain to a different quadratic form (bilinear form):

$$\tilde{q}(\boldsymbol{z}) = \boldsymbol{z}^{\mathrm{T}}\mathbf{K}\boldsymbol{z} + 2(\mathbf{K}^{1/2}\boldsymbol{\mu})\boldsymbol{z} + \boldsymbol{\mu}^{\mathrm{T}}\boldsymbol{\mu} > 0 \tag{18}$$

Now the problem is to find the probability of the standard normal $\boldsymbol{z}$ in this domain. We can start at the eigen-decomposition $\mathbf{K} = \mathbf{V}^{\mathrm{T}}\mathbf{D}\mathbf{V}$ of **K**.The transformed variable $\boldsymbol{y} = \mathbf{V}\boldsymbol{z}$ is also standard normal, and in this space the quadratic is given by the following:

$$\begin{aligned}
\hat{q}(\boldsymbol{y}) &= \boldsymbol{y}^{\mathrm{T}}\mathbf{D}\boldsymbol{y} + 2(\mathbf{K}^{1/2}\boldsymbol{\mu})\mathbf{V}\boldsymbol{y} + \tilde{q}_0 \qquad \left(\boldsymbol{b}^{\mathrm{T}} = 2(\mathbf{K}^{1/2}\boldsymbol{\mu})\mathbf{V}\right)\\
&= \sum_i \left(D_i y_i^2 + b_i y_i\right) + \sum_{i'} b_{i'} y_{i'} + \boldsymbol{\mu}^{\mathrm{T}}\boldsymbol{\mu}\\
&= \sum_i D_i \left(y_i + \frac{b_i}{2D_i}\right)^2 + \sum_{i'} b_{i'} y_{i'} + \boldsymbol{\mu}^{\mathrm{T}}\boldsymbol{\mu} - \sum_i D_i \left(\frac{b_i}{2D_i}\right)^2\\
&= \sum_i D_i \chi^2_{1,(b_i/2D_i)^2} + \mathcal{N}(m, s^2),
\end{aligned}$$

here, i and i' index the nonzero and zero eigenvalues of the eigenvalue decomposition. Finally, we obtain a weighted sum of non-central chi-square variables χ^2, each with 1 degree of freedom, and a normal variable $\mathcal{N}(m, s^2)$. So this is a generalized chi-square variable $\tilde{\chi}_{\boldsymbol{w},\boldsymbol{k},\boldsymbol{\lambda},s,m}$, where we merge the non-central chi-square variables with the same weights, so that the vector of their weights $\boldsymbol{w} = diag(\boldsymbol{D}) \quad \forall \quad D_i \neq 0$ are the unique eigenvalues among D_i, their degrees of freedom $\boldsymbol{k}$ are the numbers of times the eigenvalues occur, and their non-centralities and the normal parameters are as follows:

$$\lambda_j = \frac{1}{4w_j^2} \sum_{i=0:D_i=w_j}^{k} b_i^2, \quad s = \sqrt{\sum_{i'=0:D_i=0} b_{i'}^2}, \quad m = \boldsymbol{\mu}^{\mathrm{T}}\boldsymbol{\mu} - \boldsymbol{w}.\boldsymbol{\lambda}.$$

The : in the summation index describes that we iterate over the indices i from zero to k, only for the entries where the weight w_j and the iterated D_i are equal. The mean estimate can be described over a sum of j distinct eigenvalues occurring k_j times in the diagonal matrix $\boldsymbol{D}$

$$\mu_q = \sum_j w_j(k_j + \lambda_j) + m \tag{19}$$

and the variance estimate

$$\sigma_q^2 = 2\sum_j w_j^2(k_j + 2\lambda_j) + s^2\,. \tag{20}$$

Note that this sound power estimate can be also performed using the system matrix of the BEM. The main drawback of this method is that based on the number of points, an eigenvalue problem (algorithmic complexity of $O(n^3)$) has to be solved that slows down the prediction of the sound power estimate drastically.

2.4. Approximation of the χ^2 Expected Value and χ^2 Variance to Describe the Sound Power

In general, the expected value and the variance of the bilinear form (18) can be calculated by

$$\mu_q = E[\mathbf{z}^{\mathrm{T}}\mathbf{K}\mathbf{z} + 2(\mathbf{K}^{1/2}\boldsymbol{\mu})\mathbf{z} + \boldsymbol{\mu}^{\mathrm{T}}\boldsymbol{\mu}] = E[\mathbf{z}^{\mathrm{T}}\mathbf{K}\mathbf{z}] + \boldsymbol{\mu}^{\mathrm{T}}\boldsymbol{\mu} = \sum_i K_{ii} + \boldsymbol{\mu}^{\mathrm{T}}\boldsymbol{\mu} \tag{21}$$

and the variance by

$$VAR[\mathbf{z}^{\mathrm{T}}\mathbf{K}\mathbf{z} + 2(\mathbf{K}^{1/2}\boldsymbol{\mu})\mathbf{z} + \boldsymbol{\mu}^{\mathrm{T}}\boldsymbol{\mu}] = E[(\mathbf{z}^{\mathrm{T}}\mathbf{K}\mathbf{z} + 2(\mathbf{K}^{1/2}\boldsymbol{\mu})\mathbf{z} + \boldsymbol{\mu}^{\mathrm{T}}\boldsymbol{\mu} - \mu_q)^2]\,. \tag{22}$$

This expression can be further expanded by the expected value into

$$E[(\mathbf{z}^{\mathrm{T}}\mathbf{K}\mathbf{z} - \sum_i K_{ii} + 2(\mathbf{K}^{1/2}\boldsymbol{\mu})\mathbf{z})^2] = VAR[\mathbf{z}^{\mathrm{T}}\mathbf{K}\mathbf{z}] + VAR[2(\mathbf{K}^{1/2}\boldsymbol{\mu})\mathbf{z}]\,. \tag{23}$$

where the covariance of the normally distributed variables and the square of it is zero. Furthermore, we can utilize the details of the variance of the first and last expression for the positive definite covariance matrix $\boldsymbol{K}$

$$VAR[\mathbf{z}^{\mathrm{T}}\mathbf{K}\mathbf{z}] = 2\sum_i (\mathbf{K}^T\mathbf{K})_{ii} = 2\sum_{i,j} K_{ij}^2\,. \tag{24}$$

$$VAR[2(\mathbf{K}^{1/2}\boldsymbol{\mu})\mathbf{z}] = 4\boldsymbol{\mu}^{\mathrm{T}}\mathbf{K}\boldsymbol{\mu}\,. \tag{25}$$

Finally, we obtain a simple expression for the variance

$$\sigma_q^2 = 2\sum_{i,j} K_{ij}^2 + 4\boldsymbol{\mu}^{\mathrm{T}}\mathbf{K}\boldsymbol{\mu}\,. \tag{26}$$

The predictive uncertainty $\sigma_*^2 = \sigma_q^2/\sigma_{\mathrm{scaler}}^2$ of the ERP can be defined concerning the normalized GPR output data, such that it will have a value close to zero for low variance in the prediction and a value close to one for uncertain predictions.

2.5. Adaptive Refinement Procedure

To improve the regression quality, additional sampling points can be defined based on an adaptive refinement procedure. The procedure follows the schematic given in Figure 1. It starts by performing a variational GPR, and as long as a stopping criterion is not met, the adaptive refinement procedure is carried out. Therefore, a potential improvement function is defined to estimate the optimal locations for describing the GPR with reduced noise. The idea is to target the maxima of the function and accurately predict them using the GPR. We define the improvement function $I(x)$ at a new point x as the probability that it is located at a maximum of the absolute value of the underlying process

$$I(x) = \max(|\ f(x)\ |)\,.$$

The expectation of this improvement $EI(x)$ is defined by

$$EI(x) = \mathbb{E}[\max(|\ f(x)\ |)]$$

Based on the $Z = \frac{\mu(x)}{\sigma(x)}$, the $EI(x)$ is given by

$$EI(x) = \mu(x)(1 - 2\Phi(-Z)) + 2\sigma(x)\phi(Z)$$

where $\Phi(\cdot)$ is the Cumulative Distribution Function (CDF) and $\phi(\cdot)$ is the Probability Density Function (PDF) of the standard normal distribution. Now we select locations x that maximize this $EI(x)$ value. Finally, we select the best 500 points from all adaptive refinement samples that improve the GPR, and then randomly select 20 points. This process is carried out independently for both the real and imaginary parts. Both new locations are added to obtain new measurements, as with one measurement, we obtain both the real and the imaginary parts. With that procedure, we minimize the noise in the final ERP values.

3. Application

The method was tested using a vibrating plate benchmark test (see Figure 2a). It comprises a thin square-shaped steel plate with dimensions ($1\,\mathrm{m} \times 1\,\mathrm{m} \times 0.01\,\mathrm{m}$) and material properties (density $\rho = 7872\,\mathrm{kg\,m^{-3}}$, Young's modulus $E = 200\,\mathrm{GPa}$, and Poisson number $\nu = 0.29$) [5]. The plate was clamped at the edge Γ_{fix} and was free to move on the other edges. A time-harmonic point force of strength $F_z = 1\,\mathrm{N}$ is applied at position $\boldsymbol{x}_0 = [0.1, 0.2, 0.01]^\top$ m in the z-direction, exciting a vibrating motion in the structure.

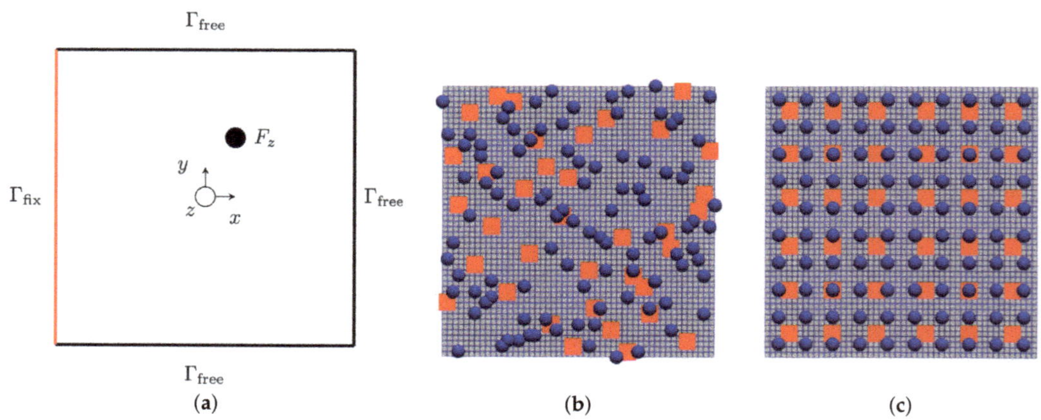

Figure 2. Top view of the investigated plate with an exemplary set of 36 (red) and 100 (blue) measurement points, based on Latin hypercube (**b**) and uniform (**c**) sampling, respectively. (**a**) Simulation setup, with force F_z and boundary conditions [5]. (**b**) Latin hypercube sampling. (**c**) Uniform sampling.

A time-harmonic finite element simulation was conducted using openCFS [36] to obtain the plate's surface vibration at each frequency. This finite element simulation served as pseudo-measurement data. At each vertex of the black grid depicted in Figure 2, the normal velocity is known and used for sampling the reference data as a training dataset. In

Figure 3a, some eigenmodes of the benchmark problem are visualized. The coincidence frequency is $f_c = 1233\,\text{Hz}$. For frequencies larger than f_c, the radiation efficiency is high, and the ERP gives a good approximation of the radiated sound power as shown in Figure 3b.

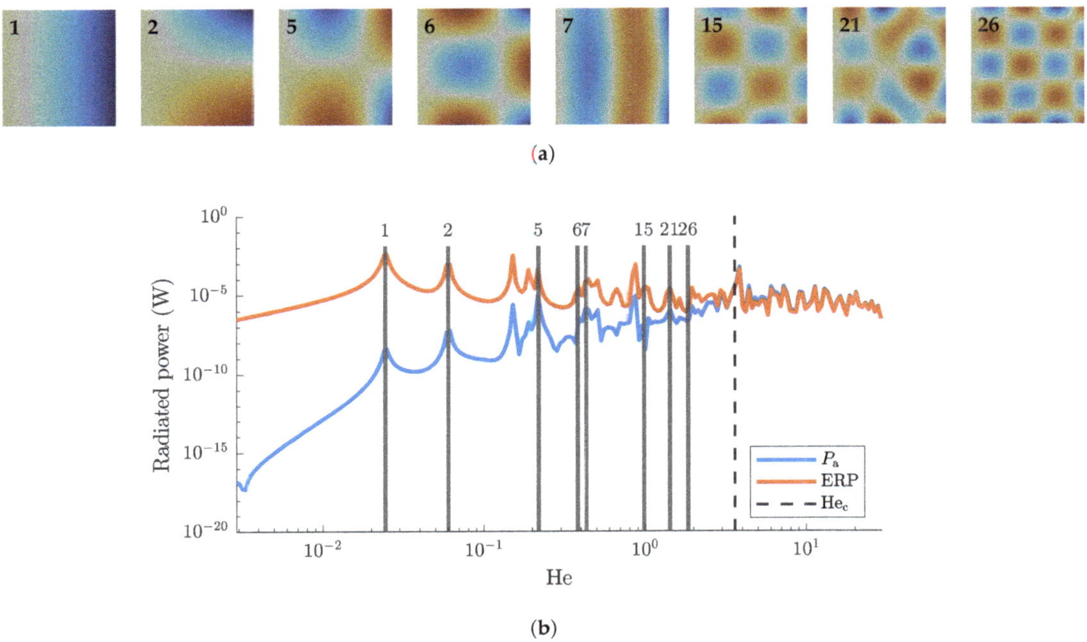

Figure 3. Solution of the benchmark problem. Indicated eigenmodes at He = 0.024, 0.06, 0.22, 0.38, 0.43, 0.98, 1.43, 1.85. The coincidence frequency for this setup is He = 3.6. (**a**) Real part of the mode shape for selected structural eigenmodes. (**b**) Radiated sound power based on BEM (P_a) and ERP.

Two sampling strategies were tested: (i) Latin hypercube (LHC) sampling and (ii) uniform grid sampling. In the case of the LHC sampling as depicted in Figure 2b, the closest node to each sample was used as a measurement point. For the uniform grid sampling depicted in Figure 2c, equally spaced nodes are selected. In Figure 2, two exemplary sets of measurement points are indicated in red and blue color, respectively. To emulate the effect of noisy observations, uncorrelated noise was added to the simulated pseudo-measurement data $\hat{v}_{n,\omega}(\boldsymbol{x}) = v_{n,\omega}(\boldsymbol{x}) + \epsilon_\omega(\boldsymbol{x})$. The added noise $\epsilon_\omega \sim N(0, \sigma^2_{\epsilon,\omega})$ was defined as spatially normally distributed noise with scaled variance based on the mean velocity amplitude $\sigma_{\epsilon,\omega} = k_{\text{noise}}\overline{v_{n,\omega}(\boldsymbol{x})}$. The factor was chosen as $k_{\text{noise}} = 0.001$.

3.1. Exact Gaussian Process Regression

In [20], the prediction capabilities of exact Gaussian process regression are discussed. It is shown that the rule of thumb, that six points per wavelength are sufficient for a respective estimate [37], can be used to give a limit of the minimum number of sampling points required for the interpolation. As shown in [20], as soon as the vibration is underresolved, it does not matter which interpolation method is used, and the result is poor. In contrast, as long as the experimental resolution is given, the radial basis function kernel GPR outperformed standard linear interpolation significantly. Similar to GPR, ordinary radial basis function interpolation [38] based on the same geometric length scale reaches a comparable level of accuracy.

At higher frequencies, the mode shapes become more complex, and the number of measurement points required to prevent under-resolution increases. Consequently, the dimensionality of the GPR gets high which first results to badly conditioned optimization problems and therefore significant numerical errors and secondly comes with substantial computational cost as the cost for inference scales at $\mathcal{O}(N^3)$ due to the need to invert the covariance matrix. Therefore, for the regression of high-frequency oscillation shapes, approximate inference can be the superior method.

3.2. Stochastic Variational Gaussian Process Regression

The exact GPRs complexity scales with the number of input data points N cubed $\mathcal{O}(N^3)$. To address this, we employ the stochastic variational Gaussian process (SVGP) framework introduced in [39]. This method combines variational inference with sparse GPs, reducing the cost from $\mathcal{O}(N^3)$ to $\mathcal{O}(NM^2)$, where $M \ll N$ is the number of inducing points.

Stochastic variational Gaussian process regression is based on variational Bayesian inference. An introduction to variational inference can be found in [40]. Bayesian inference derives the posterior distribution $p(\boldsymbol{f}|\boldsymbol{x})$ using Bayes' rule

$$p(\boldsymbol{f}|\boldsymbol{x}) = \frac{p(\boldsymbol{x},\boldsymbol{f})}{p(\boldsymbol{x})} = \frac{p(\boldsymbol{x}|\boldsymbol{f})p(\boldsymbol{f})}{p(\boldsymbol{x})} \tag{27}$$

from the prior distribution $p(\boldsymbol{f})$, the likelihood $p(\boldsymbol{x}|\boldsymbol{f})$, and the evidence also referred to as marginal likelihood $p(\boldsymbol{x})$. The evidence is defined as

$$p(\boldsymbol{x}) = \int p(\boldsymbol{x}|\boldsymbol{f})p(\boldsymbol{f})\mathrm{d}\boldsymbol{f} \tag{28}$$

To obtain computationally efficient inference, the integration in Equation (28) is typically approximated as direct integration is intractable in most cases. This can be achieved through Monte Carlo integration or by utilizing variational inference. In variational inference, an approximation

$$q(\boldsymbol{f}) \approx p(\boldsymbol{f}|\boldsymbol{x})$$

for most $\boldsymbol{f}, \boldsymbol{x}$ is desired such that $\boldsymbol{x}$ can be inferred from $\boldsymbol{f}$ cheaply. The Kullback–Leibler divergence can be used to quantify the similarity between both distributions, the truth and its approximation. The according optimization problem describes finding the best approximation $q_*(\boldsymbol{f})$

$$q_*(\boldsymbol{f}) = \underset{q(\boldsymbol{f})}{\operatorname{argmin}}\, \mathtt{KL}(q(\boldsymbol{f})||p(\boldsymbol{f}|\boldsymbol{x})) \tag{29}$$

Unfortunately, the Kullback–Leibler divergence [41] $\mathtt{KL}(q(\boldsymbol{f})\|p(\boldsymbol{f}|\boldsymbol{x}))$ comes with the same flaw as the evidence integral because it requires the evidence $\log p(\boldsymbol{x})$ in its evaluation. However, a lower bound of the objective can be stated

$$\mathtt{ELBO} = E[\log p(\boldsymbol{f},\boldsymbol{x})] - E[\log q(\boldsymbol{f})] \leq \log p(\boldsymbol{x}) \tag{30}$$

This function is called evidence lower bound (ELBO). Maximizing the ELBO is equivalent to minimizing the KL divergence [40] and ensures that the approximate posterior $q(\boldsymbol{f})$ is close to the true posterior $p(\boldsymbol{f}|\boldsymbol{x})$ while avoiding the intractable computation of the evidence.

While variational inference provides a way to efficiently approximate the posterior distribution, sparse GPs alleviate the computational bottleneck of handling all training points. Combining these two approaches yields scalable inference. Sparse Gaussian processes rely on inducing point methods [42] where the inducing variables $\boldsymbol{u}$ are used paired with the inducing inputs $\mathbf{Z}$. The distribution augmented with inducing points reads

$$p(\boldsymbol{f},\boldsymbol{u}) = \mathcal{N}\left(\begin{bmatrix} \boldsymbol{f} \\ \boldsymbol{u} \end{bmatrix} \middle| \mathbf{0}, \begin{bmatrix} \mathbf{K}_{nn} & \mathbf{K}_{nm} \\ \mathbf{K}_{nm}^\top & \mathbf{K}_{mm} \end{bmatrix}\right) \tag{31}$$

with indices n representing the data points $x_n \in \mathbf{X}$ and m the inducing point indices $z_m \in \mathbf{Z}$. Again, Bayesian inference can be written as

$$p(\boldsymbol{u}|\boldsymbol{x}) = \frac{p(\boldsymbol{x},\boldsymbol{f},\boldsymbol{u})}{p(\boldsymbol{x})} = \frac{p(\boldsymbol{x}|\boldsymbol{f})p(\boldsymbol{f}|\boldsymbol{u})p(\boldsymbol{u})}{p(\boldsymbol{x})}$$

with $p(\boldsymbol{u}) \sim \mathcal{N}(\mathbf{0}, \mathbf{K}_{mm})$, $p(\boldsymbol{f}|\boldsymbol{u}) \sim \mathcal{N}(\mathbf{K}_{nm}\mathbf{K}_{mm}^{-1}\boldsymbol{u}, \mathbf{K}_{nn} - \mathbf{Q}_{nn})$, and $\mathbf{Q}_{nn} = \mathbf{K}_{nm}\mathbf{K}_{mm}^{-1}\mathbf{K}_{nm}^\top$.

Using the Fully Independent Training Conditional (FITC) method to approximate the integration over $\boldsymbol{f}$, one arrives at a tractable bound on the marginal likelihood for the Gaussian case [24]

$$\begin{aligned} \log p(\boldsymbol{x}) \geq & \log \mathcal{N}\left(\mathbf{0}, \mathbf{K}_{nm}\mathbf{K}_{mm}^{-1}\mathbf{K}_{nm}^\top + \sigma^2\mathbf{I}\right) \\ & - \frac{1}{2\sigma^2}\operatorname{tr}(\mathbf{K}_{nn} - \mathbf{Q}_{nn}) \end{aligned} \tag{32}$$

This bound on the marginal likelihood, also referred to as *evidence*, can be used as an objective function in optimizing the covariance function parameters as well as the inducing input points $\mathbf{Z}$. The advantage of this approach is the reduced computational cost of Equation (32) to $\mathcal{O}(NM^2)$. Combining this approach of sparse GPs with the variational inference [43] yields

$$\begin{aligned} \log p(\boldsymbol{x}) \geq & \log \mathcal{N}\left(\mathbf{K}_{nm}\mathbf{K}_{mm}^{-1}\mathbf{m}, \sigma^2\mathbf{I}\right) \\ & - \frac{1}{2\sigma^2}\operatorname{tr}\left(\mathbf{K}_{nn}\mathbf{K}_{mm}^{-1}\mathbf{S}\mathbf{K}_{mm}^{-1}\mathbf{K}_{mn}\right) \\ & - \frac{1}{2\sigma^2}\operatorname{tr}(\mathbf{K}_{nn} - \mathbf{Q}_{nn}) - \mathrm{KL}[q(\boldsymbol{u})\|p(\boldsymbol{u})] \end{aligned} \tag{33}$$

with the variational parameters $\boldsymbol{m}, \boldsymbol{S}$ such that $q(\boldsymbol{u}) \sim \mathcal{N}(\boldsymbol{m}, \boldsymbol{S})$.

In the following, this combined approach of sparse GPs and variational inference will be referred to as variational GPR. Its key advantage lies in enabling scalable optimization in both stochastic [43] and distributed settings [44,45].

4. Hypotheses

The core part of this article is the investigation of the predictive capabilities of Gaussian process regression for the interpolation task specifically concerning the mean and variance of surface vibration fields. The primary interest is how the variability in terms of the mapped variance is translated into the sound emission predictions. In general, a significant variability results in a large variability in the predicted sound signal. There are two common methods to compute the standard deviation of the radiated sound power. First, a Monte Carlo simulation of the sound field using the boundary element method or the ERP. Another method, and a faster prediction method, is the estimate based on statistics of stochastic processes described in the previous sections. Both methods are suitable and can be used to update the number of sampling points and refine the underlying Gaussian process. Therefore, the following seven hypotheses are formulated to address the research questions regarding the usage of GPRs in acoustic end-of-line testing:

H1. *The algorithm derived can provide real-time capability regarding the sampling cycle of the laser scanning vibrometry system with fixed sample averaging and fixed measurement uncertainty thresholds.*

H2. *The number of training points for the Gaussian process regression positively correlates with the upper frequency limit at which the Gaussian process can accurately model the surface normal velocity and sound prediction.*

H3. *The interpolation error to the ground truth velocity correlates with the noise of the velocity prediction from the GPR.*

H4. *The Latin hypercube sampling with the same number of sampling points as regular grid sampling results in a lower level of error (of the mean compared to the ground truth) and variance of the predicted GP after the same number of training epochs.*

H5. *There exists an adaptive refinement method that reduces the (integrated) modeled noise of the velocity prediction and hence improves the accuracy in the sound power estimate.*

H6. *The ERP-based estimates based on the statistical theory have higher computational performance than the Monte Carlo with BEM, while maintaining the accuracy of the predicted sound power above a specific frequency where the radiation efficiency approaches one.*

H7. *The computational performance can be significantly increased using transfer learning, based on pre-trained models.*

H8. *The proposed method can handle different levels of noise contained in the measurement data.*

5. Results

The interpolation based on GPR has the unique advantage of quantifying uncertainty of a model, which is estimated based on experimental data. The model uncertainty is described by a mean, a covariance, and a likelihood variance estimate. This result provides the opportunity to model the variance of the surface velocity estimate, which can be translated into the variability of the radiated sound power. It serves as an informed approach to reducing uncertainty in the measurement procedure.

5.1. Computational Performance Improvement

One focus of this work was to reduce the time required for GPR training (Hypothesis 1). Thereby, the alterations from the preliminary setup [20] were twofold. First, the core framework for the training process was replaced by *GPyTorch 1.14* [18], a highly efficient and modular implementation of GPs. GPU acceleration may become attractive as we approach several tens of thousands of training points. The framework used is implemented in *PyTorch 2.6.0* [46]. On the reference setup using 3600 training points, an improvement of computational time by a factor of 60 was obtained comparing the variational GPR setup in GPyTorch compared to the exact GPR in scikit-learn (see Table 1). We tested two commonly used optimizers, the L-BFGS optimization algorithm and the Adam optimizer [47] in GPyTorch. The L-BFGS optimizer (learning rate of 0.01, with a maximum of 20 iterations and 10 previous gradients stored) took longer than the Adam optimizer (learning rate of 0.01) to reach a comparable accurate minimum. The exact GPR implementation was even faster when it converged. This was only the case at oscillations with very low frequency and using only a few training points (below 100). In other cases (when the number of training points increases), the exact GPR implementation in GPyTorch did not converge well.

Table 1. Comparison of computation time (in seconds) for $n = 3600$ uniformly distributed data points on the reference measurement grid. The mean time of an optimization run is presented in seconds. For the Monte Carlo Simulation 100 samples are drawn on a 60×60 evaluation grid. Computations were performed on a reference machine (Apple M4).

Task of Sound Prediction	**BEM**		**ERP**	
		(Monte Carlo)	**(χ^2-EV-Based)**	**(χ^2)**
Exact GPR [20] Training (L-BFGS)	scikit-learn 535.0			
Variational GPR Training (L-BFGS) Training (Adam)	GPyTorch 9.93 7.96			
Draw samples	0.20		-	-
Evaluate radiated power distribution	5.49	0.004	3.15	**0.04**
Total time (Adam)	13.65	8.16	10.11	8.00

Inspecting the computation times of the preliminary investigations [20], the drawing of samples from the GP represents a significant contribution to the overall computation time. The comparably slow drawing of samples from the GP using the scikit-learn library was due to the used algorithm in the package, which computes the samples by singular value decomposition $\boldsymbol{K} = \boldsymbol{U}\boldsymbol{\Sigma}\boldsymbol{V}^\top$ and $\boldsymbol{x} = \boldsymbol{\mu} + \boldsymbol{U}\boldsymbol{\Sigma}^{\frac{1}{2}}\boldsymbol{z}$. As the covariance matrix of any multivariate normal distribution has to be positive definite, a computationally more efficient method to draw samples is the use of Cholesky decomposition $\boldsymbol{K} = \boldsymbol{L}\boldsymbol{L}^\top$ and Equation (13). By using this modified algorithm, we were able to reduce the computational time of the sample drawing in these cases (see Table 1) from over 16.7 s (scikit-learn [20]) to 0.20 s, which is a significant reduction.

The computation of the radiated sound field using the BEM represents a significant computational cost of 5.49 s (see Table 1) and 4.9 GB of RAM. As the number of required measurement points is dominated by the high-frequency oscillation patterns showing smaller length scale mode shapes, a high-frequency ERP approximation of the radiated sound power can be used instead. Compared to the radiated sound power of the BEM, the ERP-based method assumes a uniform radiation efficiency of one for any frequency of interest. These assumptions lead to significant deviations at low frequencies (below the coincidence frequency), while minor deviations occur for high frequencies of the signal (details will be provided in Section 5.6).

Therefore, the ERP was considered as an alternative for quality assessment using Monte Carlo simulation. It reduces the computational effort required to solve a system of algebraic equations (evaluation time of radiated sound power with BEM of 9.52 s) to a matrix-vector product (evaluation time of radiated sound power with ERP of 0.004 s). Furthermore, the explicit nature of the ERP makes it possible to reformulate it in a Bayesian sense to avoid the Monte Carlo simulation altogether, as shown in Section 2.4. There exist two estimates of the mean and variance, one being an exact estimate (χ^2-EV-based) involving the eigenvalues of the covariance matrix and another approximate (χ^2) by directly acting on the covariance matrix and the mean vector. The inverse of the covariance matrix for a large number of sampling points is computationally costly and results in 3.15 s of computational time for the exact ERP estimate given in Section 2.3. In contrast, the ERP (χ^2) calculation using the covariance matrix and the mean vector directly outperforms all computations (resulting in a computational time of 0.04 s).

It then results in an overall time of 8.00 s for one prediction of a GPR and the evaluation of the sound power. In doing so, the computational time for a comparable number of support points was reduced by a factor of 60 from the previous implementation [20] to 8.00 s on the same architecture.

5.2. Expected Value and Variance of the Sound Power

In this section, we investigate the predictive capability of the GPR for estimating the sound power as a function of the frequency (Hypothesis 2). For the exact GPR, when increasing the number of training points, the numerical implementation and data fitting became unstable. The expected trend, that a higher amount of training data allows for modeling plate vibrations at higher oscillation frequencies, was not provided. Therefore, we switched to a variational Gaussian process regression method (see Section 3.2) instead of the exact Gaussian process regression method. The overall setup remains unchanged. It was implemented in GPyTorch using the algorithms described in [39]. The number of inducing points was set to $1/10$ of the total number of data points.

We selected a Gaussian prior for the length scales in each direction $\boldsymbol{\ell} \sim \mathcal{N}(\boldsymbol{\mu}_\ell, \boldsymbol{\sigma}_\ell)$ (e.g., $\boldsymbol{\mu}_\ell = (0.1, 0.1)^\top$, $\boldsymbol{\sigma}_\ell = 10^{-3}\mathbf{I}$), which is updated during the training. The homoscedastic Gaussian noise on the scaled target vibration velocity of the real and imaginary parts is learned independently. For the sparse variational inference, we provided initial M inducing points (one tenth of the provided training points) $\mathbf{Z} = \{\mathbf{z}_m\}_{m=1}^M$ selected by k-means classification on the training points. The locations of the inducing points are learned during training. A Cholesky distribution parametrizes the variational posterior. The variational ELBO specifies the loss function, and mini-batch training is used with the Adam optimizer. The model and the likelihood parameters are trained jointly. Early stopping is implemented as soon as the noise is sufficiently small and no further improvement is visible on a validation set.

In Figure 4, the radiated sound power estimate compared to the ground truth is compared to the ERP estimation based on a generalized χ^2 distribution. Several dashed lines and shaded areas are shown in the plot, describing the results of different the uniform resolution of a total of 100, 400, 1600, 3600, and 6400 points. Firstly, in blue, the relative accuracy η_{χ^2} of the (true) ERP (estimated by the reference solution data) and the ERP predicted by χ^2 distribution descriptive statistics of the velocity data from the GPR

$$\eta_{\chi^2} = 1 - \left|\frac{P_{\text{a,ERP}}}{P_{\text{a,ERP},\chi^2}} - 1\right| = 1 - \epsilon_{\chi^2}.$$

Secondly, the blue-shaded band visualizes the predictive uncertainty σ_*^2 of the GPR. The mean and variance of statistical ERP prediction methods are in good agreement with the Monte Carlo simulation η_{MC} (mean deviations less than 10^{-5} for each study), suggesting that fast computations using descriptive statistics based on the χ^2 distribution are a valuable and computationally efficient alternative.

It is noticeable that the quality of the GPR interpolation is strongly governed by the predictive uncertainty σ_*^2, which indicates how much can be described by the deterministic part of the GPR. In the case of a value of zero, the deterministic part can accurately describe the data. However, as the value increases towards 1, the descriptive capabilities of the GPR decrease, and one can see large deviations in the field plots compared to the ground truth. It means that the mean of the GPR is significantly different from the provided velocity data. In such a case, the modes of vibration cannot be explained by the GPR anymore. Figure 4 clearly shows that with an increasing number of training points, the limit where the variational GPR can still explain the surface vibration velocity rises monotonically. For a resolution of 100 points, vibration characteristics below a Helmholtz number of $\text{He}_{\text{crit}} = 0.25$ can be resolved. For 400 points, this limit increases to a Helmholtz number of $\text{He}_{\text{crit}} = 2.5$, for 1600 points to about a Helmholtz number of $\text{He}_{\text{crit}} = 13$, for 3600 and

6400 points above the maximum Helmholtz number of interest $He_{crit} > 29$. It is observed, that the predictive uncertainty is larger for 3600 in the whole frequency range compared to a 6400 points resolution.

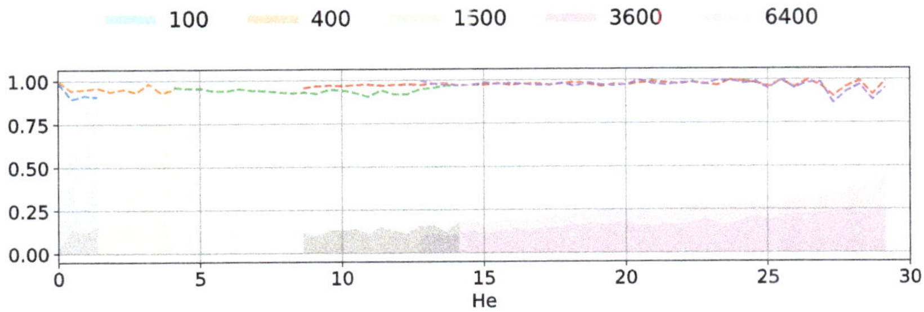

Figure 4. Evolution of the relative accuracies r_{χ^2} (dashed line) and predictive uncertainties σ_*^2 (shaded area) of the corresponding GPR as a function of the Helmholtz number, for different uniform resolutions of a total of 100 (blue), 400 (orange), 1600 (green), 3600 (magenta), 6400 (violet) points. The SNR level is 1000/1.

5.3. *Correlation Between Sound Power Error ϵ and Predicted Uncertainty σ_*^2*

In this section, we will investigate Hypothesis 3. According to Figure 4, there is no direct correlation between the interpolation error of the surface velocity and the predictive uncertainty σ_*^2 of the GPR visible. As soon as the GPR cannot explain the data by its deterministic part anymore, the predictive uncertainty σ_*^2 increases sharply, indicating that there are too few training points for the GPR. However, the error in the sound power (equal to the integrated surface velocity) increases only slightly.

Even at high GPR noise levels, the error of the predicted ERP is low. There is no clear trend whether the uniform or the Latin hypercube sampling performs better.

For a detailed analysis of the training time, the individual timings were separated into datasets, where the predictive uncertainty σ_*^2 is low and another where it is high. The separation was performed based on a critical Helmholtz number He_{crit} as a selector; everything below was judged as low noise, and everything above was regarded as a high noise region. In the respective ranges, the mean over all GPRs is computed. The means of the training times for each investigated set of are reported in Table 2, with training iterations over 1500 epochs to reach the low noise levels (Apple M4 Chip 10 Cores, 32 GB RAM, Apple Inc., Cupertino, CA, USA). The means are computed over all GPRs fulfilling the condition of the critical Helmholtz number He_{crit}. For a high number of training points and as soon as the GPR noise level increases, the training time increases substantially. There was no significant difference between the Latin hypercube sampling and the uniform sampling.

Table 2. GPR mean training times t_{tran} of the individual GPRs of the real and imaginary part.

Run	$\bar{t}_{tran,real}$ $> \mathbf{He}_{crit}$	$\bar{t}_{tran,real}$ $< \mathbf{He}_{crit}$	$\bar{t}_{tran,imag}$ $> \mathbf{He}_{crit}$	$\bar{t}_{tran,imag}$ $< \mathbf{He}_{crit}$
100, uni	2.626	0.428	2.589	0.256
400, uni	4.380	4.951	4.288	2.764
1600, uni	43.244	7.982	45.849	9.108
3600, uni	-	28.952	-	38.339
6400, uni	-	68.506	-	58.513

5.4. Uniform Sampling Versus Latin-Hypercube Sampling for the Surface Velocity

This section discusses two types of common (automated) data sampling strategies in connection with the underlying process specification (Hypothesis 4). The sampling strategies are as follows: first, a regular fit onto the geometry for uniform plate-like domains; second, a commonly used sampling strategy for arbitrary sampling spaces. The first strategy of uniform sampling is ideal in the case of uniform plate stiffness and the coordinate-sampling-aligned mode shapes. However, the results might deteriorate for inhomogeneous material, inhomogeneous plate thickness, non-rectangular geometries, non-uniform clamping at the boundaries, and other effects that produce modes with localized gradients and non-alignment with the sampling strategy. Therefore, we look into the details of the surface velocity predictions based on the two sampling strategies (using an exact GPR, which works for a low number of training points).

Figure 5 depicts the expected value and Figure 6 the standard deviation of the real part of the normal velocity for the respective sampling strategies for a frequency of 313 Hz.

The expected value is in close range to the ground truth of the reference data for both sampling strategies. For the standard deviations, uniform sampling leads to a significantly lower overall standard deviation between the sampling points compared to Latin hypercube sampling. For the Latin hypercube sampling, some blind spots on the geometry arise, where no support points of the GP are present, leading to a larger standard deviation in the prediction. These increased standard deviation spots could be used for adaptive refinement; however, they typically are located on the boundaries of the domain. This naive approach can be improved by using the variance-based refinement strategy presented in [48]. Another possibility is a modified version of the expected improvement [49].

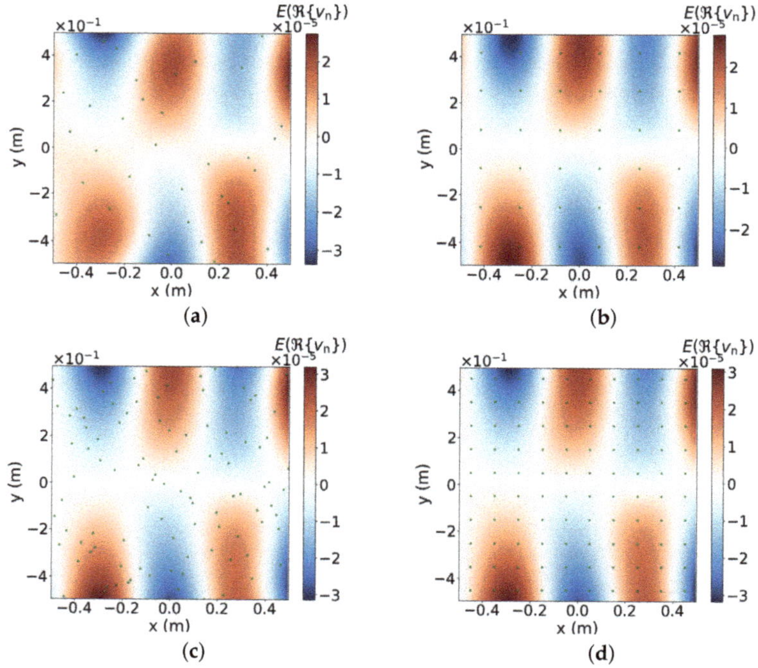

Figure 5. Mean of the real value of the normal velocity v_n at $f = 313\,\text{Hz}$, Latin hypercube sampling, and uniform sampling for $n = 36$ and $n = 100$ pseudo measurement points indicated in green. (**a**) Latin hypercube sampling with $n = 36$. (**b**) Uniform sampling with $n = 36$. (**c**) Latin hypercube sampling with $n = 100$. (**d**) Uniform sampling with $n = 100$.

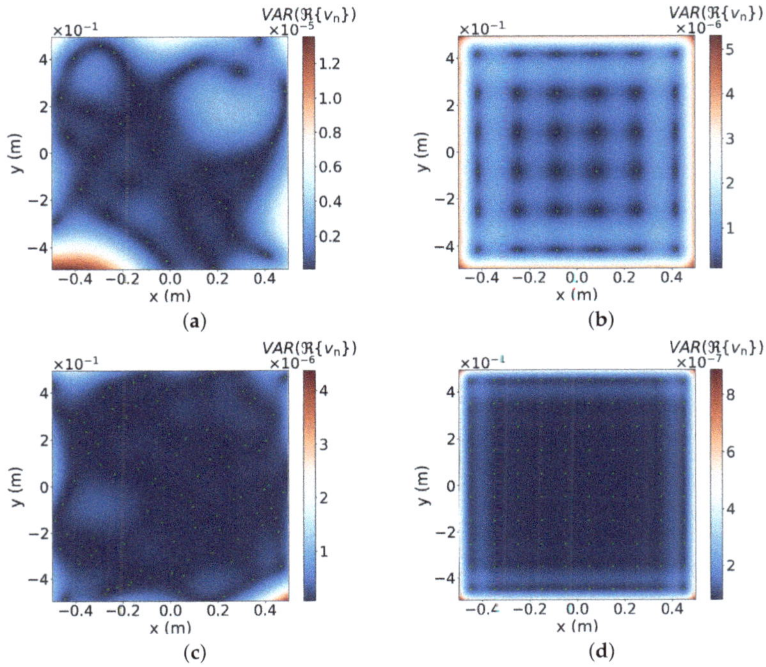

Figure 6. Standard deviation of the real value of the normal velocity v_n at $f = 313\,\text{Hz}$, latin hypercube and uniform sampling for $n = 36$ and $n = 100$ pseudo measurement points indicated in green. (**a**) Latin hypercube sampling with $n = 36$. (**b**) Uniform sampling with $n = 36$. (**c**) Latin hypercube sampling with $n = 100$. (**d**) Uniform sampling with $n = 100$.

5.5. Design of Experiement Using Adaptive Refinement

To test Hypothesis 5, an adaptive refinement procedure as described in Section 2.5 was performed. As a stopping criterion, the normalized noise of the GPR exceeds was used with a threshold of 0.01. Figure 7 shows the frequency of 1250 Hz, the $EI(x)$ at the start of the adaptive refinement iterations, and at the third stage of the adaptive refinement iterations for the real part of the surface normal velocity field. At the first stage (Figure 7a), the GP is not able to resolve the velocity field adequately, and the EI suggests adding points at the domain corners. This is expected as at this stage the field is mostly described by noise everywhere. Due to the intended randomness in the point selection, the procedure remains robust and at the third stage (Figure 7b).

Figure 8 shows the effects of the adaptive refinement procedure on the sound power error and GPR predictive uncertainty as a function of the Helmholtz number. At the initial stage, before the refinement, 400 uniform training points were considered. As a comparison, this setup without adaptive refinement predicted a low noise in the function output until a Helmholtz number of about 2.5 (see Figure 4). In comparison, with the adaptive refinement procedure, a robust prediction was possible up to a Helmholtz number of 11. This accuracy is comparable to that of predictions provided by 1600 uniform training points, despite using only 1200 data points. It is observed that during the adaptive refinement, the predictive uncertainty is lower in the converged region (He < 11) compared to the predictions using 1600 uniform training points. However, the ERP estimate is slightly less accurate compared to the estimations based on 1600 uniform training points due to the early stopping criterion selected. The estimates were robust regarding the initial training distribution; when using a Latin hypercube sampling initially, comparable results were obtained.

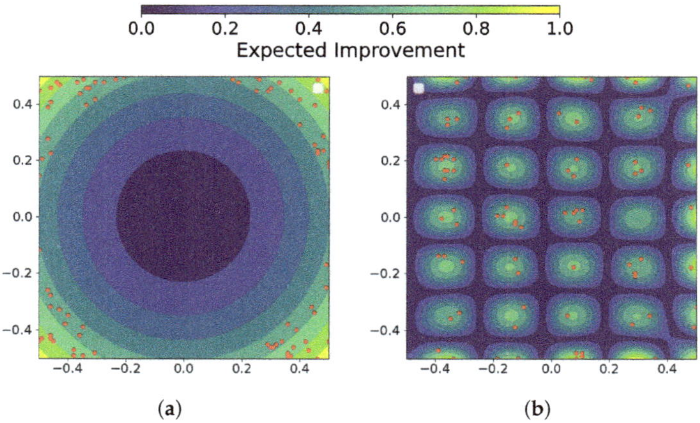

Figure 7. Two snapshots of $EI(x)$ during the adaptive refinement procedure for the real part of the surface normal velocity. The red dots indicate the added training pairs to the GPR training for both the real and imaginary parts. (**a**) First stage. (**b**) Third stage.

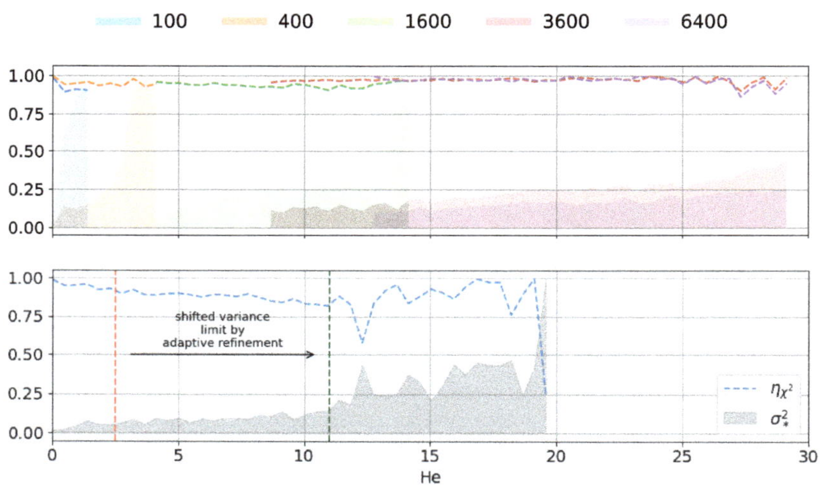

Figure 8. Evolution of the relative accuracy η_{χ^2} and the predictive uncertainty σ_*^2 as a function of the Helmholtz number. An initially uniform resolution of 400 was used, with random adaptive refinement. At the final stage, 1200 training points were considered.

5.6. Detailed Comparison of Sound Power Estimates

In Figure 9, the sound power estimate based on the ERP is compared to the one using BEM (Hypothesis 6). For the current case, below the coincidence frequency $\mathrm{He}_{\mathrm{co}}$ (red line in Figure 9), the ERP estimate is not an accurate measure for the radiated sound power. Typically, with increasing frequency, the radiation efficiency increases, and as soon as it turns to one, the ERP and the BEM estimate coincide. Under this condition, the ERP measure is preferable, as the statistical estimation presented in this article enables the statistical description and estimates to be carried out. Regarding the simulation time, at low frequencies, a relatively coarse training point distribution is sufficient, allowing for the computation of the Monte Carlo simulation within a reasonable time frame. As indicated by the results in Figure 4, the statistical values estimated by 100 simulations are sufficiently close to the analytically derived ones.

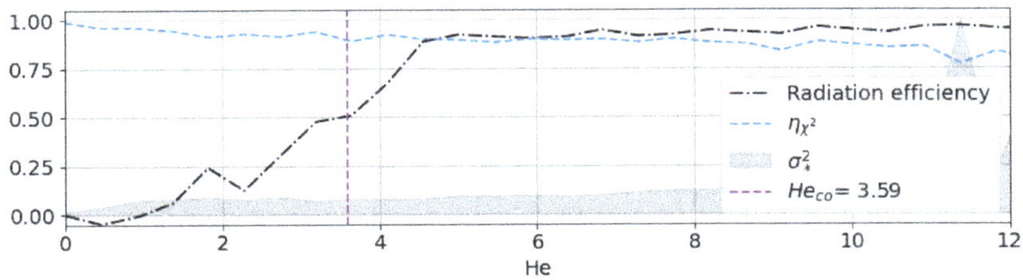

Figure 9. Comparison of the radiation efficiency, the relative ERP accuracy η_{χ^2}, and the predictive uncertainty σ_*^2 as a function of the Helmholtz number for the adaptive refinement case in Figure 8.

5.7. Computational Performance Using Pre-Trained Models

Finally, we tested if a significant speedup of the training time is possible using a pre-trained model (Hypothesis 7). Typically, during production, each product will not deviate much from the previous one (as long as it is of high quality); therefore, it might be interesting to use a pre-trained model. Table 3 compares the training times for several configurations. When using 1600 training points with the GPR setup, 1500 epochs of training, and a batch size of 1024, it took on average 5.57 s to train from scratch (in the region where convergence is achieved). When using a pre-trained GPR, the training time was reduced to 3.6 s (a nearly 36% reduction from 5.57 s to 3.6 s) with a standard deviation of 0.91 s. By relaxing the number of epochs (while still obtaining a converged GPR), the training time was reduced by approximately 68% from 3.6 s to 1.14 s. Overall, the mean training time was reduced from 5.57 s to 1.14 s, which yields an increase in computational performance of 79%.

Table 3. GPR mean training times below the critical Helmholtz number He < $\mathrm{He}_{\mathrm{crit}}$. The abbreviation uni stands for uniform sampling.

Run	$E[t_{\mathrm{tran}}]$	$\sqrt{VAR[t_{\mathrm{tran}}]}$	Training Epochs	Pre-Trained Model Used
1600, uni	5.57	1.94	1500	no
1600, uni	3.59	0.91	1500	yes
1600, uni	2.23	0.09	150	yes
1600, uni	1.14	0.12	75	yes

5.8. Influence of Measurement Noise

All previous investigations were based on a laser vibrometry measurement with a signal-to-noise ratio (SNR) of 1000/1, which represents a level of measurement quality that can be achieved for many applications. To test the effect of increased measurement noise on the proposed workflow (Hypothesis 8), the noise factor introduced in Section 3 was increased to $k_{\mathrm{noise}} = 0.1$, representing a signal-to-noise ratio (SNR) of 10/1. Figure 10 depicts the evolution of the relative accuracy η_{χ^2} and the predictive uncertainty σ_*^2 as a function of the Helmholtz number for the increased noise level. One can observe that the method remains robust despite the increased measurement noise, and the GPR can interpolate the normal velocity field accurately for an adequate number of samples. Especially at a high number of samples, the results show a decreased critical Helmholtz number. Consequently, more samples are required to describe noisy measurement data in contrast to data with low SNR.

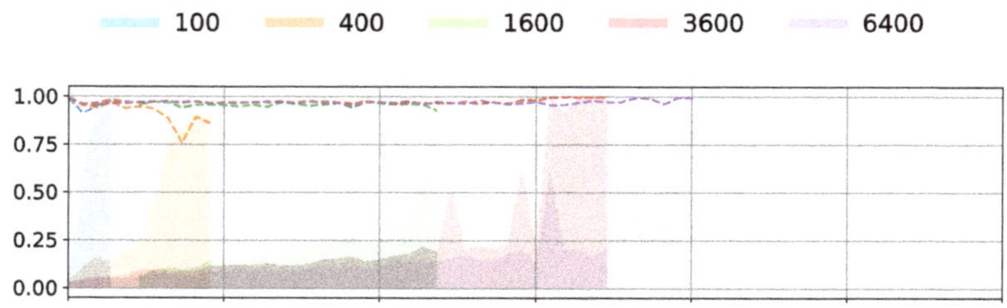

(**a**)

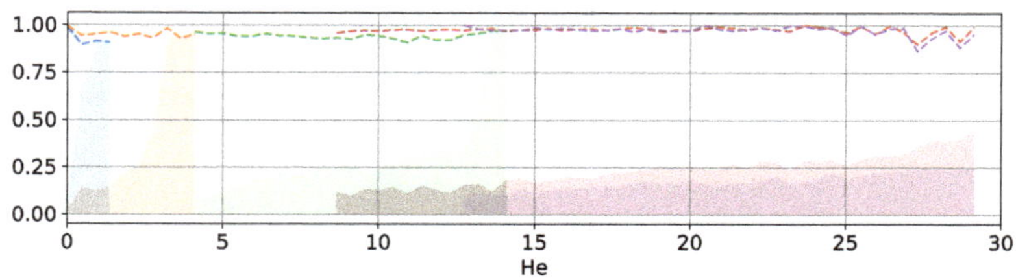

(**b**)

Figure 10. Evolution of the relative accuracy η_{χ^2} and the predictive uncertainty σ_*^2 as a function of the Helmholtz number with an increased SNR. (**a**) Increased SNR: $k_{\text{noise}} = 0.1$. (**b**) Reference SNR: $k_{\text{noise}} = 0.001$.

6. Conclusions

Initially, we identify four specifications for a measurement system for acoustic end-of-line testing to meet vibroacoustic requirements. Specification 1, to perform measurements at different locations, both contactless and without any additional assembly cost, was realized by a Laser scanning vibrometer setup. Specification 2 of the measurement system, which measures the accuracy and uncertainty of data prediction using a self-learned data-driven method, was achieved by the demonstration of the adaptive refinement method in combination with the underlying GPR. Specification 3, that the technique should provide data that give the maximum valuable insight into specific characteristics where deviations occurred over time, was not within the scope of the current investigation; however, it can be inferred through a comparative evaluation using the pre-trained models. The fourth specification that measurement and processing times should fit into the production cycle of a production line was demonstrated by the investigated hypotheses. The outcome of Hypothesis 1 is that the algorithm derived provides real-time capability regarding the sampling cycle of the laser scanning vibrometry system with fixed sample averaging and fixed measurement uncertainty thresholds. We demonstrated that the number of training points for Gaussian process regression positively correlates with the upper frequency limit at which the deterministic part of the Gaussian process can accurately model the surface normal velocity and sound prediction. We found that the ERP error with respect to the ground truth does not correlate with the noise in the velocity prediction from the GPR for the benchmark problem used. We found that Latin hypercube sampling, with the same number of sampling points, does not show better performance in training compared to uniform sampling. We also demonstrated the limitations of the ERP-based estimates by comparing them to sound power predictions using BEM. At higher oscillation frequencies, the ERP predicted sound power delivers accurate results. The computational performance was significantly increased (79% less time consumed) using transfer learning, based on pre-trained models. Overall, the use of GPyTorch over scikit-learn reduced the processing time by a factor of 60. Furthermore, we investigated the influence of uncorrelated noise on the measurement data, where we observed an increased number of measurement points to describe noisy measurement data.

Finally, we want to point out perspectives to improve the GPR modeling, including a spatially varying measurement noise distribution and improvement of the adaptive refinement strategy. The measurement uncertainty based on the local measurement point of the experimental setup can be modeled within the GPR and, therefore, considered by the sound prediction method. A direct extension to measurement noise distribution in space (variation in input locations) can be undertaken via Variational Heteroscedastic Gaussian process regression [50]. Another direction would be to develop an improved adaptive refinement strategy that eliminates oscillatory behavior as soon as the predictive uncertainty increases. Ghosh et al. [51] propose a framework that partitions prediction uncertainty based on fidelity levels, allowing for a more nuanced approach to experimental design that considers both the cost and the expected information gain from various data sources. This strategy not only enhances the efficiency of the design process but also provides a systematic method for integrating information from different fidelity levels, thereby enriching the overall understanding of the system under investigation.

Author Contributions: Conceptualization, S.S.; Methodology, A.W. and S.S.; Software, A.W. and S.S.; Validation, A.W. and S.S.; Formal analysis, A.W. and S.S.; Investigation, A.W. and S.S.; Resources, S.S.; Data curation, A.W. and S.S.; Writing—original draft, A.W. and S.S.; Writing—review and editing, A.W. and S.S.; Visualization, A.W. and S.S.; Supervision, S.S.; Project administration, S.S.; Funding acquisition, S.S. All authors have read and agreed to the published version of the manuscript.

Funding: Stefan Schoder would like to thank the Austrian Federal Ministry for Innovation, Mobility and Infrastructure and the Austrian Research Promotion Agency (FFG) for funding the bioCOMP4acoustics project under the TakeOff programme line (project number 913972). Andreas Wurzinger and Stefan Schoder acknowledge partial funding support by the COMET project ECHODA (Energy Efficient Cooling and Heating of Domestic Appliances). ECHODA is funded within the framework of COMET - Competence Centers for Excellent Technologies by BMK, BMAW, the province of Styria, as well as SFG. The COMET programme is managed by FFG.

Institutional Review Board Statement: Not applicable.

Informed Consent Statement: Not applicable.

Data Availability Statement: The models and the data presented in this study are available on request from the corresponding author.

Acknowledgments: Open Access Funding by the Graz University of Technology.

Conflicts of Interest: The authors declare no conflicts of interest.

References

Kumar, S.; Forster, H.M.; Bailey, P.; Griffiths, T.D. Mapping Unpleasantness of Sounds to Their Auditory Representation. *J. Acoust. Soc. Am.* **2008**, *124*, 3810–3817. [CrossRef]

Marburg, S. Boundary Element Method for Time-Harmonic Acoustic Problems. In *Computational Acoustics*; Kaltenbacher, M., Ed.; CISM International Centre for Mechanical Sciences; Springer International Publishing: Cham, Switzerland, 2018; pp. 69–158. [CrossRef]

Vachálek, J.; Bartalský, L.; Rovný, O.; Šišmišová, D.; Morháč, M.; Lokšík, M. The digital twin of an industrial production line within the industry 4.0 concept. In Proceedings of the 2017 21st International Conference on Process Control (PC), Štrbské Pleso, Slovakia, 6–9 June 2017; pp. 258–262.

Klippel, W. End-of-line testing. In *Assembly Line-Theory and Practice*; Grzechca, W., Ed.; Books on Demand: Norderstedt, Germany, 2011; pp. 181–206.

Wurzinger, A.; Kraxberger, F.; Maurerlehner, P.; Mayr-Mittermüller, B.; Rucz, P.; Sima, H.; Kaltenbacher, M.; Schoder, S. Experimental Prediction Method of Free-Field Sound Emissions Using the Boundary Element Method and Laser Scanning Vibrometry. *Acoustics* **2024**, *6*, 65–82. [CrossRef]

6. Rasmussen, C.E. Gaussian processes in machine learning. In *Summer School on Machine Learning*; Springer: Berlin/Heidelber Germany, 2003; pp. 63–71.
7. Wurzinger, A.; Kraxberger, F.; Mayr-Mittermüller, B.; Rucz, P.; Sima, H.; Kaltenbacher, M.; Schoder, S. Assessment of vibr acoustic sound emissions based on structural dynamics. In Proceedings of the Proceedings of DAGA 2024, Hannover, Germar 18–21 March 2024.
8. Li, J.; Wang, H. Gaussian Processes Regression for Uncertainty Quantification: An Introductory Tutorial. *arXiv* **202** arXiv:2502.03090. [CrossRef]
9. Schulz, E.; Speekenbrink, M.; Krause, A. A Tutorial on Gaussian Process Regression: Modelling, Exploring, and Exploitir Functions. *J. Math. Psychol.* **2018**, *85*, 1–16. [CrossRef]
10. Tuo, R.; Wang, W. Uncertainty quantification for Bayesian optimization. In Proceedings of the International Conference o Artificial Intelligence and Statistics, Virtual, 28–30 March 2022; pp. 2862–2884.
11. Bect, J.; Bachoc, F.; Ginsbourger, D. A Supermartingale Approach to Gaussian Process Based Sequential Design of Experimen *Bernoulli* **2019**, *25*, 2883–2919. [CrossRef]
12. Jault, D.; Gillet, N.; Schaeffer, N.; Mandéa, M. Local Estimation of Quasi-Geostrophic Flows in Earth's Core. *Geophys. J. Int.* **202** *234*, 494–511. [CrossRef]
13. Xia, G.; Han, Z.; Zhao, B.; Wang, X. Unmanned Surface Vehicle Collision Avoidance Trajectory Planning in an Uncerta Environment. *IEEE Access* **2020**, *8*, 207844–207857. [CrossRef]
14. Kocev, B.; Hahn, H.K.; Linsen, L.; Wells, W.M.; Kikinis, R. Uncertainty-Aware Asynchronous Scattered Motion Interpolatic Using Gaussian Process Regression. *Comput. Med. Imaging Graph.* **2019**, *72*, 1–12 [CrossRef]
15. Jahanandish, M.H.; Fey, N.P.; Hoyt, K. Lower Limb Motion Estimation Using Ultrasound Imaging: A Framework for Assistiv Device Control. *IEEE J. Biomed. Health Inform.* **2019**, *23*, 2505–2514. [CrossRef]
16. Omainska, M. Visual Pursuit With Switched Motion Estimation and Rigid Body Gaussian Processes. *Trans. Inst. Syst. Control Ir Eng.* **2023**, *36*, 327–335. [CrossRef]
17. Binois, M.; Huang, J.; Gramacy, R.B.; Ludkovski, M. Replication or Exploration? Sequential Design for Stochastic Simulatio Experiments. *Technometrics* **2018**, *61*, 7–23. [CrossRef]
18. Gardner, J.; Pleiss, G.; Weinberger, K.Q.; Bindel, D.; Wilson, A.G. Gpytorch: Blackbox matrix-matrix gaussian process inferen with gpu acceleration. *Adv. Neural Inf. Process. Syst.* **2018**, *31*.
19. Raychaudhuri, S. Introduction to monte carlo simulation. In Proceedings of the 2008 Winter Simulation Conference, Miami, F USA, 7–10 December 2008; pp. 91–100.
20. Wurzinger, A.; Heidegger, P.; Kraxberger, F.; Mayr-Mittermüller, B.; Sima, H.; Kaltenbacher, M.; Schoder, S. Prediction vibro-acoustic sound emissions based on mapped structural dynamics. In Proceedings of the INTER-NOISE and NOISE-CO Congress and Conference Proceedings, Nantes, France, 25–29 August 2024; Volume 270, pp. 8251–8260. [CrossRef]
21. Pedregosa, F.; Varoquaux, G.; Gramfort, A.; Michel, V.; Thirion, B.; Grisel, O.; Blondel, M.; Prettenhofer, P.; Weiss, R Dubourg, V.; et al. Scikit-Learn: Machine Learning in Python. *J. Mach. Learn. Res.* **2011**, *12*, 2825–2830.
22. Bilionis, I.; Zabaras, N. Multi-Output Local Gaussian Process Regression: Applications to Uncertainty Quantification. *J. Compu Phys.* **2012**, *231*, 5718–5746. [CrossRef]
23. Mones, L.; Bernstein, N.; Csányi, G. Exploration, Sampling, And Reconstruction of Free Energy Surfaces with Gaussian Proces Regression. *J. Chem. Theory Comput.* **2016**, *12*, 5100–5110. [CrossRef]
24. Titsias, M. Variational learning of inducing variables in sparse Gaussian processes. In Proceedings of the Artificial Intelligenc and Statistics, Clearwater Beach, FL, USA, 16–18 April 2009; pp. 567–574.
25. Maddox, W.J.; Stanton, S.; Wilson, A.G. Conditioning Sparse Variational Gaussian Processes for Online Decision-makin In *Proceedings of the Advances in Neural Information Processing Systems*; Ranzato, M., Beygelzimer, A., Dauphin, Y., Liang, I Vaughan, J.W., Eds.; Curran Associates, Inc.: New York, NY, USA, 2021; Volume 34, pp. 6365–6379.
26. Bauer, M.; Van der Wilk, M.; Rasmussen, C.E. Understanding probabilistic sparse Gaussian process approximations. *Adv. Neur Inf. Process. Syst.* **2016**, *29*.
27. Williams, C.; Rasmussen, C. Gaussian processes for regression. *Adv. Neural Inf. Process. Syst.* **1995**, *8*.
28. Rasmussen, C.E.; Williams, C.K.I. *Gaussian Processes for Machine Learning*, 3rd ed.; Adaptive Computation and Machine Learnin MIT Press: Cambridge, MA, USA, 2008.
29. Fiala, P.; Rucz, P. NiHu: An Open Source C++ BEM Library. *Adv. Eng. Softw.* **2014**, *75*, 101–112. [CrossRef]
30. Burton, A.J.; Miller, G.F. The Application of Integral Equation Methods to the Numerical Solution of Some Exterior Boundar Value Problems. *Proc. R. Soc. Lond.* **1971**, *323*, 201–210. [CrossRef]
31. Luegmair, M.; Münch, H. Advanced Equivalent Radiated Power (ERP) Calculation for Early Vibro-acoustic Product Optimizatio In Proceedings of the The 22nd International Congress on Sound and Vibration, Florence, Italy, 12–16 July 2015.
32. Fritze, D.; Marburg, S.; Hardtke, H.J. Estimation of radiated sound power: A case study on common approximation method *Acta Acust. United Acust.* **2009**, *95*, 833–842. [CrossRef]

Cremer, L.; Heckl, M.; Petersson, B. Sound Radiation from Structures. In *Structure-Borne Sound: Structural Vibrations and Sound Radiation at Audio Frequencies*; Springer: Berlin/Heidelberg, Germany, 2005; pp. 449–535. [CrossRef]

Kvist, K.; Sorokin, S.V.; Larsen, J.B. Radiation Efficiency Varying Equivalent Radiated Power. *J. Acoust. Soc. Am.* **2025**, *157*, 169–177. [CrossRef] [PubMed]

Das, A.; Geisler, W.S. Methods to integrate multinormals and compute classification measures. *arXiv* **2020**, arXiv:2012.14331.

Schoder, S.; Roppert, K. openCFS: Open Source Finite Element Software for Coupled Field Simulation—Part Acoustics. *arXiv* **2022**, arXiv:2207.04443. [CrossRef]

Langer, P.; Maeder, M.; Guist, C.; Krause, M.; Marburg, S. More Than Six Elements Per Wavelength: The Practical Use of Structural Finite Element Models and Their Accuracy in Comparison with Experimental Results. *J. Comput. Acoust.* **2017**, *25*, 1750025. [CrossRef]

Schoder, S.; Roppert, K.; Weitz, M.; Junger, C.; Kaltenbacher, M. Aeroacoustic source term computation based on radial basis functions. *Int. J. Numer. Methods Eng.* **2020**, *121*, 2051–2067. [CrossRef]

Hensman, J.; Matthews, A.; Ghahramani, Z. Scalable Variational Gaussian Process Classification. *arXiv* **2014**, arXiv:1411.2005. http://arxiv.org/abs/1411.2005. [CrossRef]

Blei, D.M.; Kucukelbir, A.; McAuliffe, J.D. Variational Inference: A Review for Statisticians. *J. Am. Stat. Assoc.* **2017**, *112*, 859–877. [CrossRef]

Kullback, S.; Leibler, R.A. On information and sufficiency. *Ann. Math. Stat.* **1951**, *22*, 79–86. [CrossRef]

Snelson, E.; Ghahramani, Z. Sparse Gaussian processes using pseudo-inputs. *Adv. Neural Inf. Process. Syst.* **2005**, *18*.

Hensman, J.; Fusi, N.; Lawrence, N.D. Gaussian Processes for Big Data. *arXiv* **2013**, arXiv:1309.6835. http://arxiv.org/abs/1309.6835. [CrossRef]

Dai, Z.; Damianou, A.; Hensman, J.; Lawrence, N. Gaussian Process Models with Parallelization and GPU acceleration. *arXiv* **2014**, arXiv:1410.4984. http://arxiv.org/abs/1410.4984. [CrossRef]

Gal, Y.; van der Wilk, M.; Rasmussen, C.E. Distributed Variational Inference in Sparse Gaussian Process Regression and Latent Variable Models. In *Proceedings of the Advances in Neural Information Processing Systems*; Ghahramani, Z., Welling, M., Cortes, C., Lawrence, N., Weinberger, K., Eds.; Curran Associates, Inc.: New York, NY, USA, 2014; Volume 27.

Paszke, A.; Gross, S.; Massa, F.; Lerer, A.; Bradbury, J.; Chanan, G.; Killeen, T.; Lin, Z.; Gimelshein, N.; Antiga, L.; et al. PyTorch: An Imperative Style, High-Performance Deep Learning Library. In *Advances in Neural Information Processing Systems 32*; Curran Associates, Inc.: New York, NY, USA, 2019; pp. 8024–8035.

Kingma, D.P.; Ba, J. Adam: A method for stochastic optimization. *arXiv* **2014**, arXiv:1412.6980.

Krause, A.; Singh, A.; Guestrin, C. Near-optimal sensor placements in Gaussian processes: Theory, efficient algorithms and empirical studies. *J. Mach. Learn. Res.* **2008**, *9*, 235–284.

Jones, D.R.; Schonlau, M.; Welch, W.J. Efficient global optimization of expensive black-box functions. *J. Glob. Optim.* **1998**, *13*, 455–492. [CrossRef]

Lázaro-Gredilla, M.; Titsias, M.K. Variational Heteroscedastic Gaussian Process Regression. In Proceedings of the ICML, Washington, DC, USA, 28 June–2 July 2011; pp. 841–848.

Ghosh, S.; Kristensen, J.; Zhang, Y.; Subber, W.; Wang, L. *A Strategy for Adaptive Sampling of Multi-Fidelity Gaussian Processes to Reduce Predictive Uncertainty*; American Society of Mechanical Engineers: New York, NY, USA, 2019. [CrossRef]

applied sciences

MDPI

Article

Analysis of the Causes of Excessive Noise and Vibrations of Live Steam Pipelines

Damian Pietrusiak *, Jerzy Czmochowski, Artur Górski, Artur Iluk, Przemysław Moczko and Michał Paduchowicz

Faculty of Mechanical Engineering, Wrocław University of Science and Technology, 50-370 Wroclaw, Poland
* Correspondence: damian.pietrusiak@pwr.edu.pl

Abstract: The article discusses the causes of excessive noise and vibrations of a live steam pipeline in a power unit. A scanning laser vibrometer was used to measure the vibrations of the live steam pipeline for two power units. Additionally, the sound (noise) level of the live steam pipeline was measured with an acoustic camera. A discrete model of the pipeline was created, and FEM modal analysis was performed. Based on experimental tests and numerical simulations, the sources of noise were identified. The final conclusions propose methods of eliminating the harmful noise.

Keywords: vibrations; steam pipeline; noise; power plant

1. Introduction

Power plants and heating power stations have a significant influence on the atmospheric air, soil, and water and, in effect, on plants, animals, and people, i.e., on the natural environment. Such influence is exerted by:

- Products of fuel combustion, i.e., produced as by-products of the power plant fuel cycle. Such products include the following: fumes containing fly ash (dust), sulfur dioxide, nitrogen oxides, carbon monoxide and dioxide, slag from boilers, and waste and wastewater from fuel desulphurization (dustiness also occurs during the transport, storage, and unloading of fuels).
- The natural environment is significantly affected by industrial wastewater, which is the by-product of water purification for steam cycles and cooling cycles and is also produced by fuel desulphurization systems, as well as systems for heating water in rivers (lakes) if turbines are cooled by means of an open cooling system. Closed cooling systems—based on ventilators and towers—produce noise [1–3], which leads to complaints from residents in nearby areas.
- Electrical networks, through the impact of electromagnetic fields, also have a detrimental effect on the natural environment.
- Noise.

With the progressing knowledge about the influence of sound on human performance, the development of countries, and the awareness of societies, noise pollution has become a regular aspect of environmental planning and protection. With that, requirements for all the industrial installations, especially those erected in past few decades, have put more focus on noise generation.

There are many places in the power-generating units of a power plant that create the following types of noise:

- Noise caused by transformers and engines;
- Noise caused by turbines [4];

- Noise caused by the unloading and crushing of coal;
- Noise produced by air and fume extraction fans and compressors;
- Noise caused by steam collectors;
- Noise from other sources.

Protection against noise has become a challenge for the entire civilization. Currently, all power plants are required to prepare inventories of noise sources and measure the average sound level. Power plants must also implement a noise reduction program by acquiring low-noise-emission equipment, building anti-noise barriers and noise dampers, and soundproofing the facility [5]. Basic investments aimed at protection against excessive noise emission include noise enclosures and sound insulation for air and fume extraction fans, acoustic protection of boiler outlet pipes, acoustic enclosures for turbine casing, acoustic protection of air fans in ash storage tanks, an anti-noise wall with a sliding door, acoustic enclosures and screens for several pieces of equipment, and others [6,7].

In power plants, the situation might be even more complicated, as the interaction of the flowing media might excite structural vibrations. It is a challenge of great importance to secure laminar flow both from the point of view of the process as well as complex aeroacoustic phenomena, often leading to resonant amplification and wideband noise emissions. Properly designed geometry of the media guiding structures is of great importance. Additionally, the application of the attenuating materials can be taken under consideration. Recent years have brought great development in sustainable damping/attenuating materials and especially great promise in the application of novel acoustic metamaterials [7]. However, one has to keep in mind that the power plant is a harsh environment with elevated or even extreme temperatures.

In one of the coal power plants (Figure 1), it was noticed that one of the live steam pipelines vibrated and generated an excessive level of noise in comparison to the other similar ducts. Additionally, that unusual noise presence was observed shortly after maintenance operations. As the general noise in the power plant hall where the power-generation unit is placed can reach up to around 90–100 dB, the noise level generated by pipeline at the level exceeding 100 dB does not make a big change in the exposure to noise. However, the fact that the pipeline used to work with an unnoticeable noise level and fact of the presence of the high-frequency noise (around 1000 Hz) raised questions about the proper and safe operation of the pipeline. This brought the necessity of the investigation of the noise/vibration cause. A schematic diagram of the power-generating unit in the power plant is shown in Figure 2.

Figure 1. General view of the power plant.

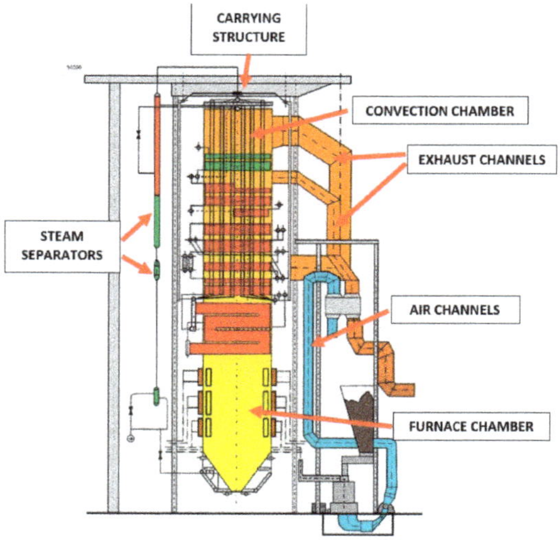

Figure 2. A schematic diagram of the power-generating unit.

2. Description and Parameters of the Pipeline

The object of measurements and analysis is the live steam pipeline in power-generating unit A of the power plant (Figures 3 and 4). The noise generated in this pipeline exceeds permissible levels and reaches up to 105 dB. In the top span above the Y-pipe, before the valves, a Ø406.4 × 50 mm pipeline was used, which is different than the pipeline used in power unit B, where the diameters of the same pipelines are smaller, i.e., Ø355.6 × 40 mm. The upper Y-pipe has a diameter of Ø508/406.4 mm (power unit A), while the Y-pipe in the same location in power unit B has a diameter of Ø508/355.6 mm. The vertical span of the piping (Figure 4) below the Y-pipe, between the levels of 12 m and 37 m, has the same diameter as the one in power unit "B", i.e., Ø508 × 55 mm. At the level of 23 m, there is a measuring nozzle with a diameter of Ø317.55 mm, which is larger than in power unit "B", where the nozzle has a diameter of Ø297.58 mm. Towards the turbine, there is the lower Y-pipe, with identical dimensions as the upper Y-pipe, i.e., Ø508/406.4 mm, and it is followed by two branches of pipelines of the same diameter as the top pipelines, i.e., Ø406.4 × 50 mm.

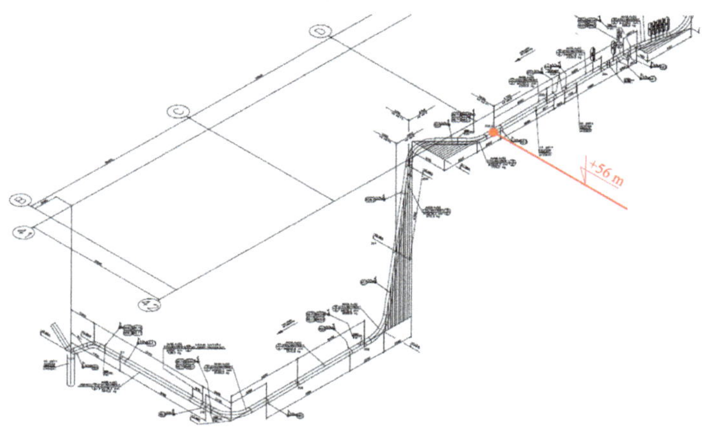

Figure 3. Live steam pipeline above the upper Y-pipe, right branch.

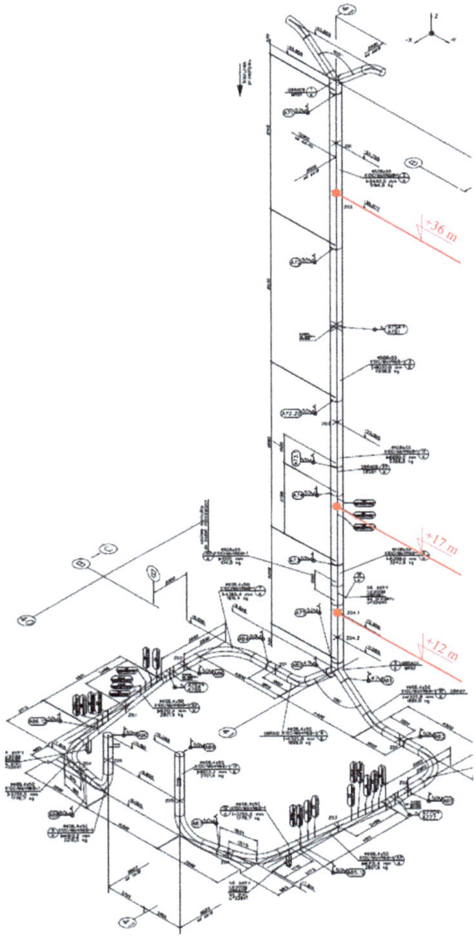

Figure 4. Live steam pipeline from the turbine to the upper Y-pipe.

3. Measurement of Vibrations of the Live Steam Pipelines

Experimental tests were performed by means of a Polytec PSV-400 scanning laser vibrometer (Polytec GmbH, Waldbronn, Germany), which allows for direct non-contact measurements of vibration velocity and displacement. The basic parameters of the measuring system were as follows:

- Bandwidth range from 0.1 to 250 kHz;
- Maximum scan speed—100 points per second;
- Vibration velocity range—1 μm/s to 10 m/s;
- Displacement range—1 μm to 160 mm;
- Laser type—633 nm (red) He-Ne laser, with power lower than 1 mW;
- Scanning range $\pm$ 20° about X, Y;
- Angular resolution < 0.002°.

Vibration measurements were taken on power unit A, in which the live steam pipeline vibrated and generated noise at the level of 105 dB. For the purposes of comparison, vibration measurements were taken in the almost identical power unit B, where such problem did not occur. Vibration measurements of both pipelines were taken by means of a laser vibrometer. In order to measure the vibrations directly in both pipelines, holes were made in the thermal insulation at the following three levels of power unit A: 12 m, 17 m, and 36 m and at the level of 12 m in the control unit B, where excessive vibration and noise does not occur. The locations of the measurement points/levels were dictated by the expected structural modal vibrations modes and were selected to avoid vibration nodes. The exact height of the measurement levels (12, 17, 36) was dictated by the floor level of the building in which the pipeline was installed. Examples of measurement points are shown in Figures 5–7. The holes were spaced at 0.40 m vertically and 45° around the circumference. Figure 6 shows the laser vibrometer system during vibration measurements.

The following parameters were measured:

- The velocity and the RMS values of vibrations at individual measurement points;
- Mode shapes at individual levels [8], where measurements were taken;
- Amplitude–frequency spectrums for individual measurement points in order to evaluate if the structure does not operate in the resonant bands.

For the time of the measurements, the control operation was responsible for keeping the operational parameters of the installation at the unchanged level to secure the stationary character of the vibrations.

Figure 5. Holes in the insulation for measuring pipeline vibrations.

Figure 6. The laser vibrometer system during vibration measurements.

Figure 7. Labeling of measurement points at the level of 17 m.

Table 1 lists the results in the form of RMS values of vibration velocity at individual measurement points, recorded at subsequent working levels in power unit A. The results of measurements taken at the level of 12 m in unit 3 are also included for comparison. Figure 7 shows the labels for measurement points used in Table 1.

Table 1. The RMS values of vibration velocity in mm/s.

Measurement Point		**V_{RMS} [mm/s]**	
Level of 12 m	unit	A	B
1		4.61	3.70
2		6.49	2.82
3		4.25	3.17
4		8.26	2.85
5		4.30	-
Level of 17 m	unit	A	
1		8.18	
2		9.15	
3		3.91	
4		10.92	
5		7.76	
Level of 36 m	unit	A	
1		4.60	
2		6.84	
3		3.99	
4		5.66	
5		5.65	

A—unit which generates high vibrations of the live steam pipeline; B—control unit, with low vibrations.

Figure 8 shows the amplitude–frequency plot for vibrations at the operating levels where measurements were made. The analysis also included the calculation of mode shapes, which are described in detail in [8], where it was concluded that they are of variable character similar to that of a sinusoidal waveform. The amplitude–frequency plot for vibrations of the live steam pipeline (Figure 8a) shows that in unit A, the dominating vibration frequency is 957 Hz, which was registered at all levels of unit A. On the other hand, the measurements taken on a similar power unit with identical parameters, except for the diameters of live steam pipeline, i.e., in power unit B, do not show this dominating frequency value, as illustrated in Figure 8b. The dominating vibration frequency in unit B is 7.5 Hz.

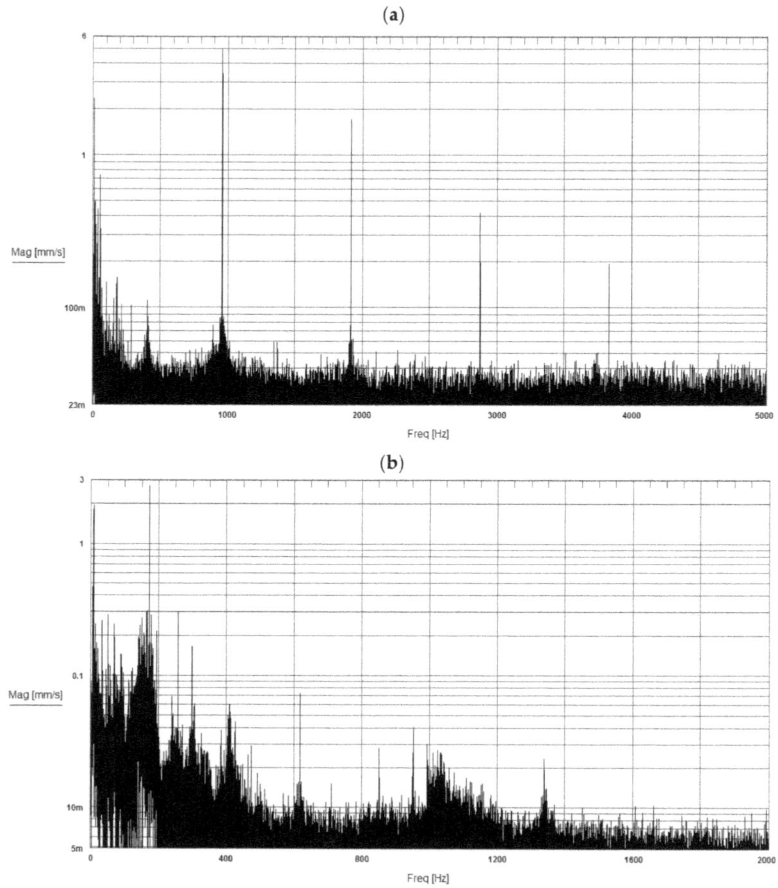

Figure 8. Amplitude–frequency plot at the level of 12 m: (**a**) power unit A, (**b**) power unit B.

Based on the obtained results of measurements of vibrations of the live steam pipeline taken by means of a laser vibrometer, the following were observed:

- The highest recorded RMS vibration velocity (Table 1) in power unit A at the level of 17 m was $V_{RMS,17,A}$ = 10.92 mm/s;
- The lowest vibration level was recorded at the level of 36 m, where the RMS value of vibration was about 50% lower than the vibrations at the level of 17 m;
- The dominating vibration frequency recorded at all levels of the noise-generating power unit A was f_A = 957 Hz, which is in close match to the structural modal modes identified in numerical simulations (see Section 6);
- In comparison, the results of measurements taken on power unit B, whose parameters are identical to those of the noise-generating unit A, show that the highest RMS value of vibration velocity (Table 1) was $V_{RMS,12,B}$ = 3.70 mm/s, with a vibration frequency of f_B = 7.5 Hz;
- The mode shape of the pipeline in unit A has characteristics of a sinusoidal-wave shape transmitted along its axis. A mode shape of this type was not observed in unit B [8]

4. Vibration Measurements Using a Handheld Dual-Channel Accelerometer

The vibration of the pipeline was measured using a Commtest VB7 dual-channel vibration analyzer. The measurement was taken using a handheld method. Due to the significant thickness of the pipe insulation, which made it impossible to mount the sensors directly on the pipe surface, the measurement resembled an indirect method and was taken by means of probes (steel rods—Figure 9). Measurements using this method were taken on supports in power unit A at the levels of 12 m, 17 m, 36 m, and 56 m. Due to the difficult access and the necessity to use probes, the measurements of the pipeline in unit B were taken only at the levels of 12 m and 17 m.

Figure 9. Pipeline vibration measurements at the level of 17 m, unit A.

The presented diagrams in Figures 10 and 11 illustrate the RMS amplitude and frequency spectrums of the vibration of the pipeline supports at the levels of 12 m and 17 m in power unit A.

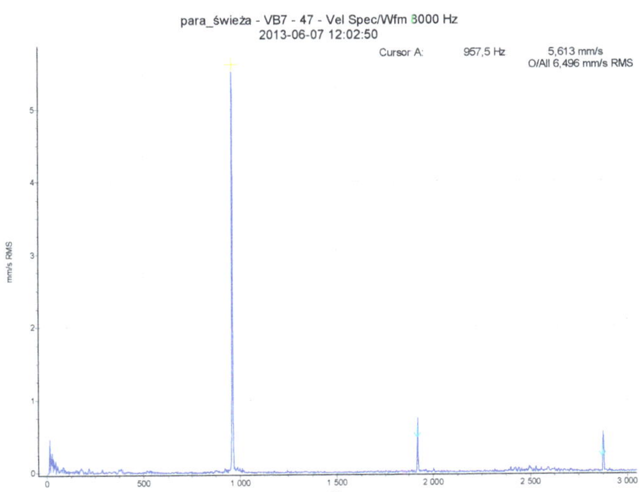

Figure 10. Pipeline vibration measurements in the horizontal axis of the support pin at the level of 17 m, unit A.

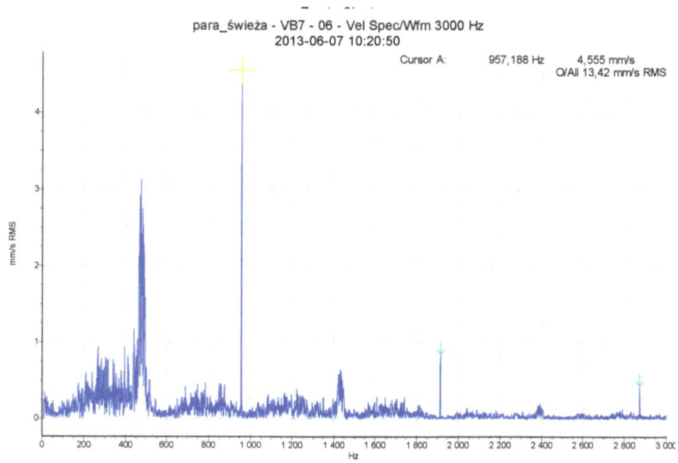

Figure 11. Pipeline vibration measurements in the second point at the level of 12 m, unit A.

5. Measurement of the Sound Level Using an Acoustic Camera

The analysis of pipelines included the measurement of the sound (noise) level in the live steam pipeline in power unit A using an acoustic camera array with 40 microphones (CAE Noise Inspector). The measurement frequency range was aiming to identify the noise source, preliminary observed roughly at the frequency of about 1 kHz. The results of such measurements are illustrated in Figures 12–14. The measurements of the sound intensity level taken at the level of 12 m indicate that the sounds in the frequency range of 929 Hz ÷ 1059 Hz originate at higher levels (Figure 12). The bottom portion of the image shows the reflections of sounds located near the microphone. The sound intensity level was approximately 101 dB.

Figure 12. Results of measurements of sound intensity for the frequency range 929 ÷ 1059 Hz at the level of 12 m at a distance of 7.39 m from the sound source.

The measurements of the sound intensity taken at the level of 17 m indicate that the sounds in the frequency range of 929 Hz ÷ 1059 Hz originate near the support above the nozzle (Figure 13). The concentration of sound intensity source is slightly away from the supports because the acoustic wave is reflected from the surrounding elements. The level of sound intensity on the support was approximately 102 dB, whereas on the pipeline, at a distance of approximately 2.4 m from the support, it was 10 dB lower.

Figure 13. Results of measurements of sound intensity for the frequency range 929 ÷ 1059 Hz at the level of 17 m at a distance of 8.1 m from the sound source.

The measurements of the sound intensity level taken at the level of 36 m indicate that the sounds in the frequency range of 929 Hz ÷ 1059 Hz originate at higher levels, where individual branches of the pipeline are located (Figure 14). The sound intensity level there was approximately 107 dB.

Figure 14. Results of measurements of sound intensity for the frequency range 929 Hz ÷ 1059 Hz at the level of 36 m at a distance of 11.48 m from the sound source.

The performed measurements of sound intensity for the live steam pipeline indicate that only at the level of 17 m was it possible to precisely locate the sound source. The level of noise generated by the support located above the nozzle in the analyzed frequency range was thus significantly lower than the level of noise produced by the surrounding elements. In the case of levels 12 m and 36 m, the sound intensity of the environment and a series of reflections from surrounding elements made it only possible to approximate the location of the sound source.

6. Numerical Analysis of Vibrations of the Live Steam Pipelines

A numerical modal analysis was performed using the finite element method [9] in order to identify the frequency and mode shape in the frequency range above 900 Hz. This range is significant because of the potential excessive noise. FEM calculations were performed on [10] geometrical models of straight pipeline spans for pipes with the following dimensions: Ø508 mm × 55 mm, Ø406.4 m × 50 mm, and Ø355.6 mm × 40 mm, as well as on models of pipeline spans near the spherical Y-pipes. Due to the fact that these are thick-walled elements, their discrete models were created with division into solid elements [4], which are shown in Figure 15.

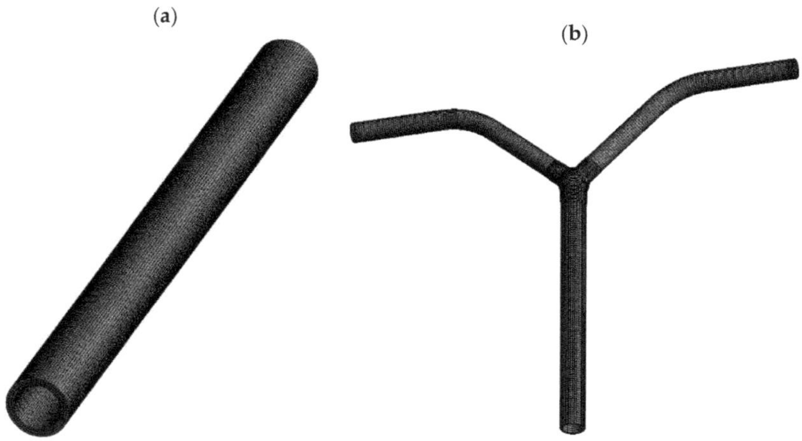

Figure 15. Discrete model of a span of the live steam pipeline: (**a**) piping span with dimensions of Ø406.4 × 50; (**b**) spherical Y-pipe with piping spans.

The modal analysis includes both the thermal loads and mechanical loads in the form of a temperature and pressure field generated by the flowing live steam. Calculations were performed using the commercial code of ANSYS Workbench 13.0 for two operating states of the power unit. The first was the nominal power state, whereas the second was related to the operating parameters of the unit on the date of measurement. The parameters of the live steam for individual cases of analysis are presented in Table 2.

Table 2. Values of live steam parameters included in the numerical analysis.

	Values of Live Steam Parameters	**Nominal Operating State**	**Operating State on 2013-06-07**
A Unit	Temperature [°C]	575	555.6
	Pressure [MPa]	19.6	18.7
B Unit	Temperature [°C]	575	
	Pressure [MPa]	19.6	

Figure 16 shows examples of the modal analysis results of FEM calculations for [1] a span of the live steam pipeline in power unit A for the natural vibrations frequency range of 900–1001 Hz in the pipeline's nominal operating state.

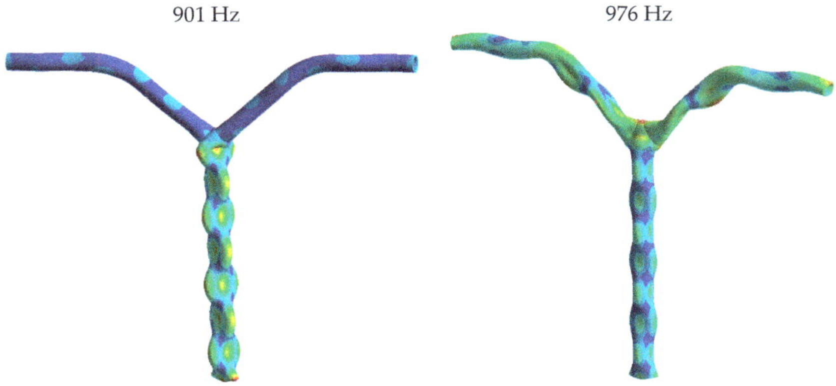

Figure 16. Examples of the circular mode shape of natural vibrations in a span of the live steam pipeline in power unit A near the top Y-pipe.

The modal analysis of a span of the live steam pipeline in power unit A near the top Y-pipe indicates that the circular mode shape of natural vibrations of the pipes connected to the Y-pipe may occur for the following frequencies: 901, 976, and 995 Hz (Figure 16). Another form of normal modes is flexural vibrations of pipes, which occurred for the following frequencies: 932 Hz, 934 Hz, 938 Hz, 945 Hz, 997 Hz, and 1001 Hz (Figure 17).

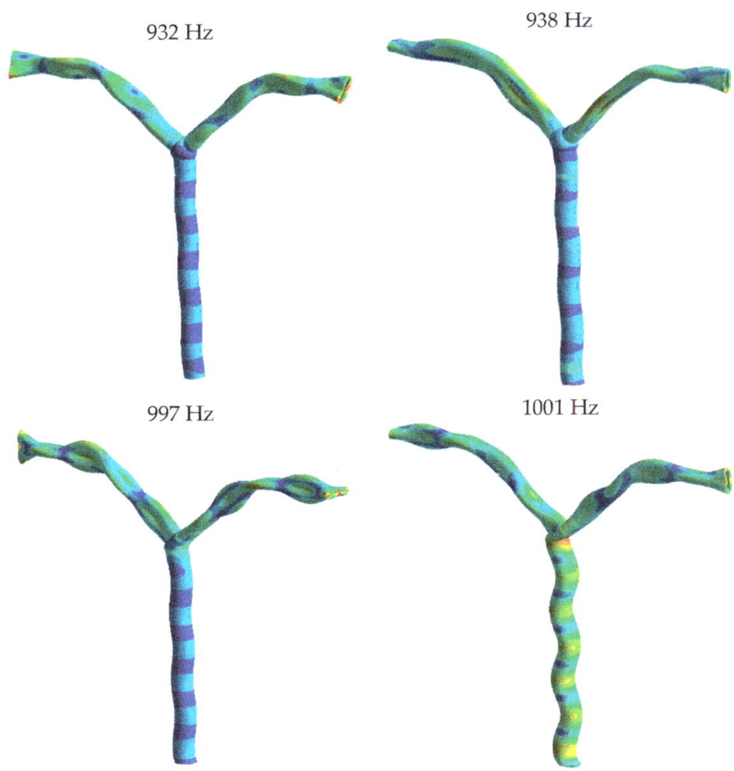

Figure 17. Examples of flexural mode shape of natural vibrations in a span of the live steam pipeline in power unit A near the top Y-pipe.

FEM numerical calculations were performed for a live steam pipeline near the top Y-pipe and for straight spans of pipes used in units A and B [2,11,12]. Due to the influence of operating parameters, i.e., temperature in particular [3,8,13–19], calculations were performed for the nominal operating state and for the current operating state on the date of measurements. Table 3 presents a comparison of vibration frequencies for corresponding mode shapes.

Table 3. Comparison of vibration frequencies for corresponding mode shapes near the top Y-pipe.

No.	Nominal State—Unit A	Measurement—Unit A	Nominal State—Unit B
	Hz	Hz	Hz
1	901	905	927
2	934	941	962
3	936	943	995
4	950	957	
5	974	981	
6	999	1002	

The comparison in Table 3 between results for unit A and unit B shows that the frequency of vibrations during operation on the date of measurements is approximately 3 ÷ 7 Hz higher than the values during nominal state of the unit. The corresponding mode shapes for unit B occur at substantially higher frequencies, i.e., 26 ÷ 49 Hz higher in comparison with those for the vibrations for unit A.

An analysis of the vibration frequencies in straight pipe segments (Table 4) for corresponding mode shapes shows that the vibration frequencies of the Ø406.4 × 50 mm pipe are lower than the vibration frequencies of the Ø355.6 × 40 mm pipe by 28, 26, 21, 14, and 6 Hz for subsequent mode shapes. In this frequency range, the Ø508 × 55 pipe has only one circular mode shape and one flexural mode shape.

Table 4. Comparison of vibration frequencies in straight pipe spans.

No.	Description of Mode Shape	Ø355.6 × 40	Ø406.4 × 50	Ø508 × 55
		Hz	Hz	Hz
1	flexural 5 half waves	905		
2	circular 1 half wave	948	920	636
3	circular 2 half waves	954	928	645
4	circular 3 half waves	963	942	663
5	circular 4 half waves	980	966	697
6	circular 5 half waves	1009	1003	753
7	circular 6 half waves			833
8	circular 7 half waves			935
9	flexural 6 half waves			998

7. Summary and Conclusions

Based on the performed tests and numerical FEM calculations for the live steam pipeline in one of the power units, it can be stated that the likely cause of the phenomenon of high-frequency vibrations, which generates the maximum noise of 101–107 dB, is as follows:

- A change in the geometry of the pipeline elements resulted in a change in the parameters of the broadband noise generated in one of those elements.
- Parameters of acoustic transmission were on the border of effective sound transmission, and as a result of the change, the effective frequency of transmission (957 Hz) overlapped with the range of generated noise. The results include an effective reinforcement of lateral vibrations of the steam column, pipe resonance, and effective transmission of sound into the environment.
- Vibrations are probably generated in the vertical segment near the nozzle and probe. They are propagated effectively for both Y-pipes. Further propagation in steam is very difficult; this frequency is strongly dampened, but vibrations may propagate in the pipe material and above the vertical segment due to the fact that the value of natural frequencies in all these pipes is approximately 957 Hz. As the distance from the 508 mm × 55 mm pipe increases, the vibration waves in the pipe material disperse, and the level of noise decreases [10,13,14,20,21].

Based on the analysis of the live steam pipeline, the potential source of noise might be one of the following four elements, listed according to decreasing probability of vibration generation:

- The nozzle located near the level of 17 m and the probe located near the nozzle;
- The Y-pipe at the level of 42 m;
- Steam valves located in pipeline branches above the top Y-pipe;
- The Y-pipe at the level of 9 m.

The maximum amplitudes of pipe vibration were recorded at the level of 17 m. At the same level, the sonometer recorded the maximum level of noise. Measurements with an acoustic camera also point to the source of noise being above the level of 12 m. This indicates that the nozzle or probe are the most probable source of noise. The frequencies generated on the probe located near the nozzles, calculated for the full range of Strouhal numbers, ranged from 372 Hz to 872 Hz. This does not mean that it could not generate vibrations with a frequency of 957 Hz. It is sufficient that the 957 Hz frequency is a multiple of the whirl generation frequency. Moreover, in reality the nozzle does not generate a single frequency but a certain range of frequencies, which increases the possibility of exciting vibrations. It is proposed to exchange the nozzle for an identical one to the nozzle in power unit B.

Another potential source is the Y-pipe at the level of 42 m. Its geometry is different in comparison to unit B, which could cause a different band of noise generation through whirls. A change in the diameter of the pipes from Ø355.6 × 40 mm to Ø406.4 × 50 mm substantially changed the character of steam flow through the Y-pipe. In the case of the solution with two Ø355.6 × 40 mm pipes entering the Y-pipe, the sum of the sections of both these pipes (A = 119.310 mm^2) was approximately equal to the section of the vertical pipe (A = 118.237 mm^2), whereas in the new solution the sum of sections of pipes entering the Y-pipe was equal to A = 147.468 mm^2, which is approximately 25% larger than the section of the (vertical) exit pipe. Therefore, the flow speed in the vertical pipe increases, and surges occur in the Y-pipe.

What makes the top Y-pipe an unlikely source of vibration is the lower levels of noise and measured vibrations of the pipe wall in the top span of the vertical 508 mm pipeline.

Additionally, the steam valves were mounted in a piping span whose diameter was reduced from 406 mm to 355 mm. This could potentially cause noise-generating whirls, but the level of noise measured near the valves was significantly lower than that in the lower span of the vertical 508 mm pipe. An experiment involving the closing of the steam valves, which substantially changed the character of flows in the top Y-pipe, did not prove any correlation between these flows and the level of vibrations. Therefore, it is unlikely that the noise is a result of changes in the diameter of the pipeline before and after the steam valves.

To explicitly identify the causes of harmful noise generation in unit A, it would be necessary to perform a full analysis of the flow of the live steam through the pipeline, examine the method of mounting and the superstructure of the power unit, and measure the vibrations on exposed elements of the live steam pipeline in unit A, which could be compared with the same spans in the live steam pipeline of unit B. It would be recommended to continuously measure the noise during power changes in the power unit, at particular points of the pipeline in both the control unit and unit A. Additionally, a numerical simulation should be performed to reconstruct the flow of the medium as well as the phenomenon of acoustic resonance for the geometry of power units A and B near levels of 17 m and 36 m. Numerical simulation should also be applied to determine the scope of alterations in the geometry that are required to eliminate the acoustic resonance. Coupled simulations combining fluid structure interactions or structural-born noise might be necessary.

Author Contributions: Software, M.P.; Validation, P.M.; Investigation, D.P., J.C., A.I., P.M. and M.P.; Resources, P.M.; Data curation, A.G.; Writing—original draft, A.I.; Writing—review & editing, D.P. and A.G.; Project administration, J.C. All authors have read and agreed to the published version of the manuscript.

Funding: This research received no external funding.

Institutional Review Board Statement: Not applicable.

Informed Consent Statement: Not applicable.

Data Availability Statement: The original contributions presented in this study are included in the article. Further inquiries can be directed to the corresponding author.

Conflicts of Interest: The authors declare no conflict of interest.

References

1. Engel, Z.; Engel, J.; Kosała, K. *Procesy Wibroakustyczne Źródła, Badania, Analiza*; WIMiR AGH: Kraków, Poland, 2009.
2. Engel, Z. *Ochrona Środowiska Przed Drganiami i Hałasem, Wydanie Drugie Poprawione i Uaktualnione*; Wydawnictwo Naukow PWN: Warszawa, Poland, 2001.
3. Engel, Z.; Piechowicz, J.; Stryczniewicz, L. *Podstawy Wibroakustyki Przemysłowej*; Uczelniane Wydawnictwa Naukow Dydaktyczne AGH: Kraków, Poland, 2003.
4. Shin, Y.S.; Wambsganss, M.W. Flow-induced vibration in LMFBR steam generators: A state-of-the-art review. *Nucl. Eng. De* **1977**, *40*, 235–284. [CrossRef]
5. Bosnjak, S.M.; Zrnic, N.D. Dynamics, failures, redesigning and environmentally friendly technologies in surface mining system *Arch. Civ. Mech. Eng.* **2012**, *12*, 348–359. [CrossRef]
6. Weber, F.; Maślanka, M. Frequency and damping adaptation of a TMD with controlled MR damper. *Smart Mater. Struc* **2012**, *21*, 055011. [CrossRef]
7. Fusaro, G.; Billi, R.; D'orazio, D. Multiphysical design for optimised ventilation and noise attenuation in ducts: An approac using metamaterials. In Proceedings of the INTER-NOISE24, Nantes, France, 25–29 August 2024; pp. 8163–8171.
8. Wójs, K.; Szulc, P.; Tietze, T.; Sitka, A. Concept of a system for waste heat recovery from flue gases in a coal-fired power plan *J. Energy Sci.* **2010**, *1*, 171–178.
9. Zienkiewicz, O.C.; Taylor, R.L. *The Finite Element Method*, 4th ed.; McGRAW-HILL Book Company: New York, NY, USA, 199 Volumes 1–2.
10. Rusiński, E.; Czmochowski, J.; Górski, A.; Iluk, A.; Moczko, P.; Paduchowicz, M.; Pietrusiak, D. *Pomiary i Analiza Nadmierneg Hałasu Oraz Drgań Rurociągu Pary Świeżej Bloków 7 i 8 w Elektrowni Bełchatów*; Raport Nr 33/2013; PWr: Wrocław, Poland, 2013.

Czmochowski, J.; Górski, A.; Paduchowicz, M.; Rusiński, E. Diagnostic method of measuring hanger rods tension forces in the suspension of the power boilers combustion chamber. *J. Vibroengineering* **2012**, *14*, 151–156.
Dobrociński, S. *Modelowanie Zagadnień Obliczania Naprężeń Cieplnych*; WNT: Warszawa, Poland, 2000.
Kostowski, E. *Promieniowanie Cieplne*; Wyd. Naukowe PWN: Warszawa, Poland, 1993.
Kostowski, E. *Przepływ Ciepła*; Wydawnictwo Politechniki Śląskiej: Gliwice, Poland, 2000.
Jabłoński, M.; Ozga, A. *Distribution of Random Pulses Acting on a Vibrating System as a Function of Its Motion*; AGH University of Science and Technology Press: Kraków, Poland, 2013; ISBN 978-83-7464-660-4.
Maślanka, M.; Sapiński, B.; Snamina, J. Experimental study of vibration control of a cable with an attached MR damper. *J. Theor. Appl. Mech.* **2007**, *45*, 893–917.
Taller, J. (Ed.) *Procesy Cieplne i Przepływowe w Dużych Kotłach Energetycznych. Modelowanie i Monitoring*; Wydawnictwo Naukowe PWN: Warszawa, Poland, 2011.
Yoshihiro, O.; Yoshinobu, T. Three-dimesional transient thermall stresses of functionally graded rectangular plate due to partial heating. *J. Therm. Stress.* **1999**, *22*, 35–55.
Ocampo Ramirez, A.; Hernández Gómez, L.H.; Núñez Carrera, A.; Armenta Molina, A.; Fernández Valdés, D.; Escalona Cambray, F.; Guzmán Escalona, M.A. Evaluation of the Acoustic Noise Inside the Main Steam Line of a BWR/5 Nuclear Reactor. *Appl. Sci.* **2025**, *15*, 3974. [CrossRef]
Jabłoński, M.; Ozga, A. Determining the distribution of values of stochastic impulses acting on a discrete system in relation to their intensity. *Acta Phys. Pol. A* **2012**, *121*, A-174–A-178. [CrossRef]
Smolnicki, T.; Stańco, M.; Pietrusiak, D. Distribution of loads in the large size bearing—Problems of identification. *Teh. Vjesn.—Tech. Gaz.* **2013**, *20*, 831–836.

applied sciences

Article

Optimization Design of Multi-Blade Centrifugal Fan Based on Variable Weight PSO-BP Prediction Model and Multi-Objective Beluga Optimization Algorithm

Wenyang Jin [1], Jiaxuan Wang [2], Junyu Li [1,3], Ren Xu [3], Ming Zhou [4] and Qibai Huang [1,3,*]

1 School of Mechanical Science and Engineering, Huazhong University of Science and Technology, Wuhan 430074, China; jinwenyang@hust.edu.cn (W.J.)
2 Wuhan Second Ship Design and Research Institute, Wuhan 430205, China
3 State Key Laboratory of Digital Manufacturing Equipment and Technology, Huazhong University of Science and Technology, Wuhan 430074, China; xuren18151310314@163.com
4 Valeo Automotive Air Conditioning Hubei Co., Ltd., Jingzhou 434000, China; ming.zhou@valeo.com
* Correspondence: qbhuang@hust.edu.cn

Abstract: Multi-blade centrifugal fans are the main workhorse of automotive air conditioners, and the performance of these fans affects riding comfort. This article proposes a prediction model and a multi-objective optimization algorithm and applies them to the optimization design of a multi-blade centrifugal fan. A prediction model between the design variables and optimization objectives, named wPSO-BP, is proposed, and the model is more effective than the BP prediction model in predicting fan performance. A multi-objective optimization algorithm, named NSGA-III-LBWO, is proposed and applied to the optimization design of the fan along with the wPSO-BP prediction model. The results indicate that the aerodynamics and noise performance of the optimized fan were improved, which provides a reference for the optimized design of these types of fans.

Keywords: multi-blade centrifugal fan; prediction model; multi-objective optimization algorithm

1. Introduction

Multi-blade centrifugal fans are an important part of automotive air conditioning, and improving their performance is crucial to ensuring good car ride comfort [1]. The core component of automobile air conditioning systems is multi-blade centrifugal fans, which have the advantages of compact structures and high flow rates, but they have the disadvantages of short blade channels, low efficiency, and a high noise level. Therefore, this paper is devoted to researching and improving the comprehensive performance of these fans in order to improve the ride comfort and energy utilization efficiency of automobiles.

The volute tongue is closest to the rotating impeller compared to other positions of the volute, and the adjustment of the structural parameters of the tongue is a key factor for improving the aerodynamic performance and reducing the noise of these fans. Wei [2] studied and analyzed the effects of different volute tongue clearances on the internal flow of a centrifugal fan through simulation and found that, after reasonable adjustment of the clearance, the flow loss near the tongue was reduced and the pressure gradient decreased, and the experimental results showed that the aerodynamic noise was reduced by 3.74 dB. Hao [3] experimentally investigated the effects of four kinds of inclined tongue structures on the aerodynamic noise of a fan and concluded that pressure pulsation near the tongue could be attenuated by the reasonable design of the tilting angle and radius of the

 https://doi.org/10.3390/app15115

tongue, such that the eddy current noise in the middle-frequency band could be decreased. Yuan [4] also investigated the use of an inclined tongue and found that the noise could be reduced to 2.33 dB after redesigning the tongue, but the aerodynamic performance of the fan was slightly reduced because of the creation of a new secondary flow near the tongue, which interfered with the impeller outflow. Lun [5] focused on the effect of adjusting the parameters of an inclined tongue on the overall aerodynamic performance of a fan, and they found that the work efficiency was increased by about 4% and the static pressure was increased by about 11 Pa. Some scholars have also borrowed designs for volute tongues from biological structures found in nature. Inspired by the wing structure of the long-eared owl, Wu [6] proposed a bionic snail tongue structure that inhibits the development of eddy currents in the vicinity of the tongue and reduces the noise radiated outward from the volute shell. Wang [7] studied and analyzed the aerodynamic properties of an owl's wing shape and applied them to the tongue, which enabled better synergy between the shell and the impeller, suppressing flow separation and resulting in improved flow.

Impellers are important parts of fans, and their structure also affects fan performance. Wu [8] designed impellers with different attack angles and obtained information on the total pressure, turbulence intensity, etc., through simulation, and they found that the attack angle affects the flow separation in the impeller channel, which, in turn, affects the energy conversion efficiency of the fan. Ding [9] investigated the effect of outlet angle variation on the flow field, and the analysis of the simulation results showed that the angle exhibits different aerodynamic characteristics when the flow rate changes. Jinho [10] optimized the design of the blade outlet angle and other parameters to improve the aerodynamic performance of an impeller. Zhang [11] grooved the blades in order to improve the flow over the blade surfaces and weaken the blade wake, which increased the total pressure of the fan by about 3.6%. Anantharaman [12] studied the effect of four impellers with different numbers of blades on aerodynamic performance and found that an appropriate increase in the number of blades reduced losses in the impeller channel and increased the efficiency of the fan by up to 5.74%. Prezelj [13] tilted the blades of a fan at a certain angle so that the shape of the blade channel was changed, the flow noise between the blades decreased, and the outer-shell radiation noise decreased more significantly in the middle- and low-frequency bands.

In recent years, the application of optimization methods has promoted the development of fluid machinery, and scholars have conducted many studies on optimization objectives and optimization algorithms. Shin [14] optimized the design of centrifugal fans for refrigerators based on the response surface method to modify the blade angle, size, and other parameters in order to lower the noise. Zhang [15] built a prediction model for a centrifugal fan with sample points obtained through experimental methods, and they used the noise and casing quality as optimization objectives, which resulted in a 7.3 dB noise reduction of the fan. Bamberger [16] obtained a performance dataset for centrifugal fans by numerical means and trained a high-precision artificial neural network, which accelerated the optimization progress of the fans. Liu [17] used the response surface method to select the inlet and outlet angles of the blades, and the simulation analysis results showed that the flow separation in the blade channel was improved, the interference of the blade wake on the airflow was weakened, and the efficiency of the fan was improved by 4.2%. Meng [18] optimized a particle swarm algorithm using a limit state machine to redesign the blade size with the pneumatic properties in mind, and the results showed that the total pressure rose by about 11 Pa. Avşar [19] used a multi-objective genetic algorithm based on data obtained from the Kriging prediction model to optimize the aerodynamic performance of the impeller for cooling, increasing the static pressure of the fan.

Many studies focus on the improvement in single parameters of the volute or impeller, while because of the compact structure of the multi-blade centrifugal fan, the matching of the volute and impeller is decisive for the comprehensive performance of the fan. In addition, when selecting the optimization objective of the fan, usually only the aerodynamic or noise performance is considered, and the multi-objective optimization method is less frequently used. In this paper, both volute and impeller parameters are considered and a prediction model named wPSO-BP is constructed for fast optimization, extracting samples based on the Latin hypercube method. The NSGA-III-LBWO algorithm is proposed and applied to the multi-objective optimization of the total pressure, efficiency, and sound pressure level of the fan. The optimization effect is demonstrated, comparing the prototype fan with the optimized fan, which provides an idea for the optimization of centrifugal fans.

2. Establishment of Prediction Model

2.1. Design Variables and Optimization Objectives

The structural parameters of the impeller and volute casing exert a decisive influence on the aerodynamic performance of the multi-wing centrifugal fan. Table 1 summarizes the key structural and operational parameters of the multi-wing centrifugal fan designed for use in the automotive air conditioning system in this study. Before constructing the predictive model, the design variables and optimization objectives should be clearly defined.

Table 1. Initial parameters of the centrifugal fan.

Category	Parameter	Value
Structural Parameters	Blade inlet angle	90°
	Blade outlet angle	139°
	Volute tongue radius	13 mm
	Number of blades	41
Operational Parameters	Impeller speed	4202 r/min
	Rated flow rate	500 m^3/h

Under the design conditions, as the outlet angle of the blades increases, the total pressure and efficiency of the fan increase, which will lead to an increase in noise, because the airflow can be sufficiently accelerated to form a "jet-wake" when the outlet angle is large. Therefore, a reasonable outlet angle can effectively improve the performance of the fan.

The match between the blade inlet angle and the airflow inlet angle determines the quality of flow in the blade channel. Flow separation in the blade channel typically produces shedding vortices that interfere with the main flow, degrade fan performance, and generate noise. Therefore, it is necessary to determine the optimal blade inlet angle to minimize flow losses in the blade channel, while also reducing the noise generated by inflowing airflow over the blades.

The single-arc blade in this paper is presented in Figure 1. The relationship between the arc radius R_c and central angle α of the blade and the inner diameter D_1, outer diameter D_2, inlet angle β_i, and outlet angle β_o of the impeller can be obtained:

$$R_c = \frac{R_2^2 - R_1^2}{2[R_2\cos(\pi - \beta_o) - R_1\cos(\pi - \beta_i)]} \quad (1)$$

$$R_{oo'} = \sqrt{{R_c}^2 + {R_2}^2 - 2R_cR_2\cos(\pi - \beta_o)} \quad (2)$$

$$\alpha = \text{acos}\left(\frac{\left|{R_c}^2 + {R_{oo'}}^2 - {R_2}^2\right|}{2R_cR_{oo'}}\right) - \text{acos}\left(\frac{\left|{R_c}^2 + {R_{oo'}}^2 - {R_1}^2\right|}{2R_cR_{oo'}}\right) \quad (3)$$

where R_c is the arc radius of the blade, R_1 and R_2 are the inner and outer diameters of the impeller, respectively, β_i and β_o are the inlet and outlet angles of the blade, respectively, $R_{oo'}$ is the distance from the center of the blade arc to the center of the impeller, and α is the blade central angle.

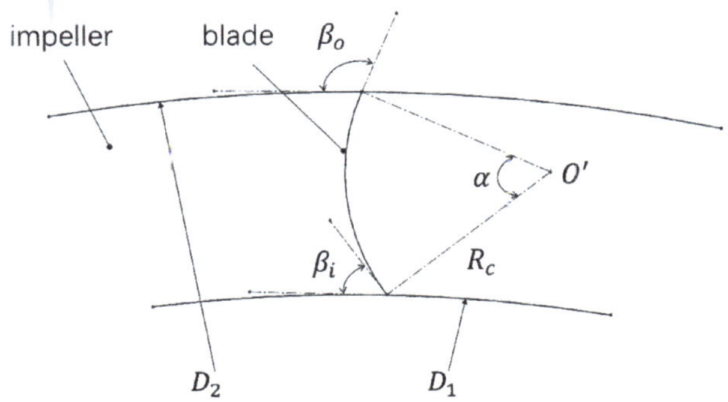

Figure 1. Single-arc blade structure.

The volute tongue prevents air recirculation within the volute during fan operation. However, residual airflow bypassing the volute tongue disrupts the impeller mainstream, inducing flow separation within the blade passage and cross-impeller flow, thereby causing performance degradation and noise generation. Furthermore, the tongue's close proximity to the impeller subjects it to periodic high-speed flow interactions, generating time-varying pressure pulsations that render the tongue structure the primary noise source in the fan system. As shown in Figure 2, the inclined tongue structure features a radius varying along the axial direction, leading to a phase difference in the airflow effects from the front to the rear disc sides of the impeller on the volute tongue. The superposition of noise from unsteady forces with different phases yields smaller amplitudes compared to forces with the same phase in constant-radius tongue structures. Consequently, the fan incorporates an inclined volute tongue design to minimize noise originating from the tongue region.

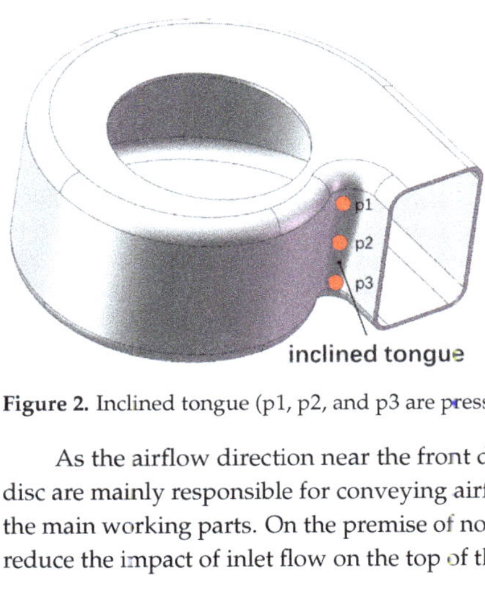

Figure 2. Inclined tongue (p1, p2, and p3 are pressure pulsation monitoring points).

As the airflow direction near the front disc is mainly axial, the blades near the front disc are mainly responsible for conveying airflow to the middle and rear discs, and are not the main working parts. On the premise of not changing the size of the collector, in order to reduce the impact of inlet flow on the top of the blade and reduce the turbulence noise, it is necessary to ensure that the outlet diameter of the collector is equal to the impeller blade inner diameter. Therefore, blades near the front disc should be chamfered (Figure 3), which can minimize the impact of the removal on the power output of the impeller.

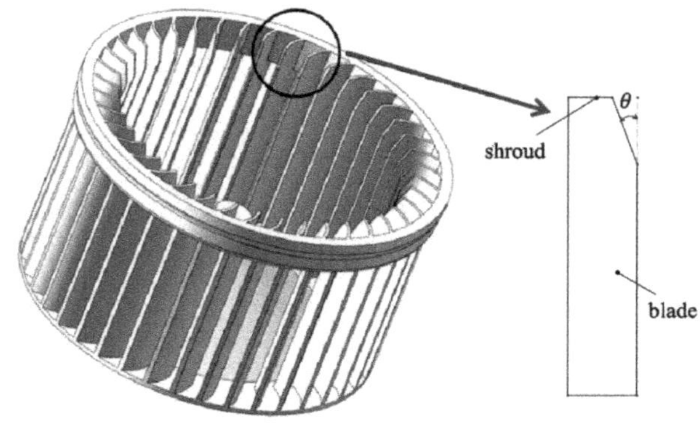

Figure 3. Beveled blade.

Based on the aforementioned analysis, the blade design variables and their corresponding boundary conditions are summarized in Table 2. The optimization objectives include enhancing total pressure P_{total}, improving fan efficiency η, and reducing noise levels L_p. A weight allocation model for each objective parameter is proposed to achieve synergistic optimization of aerodynamic performance and acoustic characteristics.

$$P_{total} = P_{total,out} - P_{total,in} \tag{4}$$

where $P_{total,out}$ and $P_{total,in}$ are the total pressure at the outlet and inlet of the fan, respectively.

$$\eta = \frac{P_{total} Q_v}{M\omega} \tag{5}$$

where Q_v is the fan flow rate, M is the impeller torque, and ω is the impeller angular velocity.

$$L_p = 20\lg(\frac{p}{p_{ref}}) \tag{6}$$

where p is the sound pressure and p_{ref} is the standard reference sound pressure, 2×10^{-5} Pa.

Table 2. Design parameters and boundary conditions.

Parameter	Symbol	Boundary Conditions
Blade Inlet Angle	β_i	80°~115°
Blade Outlet Angle	β_o	129°~149°
Volute Tongue Radius	$R_{v,s}$	16 mm~25 mm
Blade Tip Chamfer Angle	θ	10°~40°

2.2. Variable-Weight PSO-Optimized BP Neural Network (wPSO-BP) Prediction Model

The BP neural network (Figure 4) has good nonlinear processing ability and is suitable for predicting the outcomes of the fan. The network is constructed as follows: obtain the predicted values based on the inputs, adjust the node thresholds and connection weights at each layer by calculating the prediction error, and repeat the process until the error is acceptable or the iterative upper limit is reached and then the training is finished.

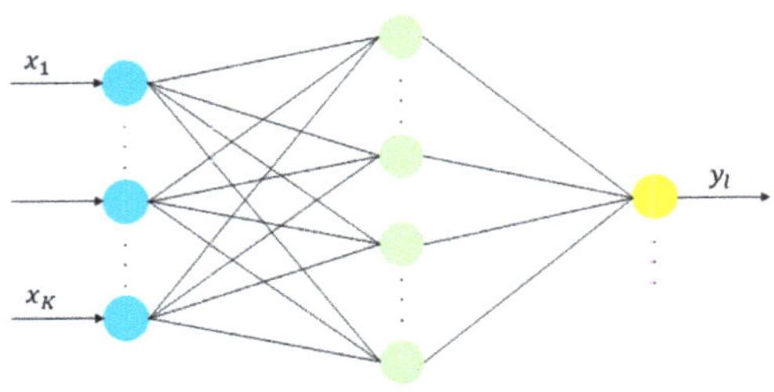

Figure 4. The structure of the BP neural network.

Despite the good predictive ability of the BP neural network, it also has problems such as slow convergence speed and difficulty in guaranteeing the global optimization of network parameters, which may not guarantee accuracy of the fan performance prediction. Therefore, this study employs the particle swarm optimization (PSO) algorithm to optimize the BP neural network's initial weights and thresholds, utilizing prediction error as the fitness function to enhance prediction accuracy

The velocity update formula for particle swarm is as follows:

$$v_i^{k+1} = wv_i^k + c_1r_1\left(p_i^k - x_i^k\right) + c_2r_2\left(g_i^k - x_i^k\right) \tag{7}$$

The formula for updating the position of the particle swarm is as follows:

$$x_i^{k+1} = x_i^k + v_i^{k+1} \tag{8}$$

where k is the current number of the iteration step, w is the inertia weight, v_i^k is the velocity of particle i in the kth iteration, which is a vector when the particle has multiple attributes, c_1 and c_2 are learning factors used to adjust the maximum step size of particle learning, r_1 and r_2 are random values within [0, 1], and x_i^k is the position of particle i in the kth iteration.

The inertia weight w controls the degree to which particles preserve their previous velocity during motion updates. A larger w in the initial phase biases the particle swarm towards global search, while a smaller w in the later phase helps in local search [20]. In order to better enhance the search ability of PSO, a calculation method for inertia weight decreasing update is proposed:

$$w = w_{start}\left(\frac{w_{end}}{w_{start}}\right)^{\frac{2}{\pi}\arcsin\left(\frac{k}{k_{max}}\right)} \tag{9}$$

where w_{start} and w_{end} are the initial and final inertia weights, respectively, and k_{max} is the upper limit of the number of iterations.

Figure 5 illustrates the workflow for constructing a centrifugal fan prediction model based on a variable-weight PSO-optimized BP neural network (wPSO-BP). The model employs a BP neural network incorporating a variable inertia weight strategy, utilizes a rectified linear unit (ReLU) activation function in the hidden layer, applies a linear function in the output layer, and adopts the mean squared error (MSE) as the training objective. The initial learning rate was set to 0.01 and dynamically optimized through the wPSO algorithm. During the data preprocessing stage, all input and output variables were normalized via the Min–Max method, and the dataset was divided into training and testing subsets at a 4:1 ratio to evaluate the model's predictive performance. For the parameter configuration of the wPSO algorithm, the population size was set to 20, the maximum number of iterations was capped at 50, and the inertia weight was linearly reduced from an initial value of 1.0

to 0.4. The maximum number of training epochs for the BP neural network was set to 1000, and the target training accuracy was defined as 0.0001, thereby ensuring the model achieved both high predictive accuracy and strong generalization capability.

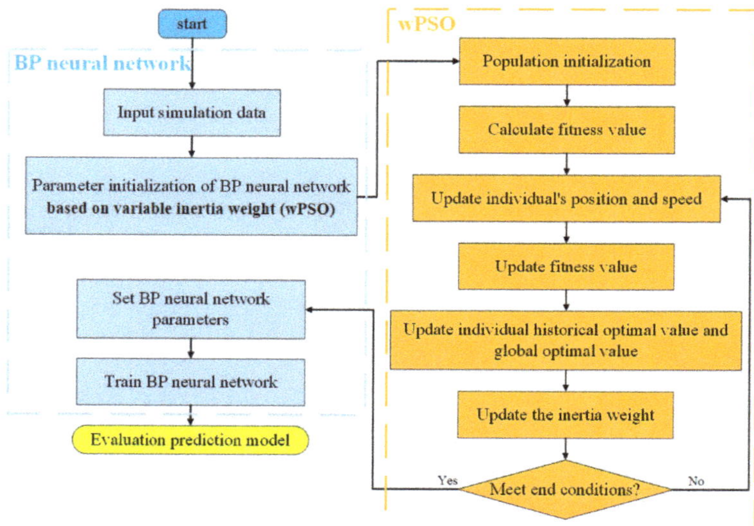

Figure 5. The construction process of the centrifugal fan prediction model based on the variable-weight PSO-optimized BP neural network (wPSO-BP).

Step 1: Input simulation data of the centrifugal fan.

Step 2: Initialize the structure and parameters of the BP neural network.

Step 3: Initialize the parameters of PSO, including the population number N, individual speed v_0 and position x_0, initial weight w_0, etc., and calculate individual fitness.

Step 4: During the iterative calculation process, use Equations (7) and (8) to calculate the speed v_k and position x_k of individuals, and update the global optimal and individual historical optimal.

Step 5: Before the end of the kth iteration, update the inertia weight w_{k+1} according to Equation (9). Determine whether the maximum number of iterations k_{max} has been reached. If so, proceed to step 6; otherwise, return to step 4.

Step 6: Output the optimal solution.

Step 7: Apply optimal solutions to BP neural network, start training, and evaluate the prediction results.

3. Establishment of Multi-Objective Optimization Algorithm

3.1. BWO Based on Logistic Chaotic Map Initialization (LBWO)

Beluga whale optimization (BWO) [21] is inspired by the behavior of beluga whales, and corresponds their swimming, hunting, and whale fall to exploration, exploitation, and whale fall, and the actions performed by individuals are determined by B_f and W_f in the algorithm. In order to enhance global convergence, the algorithm introduces Levy flight [22] during the exploitation phase and controls the behavior of individual beluga whales through adaptive balance factors and probability of whale fall. BWO can effectively control the execution of an individual's actions at different stages, which is advantageous for solving realistic problems. Therefore, BWO is selected as the basic algorithm for multi-objective optimization of the fan.

According to BWO, the beluga whale position is generated through random initialization, which can cause uneven distribution of individual positions and reduce the accuracy of the solution. The chaotic sequence based on chaos theory has the characteristics of randomness and convenience [23]. A Logistic chaotic map [24] is used to initialize the population in this paper. The expression for the Logistic chaotic map is as follows:

$$x_{i+1} = \mu \cdot x_i \cdot (1 - x_i), \quad i = 1, 2, \ldots N - 1 \tag{10}$$

where μ is a control parameter with a range of $[0, 4]$, when μ is near 4, it exhibits a pseudo random distribution, and x_i corresponds to individual i, which is used to initialize the position of the individual, with a range of $(0, 1)$.

3.2. Multi-Objective Beluga Optimization Algorithm (NSGA-III-LBWO)

Original beluga whale optimization is suitable for solving single-objective optimization problems. When there are multiple optimization objectives (total pressure, efficiency, and sound pressure level), they are usually added in a normalized and weighted manner [25] to transform into a single-objective optimization problem. However, it is not easy to achieve optimal values for each optimization variable through this means.

To address the aforementioned limitation, this study proposes a multi-objective beluga whale optimization algorithm (NSGA-III-LBWO), integrating strategies from both LBWO [26] and NSGA-III [27] (Table 3). NSGA-III is a multi-objective evolutionary algorithm that incorporates the Pareto dominance mechanism [28]. The evaluation of individuals is no longer based solely on objective value magnitudes; instead, solution quality is assessed through the dominance relationships defined by the Pareto dominance mechanism. In the population, an individual p is said to dominate another individual q if the condition specified in Equation (11) is satisfied. The Pareto front is defined as the set of objective function values corresponding to the Pareto-optimal solutions, wherein all solutions are mutually non-dominated and no external solution dominates any member of the set.

$$\forall i \in (1, 2, \ldots, \zeta), f_i(p) \leq f_i(q) \wedge \exists l \in (1.2, \ldots, \zeta), f_l(p) < f_l(q) \tag{11}$$

where $f_i(X)$ is the value of individual X on the ith objective function and ζ is the number of objective functions.

Table 3. Comparative analysis of LBWO, NSGA-III, and NSGA-III-LBWO.

Category	LBWO	NSGA-III	NSGA-III-LBWO
Core Mechanism	Logistic chaotic initialization + Levy flight search	Non-dominated sorting + Reference point mechanism	Hybrid of LBWO and NSGA-III, dynamically generates Pareto offspring
Advantages	1. Strong global search 2. High population diversity	1. High-dimensional multi-objective optimization 2. Uniform solution distribution	1. Global–local balance 2. High-quality solutions (verified in engineering applications)
Limitations	Single-objective, prone to local optima	Slow convergence, weak local search	Parameter sensitivity, moderate computational cost
Summary	NSGA-III-LBWO integrates the global search capability of single-target LBWO and the diversity maintenance mechanism of multi-target NSGA-III, realizing the complementary advantages of both.		

Compared to the single-objective optimization algorithm, NSGA-III based on non-dominated sorting enhances the exploration capability of the search space. Building upon the framework of NSGA-II, NSGA-III introduces a novel reference-point-based mechanism for evaluating individual solutions. By generating a series of uniformly distributed reference points in space, individuals and reference points are associated, so that some individuals with clustered distribution are eliminated, ensuring that the Pareto front can also maintain uniform distribution characteristics, which can ensure the uniformity and accuracy of the calculation results when analyzing nonlinear problems such as centrifugal fan performance optimization.

During the offspring generation phase in NSGA-III-LBWO, a portion of the initial population is derived from the current Pareto-optimal set, while the remainder is generated using the Logistic chaotic mapping defined in Equation (10). The positions of individuals are iteratively updated following the optimization rules of LBWO, with the final updated solutions being retained as the offspring individuals. To enhance the efficiency of the optimization process, the number of offspring individuals sampled from the non-dominated Pareto set $C_t^{\text{non-dominated}}$ will increase (Equation (12)), so as to search near the current Pareto set, which facilitates jumping out of the local optimum.

$$C_t^{\text{non-dominated}} = \alpha \cdot t \cdot S \tag{12}$$

where t is the cycle number, α is the constant scaling factor, and S is the population size.

Before generating initial positions based on the Pareto set in the LBWO algorithm, it is necessary to evaluate the individuals in the Pareto set according to Equation (13) and select the first $C_t^{\text{non-dominated}}$ non-dominated individuals to generate initial positions.

$$val_p = \sum_{i=1}^{\zeta} w_i \cdot f_i(p) \tag{13}$$

where val_p is the value of individual p and w_i is the weight of the ith objective function.

The centrifugal fan performance optimization problem in this paper can be expressed as follows:

$$find\ X^* = \{\beta_i{}^*, \beta_o{}^*, R_{v,s}{}^*, \theta^*\} \tag{14}$$

The objective functions can be described as follows:

$$\begin{cases} \max(P_{total}(X^*)) \\ \max(\eta(X^*)) \\ \min(L_p(X^*)) \end{cases} \tag{15}$$

where X^* is an ideal design variable combination that should maximize the total pressure and efficiency of the fan and, at the same time, minimize the noise. The multi-objective optimization steps of the prototype fan are based on NSGA-III-LBWO, as shown in Figure 6.

Step 1: Determine population size N, number of iterations t_{max}, individual attributes, and objective functions. Initialize the population P_0, calculate the objective functions values of each individual, and perform non-dominated sorting on the individuals.

Step 2: Based on the current Pareto set and Equation (10), generate the offspring population C_t in LBWO.

Step 3: Merge the original population P_t and the offspring population C_t to obtain population R_t.

Step 4: According to the non-dominated strategy and reference point mechanism, N individuals are selected from population R_t to join the new population P_{t+1}.

Step 5: Update the number of iterations t to determine if the end condition is met. If it is, end and output the optimization result; otherwise, return to step 2.

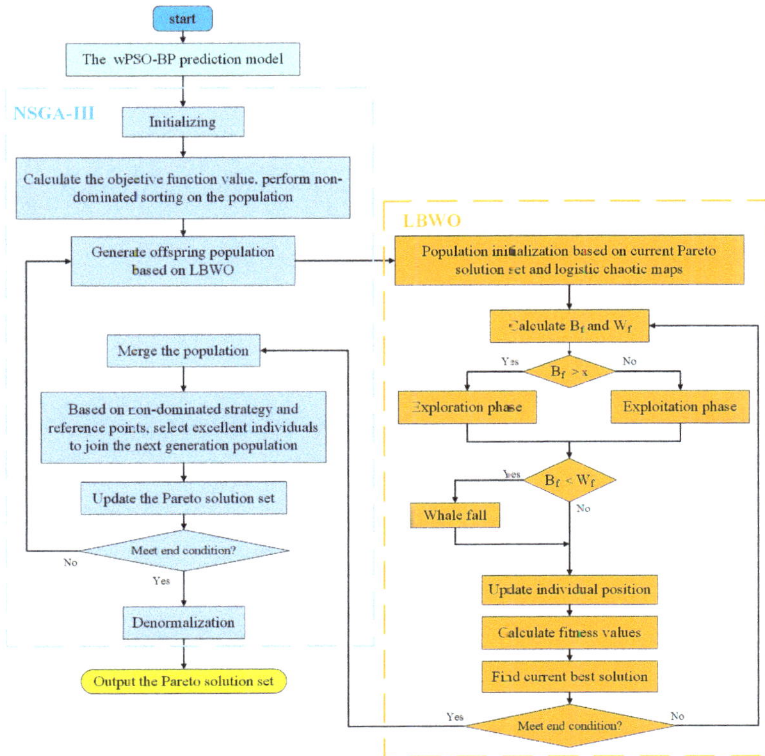

Figure 6. Optimization process of prototype fan.

4. Optimization and Analysis of Multi-Blade Centrifugal Fan

4.1. Reliability Verification of the Numerical Simulation

In order to eliminate the impact of the number and quality of meshes on the calculation results and minimize the number of meshes to ensure efficiency, mesh independence verification needs to be carried out first. The total pressure and efficiency are selected as verification indicators, and eight sets of calculation examples are calculated (Figure 7). Taking into account the accuracy and speed of the solution, a 5.99×10^6 mesh scheme is selected to carry out the subsequent simulations (Figure 8).

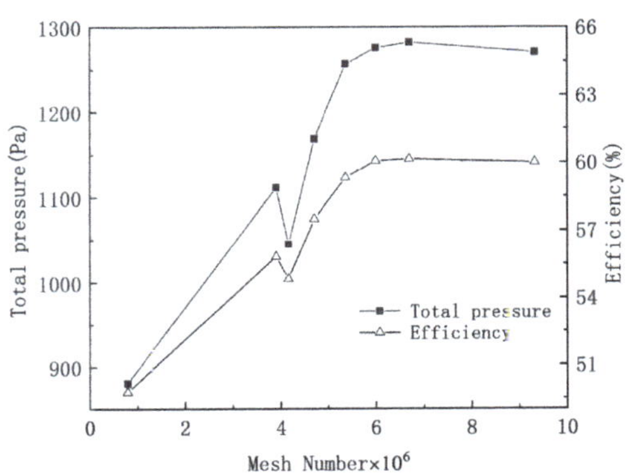

Figure 7. Result of the mesh independence verification.

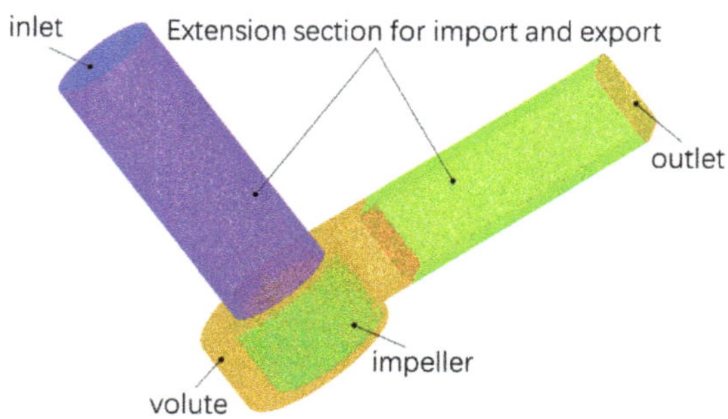

Figure 8. Mesh of the fan.

To verify the reliability of the simulation model, the total pressure and efficiency under different operating conditions are calculated and compared with experimental data, as shown in Figure 9.

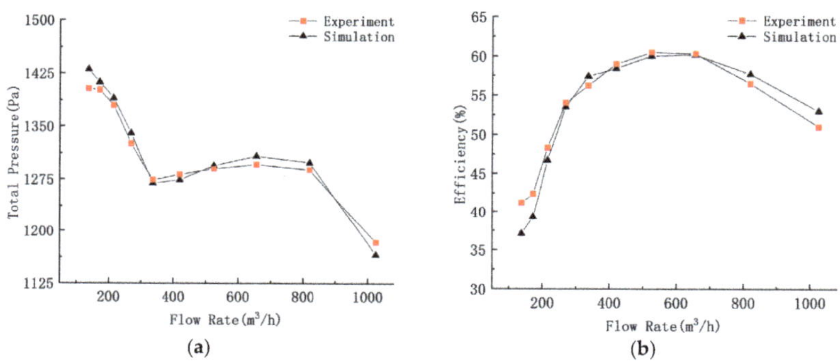

Figure 9. Comparison of total pressure and efficiency results. (**a**) Total pressure. (**b**) Efficiency.

Comparative analysis between numerical simulations and experimental measurements (Figure 9) shows that the maximum relative errors of full pressure and efficiency are 2.1% and 9.6%, respectively, which all appear under Q = 100 m^3/h (not the typical working interval of the fan), while in the typical operating flow interval of the fan, good consistency is shown between the simulation results and the experimental data, which indicates that the simulation model has good prediction accuracy.

The noise experiment of the fan is conducted in a semi-anechoic room (Figure 10a). The background noise sound pressure level is 15 dB, which is far lower than the centrifugal fan noise. The microphone is located at the fan outlet and is offset by 45° (Figure 10b) to reduce the impact of outlet airflow and motor noise on the experimental results. Aerodynamic noise calculations and experiments in this paper are conducted at a flow rate of 500 m^3/h, and the noise spectrum obtained is shown in Figure 11.

By comparing the experimental and simulation results of fan noise, it can be seen that there are some differences between the two. The reason for the error is that the noise generated by the mechanical part of the fan and the electromagnetic noise generated by the motor during operation are not considered in the simulation. Additionally, the original structure is simplified somewhat during the simulation. Under rated operating conditions, the simulated noise at the measuring point is 57.75 dB, while the experimental is 58.85 dB, with an error of 1.1 dB.

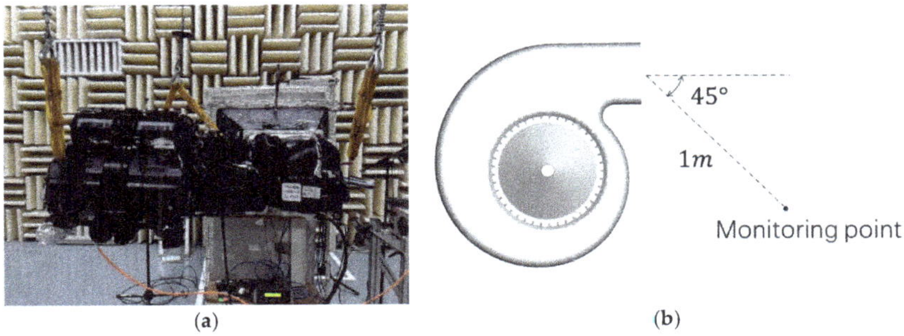

Figure 10. Experimental research on noise of the prototype fan. (**a**) Semi-anechoic room. (**b**) Microphone position.

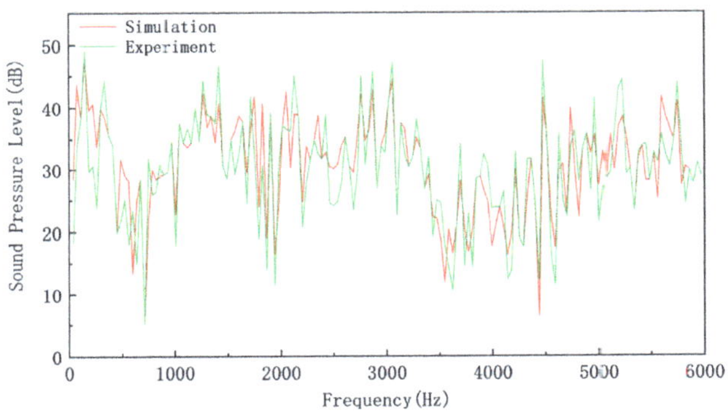

Figure 11. Noise spectrum of simulation and experiment.

Overall, the consistency between simulation and experiment is in good coincidence, indicating the rationality of model simplification, mesh partitioning, and simulation parameter settings during simulation, which can be used for subsequent calculations and optimization.

4.2. Prediction Model Results and Analysis

To establish the mapping between design variables and optimization objectives, 80 sample points are generated using the Latin hypercube sampling (LHS) method [29]. The use of LHS ensures uniform coverage of the multidimensional parameter space with a limited number of samples, thereby preventing local clustering while enhancing predictive accuracy and reducing computational costs [30]. These samples, including representative cases listed in Table 4, constitute the training and testing datasets for the prediction model. The performance metrics (e.g., total pressure, efficiency, and sound pressure level) for these samples are obtained through validated simulation techniques. Moreover, an automated batch processing workflow is implemented to handle the computational workload, which substantially improves computational efficiency.

The comparison results of wPSO-BP and BP are presented in Figure 12. Compared to the BP prediction model, the value obtained by the wPSO-BP prediction model is closer to the calculated value.

Table 4. Information of some sample points and calculations.

Design Variables				Optimization Objectives		
$\beta_i/°$	$\beta_o/°$	$R_{v,s}$/mm	$\theta/°$	P_{total}/Pa	$\eta/\%$	L_p/dB
99.72	141.49	23.65	13.25	1237.46	56.48	56.39
100.57	143.81	19.53	28.7	1268.53	57.4	56.73
102.94	133.66	17.93	22.98	1175.38	55.18	55.85
102.28	141.84	19.86	14.79	1226.4	55.47	55.63
82.98	132.66	24.39	33.03	1183.22	57.77	56.77
104.52	129.22	19.25	14.45	1074.04	52.91	53.87
93.33	135.77	19.04	38.95	1168.31	56.46	54.11
93.83	131.69	19.39	34.81	1114.82	52.79	52.26
84.12	135.42	20.68	16.18	1223.67	59.41	56.83
93.19	146.36	23.73	34.01	1314.61	59.05	57.64

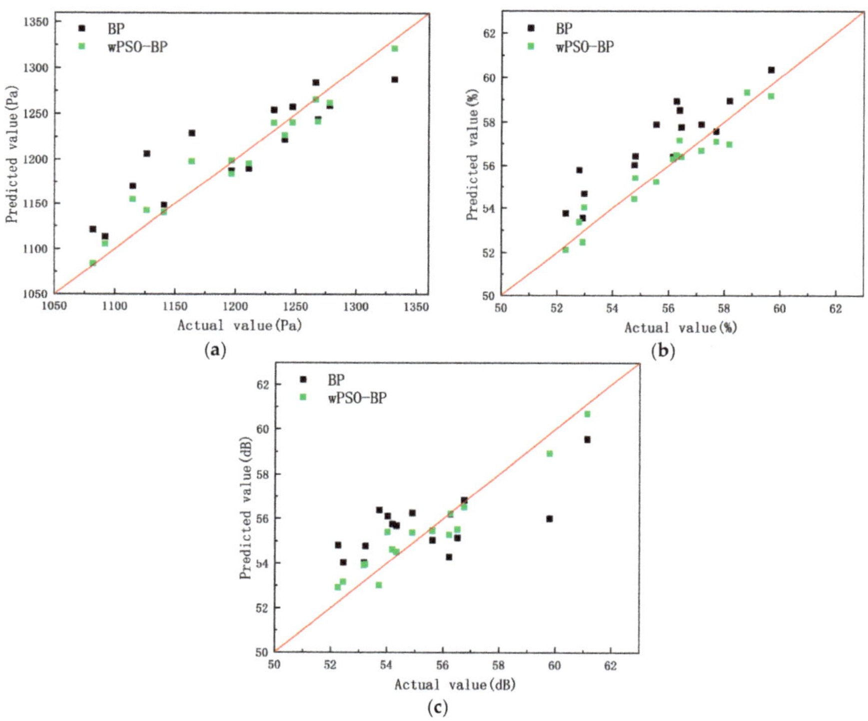

Figure 12. Comparison between predicted and calculated values. (**a**) Total pressure. (**b**) Efficiency. (**c**) Sound pressure level.

To further compare the two prediction models, quantitative analysis is conducted. The root mean square error (RMSE), mean absolute error (MAE), and coefficient of determination (R^2) are calculated according to Equation (16)–(18), respectively.

$$RMSE = \sqrt{\frac{1}{m}\sum_{i=1}^{m}(y_i - \hat{y}_i)^2} \tag{16}$$

$$MAE = \frac{1}{m}\sum_{i=1}^{m}|(y_i - \hat{y}_i)| \tag{17}$$

$$R^2 = 1 - \frac{\sum_{i=1}^{m}(y_i - \hat{y}_i)^2}{\sum_{i=1}^{m}(y_i - \overline{y})^2} \tag{18}$$

where m is the number of samples, $\hat{y}_i$ is the true value corresponding to sample i, and $\overline{y}$ is the average of true values.

Table 5 shows the evaluation indexes of the two models; it can be seen that the wPSO-BP prediction model can effectively reflect the link between the design variables and the optimization objectives, and its coefficient of determination is greater than 0.9, which can be used for subsequent optimization.

Table 5. Comparison of predicted results.

	Model	RMSE	MAE	R^2
Total pressure	BP	35.82	29.18	0.74
	wPSO-BP	17.74	13.74	0.93
Efficiency	BP	2.30	1.71	<0
	wPSO-BP	0.58	0.50	0.92
Sound pressure level	BP	1.81	1.56	0.43
	wPSO-BP	0.70	0.61	0.91

4.3. Optimization Results and Analysis

In this study, a collaborative optimization design of a prototype multi-wing centrifugal fan was carried out using the wPSO-BP prediction model and the NSGA-III-LBWO multi-objective optimization algorithm. The algorithm parameters were set as follows: the population size was set to 200, the number of iterations was 100, and the computational program was developed on the MATLAB 2022a platform. The core process includes the following:

1. Parameter initialization: 200 sets of initial samples are generated using the Latin hypercubic sampling technique and input into the wPSO-BP model for the prediction of full pressure (P_{total}), efficiency (η), and noise (L_p);
2. Pareto front search: the reference point stratification mechanism of NSGA-III is used to screen the non-dominated solutions, and the Logistic chaos mapping of LBWO is combined to enhance the global search capability.

The Pareto frontiers obtained through optimization (see Figure 13) show that the optimal solution set exhibits an obvious trade-off between full pressure enhancement, efficiency improvement, and noise suppression, thus verifying the effectiveness of the proposed multi-objective optimization framework.

As shown in Figure 13, the sound pressure level of the fan increases with both efficiency and total pressure, indicating that the total pressure, efficiency, and noise performance of the multi-blade centrifugal fan cannot be simultaneously optimized, necessitating trade-off decisions. Compared to the improvements in aerodynamic performance, noise reduction during fan operation holds higher practical significance. The optimization configuration and corresponding results are summarized in Table 6. The optimized fan achieves a total pressure increase of 34.79 Pa, an efficiency improvement of 0.67%, and a reduction in sound pressure level of 1.73 dB compared to the baseline prototype. These results demonstrate that the optimization approach based on the wPSO-BP prediction model and NSGA-III-LBWO algorithm is effective, and the optimization goal of improving aerodynamic performance while reducing noise is achieved.

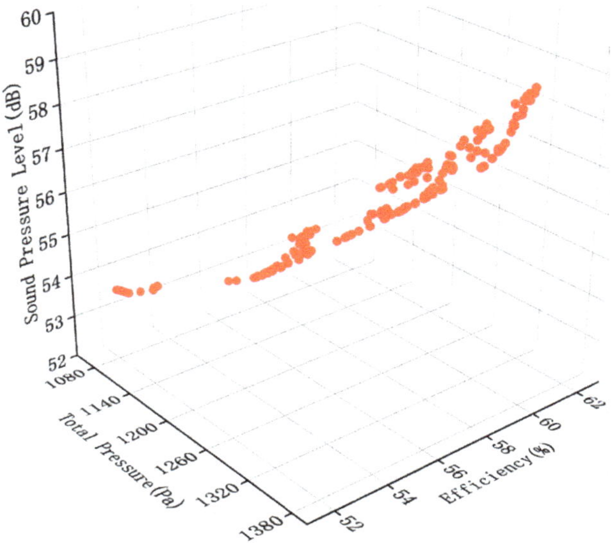

Figure 13. Pareto front.

Table 6. Comparison of results before and after optimization.

	$\beta_i/°$	$\beta_o/°$	$R_{v,s}$/mm	$\theta/°$	P_{total}/Pa	η/%	L_p/dB
Prototype fan	90	139	12.87	0	1275.89	60.07	57.75
Optimized fan	98.81	147.06	17.47	39.85	1310.68	60.74	56.02

For the convenience of analyzing the fans before and after optimization, three sections are selected, namely the front disc side (z = 75 mm), middle position (z = 50 mm), and rear disc side (z = 25 mm) (Figure 14).

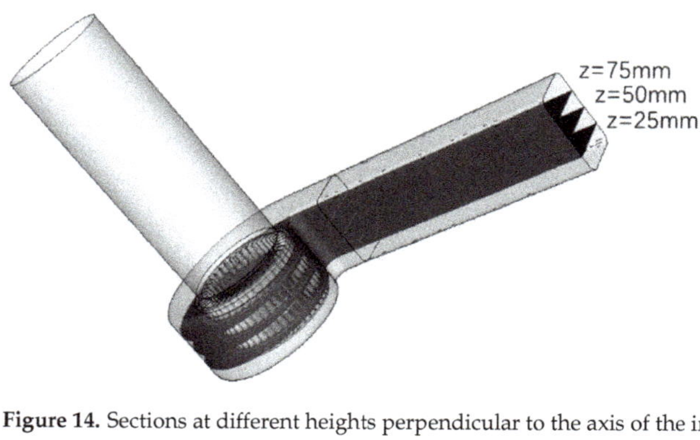

Figure 14. Sections at different heights perpendicular to the axis of the impeller.

The static pressure nephograms before and after optimization are shown in Figures 15 and 16. After optimization, the range of low static pressure near the center of the impeller in the z = 75 mm section is significantly reduced, the pressure gradient decreases, the interference of the airflow entering the blade channel is reduced, and the flow loss inside the blade channel is reduced, resulting in an improvement in aerodynamic performance. The maximum static pressure position is closer to the outlet compared to before optimization in the sections of z = 50 mm and z = 25 mm, which weakens the backflow phenomenon near the tongue, improving the impeller efficiency and reducing the fan noise. The maximum and minimum static pressure difference after optimization has increased by approximately 187 Pa compared to before, indicating an improvement in the pneumatic performance.

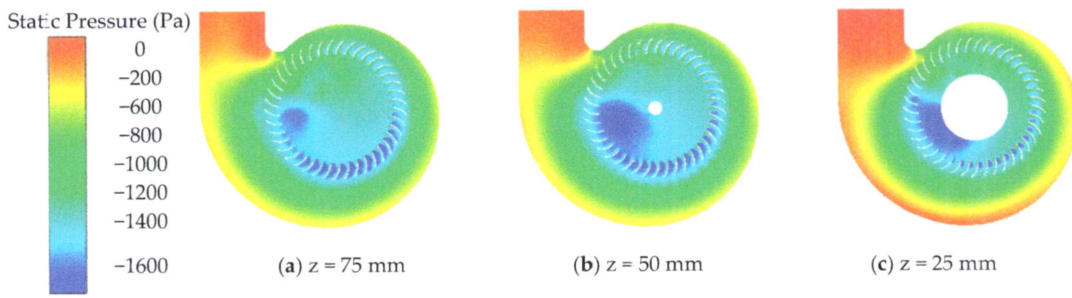

Figure 15. Static pressure nephogram of each section before optimization.

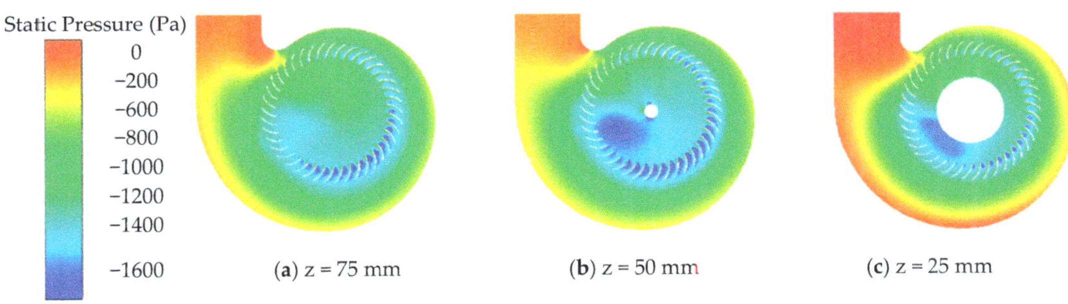

Figure 16. Static pressure nephogram of each section after optimization.

Figures 17 and 18 illustrate the velocity–streamline nephograms of the fan. Analysis shows that the airflow acceleration effect of each section of the fan is significantly promoted. Based on the turbulence kinetic energy diagram (Figures 19 and 20), it can be inferred that the matching between the airflow inlet angle and the blade inlet angle has been improved, the flow separation effect in the blade channel has been weakened, and the flow loss inside the fan has decreased. The average velocity of the airflow at the impeller outlet position has increased by about 8 m/s compared to before optimization, which means that the airflow is receiving more energy, and the fan efficiency has improved by 0.67%.

Figures 19 and 20 show the nephograms of turbulent kinetic energy before and after optimization. It can be seen that during the operation of the fan, the positions with strong turbulent kinetic energy are concentrated near the tongue, in the blade channel, and inside the impeller, all of which are the main sources of fan noise. By comparison, it can be found that the flow situation near the volute tongue with the section of z = 75 mm has significantly improved, as the tongue radius near the front disc of impeller is larger, and the unsteady interference between the tongue and airflow is weakened, manifested by a decrease in the overall fan noise. After optimization, the turbulent kinetic energy in the blade channel of the fan at the main work area z = 50 mm and z = 25 mm sections significantly decreased compared to before optimization. The mutual interference between high-speed outflow and low-speed airflow in the volute passage is reduced, manifested as a reduction in the area of the area around the blade with larger turbulent kinetic energy. Although the high turbulent kinetic energy area inside the impeller increased compared to before optimization, the overall performance of the fan was improved.

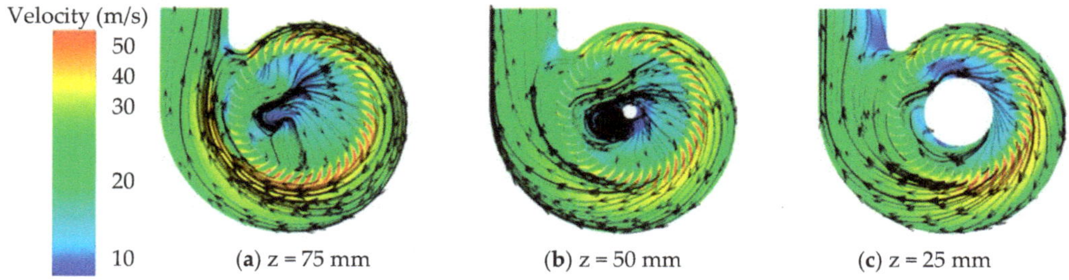

Figure 17. Velocity–streamline nephogram of each section before optimization.

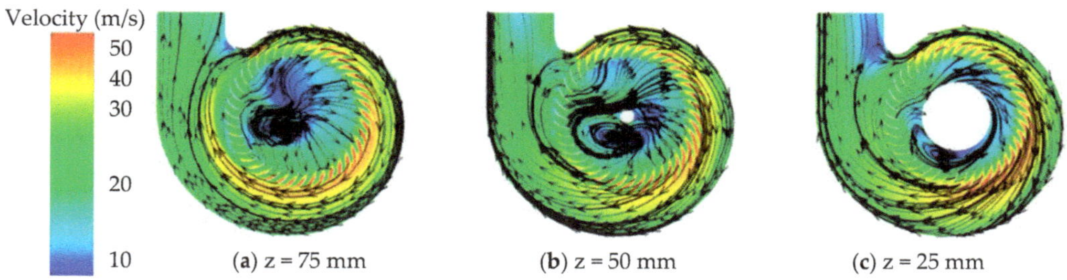

Figure 18. Velocity–streamline nephogram of each section after optimization.

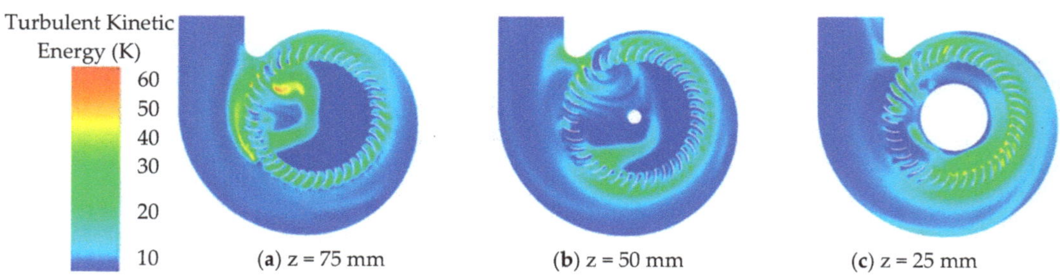

Figure 19. Turbulent kinetic energy nephogram of each section before optimization.

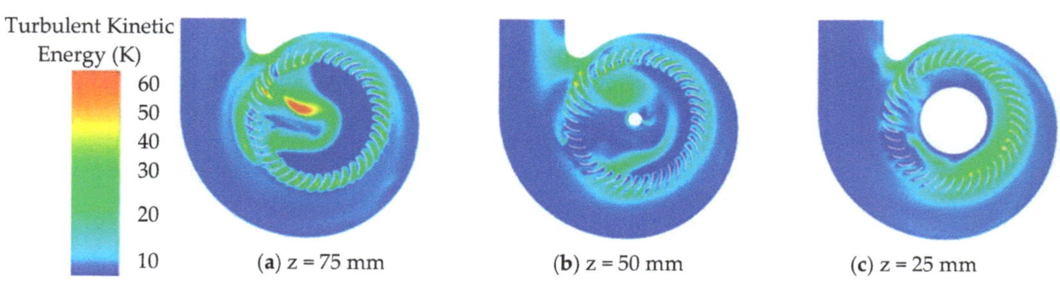

Figure 20. Turbulent kinetic energy nephogram of each section after optimization.

To further illustrate the optimization effect, three monitoring points p1, p2, and p3 near the volute tongue (Figure 2) are selected for pressure pulsation analysis, as shown in Figure 21. From the figure, it can be seen that there are obvious peaks at the rotating frequency (70 Hz) and blade frequency (2871 Hz) at each pressure pulsation monitoring point before and after optimization, indicating the accuracy of the simulation results. The optimized fan has a varying reduction in the peak pressure pulsation at three monitoring points. The reduction effect of pressure pulsation is most significant in the middle and rear disc positions of the impeller: the amplitude of the middle and rear discs decreased by 32.12 Pa and 55.82 Pa at 70 Hz, while the amplitude decreased by 30.03 Pa and 2.6 Pa at 2871 Hz, respectively.

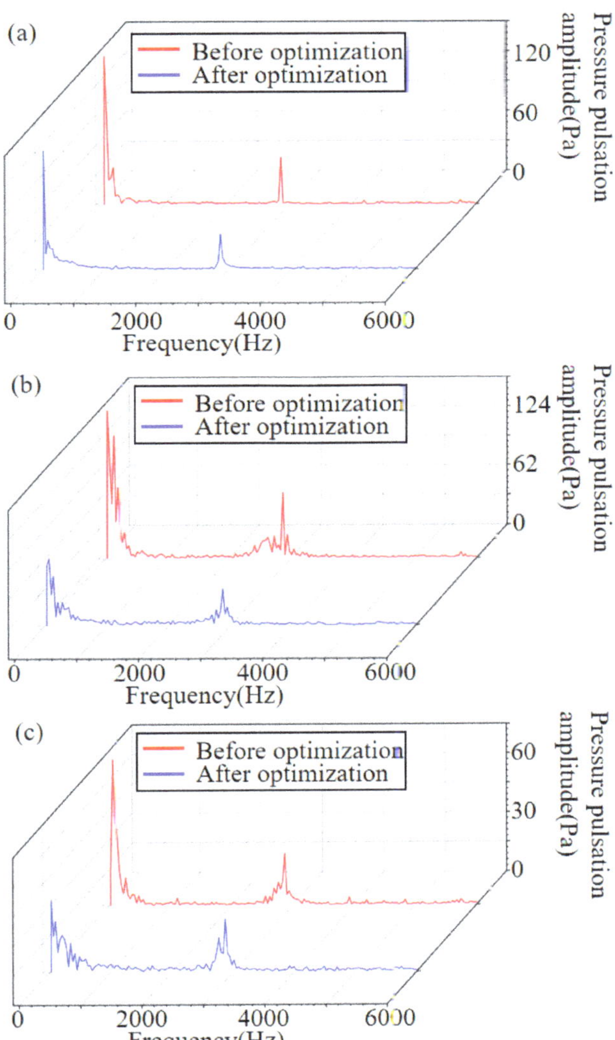

Figure 21. Pressure pulsation at detection points near the volute tongue before and after optimization. (**a**) p1 pressure pulsation. (**b**) p2 pressure pulsation. (**c**) p3 pressure pulsation.

After increasing the tongue radius at the front disc, the interference between the airflow and the tongue is weakened, and the periodic impact on the volute tongue is weakened. Moreover, due to the change in the radius of volute tongue, there is a phase difference in the unsteady force on the volute tongue at different heights. After superposition, the overall effect is weakened compared to before optimization, which is manifested as a decrease in the noise of the optimized fan (Figure 22).

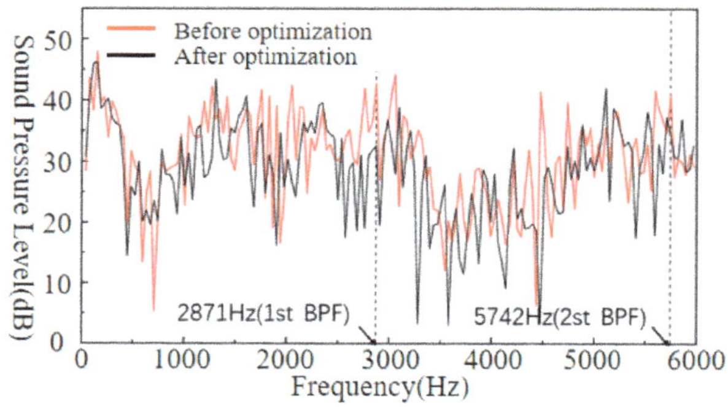

(**a**) Comparison of sound pressure level curves before and after optimization

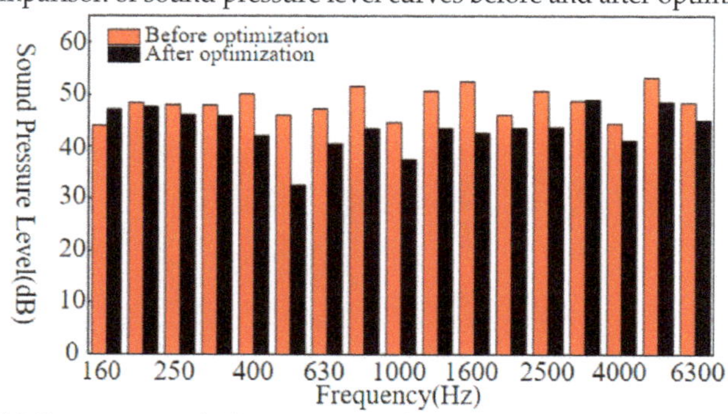

(**b**) Comparison of 1/3-octave noise before and after optimization

Figure 22. Comparison of noise at far-field monitoring point before and after optimization.

In order to observe the noise performance of the optimized fan, the noise sound pressure level of the remote field monitoring points before and after optimization are compared (Figure 22). According to the curves, it can be observed that the sound pressure level of the optimized fan has decreased to a certain extent in most frequency bands, and at the one- and two-time blade frequencies, the noise has significantly decreased by 10.24 dB and 6.46 dB, respectively. Therefore, the overall sound pressure level of the fan has reduced from 57.75 dB to 56.02 dB.

5. Conclusions

In this paper, a prediction model (wPSO-BP) and a multi-objective optimization algorithm (NSGA-III-LBWO) are proposed, and the blade inlet and outlet angle, volute tongue radius on the front disc side, and front disc side blade chamfer angle of the multi-blade centrifugal fan are optimized based on the wPSO-BP prediction model and NSGA-III-LBWO, which improves the comprehensive performance of the fan. The conclusions can be drawn as follows:

(a) A prediction model between design variables and optimization objectives called wPSO-BP is proposed and compared with the BP prediction model. The result indicates that wPSO-BP has a better effect.
(b) A Logistic chaotic map is used for population initialization in beluga whale optimization (LBWO), and a multi-objective optimization algorithm is proposed based on NSGA-III and LBWO (NSGA-III-LBWO).
(c) Based on the wPSO-BP prediction model and NSGA-III-LBWO, the prototype fan is optimized, and the result shows that the aerodynamic and noise performance of the fan improved, which provides a certain reference value for the optimization of multi-blade centrifugal fans.

Author Contributions: Conceptualization, W.J. and J.L.; methodology, W.J. and J.W.; software, W.J. and R.X.; validation, J.L., M.Z. and Q.H.; formal analysis, W.J. and J.W.; investigation, R.X. and M.Z.; resources, Q.H. and M.Z.; data curation, W.J. and J.W.; writing—original draft preparation, W.J. and J.W.; writing—review and editing, J.L. and Q.H.; visualization, W.J.; supervision, J.L. and Q.H.; project administration, J.L.; funding acquisition, Q.H. All authors have read and agreed to the published version of the manuscript.

Funding: This research was funded by the Guangxi Innovation Driven Development Special Fund Project, grant number AA22068060-6, and the Guangxi Science and Technology Major Special Project, grant number AA23062073-3.

Institutional Review Board Statement: Not applicable.

Informed Consent Statement: Not applicable.

Data Availability Statement: The original contributions presented in this study are included in the article. Further inquiries can be directed to the corresponding author.

Acknowledgments: The computation was completed on the HPC Platform of Huazhong University of Science and Technology.

Conflicts of Interest: Author Jiaxuan Wang was employed by Wuhan Second Ship Design and Research Institute. Author Ming Zhou was employed by Valeo Automotive Air Conditioning Hubei Co., Ltd. The remaining authors declare that the research was conducted in the absence of any commercial or financial relationships that could be construed as a potential conflict of interest.

References

Kamada, M.; Shimoyama, K.; Sato, F.; Washiashi, J.; Konishi, Y. Multi-objective design optimization of a high efficiency and low noise blower unit of a car air-conditioner. *Proc. Inst. Mech. Eng. Part D J. Automob. Eng.* **2019**, *233*, 3493–3503. [CrossRef]

Wei, Y.; Li, L.; Lun, Y.; Wang, Z.; Yang, H.; Zhang, W. Effect of Volute-Tongue Clearance on the Aerodynamic Performance and Noise of Multi-Wing Centrifugal Fan for Air Conditioning. *J. Appl. Fluid Mech.* **2023**, *16*, 1483–1498.

Hao, W.; Wang, J.; He, X.; Zhu, Z.; Wang, Z.; Yang, H.; Zhang, W.; Wei, Y. Reduction of aerodynamic noise of single-inlet centrifugal fan with inclined volute tongue. *Meas. Control* **2020**, *53*, 1376–1387. [CrossRef]

Yuan, Y.; Xiao, Y.; Ming, P.; Lu, H. The aerodynamic and noise characteristics of centrifugal fan with partially tilted tongue. *Phys. Fluids* **2023**, *35*, 127113. [CrossRef]

Lun, Y.; Lin, L.; He, H.; Ye, X.; Zhu, Z.; Wei, Y. Effects of vortex structure on performance characteristics of a multiblade fan with inclined tongue. *Proc. Inst. Mech. Eng. Part A J. Power Energy* **2019**, *233*, 1007–1021. [CrossRef]

Wu, L.; Liu, X.; Wang, M. Effects of bionic volute tongue on aerodynamic performance and noise characteristics of centrifugal fan used in the air-conditioner. *J. Bionic Eng.* **2020**, *17*, 780–792. [CrossRef]

Wang, K.; Ju, Y.; Zhang, C. A quantitative evaluation method for impeller-volute tongue interaction and application to squirrel cage fan with bionic volute tongue. *J. Fluids Eng.* **2019**, *141*, 081104. [CrossRef]

Wu, Y.; Dou, H.S.; Wei, Y.K.; Chen, X.P.; Chen, Y.N.; Cao, W.B. Effect of attack angle on flow characteristic of centrifugal fan. *IOP Conf. Ser. Mater. Sci. Eng.* **2016**, *129*, 012059. [CrossRef]

Ding, H.; Chang, T.; Lin, F. The influence of the blade outlet angle on the flow field and pressure pulsation in a centrifugal fan. *Process* **2020**, *8*, 1422. [CrossRef]

10. Choi, J.; Ryu, S.Y.; Cheong, C.; Kim, M.K.; Lee, K. Blade shape optimization of centrifugal fan for improving performance a reducing aerodynamic noise of clothes dryer. *J. Acoust. Soc. Korea* **2019**, *38*, 321–327.
11. Zhang, H.; Dong, F.; Zhang, X.; Chu, W. Numerical Investigation of Effect of Blade Surface Slot on the Performance and Fl Field of a Low Speed Centrifugal Fan. In Proceedings of the Turbo Expo: Power for Land, Sea, and Air. American Society Mechanical Engineers, London, UK, 22–26 June 2020; Volume 84102, p. V02ET39A011.
12. Ch, S.V.; Anantharaman, K.; Rajasekaran, G. Effect of blade number on the performance of centrifugal fan. *Mater. Today P* **2023**, *72*, 1143–1152.
13. Prezelj, J.; Novaković, T. Centrifugal fan with inclined blades for vacuum cleaner motor. *Appl. Acoust.* **2018**, *140*, 13–23. [CrossR
14. Shin, D.; Heo, S.; Cheong, C.; Kim, T.H.; Jung, J. Performance/noise optimization of centrifugal fan using response surf method. *Trans. Korean Soc. Mech. Eng. A* **2017**, *41*, 165–172.
15. Zhang, J.; Chu, W.; Zhang, J.; Lv, Y. Vibroacoustic optimization study for the volute casing of a centrifugal fan. *Appl. Sci.* **20** *9*, 859. [CrossRef]
16. Bamberger, K.; Carolus, T.; Belz, J.; Nelles, O. Development, validation, and application of an optimization scheme for impell of centrifugal fans using computational fluid dynamics-trained metamodels. *J. Turbomach.* **2020**, *142*, 111005. [CrossRef]
17. Liu, T.; Zhang, Y.; Li, K.; Wang, Y.; Li, J. Aerodynamic Optimization of a Centrifugal Fan Using Response Surface Methodol *Open J. Fluid Dyn.* **2019**, *9*, 92. [CrossRef]
18. Meng, F.; Wang, L.; Ming, W.; Zhang, H. Aerodynamics optimization of multi-blade centrifugal fan based on extreme learn machine surrogate model and particle swarm optimization algorithm. *Metals* **2023**, *13*, 1222. [CrossRef]
19. Avşar, G.; Ezertaş, A.A.; Başkan Perçin, Ö. Aerodynamic Design and Performance Optimization of a Centrifugal Fan Impel In *Turbo Expo: Power for Land, Sea, and Air*; American Society of Mechanical Engineers: Boston, MA, USA, 2023; Volume 871 p. V13DT34A008.
20. Salaria, U.A.; Menhas, M.I.; Manzoor, S. Quasi Oppositional Population Based Global Particle Swarm Optimizer With Iner Weights (QPGPSO-W) for Solving Economic Load Dispatch Problem. *IEEE Access* **2021**, *9*, 134081–134095. [CrossRef]
21. Zhong, C.; Li, G.; Meng, Z. Beluga whale optimization: A novel nature-inspired metaheuristic algorithm. *Knowl.-Based Syst.* **20** *251*, 109215. [CrossRef]
22. Chawla, M.; Duhan, M. Levy flights in metaheuristics optimization algorithms–a review. *Appl. Artif. Intell.* **2018**, *32*, 802–8 [CrossRef]
23. Yu, H.; Zhao, N.; Wang, P.; Chen, H.; Li, C. Chaos-enhanced synchronized bat optimizer. *Appl. Math. Model.* **2019**, *77*, 1201–12 [CrossRef]
24. Zhu, H.; Zhao, Y.; Song, Y. 2D logistic-modulated-sine-coupling-logistic chaotic map for image encryption. *IEEE Access* **2019** 14081–14098. [CrossRef]
25. Miettinen, K. *Nonlinear Multiobjective Optimization*; Springer: New York, NY, USA, 1998. [CrossRef]
26. Deb, K.; Jain, H. An Evolutionary Many-Objective Optimization Algorithm Using Reference-Point-Based Nondominated Sorti Approach, Part I: Solving Problems With Box Constraints. *IEEE Trans. Evol. Comput.* **2014**, *18*, 577–601. [CrossRef]
27. Hou, Y.; Liao, X.; Chen, G.; Chen, Y. Co-Evolutionary NSGA-III with deep reinforcement learning for multi-objective distribu flexible job shop scheduling. *Comput. Ind. Eng.* **2025**, *203*, 110990. [CrossRef]
28. Palakonda, V.; Mallipeddi, R. Pareto dominance-based algorithms with ranking methods for many-objective optimization. *IE Access* **2017**, *5*, 11043–11053. [CrossRef]
29. Dong, H.; Nakayama, M.K. Quantile estimation with Latin hypercube sampling. *Oper. Res.* **2017**, *65*, 1678–1695. [CrossRef]
30. Iordanis, I.; Koukouvinos, C.; Silou, I. On the efficacy of conditioned and progressive Latin hypercube sampling in supervis machine learning. *Appl. Numer. Math.* **2025**, *208*, 256–270. [CrossRef]

applied sciences

MDPI

rticle

Reducing Railway Track Vibrations by Applying Particle-Damping Systems

elipe Klein Fiorentin [1,*], Cristian Piehowiak [1], Anelize Zomkowski Salvi [1], Yesid Ernesto Asaff [1], ndrea Piga Carboni [1], Abílio Manuel Pinho de Jesus [2,3] and Thiago Antonio Fiorentin [1]

1 Department of Mobility Engineering, UFSC (Federal University of Santa Catarina), Joinville 89219-600, Brazil; cristian.piehowiak@grad.ufsc.br (C.P.); anelize.salvi@ufsc.br (A.Z.S.); yesid.a@ufsc.br (Y.E.A.); andrea.piga@ufsc.br (A.P.C.); thiago.antonio@ufsc.br (T.A.F.)
2 Institute of Science and Innovation in Mechanical and Industrial Engineering—INEGI, 4200-465 Porto, Portugal; ajesus@fe.up.pt
3 Faculty of Engineering, University of Porto, 4200-465 Porto, Portugal
* Correspondence: felipe.fiorentin@grad.ufsc.br

Featured Application: The present work focuses on the mechanical characterization of particle damper systems designed to reduce railway vibrations, reducing the negative impact of rail transit due to noise and vibrations.

Abstract: The wheel–rail contact is an intrinsic characteristic of rail transport. This contact is one of the main reasons why rails are so efficient for transportation, mainly due to the very low friction coefficient between them and the wheels. However, this strong argument also leads to a disadvantage: the wheel contact is also associated with excessive vibration and noise, which have a strong impact on the passengers' comfort and especially the surrounding community. These noises and vibrations impact the public in several ways, like disturbing sleep, increasing stress and heart-associated diseases. The main objective of the present work is to investigate the rail vibration attenuation by applying particle dampers. Four different particles will be studied, and their effectiveness in reducing the rail vibrations will be analysed. Promising results were found, where under certain conditions, the particle dampers, such as lead and magnetite particles, were able to reduce peak vibration levels by more than an order of magnitude. The application of this system may have a strong impact on the communities using and in the vicinity of rail systems by reducing the noise and vibration, consequently improving people's health and well-being.

Keywords: railroad; railway track; vibration; absorber; particle damping

1. Introduction

Noise and vibration have a severe impact on people's health and well-being, and this influence has greatly increased in recent years, mainly due to the significant increase in traffic over the years from several different modal transportation systems, like trains, cars, and planes. Wrótny et al. [1] performed extensive research regarding the impact of road and rail noise on people's lives and found that traffic has amplified severe health issues, like sleep disturbances and noise annoyance.

Although trains are well known for being very efficient and eco-friendly (when compared to other modal transportation systems), they also have a negative impact on people's health, mainly due to excessive noise and vibration levels. Regarding this topic, several interviews were conducted by Maclachlan et al. [2] about the perception of vibrations generated by rails in nearby communities. They have observed that there is a general feeling about the increase in traffic, speed, and noise. Moreover, several individuals have reported great concern regarding vibrations, with some experiencing glasses shaking in display cabinets, wall pictures moving out of place, and cracks appearing and growing in the walls. Regarding symptoms, people reported increases in stress levels, irritation, tiredness in the morning and difficulty sleeping.

Smith et al. [3] developed an interesting work investigating the effect of freight train traffic on people's health, especially regarding sleep. They have found that vibration levels have several different impacts, such as poor sleep, awakenings overnight, difficulty falling asleep, and tiredness. Another work focusing on train impacts on people's quality of sleep was developed by Croy et al. [4]. They have monitored the heart rates of individuals during sleep and have found that the vibration generated by the train had a significant impact on increasing heart rates. Moreover, they have observed that these variations remained even after dozens of seconds. Such variations reduce the rest effectiveness during sleep, increasing stress levels and other negative impacts on human health.

Some authors found strong relations between a lack of proper maintenance and the noise emitted by the trains [5]. They have measured the roughness for several train lines and found that several of them were outside the standard limits. Another work concerning wear and its impact on the noise was conducted by Höjer et al. [6]. They have developed a real-time monitoring system for rail conditions. Once more, a stronger correlation between noise levels and track wear was observed, where very high noise levels were measured in severely worn track sections. Within the noise generated by train topics, Zhang et al. [7] quantified the contribution of each train part to the total noise generated by a train. They have found that the bogie and other lower-region parts were one of the main contributors.

Regarding vibrations generated by train and their impact, a wide-ranging review study was conducted by Connolly et al. [8]. Some authors were able to successfully correlate vibration amplitude with annoyance levels in people in the vicinity of railroads [9].

They have observed that complaining reports regarding noise and vibration in areas close to railroads increased drastically over the last years. Moreover, it was found that when vibrations were measured, in more than 40% of the cases, vibration levels exceeded the national or international allowable limits. They have observed that in approximately 1/3 of the studied cases, the threshold for ground-borne noise from freight trains was exceeded, although more data are required to draw more conclusive statements. Another work focusing on the impacts of vibration generated by trains was developed by Sanayei et al. [10]. Since isolating structures that are already built from these vibrations is often too expensive, understanding and controlling these vibration levels is essential. They have measured vibrations in buildings located near surface trains and subways and found that the trains excited the surrounding buildings at certain frequencies; human comfort is strongly compromised, and this issue could be addressed in the project of new buildings. Regarding the same topic, Zou et al. [11] have studied the effect of these vibrations in tall buildings, and have observed that vibrations were amplified in certain cases, depending on which floor the measurements were performed, and could surpass the comfort levels determined by some standards and associations, like the FTA (Federal Transit Administration, Washington, DC, USA) [12].

For freight trains, when considering fuel efficiency, typical optimal speeds are around 50 km/h [13]; however, optimal values may vary according to the engine type, load, terrain, railway type, and other factors. In this speed range, the noise (and vibration levels) is dominated by the rolling phenomenon (wheel–steel rail system) [14]. While for lower speeds, the total noise's main component is associated with the traction noises [15], the train's aerodynamics dominates the noise generation at high speeds [16] (above approximately

250 km/h). Consequently, if the main objective is to reduce noise and vibration for freight trains (or other types of trains with similar average speeds), focusing on the wheel and the train track is essential. For the present work, the attenuation of the steel rail vibrations will be the main target. The vibration generated by freight trains is linked with several health conditions associated with sleep disturbance [17].

Part of the traditional railroad building components, like wooden sleepers and ballast, helps with vibration attenuation; however, they are often not enough. Passive dampers are solutions used to reduce the vibration levels. They are known to be simple and robust [18]. They are constructed using mechanical devices, and they are designed to dissipate a fraction of the system's kinetic energy [19]. Typical passive dampers are built using viscoelastic materials, tuned mass dampers (TMD), and moving particles (particle dampers) [20].

Tuned dampers were studied for applications in steel rails, like in the work proposed by Jin et al. [21], where by using a tuned mass inside a viscoelastic material, they observed increases in damping performance of up to five times (when measuring the damping coefficient). Another application for TMD, focusing on high-speed railway bridges, was developed by Lin et al. [22]. By designing and applying a group of tuned mass dampers, the authors were able to reduce the maximum acceleration of the bridge structure by as much as 50%. The authors have observed that better performance was achieved when the vibration was dominated by the structure's natural frequencies (resonance) and the train excited those frequencies (for example, by running at specific speeds that led to these excitation frequencies).

Concerning particle dampers, the working principle can be summarised as transferring kinetic energy from the structure to the particles; afterwards, part of this energy is dissipated due to collisions and friction within the particles and between the particles and the structure (or the recipient wall) [23]. Some key parameters strongly affect the efficiency of particle dampers, namely: particle size, packing ratio, position, particle overlap and excitation frequency, amplitude and orientation, for example [24]. Depending on these characteristics, the particle motion can be characterised as follows: fluid-like movement, where particles act like a liquid; collect-and-collide, where particles move similarly to a single block, colliding with the reservoir walls; and decoupled, where particles' movement displays a high level of independence from one another [25].

A very comprehensive study was performed by Xu et al. [26] regarding particle size and their damping efficiency. They have found a relation between the diameter of a specific particle material and its efficiency for a certain frequency, where larger (or heavier) particles tend to be more efficient for higher frequencies. This observation is very important in terms of designing a damper, as it can act as an initial guide for choosing the most suitable particles for reducing vibrations under certain loading conditions.

Some works studied the efficiency of particle dampers in reducing vibration for several different applications, like a wind turbine stator [27], circuit boards [28], cutting tools [29], turbines [30], and engines [31], yielding promising results. One more interesting application of particle dampers was developed by Xin [32]. In this work, deep learning methodology was applied to particle dampers for noise and vibration control of steel rails. Several materials and particle sizes were studied, and their damping efficiency was analysed. They were able to significantly reduce track vibrations in most test conditions, except for impact vibrations caused by the passing wheels.

Regarding the railway, different vibration control analyses can be applied, focusing on the control of the vehicles themselves [33] or the infrastructure [34]. An interesting study was developed by Jin et al. [35], in which a tuned particle impact (single particle confined in a reservoir) was used to minimise vibration and noise at a rail track; the vibration amplitudes and sound pressure levels were reduced by approximately half. Regarding the applications of particle dampers in rails, a comprehensive study was conducted by Lu et al. [36], where several excitation frequencies and amplitudes were studied for a certain reservoir and particles (these parameters were not changed). Solutions regarding particle dampers focusing on improving the passengers' comfort were also analysed [37], where the authors used experimental tests and the discrete element method to simulate the damping performance of the particle system. They have achieved sound level reductions by a factor of more than 2. Although scarce data can be found for railroads regarding the effect of different materials and their vibration-damping efficiency, the present research aims to address this issue.

The main goal of the present work is to explore a known damping technology, particle damping, to reduce vibration levels on a steel rail. By attenuating the vibration levels, several positive outcomes may be obtained based on the present research, like reducing track and wheel wear, enhancing passenger comfort, and reducing the railway's impact on nearby buildings and community well-being. This last topic is especially important, as noise and vibration lead to several health problems (previously discussed), and mitigating them would improve essential aspects of people's lives, like sleep quality and reducing stress levels. Moreover, attenuation in vibration amplitudes is also directly related to decreases in noise levels, but this impact will not be the subject of the present work.

An experimental development regarding different particle materials will be conducted. The following sections of the work will be divided into three main parts: Materials and Methods, where the detailed experimental procedure, equipment, and methodology used for the analyses will be detailed; Results, where the measured and processed data will be presented and discussed; Conclusion, where an analysis of the applied methodology and significance of the analysed data will be presented.

The literature review regarding particle dampers, their origins, and the impacts of railroads presented in this section will be used as a baseline for designing an experimental procedure for this type of damper, which will be detailed in the following section.

2. Materials and Methods

The present section will provide details regarding experimental analysis. Next, the details concerning data processing will be presented. The experimental procedure consists of a rail, which will be loaded by an excitation system (for the present case, a speaker, amplifier, and signal generator). Additionally, particles from several materials will be confined in a reservoir, whose main function is to act as particle dampers. Known excitation amplitudes and forces will be applied, and the system response will be measured. As previously discussed, the main goal of an efficient particle damper system is to attenuate the vibrations at the train rail, and the system's behaviour will be analysed for several different configurations of particle dampers regarding materials, mass, and filling ratio.

The testing setup is presented in Figure 1, where Figure 1a,b present an overview of the testing rig, and Figure 1c shows a schematic view of the experimental apparatus. The testing setup can be summarised by:

- Steel rail: It is the principal component of the testing apparatus to which almost all other devices are connected. The steel rail is two metres long, being a profile of an ASCE (American Society of Civil Engineers) 60 light rail, with a total mass of 60 kg. The rail was positioned sideways, and excited vertically (the original direction concerning lateral vibrations of the mounted rail). The rail is suspended by supports in two locations (discussed in the following topic) and excited at the central portion of its length. The steel rail was tested sideways (when compared to its position during use).
- Supports and ropes: In order to minimise the impact of the fixturing system on the dynamic behaviour of the system, the steel rail was suspended by a pair of racks

and ropes. The suspension region was located at the two vibration nodes of the 1st bending mode (slender beam), corresponding to a distance of 22.4% of the total length of the rail, measuring from the closest free edge.

- Speaker: This component was used to provide external excitation to the steel rail. A 6-inch speaker was used, with a power of 90 W RMS (Root Mean Square). The working range of the presented speaker extends from 50 Hz to 5 kHz. The speaker was driven by a signal generator and a 100 W amplifier. The speaker was attached to an inertia block. The entire weight of the rail is maintained by supports, and the rail is positioned to just stay over the speakers (with no force when at rest). The excitation force orientation is parallel to the gravity
- Force transducer and central accelerometer: An impedance head was used to measure the excitation force and acceleration. This measurement device was located between the speaker and the web of the steel rail, placed in the mid-section of its length.
- Accelerometer (edge location): This sensor was used to measure the steel rail's response under different excitations and with different damping systems, and it was placed 30 mm away from one of the rail ends. More details regarding the measuring system (impedance head and accelerometer) will be provided below.
- Particle reservoir: It is presented in Figure 1d. It consists of a steel box with an adjustable cover, having external dimensions of 550 × 55 × 75 mm. Only one reservoir was used for the present study, located on the web. The reservoir was attached to the rail using a structural adhesive, epoxy. Additionally, its height (75 mm) can be adjusted by two pairs of nuts. This is important since the filling ratio of the particle reservoir can be changed independently of the particle's total mass. An internal volume of approximately 2 litres is obtained when the cover is positioned at the utmost configuration. The reservoir is attached to the middle section (half length).

Regarding the measuring system, Table 1 presents more details about both the impedance head (force and acceleration sensors) and the accelerometer (located near the rail edge). The impedance head's main function is to measure the input signals (force and acceleration) at the central portion of the rail. On the other hand, the edge accelerometer is responsible for measuring the output signal. The main objective of the damping system is to minimise the excitation response of the rail. Therefore, the most efficient system will be considered the one capable of better reducing the vibration (output signal) over a wide range of frequencies and amplitudes.

Table 1. Measuring system information.

Sensor		Sensitivity	Measuring Range
Dytran 5860B—impedance head, Chatsworth, CA, USA	accelerometer	10.43 mV/(m/s^2)	1.0 to 8000 Hz
	force transducer	23.18 mV/N	1.0 to 8000 Hz
Bruel and Kjaer 4508 b, Nærum, Denmark	accelerometer	9.73 mV/(m/s^2)	0.3 to 8000 Hz

The experimental procedure consists of exciting the central section of the steel rail web with a known frequency and amplitude. For the present analysis, a sinusoidal wave sweep was used, where the frequency was modulated. Three frequency ranges and three excitation amplitudes were used, and they are presented in Table 2, resulting in a total of nine tests per condition. For simplicity, the amplitudes were often referred to as Amp1, Amp2, and Amp3, being the 1st on the smallest amplitude (4 m/s^2), while the last corresponds to the highest excitation amplitude (12 m/s^2). Each sweep test was 20 s long, starting at the lower frequency up to the higher one.

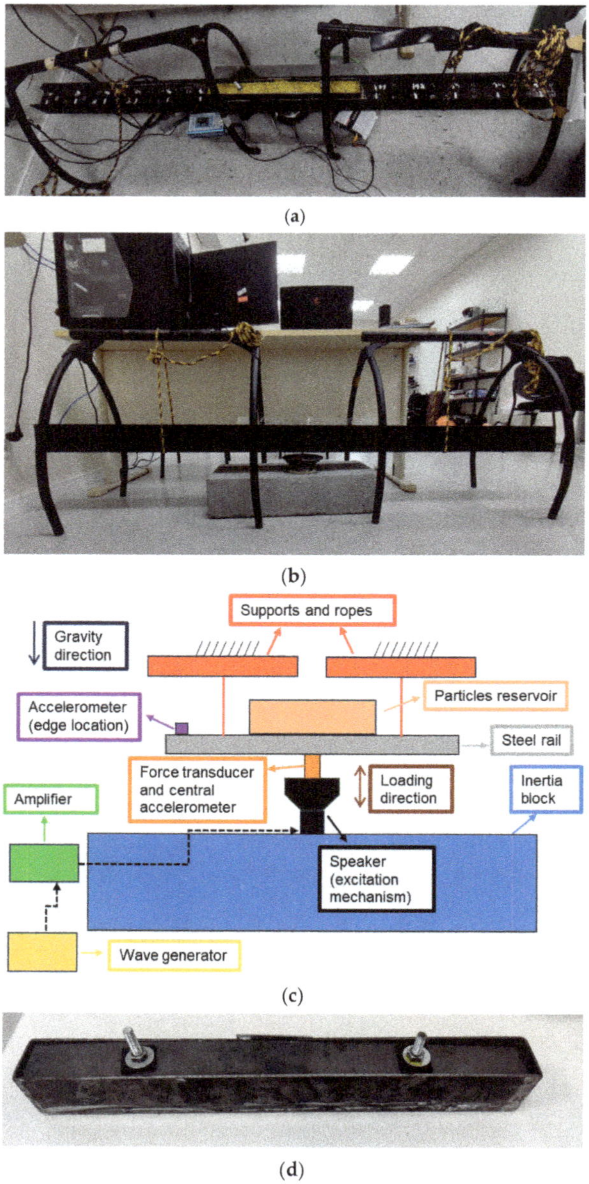

Figure 1. Steel rail and particle reservoir testing setup: (**a**) Testing setup overview, top view; (**b**) Testing setup overview, front view; (**c**) Schematic view, front view; (**d**) Reservoir.

Table 2. Loading amplitudes and excitation frequencies.

Start Excitation Frequency (Hz)	End Excitation Frequency (Hz)	Excitation Acceleration Amplitude (m/s^2)
50	800	4, 8 and 12
800	2000	4, 8 and 12
2000	4000	4, 8 and 12

Regarding the damping systems, four different damping particles were used, namely: polymer clay (FIMO®), lead spheres, magnetite powder, and natural rubber (segments of rubber bands). An overview of the particles can be seen in Figure 2. These materials were chosen in order to encompass a wide range of elasticity modulus ("hard" or "soft" materials) and bulk densities as well, which will be discussed next.

Figure 2. Types of particles used for the damping systems.

Table 3 presents the average particle dimensions and bulk densities. Materials were tested in their "as supplied" shapes and sizes, like powder for magnetite and spheres for lead. Moreover, in order to compare the efficiency of each particle type with the same total mass, natural rubber was used as the reference mass, as it was the material with the lowest bulk density. Therefore, the reference mass for comparison was considered to be the maximum natural rubber mass (entire reservoir filled with these particles), resulting in a total particle mass of 1.1 kg.

Table 3. Particle materials, size, and density.

Materials	Average Particle Size (mm)	Bulk Density (kg/m^3)	Elasticity Modulus (GPa)
Lead spheres	2.3	6500	16 [38]
Magnetite powder	0.3	2400	200 [39]
Polymer clay (FIMO)	3.0	700	4 [40]
Natural rubber	5.0	600	3 [41]

As stated earlier, all particle materials were tested under several different conditions, one of which was the same total mass (1.1 kg). All materials were tested with the maximum possible mass (entire reservoir, filled to 100%), except for the lead. Due to its high density, it was not possible to test the lead in that condition, as it would require more than 12 kg of lead spheres. Consequently, a total mass of 7 kg was used for lead. Moreover, tests were conducted for two different filling ratios, 100% and 80%. This was performed in order to analyse the effect of the free space on the particle dampers' efficiency. Additionally, a test with an empty reservoir was also performed and used as the reference (no particle damping). The combinations for testing conditions are summarised in Table 4 for all materials.

Table 4. Testing conditions, materials, total particle mass, and filling ratios.

Materials	Particles Mass (kg)	Filling Ratio (%)
Lead spheres	7.9 and 1.1	100
	7.9, 5.7 and 1.1	80
Magnetite powder	4.5 * and 1.1	100
	3.5 and 1.1	80
Polymer clay (FIMO)	1.3 * and 1.1	100
	1.1	80
Natural rubber	1.1 *	100
	0.9	80

Note: Conditions marked with an asterisk, *, represent the reservoir completely filled, with the cover at the utmost position (maximum volume).

Each test (specific material, mass, filling ratio, excitation amplitude, and start and ending frequency) was divided into 40 smaller divisions. For each of these divisions, both a time and a frequency domain were developed. Regarding the time domain, the peak excitation response (output, edge location) of each division was identified and registered. Figure 3a presents an example of the measured time-domain signal (with time as the uppermost x-axis) for the output accelerometer (response), while Figure 3b displays the respective frequency-domain data. Moreover, the excitation frequency for that time during the sine frequency sweep is also presented. For this example, all three frequency ranges were grouped for didactic purposes. Even though the signal is presented in the signal domain, the excitation frequency is known due to the sine sweep and is also presented in the chart (lower x-axis).

For the frequency domain, an analogous approach was performed, where an FFT (Fast Fourier Transformation) was performed for the input signals (force and acceleration at the central location) and output signal, and an FRF (frequency response function) was computed for each division. The FRF was obtained by simply dividing the output signal in the frequency domain by the input one (force or acceleration at the central section). In order to keep the present work succinct, only the time domain analysis will be discussed in most cases, and only the maximum excitation amplitudes will be analysed (except for the cases where the external amplitude is the focus of the analysis). The frequency-domain analysis will only be presented for the study regarding the effect of excitation amplitude, as it is the most suitable method since it normalises the input signals for different excitation amplitudes. For this analysis, the FRF using the central acceleration as an input reference will be examined.

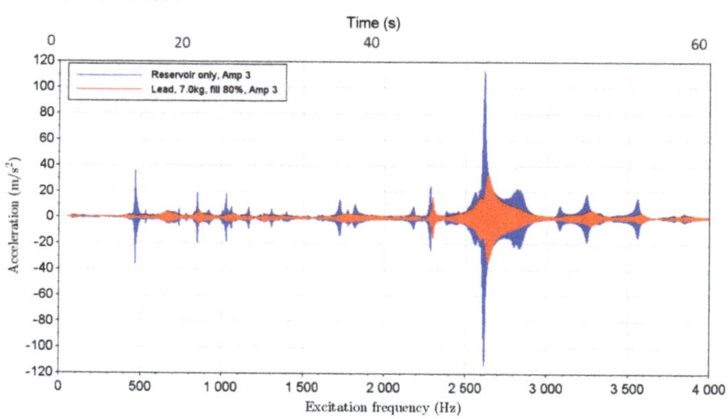

(a)

Figure 3. *Cont.*

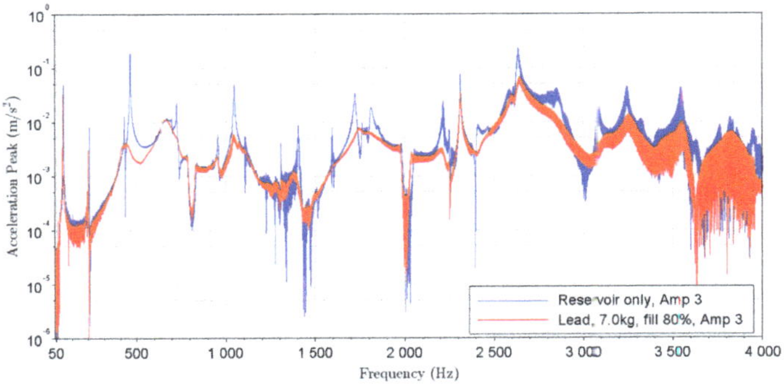

(b)

Figure 3. Example of time and frequency domain measurement, maximum excitation amplitude (12 m/s^2): (**a**) Time-domain signal; (**b**) Frequency-domain signal.

3. Results

The present section will provide the results obtained for the four tested particle materials, featuring different total masses and filling ratios. Moreover, two additional comparisons will be analysed: a comparison with all the particles of the same mass (1.1 kg) and an overview of the effect of excitation amplitude on the vibration response. As previously discussed, the case with the rail and an empty reservoir will be used as a reference in order to understand the particle dampers' performance.

3.1. Lead Particles

Lead spheres will be analysed as the first particle-damper materials. For the present analysis, five total masses and filling ratios will be combined, as presented in Table 4, namely: 7 kg, 100% filling; 7 kg, 80% filling; 5.7 kg, 80% filling; 1.1 kg (reference mass), 100% filling; and 1.1 kg, 80% filling. Once the reservoir was not completely filled with lead, it was possible to test one additional condition, the maximum mass, having an 80% filling.

Figure 4 presents the summarised results of the peak response in the time-domain analysis, with Figure 4a providing an overview of the entire frequency range. Figure 4b presents the results for the smaller excitation frequencies. It can be observed that the best results are obtained with a higher total particle mass. For example, at the highest peak for low frequencies (near 450 Hz), the three cases with more mass present (7.0 and 5.7 kg setups) showed significantly better vibration reductions than the ones with smaller masses (1.1 kg). The particle damper was able to reduce peak vibration amplitudes by 25 times (from 100 m/s^2 to 4 m/s^2, for the case of 7.0 kg and 80% filling ratio) at 470 Hz. A similar behaviour was found for peaks around 1000 and 1750 Hz.

Figure 4c presents the results obtained for the higher frequency band. For this higher frequency range, the results were different from those observed at lower frequencies. Although all damping systems were capable of significantly reducing the rail reservoir system vibration, results obtained from lower masses (both 1.1 kg systems with 100 and 80% filling ratios) presented superior vibration dampening in the higher frequency range. Considering the highest response peaks, the particles were able to reduce vibration levels by an order of magnitude.

Moreover, the effect of filling (for a fixed total mass, 7.0 kg) was presented in Figure 4d. A logarithm scale was used in this case for clarity purposes. It can be noticed that the case with free space (80% filling ratio) presents better vibration reduction for almost the entire frequency spectrum, with the difference being more noticeable at lower frequencies.

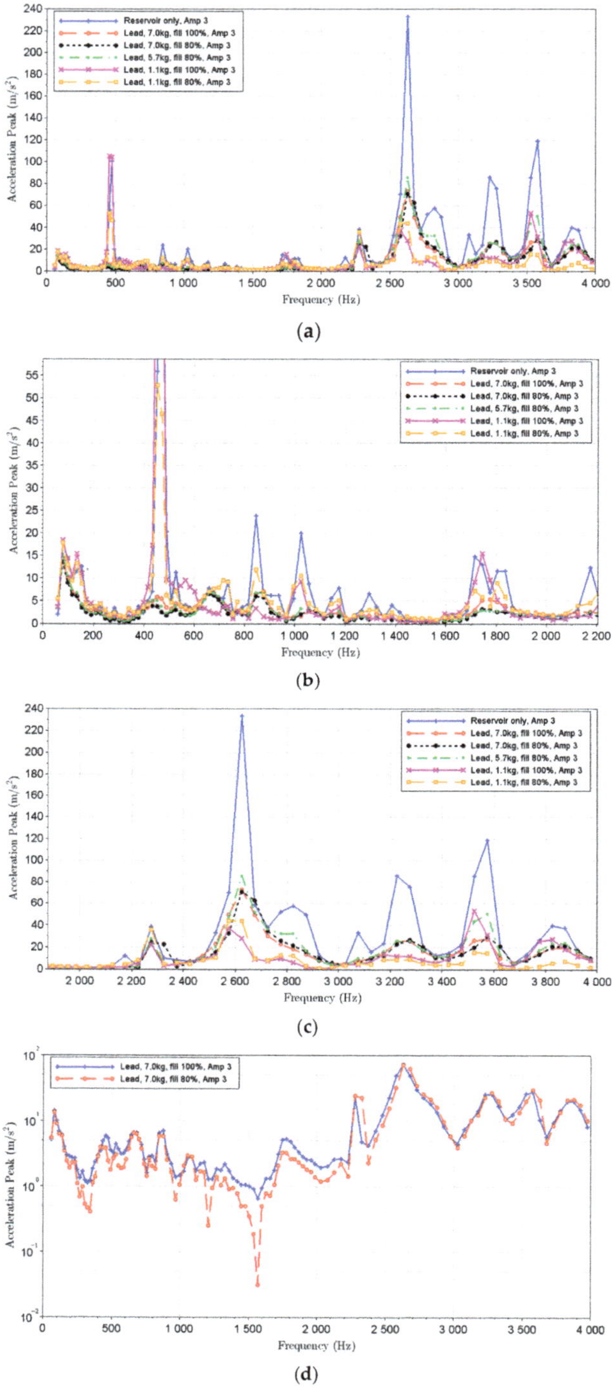

Figure 4. Lead particles, excitation amplitude of 12 m/s^2, time-domain analysis: (**a**) Overview; (**b**) Lower frequency band; (**c**) Higher frequency band; (**d**) Filling ratio comparison, equal mass.

3.2. Magnetite Particles

An analogous analysis was performed for another particle material, this time the magnetite powder. Figure 5a presents an overview of the four studied cases (Table 4), namely: 4.5 kg, fill 100% (the maximum volume of the reservoir, completely filled); 3.6 kg, fill 80%; 1.1 kg, fill 100% (reference mass); and 1.1 kg, fill 80%. The responses at lower frequencies are presented in Figure 5b. The case with the highest mass (4.5 kg) was very effective in this frequency range, except for the peak amplitude response at 450 Hz. For this case, the 3.6 kg (second highest mass) system was the one able to greatly attenuate the acceleration amplitude (from 100 m/s^2 to 7 m/s^2), although not as effectively as the best lead case.

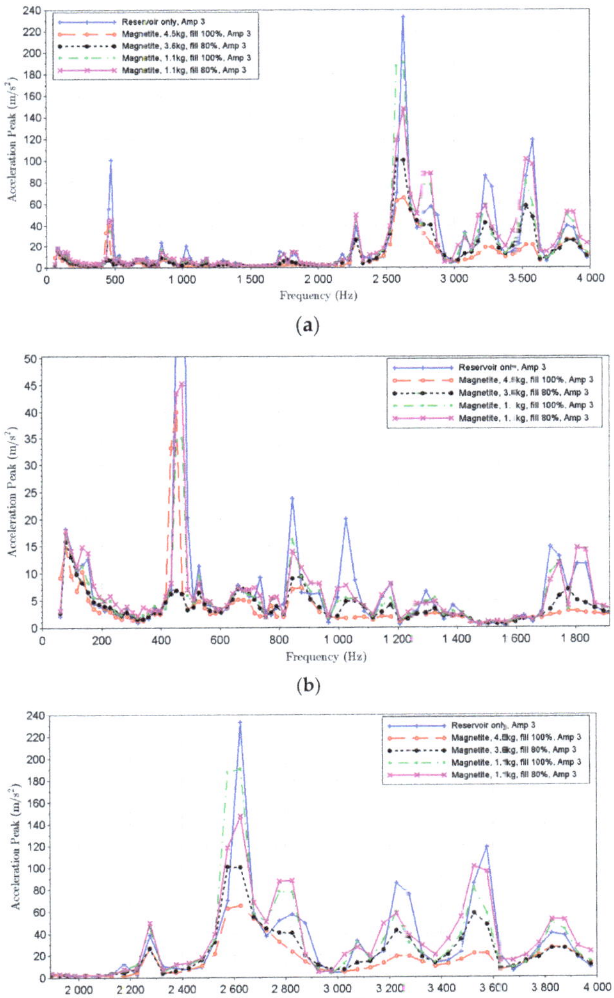

Figure 5. Magnetite particles, excitation amplitude of 12 m/s^2, time-domain analysis: (**a**) Overview; (**b**) Lower frequency band; (**c**) Higher frequency band.

Regarding the higher frequency response displayed in Figure 5c, the higher frequency systems were also the ones with better damping performances, with the heaviest case being the best-performing one for almost the entire frequency range.

3.3. FIMO and Natural Rubber Particles

Results regarding FIMO and natural rubber particles will be discussed in the present section. The summarised conditions regarding mass and filling ratio were presented in Table 4. Taking natural rubber as the reference case for mass (1.1 kg), it was only possible to test this material with the maximum mass (entire reservoir volume) of 1.1 kg and 100% filling and with a smaller filling ratio, 0.9 kg at an 80% filling ratio. For FIMO, three cases were studied: 1.3 kg, filling 100% (entire volume of the reservoir fulfilled); 1.1 kg, 100%; and 1.1 kg, 80% fill. Figure 6a presents the results for the entire frequency range. Figure 6b presents the results for the lower frequencies. It can be seen that FIMO (polymeric clay) presented better results than the rubber band (natural rubber) for almost the entire frequency range (except for very low frequencies, below 100 Hz). Peak vibrations (around 450 Hz) were attenuated by a factor of 3. It is important to emphasise that the particle's total mass is very small when compared with the total mass of the rail track, being only 1.3 kg (for FIMO, 100% filling ratio), while the rail mass is approximately 60 kg. In some cases, almost no vibration reductions were obtained from rubber band particles, and similar acceleration amplitudes were obtained when comparing the results with the empty reservoir.

Figure 6c presents the results for the higher frequency band. As it was observed in the lower frequency domain, the overall performance of FIMO was superior to that obtained from the rubber band. In this frequency range, the best case for vibration attenuation was a factor of two (for FIMO 1.3 kg, 100% fill, reducing peak vibration at around 3200 Hz from 85 m/s^2 to 40 m/s^2).

3.4. Equal Mass Comparison

This section will provide results and comparisons regarding all four particle materials, where the total particle mass (1.1 kg) was kept fixed for comparison purposes. A standard filling of 80% was used for the comparison, and it was used in all cases but one. Once the rubber band reservoir was completely filled (100%) for the reference mass, it was not possible to test this material in the partially filled condition. Figure 7a presents the results for the entire frequency range (from 50 Hz to 4000 Hz). The results containing lower frequencies are presented in Figure 7b. For this range, it can be seen that at very low frequencies, up to 250 Hz approximately, FIMO and rubber band systems yielded better results. This might be associated with the smaller individual particle mass of these cases, due to their low density, which some authors correlate with better damping at lower frequencies (and higher individual particle mass is also correlated with better efficiency at higher frequencies), as stated by Xu et al. [26]. After that range, natural rubber results are not very promising when compared with the other particles. Regarding the peak vibration for lower frequencies, around approximately 450 Hz, magnetite powder presented the greatest vibration reduction (from 100 m/s^2 to 45 m/s^2), closely followed by FIMO and lead particles. After approximately 1100 Hz, lead spheres presented the best vibration damping.

Regarding the opposite frequency spectrum, the higher ones, Figure 7c presents an overview of the behaviour of the four particle types analysed in this work. Once more, lead particles proved to be more efficient for the higher frequency spectrum, extending from 1100 Hz up to 4000 Hz (the maximum analysed frequency). After lead, FIMO particles were the ones that presented the best vibration damping (except for the peak amplitude at approximately 2600 Hz).

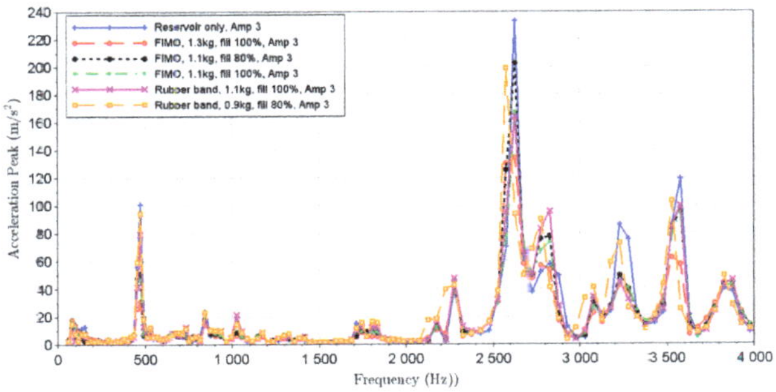

(a)

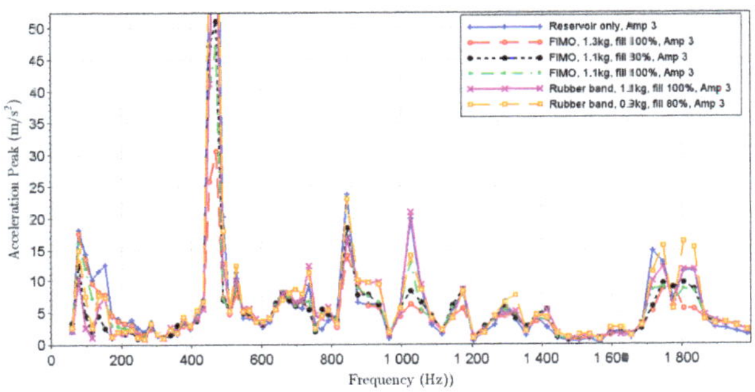

(b)

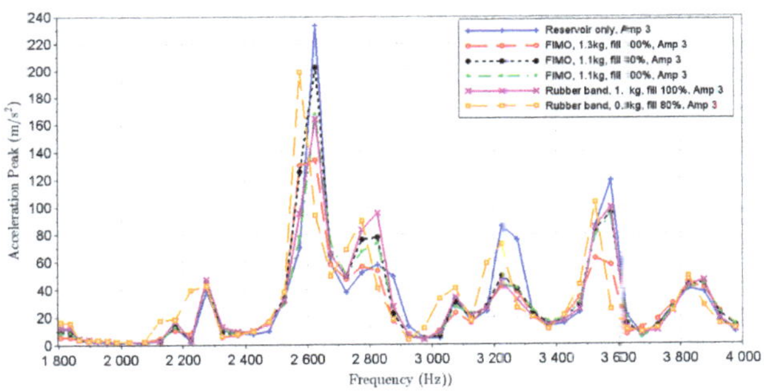

(c)

Figure 6. Polymeric clay (FIMO) and rubber band particles, excitation amplitude of 12 m/s^2, time-domain analysis: (**a**) Overview; (**b**) Lower frequency band; (**c**) Higher frequency band.

3.5. Effect of Excitation Amplitude

Additionally, besides the particle's total mass and material effect in the vibration damping of a given system, the effect of the excitation amplitude will also be analysed. It is important to emphasise that this analysis would not be required if a linear relationship between system input (excitation) and output (vibration response) were presented in the system. However, particle dampers do not present such kind of behaviour. Consequently, the presented FRF is only valid for the excitation amplitudes analysed and should not be extrapolated to other excitation magnitudes.

The amplitude effect was analysed for two materials: lead and FIMO. All three excitation amplitudes were used for comparison, and the analysis was carried out in the frequency domain. Figure 8a presents the results obtained for lead spheres. It can be observed that as the excitation amplitude increases (from Amp1, 4 m/s^2, up to Amp3,

12 m/s^2), the overall relationship between output and input (transfer function) decreases. It is important to note that, although the average amplitudes were reduced, new vibration peaks appeared for high amplitudes, like one around 1700 Hz for Amp2 and one located approximately at 2500 Hz for Amp3. In other words, for the analysed frequency and amplitude ranges, it was observed that the particle-damper efficiency increases with the increment of the excitation amplitude.

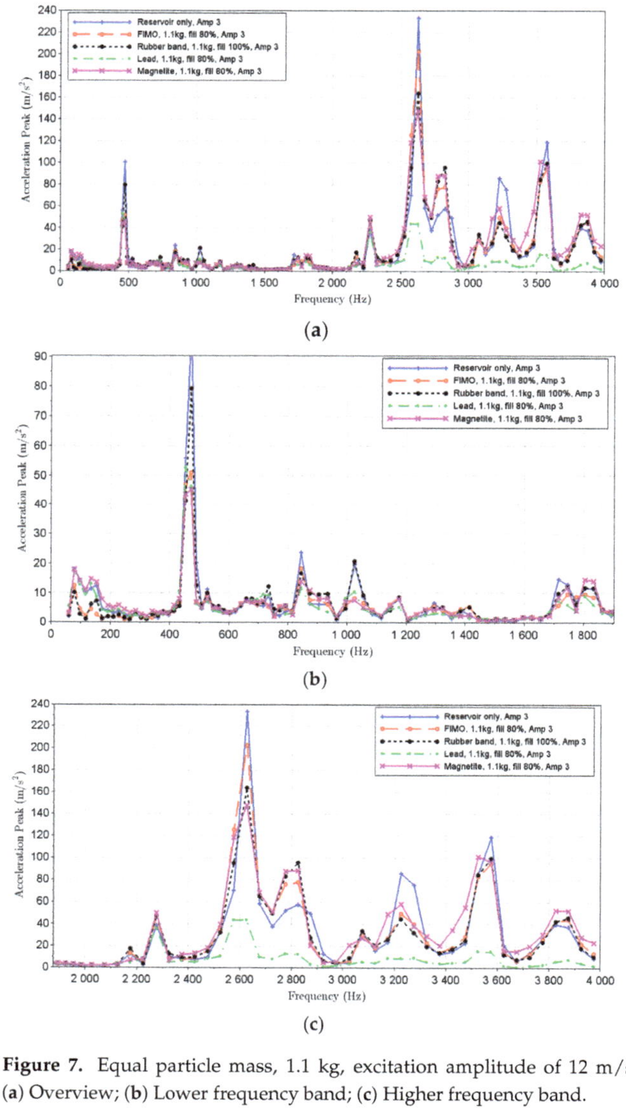

Figure 7. Equal particle mass, 1.1 kg, excitation amplitude of 12 m/s^2, time-domain analysis: (**a**) Overview; (**b**) Lower frequency band; (**c**) Higher frequency band.

A similar behaviour was observed for FIMO, presented in Figure 8b. Once more, when excited with the smallest amplitude, the system presented a higher proportional response when compared to higher external excitations (like the intermediate or highest amplitude).

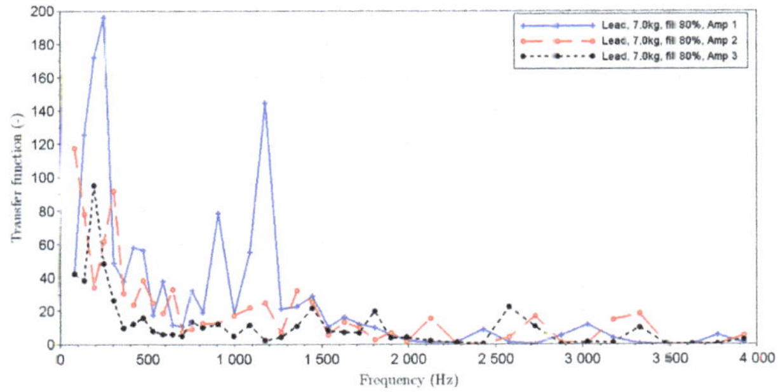

(**a**)

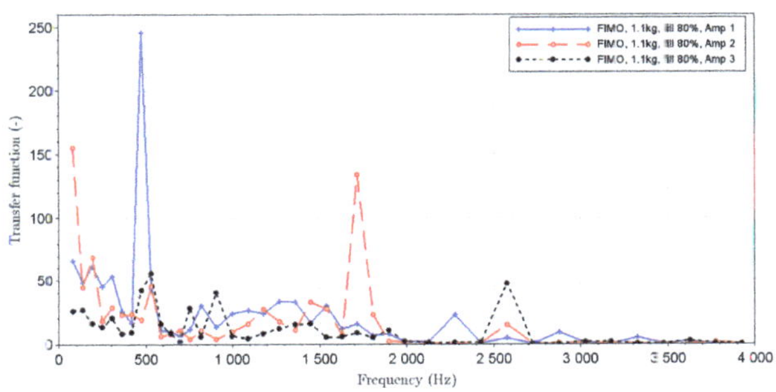

(**b**)

Figure 8. Effect of excitation amplitude on vibration response, comparison of the lowest and highest excitation amplitudes, frequency-domain analysis: (**a**) Lead particles; (**b**) FIMO particles.

3.6. Summary

The present section will provide a summary of the results. As discussed before, three frequency ranges were used. For each frequency range, average values regarding peak values will be presented for each material. Two comparisons will be performed, one presenting the same total particle mass for all four materials, while the remaining case will showcase the best configuration for each material. Although some mass configurations performed better than others in specific frequency ranges and amplitudes, the overall best will be used.

Figure 9 presents the summary results for the same total mass comparison, 1.1 kg, across the three frequency ranges and amplitudes. All cases were analysed with an 80% filling ratio, except for the rubber band, which was tested at 100% (once the reservoir was completely full). Figure 9a presents the results for the lowest excitation amplitude. Regarding the lowest frequency range, 50 to 800 Hz, the FIMO presents the highest attenuation, while lead shows the worst results. On the other hand, for intermediate and higher frequencies, lead presents the best behaviour, attenuating the vibrations' average amplitudes by approximately 6.0 and 2.5 times for the intermediate and highest frequencies, respectively.

Figure 9b,c presents the results for the intermediate and highest excitation amplitudes. It can be observed that the overall damping behaviour of lead particles has improved, even for the lowest frequency (where lead presented the worst results for the lowest excitation amplitude). One hypothesis is that, when the excitation amplitude is very small, not enough energy is provided to generate significant movement of the lead particles (which are the heaviest among the analysed ones). Moreover, regarding the lowest frequency range, FIMO presented the best behaviour for all three analysed excitation amplitudes. Additionally, rubber bands present good results for low excitation amplitudes and frequencies, probably associated with their low particle mass (which requires less energy to move and results in more frequent collisions with other particles).

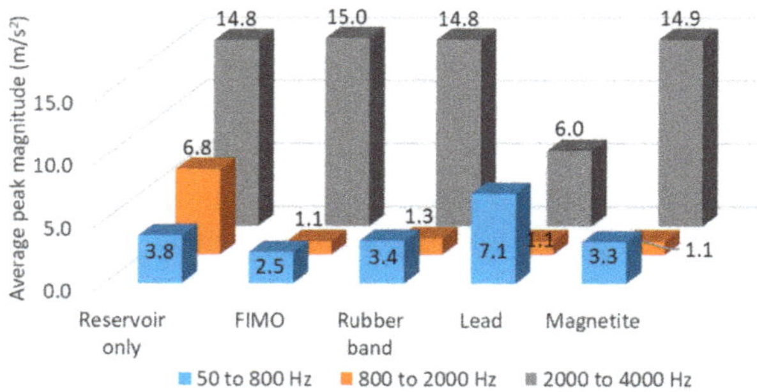

(a)

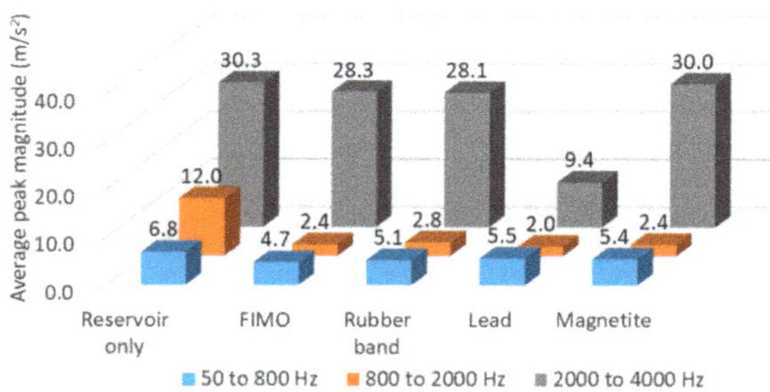

(b)

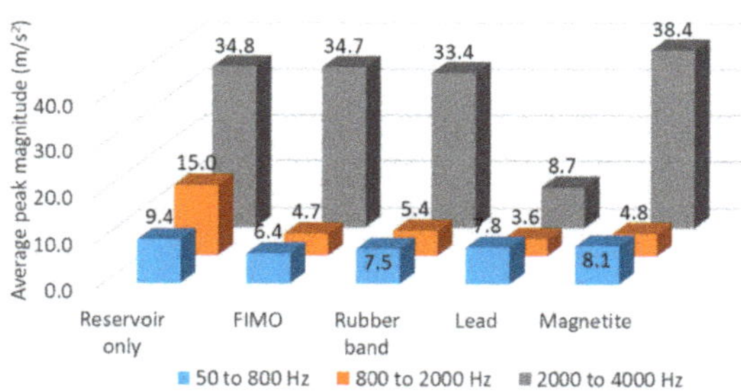

(c)

Figure 9. Equal mass comparison for all materials: (**a**) Lowest excitation amplitude; (**b**) Intermediate excitation amplitude; (**c**) Highest excitation amplitude.

Regarding the comparison presenting the best results for each configuration, Figure 10 shows a summary of these data. The lowest excitation amplitude is presented in Figure 10a. This time, lead presents the best results for all analysed frequencies. It is important to emphasise that this mass configuration of lead had 7.0 kg of particles, nearly six times more than FIMO and a rubber band. By using lead particles, attenuation factors of 3, 20 and 2.5 times were obtained for the lowest, intermediate, and highest frequencies, respectively. Magnetite also presented good results. Once again, magnetite was the second heaviest configuration, with a particle mass of 3.6 kg. Next, FIMO presented good attenuation factors, especially for the lowest and intermediate frequency ranges.

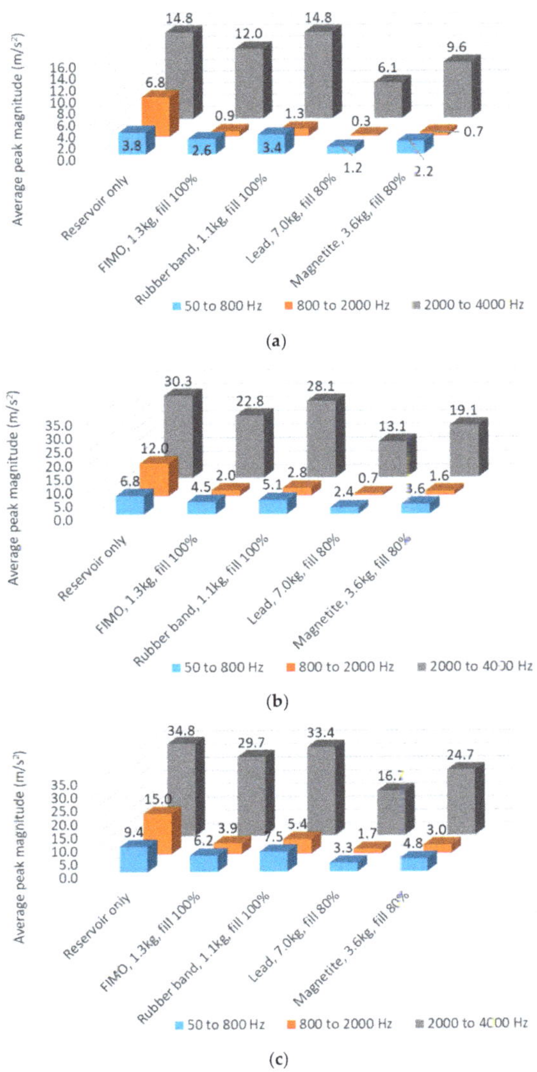

Figure 10. Best case comparison for all materials: (**a**) Lowest excitation amplitude; (**b**) Intermediate excitation amplitude; (**c**) Highest excitation amplitude.

Figure 10b,c presents the results regarding intermediate and highest excitation amplitudes. Once again, the best results were obtained using lead particles (heaviest particles and total particle mass), followed by magnetite configuration. In some cases, attenuation factors of approximately 10 were obtained, like in the case of intermediate frequencies and highest amplitudes. As was observed before, FIMO and rubber band particles presented low attenuation for the highest excitation frequencies.

Figure 11a–c displays the analysis regarding the impact of filling ratio. As discussed before, the same particle mass of 1.1 kg was used for all cases, and filling ratios of 100% and 80% were analysed. Once it was not possible to perform tests using natural rubber for 1 kg and an 80% filling ratio, this material was not used for the present comparison. It can be observed that for the lowest and highest frequency ranges analysed, a partial filling ratio (80%) presented an overall better damping performance than the counterpart (100% filling). This can be explained by the operating principle of the particle dampers, which relies on the movement and impact of the particles, being less prominent on a completely full reservoir. For the intermediate particle range (800 to 2000 Hz), no noticeable difference was found regarding different filling rates. It is important to emphasise that, for the present study, this frequency range also presented the lowest vibration amplitudes, which might not be sufficient to create significant particle motion, resulting in the particles behaving like a fixed mass (without relevant collisions between the particles and the reservoir).

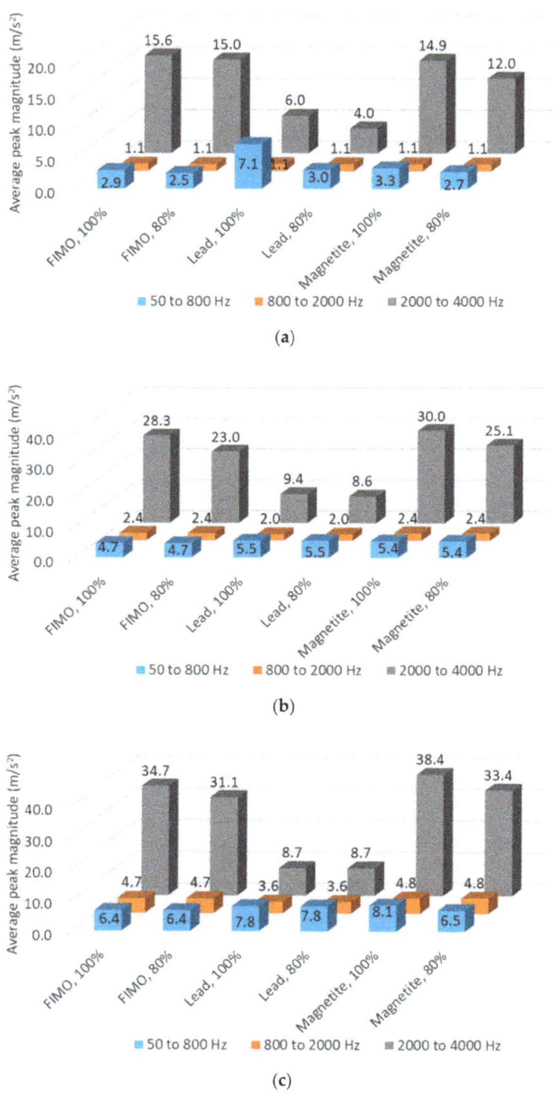

Figure 11. Impact of filling ratio on vibration: (**a**) Lowest excitation amplitude; (**b**) Intermediate excitation amplitude; (**c**) Highest excitation amplitude.

4. Conclusions and Future Work

It was observed that the particle damper systems were capable of efficiently reducing the vibration levels for the frequency ranges and excitation amplitudes studied in the present work. When comparing the performance of different particle materials, the lead spheres proved to be the most efficient solution for the conditions analysed. In some cases, the particle dampers were capable of reducing peak vibrations by more than 20 times.

Moreover, it was observed that the studied particle-damping systems were more efficient when larger levels of vibrations were present (for example, in the natural frequencies of the railway track), especially for denser particles like lead and magnetite. Additionally, it was detected that the total particle mass has a stronger impact on reducing vibration levels at lower frequencies. Finally, in cases where the reservoir was completely filled with particles (100% fill), it was noticed that the particle-damping efficiency was reduced when compared to partially filled reservoirs (for the present study, 80%). This observation was in good agreement with the literature. Once the reservoir is completely filled, the particles do not have enough space to move and collide with each other. Since the collisions and friction between particles are intrinsic characteristics, they affect the particle dampers' efficiency and are the main components for energy dissipation. This loss in efficiency can be easily explained.

As it was observed in the literature, each type of particle might be very effective at a specific frequency and amplitude range. In the present study, it was observed that FIMO and rubber bands (the lightest particles) presented good vibration attenuation for low excitation amplitudes and low frequencies. On the other hand, lead particles proved to be very effective in attenuating vibration levels at higher frequencies. Consequently, the best material must be chosen by taking into account the target frequency range, and even a combination of materials might be used to cover different frequency ranges. Analysing the average amplitude values for the entire set of frequency ranges and amplitudes, lead particles showed to result in the best damping behaviour.

Regarding future work, a wide range of different solutions could be addressed, like analysing the reservoir design and materials, which is an essential step for a better understanding of the particle-damping systems and enhancing their performance. Studying the effects of different reservoir materials, like building and testing an acrylic reservoir, would provide interesting information. Additionally, a combination of transparent reservoir materials and high-speed cameras would provide important insights into the vibration behaviour for each material and volume filling. Moreover, studying the distribution of several smaller reservoirs and how they compare with a single one could improve the overall damper's efficiency without the need to increase the system's total mass. Furthermore, an analysis encompassing the particles' granulometry (like average particle size and distribution effect) and the impact of reservoir internal divisions might help intensify the particle-damping system's effectiveness. Lastly, the application of hybrid damping systems, like particle dampers and tuned mass dampers, could be analysed, and their efficiency compared with single-damper solutions.

Later, studies regarding the feasibility of applying the present solution in a real-case scenario would be vital, where factors like economic viability and long-term duration of the particles would be addressed.

Author Contributions: Conceptualization: A.Z.S. and A.P.C.; Methodology: A.Z.S. and Y.E.A.; Investigation: F.K.F., C.P. and A.P.C.; Writing—Original Draft: F.K.F., C.P. and T.A.F.; Software: F.K.F.; Formal analysis: F.K.F. and A.M.P.d.J. Writing—Review and Editing: Y.E.A., A.P.C. and A.M.P.d.J.; Funding Acquisition: A.M.P.d.J. and T.A.F.; Resources: A.Z.S. and Y.E.A.; Supervision: C.P., A.M.P.d.J. and T.A.F. All authors have read and agreed to the published version of the manuscript.

Funding: The authors would like to acknowledge FUNDEP for funding the present research.

Institutional Review Board Statement: Not applicable.

Informed Consent Statement: Not applicable.

Data Availability Statement: The data presented in this study are available on request from the corresponding author. The data are not publicly available due to privacy.

Conflicts of Interest: The authors declare no conflicts of interest.

References

1. Wrótny, M.; Bohatkiewicz, J. Traffic noise and inhabitant health—A comparison of road and rail noise. *Sustainability* **2021**, *13*, 7[illegible] [CrossRef]
2. Maclachlan, L.; Waye, P.K.; Pedersen, E. Exploring perception of vibrations from rail: An interview study. *Int. J. Environ. [illegible] Public Health* **2017**, *14*, 1303. [CrossRef] [PubMed]
3. Smith, M.G.; Croy, I.; Ögren, M.; Waye, P.K. On the influence of freight trains on humans: A laboratory investigation of the imp[illegible] of nocturnal low frequency vibration and noise on sleep and heart rate. *PLoS ONE* **2013**, *8*, e55829. [CrossRef] [PubMed]
4. Croy, I.; Smith, M.G.; Waye, K.P. Effects of train noise and vibration on human heart rate during sleep: An experimental stu[illegible] *BMJ Open* **2013**, *3*, e002655. [CrossRef]
5. Croft, B.; Miller, A.; Küpper, A. Maintenance effects on rolling noise–metro and light rail. *Proc. Acoust.* **2021**, *21*, 2022.
6. Höjer, M.; Bergseth, E.; Olofsson, U.; Nilsson, R.; Lyu, Y. A noise related track maintenance tool for severe wear detection[illegible] wheel–rail contact. In Proceedings of the Third International Conference on Railway Technology: Research, Development a[illegible] Maintenance, Caglinari, Italy, 5–8 April 2016; Civil-Comp Press: Stirlingshire, UK, 2016.
7. Zhang, J.; Xiao, X.; Wang, D.; Yang, Y.; Fan, J. Source Contribution Analysis for Exterior Noise of a High-Speed Train: Experime[illegible] and Simulations. *Shock Vib.* **2018**, *1*, 5319460. [CrossRef]
8. Connolly, D.P.; Marecki, G.P.; Kouroussis, G.; Thalassinakis, I.; Woodward, P.K. The growth of railway ground vibrat[illegible] problems—A review. *Sci. Total Environ.* **2016**, *568*, 1276–1282. [CrossRef]
9. Ogran, M.; GIdlof-Gunnarsson, A.; Smith, M.; Gustavsson, S.; Waye, K.P. Comparison of annoyance from railway noise a[illegible] railway vibration. *Int. J. Environ.* **2017**, *14*, 805.
10. Sanayei, M.; Maurya, P.; Moore, J.A. Measurement of building foundation and ground-borne vibrations due to surface trains a[illegible] subways. *Eng. Struct.* **2013**, *53*, 102–111. [CrossRef]
11. Zou, C.; Wang, Y.; Moore, J.A.; Sanayei, M. Train-induced field vibration measurements of ground and over-track buildings. [illegible] *Total Environ.* **2017**, *575*, 1339–1351. [CrossRef]
12. Hanson, C.E.; Towers, D.A.; Meister, L.D. *Transit Noise and Vibration Impact Assessment*; Federal Transit Administration (US[illegible] Washington, DC, USA, 2006.
13. Abramov, A.; Podorozkina, A.; Bilenko, G.; Ivankova, L.; Okulova, M. Optimization of Freight Train Speeds on Railway Transp[illegible] *Transp. Res. Procedia* **2022**, *61*, 371–375. [CrossRef]
14. Thompson, D.J.; Jones, C.J.C. A review of the modelling of wheel/rail noise generation. *J. Sound Vib.* **2008**, *231*, 519–536. [CrossR[illegible]
15. Thompson, D.J. On the relationship between wheel and rail surface roughness and rolling noise. *J. Sound Vib.* **1996**, *193*, 149–1[illegible] [CrossRef]
16. Jeong, D.; Choi, H.S.; Choi, Y.J.; Jeong, W. Measuring Acoustic Roughness of a Longitudinal Railhead Profile Using a Multi-Sen[illegible] Integration Technique. *Sensors* **2019**, *19*, 1610. [CrossRef]
17. Smith, M.G.; Croy, I.; Hammar, O.; Wayer, K.P. Vibration from freight trains fragments sleep: A polysomnographic study. *Sci. R[illegible]* **2016**, *6*, 24717. [CrossRef]
18. Elias, S.; Matsagar, V. Research developments in vibration control of structures using passive tuned mass dampers. *Annu. R[illegible] Control* **2017**, *44*, 129–156. [CrossRef]
19. Jangid, R.S.; Datta, T.K. Seismic behaviour of base-isolated buildings: A state-of-the art-review. *Proc. Inst. Civ. Eng. Struct. Bu[illegible]* **1995**, *110*, 186–203. [CrossRef]
20. Saidi, I.; Mohammed, A.D.; Gad, E.F.; Wilson, J.L.; Haritos, N. *Optimum Design for Passive Tuned Mass Dampers Using Viscoelas[illegible] Materials*; Australian Earthquake Engineering Society: Wollongong, Australia, 2007.
21. Jin, J.; Yang, W.; Koh, H.; Park, J. Development of tuned particle impact damper for reduction of transient railway vibratio[illegible] *Appl. Acoust.* **2020**, *169*, 107487. [CrossRef]
22. Lin, C.C.; Wang, J.F.; Chen, B.L. Train-induced vibration control of high-speed railway bridges equipped with multiple tun[illegible] mass dampers. *J. Bridge Eng.* **2005**, *10*, 398–414. [CrossRef]
23. Gagnon, L.; Morandini, M.; Ghiringhelli, G.L. A review of particle damping modeling and testing. *J. Sound Vib.* **2019**, *459*, 1148[illegible] [CrossRef]

4. Friend, R.D.; Kinra, V.K. Particle impact damping. *J. Sound Vib.* **2000**, *233*, 93–118. [CrossRef]
5. Meyer, N.; Seifried, R. Design of robust particle dampers using inner structures and coated container walls. *Granul. Matter* **2023**, *25*, 10. [CrossRef]
6. Xu, Z.W.; Chan, K.W.; Liao, W.H. An empirical method for particle damping design. *Shock Vib.* **2004**, *11*, 647–664. [CrossRef]
7. Prasad, B.B.; Duvigneau, F.; Woschke, E.; Juhre, D. Application and damping mechanism of particle dampers. *Proc. Appl. Math. Mech.* **2023**, *22*, e202200116. [CrossRef]
8. Veeramuthuvel, P.; Shankar, K.; Sairajan, K.K. Experimental investigation of particle damper-based vibration suppression in printed circuit board for spacecraft applications. *Proc. Inst. Mech. Eng. Part G J. Aerosp. Eng.* **2015**, *230*, 1299–1311. [CrossRef]
9. Paul, P.S.; Raja, P.; Aruldhas, P.; Pringle, S.; Shaji, E. Effectiveness of particle and mass impact damping on tool vibration during hard turning process. *Proc. Inst. Mech. Eng. Part B J. Eng. Manuf.* **2018**, *232*, 776–786. [CrossRef]
0. Panossian, H.V. Structural Damping Enhancement Via Non-Obstructive Particle Damping Technique. *J. Vib. Acoust.* **1992**, *114*, 101–105. [CrossRef]
1. Prasad, B.B.; Luft, T.; Michaelsen, C.; Rottengruber, H.S. Enhancing Vibroacoustic Performance of Power Electronic Subsystem in Electric Drives Using Particle Dampers. In Proceedings of the DAGA 2024, Hannover, Germany, 18–21 March 2024.
2. Xin, Y. Deep learning-based investigation of an innovative rail damper using particle damping technology for noise and vibration control. Ph.D. Thesis, The Hong Kong Polytechnic University, Hong Kong, 2024.
3. Liu, C.; Lai, S.; Ni, Y.; Chen, L. Dynamic modelling and analysis of a physics-driven strategy for vibration control of railway vehicles. *Veh. Syst. Dyn.* **2024**, 1–31. [CrossRef]
4. Zhang, C.; Kordestani, H.; Shadabfar, M. A combined review of vibration control strategies for high-speed trains and railway infrastructures: Challenges and solutions. *J. Low Freq. Noise Vib. Act. Control.* **2023**, *42*, 272–291. [CrossRef]
5. Jin, J.; Kim, H.; Koh, H.I.; Park, J. Railway noise reduction by periodic tuned particle impact damper with bounce and pitch-coupled vibration modes. *Compos. Struct.* **2022**, *284*, 115230. [CrossRef]
6. Lu, Z.; Zhang, Q.; Fan, Q.; Li, Q. Studies on dissipative characteristics and equivalent model of particle damper in railway application. *J. Sound Vib.* **2023**, *560*, 117788. [CrossRef]
7. Yanning, T.; Yu, D.; Wangqiang, X.; Kun, X. Particle damping-based design for vibration and noise reduction of interior wooden flooring in high-speed railway trains. *Railw. Roll. Stock* **2024**, *1*, 85–92.
8. Cuenot, S.; Frétigny, C.; Demoustier-Champagner, S.; Nysten, B. Surface tension effect on the mechanical properties of nanomaterials measured by atomic force microscopy. *Phys. Rev. B* **2004**, *69*, 165410. [CrossRef]
9. Chicot, D.; Mendoza, J.; Zaoui, A.; Louis, G.; Lepingle, V.; Roudet, F.; Lesage, J. Mechanical properties of magnetite (Fe_3O_4), hematite (α-Fe2O3) and goethite (α-FeO·OH) by instrumented indentation and molecular dynamics analysis. *Mater. Chem. Phys.* **2011**, *129*, 862–870. [CrossRef]
0. Vo, V.S.; Nguyen, V.; Mahouche-Chegui, S.; Carbonnier, B.; Naili, S. Estimation of effective elastic properties of polymer/clay nanocomposites: A parametric study. *Compos. Part B Eng.* **2018**, *152*, 139–150. [CrossRef]
1. Koblar, D.; Škofic, J.; Boltežar, M. Evaluation of the Young's Modulus of Rubber-Like Materials Bonded to Rigid Surfaces with Respect to Poisson's Ratio. *J. Mech. Eng.* **2014**, *60*, 506–611. [CrossRef]

applied sciences

MDPI

Article

Novel Real-Time Acoustic Power Estimation for Dynamic Thermoacoustic Control

Eduardo Pilo de la Fuente , Jaime Gros, María Antonia Simón Rodríguez , Ana-Isabel Velasco and Carmen Iniesta

Escuela Politécnica Superior, Universidad Francisco de Vitoria, Ctra. Pozuelo-Majadahonda KM 1.800, 28223 Pozuelo de Alarcón, Madrid, Spain; eduardo.pilo@ufv.es (E.P.d.l.F.); jaime.gros@gmail.com (J.G.); mariaantonia.simon@ufv.es (M.A.S.R.); anaisabel.velasco@ufv.es (A.-I.V.)

* Correspondence: carmen.iniesta@ufv.es

Abstract: This paper presents a new procedure for the real-time processing and analysis of data from thermoacoustic systems. The approach focuses on continuously acquiring and adjusting measurements of acoustic wave pressure, enabling the instantaneous estimation of acoustic power. This is crucial for real-time control and decision-making, especially in applications that require rapid power estimation, such as the control loop implementation in thermoacoustic engines, where conditions are constantly changing and dynamic adaptation is essential. Two methods for estimating the power delivered to the load are proposed: (method 1) instantaneous power evaluation, which calculates the power consumed by the resistance in the resistance–capacitance (RC) load, and (method 2) one-period average power calculation using the well-established two-microphones method. These methods are validated with both different synthetic signals and experimental measurements. The results reveal that the new method provides real-time accurate estimations of the power delivered to the acoustic load and, thus, has shown potential for control-based applications.

Keywords: data processing; acoustic power; instantaneous versus average estimation; thermoacoustic engines

1. Introduction

The thermoacoustic Stirling-like cycle engine (TA-SLiCE) represents an innovative class of external combustion engines designed to convert thermal energy into mechanical work and ultimately into direct current (DC) electrical energy [1]. These systems feature a thermoacoustic core with a regenerator between two heat exchangers, integrated into a looped acoustic network modelled as a lumped-element circuit due to its short-length component dimensions [2]. Over the years, the scientific community has extensively investigated the underlying thermoacoustic phenomena governing the operation of thermoacoustic engines, primarily aiming to improve the efficiency and performance of these systems [3]. Rott [4] established the fundamental theoretical framework for studying low-amplitude thermoacoustic phenomena under laminar flow conditions, providing the governing equations that describe the propagation of acoustic waves coupled with thermal effects in confined fluids. Later, Ceperley introduced the analogy between a traveling-wave thermoacoustic engine and a lumped-element electrical circuit [5], recognizing that the working fluid undergoes a thermodynamic cycle analogous to that of a Stirling engine [6]. This perspective facilitated the development of more efficient configurations and simplified the mathematical representation of these systems. More recently, Swift [7] refined and extended this approach through lumped-parameter models, providing more accessible and practical tools for the design and optimization of real thermoacoustic engines [8].

Thermoacoustic measurements often provide high signal-to-noise ratios, making the need for statistical analysis unnecessary [1]. While significant progress has been made in understanding the theoretical foundations and in optimizing the design of thermoacoustic engines [9,10], a variety of passive and active control strategies have been explored to improve the acoustic wave quality of these systems [11]. In this context, acoustic power is relatively easy to measure when volumetric velocity can be reliably inferred, with simpler techniques based on pressure measurements [12] or the motion of a solid object [13] being widely adopted in practice. More high-cost and sophisticated methods for direct velocity measurement, such as hot-wire anemometry particle, image velocimetry, or laser Doppler anemometry techniques, fall beyond the scope of this study and are covered in detail elsewhere [14]. The two-microphone measurement technique [15,16] is widely used to determine acoustic power from pressure amplitude and phase measurements at two locations in a resonator. This well-established method has been widely validated, particularly under laminar flow conditions, where it aligns with the analytical model developed by Fusco et al. [17], the so-called resistance–capacitance (RC) load method. These methodologies, supported by extensive and rigorous work [2], ensure reliable and robust power estimation across varying operational parameters (e.g., loads [18], temperatures, and pressures [19]), reinforcing the applicability of the proposed measurement framework to real-world thermoacoustic systems [20]. In all those studies, the measurement of acoustic power in thermoacoustic engines has been constrained by methods that rely on time-averaged estimations [21,22]. Although effective in many contexts, these methods do not account for potential fluctuations in acoustic amplitude within the mechanical resonator, which can reduce their effectiveness in applications such as control systems [23]. The ability to dynamically estimate acoustic power [24] and make immediate adjustments has been a long-standing challenge in thermoacoustic systems, where traditional optimization methods have typically relied on structural modifications [25] or temperature-based estimates [26]. Integrating real-time acoustic power measurements enables the system to respond to changes in performance as they occur, thereby ensuring more precise and adaptive control. Additionally, experimental constraints imposed by working within the low-amplitude regime required by linear theory, such as the subtle pressure oscillations, demand high-precision sensors or signal amplification lock-in systems [27], which significantly impact the cost and complexity of the data acquisition setup. In this context, recent studies have demonstrated that low-cost systems, such as those based on the Arduino platform, can achieve promising results in dynamic applications, ensuring reliability at reasonably high sampling rates when a reduced number of sensors are used [28]. The development of a robust yet affordable acquisition system requires optimizing sampling frequency, data transmission, and error mitigation, as demonstrated by Moreno [29], who enhanced acquisition rates and minimized errors in Arduino-based platforms. Building on these findings, this study utilizes the previously validated low-cost Arduino-based acquisition system designed for thermoacoustic Stirling engines [30]. This system has been optimized to reduce noise-related errors and enhance dynamic response, ensuring both accurate real-time thermoacoustic power estimation and reliable measurements.

This study presents a novel approach for the real-time estimation of instantaneous acoustic power in thermoacoustic engines, addressing the limitations of conventional time-averaged power estimation methods. The measurements are performed within a laminar regime, using the RC load-based method [30], where a resonator and a variable acoustic load are utilized to replicate the lossless acoustic behaviour of a piston in a linear alternator while accounting for parasitic losses due to piston motion. Unlike traditional methods that rely on time-averaged estimations, our procedure offers a way to measure instantaneous power by continuously acquiring and adjusting data on acoustic waves and system parameters. This allows real-time monitoring of the power dissipated in the RC load within the TA-SLiCE power extraction branch (see Figure 1), providing a more accurate and responsive approach for evaluating thermoacoustic power. Furthermore, the methodology is versatile and can be applied to various data acquisition systems, independent of their cost or complexity.

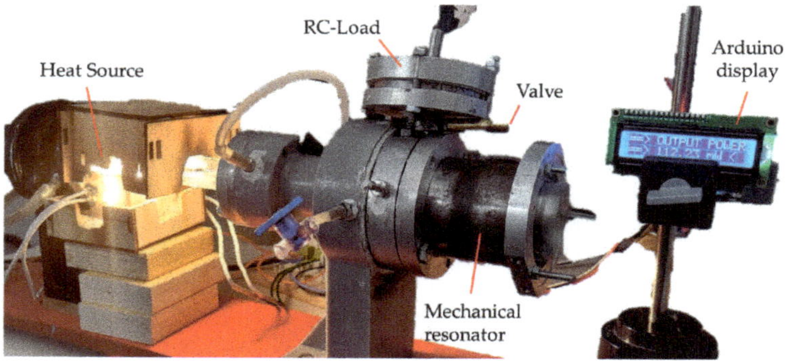

Figure 1. Illustration of the acoustic power visualization through a low-cost display.

The approach presented in this paper offers several advantages over traditional methods. A comparison between the real-time estimation technique and the widely used RC load-based method, which relies on averaged measurements, demonstrates that the proposed method provides accurate and timely results, even with a low-cost acquisition system. The effects of sampling rates and acquisition frequencies on measurement accuracy are also examined, showing that a higher resolution leads to reduced errors and greater precision in real-time applications. The obtained results emphasize the potential of real-time power measurement as a crucial tool for enhancing thermoacoustic engine performance, enabling new opportunities for control and optimization, such as the control algorithm developed by Callanan et al. [31], which improves efficiency and power density in thermoacoustic energy harvesters, making them more effective for practical applications in refrigeration and energy conversion.

The paper is organized as follows: In Section 2, the theoretical background and methodology for real-time power estimation in thermoacoustic engines is outlined. Section 3 describes the experimental setup, measurements, and results. Section 4 includes the experimental validation of the estimation procedure, comparison with traditional approaches, and discussion. Section 5 provides the main conclusions of this work.

2. Materials and Methods

In this section, the analogy between different acoustic and electrical magnitudes will be presented, which will allow the development of an equivalent electrical model. From this model, it will be possible to calculate the electrical power consumed and, by analogy of the models, to estimate the acoustic power provided by the engine. On the other hand, different acoustic power measurement methods will be explored, both for the calculation of the average value and for its measurement in real time, and various comparisons will be made between these methods, including the RC load method, which is firmly established.

2.1. RC Equivalent Model in Electrical Analogy

The acoustic wave interactions in thermoacoustic devices are difficult to analyse, either because of their physical complexity or because of their dependence on the medium in which the wave propagates, in many cases requiring the use of very advanced tools. It is possible to establish an electric-acoustic correspondence thanks to the similarity of the fundamental equations that govern both disciplines [1,32]. The analogies relevant to this article are shown in Table 1. This similarity enables the representation of complex acoustic systems as simplified electrical circuits, facilitating the use of electrical analysis tools and simulators for efficient system evaluation and optimization.

Table 1. Electro-Acoustic analogous variables.

Physical Variable	Electrical Analogy
Acoustic pressure (P)	Electrical voltage (V)
Volume flow rate (U)	Current (I)
Resistance (R)	Resistance (R)
Compliance (C)	Capacitance (C)
Acoustic power $\left(\dot{E}_{load}\right)$	Electric power (P_{elec})

The acoustic RC load in the power extraction branch of a TA-SLiCE, depicted in Figure 2, consists of a small tank of volume V_C (compliance) connected through a needle valve to the mechanical branch resonator.

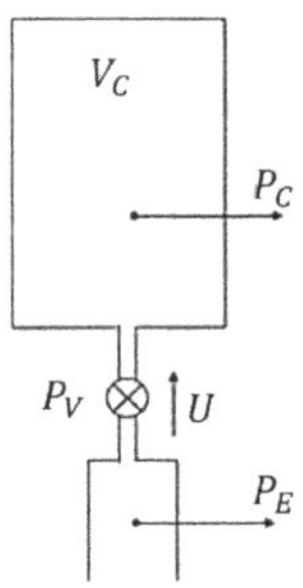

Figure 2. Diagram of a thermoacoustic resistance–capacitance (RC) load. P_C, P_E, and P_V are the pressures at the compliance, the resonator, and the valve, respectively. U is the volume flow rate through the valve.

The expression describing the process is given by Equation (1):

$$P_E(t) = P_V(t) + P_C(t), \tag{1}$$

According to the electro-acoustic analogies shown in the table above and the physical problem under consideration, the pressure in the resonator, $P_E(t)$, is analogous to the total voltage or source voltage, $V_g(t)$. Similarly, the pressure in the capacitor $P_C(t)$ corresponds to the capacitor voltage $V_C(t)$ and the pressure in the valve, $P_V(t)$, is analogous to the resistor voltage $V_g(t)$. On the other hand, the analogue to the volume flow rate, $U(t)$, is the circuit current, $I(t)$. This results in Equation (2) and the corresponding electrical model shown in Figure 3.

$$V_g(t) = V_R(t) + V_C(t), \tag{2}$$

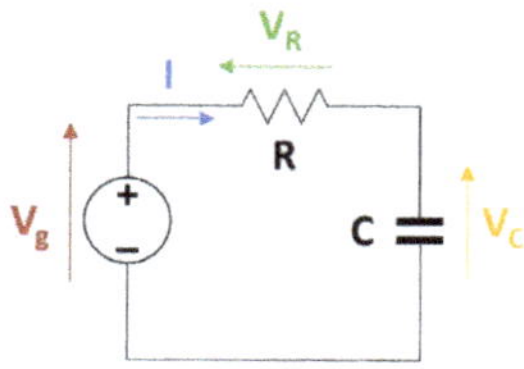

Figure 3. Electric RC load, where V_C, V_g, and V_R are the voltages at the capacitor, the source, and the resistor and I is the current though the circuit.

On the other hand, the characteristic equation of a capacitor is

$$i_C(t) = C\frac{dV_C(t)}{dt}, \tag{3}$$

where C is the capacitance of the capacitor and $i_C(t)$ is the current flowing through it. As the elements are in series, the current flowing through the whole circuit would be the same:

$$I(t) = i_C(t) = C\frac{dV_C(t)}{dt}, \tag{4}$$

If the circuit analysis is performed in steady state, phasor notation can be used, leading to

$$\vec{V_g} = \vec{V_R} + \vec{V_C}, \tag{5}$$

where $\vec{V_g}$, $\vec{V_R}$, and $\vec{V_C}$ are the voltage phasors of the source, the resistor, and the capacitor, respectively.

$$\vec{I} = jwC\vec{V_C}, \tag{6}$$

The $\vec{I}$ denotes the current phasor. The capacitor voltage, as a function of the current flowing through it, is expressed in Equation (7):

$$\vec{V_C} = \frac{1}{jwC}\vec{I} = -\frac{j}{wC}\vec{I}, \tag{7}$$

The phasor of a number in polar form is expressed by its magnitude and phase, such that $\vec{I} = I\angle\varphi_I$, $\vec{V_R} = V_R\angle\varphi_{VR}$, and $\vec{V_C} = V_C\angle\varphi_{VC}$ are the phasors, expressed in polar form, of the current, the voltage across the resistor, and the voltage across the capacitor, respectively. As the circuit is in series, considering the current as the phase reference, $\vec{I} = I\angle 0°$ the voltage at the terminals of the resistor will be in phase with the current passing through it, $\vec{V_R} = V_R\angle 0$ and the voltage at the capacitor will be delayed by 90° with respect to the same current, $\vec{V_C} = V_C\angle -90°$ as illustrated in the phasor diagram in Figure 4.

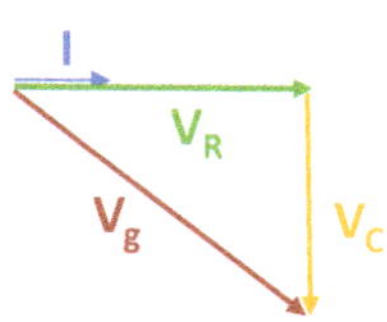

Figure 4. Phasor diagram of an RC load.

2.2. Average Power Estimation

The RC load method has been widely adopted as a reliable approach for measuring acoustic power in thermoacoustic systems [17]. This method utilizes the phasor representation of the volumetric flow rate across the resistance, derived from the pressure oscillations within the compliance, C, assuming the short duct length approximation:

$$U = j\omega CP_C = j\omega \frac{V}{\gamma P_m} P_C, \tag{8}$$

where U represents the volumetric flow rate, P_C the pressure measured at the compliance and V, P_m, and γ correspond to the compliance volume, mean pressure, and specific heat ratio, respectively [1].

Using this relationship, the dissipated acoustic power at the resistance is determined by analysing the two key pressure signals, P_C and P_E, in terms of their amplitude, phase, and angular frequency:

$$\dot{E}_{load} = \frac{1}{2}\frac{\omega V}{\gamma P_m} Im\left(P_E \widetilde{P}_C\right) = \frac{1}{2}\frac{\omega V}{\gamma P_m} |P_E||P_C| sin\theta_{EC}, \tag{9}$$

where θ_{EC} is the phase angle between the P_C and P_E pressure signals. The short duct length approximation allows this method to be consistently expressed in terms of the compliance of geometric and thermodynamic parameters [33].

The RC load method determines the dissipated acoustic power as the time-averaged product of the volumetric flow rate through the valve and the pressures P_C and P_E across it [30].

2.3. Instantaneous Power Estimation

By measuring the pressure difference in the resonator and in the small tank, it will be possible to determine the acoustic power lost, $\dot{E}_{load}$, by simply multiplying this difference by the flow rate through the valve.

$$\dot{E}_{load} = P_V \cdot U = (P_E - P_C) \cdot U, \tag{10}$$

where P_V is the pressure in the valve.

Using the electro-acoustic analogy to the electrical power equation would leave

$$\dot{E}_{load} = P_{elec} = V_R \cdot I = (V_g - V_C) \cdot I, \tag{11}$$

To calculate the power at each time instant, the following expression for the instantaneous power $P_{elec}(t)$ is employed:

$$P_{elec}(t) = V_R(t) \cdot I(t) = (V_g(t) - V_C(t)) \cdot I(t) = (V_g(t) - V_C(t)) \cdot C \frac{dV_C(t)}{dt}, \tag{12}$$

where $V_R(t)$, $V_g(t)$, and $V_C(t)$ are the instantaneous voltages across the resistor, the source, and the capacitor, respectively, and $I(t)$ is the instantaneous current flowing through the circuit. Under the assumption of a short duct length, the expression for the electrical power is derived as

$$P_{elec}(t) = \frac{V}{\gamma P_m} \cdot (V_g(t) - V_C(t)) \cdot \frac{dV_C(t)}{dt}, \tag{13}$$

Applying the electro-acoustic analogy to the acoustic power equation would leave

$$\dot{E}_{load}(t) = \frac{V}{\gamma P_m} \cdot (P_E(t) - P_C(t)) \cdot \frac{dP_C(t)}{dt}, \tag{14}$$

The instantaneous power in any element of an alternating current circuit is expressed as $p(t) = v(t) \cdot i(t)$, where $v(t)$ and $i(t)$ represent the voltage and current at each moment, respectively. If the source supplying the circuit produces a sinusoidal alternating current, both the voltage and current of each element will be represented by sinusoidal waves. These waves will exhibit a relative phase shift, determined by the specific characteristics of the element where the instantaneous power is being evaluated.

The expression for instantaneous power, $P_{elec}(t)$, as a function of the voltage and current of an element of an electrical circuit is defined as

$$P_{elec}(t) = v(t) \cdot i(t) = 2 \cdot V \cdot I \cdot \cos(w \cdot t) \cos(w \cdot t - \varphi), \tag{15}$$

where V and I represent the root mean square (RMS) voltage and current of that element. w represents the angular frequency and φ is the phase angle between the voltage and the current of the element.

By applying the trigonometric identities for sine and cosine of a double angle, this expression can be reformulated, as follows:

$$P_{elec}(t) = P \cdot (1 + \cos(2 \cdot w \cdot t)) + Q \cdot sen(2 \cdot w \cdot t), \tag{16}$$

where P and Q are the active and reactive power, respectively, consumed by the passive element.

The average value of this instantaneous power is the active power, P, the power that provides the energy that is converted into effective or useful work, either in the form of heat, light, or motion.

$$\overline{P_{elec}(t)} = P, \tag{17}$$

In this case, the instantaneous power to be measured and calculated is that of the resistive element of the circuit, where the voltage at the terminals of the resistor and the current flowing through it are in phase. Figure 5 shows a singular case of the voltage and current in a resistive element, as well as the instantaneous power.

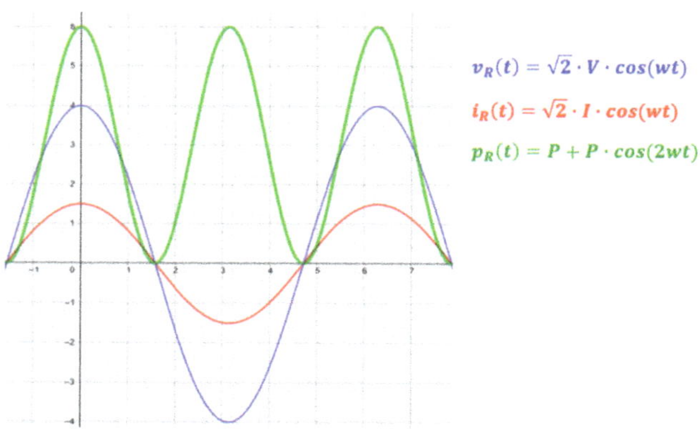

Figure 5. Voltage, current, and instantaneous power in a resistive element.

3. Results

The acoustic power measurement system described in this paper has two main components: (i) the real-time data-acquisition system that measures the pressure both in the compliance (P_C) and the resonator (P_E) and (ii) the data-processing system, which scales and filters the measurements (Section 3.1) and then calculates the power delivered to the load (Sections 3.2 and 3.3).

The former, which builds upon a thoroughly validated setup, described in previous research [30], is based on an Arduino platform designed to accurately calculate the acoustic power of the TA-SLiCE. In that earlier work, the performance of this setup was shown to be both reliable and accurate, confirming its suitability for measuring acoustic power in thermoacoustic engines. Integrated with piezoelectric low-cost pressure sensors, the system enables the real-time measurement and transmission of sensor data, ensuring continuous monitoring of pressure variations in two key components of the system: the compliance, which functions as a dynamic capacitor, and the resonator, responsible for the acoustic oscillations.

The latter is described in this section of the paper. Two different approaches for estimating the power delivered to the load are proposed:

- Instantaneous power evaluation (method 1), which consists of using the instantaneous power consumed in the resistance of the equivalent RC model of the load;
- One-period average power calculation (method 2), in which the procedure established by Fusco et al. [17] is adapted to be used each single period for each single period of the signal.

3.1. Measurements Conditioning

The data-acquisition system described in [30] provides pressure measurements that are already expressed in mbar. However, the following steps are needed prior to the calculation of the power delivered to the load.

First, the acoustic pressure wave and the average pressure value need to be split up. Alternatively, expressing this idea with electrical terms, the alternating current (AC) wave and the DC operation point need to be separated. To do so, the DC component of cycle c is calculated based on the maximum and minimum values of the signal in cycle c − 1:

$$X_{DC}(c) = \frac{X_{max}(c-1) + X_{min}(c-1)}{2}, \tag{18}$$

where $X_{DC}(c)$ refers to the DC component of signal X in cycle c, whereas $X_{max}(c-1)$ and $X_{min}(c-1)$ are the maximum and minimum values of the signal X in cycle c − 1, respectively (see Figure 6).

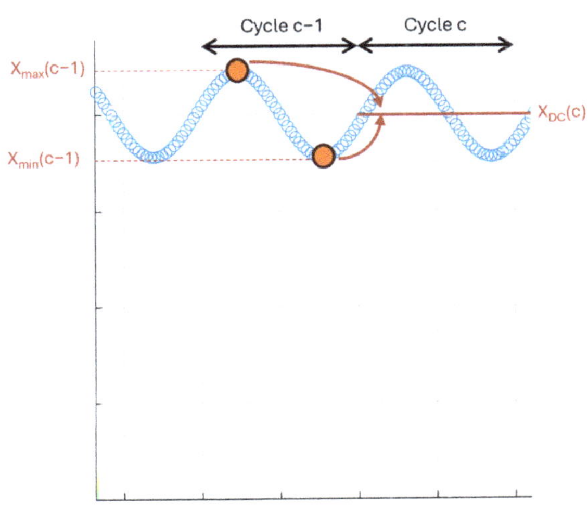

Figure 6. Estimation of the average value of the signal based on the previous cycle.

This procedure is simple and provide a good estimation of the DC component of the signal, but it cannot be used to calculate the DC component of the first cycle. Therefore, the following expression is used to calculate the DC component for each time step k:

$$X_{DC}(k) = \frac{\sum_{j=1}^{k} X(j)}{k}, \tag{19}$$

where $X_{DC}(k)$ and $X(k)$ refer to the DC component and the value of signal X in time step k, respectively.

Figure 7 shows the response of the DC component estimation algorithms in the initial cycle (see Equation (19)) and the rest of the cycles (see Equation (18)).

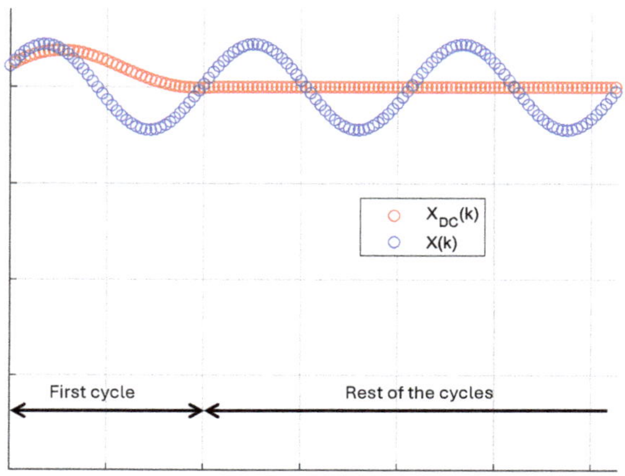

Figure 7. Estimation of the average value of the signal based on the first cycle.

Once the AC and DC components have been split up, the AC signal is filtered to reduce the noise using a moving average:

$$X_{filt}(k) = \frac{\sum_{j=0}^{W-1} X(k-j)}{W}, \tag{20}$$

where $X_{filt}(k)$ is the filtered value of the signal and W is the size of the moving window.

As shown in Figure 8, this filtering technique causes some delay in the filtered signal compared to the original one and, therefore, the size of the moving windows needs to be selected as a trade-off between the noise reduction and the admissible delay.

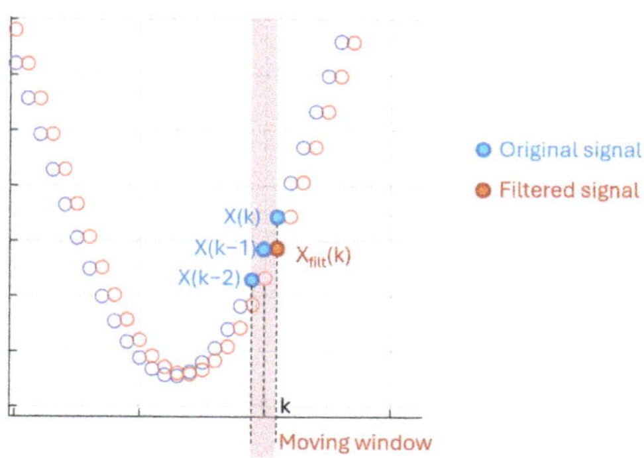

Figure 8. Moving-average-based filtering of the drawing, with W = 3.

3.2. Instantaneous Power Calculation by Method 1

In this section, the instantaneous power calculation by method 1 is presented, relying on Equation (8) to evaluate the power consumed by the resistance of the RC load at each time lapse.

The derivative of $P_C(t)$ for a given time step k can be approximated as follows:

$$\frac{dP_C(k)}{dt} \approx \frac{P_{C,filt}(k) - P_{C,filt}(k-1)}{T_S}, \quad (21)$$

where T_S is the sampling period and $P_{C,filt}(k)$ is the filtered value of the pressure at the compliance at time step k.

Therefore, the power delivered to the load at a time step k can be expressed as

$$\dot{E}_{load}(k) = \frac{V}{\gamma P_m} \cdot \left(P_{E,filt}(k) - P_{C,filt}(k)\right) \cdot \frac{P_{C,filt}(k) - P_{C,filt}(k-1)}{T_S}, \quad (22)$$

where $P_{E,filt}(k)$ is the filtered value of the pressure in the resonator at time step k.

To determine the average value of the power delivered to the load, the following expression can be used:

$$\overline{\dot{E}_{load,method1}} = \frac{\sum_{j=1}^{N_S} P_{ac}(j)}{N_S}, \quad (23)$$

where N_S is the number of samples considered for averaging.

According to Equation (17), the average value of $P_{ac}(t)$ can alternatively also be calculated as

$$\overline{\dot{E}_{load,method1}} = \frac{\dot{E}_{load,max}}{2}, \quad (24)$$

where $\dot{E}_{load,max}$ is the maximum value of $\dot{E}_{load}(k)$.

3.3. One-Period Average Power Calculation by Method 2

The one-period average power calculation (method 2) uses Equation (22) to calculate the average power delivered to the load but, instead of determining P_E, P_C, and θ_{EC} over a large number of periods by means of the Fast Fourier Transform (FFT) and least-squares fitting, they are obtained by identification over a single period (see Figure 9).

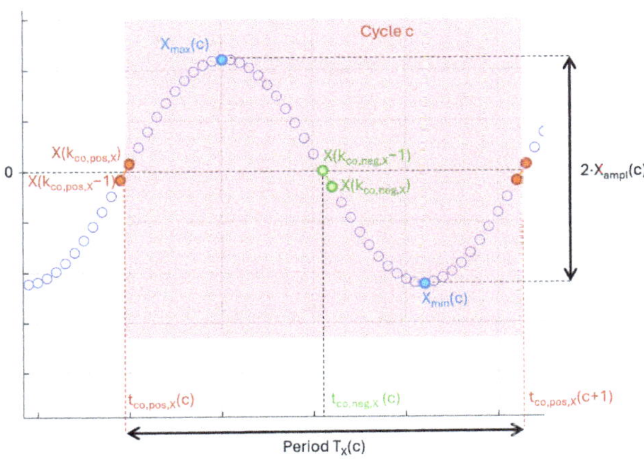

Figure 9. Identification of relevant quantities of the signal for method.

Given a signal X(k), the maximum and minimum values measured in a cycle c (referred to as $X_{max}(c)$ and $X_{min}(c)$, respectively) are used to calculate the amplitude $X_{ampl}(c)$ of the signal:

$$X_{ampl}(c) = \frac{X_{max}(c) - X_{min}(c)}{2}, \tag{25}$$

For a cycle c, the crossover time with a positive slope $t_{co,pos,X}(c)$ is obtained by (i) detecting the time step $k_{co,pos,X}$ at which the signal X becomes positive after being negative and (ii) conducting a linear interpolation to determine $t_{co,pos,X}(c)$ at which X(t) equals 0. If needed, the crossover time with a negative slope $t_{co,neg}(c)$ can also be determined by detecting the time step $k_{co,neg.X}$ at which the signal X becomes negative after being positive.

The period $T_X(c)$ of a signal X can then be calculated as

$$T_X(c) = t_{co,pos,X}(c) - t_{co,pos,X}(c-1), \tag{26}$$

The acquisition system just described allows to measure this expression and can also be reformulated in terms of the active and reactive power consumed by the element, as follows:

$$\dot{E}_{load}(c) = \frac{1}{2}\frac{\omega V}{\gamma P_m} P_E(c)\cdot P_C(c)\cdot sin\theta_{EC}(c), \tag{27}$$

where $P_E(c)$ is the amplitude of $P_{E,filt}(k)$ in cycle c, $P_C(c)$ is the amplitude of $P_{C,filt}(k)$ in cycle c, and $\theta_{EC}(c)$ is the phase difference between $P_{E,filt}$ and $P_{C,filt}$.

The phase difference $\theta_{EC}(c)$, expressed in radians, can be calculated as

$$\theta_{EC}(c) = \frac{2\pi}{T_{PE}(c)}\left(t_{co,pos,Pc}(c) - t_{co,pos,Pe}(c)\right), \tag{28}$$

where $T_{PE}(c)$ is the period of $P_{E,filt}(k)$ in cycle c, $t_{co,pos,Pc}(c)$ is the crossover time with a positive slope of $P_{C,filt}$ in cycle c, and $t_{co,pos,Pe}(c)$ is the crossover time with a positive slope of $P_{E,filt}$ in cycle c.

4. Discussion

To evaluate the accuracy of the proposed methods, the following studies are carried out:

- First, simulated values of $P_E(k)$ and $P_C(k)$ with no noise and a good sampling frequency are considered. The average power delivered to the load is calculated using the proposed methods and compared to the results obtained with the reference procedure [17].
- Then, the sensitivity to the noise is analysed, for which a random noise is added to the simulated of $P_E(k)$ and $P_C(k)$;
- Afterwards, the sensitivity to the measurement frequency is analysed, for which the sampling frequency of $P_E(k)$ and $P_C(k)$ is reduced;
- Finally, real measurements of $P_E(k)$ and $P_C(k)$ are used to conduct the analysis.

4.1. Results Using Ideal Signals

For this analysis, the following functions $P_E(t)$ and $P_C(t)$ were considered over the interval from 0 to 10 s, with a sampling time of 1 ms:

$$P_E(t) = 78309 + 4421.3\cdot \cos(145.76\cdot t), \tag{29}$$

and

$$P_C(t) = 78359 + 2218.7\cdot \cos(145.76\cdot t - 1.0451), \tag{30}$$

Figure 10 shows the convergence of the DC component estimation for both $P_E(\mathrm{t})$ and $P_C(\mathrm{t})$. The DC component estimation algorithm shows good convergence, stabilizing after approximately three cycles.

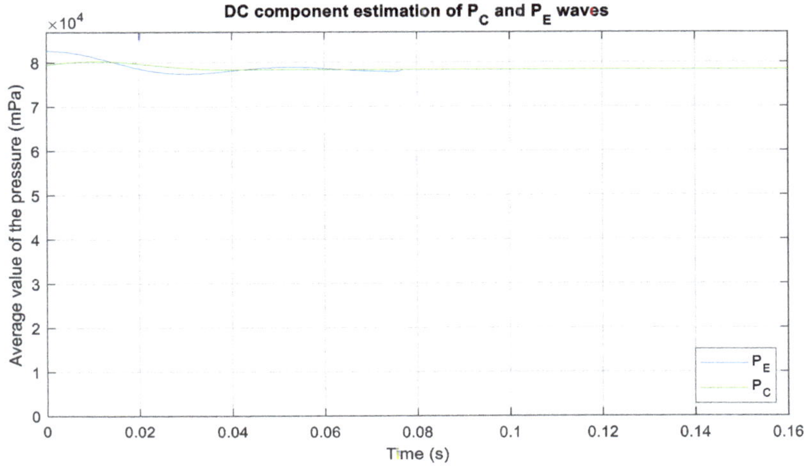

Figure 10. Estimation of the direct current (DC) component of the signal of $P_E(k)$ and $P_C(k)$ (ideal signals).

Figure 11 compares the AC component of $P_E(\mathrm{t})$ and $P_C(\mathrm{t})$, both filtered and non-filtered. The moving window size for the filtering is W = 3 in all the study cases.

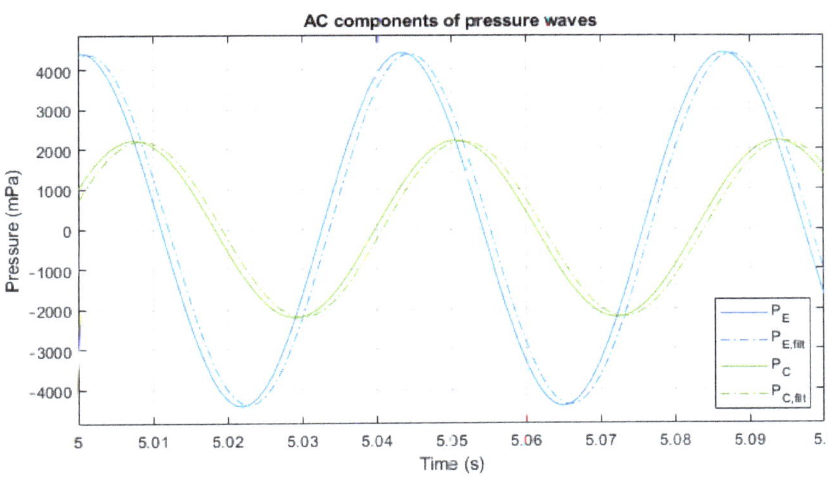

Figure 11. Alternating current (AC) component of $P_E(k)$ and $P_C(k)$ analyzed for ideal signals, considering both non-filtered and filtered cases.

Figure 12 shows the instantaneous power obtained using method 1.

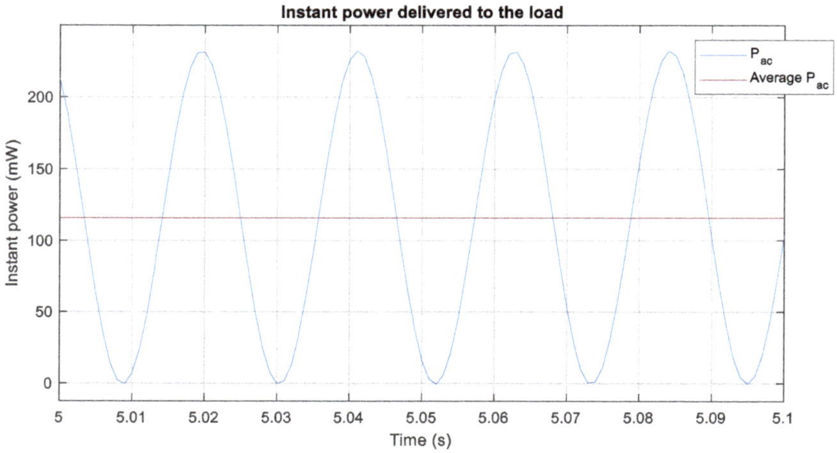

Figure 12. Instantaneous power obtained using Equation (22) for ideal signals.

Table 2 shows the average power obtained with the proposed methods and compares them to the average power obtained with the reference procedure [17]. The error is defined as follows:

$$Error(\%) = \frac{\dot{E}_{load,ref} - \dot{E}_{load,method}}{\dot{E}_{load,ref}} \cdot 100, \tag{31}$$

where $\dot{E}_{load,ref}$ is the average power obtained with the reference procedure and $\dot{E}_{load,method}$ refers to the average power obtained with the proposed methods (1 or 2).

Table 2. Comparison of the results obtained using different methods (ideal signals).

Method	Average Power (mW)	Error (%)
Reference method	118.05	--
Instantaneous power (method 1)	115.97	1.75
One-period average (method 2)	116.69	1.15

The first three cycles (needed to stabilize the DC components) have not been considered in calculating the averages.

These results show that good correspondence is obtained when using the three methods with an ideal synthesis signal sampled at approximately 40 measurements per period: the difference is lower than 1.8%.

4.2. Sensitivity to Noise

For this analysis, the following functions $P_E(\mathrm{t})$ and $P_C(\mathrm{t})$ have been considered in the interval between 0 a 10 s (sampling time is 1 ms):

$$P_E(\mathrm{t}) = 78309 + 4421.3 \cdot (\cos(145.76 \cdot \mathrm{t}) + \mathrm{NoiseLevel} \cdot \mathrm{Noise}()), \tag{32}$$

and

$$P_C(\mathrm{t}) = 78359 + 2218.7 \cdot (\cos(145.76 \cdot \mathrm{t} - 1.0451) + \mathrm{NoiseLevel} \cdot \mathrm{Noise}()), \tag{33}$$

where NoiseLevel is the amplitude of the noise expressed in per unit and Noise() is a noise function which will vary depending on the type of noise to be analysed.

4.2.1. Uniformly-Distributed Random Noise

In this case, Noise() is a function which follows a uniform distribution from −1 to 1. Figure 13 represents the functions $P_E(t)$ and $P_C(t)$ obtained using Equations (32) and (33) with different noise levels.

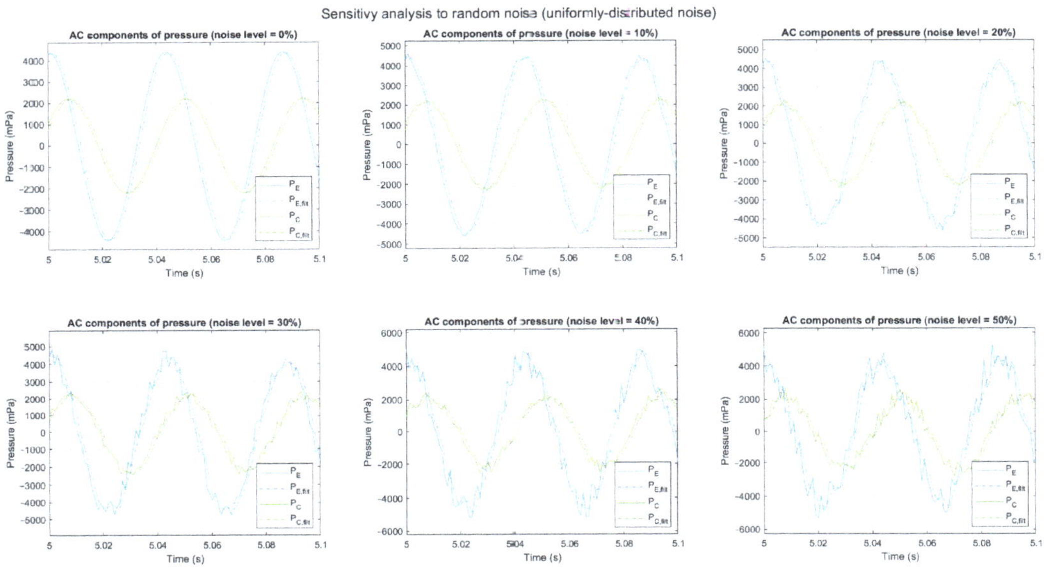

Figure 13. AC component of $P_E(k)$ and $P_C(k)$, filtered and non-filtered, with different noise levels (uniformly distributed noise).

Table 3 shows how adding a uniformly-distributed noise to $P_E(t)$ and $P_C(t)$ impacts into the calculated power depending on the method.

Table 3. Comparison of the results obtained with different levels of noise (uniformly distributed noise).

Method	Average Power (mW) for Different Levels of Noise (Uniformly Distributed Noise)					
	0%	5%	10%	15%	20%	25%
Reference method	118.05	117.969	118.377	117.987	118.310	117.931
Instantaneous power (method 1)	115.983	115.814	115.788	115.216	114.332	113.789
One-period average (method 2)	116.691	117.355	119.879	122.161	126.007	128.734

The results of this analysis show some degradation of the accuracy of the result when noise increases. When the noise level is 25%, the average power obtained is 113.789 mW (which corresponds to an error of 3.5%) and 128.734 mW (which corresponds to an error of −9.2%) using methods 1 and 2, respectively. In general, method 1 tends to underestimate the average power, whereas method 2 tends to overestimate it.

Although method 2 has shown better accuracy with lower noise levels, method 1 has shown better robustness when noise increases. This is mainly because method 2 relies on the peak values of the filtered signals, which are more sensitive to the noise, to determine the averaged power.

4.2.2. Gaussian Random Noise

In this case, Noise() is a function which follows a Gaussian distribution with a mean of 0 and standard deviation of 1. Since the Gaussian noise is not mathematically bounded, the amplitude of the noise has been assumed to be equal to two times the standard deviation (which is a bound for 95.4% of the possible values). Figure 14 represents the functions $P_E(\mathrm{t})$ and $P_C(\mathrm{t})$ obtained using Equations (32) and (33) with different noise levels.

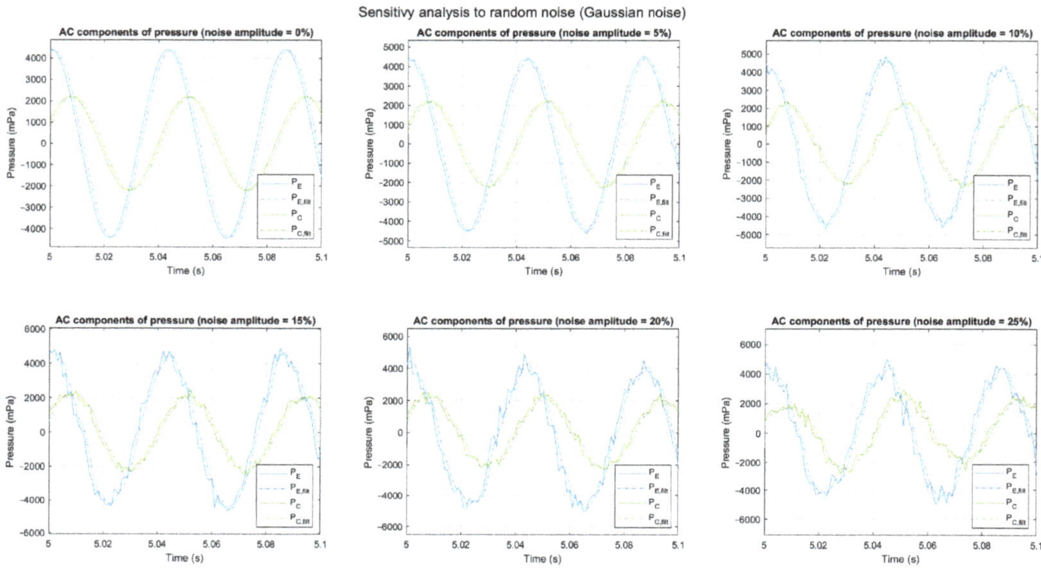

Figure 14. AC component of $P_E(k)$ and $P_C(k)$, filtered and non-filtered, with different noise levels (gaussian noise).

Table 4 shows how adding a gaussian noise to $P_E(\mathrm{t})$ and $P_C(\mathrm{t})$ impacts into the calculated power depending on the method.

Table 4. Comparison of the results obtained with different levels of noise (Gaussian noise).

Method	Average Power (mW) for Different Levels of Noise (Gaussian Noise)					
	0%	5%	10%	15%	20%	25%
Reference method	118.05	117.924	118.086	117.418	118.265	117.952
Instantaneous power (method 1)	115.983	115.817	115.665	115.065	115.022	114.140
One-period average (method 2)	116.691	117.288	119.136	121.281	124.101	126.584

The results of this analysis show a degradation of the accuracy of the result when noise increases. When the noise level is 15%, the average power obtained is 114.140 mW (which corresponds to an error of 3.2%) and 126.584 mW (which corresponds to an error of −7.3%) using methods 1 and 2, respectively. In general, method 1 tends to underestimate the average power, whereas method 2 tends to overestimate it. As observed with uniformly distributed noise, method 1 has shown better robustness when noise increases.

4.2.3. Harmonic Noise

In this case, Noise() is a cosine function with a given frequency (for this analysis, a noise frequency of 400 Hz has been considered, a frequency one decade larger than the measured signals). Figure 15 represents the functions $P_E(\mathrm{t})$ and $P_C(\mathrm{t})$ obtained using Equations (32) and (33) with different noise levels.

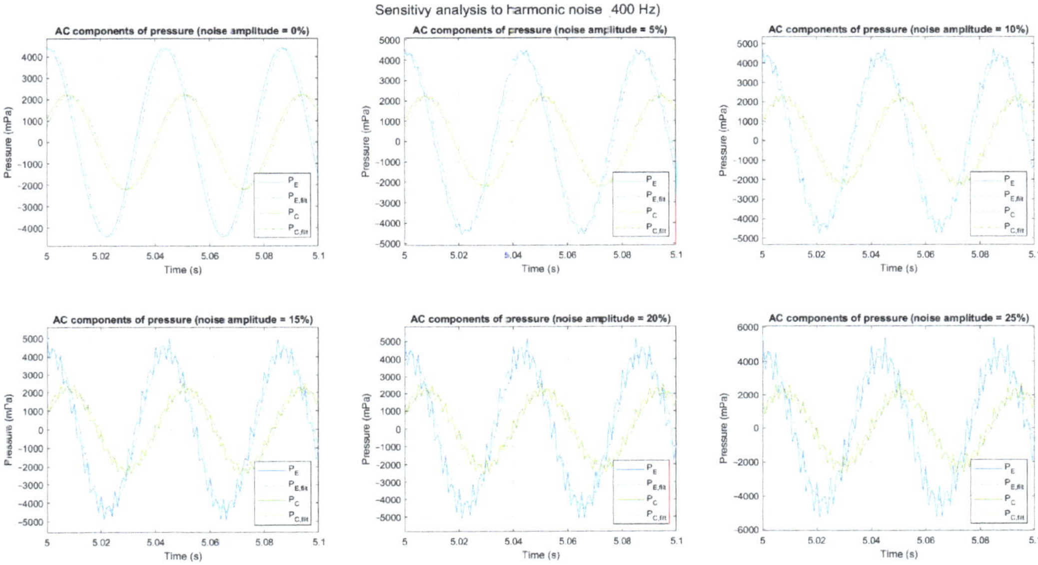

Figure 15. AC component of $P_E(k)$ and $P_C(k)$, filtered and non-filtered, with different noise levels (harmonic noise, 400 Hz).

Table 5 shows how adding a gaussian noise to $P_E(\mathrm{t})$ and $P_C(\mathrm{t})$ impacts into the calculated power depending on the method.

Table 5. Comparison of the results obtained with different levels of noise (harmonic noise, 400 Hz).

Method	Average Power (mW) for Different Levels of Noise (Harmonic Noise, 400 Hz)					
	0%	5%	10%	15%	20%	25%
Reference method	118.05	118.052	118.053	118.054	118.055	118.056
Instantaneous power (method 1)	115.983	116.015	116.281	116.727	117.351	118.155
One-period average (method 2)	116.691	117.751	119.426	121.266	123.170	125.137

The results of this analysis show a degradation of the accuracy of the result when noise increases. When the noise level is 15%, the average power obtained is 118.155 mW (which corresponds to an error of −0.08%) and 125.137 mW (which corresponds to an error of −6%) using methods 1 and 2, respectively. As observed with uniformly distributed noise, method 1 has shown better robustness when noise increases.

4.3. Sensitivity to the Sampling Frequency

For this analysis, the functions $P_E(\mathrm{t})$ and $P_C(\mathrm{t})$ have been used as in Equations (29) and (30), but the sampling time is swept between 0.1 ms and 5 ms. As a reference, both $P_E(\mathrm{t})$ and $P_C(\mathrm{t})$ have a period equal to 43.1 ms.

Figure 16 represents the functions $P_E(\mathrm{t})$ and $P_C(\mathrm{t})$ obtained using Equations (32) and (33) with different sampling periods from 0.5 ms to 5 ms. In the latter, the piecewise aspect can easily be observed.

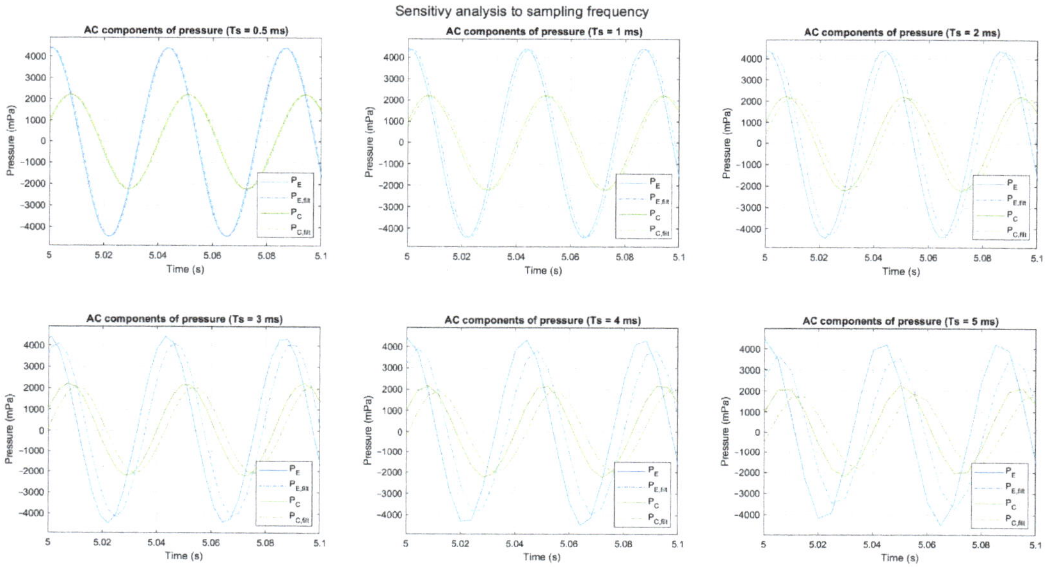

Figure 16. AC component of $P_E(k)$ and $P_C(k)$, filtered and non-filtered, with different sampling periods.

Table 6 shows how the sampling time impacts in the average power calculated using the proposed methods.

Table 6. Comparison of the results obtained with different sampling times.

Method	Average Power (mW) for Different Sampling Periods Ts						
	0.1 ms	0.5 ms	1 ms	2 ms	3 ms	4 ms	5 ms
Reference method	118.050	118.050	118.050	118.050	118.050	118.050	118.050
Instantaneous power (method 1)	118.025	117.530	115.983	109.957	100.417	88.3360	74.2730
One-period average (method 2)	118.551	118.097	116.691	111.200	102.506	91.3430	77.9310

These results show that the estimation error observed when using ideal synthesis signals of $P_E(\mathrm{t})$ and $P_C(\mathrm{t})$ (see Table 2) is partially due to the sampling frequency. In fact, a noticeable degradation of the results (more than 10%) has been remarked when the number of measurements falls under 15 samples per cycle of the signal (i.e., with sampling time is longer than 3 ms).

4.4. Analysis Using Experimental Measurements

In this analysis, real measurements of $P_E(t)$ and $P_C(t)$ were taken with the experimental setup described in [30]. As shown in Figure 17, both signals show small fluctuations, especially in their amplitude, but also in their phase and frequency. Some noise has also been observed.

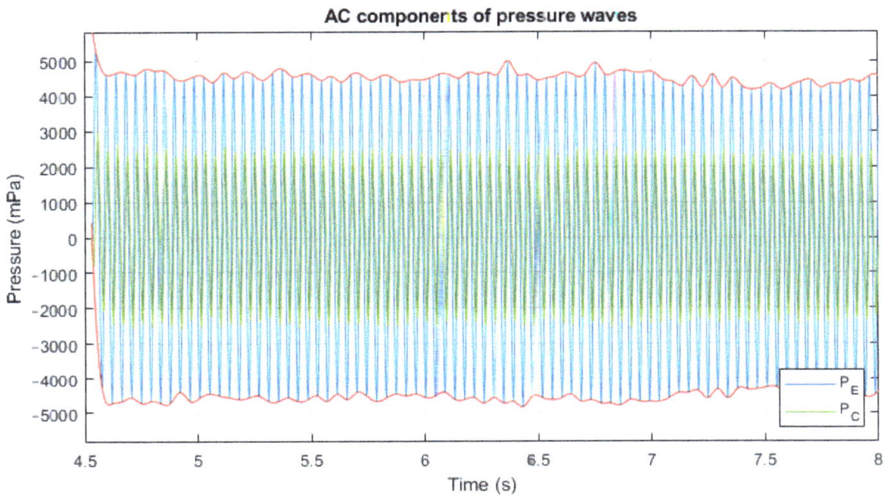

Figure 17. Experimental values of $P_E(k)$ and $P_C(k)$ for measured signals, showing amplitude variations (red line).

Figure 18 shows the convergence of the DC component estimation for both $P_E(t)$ and $P_C(t)$. The DC component estimation algorithm shows good convergence, stabilizing after approximately three cycles, showing some small fluctuations afterwards.

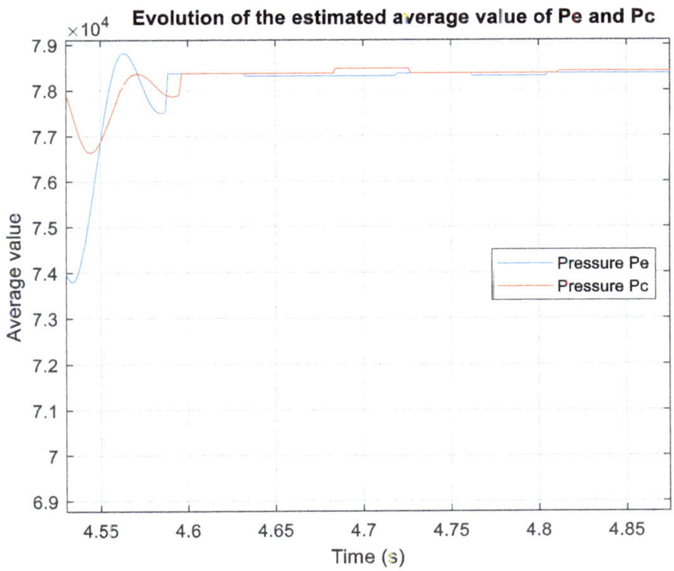

Figure 18. Estimation of the DC component of the signal of $P_E(k)$ and $P_C(k)$ for measured signals.

Figure 19 compares the AC component of $P_E(\mathrm{t})$ and $P_C(\mathrm{t})$, both filtered and non-filtered. The moving window size for the filtering is W = 3 in all the study cases.

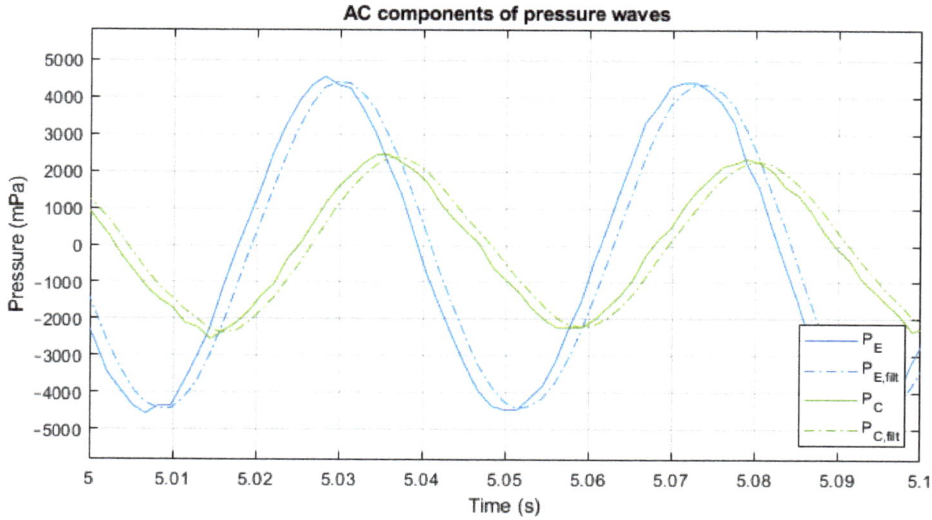

Figure 19. AC component of $P_E(k)$ and $P_C(k)$: non-filtered and filtered for measured signals.

Figure 20 shows the instantaneous power obtained using method 1:

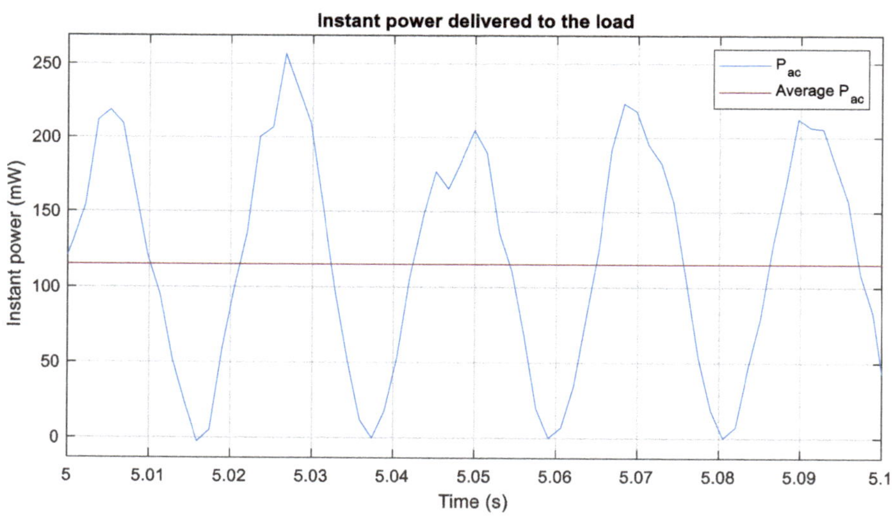

Figure 20. Instantaneous power obtained using Equation (22) using measured signals.

Figure 21 shows how the estimation algorithms respond to the fluctuations observed in $P_E(\mathrm{t})$ and $P_C(\mathrm{t})$:

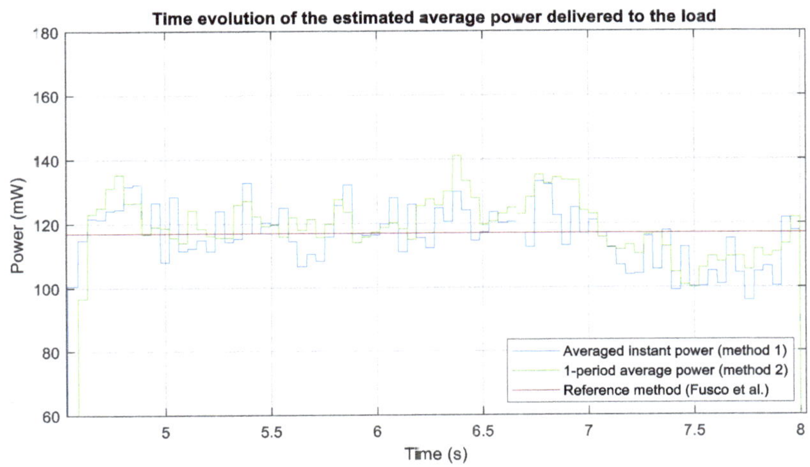

Figure 21. Evolution of the estimated average power using measured signals.

Table 7 shows the average power obtained with the proposed methods and compares them to the average power obtained with the reference procedure [17].

Table 7. Comparison of the results obtained using different methods (measured signals).

Method	Average Power (mW)	Error (%)
Reference method	116.962	--
Instantaneous power (method 1)	115.735	1.295
One-period average (method 2)	121.236	−3.654

These results show also that a good correspondence is obtained when using the three methods when using real measurements (sampled at approximately 30 measurements per period): the difference is lower than 1.3% (method 1) and 3.7% (method 2).

5. Conclusions

This paper has introduced a novel methodology for the real-time estimation of acoustic power in thermoacoustic systems, overcoming the limitations of traditional methods based on temporal averaging. The approach focuses on continuously acquiring and adjusting measurements of acoustic wave pressure, enabling the instantaneous estimation of acoustic power.

Two methods for estimating the power delivered to the load have been evaluated: (method 1) instantaneous power evaluation, which calculates the power consumed by the resistance in the RC load, and (method 2) one-period average power calculation using the well-established two-microphones method.

These methods have been validated with both different synthetic signals and experimental measurements. The results reveal that the new method provides real-time accurate estimations of the power delivered to the acoustic load and, thus, has shown potential for control-based applications.

The average power calculated by the proposed methods, compared with that obtained by the reference procedure [17], shows excellent concordance both with synthetic signals (see Table 2) and experimental measurements (Table 7).

The sensitivity analysis performed against uniformly distributed noise (see Table 3), Gaussian noise (see Table 4) and harmonic noise (see Table 5) shows that the power estimation accuracy degrades as the noise level increases. Although method 2 shows better accuracy at low noise levels, method 1 shows better robustness when the noise increases.

Another factor that has been studied is the influence of the sampling time on the average power calculated (see Table 6). The results degrade significantly when insufficient sampling (less than eight samples per cycle of the observed signals) is used. Although method 2 presents better accuracy with fine sampling, method 1 shows better robustness against coarser sampling.

This methodology allows for adaptive adjustments during operation in terms of system design and control, enhancing the overall system efficiency. Furthermore, real-time power measurement facilitates the implementation of more precise control systems, improving system performance across a range of applications.

The practical implications of this work are significant, as the methodology can be adapted for low-cost data acquisition systems, making it accessible for both commercial and research applications. The approach outlined here also offers a foundation for the development of advanced controllers in thermoacoustic engines and other similar systems, potentially paving the way for their use in sustainable energy applications.

Author Contributions: Conceptualization, J.G. and C.I.; methodology, J.G., E.P.d.l.F. and M.A.S.R.; software, J.G. and E.P.d.l.F.; validation, M.A.S.R., E.P.d.l.F. and A.-I.V.; formal analysis, M.A.S.R. and E.P.d.l.F.; investigation, J.G., E.P.d.l.F., M.A.S.R., A.-I.V. and C.I.; resources, J.G. and C.I.; data curation, E.P.d.l.F. and M.A.S.R.; writing—original draft preparation, E.P.d.l.F., M.A.S.R., A.-I.V. and C.I.; writing—review and editing, E.P.d.l.F., M.A.S.R., A.-I.V. and C.I.; visualization, E.P.d.l.F., M.A.S.R., A.-I.V. and C.I.; supervision, J.G., E.P.d.l.F., M.A.S.R., A.-I.V. and C.I.; project administration, C.I.; funding acquisition, C.I. All authors have read and agreed to the published version of the manuscript.

Funding: This research is part of the project PID2022-138700OB-I00 funded by MICIU/AEI/10.13039/501100011033 and FEDER, UE.

Institutional Review Board Statement: Not applicable.

Informed Consent Statement: Not applicable.

Data Availability Statement: The original data presented in the study are openly available in Mendeley Data at doi: 10.17632/h9zhph34k5.2.

Acknowledgments: The authors gratefully acknowledge the valuable technical support provided by Juan Manuel Díaz Montalvo.

Conflicts of Interest: The authors declare no conflicts of interest.

Abbreviations

The following abbreviations are used in this manuscript:

TA-SLiCE	thermoacoustic Stirling-like cycle engine
RC	resistance–capacitance
DC	direct current
RMS	root mean square
FFT	Fast Fourier Transform
AC	alternating current

ferences

Swift, G.W. *Thermoacoustics: A Unifying Perspective for Some Engines and Refrigerators*, 2nd ed.; ASA Press/Springer: Cham, Switzerland, 2017; ISBN 978-3-319-66932-8.

Backhaus, S.; Swift, G.W. A Thermoacoustic-Stirling Heat Engine: Detailed Study. *J. Acoust. Soc. Am.* **2000**, *107*, 3148–3166. [CrossRef] [PubMed]

Farikhah, I.; Ueda, Y. Numerical Calculation of the Performance of a Thermoacoustic System with Engine and Cooler Stacks in a Looped Tube. *Appl. Sci.* **2017**, *7*, 672. [CrossRef]

Rott, N. Damped and Thermally Driven Acoustic Oscillations in Wide and Narrow Tubes. *J. Appl. Math. Phys.* **1969**, *20*, 230–243. [CrossRef]

Ceperley, P.H. A Pistonless Stirling Engine—The Traveling Wave Heat Engine. *J. Acoust. Soc. Am.* **1979**, *66*, 1508–1513. [CrossRef]

Ceperley, P.H. Resonant Travelling Wave Heat Engine. U.S. Patent 4355517, 26 October 1982.

Swift, G.W. Thermoacoustic Engines. *J. Acoust. Soc. Am.* **1988**, *84*, 1145–1180. [CrossRef]

Ward, W.C.; Swift, G.W. Design Environment for Low-Amplitude Thermoacoustic Engines. *J. Acoust. Soc. Am.* **1994**, *95*, 3671–3672. [CrossRef]

Zare, S.; Tavakolpour-Saleh, A.R.; Aghahosseini, A.; Mirshekari, R. Thermoacoustic Stirling Engines: A Review. *Int. J. Green Energy* **2023**, *20*, 89–111. [CrossRef]

Iniesta, C.; Olazagoitia, J.L.; Vinolas, J.; Aranceta, J. Review of Travelling-Wave Thermoacoustic Electric-Generator Technology. *Proc. Inst. Mech. Eng. Part A J. Power Energy* **2018**, *232*, 940–957. [CrossRef]

Chen, G.; Tang, L.; Mace, B.; Yu, Z. Multi-Physics Coupling in Thermoacoustic Devices: A Review. *Renew. Sustain. Energy Rev.* **2021**, *146*, 111170. [CrossRef]

Backhaus, S.; Swift, G. A Thermoacoustic Stirling Heat Engine. *Nature* **1999**, *399*, 335–338. [CrossRef]

Iniesta, C.; Olazagoitia, J.; Vinolas, J.; Gros, J. Assessing the Performance of Design Variations of a Thermoacoustic Stirling Engine Combining Laboratory Tests and Model Results. *Machines* **2022**, *10*, 958. [CrossRef]

Nabavi, M.; Siddiqui, K. A Critical Review on Advanced Velocity Measurement Techniques in Pulsating Flows. *Meas. Sci. Technol.* **2010**, *21*, 042002. [CrossRef]

Clapp, C.W.; Firestone, F.A. The Acoustic Wattmeter, an Instrument for Measuring Sound Energy Flow. *J. Acoust. Soc. Am.* **1941**, *13*, 124–136. [CrossRef]

Seybert, A.F. Two-Sensor Methods for the Measurement of Sound Intensity and Acoustic Properties in Ducts. *J. Acoust. Soc. Am.* **1988**, *83*, 2233–2239. [CrossRef]

Fusco, A.M.; Ward, W.C.; Swift, G.W. Two-Sensor Power Measurements in Lossy Ducts. *J. Acoust. Soc. Am.* **1992**, *91*, 2229–2235. [CrossRef] [PubMed]

Luo, E.C.; Ling, H.; Dai, W.; Yu, G.Y. Experimental Study of the Influence of Different Resonators on Thermoacoustic Conversion Performance of a Thermoacoustic-Stirling Heat Engine. *Ultrasonics* **2006**, *44*, 1507–1509. [CrossRef]

Hamood, A.; Jaworski, A.J.; Mao, X. Development and Assessment of Two-Stage Thermoacoustic Electricity Generator. *Energies* **2019**, *12*, 1790. [CrossRef]

Backhaus, S. *Initial Tests of a Thermoacoustic Space Power Engine*; AIP Publishing: Melville, NY, USA, 2003; pp. 641–647.

Tijani, M.E.H.; Spoelstra, S. A Hot Air Driven Thermoacoustic-Stirling Engine. *Appl. Therm. Eng.* **2013**, *61*, 866–870. [CrossRef]

Yang, P.; Liu, Y.-W. Computation of the Influence of a Phase Adjuster on Thermo-Acoustic Stirling Heat Engine. *J. Power Energy* **2015**, *229*, 73–87. [CrossRef]

Olivier, C.; Penelet, G.; Poignand, G.; Lotton, P. Active Control of Thermoacoustic Amplification in a Thermo-Acousto-Electric Engine. *J. Appl. Phys.* **2014**, *115*, 174905. [CrossRef]

Chen, G.; Tang, L.; Yang, Z.; Tao, K.; Yu, Z. An Electret-Based Thermoacoustic-Electrostatic Power Generator. *Int. J. Energy Res.* **2020**, *44*, 2298–2305. [CrossRef]

Iniesta, C.; Olazagoitia, J.L.; Vinolas, J.; Gros, J. New Method to Analyse and Optimise Thermoacoustic Power Generators for the Recovery of Residual Energy. *Alex. Eng. J.* **2020**, *59*, 3907–3917. [CrossRef]

Chakradeo, A.P.; Anagolkar, S.P.; Shendge, A.B.; Pawar, P.M.; Ganeshkar, J.D. Design, Development and Manufacturing of Thermoacoustic Cooler. *Int. J. Eng. Res. Technol.* **2019**, *8*, 576–582.

Tijani, M.E.H.; Lycklama à Nijeholt, J.A.; Spoelstra, S. Amplifying the Power Density in Thermoacoustic Systems Using a Spring Component. *J. Acoust. Soc. Am.* **2024**, *156*, 202–213. [CrossRef] [PubMed]

Moreno, C.; González, A.; Olazagoitia, J.L.; Vinolas, J. The Acquisition Rate and Soundness of a Low-Cost Data Acquisition System (LC-DAQ) for High Frequency Applications. *Sensors* **2020**, *20*, 524. [CrossRef]

Moreno-Ramírez, C.; Iniesta, C.; González, A.; Olazagoitia, J.L. Development and Characterization of a Low-Cost Sensors System for an Acoustic Test Bench. *Sensors* **2020**, *20*, 6663. [CrossRef]

Iniesta, C.; Vinolas, J.; Prieto, F.; Olazagoitia, J.L.; Soliverdi, L. Experimental Performance Evaluation of a Thermoacoustic Stirling Engine with a Low-Cost Arduino-Based Acquisition System. *Appl. Sci.* **2024**, *14*, 6049. [CrossRef]

31. Callanan, J.; Nouh, M. Optimal Thermoacoustic Energy Extraction via Temporal Phase Control and Traveling Wave Generat *Appl. Energy* **2019**, *241*, 599–612. [CrossRef]
32. Bertuccio, G. On the Physical Origin of the Electro-Mechano-Acoustical Analogy. *J. Acoust. Soc. Am.* **2022**, *151*, 2066–2 [CrossRef]
33. Al-Kayiem, A.; Yu, Z. Using a Side-Branched Volume to Tune the Acoustic Field in a Looped-Tube Travelling-Wave Thermoac tic Engine with a RC Load. *Energy Convers. Manag.* **2017**, *150*, 814–821. [CrossRef]

applied sciences

MDPI

rticle

Effects of Installation Angle on Energy Harvesting Performance of Airfoil-Based Piezoelectric Energy Harvester

ongjiang Tang, Dianliang Li, Yanhong Wei, Enze Li and Zeyu You *

School of Mechanical and Electrical Engineering, Guilin University of Electronic Technology, Guilin 541004, China; tangrongjiang@guet.edu.cn (R.T.)
* Correspondence: youzeyv@163.com

Abstract: This study introduces a novel optimization approach for airfoil-based flutter energy harvesters through installation angle adjustment, addressing a critical research gap in the field where previous studies have primarily focused on structural modifications. To investigate this unexplored avenue, we developed a flutter energy harvester with an adjustable installation angle mechanism, aiming to reduce critical flutter velocity, broaden operational bandwidth, and improve energy harvesting efficiency under low-speed airflow conditions. The performance characteristics of the harvester were comprehensively evaluated through both numerical simulations incorporating fluid–structure-electrical coupling and wind tunnel experiments conducted at four distinct installation angles (0°, 3°, 6°, and 9°). The experimental results demonstrated a significant correlation between installation angle and critical flutter velocity, showing a consistent reduction from 7.8 m/s at 0° to 7.2 m/s at 6°, and further decreasing to 6.3 m/s at 9°. Notably, optimal performance was achieved at a moderate installation angle of 3°, yielding a maximum output voltage of 12.0 V and power output of 0.58 mW, which substantially exceeded the baseline performance at 0° (10.9 V, 0.48 mW). However, further increasing the installation angle to 9° led to performance degradation, attributed to a premature aerodynamic stall, resulting in reduced output metrics of 7.9 V and 0.25 mW for voltage and power, respectively. These findings demonstrate a simple yet effective method for enhancing flutter energy harvesting performance in low-speed airflow conditions.

Keywords: wind-induced vibration; futter; piezoelectric energy harvester; numerical analysis

1. Introduction

Flow-induced vibration (FIV) is a common source of vibration in nature. Since its discovery by von Kármán, this phenomenon—which is widely observed in flow environments—has attracted significant attention from researchers. FIV occurs when periodic vortices are generated as fluid flows past bluff bodies, creating alternating low-pressure regions behind them and resulting in vibrations. Numerous studies have investigated this phenomenon [1–3]. The main forms of FIV include vortex-induced vibration (VIV), galloping, and flutter. Flutter, as a self-excited vibration characterized by large amplitude oscillations [4,5], occurs when the flow velocity surpasses a critical threshold and has been extensively studied due to its significant impact on the stability of aircraft wings and blades [6,7].

In recent decades, driven by the pursuit of clean energy, researchers have investigated utilizing specialized devices to convert the mechanical energy from flow-induced vibrations into electrical energy, thereby exploring novel energy harvesting methods [8–10]. The common methods for converting vibration energy into electrical energy include piezoelectric energy harvesters [11,12], electromagnetic energy harvesters [13,14], electrostatic energy harvesters [15,16], and triboelectric energy harvesters [17,18]. Among these, piezoelectric harvesters have emerged as a prominent research focus due to their simplicity and high-power output [19,20].

Given that flutter possesses substantial energy potential, it has been investigated for possible applications in energy harvesting [21,22]. To understand the mechanisms of flutter-based piezoelectric energy harvester systems, researchers have employed theoretical analyses, experiments, and numerical simulations to explore the impact of various physical parameters on harvester performance. Zhen [23] utilized the lattice method and beam theory to establish a fluid–solid coupling model, examining the influence of the airfoil-based's aspect ratio on harvester performance and validating the findings through experiments. Their results indicated that a wider airfoil-based harvester accelerates the onset of limit cycle oscillations (LCOs). Elahi [24] compared the effects of steady aerodynamics, unsteady formulations, and unsteady-state aerodynamics on computational accuracy, demonstrating that unsteady-state aerodynamics yield the highest accuracy. Tian [25] compared the accuracy of quasi-steady representations, unsteady formulations, and dynamic stall models, concluding that unsteady formulations offer superior accuracy. Furthermore, Tian studied the impact of elastic coefficients on the performance of airfoil-based flutter energy harvester systems, revealing that lower pitch elastic coefficients and moderate plunge elastic coefficients enhance system performance.

To further enhance the performance of airfoil-based piezoelectric energy harvester systems, researchers have explored innovative approaches by incorporating strategic accessories to optimize system performance. Shan et al. [26] developed a novel configuration by integrating a cantilever beam and a cylindrical bluff body into an airfoil-based flutter energy harvester system. The researchers strategically placed a piezoelectric ceramic transducer (PZT) on the cantilever beam to expand the system's operational capabilities. Their proposed design demonstrates remarkable versatility: at velocities below the critical threshold, the cylindrical bluff body effectively induces VIV; while at velocities exceeding the critical point, it triggers limit cycle oscillations (LCOs) in the flutter energy harvester system. This dual functionality significantly improves output power generation during both VIV and LCO conditions. Following this approach, Li et al. [27] developed an innovative piezoelectric energy harvester system featuring a centrally positioned cylindrical bluff body and symmetrically arranged airfoil-based structures. This design effectively achieves a synergistic coupling of VIV and flutter energy harvesting mechanisms, resulting in superior performance compared to individual system configurations. Wang et al. [28] advanced the field by comprehensively investigating airfoil-based flutter energy harvester systems equipped with flaps. Through a multi-methodological approach that included theoretical derivations, computational simulations, and experimental validation, their study revealed an important insight: the implementation of inelastic constraint flaps fundamentally alters the vibration characteristics of the harvester. Specifically, the system transitions from flutter behavior at low velocities to VIV as the velocity increases, thereby reducing the critical flutter velocity. In a related study, Tian et al. [29] conducted a detailed examination of flap installation angles, demonstrating that these angles significantly influence the vortex-shedding dynamics of the airfoil-based harvesters. Their findings confirmed that smaller installation angles consistently enhance system performance, providing valuable design guidance for future energy harvester configurations.

Beyond integrating mechanical accessories, researchers have investigated the incorporation of magnetic forces as an alternative strategy to improve energy harvester efficiency. Iqbal [30] introduced a novel airfoil-based flutter energy harvester system that simultaneously integrates piezoelectric and electromagnetic energy conversion modes.

This innovative approach enables concurrent energy extraction from both structural- and flow-induced vibrations, thus substantially enhancing the system's overall performance potential. Li et al. [31] extended this concept by designing a piezoelectric–electromagnetic hybrid flutter energy harvester. By utilizing a semi-empirical nonlinear aerodynamic model and a magnetic dipole model, they observed that when magnets are positioned in close proximity, an amplitude jump occurs, significantly amplifying the output power of the electromagnetic component near a critical point. Building upon these approaches, Tian et al. [32] conducted a comprehensive investigation of airfoil-based flutter energy harvesting devices, systematically analyzing the effects of various magnet installation distances through theoretical derivations, computational simulations, and experimental methods. Their findings demonstrated the profound impact of a strategic magnet arrangement, showing that an optimized configuration can reduce the critical flutter velocity by up to 80% while achieving an 82.6% increase in output power generation, marking a significant advancement in energy harvester design and performance optimization.

Previous research on airfoil-based flutter piezoelectric energy harvester systems has primarily concentrated on structural design and theoretical foundations, with relatively limited scope. The mounting angle, despite being a crucial parameter in these systems, has received insufficient attention in existing literature. Given that the mounting angle is an essential installation parameter in practical applications, there is a critical need to investigate its effects systematically. To address this research gap, we employ numerical simulation methods to examine the influence of mounting angles on both the vibration dynamics and energy harvesting performance of the airfoil-based flutter piezoelectric energy harvester system. To validate our computational approach, we conduct empirical experiments using a prototype system in a specialized wind tunnel setup. This study aims to comprehensively investigate the impact of mounting angle variations on the system's vibration characteristics and energy harvesting efficiency. Based on established aerodynamic principles for determining wing angle of attack, we systematically selected three mounting angles: 3°, 6°, and 9°, representing a progressive range from small to large angles. A system configuration with a 0° mounting angle serves as the baseline control case. Through this comparative analysis of four distinct configurations of the airfoil-based flutter piezoelectric energy harvester system, we seek to provide a detailed understanding of how mounting angle variations affect system performance.

The manuscript follows a logical and thorough progression of scientific investigation. Section 2 presents an in-depth introduction to the system's structural configuration and the fundamental control equations, establishing the theoretical foundation for subsequent analyses. Section 3 details the numerical simulation methodology, including a comprehensive exposition of the computational approach and a rigorous analysis of the computational outcomes. In Section 4, we present empirical investigations of the vibration response characteristics and output performance of the airfoil-based flutter energy harvester system through systematic wind tunnel experiments. Finally, Section 5 synthesizes the key findings, presents substantive conclusions, and suggests potential future research directions, providing a comprehensive overview of the study's scientific contributions.

2. Airfoil-Based Flutter Energy Harvester System Design and Control Equations

2.1. Conceptual Designing

In airfoil-based flutter piezoelectric energy harvester systems, when the airflow velocity exceeds a critical threshold, aeroelastic coupling induces flutter motion characterized by coupled plunge–pitch oscillations. Based on this fundamental principle and the structural designs reported in [28,29], we designed a novel energy harvesting system, as illustrated in Figure 1. The proposed system consists of several key components: an airfoil-based structure for aerodynamic force capture, a rotating pitch mechanism enabling controlled pitch motion, two fixed brackets for structural support, and dual elastic beams that facilitate plunge motion through their bending deformation. The system's restoration mechanism is achieved through two spring rods connecting the rotating pitch component to the brackets, while energy conversion is accomplished by two PZTs mounted on the elastic beams. The material properties and structural dimensions of all components are listed in Table 1.

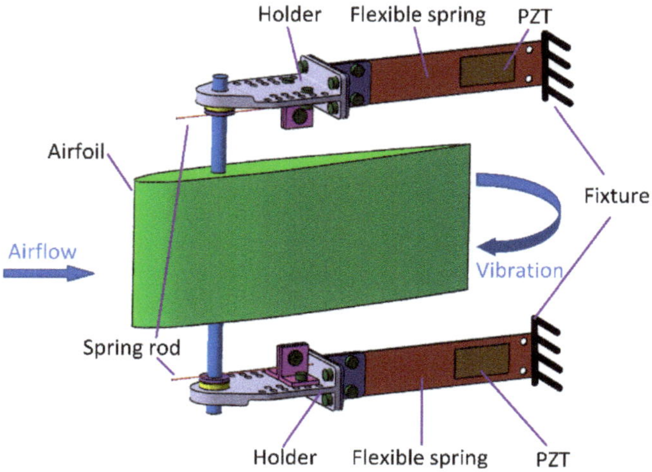

Figure 1. Schematic diagram of airfoil-based flutter piezoelectric energy harvester system.

Table 1. Materials and dimensions parameters of the harvester system.

Parameters	Flexural Spring	Piezoelectric Patch	Holder	Spring Rod
Materials	Spring steel	PZT-5H	Aluminum alloy	Glass fiber
Density (kg/m^3)	7850	7500	2810	2500
Young's modulus (GPa)	210	66	72	73
Poisson's ratio	0.29	0.3	0.33	0.22
Length (mm)	180	40	90	50
Width/Radius (mm)	30	20	60	0.3
Thickness (mm)	0.8	0.2	4	-

The working principle can be described as follows: As the ambient fluid velocity increases, the system experiences growing aerodynamic negative damping effects. When this negative damping overcomes the system's inherent structural damping, the harvester enters a LCO state. During this state, the airfoil-based harvester undergoes sustained plunge–pitch oscillations: the plunge motion is facilitated by the elastic beam deformation, while the pitch motion is regulated by the spring-loaded rotating mechanism. These coupled oscillations induce cyclic strain in the PZTs, effectively converting the mechanical energy of flutter vibrations into electrical energy. This self-sustained oscillation mechanism enables continuous energy harvesting without external mechanical excitation, making it particularly suitable for sustained power generation in fluid flow environments.

2.2. Governing Equations

Figure 2 illustrates a schematic diagram depicting the aerodynamic loads acting on the airfoil-based flutter piezoelectric energy harvester system. The motion model of this system is simplified to a "spring-mass-damping" system for descriptive purposes. The control equations governing the two-degree-of-freedom dive-pitch flutter piezoelectric energy harvester are derived, taking into account the piezoelectric effect. These control equations are formulated as follows [25,32]:

$$\mathrm{m}_T\ddot{h} + S_\alpha\ddot{\alpha} + C_h\dot{h} + (k_{h0} + k_{h2}\mathrm{h}^2)\mathrm{h} + \theta V = L \quad (1)$$

$$S_\alpha\ddot{h} + I_\alpha\ddot{\alpha} + C_\alpha\dot{\alpha} + (\mathrm{k}_{\alpha 0} + \mathrm{k}_{\alpha 2}\alpha^2)\alpha = M \quad (2)$$

$$C_p\dot{V} + \frac{V}{R} - \theta\dot{h} = 0 \quad (3)$$

where L is the longitudinal force, positive in the upward direction, M is the moment, positive in the counterclockwise direction, and h is the sudden displacement, positive in the downward direction; α represents the pitch displacement, positive in the clockwise direction; m_t represents the total mass, including the airfoil-based components, plunge spring, spring rod, and holder; m_f denotes solely the mass of the wing; I_a is the mass moment of inertia about the elastic axis. C_h and C_α are the damping coefficients of the pitch and roll degrees of freedom, respectively; k_{h0} and $\mathrm{k}_{\alpha 0}$ represent the linear structural stiffness coefficients associated with the pitch and roll degrees of freedom, respectively; k_{h2} and $\mathrm{k}_{\alpha 0}$ represent the linear structural stiffness coefficients related to the cubic nonlinear pitch and roll degrees of freedom, respectively; θ is the harvester electromechanical coupling term; R represents the external load resistance connected to the piezoelectric sheet of the collector; V is the output voltage generated by the external resistor; C_p represents the capacitance of the piezoelectric sheet; $S_\alpha = m_f X_a b$ is the mass moment of the airfoil-based body about the rigid center; b represents the half chord of the airfoil-based -based; a denotes the dimensionless offset of the airfoil-based elastic axis measured from the half chord; X_a is the dimensionless distance from the center of gravity to the elastic axis.

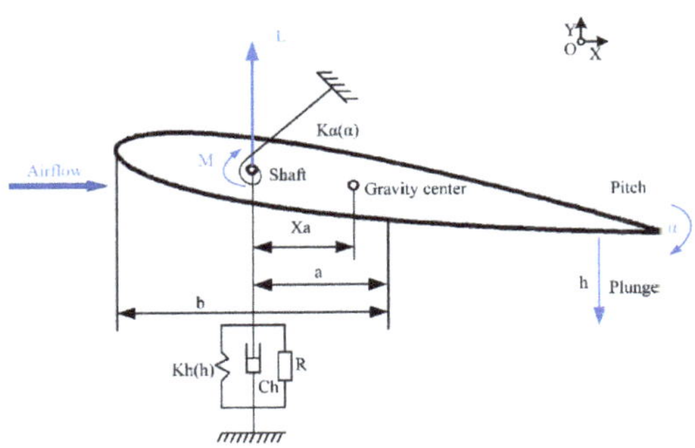

Figure 2. Schematic of a piezoelectric harvester.

Table 2 presents a comprehensive summary of the parameters for the airfoil-based flutter piezoelectric energy harvesting system. These parameters can be classified into four distinct categories: (1) designated design parameters (s, b and R); (2) directly measured parameters (m_t, m_f, a and X_a) obtained using standard measurement instruments; (3) dynamic parameters (k_{h0}, $\mathrm{k}_{\alpha 0}$, C_h, and C_α) determined through free vibration experiments following Chen's methodology [33]; and (4) theoretical parameters (C_p and θ) of the PZT-5H piezoelectric material as provided by the manufacturer.

Table 2. Dimensional parameters of the harvester.

Properties	Value
Span, s (m)	0.1
Total mass, m_t (kg)	0.6
Airfoil-based mass, m_f (kg)	0.18
Semi-chord, b (m)	0.125
Position of the airfoil-based pitch relative to the semi-chord, a	0.5
Offset of airfoil-based gravity center, X_a	0.335
Stiffness coefficient in plunge, k_{h0} (N/m)	240
Stiffness coefficient in pitch, $k_{\alpha 0}$ (0.28 Nm)	0.28
Damping coefficient in plunge, C_h (kg/s)	0.056
Damping coefficient in pitch, C_α (kg/s)	0.056
Resistance, R (KΩ)	250
Capacitance, C_p (F)	0.0000007
electromechanical coefficient of the harvester, θ (N/V)	2.7×10^{-4}

3. Multi-Physical Coupled Fields Simulation Analyses

3.1. Equations for Rigid Body Motion and Solution Methodology

In this study, a dual-degree-of-freedom model is employed to characterize the system's motion. Given that the operational velocity of the system does not exceed 0.1 Mach, air is assumed to behave as an incompressible fluid. The numerical simulations are conducted using ANSYS FLUENT 2020R2. The computer's CPU model utilized for the simulations is the Intel Xeon Silver 4216 with 16 cores (Intel, Santa Clara, CA, USA).

Since flow-induced vibration represents a typical transient problem, it is essential to account for the flow field phenomenon at each moment within a time period. Consequently, the unsteady Navier–Stokes equations are utilized to describe the flow. The control equation is expressed in dimensionless form as follows:

$$\frac{\partial \overline{u_i}}{\partial \overline{x_i}} = 0 \tag{4}$$

$$\rho\frac{\partial \overline{u_i}}{\partial t} + \rho\frac{\partial \overline{u_i u_j}}{\partial t} = -\frac{\partial p}{\partial x_i} + \mu\nabla^2\overline{u_i} - \rho\frac{\overline{u_i' u_j'}}{\partial x_j} \tag{5}$$

where x_i and x_j are the Cartesian coordinates in the i and j directions, $\overline{u_i}$ and $\overline{u_i'}$ are the time-averaged values of the corresponding instantaneous components of velocity and velocity wave term, ρ is the density of the fluid, μ is the dynamic viscosity of the fluid, p is the pressure, and $\rho\overline{u_i' u_j'}$ is the Reynolds stress tensor. To enhance the accuracy of the computational results, we employ the turbulence model proposed by Menter [31,32] to address the issue. This model incorporates a turbulent viscosity limit, which enhances the accuracy of calculations, particularly for backflow scenarios [34,35].

The pressure–velocity coupling in this study is achieved through the Coupled algorithm in FLUENT. This solver employs a fully implicit approach where pressure and velocity fields are solved simultaneously. Compared to the segregated solver, the Coupled algorithm demonstrates superior convergence characteristics and enhanced numerical stability. Although it requires more computational memory per iteration, this approach significantly reduces the total number of iterations needed for convergence, thereby improving overall computational efficiency.

In this paper, FLUENT User Defined Functions (UDFs) are employed to establish mesh motion, while the fourth-order Runge–Kutta method is utilized to solve the motion dynamics of the airfoil-based flutter energy harvester system. This approach enables the computation of linear displacement, linear velocity, angular displacement, and angular velocity of the system at each time step. The solution from the preceding iterative calculation serves as the initial condition for the subsequent step, facilitating mesh updates. The Runge–Kutta algorithm is implemented as follows:

$$y_{n+1} = y_n + \dot{y}\Delta t + \frac{\Delta t^2}{12}(S_1 + 2S_2 + 2S_3 + S_4) \tag{6}$$

$$S_1 = f(x_n, y_n) \tag{7}$$

$$S_2 = f(x_{n+1/2}, y_n + \frac{\Delta t}{2}S_1) \tag{8}$$

$$S_3 = f(x_{n+1/2}, y_n + \frac{\Delta t}{2}S_2) \tag{9}$$

$$S_4 = f(x_{n+1}, y_n + \Delta t S_3) \tag{10}$$

where x_n represents a series of discrete nodes; y_n represents the approximate solution corresponding to x_n.

Since the airfoil-based flutter energy harvester system is 0 at the initial position h, $\dot{h}$, $\dot{\alpha}$, α and V, the initial value problem of the second-order differential Equations (1)–(3) has the following expression

$$\begin{aligned}\ddot{h} = \; & [(L + V\theta)I_\alpha/S_\alpha - (M - C_\alpha\dot{\alpha} - (k_{\alpha 0} + k_{\alpha 2}\alpha^2)\alpha)]/(m_T I_\alpha/S_\alpha - S_\alpha) \\ & -I_\alpha/(m_T I_\alpha - S_\alpha^2)\cdot(C_h\dot{h} + (k_{h0} + k_{h2}h^2)h)\end{aligned} \tag{11}$$

$$\begin{aligned}\ddot{\alpha} = \; & [Mm_T/S_\alpha - (L - C_h\dot{h} - (k_{h0} + k_{h2}h^2)h - \theta V)]/(m_T I_\alpha/S_\alpha - S_\alpha) \\ & -m_T/(m_T I_\alpha - S_\alpha^2)\cdot(C_\alpha\dot{\alpha} + (k_{\alpha 0} + k_{\alpha 2}\alpha^2)\alpha)\end{aligned} \tag{12}$$

$$\dot{V} = -(\dot{h}\cdot\theta) - V/(C_P R) \tag{13}$$

As depicted in Figure 3, the solution process proceeds as follows: (1) initialize the flow field; (2) use UDFs to calculate amplitude, velocity, angular velocity, and angular acceleration; (3) update the dynamic mesh; (4) when the calculation is completed, return to step (2) until the calculation is completed.

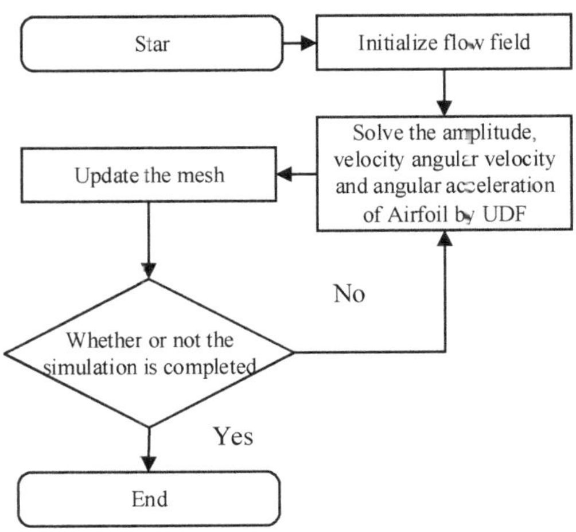

Figure 3. The process of the numerical simulation.

The numerical simulation domain consists of a rectangular region measuring 20b × 12b, as illustrated in Figure 4a. The boundary conditions are configured as follows: velocity inlet at the upstream boundary; pressure outlet at the downstream boundary; symmetric conditions at both upper and lower boundaries; and no-slip wall condition on the airfoil-based surface. To ensure mesh quality and capture flow characteristics accurately, a structured mesh strategy is employed, as shown in Figure 4b. Special attention is paid to the boundary layer region around the airfoil, where mesh refinement is implemented to resolve the near-wall flow physics. To handle the airfoil-based motion and prevent mesh distortion, a dynamic mesh technique is adopted, ensuring that the boundary layer mesh moves synchronously with the airfoil-based surface. The mesh update is performed at each time step according to the displacement calculated through the UDF framework.

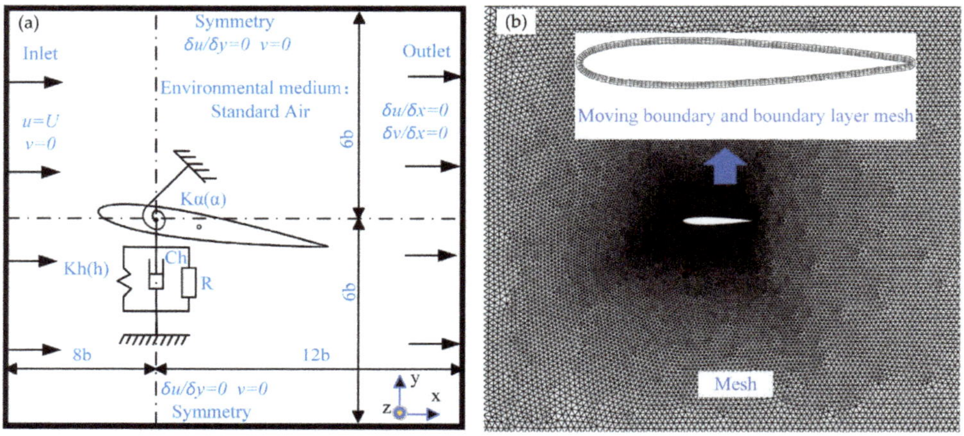

Figure 4. (**a**) Schematic diagram of the physical model; (**b**) meshing diagram of system.

For spatial discretization, the Green–Gauss node-based gradient method available in FLUENT is selected. This approach demonstrates superior accuracy for unstructured meshes, particularly in cases involving triangular elements and significant mesh size variations. The method proves especially effective in handling mesh deformation during boundary motion simulations.

In this study, ICEM CFD is utilized to generate a grid for computations. The grid's Element Quality surpasses 0.4, while the skewness remains below 0.6. To guarantee calculation accuracy and efficiency, we examine grid independence for the airfoil-based flutter energy harvesting system at a mounting angle of 0° under a wind speed of 9 m/s. Three varying grid resolutions are established sequentially, with an increase in the number of grids. The first boundary layer mesh height strictly adheres to the criteria of $y^+ \leq 30$, where the boundary layer mesh growth rate is set at 1.2. The relationship between y^+ and y_H is maintained as follows:

$$y_H = \frac{2y^+\sqrt{0.0288Re^{-0.2}U^2}}{\mu} \tag{14}$$

The calculation outcomes for the root mean square value of the lift coefficient and the root mean square value of the lift coefficient are detailed in Table 3. Analysis of the data reveals that the variance between the values of M2 and M3 is under 1.0%, signifying that the M2 grid has achieved full convergence. Consequently, we adopt the M2 grid strategy for grid construction in this research.

Table 3. Mesh independence validation.

Mesh	Elements	A,rms (m)	Change Rate	Cl,rms	Change Rate
M1	57,344	0.0164	---	0.5445	---
M2	81,097	0.0167	1.80%	0.5594	2.66%
M3	114,689	0.0168	0.63%	0.5628	0.61%

3.2. Aerodynamic Performance

Figure 5 presents a comprehensive analysis of the dynamic characteristics and energy harvesting performance of the airfoil-based piezoelectric flutter energy harvester under various installation angles and wind speeds. The experimental results reveal that the installation angle plays a crucial role in determining the system's performance characteristics. Notably, the critical flutter speed demonstrates a consistent decreasing trend as the installation angle increases from 7.8 m/s at 0° to 7.6 m/s at 3°, further reducing to 7.2 m/s at 6°, and reaching 6.3 m/s at 9°. This systematic reduction in critical flutter speed significantly broadens the effective operating range of the energy harvester.

Figure 5a,b demonstrate the displacement and pitch angle characteristics of the airfoil-based flutter piezoelectric energy harvesting system at various installation angles (0°, 3°, 6°, and 9°). The analysis reveals that at wind speeds below 7.5 m/s, the system installed at 9° exhibits the highest displacement and pitch angle among all configurations; however, these performance parameters progressively decrease as wind speeds exceed 7.5 m/s, with a significant reduction observed beyond 8.5 m/s. The system behavior at the 3° installation angle closely mirrors that of the 0° configuration, particularly in terms of displacement characteristics, while their pitch angles remain similar at wind speeds below 10 m/s, though the 3° configuration demonstrates higher pitch angles at speeds exceeding 10 m/s. Within the specific wind speed range of 7.5–8.5 m/s, the 6° installation angle configuration achieves maximum displacement and pitch angle values; as wind speeds surpass 8.5 m/s, the performance metrics of the 6° configuration converge with those of the 3° setup.

Figure 5c presents the lift characteristics of the airfoil-based flutter piezoelectric energy harvesting system at various installation angles. The results demonstrate that as the installation angle increases, the wind speed required for the system to achieve greater lift decreases. However, as the wind speed continues to increase, the lift obtained by systems with different installation angles tends to converge. This phenomenon, when analyzed in conjunction with Figure 5a, explains why systems with larger installation angles can experience fluttering at lower wind speeds. Figure 5d illustrates the torque characteristics under different installation angles, showing that the torque generated by the system increases proportionally with the installation angle. The analysis reveals that the system with a 9° installation angle generates torque significantly higher than that of the 6° angle configuration, while the torque for the 6° installation angle is substantially higher than those observed at 3° and 0° angles. At wind speeds below 8.5 m/s, the torques generated by systems with 3° and 0° installation angles remain comparable; however, beyond this wind speed threshold, the torque for the 3° angle configuration becomes significantly higher than that of the 0° angle. Analysis of Figure 5b,c reveals that at higher wind speeds, the system with a 9° installation angle, despite generating higher torque, does not achieve larger pitch angles or lift.

Figure 5e,f demonstrate the energy output characteristics of the airfoil-based flutter piezoelectric energy harvesting system at different installation angles under varying wind speeds. At wind speeds below 7.5 m/s, the configuration with a 9° installation angle exhibits superior energy output capacity. However, this configuration's performance significantly deteriorates when wind speeds exceed 8.5 m/s, resulting in the lowest energy output among all tested configurations. The 6° installation angle configuration generates higher energy output compared to the 3° and 0° configurations at wind speeds below 8.5 m/s, but its performance converges with that of the 0° configuration at higher wind speeds. The 3° installation angle configuration shows energy output characteristics comparable to the 0° configuration at wind speeds below 9 m/s; notably, it achieves the highest energy output capacity among all configurations when wind speeds surpass 9 m/s. These experimental results clearly indicate that configurations with smaller installation angles enhance the energy harvesting efficiency of the airfoil-based flutter energy harvesting system under high wind speed conditions.

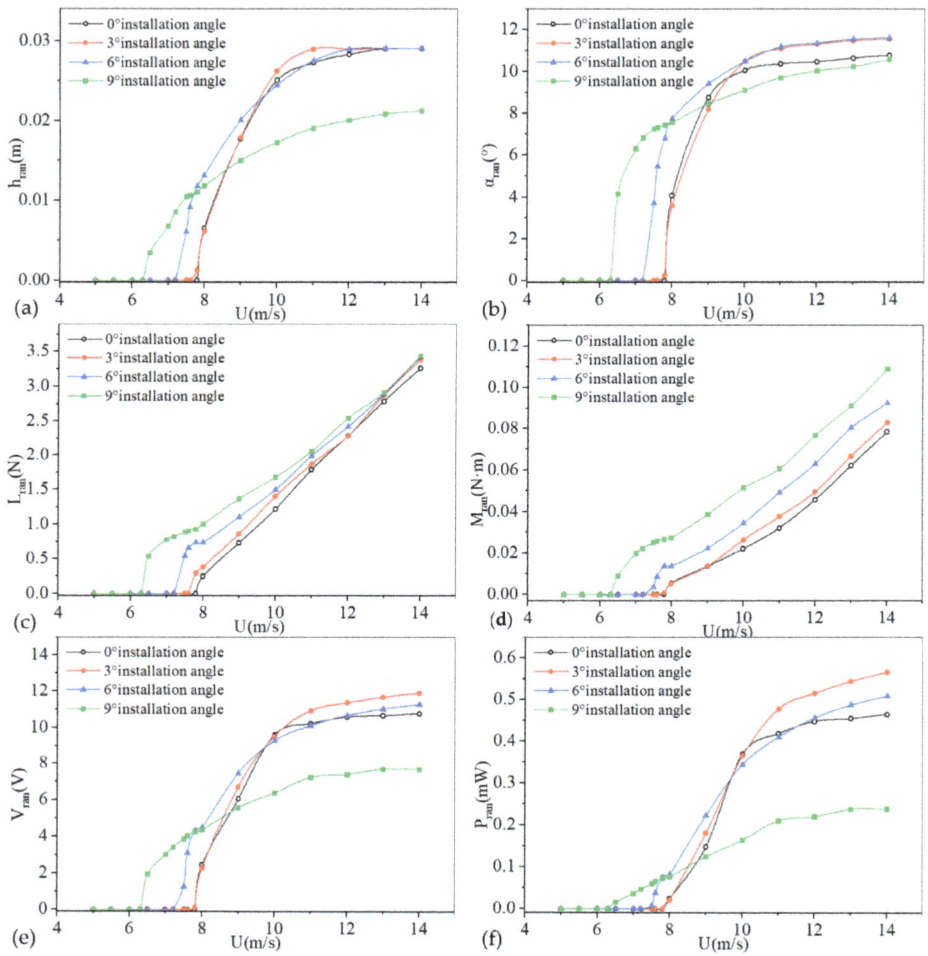

Figure 5. Variation in output characteristics with the installation angle: (**a**) root mean square displacement; (**b**) root pitch angle; (**c**) root mean square output lift; (**d**) root mean square moment; (**e**) root mean square output voltage; (**f**) root mean square output power.

Figure 6 illustrates the phase diagrams and time histories of displacement and pitch angle for the airfoil-based flutter piezoelectric energy harvesting system at 8 m/s wind speed under varying installation angles. The results demonstrate that increasing installation angles leads to a progressive shift in neutral points away from zero for both displacement and pitch angle measurements. Notably, the system exhibits significantly larger displacement and pitch angle amplitudes at 6° and 9° installation angles compared to those at 0° and 3°. At the 3° installation angle, the maximum positive displacement shows an increment of 0.0007 m relative to the 0° configuration, while the maximum negative displacement decreases by 0.0018 m, resulting in a larger overall displacement amplitude at 0° installation angle. Interestingly, at the 9° installation angle, while the displacement magnitude decreases compared to the 6° configuration, the pitch angle demonstrates a larger amplitude. This observation aligns with the trends presented in Figure 5, where the displacement at the 9° installation angle becomes progressively smaller than that at 6° as wind speed increases. This phenomenon can be attributed to stall occurrence at this specific wind speed under a 9° installation angle, effectively limiting the displacement. Stall, characterized by a sudden reduction in lift force despite increasing pitch angle beyond the critical stall angle, fundamentally alters the system's aerodynamic behavior.

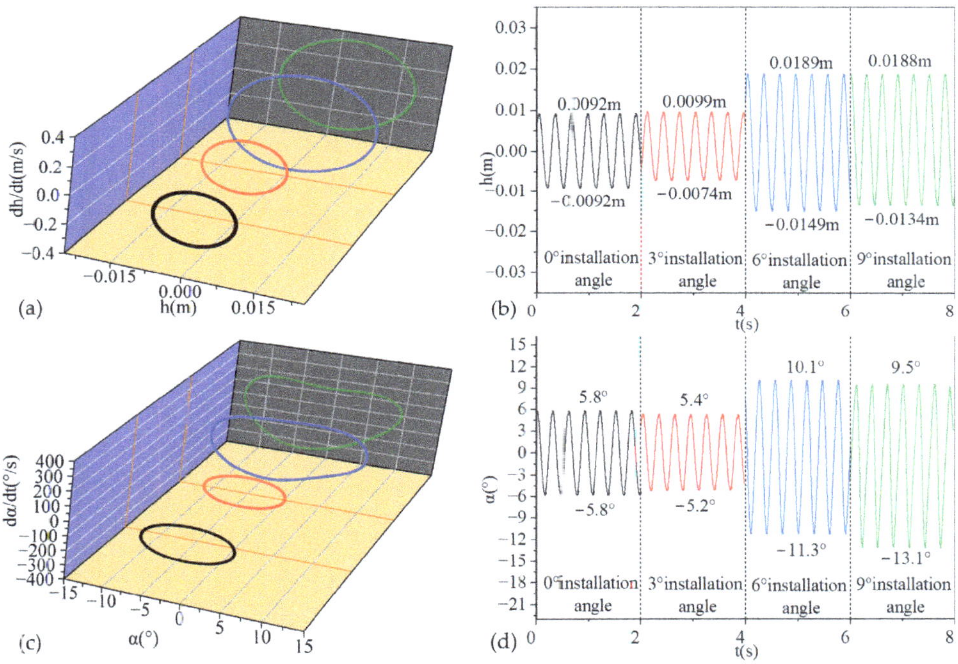

Figure 6. Variation in output characteristics with the installation angle under wind velocity of 8 m/s: (**a**) phase diagram of displacement; (**b**) time history of displacement; (**c**) phase diagram of pitch angle; and (**d**) time history of pitch angle.

Figure 7 illustrates the phase diagrams and time histories of lift and moment magnitudes for the airfoil-based flutter piezoelectric energy harvesting system operating at a wind speed of 8 m/s under varying installation angles. The analysis reveals that the lift and moment magnitudes at the installation angles of 6° and 9° substantially exceed those observed at 0° and 3°. Within each oscillation cycle, the systems with 6° and 9° installation angles demonstrate distinct characteristics, manifesting in sharp fluctuations of both lift and moment. These abrupt variations effectively constrain the pitch angle increment, which explains the observed phenomenon in Figure 5b,d, where despite experiencing larger moments, the systems with 6° and 9° installation angles did not achieve correspondingly higher pitch angles. Furthermore, the system configured at a 9° installation angle exhibits more pronounced moment fluctuations, consequently resulting in a reduced pitch angle compared to the 6° configuration.

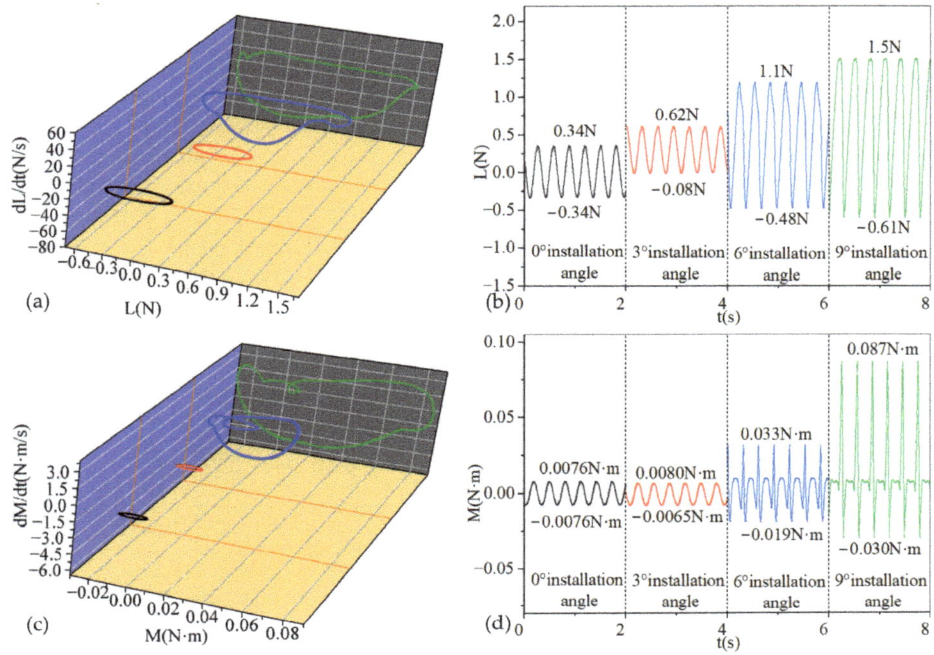

Figure 7. Variation in output characteristics with the installation angle under wind velocity of 8 m/s: (**a**) phase diagram of lift; (**b**) time history of lift; (**c**) phase diagram of moment; and (**d**) time history of moment.

Figure 8 presents the phase diagrams and time histories of the output voltage for the airfoil-based flutter piezoelectric energy harvesting system operating at a wind speed of 8 m/s under different installation angles. The analysis reveals that the output voltage waveforms exhibit predominantly sinusoidal characteristics. Under these operating conditions, the output voltage magnitudes show that the system with a 6° installation angle produces the highest output, followed by the 9°, 0°, and 3° configurations. This voltage magnitude relationship corresponds to the displacement and pitch angle trends observed in Figures 6 and 7.

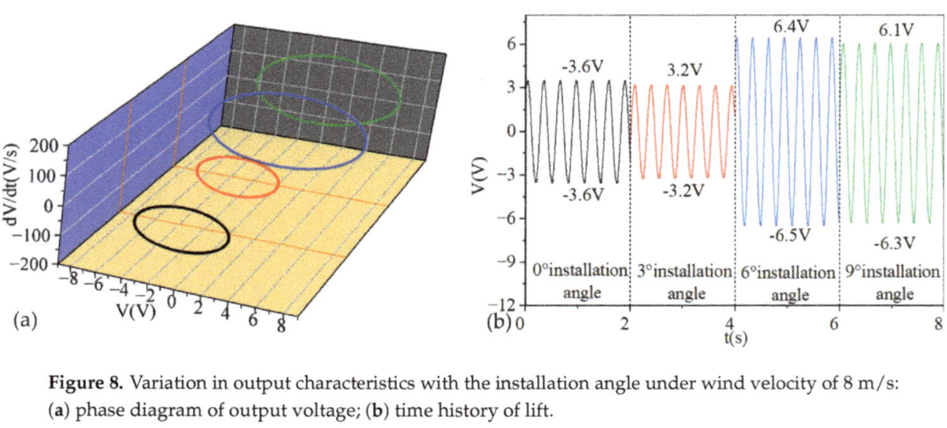

Figure 8. Variation in output characteristics with the installation angle under wind velocity of 8 m/s: (**a**) phase diagram of output voltage; (**b**) time history of lift.

3.3. Visualized Analysis

To further investigate the aerodynamic mechanism and elucidate the phenomena observed in Section 3.2, a comprehensive comparative analysis was conducted on the flow characteristics of the airfoil-based flutter piezoelectric energy harvester system under a constant incoming flow velocity of 8 m/s. Figures 9 and 10 illustrate the pressure distributions and velocity profiles under four mounting angles during one vibration cycle.

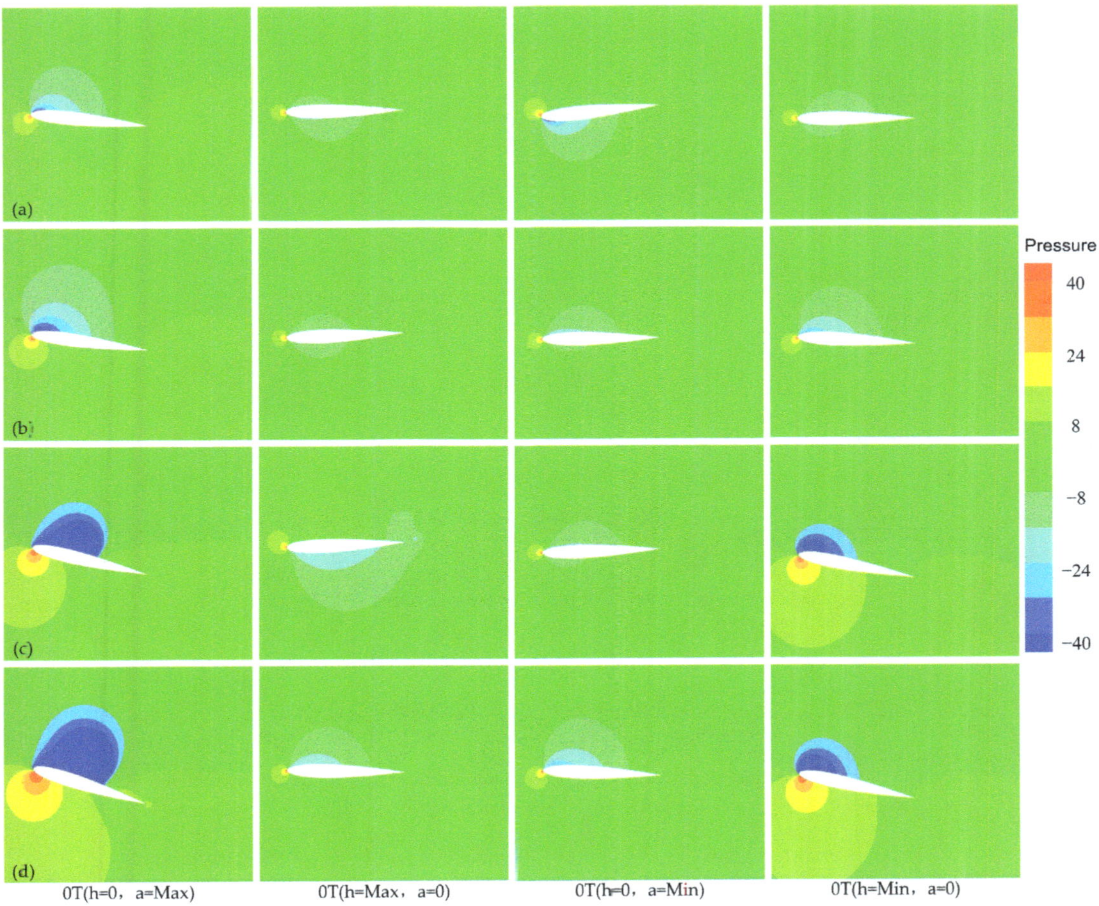

Figure 9. Pressure distribution diagram with the installation angle: (**a**) 0° installation angle; (**b**) 3° installation angle; (**c**) 6° installation angle; (**d**) 9° installation angle.

For the case of the 0° mounting angle (Figures 9a and 10a), the flow field exhibits symmetric characteristics. A low-pressure region coupled with high-velocity flow alternately develops near the leading edge of the upper and lower surfaces at maximum and minimum angles of attack, respectively, corresponding to peak aerodynamic force generation. In contrast, at a 3° mounting angle (Figures 9b and 10b), the flow field demonstrates significant asymmetry, with more pronounced low-pressure regions and higher flow velocities at the maximum angle of attack, while these effects are substantially weakened during the downward motion. This asymmetric behavior aligns with the kinematic data in Figure 6, where the energy harvester achieves an 8.4° maximum angle of attack during upward motion but only 2.2° during downward motion, resulting in predominant energy harvesting during the upward phase.

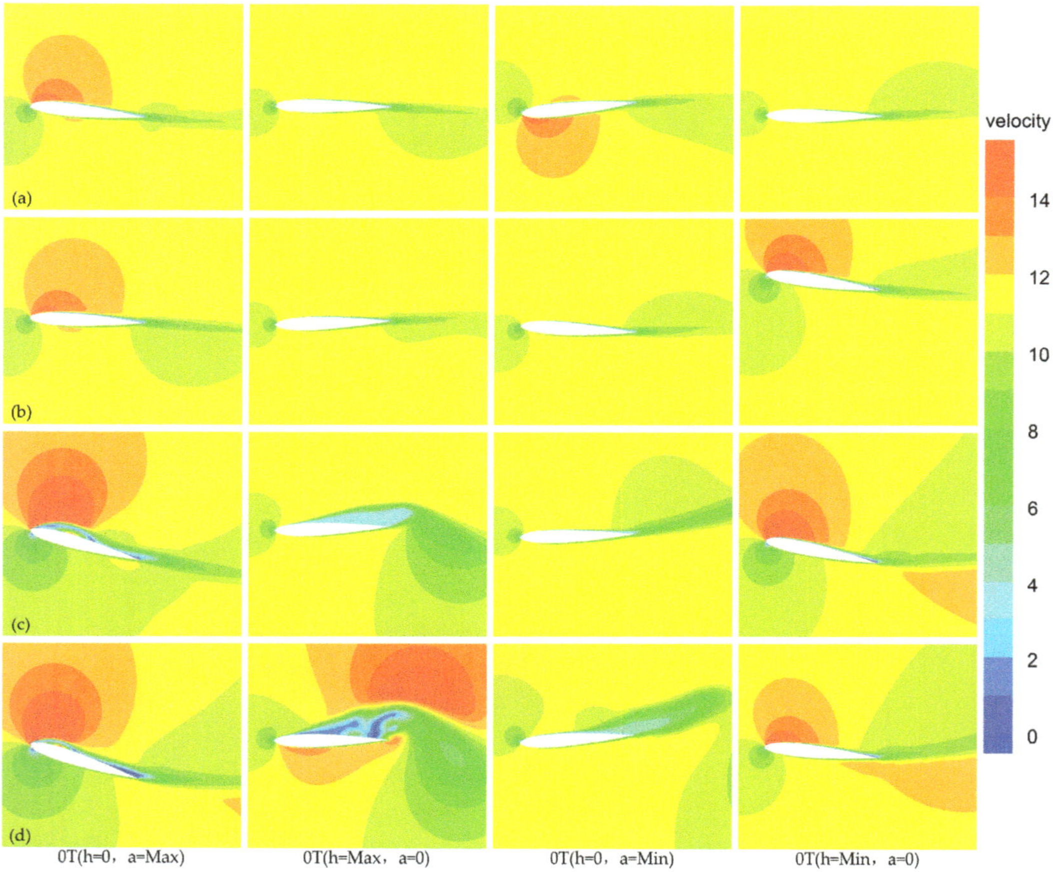

Figure 10. Velocity distribution diagram with the installation angle: (**a**) 0° installation angle; (**b**) 3° installation angle; (**c**) 6° installation angle; (**d**) 9° installation angle.

At higher mounting angles of 6° and 9° (Figure 9c,d and Figure 10c,d), the system experiences a local stall during its motion cycle, with notable flow separation at maximum angle of attack. This phenomenon is particularly severe at a 9° mounting angle, where flow separation persists even as the angle of attack decreases toward 0°, leading to reduced displacement and voltage output capabilities compared to the 6° configuration. However, comparative analysis of Figure 9a–d reveals that increasing mounting angles generate greater lift at 0° angle of attack, providing enhanced excitation for flutter initiation, which explains the observed decrease in critical velocity with increasing mounting angle as shown in Figure 5.

4. Experimental Investigation of Aeroelastic Vibration and Harvesting Performance

4.1. Experimental Setup

The experimental apparatus for the airfoil-based flutter piezoelectric energy harvester systems was constructed in a controlled laboratory environment, as illustrated in Figure 11.

The core component—an energy collection system—was mounted vertically in the test section using a specialized support mechanism to ensure stability and precise positioning.

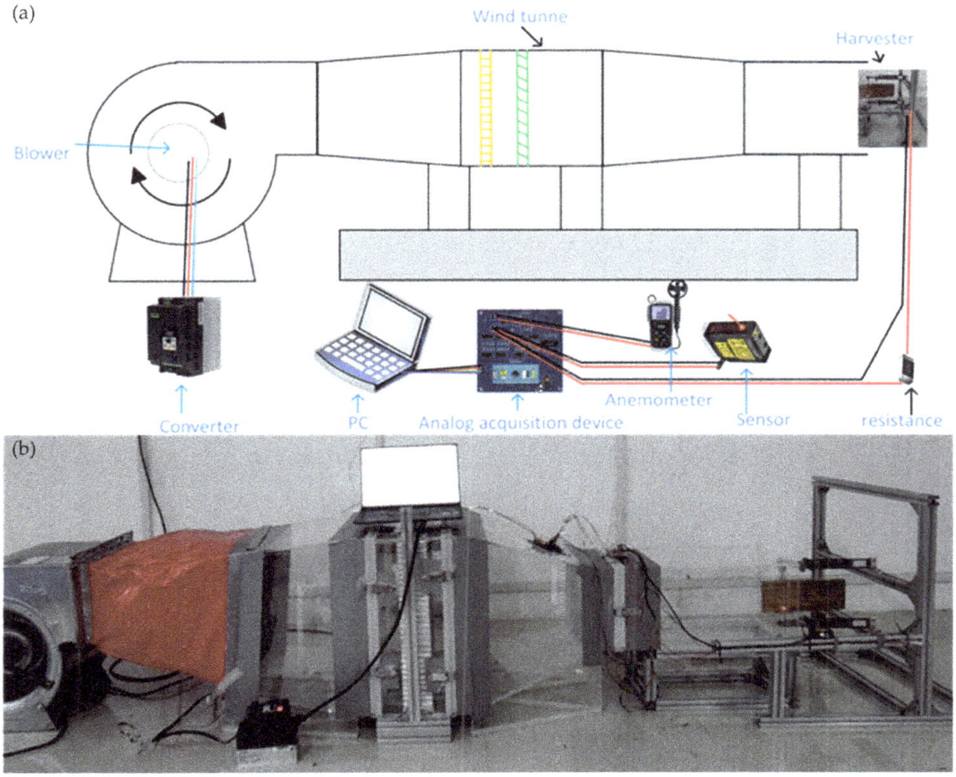

Figure 11. Wind tunnel experimental setup: (**a**) schematic diagram; (**b**) physical device.

The experiments were conducted in an open-circuit wind tunnel facility housed within an enclosed laboratory space. To maintain accurate flow conditions, a calibrated pitot-static tube was installed at the tunnel inlet for continuous velocity monitoring. The experimental configuration was carefully designed to minimize flow interference, with adequate downstream distance between the test section and the laboratory wall to prevent flow recirculation. The energy harvesting system was installed in the test section through the access panel, with precise alignment relative to the freestream flow direction. To ensure reliable results and minimize wall interference effects, the system was designed with a blockage ratio below 5%, and no-slip boundary conditions were implemented on both the tunnel walls and airfoil-based surfaces.

To validate the computational results presented in Section 3, the experimental protocol began with constraining the movable components of the energy harvester. Upon establishing steady-state flow conditions at the designated test velocity, the constraints were systematically removed to allow free oscillation of the system. The measurement apparatus consisted of a high-precision laser displacement sensor with a 0.1 mm resolution for tracking instantaneous motion, coupled with a microcontroller-based data acquisition system providing a 0.00081 V voltage resolution. This integrated system simultaneously recorded both displacement measurements from the laser sensor and voltage output from the piezoelectric sheet, with all experimental data continuously acquired and stored in a digital format for subsequent analysis and comparison with computational results.

4.2. Experimental Validation

To validate the effectiveness of the numerical simulation methodology presented in Section 3, a comprehensive comparison between numerical and experimental results was conducted. Figure 12 presents the comparative analysis at installation angles of 0° and 9°. The results demonstrate excellent agreement between numerical predictions and experimental measurements, as shown in Figure 12a–f. However, some minor discrepancies were observed between the simulated and experimental values.

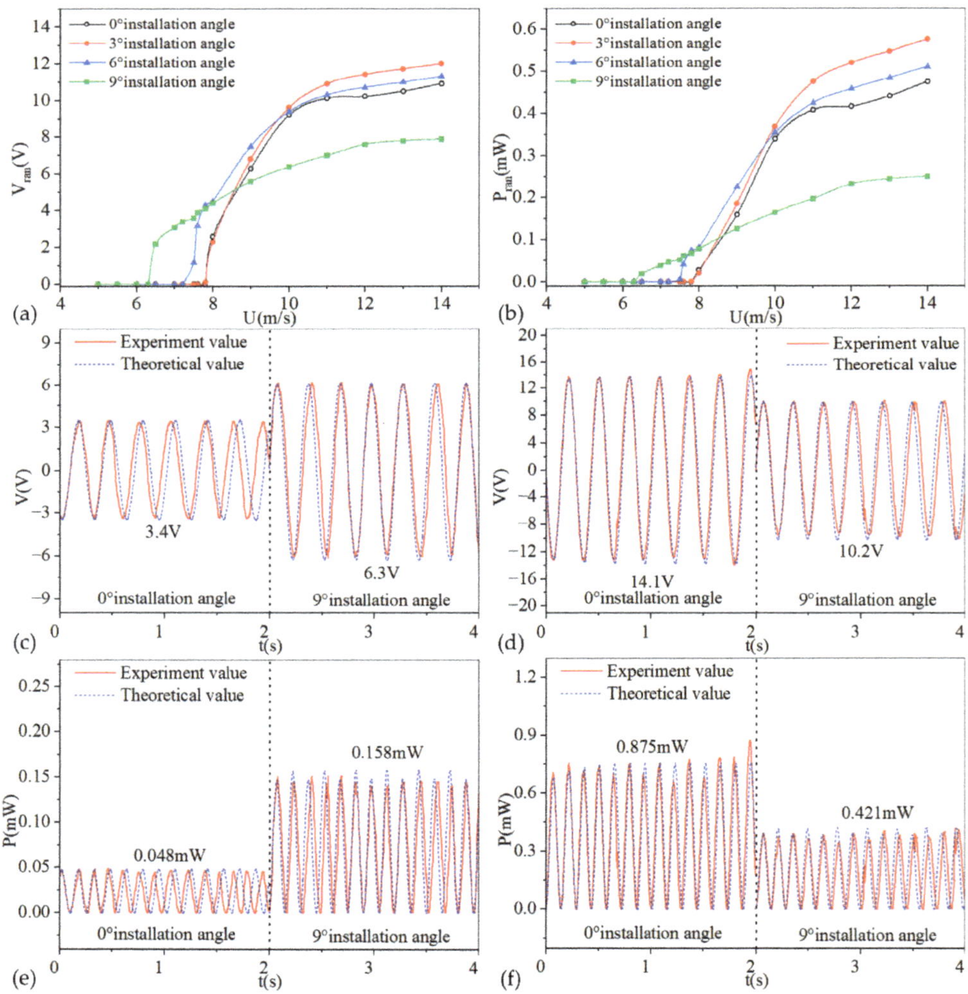

Figure 12. Output performance of the harvester system with and without installation angle obtained theoretically and experimentally: (**a**) output voltage versus airflow velocity; (**b**) output power versus airflow velocity; (**c**) time history of the output voltage at 8 m/s; (**d**) time history of the output voltage at 11 m/s; (**e**) time history of the output power at 8 m/s; (**f**) time history of the output power at 11 m/s.

These differences can be attributed to several factors, primarily the inherent challenges in precisely replicating experimental conditions in numerical simulations, particularly regarding environmental parameters such as airfoil-based geometry and surface roughness characteristics. Furthermore, the flow field exhibits increasingly complex behavior at higher air velocities, characterized by significant deformations and pronounced nonlinear effects. These combined factors account for the slight variations observed in Figure 12a–d. Despite these minor discrepancies, the strong correlation between numerical and experimental results substantiates the reliability and accuracy of our simulation methodology.

4.3. *Aeroelastic Vibration and Harvesting Performance*

The experimental results highlight the substantial influence of the installation angle on the voltage output and overall performance of the airfoil-based flutter piezoelectric energy harvester systems. Figure 13 displays the voltage output and power curves of the airfoil-based energy harvester system as the velocity increases at various installation angles, including 0°, 3°, 6°, and 9°. Observations from the figure reveal that installation angles of 6° and 9° can lower the critical velocity. Specifically, the critical velocity at a 9° installation angle decreases to 6.3 m/s, while at a 6° installation angle, it decreases to 7.2 m/s. However, the 9° installation angle reduces the maximum output voltage and power. In comparison to the maximum output voltage of 10.9 V and maximum output power of 0.48 mW at a 0° installation angle, the maximum output voltage and power at a 9° installation angle decrease to 7.9 V and 2.5 mW, respectively. Conversely, installation angles of 3° and 6° can enhance the maximum output voltage and power. At a 3° installation angle, the system achieves an output voltage of 12.0 V and power of 0.58 mW, while at a 6° installation angle, it reaches an output voltage of 11.3 V and power of 0.51 mW. These results indicate that incorporating a moderate installation angle in the airfoil-based flutter energy harvester system can enhance its overall performance.

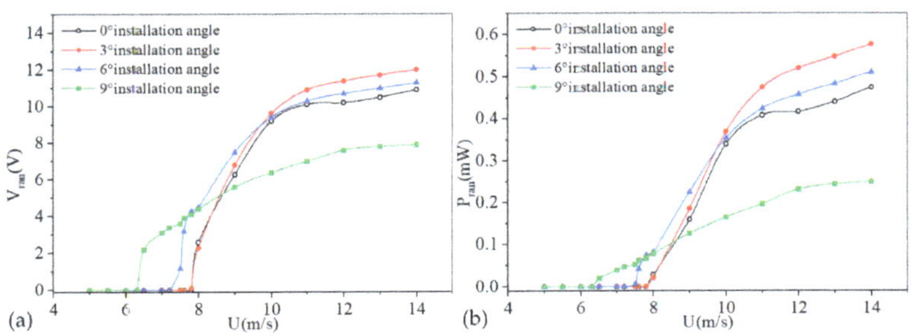

Figure 13. Experimental results of output characteristics changing with installation angle: (**a**) output voltage versus airflow velocity; (**b**) output power versus airflow velocity.

4.4. *Field Harvesting Performance*

To validate the energy harvesting capabilities of the airfoil-based flutter energy harvester system and to pave the way for its practical application, an energy harvesting circuit was meticulously designed, and experiments were conducted. The energy harvesting circuit, as illustrated in Figure 14, consists of a rectifier and a light-emitting diode (LED). The current generated by the airfoil-based flutter energy harvester system is rectified by the rectifier and subsequently utilized to power the LED. In Figure 14b, an experimental image showcases the airfoil-based flutter energy harvester system successfully powering six LED lamps at a velocity of 11 m/s. This demonstration serves as concrete evidence of the feasibility and functionality of the airfoil-based flutter energy harvester system, indicating its potential for practical applications in the future.

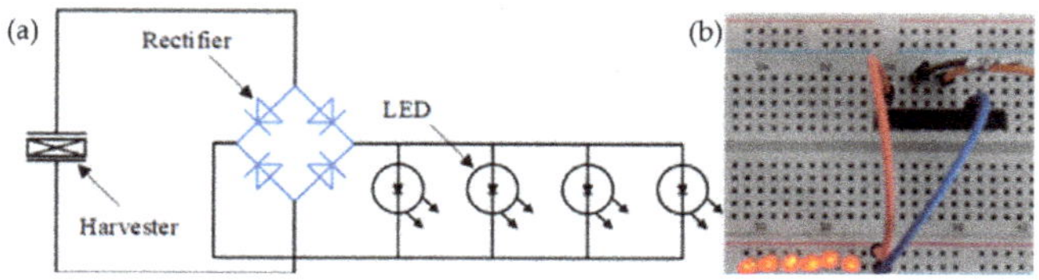

Figure 14. Energy collecting and physical device of powering directly. (**a**) schematic diagram; (**b**) physical device.

5. Conclusions

This study systematically investigates the performance characteristics of airfoil-based flutter piezoelectric energy harvesting systems at the installation angles of 3°, 6°, and 9°, using both numerical calculations and experimental methods. Taking the 0° configuration as the baseline, a detailed analysis is conducted to evaluate the effect of installation angle on system performance. The research, while conducted under controlled conditions, identifies several critical aspects that warrant further investigation for practical applications, including the influence of environmental factors (temperature and humidity) on energy harvesting efficiency, system resilience to disturbances in actual wind fields, and the impact of structural and material fatigue on long-term performance. Although these practical considerations require additional research, this study successfully establishes the fundamental relationship between installation angle and system performance under controlled conditions, providing a solid theoretical foundation for practical implementations. The main conclusions are as follows:

(1) The installation angle is a crucial parameter influencing the critical flutter velocity of the airfoil-based piezoelectric energy harvester system. A clear inverse relationship exists between the installation angle and critical flutter velocity, with the latter decreasing from 7.8 m/s at 0° to 6.3 m/s at 9°. This systematic reduction in critical velocity can be attributed to enhanced initial lift generation at higher installation angles, which facilitates the earlier onset of flutter oscillations.

(2) Moderate installation angles (3° and 6°) yield optimal energy harvesting performance. The system achieves maximum efficiency at a 3° installation angle, producing a peak output voltage of 12.0 V and power output of 0.58 mW, marking a substantial improvement over the baseline configuration at 0° (10.9 V, 0.48 mW). This enhanced performance stems from the development of favorable asymmetric flow field characteristics at moderate angles, enabling more efficient energy extraction from the airflow.

(3) At higher installation angles, particularly at 9°, significant performance degradation occurs. Although this configuration achieves the lowest critical flutter velocity, it exhibits markedly reduced performance metrics (7.9 V voltage, 0.25 mW power). This deterioration is primarily due to the premature aerodynamic stall and persistent flow separation, highlighting a fundamental trade-off between reduced critical flutter velocity and maintained aerodynamic stability.

(4) Installation angle adjustment represents an effective and practical approach to optimizing airfoil-based flutter energy harvesters, particularly in low-speed wind conditions. However, successful implementation necessitates careful consideration of the balance between reducing critical velocity and avoiding stall conditions. The results suggest that optimal performance can be achieved with moderate installation angles around 3° to 6°, providing valuable guidance for practical applications.

Author Contributions: R.T.: Writing—original draft, preparation, methodology, and software. D.L.: Formal analysis and writing—review and editing. Y.W.: Formal analysis and writing—review and editing. E.L.: Formal analysis and writing—review and editing. Z.Y.: Conceptualization and writing—original draft, preparation, Validation, methodology, and software. All authors have read and agreed to the published version of the manuscript.

Funding: This research was funded by the National Natural Science Foundation of China (Grant No. 52165010), and Guangxi Science and Technology Major Project (Grant No. GuiKeAA24206038).

Institutional Review Board Statement: Not applicable.

Informed Consent Statement: Not applicable.

Data Availability Statement: The raw data supporting the conclusions of this article will be made available by the authors on request.

Conflicts of Interest: The authors declare no conflicts of interest.

eferences

Tang, R.; Wang, Q.; Gu, Y.; Wang, J.; You, Z.; Zhao, Y. Numerical study of wake induced vibration(WIV) and energy harvesting characteristics under different stable conditions. *Energy* **2024**, *289*, 129908. [CrossRef]

Wang, J.; Sun, S.; Tang, L.; Hu, G.; Liang, J. On the use of metasurface for Vortex-Induced vibration suppression or energy harvesting. *Energy Convers. Manag.* **2021**, *235*, 113991. [CrossRef]

Gu, Y.; Yurchenko, D.; Wang, J.; Li, S.; Wei, S.; Tang, R. Numerical analysis of reverse wake-induced vibration at low Reynolds number. *Phys. Fluids* **2023**, *35*. [CrossRef]

Tian, H.; Shan, X.; Cao, H.; Xie, T. Enhanced performance of airfoil-based piezoaeroelastic energy harvester: Numerical simu-lation and experimental verification. *Mech. Syst. Signal Process.* **2022**, *162*, 108065. [CrossRef]

Goyaniuk, L.; Poirel, D.; Benaissa, A.; Amari, H. The energy extraction potential from pitch-heave coupled flutter. *J. Sound Vib.* **2023**, *555*, 117714. [CrossRef]

Chai, Y.; Gao, W.; Ankay, B.; Li, F.; Zhang, C. Aeroelastic analysis and flutter control of wings and panels: A review. *Int. J. Mech. Syst. Dyn.* **2021**, *1*, 5–34. [CrossRef]

Yuan, W.; Zhang, X. Numerical Stabilization for Flutter Analysis Procedure. *Aerospace* **2023**, *10*, 302. [CrossRef]

Ma, X.; Zhou, S. A review of flow-induced vibration energy harvesters. *Energy Convers. Manag.* **2023**, *254*, 115223. [CrossRef]

Ma, X.; Li, Z.; Zhang, H.; Zhou, S. Dynamic modeling and analysis of a tristable vortex-induced vibration energy harvester. *Mech. Syst. Signal Process.* **2023**, *187*, 109924. [CrossRef]

Li, J.; Wang, G.; Yang, P.; Wen, Y.; Zhang, L.; Song, R.; Hou, C. An orientation-adaptive electromagnetic energy harvester scavenging for wind-induced vibration. *Energy* **2024**, *286*, 129578. [CrossRef]

Ali, A.; Ali, S.; Shaukat, H.; Khalid, E.; Behram, L.; Rani, H.; Altabey, W.; Kouritem, S.; Noori, M. Advancements in piezoelectric wind energy harvesting: A review. *Results Eng.* **2024**, *21*, 101777. [CrossRef]

Naqvi, A.; Ali, A.; Altabey, W.A.; Kouritem, S.A. Energy harvesting from fluid flow using piezoelectric materials: A review. *Energies* **2022**, *15*, 7424. [CrossRef]

Miao, G.; Fang, S.; Wang, S.; Zhou, S. A low-frequency rotational electromagnetic energy harvester using a magnetic plucking mechanism. *Appl. Energy* **2022**, *305*, 117838. [CrossRef]

Fan, B.; Fang, J.W.; Zhao, J.C.; Li, C.; Wang, J.; Lv, M.M. Bionic flutter wing piezoelectric-electromagnetic composite energy harvesting system. *Energy Convers. Manag.* **2022**, *271*, 116319. [CrossRef]

Chen, Y.; Cheng, Y.; Jie, Y.; Cao, X.; Wang, N.; Wang, Z.L. Energy harvesting and wireless power transmission by a hybridized electromagnetic–triboelectric nanogenerator. *Energy Environ. Sci.* **2019**, *12*, 2678–2684. [CrossRef]

Tcho, I.-W.; Kim, W.-G.; Kim, J.-K.; Kim, D.-W.; Yun, S.-Y.; Son, J.-H.; Choi, Y.-K. A flutter-driven triboelectric nanogenerator for harvesting energy of gentle breezes with a rear-fixed fluttering film. *Nano Energy* **2022**, *98*, 107197. [CrossRef]

Wang, J.; Geng, L.; Ding, L.; Zhu, H.; Yurchenko, D. The state-of-the-art review on energy harvesting from flow-induced vi-brations. *Appl. Energy* **2020**, *267*, 114902. [CrossRef]

Lensvelt, R.; Fey, R.H.; Mestrom, R.M.C.; Nijmeijer, H. Design and numerical analysis of an electrostatic energy harvester with impact for frequency up-conversion. *J. Comput. Nonlinear Dyn.* **2020**, *15*, 051005. [CrossRef]

Sezer, N.; Koç, M. A comprehensive review on the state-of-the-art of piezoelectric energy harvesting. *Nano Energy* **2021**, *80*, 105567. [CrossRef]

20. Sitharthan, R.; Yuvaraj, S.; Padmanabhan, S.; Holm-Nielsen, J.B.; Sujith, M.; Rajesh, M.; Prabaharan, N. Piezoelectric ener harvester converting wind aerodynamic energy into electrical energy for microelectronic application. *IET Renew. Power Ge* **2021**, *15*, 1968–1975. [CrossRef]
21. Li, Z.; Zhou, S.; Yang, Z. Recent progress on flutter-based wind energy harvesting. *Int. J. Mech. Syst. Dyn.* **2022**, *2*, 82– [CrossRef]
22. Li, S.; Chen, Z.; He, X.; Ye, Y.; Wan, S.; Dong, L. High performance hybrid omnidirectional wind energy harvester based on flut for wireless sensing and hydrogen production applications. *Nano Energy* **2024**, *132*, 110403. [CrossRef]
23. Rong, Z.; Cao, B.; Hu, J. Stability analysis on an aeroelastic system for design of a flutter energy harvester. *Aerosp. Sci. Techn* **2017**, *60*, 203–209. [CrossRef]
24. Elahi, H.; Eugeni, M.; Gaudenzi, P. Design and performance evaluation of a piezoelectric aeroelastic energy harvester based the limit cycle oscillation phenomenon. *Acta Astronaut.* **2019**, *157*, 233–240. [CrossRef]
25. Tian, H.; Shan, X.; Cao, H.; Song, R.; Xie, T. A method for investigating aerodynamic load models of piezoaeroelastic ener harvester. *J. Sound Vib.* **2021**, *502*, 116084. [CrossRef]
26. Shan, X.; Tian, H.; Cao, H.; Xie, T. Enhancing performance of a piezoelectric energy harvester system for concurrent flutter a vortex-induced vibration. *Energies* **2020**, *13*, 3101. [CrossRef]
27. Li, X.; Wang, X.; Tian, H.; Wang, C.; Liu, B. Experimental research of symmetrical airfoil-based piezoelectric energy harves excited by vortex-induced flutter coupling. *Appl. Sci.* **2022**, *12*, 12514. [CrossRef]
28. Wan, C.; Tian, H.; Shan, X.; Xie, T. Enhanced performance of airfoil-based piezoelectric energy harvester under coupled flut and vortex-induced vibration. *Int. J. Mech. Sci.* **2023**, *241*, 107979. [CrossRef]
29. Tian, H.; Shan, X.; Wang, H.; Li, X.; Su, Y.; Wang, J. Enhanced piezoelectric energy harvesting performance using trailing-ed flap. *Ocean Eng.* **2023**, *285*, 115443. [CrossRef]
30. Iqbal, M.; Khan, F.U. Hybrid vibration and wind energy harvesting using combined piezoelectric and electromagnetic con-versi for bridge health monitoring applications. *Energy Convers. Manag.* **2018**, *172*, 611–618. [CrossRef]
31. Li, Z.; Zhou, S.; Li, X. A piezoelectric–electromagnetic hybrid flutter-based wind energy harvester: Modeling and nonline analysis. *Int. J. Non-Linear Mech.* **2022**, *144*, 104051. [CrossRef]
32. Tian, H.; Shan, X.; Li, X.; Wang, J. Enhanced airfoil-based flutter piezoelectric energy harvester via coupling magnetic force. *Ap Energy* **2023**, *340*, 120979. [CrossRef]
33. Chen, Z.; Shi, Z.; Chen, S.; Yao, Z. Stall flutter suppression of NACA 0012 airfoil-based based on steady blowing. *J. Fluids Stru* **2022**, *109*, 103472. [CrossRef]
34. Menter, F.R. 2-EQUATION eddy-viscosity turbulence models for engineering applications. *AIAA J.* **1994**, *32*, 1598–1605. [CrossR
35. Menter, F.R. A comparison of some recent eddy-viscosity turbulence models. *J. Fluids Eng.* **1996**, *118*, 514–519. [CrossRef]

applied sciences

MDPI

rticle

Optimization of the Geometric Characteristics of Damping Layers for Acoustic Black Hole Beams Based on the Backpropagation Algorithm

ijun Ouyang, Jiahao Zhang and Bin Zhen *

School of Environment and Architecture, University of Shanghai for Science and Technology, Shanghai 200093, China; ouyang@usst.edu.cn (L.O.); 223382086@st.usst.edu.cn (J.Z.)
* Correspondence: zhenbinshea@usst.edu.cn

Abstract: In real-world scenarios, it is common to apply a damping layer of a specific thickness to the surface of an acoustic black hole (ABH) beam to boost its energy dissipation capacity. However, it has become apparent that excessive damping layers might result in negative consequences. The present study suggests employing the backpropagation (BP) algorithm to refine the positioning, thickness, and contour of the damping layer for optimal results. This study begins with the derivation of a semi-analytical solution for the vibration characteristics of an ABH beam under a harmonic load using the Gaussian expansion method (GEM). This process results in the preliminary identification of a thickness profile for the damping layer that exhibits significant potential for energy dissipation. Subsequently, a BP neural network is trained on the data produced by the semi-analytical solution to further optimize this thickness variation function. The findings reveal that the geometry of the damping layer has a more complex influence on performance than previously recognized. The optimization guided by the BP neural network suggests that achieving a strong ABH effect does not require uniform application of the damping layer across the entire ABH section. Rather, the most effective approach is to concentrate the damping layer thickness at the ABH tip, with a rapid decrease in thickness as one moves away from this point. It is also determined that applying a damping layer in areas far from the tip is unnecessary. Additionally, an innovative strategy is proposed to enhance the system's energy dissipation capabilities without changing the truncation thickness of the ABH beam. This research contributes to a deeper understanding of how the damping layer affects the energy dissipation performance of ABH beams.

Keywords: ABH beam; damping layers; BP algorithm; optimization; Gaussian expansion method

1. Introduction

Acoustic black holes (ABHs) are a unique type of acoustic structure, defined by a continuous reduction in material thickness along the length of the structure, following a power-law distribution. This design leads to a gradual slowing down of the phase velocity of waves as they move towards the end of the ABH. In theory, when the thickness reaches zero, the wave velocity should drop to zero as well, preventing the waves from spreading further and achieving nearly perfect sound isolation [1–3]. The applications of ABHs are broad, including reducing mechanical vibrations, enhancing the efficiency of acoustic devices, and serving as energy conversion devices that convert kinetic energy into electrical energy [4–9].

While ABHs are lauded for their exceptional theoretical capabilities, the challenge of crafting a perfect ABH for real-world applications is fraught with difficulties. These challenges stem from not just the constraints of manufacturing accuracy and the inherent properties of materials, but also from the requirement to preserve a certain level of truncation thickness, which can negatively impact the system's efficiency. Two main strategies have been recognized for using ABHs to reduce vibrations and noise. The first strategy involves altering the geometric design of a critical structural component, such as a beam [10–12], plate [13–15], rotating disk [16], or shell [17], to create a segment that can accommodate an ABH. Although integrating ABHs can lead to weight reduction, implementing this approach in practical settings is complicated by the potential compromise to the structural strength. To successfully integrate ABH technology into practical scenarios, it is crucial to develop practical strategies that address current limitations. An alternative and promising approach is to incorporate an ABH layer on the outside of the main structure, rather than integrating it internally. This idea eliminates the need to change the thickness of the main structure, thus minimizing any risks to its structural integrity. The resulting hybrid structure exhibits enhanced vibration damping capabilities, which can significantly improve its operational performance [18–21]. However, the additional ABHs discussed above are typically considered as separate or multiple absorbers, without considering their potential for periodic arrangement. In reality, the periodic arrangement of additional ABHs offers the unique advantage of activating both localized resonance and Bragg scattering bandgaps simultaneously. Furthermore, their strong damping characteristics lead to a substantial reduction in vibrations across the passbands [22–24]. Given the intricate composite structure found in additional ABHs, the existing literature suggests that the finite element method (FEM), when combined with experimental studies, is virtually the sole technique that has been utilized. In fact, studying individual ABH units within periodic structures is very helpful for enhancing the overall damping characteristics and is still worth further investigation.

To address the challenge of truncation, studies have indicated that the application of a thin layer of viscoelastic damping material to the ABH region is crucial for energy extraction from the system [3], as supported by further research [25–27]. Recent investigations have revealed that the incorporation of damping layers can significantly enhance the acoustic emission efficiency of an ABH panel, primarily due to the additional rigidity these layers offer [28]. The inclusion of damping layers is essential for achieving the optimal ABH effect, which can operate independently [29] or in tandem with other constraints [30]. However, excessive use of damping layers has been identified as potentially detrimental. For example, the addition of a coating layer could introduce excessive stiffness to the underlying structure, thereby altering the expected ABH effect [31]. The influence of added mass is particularly relevant when the damping layer thickness is substantial compared to the ABH wedge's thickness near the tip area. Furthermore, applying a coating to the central part of an indentation in a less-than-ideal ABH plate, designed for a specific ABH thickness profile, could lead to an increase in the minimum thickness, thereby disrupting the intended energy concentration. By using laser-induced excitation combined with wave analysis techniques, the optimal damping layer thickness that minimizes wave reflections was determined experimentally [32]. It was found that an excessive amount of coating could counteract or even damage the intended energy focusing due to the dynamic disturbances it induces within the host structure, leading to a decrease in energy dispersion efficiency. These findings underscore the significance of a deliberate and strategic design approach for the placement of damping layers, which is vital for maintaining a balance between the opposing yet interconnected effects of the layers: enhancing damping on one hand, and increasing wave reflection on the other.

Investigations have demonstrated that the effectiveness of damping layers in dissipating energy is significantly influenced by their geometric properties, material characteristics, and placement [33,34]. To attain a more accurate representation of practical scenarios, it is imperative to account for the intricate interplay between the damping layer and the wedge with a power-law profile. The Ross–Unar–Kerwin (RUK) model [35] is commonly utilized to evaluate the impact of thin damping layers, assuming that their thickness is considerably less than that of the wedge. However, in real-world applications, even the thinnest damping layer's thickness might be similar to the wedge's tip. A significant concern is the increasing relevance of the added mass effect, which has been recognized in previous studies for layers with uniform thickness [36]. Enhancing the performance of a damping layer might require precise adjustments to its positioning and setup. This necessitates a more flexible methodology to address the layer's additional mass and stiffness implications. In [29], a semi-analytical technique was devised to examine the impact of varying the thickness of damping layers with constant mass on the system's damping loss factor across different linear distributions. The research indicated that altering the thickness of damping layers could offer a distinct avenue for optimizing energy dissipation efficiency. However, there remains a void in the field as comprehensive studies on this topic and the creation of critical optimization tools have not been adequately addressed.

The present study zeroes in on an individual ABH element and utilizes a backpropagation (BP) neural network for an in-depth examination of the effects exerted by damping layers. Renowned in artificial intelligence circles, the BP algorithm boasts exceptional error tolerance, formidable learning capabilities, and steadfast performance. It stands out in managing intricate nonlinear dynamics, showcasing its adaptability and applicability across diverse scenarios [37,38]. The investigation commences with the construction of a mathematical model for a symmetric ABH beam, leveraging Lagrangian mechanics. Subsequently, a semi-analytical solution is derived through the Gaussian expansion method (GEM) [17], validated by aligning it with FEM outcomes. A function is introduced to delineate the thickness gradient of damping layers. Following this, a BP neural network, informed by the semi-analytical solution data, is tasked with refining the damping layers' positioning, thickness, and geometry. The findings indicate that the damping layer's geometry has a more intricate impact than previously acknowledged. The BP algorithm emerges as a potent instrument for amplifying the performance analysis of ABH structures amidst a multitude of variables. In addition, an innovative strategy has been put forward to augment the system's energy dissipation capabilities without changing the ABH beam's truncation thickness.

The structure of the remainder of this paper is as follows: Section 2 provides a detailed account of the establishment and analytical solution of the governing equation for a symmetric ABH beam. Subsequently, Section 3 examines the impact of damping layer parameters on the energy dissipation efficiency of the ABH beam, determining the expression form of the thickness function with higher energy dissipation efficiency by comparing the energy consumption effects of various damping layer thickness functions. Based on this expression form, Section 4 outlines the deployment and training procedures of the BP neural network model, presents the expression form of the optimal damping layer thickness function, and verifies it through numerical results. In Section 5, the BP algorithm is applied to optimize the analysis of the thickness function of the damping layer for an altered symmetric ABH beam, suggesting an innovative method to boost the system's energy dissipation efficiency without modifying the truncation thickness of the ABH beam. In the last section, the pivotal conclusions drawn from this research are synthesized.

2. A Mathematical Framework and Its Corresponding Solution for a Symmetric ABH Beam

Referencing Figure 1, we examine a symmetric Euler–Bernoulli beam that experiences bending oscillations due to a localized force F_t applied at position $x = x_f$. The beam's structure includes a segment with a uniform thickness h_b extending between $[0, x_{b1}]$ and $[x_{b3}, x_{b4}]$, as well as a section with an ABH profile that features a thickness varying according to a power law from x_{b1} to x_{b3}, i.e.,

$$h(x) = \epsilon(x - x_{b2})^m + h_0, \quad x \in [x_{b1}, x_{b3}] \tag{1}$$

where h_0 is the thickness of the ABH structure at the location $x = x_{b2}$, ϵ and m represent the slope and the ABH order, respectively. Both the lines $x = x_{b2}$ and $z = 0$ are axes of symmetry for the structure in Figure 1. To enhance the wave trapping capability of the structure, damping material is affixed to both sides of the beam within the coordinates $[x_{d1}, x_{d4}]$, with a thickness designated as $h_d(x)$. The beam's edges are secured by a rotational spring with stiffness K_1 and a translational spring with stiffness K_2, and a variety of distinct boundary conditions are emulated by varying the values assigned to K_1 and K_2. The structure presented in Figure 1 usually is considered as a unit cell in a periodic ABH beam. Considering the inherent damping dissipation of the beam and the additional damping material, the complex modulus of elasticity can be articulated as follows:

$$E_{b,d} = E(1 + i\eta_{b,d}), \tag{2}$$

where $\eta_{b,d}$ are the damping factors of the beam and the damping layers, respectively.

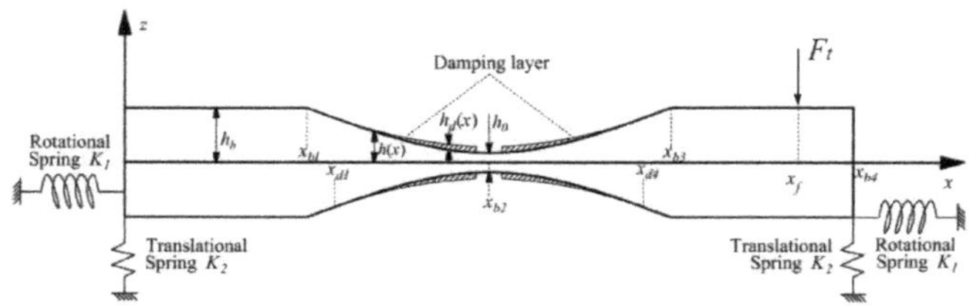

Figure 1. The diagrammatic representation of a symmetric ABH beam.

2.1. The Governing Equation

In this context, the displacement vector of the beam represents the movement along the x-axis and z-axis at every point along the beam, including the damping layer. It should be noted that the assumption presupposes an ideal adhesion between the damping layer and the primary beam, which is crucial for maintaining displacement continuity. $w(x, t)$ denotes the flexural displacement of any point on the beam in relation to time t. According to Euler–Bernoulli beam theory, the displacement field of the beam can be expressed as follows:

$$[-z\frac{\partial w}{\partial x}, w]. \tag{3}$$

Assume that $w(x, t)$ can be expanded as

$$w = \sum_k^n a_k(t)\varphi_k(x) = \mathbf{a}^T\boldsymbol{\varphi}, \tag{4}$$

where $\boldsymbol{a}$ is a series of time-dependent coefficients to be determined and $\boldsymbol{\varphi}$ the admissible shape functions

$$\begin{aligned} \boldsymbol{a(t)} &= [a_1(t), a_2(t), \cdots, a_n(t)]^T, \\ \boldsymbol{\varphi(x)} &= [\varphi_1(x), \varphi_2(x), \cdots, \varphi_n(x)]^T. \end{aligned} \tag{5}$$

From classical Lagrange theory, the Lagrange quantity L for the system depicted in Figure 1 is given by

$$L = E_k - E_s + W. \tag{6}$$

where E_k and E_s are the kinetic energy and potential energy of the structure, respectively, and W is the work done on the ABH structure by external forces F_t,

$$E_k = \frac{1}{2} \int \rho_b \left(\frac{\partial w}{\partial t} \right)^2 dV, \tag{7}$$

$$E_s = \frac{1}{2} \int E_b I \left(\frac{\partial^2 w}{\partial x^2} \right)^2 dx + E_e, \tag{8}$$

$$E_e = \frac{1}{2} K_1 [\left(\frac{\partial w(x_{b4}, t)}{\partial x} \right)^2 + \left(\frac{\partial w(0, t)}{\partial x} \right)^2] - \frac{1}{2} K_2 [w^2(x_{b4}, t) + w^2(0, t)], \tag{9}$$

$$W = F_t w(x_f, t). \tag{10}$$

where E_e is the potential energy generated by the four springs at the boundary of the ABH beam, and ρ_b and $E_b I$ are the density and the flexural rigidity of the beam, respectively. The integration process in Equations (7) and (8) must encompass both the beam and its associated damping layers. From [29], the damping layers are assumed to be fully integrated with the beam and are conceptualized as integral components of the system, characterized by their inherent material attributes, namely, the modulus of elasticity E_d and the density ρ_d. Substituting Equations (4)–(10) into the Lagrange equation

$$\frac{d}{dt} \left[\frac{\partial L}{\partial \dot{\boldsymbol{a}}(t)} \right] - \left[\frac{\partial L}{\partial \boldsymbol{a}(t)} \right] = 0, \tag{11}$$

one can obtain the following governing equations of the ABH beam in matrix form:

$$\boldsymbol{M} \ddot{\boldsymbol{a}}(t) + \boldsymbol{K} \boldsymbol{a}(t) = \boldsymbol{f}(t), \tag{12}$$

where $\boldsymbol{M}$ and $\boldsymbol{K}$ stand for the mass and stiffness matrices, $\boldsymbol{f}(t) = F_t \boldsymbol{\varphi}(x_f)$ for the external force vector, and $\boldsymbol{a}(t)$ for the response vector, as defined in Equation (5). The matrix $\boldsymbol{M}$ can be broken down into three components that correspond to the uniformity ($\boldsymbol{M}_{uni}$), the ABH elements of the beam ($\boldsymbol{M}_{ABH}$), and the damping layers ($\boldsymbol{M}_d$), while the matrix $\boldsymbol{K}$ can be dissected into four distinct segments, each associated with the aforementioned trio of components ($\boldsymbol{K}_{uni}, \boldsymbol{K}_{ABH}, \boldsymbol{K}_d$) as well as the springs ($\boldsymbol{K}_e$). The expressions of matrices $\boldsymbol{M}$ and $\boldsymbol{K}$ are given below:

$$\begin{aligned} \boldsymbol{M} &= \int \rho_b A(x) \boldsymbol{\varphi} \boldsymbol{\varphi}^T dx = \boldsymbol{M}_{uni} + \boldsymbol{M}_{ABH} + \boldsymbol{M}_d \\ &= 2[\int_0^{x_{b1}} \rho_b h_b(x) \boldsymbol{\varphi} \boldsymbol{\varphi}^T dx + \int_{x_{b1}}^{x_{b2}} \rho_b h(x) \boldsymbol{\varphi} \boldsymbol{\varphi}^T dx + \int_{x_{d1}}^{x_{d2}} \rho_d h_d(x) \boldsymbol{\varphi} \boldsymbol{\varphi}^T dx] \end{aligned} \tag{13}$$

$$\begin{aligned}
\boldsymbol{K} &= \int E_b I(x)\left(\frac{d^2\boldsymbol{\varphi}}{dx^2}\right)\left(\frac{d^2\boldsymbol{\varphi}}{dx^2}\right)^T dx + \boldsymbol{K_e} = \boldsymbol{K_{uni}} + \boldsymbol{K_{ABH}} + \boldsymbol{K_d} + \boldsymbol{K_e} \\
&= \frac{2}{3}\left[\int_0^{x_{b1}} E_b\, h_b^3(x)\left(\frac{d^2\boldsymbol{\varphi}}{dx^2}\right)\left(\frac{d^2\boldsymbol{\varphi}}{dx^2}\right)^T dx + \int_{x_{b1}}^{x_{b2}} E_b\, h_b^3(x)\left(\frac{d^2\boldsymbol{\varphi}}{dx^2}\right)\left(\frac{d^2\boldsymbol{\varphi}}{dx^2}\right)^T dx\right] \\
&+ \frac{2}{3}\int_{x_{d1}}^{x_{d2}} E_d[h_d^3(x) + 3h_d^2(x)h(x) + 3h_d(x)h^2(x) + h^3(x)]\left(\frac{d^2\boldsymbol{\varphi}}{dx^2}\right)\left(\frac{d^2\boldsymbol{\varphi}}{dx^2}\right)^T dx \\
&+ K_1\left(\frac{d^2\boldsymbol{\varphi}(\boldsymbol{0})}{dx^2}\right)\left(\frac{d^2\boldsymbol{\varphi}(\boldsymbol{0})}{dx^2}\right)^T + K_2\boldsymbol{\varphi}(\boldsymbol{0})\boldsymbol{\varphi}(\boldsymbol{0})^T + K_1\left(\frac{d\boldsymbol{\varphi}(\boldsymbol{x_{b4}})}{dx}\right)\left(\frac{d\boldsymbol{\varphi}(\boldsymbol{x_{b4}})}{dx}\right)^T \\
&+ K_2\boldsymbol{\varphi}(\boldsymbol{x_{b4}})\boldsymbol{\varphi}(\boldsymbol{x_{b4}})^T
\end{aligned} \tag{14}$$

2.2. The Solution of the Model Using the GEM

Given that the ABH beam is subjected to a harmonic external excitation with the circle frequency ω, it follows that the structure's steady-state response will also be harmonic. These can be mathematically represented as

$$\boldsymbol{f(t)} = \boldsymbol{F}e^{i\omega t}, \quad \boldsymbol{F} = F_t \cdot [\varphi_1(x_f), \cdots, \varphi_n(x_f)], \tag{15}$$

$$\boldsymbol{a(t)} = \boldsymbol{A}e^{i\omega t}, \quad \boldsymbol{A} = [a_1, a_2, \cdots, a_n], \tag{16}$$

where $\boldsymbol{F}$ represents the amplitude vector of the external force and $\boldsymbol{A}$ the amplitude vector of the response. Substituting Equations (15) and (16) into Equation (12) yields

$$[\boldsymbol{K} - \omega^2\boldsymbol{M}]\boldsymbol{A} = \boldsymbol{F}. \tag{17}$$

When there is no external force applied, it translates into a generalized eigenvalue problem characterized by the presence of damped angular eigenfrequencies

$$\omega_d^2 = \omega_n^2(1 + i\eta) \tag{18}$$

where ω_n is the natural frequency of the system and η denotes the modal loss factor, derived from the modal strain energy method (MSEM) [39], which employs a complex Young's modulus, as detailed in Equation (2). The modal loss factor is the ratio of energy dissipated per cycle to the maximum energy stored within a cycle. It represents the viscoelastic properties of a material; a higher loss factor indicates greater viscosity, while a lower loss factor indicates greater elasticity. The modal loss factor plays a crucial role in evaluating how a structure dissipates energy when subjected to dynamic forces. It is especially valuable for determining the energy absorption capacity of damping layers due to the ABH effect.

The key to solving Equation (17) is to determine the shape functions in Equations (4) and (5). Research presented in [17,21,29] indicates that employing power series and polynomial expansions for shape functions may result in matrix singularities and poorly conditioned problems, thereby potentially reducing the solution's accuracy. This is particularly relevant in the context of the ABH beam, where there are significant variations in wave numbers and wave velocities at the beam's ends. The Gaussian function is proposed as the shape function due to its effectiveness in reducing the likelihood of singularities in the mass matrix calculations. The Gaussian function has the standard form below:

$$g(x) = \frac{1}{\sigma\sqrt{2\pi}} exp\left(-\frac{(x-\mu)^2}{2\sigma^2}\right) \tag{19}$$

The function is symmetric with respect to the line $x = \mu$, and it reaches its peak at $x = \mu$. The value of σ controls the width of the function. The larger the σ, the flatter the function and the more spread out the distribution: the smaller the σ, the sharper the function and the more concentrated the distribution. In this paper, we choose the following series of Gaussian functions as the shape functions:

$$\varphi_{i,k}(x) = \frac{1}{\sqrt{2\pi}} 2^{\frac{a}{2}} exp\left(-\frac{(2^a x - k)^2}{2}\right), \tag{20}$$

where the integer a serves as a scaling factor, while the integer k acts as a translation factor. By selecting appropriate values for a and k in Equation (20), the vibration of the entire ABH beam can be recovered [30]. a acts as a regulatory parameter that dictates the precision of the model. With an increasing number of recoverable modes as the value of a gets larger, the computational cost correspondingly rises. According to the suggestion in [30], we limit the range of k to $[-8, 8]$ for the ABH beam considered in this paper. a is determined by the following relation:

$$a \geq ceil\left(\log_2 \left(\frac{8}{x_{b4}}\right)\right), \tag{21}$$

where $ceil(x)$ denotes the smallest integer that is greater than or equal to x. For every given a, the range of k is limited to

$$k \in [-4, ceil(2^a x_{b4}) - 4] \tag{22}$$

2.3. Numerical FEM Validation

It is crucial to ascertain whether the GEM faithfully captures the deformation of a beam that incorporates a truncated ABH. This validation will be accomplished through comparative studies with FEM results within this subsection. The numerical simulation parameters for the ABH beam are specified in Table 1.

Table 1. Parameters of the symmetric ABH structure.

Geometrical Parameters	Material Parameters
$x_{b1} = 0.1$ m	Beam
$x_{b2} = 0.2$ m	$\rho_b = 7800$ kg/m^3
$x_{b3} = 0.3$ m	$E_b = 210$ GPa
$x_{b4} = 0.4$ m	$\eta_b = 0.005$
$x_f = 0.35$ m	Damping layer
$\epsilon = 0.5$ m^{-1}, m = 2	$\rho_d = 950$ kg/m^3
$h_0 = 0.0002$ m	$E_d = 5$ GPa
$h_b = 0.0052$ m	$\eta_d = 0.3$

The eigenfrequencies and eigenvectors of the ABH beam are determined utilizing two distinct approaches: the first employs the GEM in conjunction with Equation (17), while the second approach relies on a 2D planar finite element model that encompasses 19,204 elements, all within the COMSOL software environment. Figure 2 illustrates a comparative analysis of the first 25 eigenvalues obtained from both the GEM and FEM, with the scaling factor (as defined in Equation (20)) taken as $a = 7, 8, 9$, respectively. It is evident that the GEM results quickly align with the FEM results as the value of a increases. As depicted in Figure 2b, selecting $a = 9$ results in a residual discrepancy of approximately 3% for the first 25 resonant sequences. Figure 3 displays the modal shapes corresponding to various resonant frequencies, as determined by the FEM and GEM outlined in this study. The results indicate that the analytical model using the GEM is capable of accurately capturing the substantial deformations at the tip of the ABH beam.

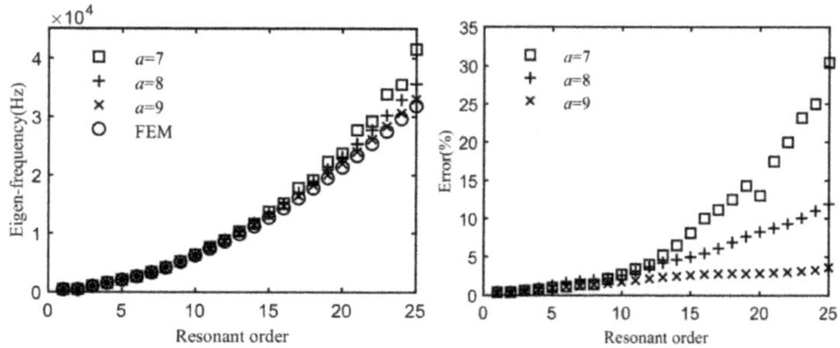

(a) Resonance frequency

(b) Relative error

Figure 2. The comparison of (a) resonance frequency and (b) relative error, as derived from the FEM and GEM for varying values of the scaling factor defined in Equation (20).

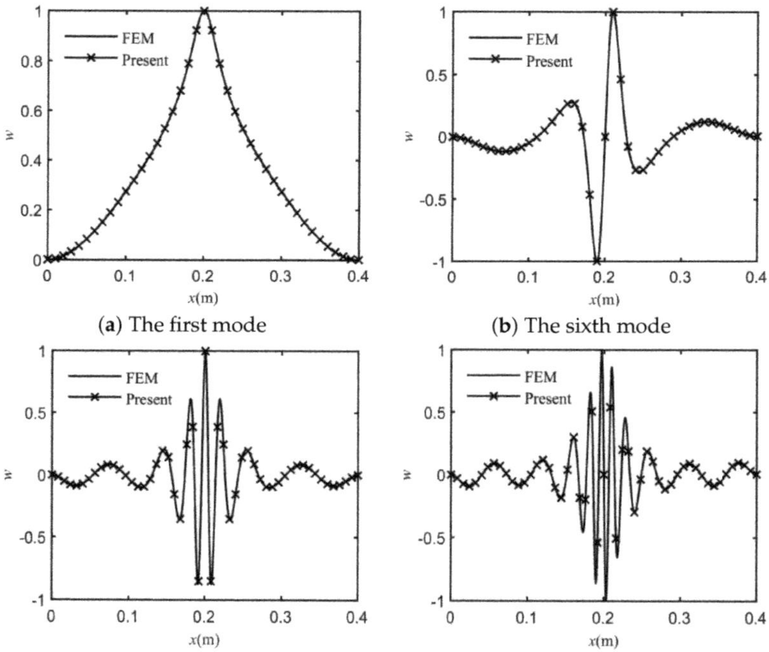

(a) The first mode

(b) The sixth mode

(c) The fifteenth mode

(d) The twentieth mode

Figure 3. The comparison of the modal shapes for the symmetric ABH structure, as obtained through the FEM and GEM presented in this paper across various modes: (a) the first mode, (b) the sixth mode, (c) the fifteenth mode, and (d) the twentieth mode.

3. Analysis of Damping Layer Parameters

In this section, we analyze the impact of the damping layer's parameters, such as position, thickness, and shape, on the system's energy dissipation efficiency, characterized by the modal loss factor as defined by Equation (18), using the semi-analytical solutions obtained from the GEM.

3.1. The Effect of the Damping Layer's Position

We fix the thickness of the damping layer at $h_d = 0.0002\,m$, and consider four different scenarios of adhesive attachment positions:

$$\begin{aligned} &Case \quad 1: \quad x_{d1} = 0.14\,m, \quad x_{d4} = 0.26\,m, \\ &Case \quad 2: \quad x_{d1} = 0.15\,m, \quad x_{d4} = 0.25\,m, \\ &Case \quad 3: \quad x_{d1} = 0.16\,m, \quad x_{d4} = 0.24\,m, \\ &Case \quad 4: \quad x_{d1} = 0.18\,m, \quad x_{d4} = 0.22\,m. \end{aligned} \tag{23}$$

Other parameter values of the damping layers continue to utilize those listed in Table 1. Figure 4 illustrates the effect of various placements of damping layers on the modal loss factor. It can be observed from Figure 4 that although Case 1 has the longest adhesive length, the variation in the system's damping coefficient is not pronounced compared to other adhesive lengths. As the mode shape order increases, the impact of different adhesive lengths gradually converges. This suggests that the adhesive length has a minimal influence on the ABH effect in this case and can be disregarded.

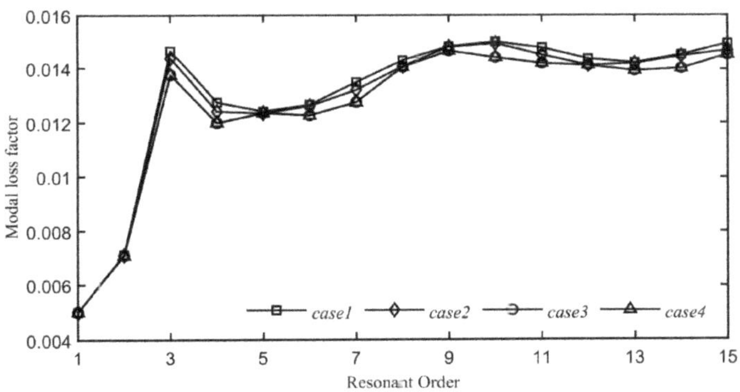

Figure 4. The impact of different damping layer positions on the system's modal loss factor when the damping layer thickness is fixed at $h_d = 0.0002\,m$.

3.2. The Effect of the Damping Layer's Thickness (h_d Remains Unchanged)

Consider that the position of the damping layer is confined between $x_{d1} = 0.14\,m$ and $x_{d4} = 0.26\,m$, and the thickness is taken as $h_d = 0.0002\,m$, $0.0005\,m$, $0.001\,m$, $0.005\,m$, respectively. The comparative outcomes are depicted in Figure 5. An examination of Figure 5 reveals that for low-order modes, the modal loss factor is very sensitive to the thickness of the damping layer, with the maximum increase in the modal loss factor being 16 times when the thickness is increased by 25 times. As the order of the vibration mode increases, the increase in the modal loss factor caused by the increase in damping layer thickness will exhibit a more pronounced fluctuation phenomenon. This indicates that increasing the thickness of the damping layer does not always enhance system performance. When the damping layer becomes too thick to the point where it significantly affects the mass and stiffness of the truncated section, it may actually have an adverse effect by resonating with a specific order of frequency.

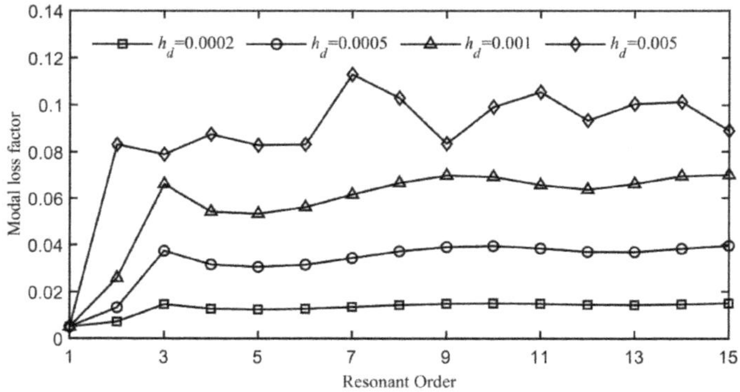

Figure 5. The influence of various damping layer thicknesses ($h_d = 0.0002\,m, 0.0005\,m, 0.001\,m, 0.005\,m$) on the modal loss factor when the position is limited between $x_{d1} = 0.14\,m$ and $x_{d4} = 0.26\,m$.

3.3. The Effect of the Damping Layer's Thickness (h_d Is Variable)

In this subsection, the impact of the damping layer thickness distribution on the overall system damping is explored through the establishment of various functions representing changes in damping layer thickness. The damping layer is positioned within the range $[x_{d1}, x_{d4}] = [0.14, 0.26]$. For ease of comparison, the effect of a damping layer with a constant thickness of $0.0002\,m$ is used as the reference. The thickness of the damping layer, h_d, is considered as a function of x. For the sake of comparison, two restrictions for $h_d(x)$ are assumed as follows:

- The mass of the damping layer remains constant during the variation in $h_d(x)$:

$$\int_{x_{d1}}^{x_{d4}} h_d(x)dx = \int_{x_{d1}}^{x_{d4}} 0.0002\,dx \tag{24}$$

- The thickness variation function $h_d(x)$ is symmetric about $x = x_{b2}$, and it satisfies

$$h_d(x_{b2}) = 0, \quad or \quad h_d(x_{d1}) = h_d(x_{d4}) = 0. \tag{25}$$

3.3.1. Case of $h_d(x_{b2}) = 0$

The thickness $h_d(x)$ varies according to the following different functional patterns:

$$\begin{aligned}
h_{d1}(x) &= \frac{1}{150}|x - 0.2|, \\
h_{d2}(x) &= -\frac{1}{36}(|x - 0.2| - 0.14)^2 + \frac{49}{90000}, \\
h_{d3}(x) &= -\frac{1}{12}(|x - 0.2| - 0.06)^2 + \frac{3}{10000}, \\
h_{d4}(x) &= \frac{100}{27}|x - 0.2|^3, \qquad\qquad x \in [0.14, 0.26]
\end{aligned} \tag{26}$$

The graphs of functions in Equation (26) are illustrated in Figure 6. Figure 7 demonstrates how different functions, $h_d(x) = h_{d1}, \cdots, h_{d4}$, respectively, for varying the thickness of the damping layer affect the modal loss factor. From Figure 7, it is observed that positioning the damping layer's maximum thickness away from the ABH tip results in a less effective enhancement of the ABH effect compared to a damping layer with uniform thickness. The damping layer that varies in thickness according to the function h_{d3} shows the most pronounced effect in enhancing the ABH effect, followed by the functions h_{d1} and h_{d2}, with the least effective being the variation according to the function h_{d4}. Figure 7 demonstrates that the choice of damping layer thickness variation function has a very significant impact on the ABH effect.

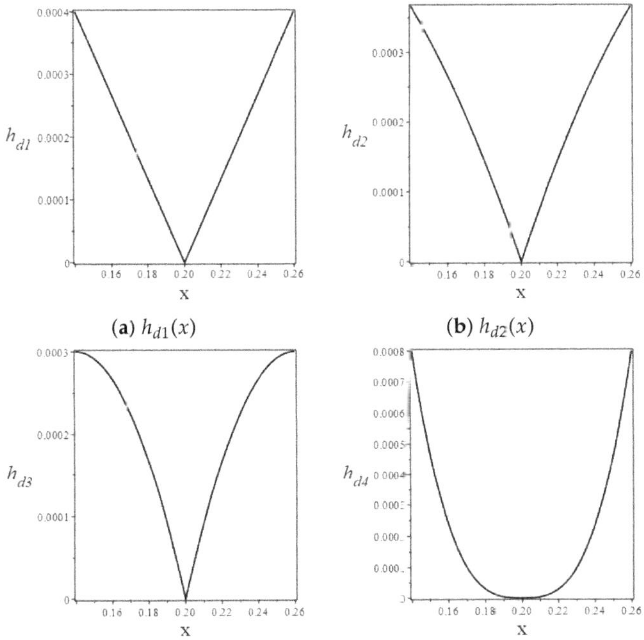

(a) $h_{d1}(x)$ (b) $h_{d2}(x)$ (c) $h_{d3}(x)$ (d) $h_{d4}(x)$

Figure 6. The graphs of functions $h_{d1}, \cdots, h_{d4}$ given in Equation (26).

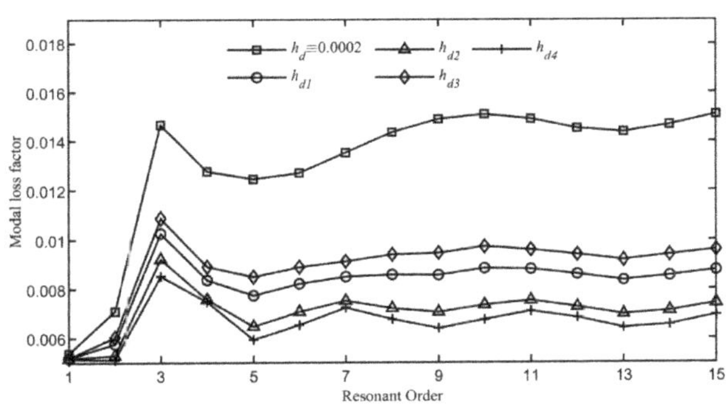

Figure 7. The impact of damping layer thickness variation on the system modal loss factor. The damping layer position is limited between $x_{d1} = 0.14\,m$ and $x_{d4} = 0.26\,m$ and $h_d(x)$ is taken as 0.0002, $h_{d1}, \cdots, h_{d4}$, respectively. $h_{d1}, \cdots, h_{d4}$ are given in Equation (26).

3.3.2. Case of $h_d(x_{d1}) = h_d(x_{d4}) = 0$

Consider that the thickness $h_d(x)$ fluctuates in accordance with several distinct functional forms:

$$
\begin{aligned}
h_{d5}(x) &= -\frac{1}{150}|x-0.2| + \frac{1}{2500}, \\
h_{d6}(x) &= -\frac{1}{12}(x-0.2)^2 + \frac{3}{10000}, \\
h_{d7}(x) &= \frac{1}{6}(|x-0.2| - 0.06)^2, \\
h_{d8}(x) &= -\frac{100}{81}|x-0.2|^3 + \frac{1}{3750}, \qquad x \in [0.14, 0.26]
\end{aligned} \tag{27}
$$

The plots of the functions given in Equation (27) are depicted in Figure 8. Figure 9 illustrates the improvement in the ABH effect achieved through various thickness variation functions, with the damping layer's maximum thickness positioned at the ABH tip. Varying the damping layer's thickness based on the functions h_{d5} through h_{d8} achieves better outcomes than maintaining a constant thickness throughout. This demonstrates that a uniform application of damping material across the entire region $[x_{d1}, x_{d4}]$ is not optimal. With a fixed total amount of damping material, concentrating more damping at the ABH tip and tapering off as we move away from it leads to a markedly improved performance over a uniform distribution. Figure 9 shows that among the different thickness variation functions, the ABH effect is most significant when the thickness of the damping layer is adjusted according to the function $h_{d7}(x)$. The findings from this subsection reveal that selecting the appropriate thickness variation function for the damping layer has a substantial influence on the ABH effect, warranting further investigation into optimizing the shape of the function.

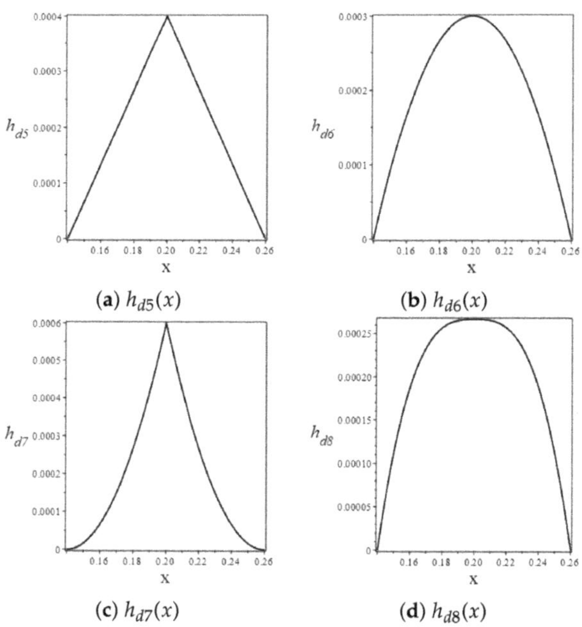

Figure 8. The graphs of functions $h_{d5}, \cdots, h_{d8}$ given in Equation (27).

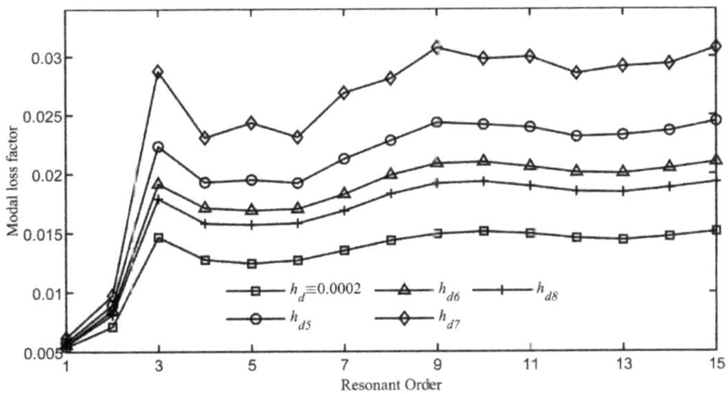

Figure 9. The impact of damping layer thickness variation on the system modal loss factor. The damping layer position is limited between $x_{d1} = 0.14\,m$ and $x_{d4} = 0.26\,m$ and $h_d(x)$ is taken as 0.0002, $h_{d5}, \cdots, h_{d8}$, respectively. $h_{d5}, \cdots, h_{d8}$ are given in Equation (27).

4. Optimization of the Damping Layer's Position and Thickness

From the analysis in the previous section, we consider that the thickness of the damping layer varies as follows:

$$h_d(x) = c_1(|x - c_0| + c_2)^n + c_3, \tag{28}$$

where $c_{0,1,2,3}$ and n are the parameters that need to be optimized for determining the best damping layer thickness variation function under conditions (24) and (25). In this section, we will find the optimal form of the damping layer thickness variation function based on BP neural networks. BP neural networks are a class of artificial neural networks that are widely used for various tasks such as pattern recognition, prediction, and data classification. A BP neural network typically consists of an input layer, one or more hidden layers, and an output layer. Each layer is composed of a set of neurons, and each neuron is connected to the neurons in the next layer through weights. A typical BP neural network structure is shown in Figure 10.

When a training example is presented, the input is passed through the network. Each neuron in the hidden layers computes a weighted sum of its inputs and applies an activation function to it. The activation function introduces nonlinearity into the model, allowing it to learn complex relationships. Common activation functions used in BP neural networks include the Sigmoid function, hyperbolic tangent (tanh), and the rectified linear unit (ReLU). The choice of activation function can have a significant impact on the network's performance. After the forward pass, the network's prediction is compared to the actual target value, and the error is calculated. The choice of loss function depends on the specific task. Common loss functions include mean squared error for regression tasks and cross-entropy loss for classification tasks. This error is then propagated back through the network, adjusting the weights to minimize the error. The process involves the calculation of gradients using the chain rule of calculus. The learning in a BP neural network is achieved through iterative training. During each iteration, the network processes a batch of training data, calculates the error, and updates the weights. This process is repeated over many epochs until the network's performance on a validation set is satisfactory.

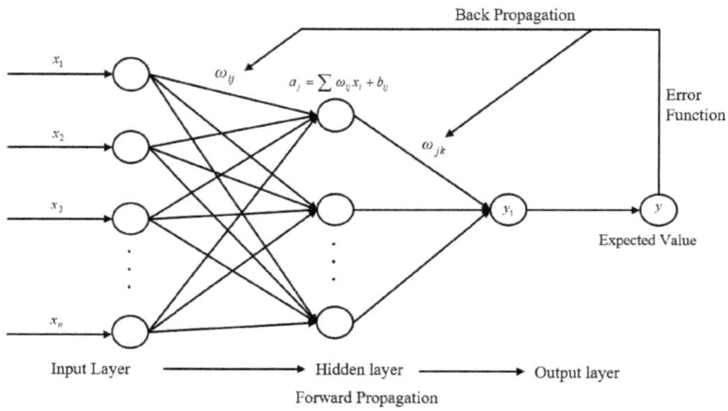

Figure 10. A BP neural network structure diagram with one hidden layer.

The parameters $c_{0,1,2,3}$ and n in Equation (28) and the position of the damping layer $[x_{d1}, x_{d4}]$ are used as six different indicator inputs for the BP neural network. The values of the output layer represent the desired results of the prediction, signifying the functional purpose that the network aims to achieve. In this model, the damping coefficients of the system at different vibration orders need to be predicted. Considering the practical needs of engineering, this paper predicts the damping coefficients for the first ten orders of the system; hence, the number of nodes in the output layer is 10. We set up two hidden layers through the design of network architecture, cross-validation, and performance evaluation. Determining the appropriate number of neurons in each hidden layer is crucial for neural network design. Insufficient neurons may result in underfitting, preventing the network from capturing the full complexity of the training data and thus weakening its predictive capabilities. Conversely, an excess of neurons can cause overfitting, where the network performs well on training data but poorly on unseen data, and also prolongs the training process. For networks with multiple hidden layers, the number of nodes in the hidden layers can be determined using the following empirical formula:

$$m = \sqrt{n + l} + \alpha, \quad m = \sqrt{nl}, \tag{29}$$

where the number of nodes in the hidden layer is denoted by m, the number of nodes in the input layer by n, and the number of nodes in the output layer by l. The constant α is greater than 1 and less than 10. According to the empirical formula, this paper sets the number of hidden layer nodes to be eight and nine, respectively. Considering that the output value of the Sigmoid function ranges from 0 to 1, and the derivative ranges from 0 to 0.25, it can conveniently control the magnitude of weight updates during the backpropagation process and avoid the problem of gradient vanishing. The choice of activation function is the Sigmoid function.

When seeking the minimum value of the error function, the Levenberg–Marquardt algorithm [40] is used for iteration. The algorithm is an improved method that lies between the Gauss–Newton method and the gradient descent method [41]. The algorithm incorporates a step-size adjustment parameter. In situations where the error function decreases sharply in the direction of the gradient, a reduced step-size factor is applied, thereby aligning the method more closely with the Gauss–Newton approach. Conversely, when the descent is slower, a larger step-size factor is used, making the algorithm more similar to the gradient descent method.

We set the following range for the six input parameters separately,

$$c_0 \in [0, 0.2], \quad c_1 \in [-2, 2], \quad c_2 \in [-0.06, 0]$$
$$c_3 \in [0, 0.005], \quad n \in [0, 3], \quad [x_{d1}, x_{d4}] \subseteq [0.1, 0.3],$$

and use the larger mean of output data and the smaller variance as the evaluation criteria. The training samples and validation samples both originate from theoretical computational results. Figure 11 illustrates the degree of fit of the BP network after being trained with Matlab software. It is evident that the linear correlation between the output data of the BP model and the training, validation, and test datasets exceeds 0.84 in each case. The overall fit rate of the entire model is 0.98657, indicating a high degree of fit, making the model acceptable and suitable as a predictive network model. The optimal damping layer thickness variation function predicted by the BP network is

$$h_{dp}(x) = \frac{4}{3}(|x - 0.2| - 0.03)^2, \quad x \in [0.17, 0.23] \tag{30}$$

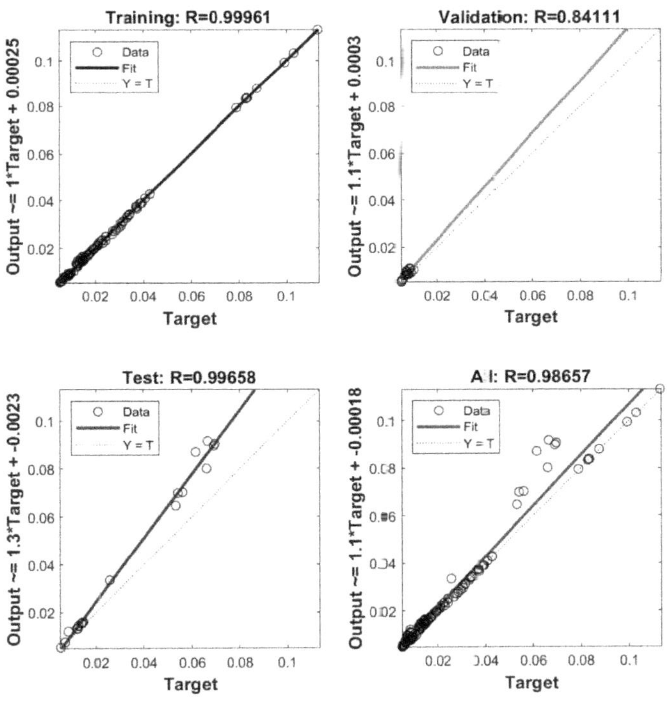

Figure 11. The BP neural network regression analysis chart.

Figure 12 displays the graphical representations of the functions h_{dp}, as defined by Equation (30), and h_{d7}, as defined by Equation (27). The comparison of the effect of different damping layer thicknesses (varying according to the functions h_{dp} and h_{d7}) on the ABH effect is shown in Figure 13. It is clear that as the resonance order increases, the modal loss factors of the system with damping layer thickness set according to the function h_{d7} gradually stabilize around 0.029, whereas with the damping layer thickness set according to the function h_{dp}, the modal loss factors gradually stabilize around 0.035. The average value of the modal loss factors for the first fifteen modes of the system with damping layer thickness set according to the function h_{d7} is 0.0252, while for the function h_{dp} it is 0.0293, representing an approximate 16.2% increase compared to the h_{d7} scenario. Figure 13 shows the effectiveness of optimization using the BP neural network.

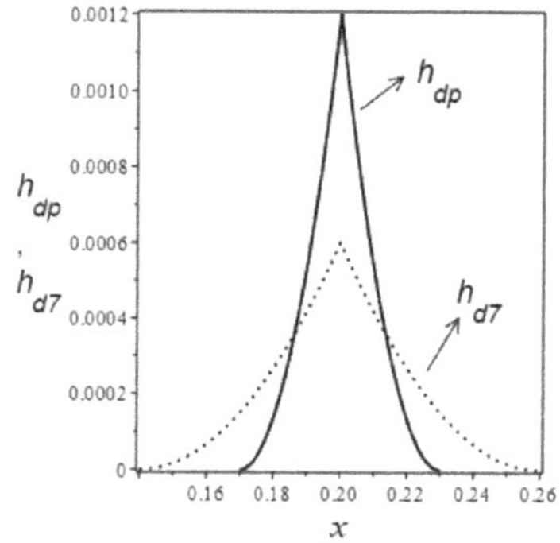

Figure 12. The graph of functions $h_{dp}(x)$ and $h_{d7}(x)$ given in Equations (27) and (30), respectively. The areas enclosed by the two function curves and the x−axis are the same.

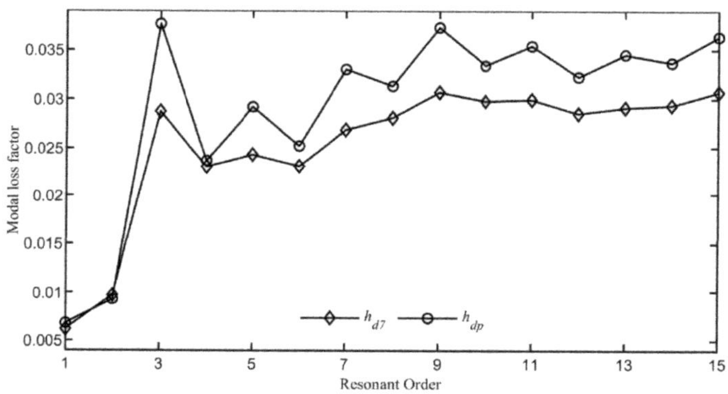

Figure 13. The comparison of the impact of damping layer thicknesses set according to the functions $h_{dp}(x)$ and $h_{d7}(x)$, as defined in Equations (27) and (30), on the ABH effect.

The analysis based on BP neural network optimization indicates that to achieve a good ABH effect, it is not necessary to apply the damping layer over the entire ABH section. The thickness of the damping layer should be maximized at the ABH tip, with a swift reduction as one moves away from the tip. Additionally, it is unnecessary to apply a damping layer in regions that are distant from the tip.

Given that the thickness of the damping layer significantly affects the vibration reduction performance of the system, precise control over the damping layer thickness on the ABH beam is essential in practical applications. To further elucidate the impact of the damping layer thickness tolerances on the ABH effect, we consider the damping layer thickness varying according to the following two functions:

$$\begin{aligned} h_{dpa}(x) &= \frac{4}{3}(|x-0.2|-0.031)^2, \\ h_{dps}(x) &= \frac{4}{3}(|x-0.2|-0.029)^2, \qquad x \in [0.17, 0.23]. \end{aligned} \tag{31}$$

The two functions above are employed to simulate the manufacturing tolerances that arise in the optimized function $h_{dp}(x)$, presented in Equation (30). The impact of manufacturing tolerances in the damping layer thickness on the ABH effect is illustrated in Figure 14.

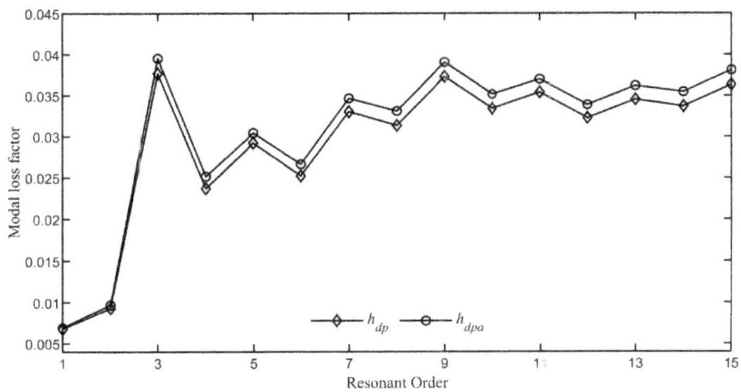

(**a**) The impact of the increased thickness.

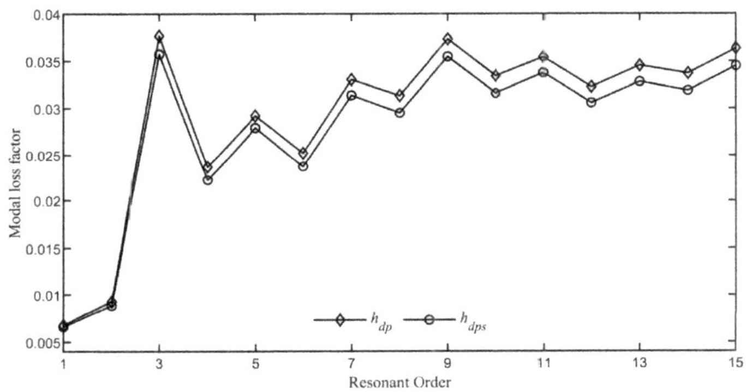

(**b**) The impact of thickness reduction

Figure 14. The impact of manufacturing tolerances in the damping layer thickness on the ABH effect: (**a**) the impact of the increased thickness; (**b**) the impact of thickness reduction.

As can be seen from Figure 14, when the optimized shape of the thickness does not undergo significant changes, minor manufacturing tolerances in the damping layer thickness only cause minor variations in the system's vibration reduction performance. When the damping layer thickness is slightly increased, the system's vibration reduction performance is also slightly enhanced, and vice versa. This indicates that optimizing the thickness profile of the damping layer is feasible in practical applications.

To achieve more precise control over the thickness of the damping layer in actual manufacturing, the following strategies and methods can be considered [42,43]: Firstly, the thickness of damping materials can be controlled through optimized design. For instance, the surface of the structure can be divided into multiple zones, with the thickness of the damping material in each zone treated as a design variable for optimization. This approach allows the damping layer to meet specific requirements for vibration reduction. Secondly, the performance of damping materials can be enhanced through methods such as blending and copolymerization. These techniques help minimize tolerance issues arising from material inhomogeneity. Additionally, a multi-layer structural design can be employed, with the overall thickness uniformity controlled by adjusting the thickness and number of layers. Moreover, to maximize the effectiveness of the damping layer, the bonding area of the damping material should be as extensive as possible. Considering the entire construction process, a bonding area exceeding 80% can serve as a process indicator to ensure the quality of damping material installation.

5. Further Discussion

In this section, we examine the alterations made to the ABH beam illustrated in Figure 1, which are detailed in Figure 15. The beam comprises three distinct segments: The initial segment extends across the intervals $[0, x_{b1}]$ and $[x_{b3}, x_{b4}]$, with a consistent thickness of h_b. The second segment, which spans $[x_{y1}, x_{y2}]$, maintains a uniform thickness of h_0. The third segment features an ABH profile, with its thickness varying according to a power law between the points x_{b1} and x_{y1}, as well as between x_{y2} and x_{b3}. The thickness variation of the beam can be expressed as follows:

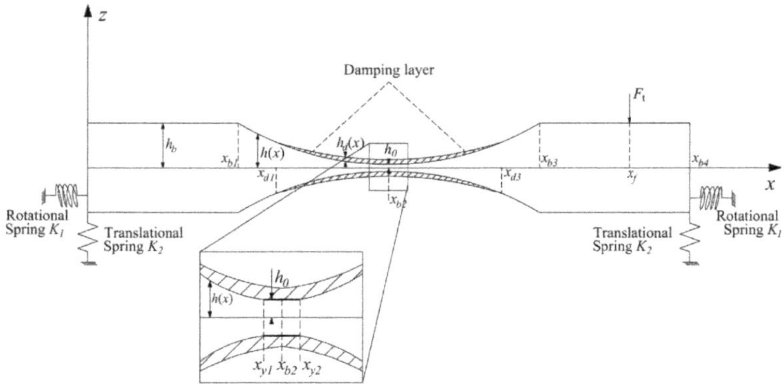

Figure 15. The schematic diagram of a modified symmetric ABH beam.

$$h(x) = \begin{cases} \epsilon(x - x_{y1})^m + h_0, & x \in [x_{b1}, x_{y1}] \\ h_0, & x \in [x_{y1}, x_{y2}] \\ \epsilon(x - x_{y2})^m + h_0, & x \in [x_{y2}, x_{b3}] \end{cases} \quad (32)$$

where ϵ and m represent the slope and the ABH order, respectively. The structure depicted in Figure 15 exhibits symmetry about both the line $x = x_{b2}$ and the plane $z = 0$. Damping material is attached to both flanges of the beam, spanning the region $[x_{d1}, x_{d3}]$, with a variable thickness denoted by $h_d(x)$. The beam's ends are supported by rotational springs of stiffness K_1 and translational springs of stiffness K_2, allowing for a range of boundary conditions to be simulated by adjusting the values of K_1 and K_2. The parameters for the modified ABH beam are given in Table 2. The difference between Figures 1 and 15 is that the structure in Figure 15 includes an additional segment in $[x_{y1}, x_{y2}]$, where the beam's thickness remains constant at h_0. In this section, we focus on discussing the impact of adding a segment with constant thickness h_0 on the system's ABH effect over the interval $[x_{y1}, x_{y2}]$.

Table 2. Parameters of the modified symmetric ABH structure

Geometrical Parameters	Material Parameters
$x_{b1} = 0.1$ m	Beam
$x_{b2} = 0.22$ m	$\rho_b = 7800$ kg/m^3
$x_{b3} = 0.34$ m	$E_b = 210$ Gpa
$x_{b4} = 0.44$ m	$\eta_b = 0.005$
$x_f = 0.39$ m	Damping layer
$\epsilon = 0.5$ m^{-1}, $m = 2$	$\rho_d = 950$ kg/m^3
$x_{y1} = 0.2$ m, $x_{y2} = 0.24$ m	$E_d = 5$ Gpa
$h_0 = 0.0002$, $h_b = 0.0052$ m	$\eta_d = 0.3$

5.1. The Effect of the Damping Layer's Position

We set the thickness of the damping layer to a constant value of $h_d = 0.0002\,m$ and explore four distinct scenarios regarding the placement of adhesive bonds:

$$\begin{aligned} &Case\quad 1: && x_{d1} = 0.18\,m, && x_{d3} = 0.26\,m, \\ &Case\quad 2: && x_{d1} = 0.16\,m, && x_{d3} = 0.28\,m, \\ &Case\quad 3: && x_{d1} = 0.14\,m, && x_{d3} = 0.3\,m, \\ &Case\quad 4: && x_{d1} = 0.12\,m, && x_{d3} = 0.32\,m. \end{aligned} \tag{33}$$

Figure 16 illustrates the effects of different damping layer configurations on the modal loss factor. As shown in Figure 16, even though Case 4 has the longest adhesive length, the changes in the modal loss factor of the system are not markedly different from those with shorter adhesive lengths. As the mode shape order increases, the impact of varying adhesive lengths becomes less pronounced. This suggests that the length of the adhesive has a minimal effect on the ABH effect in this context and can be considered insignificant.

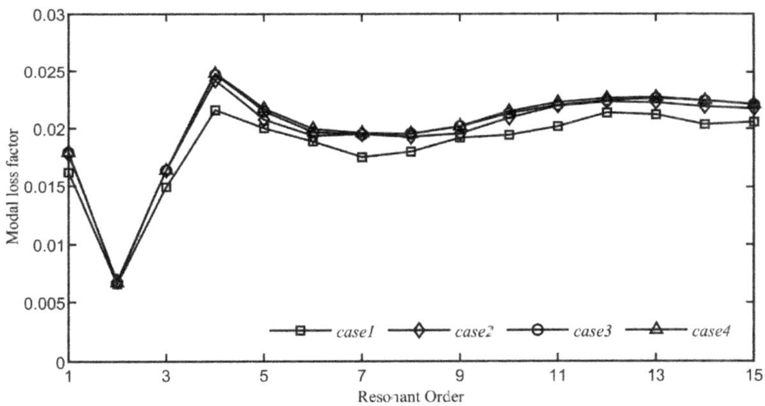

Figure 16. The comparison of the effects of different damping layer positions on the system's modal loss factor. The damping layer thickness consistently is set at $h_d = 0.0002\,m$.

5.2. The Effect of the Damping Layer's Thickness (h_d Is Variable)

In this subsection, we delve into the influence of the distribution of damping layer thickness on the system's overall damping by defining several functions that model variations in damping layer thickness under the conditions specified by Equations (24) and (25). The damping layer is situated within $[x_{d1}, x_{d3}] = [0.16, 0.28]$. Additionally, the impact of a damping layer with a uniform thickness of $0.0002\,m$ serves as a benchmark for comparison. Following the findings from Section 3, which suggest that increased damping at the ABH tip yields better outcomes, we now contemplate the thickness $h_d(x)$ that alters according to various specific mathematical expressions:

$$\begin{aligned} h_{d10}(x) &= -\frac{1}{150}|x - 0.22| + \frac{1}{2500}, \\ h_{d11}(x) &= -\frac{1}{12}(x - 0.22)^2 + \frac{3}{10000}, \\ h_{d12}(x) &= \frac{1}{6}(|x - 0.22| - 0.06)^2, \\ h_{d13}(x) &= -\frac{100}{81}|x - 0.22|^3 + \frac{1}{3750}, \qquad x \in [0.16, 0.28] \end{aligned} \tag{34}$$

The graphical representations of the functions from Equation (34) closely resemble those shown in Figure 8; therefore, no further graphics are provided here. Figure 17 demonstrates the intensified ABH effect achieved by employing diverse thickness variation functions, as defined in Equation (34). The results obtained by customizing the damping layer's thickness with functions h_{d10} to h_{d13} are superior to those of a uniform thickness. Notably, Figure 17 reveals that the function h_{d12} yields the most significant ABH effect among the thickness variation functions. This indicates that focusing a higher concentration of damping material at the ABH tip and diminishing it as we move away from the tip significantly boosts the performance compared to an even distribution.

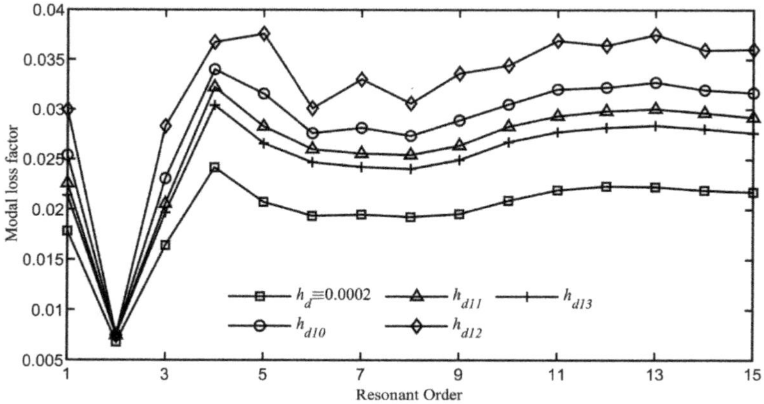

Figure 17. The effect of varying the thickness of the damping layer on the system's modal loss factor. The damping layer is confined to the interval between $x_{d1} = 0.16\,m$ and $x_{d3} = 0.28\,m$, with $h_d(x)$ taking on the values of 0.0002, $h_{d10}, \ldots, h_{d13}$. The values for h_{d10} through h_{d13} are specified in Equation (34).

5.3. Optimization of the Damping Layer's Position and Thickness

Employing the optimization technique for the damping layer thickness function, as detailed in the preceding section, Figure 18 depicts the fitting accuracy of the BP network post-training with Matlab software. The BP neural network has determined the following optimal thickness variation function for the damping layer:

$$h_{dp}(x) = \frac{9}{16}(|x - 0.22| - 0.04)^2, \quad x \in [0.18, 0.26]. \tag{35}$$

Figure 18 displays the graphical depictions of the functions h_{dp} and h_{d12}, which are specified by Equations (34) and (35), respectively. Figure 19 presents a comparison of the impact on the ABH effect exerted by damping layer thicknesses varied according to the functions h_{dp} and h_{d12}. It is evident that with the increase in resonance order, the modal loss factors for the system with the damping layer thickness following the function h_{d12} tend to stabilize at approximately 0.036, while for the system with the damping layer thickness following the function h_{dp}, these factors stabilize at around 0.038. The mean modal loss factor for the first fifteen modes of the system with the damping layer thickness set by the function h_{d12} is 0.0323, whereas for the function h_{dp}, it is 0.0338, which is roughly 4.6% higher compared to the scenario with h_{d12}.

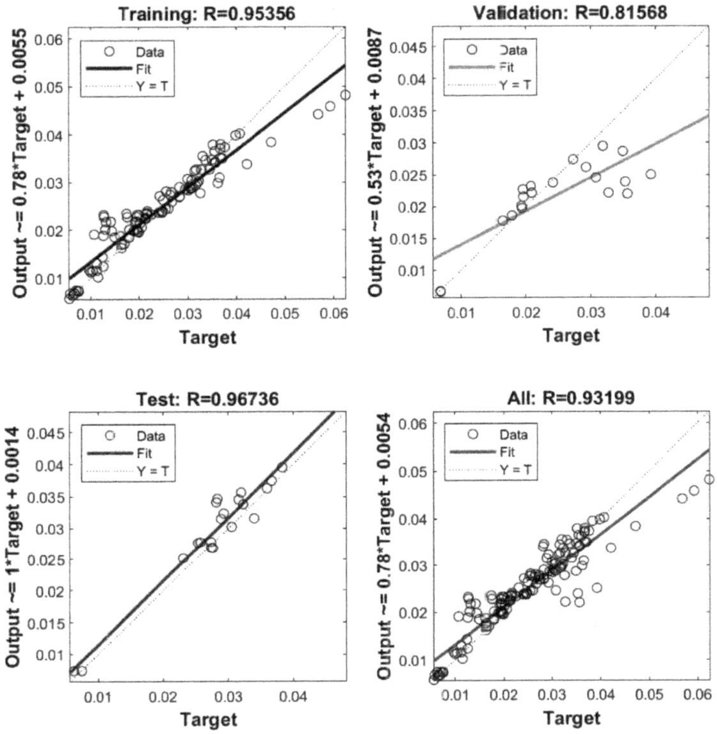

Figure 18. The BP neural network regression analysis graph.

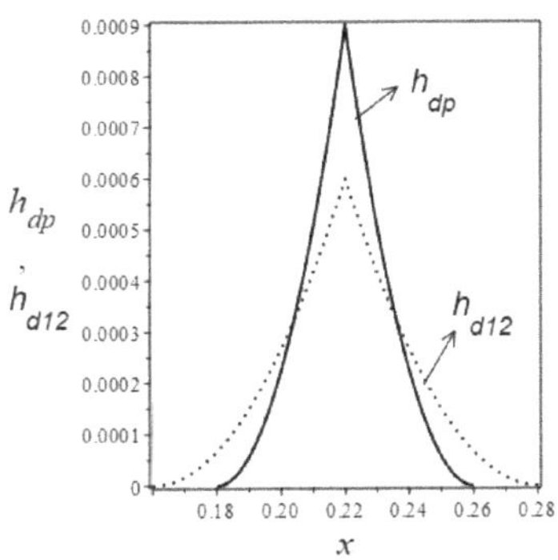

Figure 19. The graph of functions $h_{dp}(x)$ and $h_{d12}(x)$, as defined in Equations (34) and (35), respectively. The regions bounded by these two function curves and the x−axis are identical.

Comparing Figure 20 with Figure 13, it can be observed that when the same mass of damping layer material is applied (after optimizing the thickness of the damping layer using the BP algorithm), the average value of the first fifteen modal loss factors of the modified ABH beam structure (as shown in Figure 15) increases by approximately 15% compared to before the modification (as shown in Figure 1). This indicates that when the truncation thickness h_0 of the ABH beam shown in Figure 15 cannot be reduced, the ABH effect can be enhanced by adding a segment with constant thickness h_0 within $[x_{y1}, x_{y2}]$. To achieve better effects, the length of the segment $[x_{y1}, x_{y2}]$ can be further optimized using the BP algorithm.

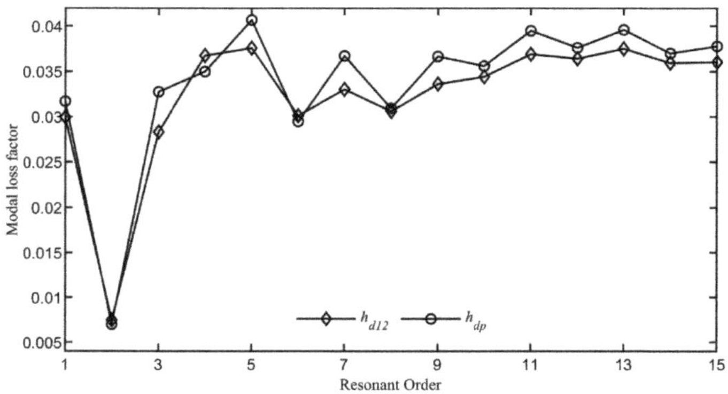

Figure 20. The comparison of the impact on the ABH effect by the thicknesses of the damping layer set according to functions $h_{dp}(x)$ and $h_{d12}(x)$, as defined in Equations (34) and (35), respectively.

6. Conclusions

This paper investigates the impact of changing the geometric characteristics of damping layers on the energy dissipation capabilities of a symmetric ABH beam. The utilization of the BP algorithm is proposed to optimize the shape variation of the damping layer. Initially, a semi-analytical solution for the ABH beam's vibration behavior is derived using the GEM, and the accuracy of this solution is confirmed by comparing it against results from the FEM. Next, leveraging the semi-analytical solution, an analysis of the impact of damping layer parameters, including position, thickness, and shape, on the ABH effect is conducted. Under the premise of maintaining a constant mass of the damping layer, a thickness variation function with a good energy dissipation effect is preliminarily selected. Subsequently, a BP neural network is trained based on the database generated by the semi-analytical solution to optimize the thickness variation function. This study reveals that the damping layer's geometry has a more intricate impact on performance than previously understood. The BP algorithm stands out as a powerful tool for enhancing the performance evaluation of ABH structures amidst a variety of factors. The optimization analysis conducted using the BP neural network suggests that achieving an effective ABH effect does not require the application of a damping layer across the entire ABH section. The optimal configuration involves maximizing the damping layer thickness at the ABH tip, followed by a rapid decrease in thickness as one moves away from the tip. It is deemed unnecessary to apply a damping layer in areas that are far from the tip.

By appropriately stretching the ABH beam along the truncation thickness while keeping the thickness constant, this paper also optimizes the thickness of the damping layer for the modified ABH beam structure. This study finds that with the same mass of damping layer attached, the modified ABH beam structure can exhibit better energy dissipation effects. This is a novel approach that further enhances the energy dissipation performance of ABH beams without reducing the truncation thickness. Based on the research approach of this paper, the length of the stretched section in the ABH beam can be further optimized using the BP algorithm to achieve better energy dissipation effects. The research in this paper helps to gain a deeper understanding of the impact of the damping layer on the energy dissipation effect of ABH beams.

Author Contributions: Conceptualization, B.Z.; methodology, B.Z.; software, J.Z.; investigation, L.O. and J.Z.; writing—original draft preparation, L.O. and J.Z.; writing—review and editing, L.O. and

B.Z.; visualization, J.Z.; supervision, B.Z.; project administration, B.Z.; funding acquisition, B.Z. All authors have read and agreed to the published version of the manuscript.

Funding: This research was funded by the National Natural Science Foundation of China grant number 11672185.

Institutional Review Board Statement: Not applicable

Informed Consent Statement: Not applicable

Data Availability Statement: Data are contained within the article.

Conflicts of Interest: The authors declare no conflicts of interest.

References

1. Mironov, M.A. Propagation of a flexural wave in a plate whose thickness decreases smoothly to zero in a finite interval. *Sov. Phys. Acoust.* **1988**, *34*, 318–319.
2. Vemula, C.; Norris, A.N. Attenuation of waves in plates and bars using a graded impedance interface at edges. *J. Sound Vib.* **1996**, *196*, 107–127. [CrossRef]
3. Krylov, V.V.; Tilman, F.J.B.S. Acoustic black holes' for flexural waves as effective vibration dampers. *J. Sound Vib.* **2004**, *274*, 605–619. [CrossRef]
4. Pelat, A.; Gautier, F.; Conlon, S.C.; Semperlotti, F. The acoustic black hole: A review of theory and applications. *J. Sound Vib.* **2020**, *476*, 115316. [CrossRef]
5. Xiao, Y.; Shen, W.N.; Zhu, H.P.; Du, Y.L. An acoustic black hole absorber for rail vibration suppression: Simulation and full-scale experiment. *Eng. Struct.* **2024**, *304*, 117647. [CrossRef]
6. Zenkour, A.M.; Aljadani, M.H. Thermo-electrical buckling response of actuated functionally graded piezoelectric nanoscale plates. *Results Phys.* **2019**, *13*, 102192. [CrossRef]
7. Xiong, D.F.; Liang, J.F.; Qiao, Y.P.; Qi, S.B. Enhanced acoustic black hole energy harvesters with multipiezoelectric array designs. *Appl. Phys. Express* **2023**, *16*, 045502. [CrossRef]
8. Yang, C.; Yuan, Y.; Wang, H.; Tang, Y.; Gui, J. Research on vibration energy harvester based on two-dimensional acoustic black hole. *Micromachines* **2023**, *14*, 538. [CrossRef] [PubMed]
9. Gao, W.; Hu, J.; Qin, Z.; Chu, F. Flexural wave manipulation in perforated metamaterial plates with acoustic blackholes interconnected by piezoelectric studs. *Compos. Struct.* **2023**, *321*, 117224. [CrossRef]
10. Zhao, L.; Conlon, S.C.; Semperlotti, F. Broadband energy harvesting using acoustic black hole structural tailoring. *Smart Mater. Struct.* **2014**, *23*, 065021. [CrossRef]
11. Tang, L.; Cheng, L. Broadband locally resonant band gaps in periodic beam structures with embedded acoustic black holes. *J. Appl. Phys.* **2017**, *121*, 605. [CrossRef]
12. Gao, N.; Wei, Z.; Zhang, R.; Hou, H. Low-frequency elastic wave attenuation in a composite acoustic black hole beam. *Appl. Acoust.* **2019**, *154*, 68–76. [CrossRef]
13. O'boy, D.; Krylov, V.V. Damping of flexural vibrations in circular plates with tapered central holes. *J. Sound Vib.* **2011**, *330*, 2220–2236. [CrossRef]
14. Ma, L.; Zhang, S.; Cheng, L. Vibration of a plate with power-law-profiled thickness variation by wavelet decomposed Rayleigh-Ritz method. *Int. Congr. Expo. Noise Control Eng.* **2018**, *255*, 1014–1021.
15. Zhao, C.; Zheng, J.; Sang, T.; Wang, L.; Yi, Q.; Wang, P. Computational analysis of phononic crystal vibration isolators via FEM coupled with the acoustic black hole effect to attenuate railway-induced vibration. *Constr. Build. Mater.* **2021**, *283*, 122802. [CrossRef]
16. Zhu, R.; Liu, Y.; Bojja, N.; Qin, Z.; Chu, F. Vibration attenuation of rotating disks via acoustic black holes. *Int. J. Mech. Sci.* **2023**, *242*, 10802. [CrossRef]
17. Deng, J.; Zheng, L.; Guasch, O.; Wu, H.; Zeng, P.; Zuo, Y. Gaussian expansion for the vibration analysis of plates with multiple acoustic black holes indentations. *Mech. Syst. Signal Process.* **2019**, *131*, 317–334. [CrossRef]
18. Pu, H.E.; Zhu, J.; Sun, X.; Ji, H.; Qiu, J. Energy focusing effect of a novel acoustic black hole absorber on flexural waves in box-type structure. In Proceedings of the 2020 15th Symposium on Piezoelectrcity, Acoustic Waves and Device Applications (SPAWDA), Zhengzhou, China, 16–19 April 2021; pp. 334–337.
19. Ji, H.; Wang, N.; Zhang, C.; Wang, X.; Cheng, L.; Qiu, J. A vibration absorber based on two-dimensional acoustic black holes. *J. Sound Vib.* **2021**, *500*, 116024. [CrossRef]
20. Li, M.Y.; Deng, J.; Zheng, L.; Xiang, S.H. Vibration mitigation via integrated acoustic black holes. *Appl. Acoust.* **2022**, *198*, 109001. [CrossRef]

21. Deng, J.; Ma, J.F.; Chen, X.; Yang, Y.; Gao, N.S.; Liu, J. Vibration damping by periodic additive acoustic black holes. *J. Sound V* **2024**, *574*, 118235. [CrossRef]
22. Deng, J.; Gao, N.S.; Chen, X.; Han, B.; Ji, H. Evanescent waves in a metabeam attached with lossy acoustic black hole pill *Mech. Syst. Signal Process.* **2023**, *191*, 110182. [CrossRef]
23. Deng, J.; Gao, N.S.; Chen, X. Ultrawide attenuation bands in gradient metabeams with acoustic black hole pillars. *Thin-Wa Struct.* **2023**, *184*, 110459. [CrossRef]
24. Chen, X.; Jing, Y.; Zhao, J.L.; Deng, J.; Cao, X.J.; Pu, H.Y.; Cao, H.J.; Huang, X.X.; Luo, J. Tunable shunting periodic acoustic bla holes for low-frequency and broadband vibration suppression. *J. Sound Vib.* **2024**, *580*, 118384. [CrossRef]
25. Ma, L.; Zhang, S.; Cheng, L. A 2D Daubechies wavelet model on the vibration of rectangular plates containing strip indentatic with a parabolic thickness profile. *J. Sound Vib.* **2018**, *429*, 130–146. [CrossRef]
26. Conlon, S.C.; Fahnline, J.B.; Semperlotti, F. Numerical analysis of the vibroacoustic properties of plates with embedded grids acoustic black holes. *J. Acoust. Soc. Am.* **2015**, *137*, 447–457. [CrossRef] [PubMed]
27. O'Boy, D.; Krylov, V.V. Vibration of a rectangular plate with a central power-law profiled groove by the Rayleigh-Ritz meth *Appl. Acoust.* **2016**, *104*, 24–32. [CrossRef]
28. Ma, L.; Cheng, L. Sound radiation and transonic boundaries of a plate with an acoustic black hole. *J. Acoust. Soc. Am.* **2019**, *1* 164–172. [CrossRef]
29. Tang, L.; Cheng, L.; Ji, H.; Qiu, J. Characterization of acoustic black hole effect using a one-dimensional fully-coupled a wavelet-decomposed semi-analytical model. *J. Sound Vib.* **2016**, *374*, 172–184. [CrossRef]
30. Deng, J.; Zheng, L.; Zeng, P.; Zuo, Y.; Guasch, O. Passive constrained viscoelastic layers to improve the efficiency of truncat acoustic black holes in beams. *Mech. Syst. Signal Process.* **2019**, *118*, 461–476. [CrossRef]
31. Huang, W.; Ji, H.; Qiu, J.; Cheng, L. Wave energy focalization in a plate with imperfect two-dimensional acoustic black h indentation. *J. Vib. Acoust.* **2016**, *138*, 061004. [CrossRef]
32. Ji, H.; Luo, J.; Qiu, J.; Cheng, L. Investigations on flexural wave propagation and attenuation in a modified one-dimensior acoustic black hole using a laser excitation technique. *Mech. Syst. Signal Process.* **2018**, *104*, 19–35. [CrossRef]
33. Georgiev, V.B.; Cuenca, J.; Gautier, F.; Simon, L.; Krylov, V.V. Damping of structural vibrations in beams and elliptical plates usi the acoustic black hole effect. *J. Sound Vib.* **2011**, *330*, 2497–2508. [CrossRef]
34. Bowyer, E.P.; O'Boy, D.J.; Krylov, V.V.; Horner, J.L. Effect of geometrical and material imperfections on damping flexural vibratio in plates with attached wedges of power law profile. *Appl. Acoust.* **2012**, *73*, 514–523. [CrossRef]
35. Ross, D.; Kerwin, E.E.; Ungar, E.M. Damping of plate flexural vibrations by means of viscoelastic laminae. In *Structural Dampi* Pergamon Press: Oxford, UK, 1960.
36. Krylov, V.V. New type of vibration dampers utilizing the effect of acoustic black holes. *Acta Acust. United Acust.* **2004**, *90*, 830–8
37. Goodfellow, I.; Bengio, Y.; Courville, A.; Bengio, Y. *Deep Learning*; MIT Press: Cambridge, CA, USA, 2016.
38. Jahn, M. Artificial neural network regression models in a panel setting: Predicting economic growth. *Econ. Model.* **2020**, 148–154. [CrossRef]
39. Mrinal, K. Non-Classical Damping Properties and Modal Correlation Coefficient for Dynamic Analysis of Structures. Doctor Dissertation, North Carolina State University, Raleigh, NC, USA, 2001.
40. Gavin, H. *The Levenberg-Marquardt Algorithm for Nonlinear Least Squares Curve-Fitting Problems*; Department of Civil and Envirc mental Engineering, Duke University: Durham, NC, USA, 2020.
41. Amari, S.I. Backpropagation and stochastic gradient descent method. *Neurocomputing* **1993**, *5*, 185–196. [CrossRef]
42. Xie, Y.M.; Steven, G.P. *Evolutionary Structural Optimization*; Springer: London, UK, 1997.
43. *ASTM E756-04*; Standard Test Method for Measuring Vibration-Damping Properties of Materials. American Society for Testi and Materials: West Conshohocken, PA, USA, 2004.

applied sciences

MDPI

rticle

Acoustic Emission Analysis of the Cracking Behavior in ECC-LWSCC Composites

ara Zaki [1], Ahmed Abouhussien [2,*] and Assem Hassan [1]

[1] Department of Civil Engineering, Faculty of Engineering and Applied Science, Memorial University of Newfoundland, St. John's, NL A1B 3X5, Canada; azakielsayed@mun.ca (Y.Z.); ahassan@mun.ca (A.H.)
[2] Kinectrics, 393 University Ave, Toronto ON M5G 1E6, Canada
* Correspondence: aabouhussien@mun.ca; Tel.: +1-416-200-7149

Abstract: Acoustic emission (AE) analysis was utilized to assess the cracking behavior of six lightweight self-consolidating concrete (LWSCC)–engineering cementitious composite (ECC) beams under flexural loading. Two control beams were fully cast with ECC containing either polyvinyl alcohol (PVA) fibers or steel fibers (SF). The remaining four beams were ECC-LWSCC composite beams, with the ECC layer containing PVA fibers or SF placed on either the tension or compression side. The results showed that the control beams had the highest ultimate load capacity, followed by beams repaired in tension, and then beams repaired in compression. PVA fibers exhibited higher performance compared to steel fibers at the first crack load, while steel fibers enhanced the beam's performance at the ultimate load stage. During the flexural testing, AE parameters such as the number of hits, signal amplitude, and cumulative signal strength (CSS) were collected until failure. The analysis of these AE parameters was effective in detecting the first crack and evaluating cracking propagation in all beams. Changing the type of fibers (PVA and SF) in the ECC layer showed a significant effect on AE parameters. Moreover, adding a new ECC layer to an existing LWSCC layer resulted in variations in the signal amplitude. Finally, the flexural failure mode was confirmed with the aid of the rise time/maximum amplitude vs. average frequency analysis.

Keywords: acoustic emission analysis; ECC-LWSCC composite beams; first crack detection; damage quantification; failure modes

1. Introduction

In recent years, there has been growing interest in the application of lightweight concrete (LWC) within the construction industry due to its cost-effectiveness and structural advantages. LWC is designed by fully or partially replacing normal weight aggregates with lightweight aggregates, which have low density. This reduction in self-weight results in smaller concrete cross-sections and decreased dead loads [1–3]. Additionally, lightweight aggregates in concrete offer benefits such as reduced thermal conductivity and improved insulation properties due to air voids [4]. The incorporation of lightweight aggregates into self-consolidating concrete (SCC) creates lightweight self-consolidating concrete (LWSCC), which flows easily into congested reinforcements and complex formwork [4].

Concrete structures face degradation from aging and environmental factors, leading to cracks, spalling, deflections, and steel reinforcement corrosion [5]. These problems can also stem from construction defects and increased structural loads [6]. Therefore, aging structures often require repairs to maintain design integrity, resist higher loads, ensure serviceability, and prevent sudden failures [5–7]. Typically, repair involves removing damaged concrete and applying a new repair layer [8], making the selection of high-performance, economical repair materials critical for effective rehabilitation.

Rehabilitating concrete structures demands materials with superior properties such as high ductility, strength, energy absorption, and durability [9]. Fiber-reinforced cement-based composites, like engineering cementitious composites (ECCs), offer these attributes. ECCs exhibit enhanced tensile strength, high ductility, and minimal crack widths [10]. Compared to regular concrete, ECC can achieve 600 times the tensile ductility [11,12], with a 2% fiber content enhancing its tensile capacity by 3–5% and showing pseudo strain hardening [12,13]. Polyvinyl alcohol (PVA) and steel fibers (SFs) notably improve ECC's cracking behavior, with SF contributing to superior ductility, crack load, ultimate load, and energy absorption [14]. ECCs typically exhibit tensile strengths of 4–6 MPa, compressive strengths of 30–80 MPa, and strain capacities of 0.4% to 0.65% [15], allowing repaired structures to perform well under fatigue and impact loads [9].

Combining ECC and SCC has enhanced structural performance in various studies. For example, Hossain et al. [16] analyzed hybrid composite beams of SCC and ECC, noting improved ductility and energy absorption without shear reinforcement. Batran et al. [17] tested lightweight ECC composites with PVA or SF under impact loading, demonstrating superior impact resistance. Ismail et al. [18] studied ECC in beam–column joints, finding SF ECC provided the highest ductility and load capacities.

Acoustic emission (AE) monitoring is valuable for the health monitoring of materials and structures, detecting transient waves emitted by damage events [19]. AE's high sensitivity enables the detection of micro-cracking and other low-energy sources in concrete structures [19]. AE has proven effective in characterizing fracture processes in fiber-reinforced concrete [20], assessing bridge integrity [21], monitoring crack propagation in shear walls [22], and evaluating pre-stressed concrete beams [23]. AE analysis in composite beams includes damage detection, classification, and quantification. For example, studies have used parameters like average frequency versus rise time and AE hits versus test time to analyze fracture mechanisms in lightweight composite beams [24]. Rise time/amplitude (RA) analysis has differentiated flexural and shear failures in multi-layered beams [25]. AE ringing counts, energy, and *b*-value (the ratio of amplitude to the number of hits) analyses have investigated crack propagation in ultra-high-performance concrete (UHPC) hybrid composite beams [26], and *Ib*-value (improved *b*-value) analysis has examined crack development in ECC–normal concrete beams and failures of steel plate reinforcements [27].

However, AE applications in evaluating crack development and failure modes in ECC-LWSCC composite beams are limited. Specifically, research gaps exist regarding *b*-value analysis, *Ib*-value analysis, and rise time/amplitude analysis for categorizing cracking mechanisms and damage stages in large-scale ECC-LWSCC composite beams. The combination of ECC and LWSCC materials is expected to affect wave propagation characteristics due to the potential signal attenuation [28], necessitating further exploration of AE parameters' response to different fiber types (PVA or SF) in ECC layers. This study aims to assess ECC-LWSCC composite beam cracking behavior using AE parameters such as RA, *b*-value, and *Ib*-value analyses.

2. Research Significance

The exploitation of AE monitoring has proven effective in evaluating cracking behavior in both normal concrete and fiber-reinforced concrete beams. However, the literature still lacks information regarding the application of AE analysis for crack characterization, quantification, and evaluation in ECC-LWSCC composite beams. Further investigations are required to understand the effect of incorporating different fiber types in ECC on the cracking activity of ECC-LWSCC composite beams. Specifically, the literature lacks information regarding the effect of different concrete densities on AE wave propagation characteristics. This paper aims to address these gaps by utilizing AE analyses such as RA, *b*-value and *Ib*-value analyses to detect cracking activities and evaluate damage progression beyond the first crack.

3. Experimental Program

3.1. Material Properties and Mix Design of ECC and LWSCC

This study included three main mixtures: lightweight self-consolidating concrete (LWSCC), engineering cementitious composites with PVA or steel fibers (ECCP and ECCS). The design and proportions for these three main mixtures are summarized in Table 1. In the LWSCC mixture, slate lightweight coarse aggregate and fine aggregate were used. Their maximum aggregate sizes were 12.5 mm and 4.75 mm, respectively. The aggregates had specific gravities of 1.53 and 1.8 and water absorption rates of 7.1% and 10%, respectively. The LWSCC mixture had a density of 1727 kg/m^3, which classifies it as lightweight concrete according to the ACI [28] and CSA [29]. Details on the development of the LWSCC mixture are discussed elsewhere [9].

Table 1. Mixture designs and proportions for all tested beams [9].

Mixture	BC	C/BC	SCM Type	FA/BC	MK/BC	S/BC	CA/BC	W/BC	Fibers %	Fibers Type	Dry Density (kg/m^3)	fc/ (MPa)	STS (MPa)
LWSCC	1	0.40	FA+MK	0.40	0.20	0.94	0.8	0.40	-	-	1727	42.5	2.6
ECCP	1	0.45	FA+MK	0.35	0.20	0.36	-	0.27	2	PVA	2091	77.5	8.8
ECCS	1	0.45	FA+MK	0.35	0.20	0.36	-	0.27	2	SF	2222	82.5	10.5

Of the ECCP and ECCS mixtures, ordinary Portland cement type 1 (ASTM C150 [30]) constituted 45%, Class F fly ash (ASTM C618 [31]) constituted 35%, and Class N metakaolin (ASTM C618 [31]) constituted 20% and were used as binders. The ECC mixtures also included silica sand as a fine aggregate, with a maximum aggregate size of 400 μm and a specific gravity of 2.65. The fibers used in the ECC mixtures were 8 mm PVA fibers and 35 mm hooked-end steel fibers (SFs). According to the manufacturer's specifications, the PVA fibers were 8 mm in length, had an aspect ratio of 210, a diameter of 38 μm, a tensile strength of 1600 MPa, a Young's modulus of 40 GPa, and a density of 1300 kg/m^3. The SFs were 35 mm in length, had an aspect ratio of 65, a diameter of 0.55 mm, a tensile strength of 1050 MPa, and a density of 7850 kg/m^3. Metakaolin was used in this study to achieve an ECC compressive strength exceeding 70 MPa and to improve the viscosity of the cementitious paste, thereby enhancing the distribution of fibers [9].

3.2. Tested Beams

To evaluate their structural performance, a total of six beams were cast and subjected to four-point loading tests. Figure 1 illustrates the dimensions and reinforcement details of the tested beams. All the beams had a total length of 2160 mm, with a square cross-section of 250 × 250 mm and a concrete cover of 30 mm. The tensile reinforcement used consisted of three deformed steel bars with a diameter of 25 mm, while the compression reinforcement used consisted of two deformed steel bars with a diameter of 10 mm. Since all the beams were designed to fail in flexure, 10 mm stirrups were spaced at 100 mm intervals to prevent shear failure. The six tested beams are described as follows:

- The first two beams were fully cast with ECC containing either PVA fibers or SFs. These beams are referred to as ECCP and ECCS, respectively, and were used as control beams for comparison;

- The third and fourth beams were repaired in compression. The top layer was either ECCP or ECCS and was 85 mm in depth, while the bottom layer was LWSCC and was 165 mm in depth. These beams are referred to as ECCP-C and ECCS-C, respectively;
- The fifth and sixth beams were repaired in tension. The top layer was LWSCC and was 165 mm in depth, while the bottom layer was either ECCP or ECCS and was 85 mm in depth. These beams were designated as ECCP-T and ECCS-T, respectively.

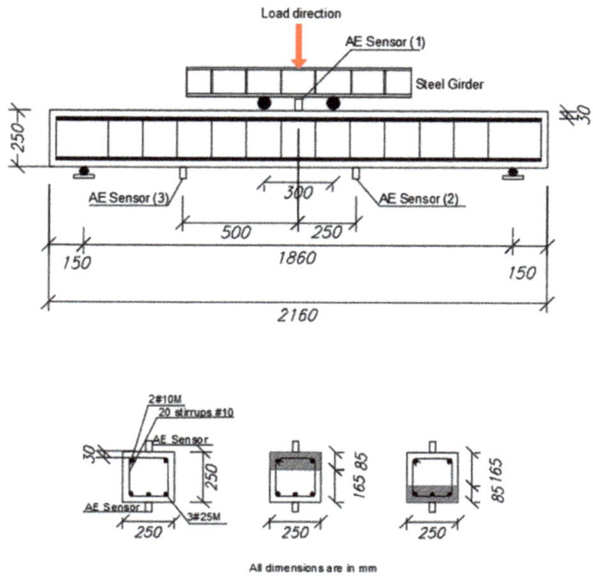

Figure 1. Test setup for all the tested beams.

The repaired depth for all the beams was selected to be 85 mm, which provided adequate space for the concrete around the longitudinal bars in the tension or compression zone. Specifically, the depth of the repaired layer was chosen to maintain a depth equal to the covering (30 mm) above and below the longitudinal bars. The bond between the ECC layer and the LWSCC layer was achieved through the placement of shear stirrups and the roughening of the surface of the interface between the two layers [9].

4. Flexural Test Setup

As illustrated in Figure 1, all the beams were simply supported using two round steel bars placed at a span of 1860 mm. A 500 kN hydraulic jack mounted on a steel girder was used to apply the loading for all the tested beams. The load was distributed using two points that were spaced 300 mm apart. Initially, the load was applied until a visible crack occurred at the beam's midspan. After the first visible crack was detected, the load was applied in increments of 45 kN. After each load increment, the widths of the cracks were measured using a microscope with 60× magnification. To measure any potential slippage between the two layers, two linear variable differential transformers (LVDTs) were placed at each end of the beam [9].

5. AE Monitoring Setup

The acoustic emission (AE) data collected for this study were continuously acquired throughout the tests using three sensors. As illustrated in Figure 1, one sensor (sensor 1) was attached to the compression zone of the beam at the midspan, while two other sensors

(sensors 2 and 3) were attached to the tension zone of the beam, spaced at 250 mm and 500 mm from sensor 1, respectively. All AE sensors were affixed to the beams using epoxy before the tests. The sensors used were piezoelectric AE sensors (model R61-AST [32]) with integral preamplifiers (incorporating a low-noise input, 40 dB preamplifier). These sensors are specifically engineered to attain high sensitivity (a peak sensitivity of 117 dB with reference V/(m/s)) and low resonant frequency properties (a resonant frequency of 55 kHz with reference V/(m/s)). To record the raw data and signals emitted during testing, AEwin for USB^{TM} software, Version E3.32 [33] was utilized. An amplitude magnitude of 40 dB was maintained, with the other parameters detailed in Table 2. The AE acquisition system recorded several parameters, including signal amplitude, absolute energy, rise time, count, peak frequency, and average frequency. Further details of these parameters can be found in ASTM E1316 [34].

Table 2. Constants for AE parameters set pre-testing.

AE Data-Monitoring Setup	
Threshold	40 dBAE
Sample rate	1 MSPS
Pre-trigger	256 μs
Length	1 k points
Preamp gain	40 dB
Peak definition	200 μs
Hit definition	800 μs
Hit lockout time	1000 μs
Maximum duration	1000 μs

6. Post-Testing AE Filtering

The AE raw data obtained during the four-point loading tests underwent a filtering process to eliminate noise or unwanted signals, using either an amplitude–duration-based filter or the Swansong II filter [35,36]. The filtering process is based on the principle that signals with high amplitudes and long durations, and vice versa, are considered authentic AE signals [37,38]. The acceptance/rejection criteria for amplitudes and durations are detailed in Table 3. Signals with amplitudes ranging from 40 to 45 dB were classified as noise and subsequently filtered out [39]. This filtering approach has been successfully employed in previous studies [40,41]. Following the filtering process, all remaining AE signals were attributed to actual cracking activities that occurred during the testing process.

Table 3. Rejection ranges for the filtering process.

Amplitude (dB)	Duration (μs)	
	Lower	Upper
$40 \leq A < 45$	0	400
$45 \leq A < 48$	0	500
$48 \leq A < 52$	0	600
$52 \leq A < 56$	0	700
$56 \leq A < 60$	100	800
$60 \leq A < 65$	300	1000
$65 \leq A < 70$	500	2000
$70 \leq A < 80$	1000	4000
$80 \leq A < 90$	2000	7000
$90 \leq A < 100$	3000	10,000

7. Results and Discussion

7.1. Cracking Behavior, Failure Mode, and Ultimate Load of the Tested Beams

Figure 2 illustrates the cracking pattern of the six tested beams. All the beams failed in flexural mode when the steel reinforcement in the tension zone reached the yield point and concrete crushing occurred at the compression zone. For the control beams (ECCP and ECCS), the first crack developed when the tensile strength at the tension zone of the beam reached its maximum due to the applied load. After the formation of the first crack, vertical cracks on the tension side of the beam started to form. As the load increments increased, diagonal cracks in the shear span (the distance between the point load and support) started to develop towards the compression zone. The number of cracks and their widths increased further with higher loads. ECCP and ECCS exhibited 34 and 37 visible cracks, respectively. Table 4 shows the ultimate loads obtained for all beams. ECCP and ECCS had failure loads of 349.8 kN and 358.7 kN, respectively. The failure loads for both beams were very comparable, which could be attributed to the fact that SFs enhanced both the compressive and pullout strength of the ECCs, neutralizing the high dispersion effect of PVA fibers (a lower fiber density and consequently higher fiber count and dispersion) [9].

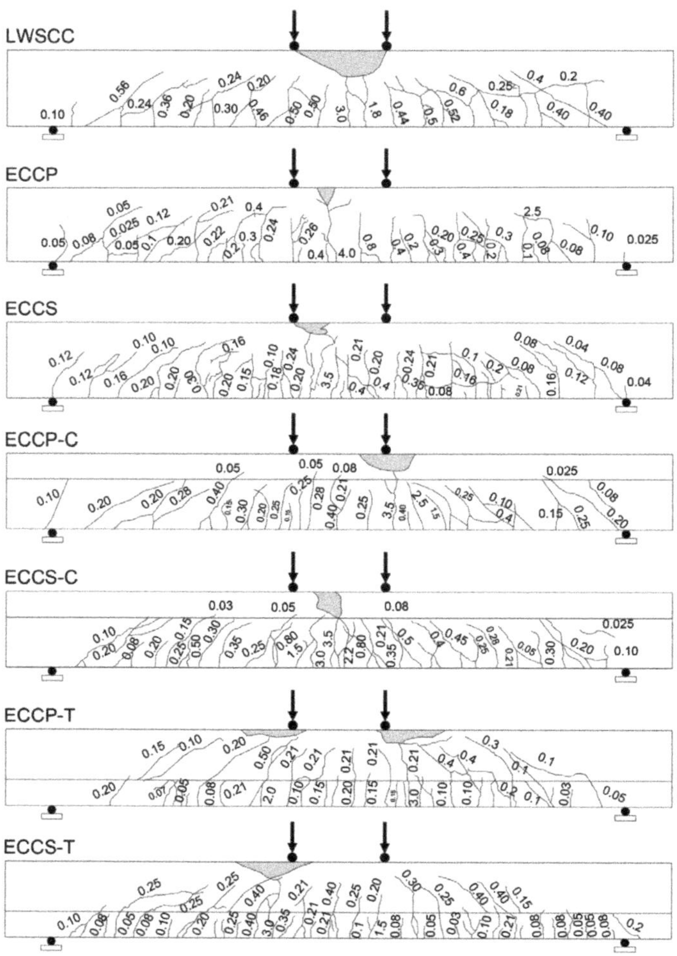

Figure 2. Cracking pattern for all tested beams [9].

Table 4. Experimental results obtained from the flexural tests.

Beam	First Crack Load (kN)	Maximum Crack Width at Service Load	Failure Load (kN)	Failure Mode
ECCP	27.6	0.18	349.8	Flexural
ECCS	23.1	0.24	358.7	Flexural
ECCP-C	14.5	0.35	301.9	Flexural
ECCS-C	15.1	0.40	308.0	Flexural
ECCP-T	28.3	0.20	313.7	Flexural
ECCS-T	26.2	0.22	330.4	Flexural

Regarding beams repaired in the compression zone (ECCP-C and ECCS-C), cracks began developing in the LWSCC layer (tension zone) during the loading process. As the load increased, some cracks formed horizontally at the LWSCC-ECC interface, while others perforated the interface with very small widths (less than 0.1 mm). ECCP-C displayed 27 cracks, while ECCS-C displayed 30 cracks. The failure loads for ECCP-C and ECCS-C were 301.9 kN and 308.0 kN, respectively (Table 4). The failure load values were comparable to each other and lower than those of the control beams, likely due to the repair in the compression zone and the absence of fibers in the tension zone (LWSCC), which contributed to delaying crack formation [9].

Crack development in beams repaired in the tension zone (ECCP-T and ECCS-T) was characterized by very fine vertical cracks in the ECC layer (tension zone). As the load increased, additional cracks developed at the ECC-LWSCC interface. These cracks initially propagated into the LWSCC layer and, with further loading, extended downward into the ECC layer with narrower widths due to the presence of fibers. ECCP-T and ECCS-T exhibited 30 and 37 visible cracks. These beams displayed failure loads of 313.7 kN and 330.4 kN, respectively, which were lower than those of the control beams. These results were attributed to the fact that the control beams were fully cast with ECC and lacked the LWSCC layer (42.5 MPa), compared to the high-strength layer of ECC (77.5 MPa to 82.5 MPa) [9].

7.2. *Crack Progression Investigation Using b-Value and Ib-Value Analyses*

7.2.1. Calculation of *b*-Value and *Ib*-Value Parameters

A *b*-value analysis was carried out on the AE signals collected throughout the testing. The *b*-value parameter was calculated as the ratio of amplitude to the number of hits. A *b*-value analysis has been successfully implemented in several previous investigations [42–44]. The application of the *b*-value was originally used in seismic magnitude–frequency equations and later expanded to the analysis of AE data [45]. The *b*-value was calculated using Equation (1):

$$\log N = a - b \log A \tag{1}$$

where N = the number of hits having an amplitude larger than A; A = signal amplitude (dB); a = the empirically derived constant; and b = the *b*-value [43,46]; the value 'a' was obtained by plotting log N (y-axis) versus log A (x-axis) for all the six beams. The average value of 'a' for all the beams was then calculated and applied in Equation (1).

Furthermore, an improved *b*-value (*Ib*-value) analysis was also carried out. The *Ib*-value, initially proposed by Shiotani [47], has been successfully utilized in similar previous investigations [48,49]. The *Ib*-value is calculated using Equation (2):

$$\mathrm{Ib} = \frac{\log_{10} N(\mu - \alpha_1 \sigma) - \log_{10} N(\mu + \alpha_2 \sigma)}{(\alpha_1 + \alpha_2)\sigma} \tag{2}$$

where N = the number of hits having an amplitude larger than A; A = signal amplitude (dB); σ = the standard deviation of the amplitude distribution of the AE event group; α = mean values of the amplitude distribution of the AE event group; and α_1 and α_2 are user-defined constants obtained from the upper and lower limits of the amplitude. All of the previously mentioned constants are calculated based on 100 hits [50].

7.2.2. Evaluation of Crack Development by *b*-Value and *Ib*-Value Analyses

The ECCP-T (sensor 1) beam was chosen as a typical example for all beams and sensors. Figure 3 shows the trends resulting from both the *b*-value and *Ib*-value analyses for the ECCP-T beam (sensor 1). Referring to Figure 3a, the *b*-value followed a generally decreasing trend. The decrease in *b*-value magnitudes indicates crack propagation leading to failure throughout the test duration. Generally, lower *b*-values correspond to higher cracking activity. Furthermore, the first noticeable decrease, around 120 s, represents the occurrence of the first crack. The sudden drops in *b*-value were also correlated with changes in the AE parameters' slopes.

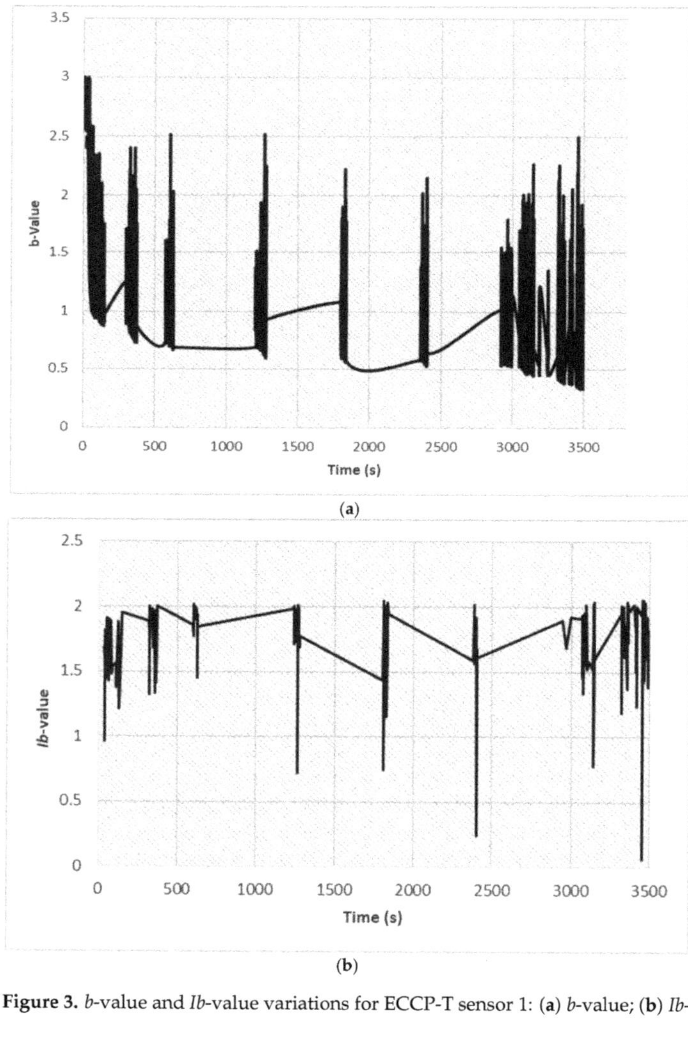

(b)

Figure 3. *b*-value and *Ib*-value variations for ECCP-T sensor 1: (**a**) *b*-value; (**b**) *Ib*-value.

In Figure 3b, the *Ib*-value does not follow a clear trend, unlike the *b*-value. However, the sudden fluctuations (vertical drops) in Figure 3b indicate high cracking activity [50]. To pinpoint the periods of highest cracking activity, the difference between the maximum and minimum points of fluctuation is calculated. For example, in Figure 3b, the highest cracking activity (ultimate load) is observed around 3450 s (*Ib*-value of 2.052 − 0.069 = 1.983). The first significant vertical drop (first crack) in Figure 3b is also around 120 s, similar to the *b*-value analysis for the first crack. Moreover, the fluctuation trends in Figure 3b resemble those in Figure 3a, showing similar cracking activities at corresponding time intervals.

Table 5 presents the *b*-values and *Ib*-values for all the beams. The ECCP and ECCS beams showed average *b*-values and *Ib*-values of 2.19, 1.39, 1.516, and 1.62 at the first crack, respectively. The ECCP-C and ECCS-C beams exhibited average *b*-values and *Ib*-values of 2.44, 1.39, 1.74, and 1.85 at the first crack, respectively. ECCP-T and ECCS-T resulted in average *b*-values and *Ib*-values of 0.84, 0.95, 1.84, and 1.74 at the first crack, respectively. Both b-values and *Ib*-values yield promising results for understanding and analyzing crack onset and development throughout the testing process.

Table 5. *b*-value and *Ib*-value at first crack and ultimate load.

Beam	Sensor	*b*-Value		*Ib*-Value	
		First Crack	Ultimate Load	First Crack	Ultimate Load
ECCP	CH-1	2.78	0.86	1.47	1.79
	CH-2	1.14	0.24	1.45	1.82
	CH-3	2.64	0.41	1.63	2.08
ECCS	CH-1	1.77	0.20	1.48	2.09
	CH-2	0.96	0.09	1.73	1.96
	CH-3	1.44	0.12	1.65	2.05
ECCP-C	CH-1	2.76	1.02	1.67	1.74
	CH-2	1.86	0.61	1.79	1.66
	CH-3	2.71	0.74	1.77	1.65
ECCS-C	CH-1	1.52	0.97	1.85	1.96
	CH-2	1.51	0.69	1.88	1.97
	CH-3	1.16	0.78	1.82	1.95
ECCP-T	CH-1	0.93	0.51	1.88	2.052
	CH-2	0.74	0.36	1.88	2.042
	CH-3	0.84	0.46	1.75	2.064
ECCS-T	CH-1	1.08	0.63	1.82	1.62
	CH-2	0.82	0.38	1.68	1.89
	CH-3	0.96	0.52	1.72	1.86

7.3. Impact of Fiber Type on AE Parameters

Table 6 shows the values of the AE parameters, including the number of hits and cumulative signal strength (CSS) at the first crack and ultimate load.

As observed from Table 6, the effect of fiber type (PVA or SF) was most evident in the number of hits and CSS. It can be concluded that beams repaired or fully cast with PVA fibers generally displayed a higher number of hits compared to beams repaired or fully cast with SFs, specifically at the first crack. For ECCP and ECC, the average number of hits and CSS at the first crack were 2859 hits, 2.92×10^7 pV.s and 2384 hits, 2.46×10^7 pV.s, respectively. ECCP-T and ECCS-T showed an average number of hits of 2990 and 2666 hits, respectively, and CSS values of 3.07×10^7 pV.s and 3.01×10^7 pV.s, respectively.

Beams repaired in compression, however, were not significantly affected by these phenomena, as the material existing on the tension side was LWSCC. The rationale behind the higher number of hits and CSS in beams incorporated with PVA fibers is that PVA fibers generally have a lower density than SFs. The lower density and smaller size of PVA fibers allow for more dispersion in the ECCS at the same fiber volume as SFs. Therefore, a higher number of PVA fibers are present, which delay crack formation compared to SFs [9].

Table 6. CSS and number of hits at first crack and ultimate load.

Beam	Sensor	CSS × 10^7		Number of Hits	
		First Crack	Ultimate Load	First Crack	Ultimate Load
ECCP	CH-1	2.42	35.1	2705	25162
	CH-2	3.59	48.7	2964	27902
	CH-3	2.75	38.6	2910	27140
ECCS	CH-1	2.03	40.2	2245	25902
	CH-2	3.05	45.6	2492	28690
	CH-3	2.30	43.9	2417	27910
ECCP-C	CH-1	1.36	12.8	1514	21925
	CH-2	2.03	33.7	1669	24305
	CH-3	1.58	31.4	1621	23650
ECCS-C	CH-1	0.33	22.7	1617	22290
	CH-2	1.12	5.64	1789	24705
	CH-3	0.45	19.9	1750	24050
ECCP-T	CH-1	2.55	30.3	2816	22644
	CH-2	3.77	34.8	3120	25102
	CH-3	2.89	32.4	3035	24420
ECCS-T	CH-1	2.94	32.5	2453	24090
	CH-2	3.12	37	2810	26695
	CH-3	2.99	34.5	2736	25971

Conversely, at ultimate load, the number of hits displayed by beams incorporating/ repaired with PVA fibers is very comparable to those repaired with steel fibers. For instance, ECCP and ECCS displayed an average number of hits of 26734 and 27500 hits, respectively, and CSS values of 40.8 × 10^7 pV.s and 43.2 × 10^7 pV.s at ultimate load, respectively. ECCP-T and ECCS-T exhibited average values of number of hits and CSSs of 24055 and 25585 hits, 32.5 × 10^7 pV.s and 34.6 × 10^7 pV.s at ultimate load, respectively. These parameters correlated well with the number of cracks in the ECCS-T and ECCP-T beams (30 and 37 cracks, respectively) [9]. A similar trend was also observed in the cracking activities of ECCP and ECCS beams at ultimate load (34 and 37 cracks, respectively) [9]. Therefore, the number of hits and the CSS were found to be useful in demonstrating the impact of the different fiber types used in this study.

7.4. Evaluation of Wave Propagation Characteristics Among the Tested Beams

The wave propagation characteristics across all beams were best illustrated by variations in signal amplitude, which were influenced by the sensor placements at different locations (top and bottom) relative to the repair area (Figure 1).

Figure 4 depicts the signal amplitudes at the time of the first crack detection in all the beams. It can be observed that beams repaired under compression or tension experienced variations due to wave propagation. These variations were caused by differences in the density of the ECC and LWSCC, which affected the signal amplitude depending on the sensor location. Specifically, the signal amplitude at sensor 1 differed significantly from those at sensors 2 and 3, indicating signal attenuation due to the differing material densities (lack of homogeneity) [51,52].

For the ECCP-T beam, sensor 1 showed a signal amplitude of 40 dB, while sensors 2 and 3 displayed 47 dB and 46 dB, respectively (Figure 4). Conversely, beams entirely cast in ECCP or ECCS showed negligible signal propagation, resulting in very similar amplitude values (Figure 4). For instance, in ECCP, the signal amplitudes at sensors 1, 2, and 3 were 56 dB, 56 dB, and 55 dB, respectively at the first crack detection.

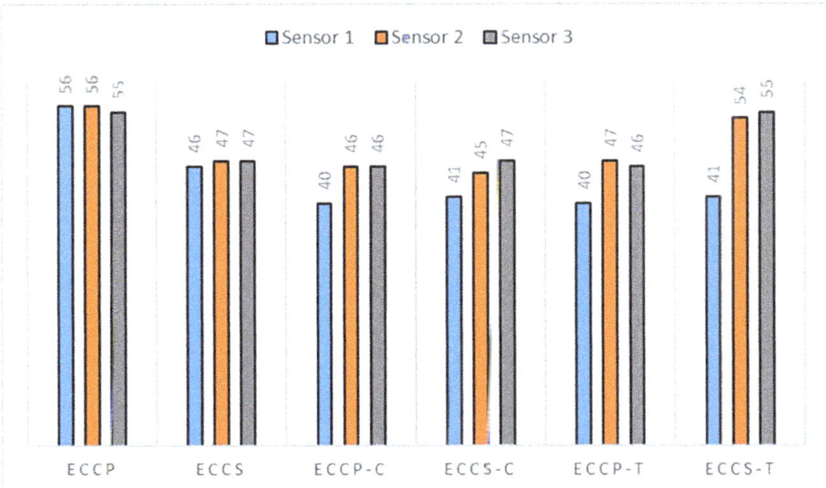

Figure 4. Signal amplitude variations at the first crack for the three sensors of all the tested beams.

7.5. Failure Mode Characterization Using Rise Time/Maximum Amplitude (RA) Analysis

The rise time/maximum amplitude (RA) versus average frequency (AF) are crucial acoustic emission (AE) parameters that effectively distinguish between flexural and shear failure modes [25,53–55]. The flexural failure mode is typically characterized by tensile cracking, whereas the shear failure mode involves shear cracking. Studies have shown that, initially, AF values are significantly higher compared to RA values, whereas towards the end of the test, RA values become higher than AF values. This disparity arises because tensile cracks predominantly occur during the early stages of flexural testing, while shear cracks tend to appear later in the process [56–58]. RA analysis has been successfully employed in previous studies to identify fracture modes in concrete structures [25,53–55]. RA and AF values are determined using Equations (3) and (4) [55]:

$$RA = \text{Rise time/maximum amplitude} \quad (3)$$

$$AF = \text{counts/duration time} \quad (4)$$

According to the JSCM-111 [59] code, RA analysis was implemented by obtaining the average of RA and AF values based on 50 hits. In this study, the average values of rise time, maximum amplitude, and average frequency were acquired from the three sensors for each beam. Furthermore, the average of RA and AF of the 50 hits was obtained to construct the charts in Figure 5 for all the tested beams. The diagonal line was constructed by drawing a horizontal line at the farthest AF point and a vertical line at the farthest RA point (Figure 5). The intersection point is then determined by constructing the two lines. The slope of each diagonal point was then calculated and presented in Figure 5. This method has been used in previous papers with similar research investigations [60–62].

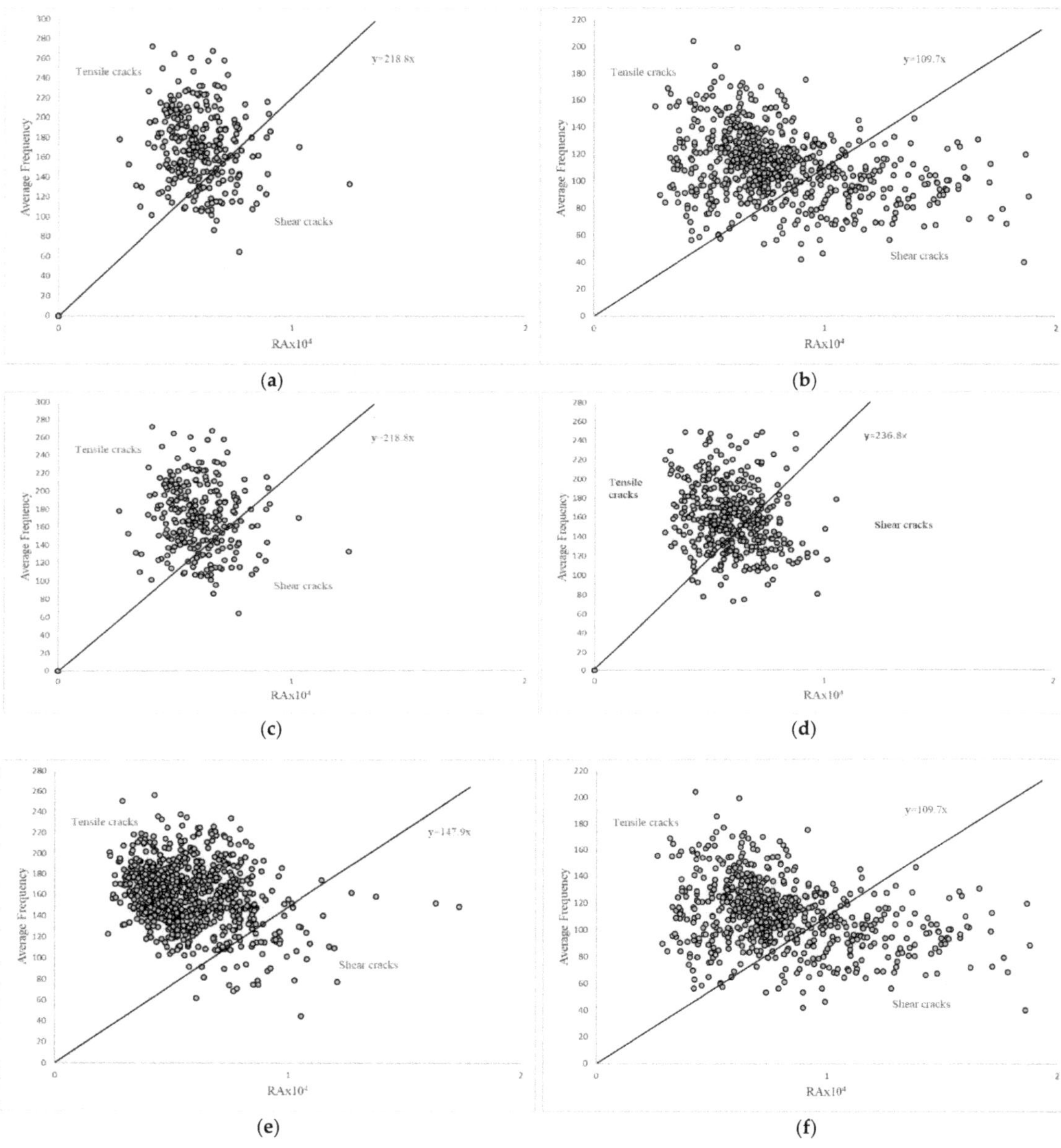

Figure 5. RA vs. AF analysis for all six beams: (**a**) ECCS; (**b**) ECCP; (**c**) ECCP-C; (**d**) ECCS-C; (**e**) ECCP-T; (**f**) ECCS-T.

By observing the charts in Figure 5, it is evident that in all the beams, the majority of the points dominate the left side of the diagonal line, although some points lie on the right side of the line. Consequently, the majority of the cracks are tensile cracks, and therefore, all the beams are depicted as failed in flexural mode. Based on the aforementioned results, RA vs. AF analysis proved to be an effective tool in identifying the failure mode of the tested beams.

8. Conclusions

For the purpose of the damage characterization of ECC-LWSCC composite beams under flexural loading, an experimental study was conducted using several AE analyses. Six beams were tested, each constructed with different fibers (PVA or SF) and repaired in various locations: two beams were fully cast with ECC (ECCP and ECCS), two beams were repaired in compression (ECCP-C and ECCS-C), and two beams were repaired in tension (ECCP-T and ECCS-T). Three sensors monitored the changes resulting from crack development until failure. The post-testing analysis of AE data yielded the following conclusions:

- All six beams failed in flexural mode after reinforcement bars in the tension zone yielded and the concrete in the compression zone was crushed. The control beams (ECCP and ECCS) showed the highest ultimate load capacity, followed by beams repaired in tension (ECCP-T and ECCS-T), and then beams repaired in compression (ECCP-C and ECCS-C). PVA fibers exhibited superior performance compared to steel fibers at the first crack load. However, steel fibers enhanced beam performance at the ultimate load stage;
- Analysis of both the *b*-value and *Ib*-value proved useful in evaluating crack growth throughout the testing. A general decrease in *b*-value after the detection of the first crack reflected ongoing crack development. The *Ib*-value exhibited a fluctuating trend, with sudden vertical drops indicating high cracking activity. The first crack was consistently detected, coinciding with the first decreasing trend in *b*-value and the first increase in *Ib*-value across all beams.
- Different fiber types impacted the number of hits and CSS among the tested beams. Beams fully cast or repaired with PVA fibers displayed higher hits and CSSs at the first crack due to dispersion effects. However, at the ultimate load stage, beams with SFs demonstrated higher hits and CSSs due to enhanced compressive and pullout strengths balancing the dispersion effect of the PVA fibers;
- Variations in sensor location significantly affected wave propagation characteristics in ECC-LWSCC composite beams, specifically signal amplitude. Signal amplitude values varied between sensors due to signal attenuation and was particularly evident in all composite beams due to material homogeneity. Fully cast ECC beams did not experience signal attenuation, with signal amplitude values closely aligned across the three sensors;
- RA vs. AF analysis successfully characterized the failure modes in all the beams, predominantly in the tensile cracking zone indicating flexural failure. RA analysis effectively determined the failure modes, corroborating the experimental results;
- Overall, these findings confirmed the usefulness of AE analysis in understanding the behavior of ECC-LWSCC composite beams under flexural loading, highlighting the influence of fiber type, repair location, and sensor placement on structural performance and failure characteristics. The practical application of these results includes the implementation of AE monitoring in assessing LWSCC repaired with ECCs. In particular, AE analysis can be used as a useful tool for evaluating the structural performance of LWSCC beams repaired with an ECC layer.

Author Contributions: Conceptualization, A.H. and A.A.; methodology, Y.Z.; software, Y.Z.; validation, Y.Z., A.A. and A.H.; formal analysis, Y.Z.; investigation, Y.Z.; resources, A.H.; data curation, A.A.; writing—original draft preparation, Y.Z.; writing—review and editing, A.A. and A.H.; visualization, A.A.; supervision, A.A. and A.H.; project administration, A.H.; funding acquisition, A.H. All authors have read and agreed to the published version of the manuscript.

Funding: This research received no external funding.

Institutional Review Board Statement: Not applicable.

Informed Consent Statement: Not applicable.

Data Availability Statement: The original contributions presented in this study are included in the article. Further inquiries can be directed to the corresponding author.

Conflicts of Interest: The authors declare no conflicts of interest.

References

1. Grosse, C.U.; Ohtsu, M.; Aggelis, D.G.; Shiotani, T. (Eds.) *Acoustic Emission Testing: Basics for Research–Applications in Engineerin* Springer Nature: Berlin/Heidelberg, Germany, 2021.
2. Umehara, H.; Uehara, T.; Enomoto, Y.; Oka, S. Development and usage of lightweight high performance concrete. In Proceeding of the International Conference on high Performance Concrete (Supplementary Papers), Singapore, 21–22 November 199 American Concrete Institute: Detroit, MI, USA, 1994.
3. Yao, S.X.; Gerwick, B.C.; Gerwick, B. *Development of Self-Compacting Lightweight Concrete for Rfp Reinforced Floating Concret Structures*; Technical Report; US Army Corps of Engineers Research and Development Center: San Francisco, CA, USA, 2006.
4. Omar, A.T.; Ismail, M.K.; Hassan, A.A. Use of polymeric fibers in the development of semilightweight self-consolidating concret containing expanded slate. *J. Mater. Civ. Eng.* **2020**, *32*, 04020067. [CrossRef]
5. Murthy, A.R.; Karihaloo, B.; Rani, P.V.; Priya, D.S. Fatigue behaviour of damaged RC beams strengthened with ultra hig performance fibre reinforced concrete. *Int. J. Fatigue* **2018**, *116*, 659–668. [CrossRef]
6. Deng, M.; Ma, F.; Ye, W.; Li, F. Flexural behavior of reinforced concrete beams strengthened by HDC and RPC. *Constr. Build. Mate* **2018**, *188*, 995–1006. [CrossRef]
7. Kim, J.-H.J.; Lim, Y.M.; Won, J.-P.; Park, H.-G.; Lee, K.-M. Shear capacity and failure behavior of DFRCC repaired RC beams a tensile region. *Eng. Struct.* **2007**, *29*, 121–131. [CrossRef]
8. Engindeniz, M.; Kahn, L.F.; Abdul-Hamid, Z. Repair and strengthening of reinforced concrete beam-column joints: State of th art. *ACI Struct. J.* **2005**, *102*, 1.
9. Batran, T.Z.; Ismail, M.K.; Hassan, A.A. Flexural behavior of lightweight self-consolidating concrete beams strengthened wit engineered cementitious composite. *ACI Mater. J.* **2021**, *118*, 39–50.
10. Li, V.C. Tailoring ECC for Special Attributes: A Review. *Int. J. Concr. Struct. Mater.* **2012**, *6*, 135–144. [CrossRef]
11. Li, V.C. Engineered cementitious composites (ECC)-tailored composites through micromechanical modeling. In *Fiber Reinforce Concrete: Present and the Future*; Banthia, N., Bentur, A., Mufti, A., Eds.; Canadian Society for Civil Engineering: Montreal, QC Canada, 1998.
12. Kong, H.-J.; Bike, S.G.; Li, V.C. Development of a self-consolidating engineered cementitious composite employing electrosteri dispersion/stabilization. *Cem. Concr. Compos.* **2003**, *25*, 301–309. [CrossRef]
13. Li, V.C.; Wu, C.; Wang, S.; Ogawa, A.; Saito, T. Interface tailoring for strain-hardening polyvinyl alcohol-engineered cementitiou composite (PVA-ECC). *Mater. J.* **2002**, *99*, 463–472.
14. Mustafa, S.; Li, V. Engineered cementitious composites, transportation research record. *J. Transp. Res. Board.* **2010**, *2164*, 1–8.
15. Said, S.H.; Razak, H.A. The effect of synthetic polyethylene fiber on the strain hardening behavior of engineered cementitiou composite (ECC). *Mater. Des.* **2015**, *86*, 447–457. [CrossRef]
16. Hossain, K.; Hasib, S.; Manzur, T. Shear behavior of novel hybrid composite beams made of self-consolidating concrete an engineered cementitious composites. *Eng. Struct.* **2020**, *202*, 109856. [CrossRef]
17. Batran, T.Z.; Ismail, M.K.; Hassan, A.A. Behavior of novel hybrid lightweight concrete composites under drop-weight impac loading. *Structures* **2021**, *34*, 2789–2800. [CrossRef]
18. Ismail, M.K.; Abdelaleem, B.H.; Hassan, A.A. Effect of fiber type on the behavior of cementitious composite beam-column joint under reversed cyclic loading. *Constr. Build. Mater.* **2018**, *186*, 969–977. [CrossRef]
19. Aggelis, D.; De Sutter, S.; Verbruggen, S.; Tsangouri, E.; Tysmans, T. Acoustic emission characterization of damage sources o lightweight hybrid concrete beams. *Eng. Fract. Mech.* **2019**, *210*, 181–188. [CrossRef]
20. Aggelis, D.; Soulioti, D.; Sapouridis, N.; Barkoula, N.; Paipetis, A.; Matikas, T. Acoustic emission characterization of the fractur process in fibre reinforced concrete. *Constr. Build. Mater.* **2011**, *25*, 4126–4131. [CrossRef]
21. Shigeishi, M.; Colombo, S.; Broughton, K.; Rutledge, H.; Batchelor, A.; Forde, M. Acoustic emission to assess and monitor th integrity of bridges. *Constr. Build. Mater.* **2001**, *15*, 35–49. [CrossRef]
22. Farhidzadeh, A.; Dehghan-Niri, E.; Salamone, S.; Luna, B.; Whittaker, A. Monitoring crack propagation in reinforced concret shear walls by acoustic emission. *J. Struct. Eng.* **2013**, *139*, 04013010. [CrossRef]
23. Abdelrahman, M.; ElBatanouny, M.K.; Ziehl, P.H. Acoustic emission based damage assessment method for prestressed concret structures: Modified index of damage. *Eng. Struct.* **2014**, *60*, 258–264. [CrossRef]

Aggelis, D.G.; De Sutter, S.; Verbruggen, S.; Tysmans, T. Fracture monitoring of lightweight composite-concrete beams with acoustic emission. In Proceedings of the 14th International Conference on Fracture, ICF 2017, Rhodes, Greece, 18–23 June 2017.

Ranjbar, N.; Behnia, A.; Chai, H.K.; Alengaram, U.J.; Jumaat, M.Z. Fracture evaluation of multi-layered precast reinforced geopolymer-concrete composite beams by incorporating acoustic emission into mechanical analysis. *Constr. Build. Mater.* **2016**, *127*, 274–283. [CrossRef]

Li, S.; Zhang, L.; Guo, P.; Zhang, P.; Wang, C.; Sun, W.; Han, S. Characteristic analysis of acoustic emission monitoring parameters for crack propagation in UHPC-NC composite beam under bending test. *Constr. Build. Mater.* **2021**, *278*, 122401. [CrossRef]

Li, S.; Hou, J.; Guo, P.; Zhang, X.; Zhang, P. Analysis of acoustic emission parameters of steel plate reinforcement effect on shearing zone of ECC-NC composite beams. *Eng. Struct.* **2022**, *266*, 114505. [CrossRef]

ACI Committee 318. *Building Code Requirements for Structural Concrete (ACI 318-08) and Commentary*; American Concrete Institute: Detroit, MI, USA, 2008.

CSA A23.3-04; Design of Concrete Structures. Canadian Standards Association: Rexdale, ON, Canada, 2004.

ASTM C150/C150M; Standard Specification for Portland Cement. ASTM International: West Conshohocken, PA, USA, 2012; p. 9.

ASTM C618; Standard Specification for Coal Fly ash and Raw or Calcined Natural Pozzolan for Use in Concrete. ASTM International: West Conshohocken, PA, USA, 2012.

MISTRAS Group. *R6I-AST Sensor*; Physical Acoustics Corporation: Princeton Junction, NJ, USA, 2005.

MISTRAS Group. *PCI-2 Based AE System 1 User's Manual*; Physical Acoustics Corporation: Princeton Junction, NJ, USA, 2007.

ASTM E1316; ASTM, Standard Terminology for Nondestructive Examinations. ASTM International: West Conshohocken, PA, USA, 2014.

Abouhussien, A.A.; AHassan, A.; AbdelAleem, B.H. Acoustic Emission Analysis of Self-Consolidating Rubberized Concrete Beam-Column Connections under Cyclic Loading. *ACI Struct. J.* **2019**, *116*, 41. [CrossRef]

Abouhussien, A.A.; Hassan, A.A. Acoustic emission monitoring for bond integrity evaluation of reinforced concrete under pull-out tests. *Adv. Struct. Eng.* **2017**, *20*, 1390–1405. [CrossRef]

Abouhussien, A.A.; Hassan, A.A.; Ismail, M.K.; AbdelAleem, B.H. Evaluating the cracking behavior of ECC beam-column connections under cyclic loading by acoustic emission analysis. *Constr. Build. Mater.* **2019**, *215*, 958–968. [CrossRef]

Abouhussien, A.A.; Hassan, A.A. Crack Growth Monitoring in Fiber-Reinforced Self-Consolidating Concrete via Acoustic Emission. *ACI Mater. J.* **2019**, *116*, 181–191. [CrossRef]

Abouhussien, A.A.; Hassan, A.A. The use of acoustic emission intensity analysis for the assessment of cover crack growth in corroded concrete structures. *J. Nondestruct. Eval.* **2016**, *35*, 52. [CrossRef]

ElBatanouny, M.K.; Mangual, J.; Ziehl, P.H.; Matta, F. Early corrosion detection in prestressed concrete girders using acoustic emission. *J. Mater. Civ. Eng.* **2014**, *26*, 504–511. [CrossRef]

Abouhussien, A.A.; Hassan, A.A.A. Evaluation of damage progression in concrete structures due to reinforcing steel corrosion using acoustic emission monitoring. *J. Civ. Struct. Health Monit.* **2015**, *5*, 751–765. [CrossRef]

Li, D.; Chen, Z.; Feng, Q.; Wang, Y. Damage analysis of CFRP-confined circular concrete-filled steel tubular columns by acoustic emission techniques. *Smart Mater. Struct.* **2015**, *24*, 085017. [CrossRef]

Colombo, I.S.; Main, I.; Forde, M. Assessing damage of reinforced concrete beam using "b-value" analysis of acoustic emission signals. *J. Mater. Civ. Eng.* **2003**, *15*, 280–286. [CrossRef]

Sagar, R.V.; Prasad, B.R.; Kumar, S.S. An experimental study on cracking evolution in concrete and cement mortar by the b-value analysis of acoustic emission technique. *Cem. Concr. Res.* **2012**, *42*, 1094–1104. [CrossRef]

ElBatanouny, M.K.; Larosche, A.; Mazzoleni, P.; Ziehl, P.H.; Matta, F.; Zappa, E. Identification of cracking mechanisms in scaled FRP reinforced concrete beams using acoustic emission. *Exp. Mech.* **2014**, *54*, 69–82. [CrossRef]

Ohtsu, M.; Tomoda, Y. Phenomenological model of corrosion process in reinforced concrete identified by acoustic emission. *ACI Mater. J.* **2008**, *105*, 194–199.

Shiotani, T.; Fujii, K.; Aoki, T.; Amou, K. Evaluation of Progressive Failure Using AE Sources/Improved *b*-Value on Slope Model Tests. *Prog. Acoust. Emiss.* **1994**, *7*, 529–534.

Shiotani, T.; Ohtsu, M. Prediction of slope failure based on AE activity. *ASTM Spec. Tech. Publ.* **1999**, *1353*, 156–174.

Shiotani, T. Application of the AE Improved b-Value to Quantiative Evaluation of Fracture Process in Concrete-Materials. *J. Acoust. Emiss.* **2001**, *19*, 118–133.

Han, Q.; Yang, G.; Xu, J.; Fu, Z.; Lacidogna, G.; Carpinteri, A. Acoustic emission data analyses based on crumb rubber concrete beam bending tests. *Eng. Fract. Mech.* **2019**, *210*, 189–202. [CrossRef]

Ervin, B.L.; Bernhard, J.T.; Kuchma, D.A.; Reis, H. Monitoring general corrosion of rebar embedded in mortar using high-frequency guided mechanical waves. In Proceedings of the Sensors and Smart Structures Technologies for Civil, Mechanical, and Aerospace Systems 2007, San Diego, CA, USA, 19–22 March 2007.

Schumacher, T.; Higgins, C.C.; Lovejoy, S.C. Estimating operating load conditions on reinforced concrete highway bridges with b-value analysis from acoustic emission monitoring. *Struct. Health Monit.* **2011**, *10*, 17–32. [CrossRef]

53. Prem, P.R.; Murthy, A.R. Acoustic emission monitoring of reinforced concrete beams subjected to four-point-bending. *Appl. Aco* **2017**, *117*, 28–38. [CrossRef]
54. Behnia, A.; Chai, H.K.; Shiotani, T. Advanced structural health monitoring of concrete structures with the aid of acoustic emissi *Constr. Build. Mater.* **2014**, *65*, 282–302. [CrossRef]
55. Ohno, K.; Ohtsu, M. Crack classification in concrete based on acoustic emission. *Constr. Build. Mater.* **2010**, *24*, 2339–23 [CrossRef]
56. Aggelis, D.G. Classification of cracking mode in concrete by acoustic emission parameters. *Mech. Res. Commun.* **2011**, *38*, 153–1 [CrossRef]
57. Grosse, C.U.; Ohtsu, M. *Acoustic Emission Testing*; Springer Science & Business Media: Berlin/Heidelberg, Germany, 2008.
58. Shahidan, S.; Pulin, R.; Bunnori, N.M.; Holford, K.M. Damage classification in reinforced concrete beam by acoustic emissi signal analysis. *Constr. Build. Mater.* **2013**, *45*, 78–86. [CrossRef]
59. *JCMS-III B5706*; Monitoring Method for Active Cracks in Concrete by Acoustic Emission. Federation of Construction Mater Industries: Tokyo, Japan, 2003; pp. 23–28.
60. Soulioti, D.; Barkoula, N.; Paipetis, A.; Matikas, T.; Shiotani, T.; Aggelis, D. Acoustic emission behavior of steel fibre reinforc concrete under bending. *Constr. Build. Mater.* **2009**, *23*, 3532–3536. [CrossRef]
61. Behnia, A.; Chai, H.; Yorikawa, M.; Momoki, S.; Terazawa, M.; Shiotani, T. Integrated non-destructive assessment of concre structures under flexure by acoustic emission and travel time tomography. *Constr. Build. Mater.* **2014**, *67*, 202–215. [CrossRef]
62. Prem, P.R.; Murthy, A.R. Acoustic emission and flexural behaviour of RC beams strengthened with UHPC overl *Constr. Build. Mater.* **2016**, *123*, 481–492. [CrossRef]

applied sciences

MDPI

Article

Deep Learning-Based Low-Frequency Passive Acoustic Source Localization

Arnav Joshi * and Jean-Pierre Hickey

Department of Mechanical and Mechatronics Engineering, University of Waterloo, Waterloo, ON N2L 3G1, Canada; j6hickey@uwaterloo.ca
* Correspondence: a5joshi@uwaterloo.ca

Abstract: This paper develops benchmark cases for low- and very-low-frequency passive acoustic source localization (ASL) using synthetic data. These cases can be potentially applied to the detection of turbulence-generated low-frequency acoustic emissions in the atmosphere. A deep learning approach is used as an alternative to conventional beamforming, which performs poorly under these conditions. The cases, which include two- and three-dimensional ASL, use a shallow and inexpensive convolutional neural network (CNN) with an appropriate input feature to optimize the source localization. CNNs are trained on a limited dataset to highlight the computational tractability and viability of the low-frequency ASL approach. Despite the modest training sets and computational expense, detection accuracies of at least 80% and far superior performance compared with beamforming are achieved—a result that can be improved with more data, training, and deeper networks. These benchmark cases offer well-defined and repeatable representative problems for comparison and further development of deep learning-based low-frequency ASL.

Keywords: acoustic source localization; convolutional neural network; turbulence-generated low-frequency acoustic emissions

1. Introduction

The detection of low-frequency acoustic sources is an important topic in the field of acoustic source localization (ASL). Low-frequency sources (30–300 Hz) and their detection are common in the fields of aeroacoustics, underwater acoustics [1–3], seismology [4–6], and other related fields [7]. Here, we are primarily interested in applications in aeroacoustics, specifically in the turbulence-generated low-frequency acoustic emissions. Wake turbulence, which is characterized by wake vortices, has been shown to emit a characteristic low-frequency noise [8] that can be used to locate wake vortices in an effort to minimize wake turbulence encounters [9] and increase airport efficiency and throughput [10]. Other applications include large-scale atmospheric turbulence detection [11] using ground-based microphone arrays and the characterization of volcano jets through their aeroacoustics information [12].

Acoustic sources at low frequencies cause methods such as conventional beamforming [13–15] to suffer from poor resolution. Figure 1 shows the increasingly poor localization predictions as the source frequency decreases. The resolution is even poorer for the low-frequency range we are interested in. This can be attributed to the Rayleigh resolution criterion, originally given for the angular resolution of an optical system [16] but can be applied analogously to an acoustical system. The source map obtained from conventional beamforming can be improved through post-processing by deconvolution algorithms such as DAMAS [17] and CLEAN-SC [14]; however, a perfectly clean and accurate source map is difficult to obtain [18]. Due to this limitation of beamforming, other approaches for low-frequency source localization have to be explored.

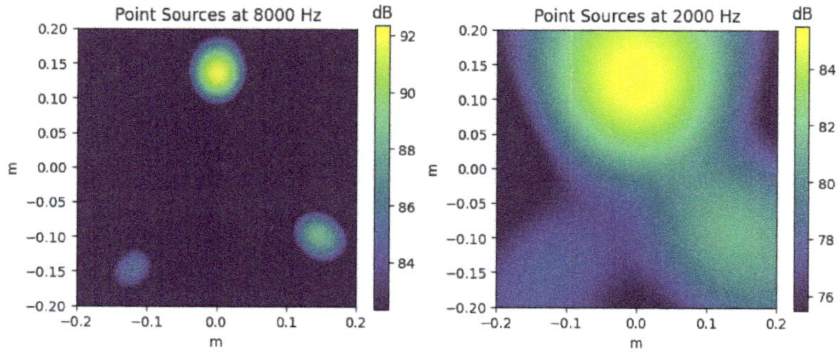

Figure 1. Comparison of beamforming result for point sources (located at (0, 0.14, 0.3), (0.15, −0.1, 0.3), and (−0.12, −0.15, 0.3)) emitting white noise signals over 1/3 octave bands with center frequencies of 8000 Hz and 2000 Hz, obtained using the open-source beamforming framework developed by Sarradj and Herold [19].

Machine learning (ML), and deep learning (DL) in particular, have shown great promise in the field of acoustics [20–22]. Deep learning algorithms involve the use of neural networks that process data in multiple layers to perform regression, classification, and many other such tasks.

Despite the limitations of these methods, such as requiring large numbers of data and not being physically intuitive, the ability of deep learning algorithms to extract features from data in any shape or form provides much scope for their application in ASL. Thus, the goal of this paper is to build deep learning models for low-frequency ASL as an alternative to beamforming.

A general study of the literature on deep learning-based ASL offers insights into the different kinds of input features and network architectures used, which can then be applied to low-frequency source localization. Most research in deep learning-based ASL is focused on the localization of speech signals. While most works process the acoustic data before feeding them to a network, Vera-Diaz et al. [23] were the first to use raw audio signals as input to a convolutional neural network (CNN) [24] to predict the position of the three-dimensional source. Chakrabarty and Habets [25] and Xiao et al. [26] used the phase component of the short-time Fourier transform (STFT) and Generalized Cross-Correlation with Phase Transform (GCC-PHAT), respectively, as input for estimating the direction of arrival (DoA) of speech signals.

Studies focusing on a source frequency range such as Ma and Liu [27] simulated a phased microphone array and monopole sources at high frequencies (3000–8000 Hz) on a scanning plane, and used the cross-spectral matrix (CSM) as input to a CNN for localization of these sources. They were able to demonstrate excellent spatial resolution, comparable to that of DAMAS, and much better than conventional beamforming. However, they did not address the challenges at lower source frequencies. Xu et al. [18] employed a similar setup and methodology, but focused on a wider source frequency range of 200–20,000 Hz and were able to predict the source distribution, even for low frequencies. However, they used a densely connected convolutional network (DenseNet) [28] that required large numbers of data and a large amount of memory for training. Niu et al. [29] carried out ocean source localization in the frequency range of 100–200 Hz using a single hydrophone and the discrete Fourier transform of the raw pressure data. Fifty-layer residual networks (ResNet-50), which also needed a significant number of training data, were separately trained to determine the range and depth of the source.

The literature has broadly explored the viability of deep learning techniques for low-frequency acoustic source localization. Most of it, however, does not focus exclusively on low-frequency sound, and infrasound (below 20 Hz). The works that do [18,30] use very deep and computationally expensive network architectures. Thus, in this paper, we present deep learning models for three reproducible test cases covering two-dimensional and three-dimensional ASL, as a proof-of-concept for the viability of deep learning methods exclusively in low- and very-low-frequency ASL. The models are built using limited data and computationally inexpensive networks. These test cases, which contain key features of applied ASL problems, seek to optimize low-frequency ASL under imposed computational limits and are intended to serve as benchmark cases for studying and further developing low-frequency ASL using deep learning. We adopted a relatively shallow CNN (fewer numbers of layers as compared with a deep neural network such as DenseNet), which was inexpensive and capable of being trained on limited data, for all the cases with an appropriate input feature. Section 2 gives a comprehensive description of the method. Section 3 provides the details of all test cases. Section 4 discusses the results obtained from the cases, followed by the conclusion.

2. Method

The methodology used for low-frequency ASL in this paper can be described in three steps. The first step involves collecting the synthetic acoustic pressure data using a simulated microphone array. These data are then processed, either in the time or frequency domain, to generate an input feature capable of being fed to a CNN. Finally, the CNN is trained with the generated input feature against the ground truth and is used to make predictions. The method is summarized in Figure 2.

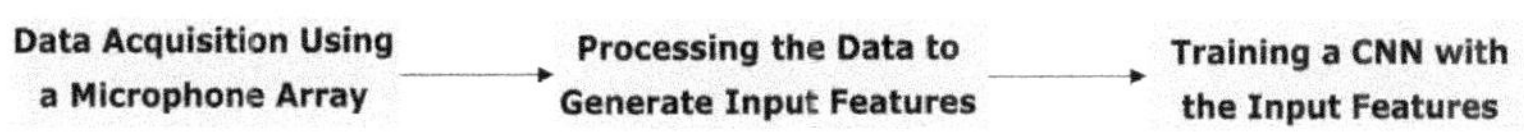

Figure 2. Flow of data in the method. This structure is followed by all the test cases developed in this paper.

Figure 3 shows a flowchart of the three test cases for low-frequency ASL developed in this paper. Case 1 (inspired by Xu et al. [18], Ma and Liu [27]) is regression-based two-dimensional ASL on a scanning plane parallel to the microphone array plane. This setup can be applied to the detection of aeroacoustic sources, such as wake vortices that emit low-frequency noise. Case 2 (source localization on the horizon), also two-dimensional, tackles ASL as a direction-of-arrival (DoA) estimation problem through a classification approach. Case 3, which is an extension of case 2, deals with three-dimensional ASL. Cases 2 and 3 are inspired by the work of Shams et al. [11] on the development of an early-warning clear-air turbulence (CAT) detection system using a ground-based microphone array. All the cases are discussed in detail in Section 3.

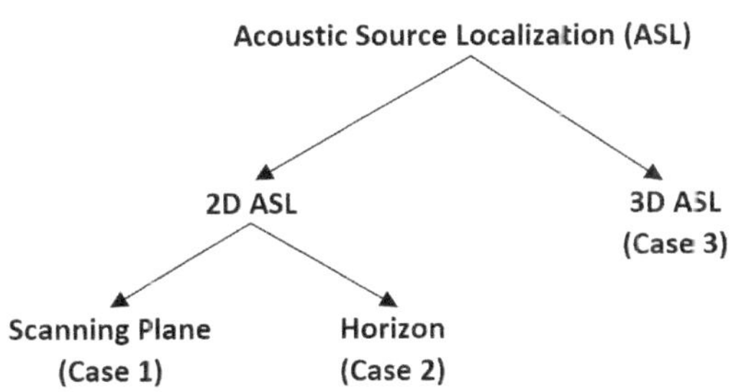

Figure 3. Summary of the test cases. All the cases use the framework shown in Figure 2.

2.1. Microphone Array and Source Simulation

Two types of microphone arrays and sources are simulated. The first type of array, used for case 1, is a 64-microphone array in the shape of a logarithmic spiral. A spiral is naturally irregular and has unique inter-microphone spacing, which is needed to avoid spatial aliasing, thus making it a popular architecture for microphone arrays [31]. The specific type of logarithmic spiral used in this paper is called the *Arcondoulis* spiral, which performs well over a range of frequencies. The equation of the spiral is $r = ae^{b\theta}$, wherein the parameters a and b are set as $a = 0.018$ and $b = 0.002$ to obtain the microphone array as shown in Figure 4, similar to the array used by Xu et al. [18].

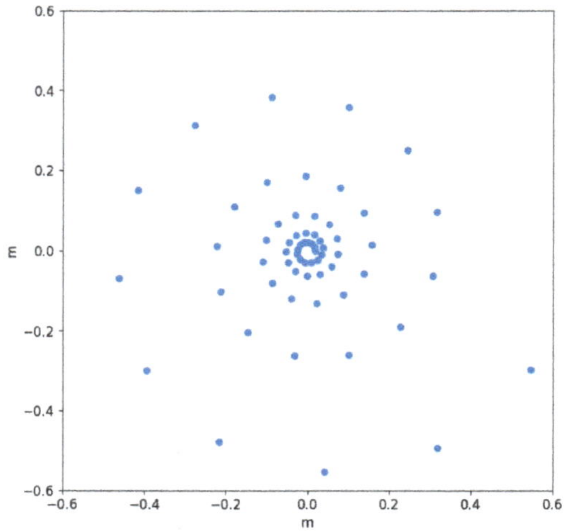

Figure 4. A 64-channel, simulated, logarithmic spiral-shaped microphone array.

Using a large number of microphones may not always be economically viable nor is it necessary to capture low-frequency content, thus we also simulated a more minimalistic array. The microphone array used for cases 2 and 3 is a four-microphone array, as shown in Figure 5. The design is inspired by the triangular array used by Shams et al. [11]. The addition of a fourth microphone introduces variation in inter-microphone spacing and provides more data and a better-sized input feature to work with. The chosen array depends on whether the case is modeled as a regression or classification task. Case 1 is modeled as a regression problem to accurately predict the location of the sources. Due to its complexity, the array with more microphones is chosen. Cases 2 and 3 are classification tasks that involve estimating the DoA of the signal. They are relatively less complex and thus use the four-microphone array.

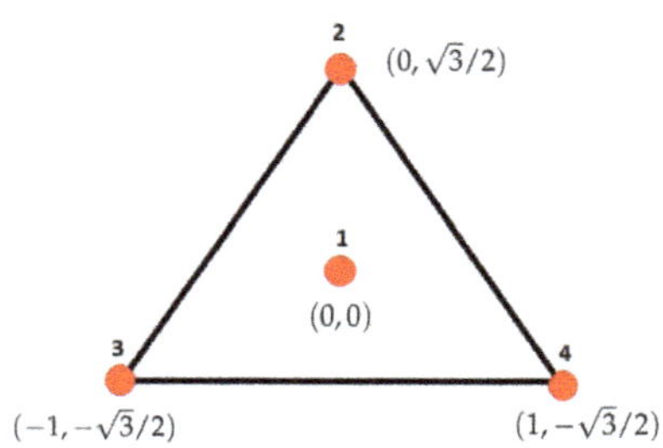

Figure 5. Four microphone array. All coordinates are in meters. The three outer microphones form an equilateral triangle while the fourth microphone is at the midpoint of the altitude.

We simulated two types of sources with different levels of complexity. Source 1 (S1) (Equation (1)) is an analytically-defined monopole that oscillates at a fixed frequency, f. $P_s(m)$ (Equation (1)) shows the complex acoustic pressure due to a monopole, s, as detected by a microphone, m, located at a distance r_s from the source. Here, Q is the complex source strength, and c_0 is the speed of sound in the air, both assumed to be constant. S1 exhibits geometric decay through distance-based attenuation of the complex pressure signal. It is computationally inexpensive and allows us to test models rapidly.

$$P_s(m) = Q\,\frac{e^{-j2\pi f r_s/c_o}}{4\pi|r_s|} \tag{1}$$

The second type of source, source 2 (S2) (Equation (2)), is also an analytical source: a time-domain sinusoidal plane wave of amplitude A, frequency f, and phase difference ϕ. The phase difference for one microphone with respect to another is given in terms of the time delay (Δt) in the signal received by the pair of microphones. The plane wave signal is defined at the microphone location, which is fixed, and thus varies sinusoidally with time. The signal is polluted with noise that can be correlated, uncorrelated noise, or a combination of both:

$$P(t) = A\sin(2\pi f t + \phi) + Noise \tag{2}$$

where $\phi = 2\pi f \Delta t$. Being a plane wave, S2 does not undergo any geometric or viscous decay. Unlike S1, which is strictly defined in the frequency domain, S2 can be used for both time- and frequency-domain processing.

2.2. Convolutional Neural Network

A shallow convolutional neural network (CNN) similar to the generic network shown in Figure 6 is adopted for all cases in this paper. Figure 6 shows the working of a CNN through convolution and pooling operations performed on a 32 × 32 × 1 image. The stride values for the convolution and pooling layers are 1 and 2, respectively. Once the image is fed to the CNN, the convolution layer applies a series of filters to help the network capture the various characteristics of the image. The image size thus changes after the convolution operation. For an image of dimensions $I \times I$, filter width $F \times F$, zero-padding P, and stride S, the output dimensions of the image are $\left[\frac{(I-F+2P)}{S}+1\right] \times \left[\frac{(I-F+2P)}{S}+1\right]$ [32]. This is followed by a pooling layer that downsamples the image, thereby reducing its size while preserving the dominant features. The dimensions of an $I \times I$ image after a $F \times F$ max-pooling filter operation are $\left[\frac{(I-F)}{S}+1\right] \times \left[\frac{(I-F)}{S}+1\right]$. The resulting image is flattened to a vector and fed to a fully connected layer as part of a regular feed-forward network. The loss and activation functions in the final layer are chosen depending on the nature of the case, i.e., whether it is a regression problem or a classification problem. The CNN compares its prediction with the ground truth, calculates the loss/error, and adjusts its learnable parameters to minimize the loss.

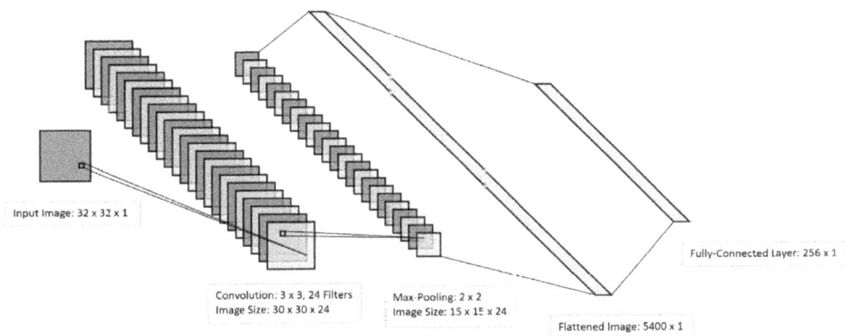

Figure 6. An example showing a convolutional neural network and the impact of convolution and pooling layers on the image size and information transfer.

3. Test Case Setups

3.1. Case 1: Stationary Source Localization on a Scanning Plane

This case takes inspiration from the work by Xu et al. [18], Ma and Liu [27]. Xu et al. [18], in particular, carried out source localization on a scanning plane parallel to the microphone array plane for a wide frequency range of 200 to 20,000 Hz, using a deep neural network called DenseNet-201. They were able to show the superiority of DenseNet-201 over other classic acoustic imaging methods. However, DenseNet needed a significant amount of simulated data, memory, and processing power to train. In this paper, we focused on ASL at two frequencies in the low-frequency range (100 Hz and 300 Hz) using limited training data and a shallow CNN to prove that ASL is possible using a computationally less expensive approach. The setup is shown in Figure 7.

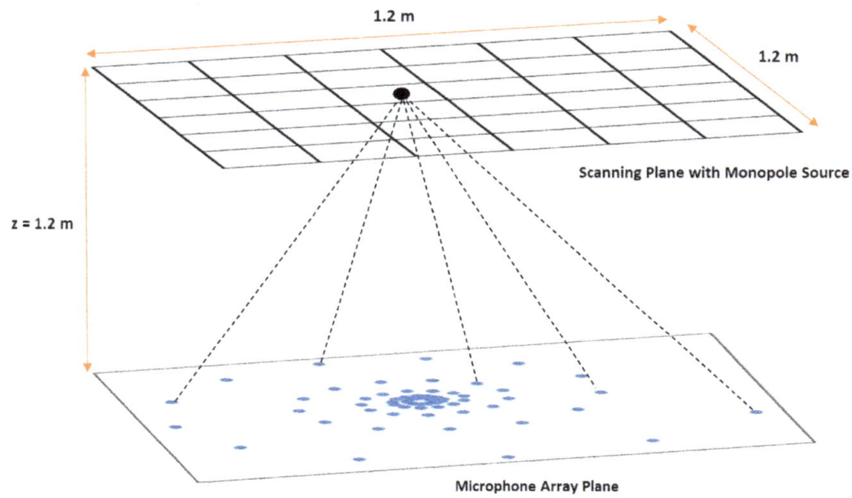

Figure 7. Case 1: Acoustic source localization on a scanning plane. The scanning plane is discretized into an $N \times N$ grid of uniform resolution. The finer the grid size is, the higher is the computational cost.

We used a scanning plane of dimensions 1.2 m × 1.2 m. The scanning plane was located 1.2 m above the array plane containing the 64-microphone logarithmic spiral array, as described in the previous section. To generate the training dataset, S monopole sources (S1, Equation (1)) with unit source strength were randomly distributed throughout the $N \times N$ scanning grid. The acoustic pressure of all sources was calculated at all the microphones (M) to form the combined pressure vector, P, given as:

$$P = \left[\sum_{s=1}^{S} P_s(1), \sum_{s=1}^{S} P_s(2), \sum_{s=1}^{S} P_s(3), \ldots, \sum_{s=1}^{S} P_s(M) \right] \tag{3}$$

Vector P, in turn, was used to obtain the cross-spectral matrix (CSM) as:

$$\mathrm{CSM} = PP^H \tag{4}$$

where P^H is the conjugate transpose of P. The dimensions of the CSM are $M \times M$, which in this case is 64×64. The CSM represents the power distribution over frequency, and we used the real part of it as an input feature to the CNN. The CSM here serves a different purpose than what it traditionally serves in signal processing. In the context of deep learning, the CSM is an image-like input feature that encapsulates the acoustic pressure information needed to train our CNN. The CNN was trained against the ground truth, i.e., the source distribution from which the CSM was derived, to predict the strength and location of the sources. For the ground truth, the $N \times N$ scanning grid was converted to a $N^2 \times 1$ binary vector in which the elements corresponding to the sources were assigned the value 1 (equal to the source strength), and the elements without a source were assigned the value 0. We defined the output layer as a dense layer with N^2 nodes without an activation function, thus treating this as a regression problem. We use the Rectified Linear Unit (ReLU) activation function everywhere throughout the network. The network prediction was a vector of output layer dimensions ($N^2 \times 1$) that was compared against the ground truth vector to calculate the loss. The loss function used was the mean squared error (MSE), defined as:

$$MSE = \frac{\sum_{i=1}^{n}(y_{pred} - y_{gt})^2}{n} \tag{5}$$

where, y_{pred} is the predicted vector given by the network, y_{gt} is the ground truth vector, and n is the length of the two vectors, which in this case is N^2. The optimizer used was *ADAM* [33] with the default values of the hyperparameters. Details of the CNN and the training process are given in Section 4.

3.2. Case 2: Two-Dimensional ASL on the Horizon

This case used a classification approach to determine the direction of arrival (DoA) of the acoustic signal from a source located on the horizon. The four-microphone array was used for this case and the azimuth angle (θ) had to be determined. The range of possible values of θ (0–180°) was discretized into N classes. The output of the network is the probability distribution of all the classes, and the class with the highest probability is the estimated DoA. The setup is shown in Figure 8.

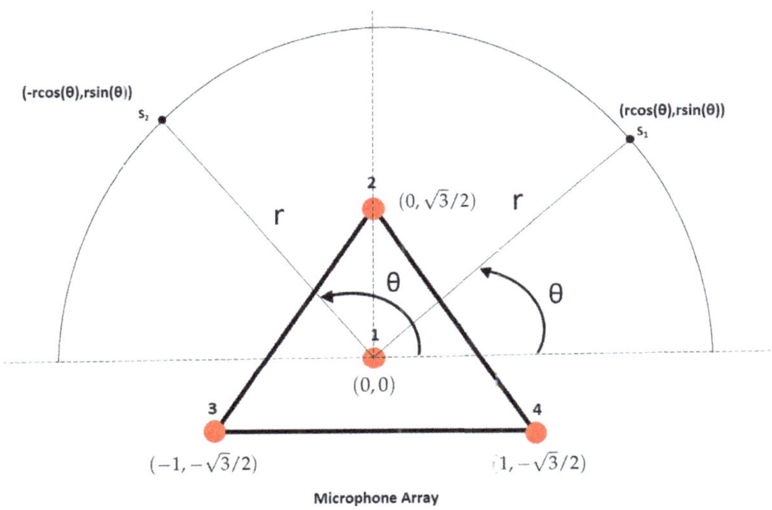

Figure 8. Case 2: Two-dimensional ASL on the horizon. Two possible source configurations S_1 and S_2 are shown. $\theta < 90°$ for S_1 while $\theta > 90°$ for S_2. $r = 10$. The source coordinates for these two positions are $(r\cos\theta, r\sin\theta)$ and $(-r\cos\theta, r\sin\theta)$, respectively.

Since this case uses a classification approach, the final dense layer of the network had the softmax activation function, which normalized the output of the network to give the probability distribution over N classes. ReLU activation was used everywhere else. *ADAM* was used as the optimizer while the loss function was cross-entropy, which is the standard loss function for classification problems [34]. We used both types of sources in this case, the monopole and the sinusoidal plane wave signal, and they have been discussed separately.

3.2.1. Case 2 (i): Monopole (S1)

To generate the training set, a monopole with unit source strength was placed at a real, random value of θ (in the range of θ) from the center of the four-microphone array and at a fixed radial distance r (=10 m). The cross-spectral matrix was calculated with the same procedure as in case 1 and its real part was used as an input to a CNN. The value of θ falls into a certain class and the index of this class was the ground truth against which the network was trained.

3.2.2. Case 2 (ii): Sinusoidal Plane Wave (S2)

A sinusoidal plane wave signal (Equation (2)) was generated from a random direction (real, random value of θ) and fixed r (=10 m) from the origin. The signal was polluted with white Gaussian noise. The amplitude of the pressure signal and the white noise were equal and set to 10 Pa. We applied the generalized cross-correlation (GCC) algorithm to all microphone pairs to generate an input feature. GCC is a time delay of arrival (TDOA) approach and is known to be robust to noise and reverberation. The GCC vector between two signals $r_1(t)$ and $r_2(t)$ is defined as the inverse Fourier transform (IFFT) of the cross-power spectrum [35]:

$$\mathrm{GCC} = \mathrm{IFFT}\,(R_1 \odot R_2^*)$$

where, R_1 and R_2 are the STFT vectors for r_1 and r_2, $\odot$ represents element-wise multiplication, and * represents the complex conjugate.

Figure 9 shows a sample GCC pattern obtained using a pair of microphone signals polluted with uncorrelated noise. It can be seen that, while the signals are distorted, the GCC pattern is still very evident. The entire GCC vector was not used as input. For each microphone pair, there are a certain number of correlation coefficients near the center that contain useful information. These coefficients were extracted from the GCC feature map to be used as input to the CNN. The calculation for the number of coefficients is as follows. The maximum possible time delay (τ) between two microphones for the four-microphone array shown in Figure 5 is given by the distance between two microphones (2 m) and the speed of sound (343 m/s) as $\tau = 2/343 = 5.83$ ms. For a sampling frequency of 16,000 Hz, the maximum delay in samples is $n = 16{,}000\tau \approx 93$. So it is only the first 93 coefficients from the center of the GCC that contain useful information for each microphone pair. The first 93 GCC coefficients from the GCC of all microphone pairs (6) were concatenated to form a vector of size (558×1) and then reshaped into a matrix of dimensions (31×18). This reshaped matrix was used as input to the CNN. Of course, the vector of GCC coefficients can be directly fed to a multi-layer perceptron (MLP); however, a CNN is generally more powerful and accurate for classification problems. The CNN also has fewer learnable parameters compared with MLP, which reduces the risk of overfitting.

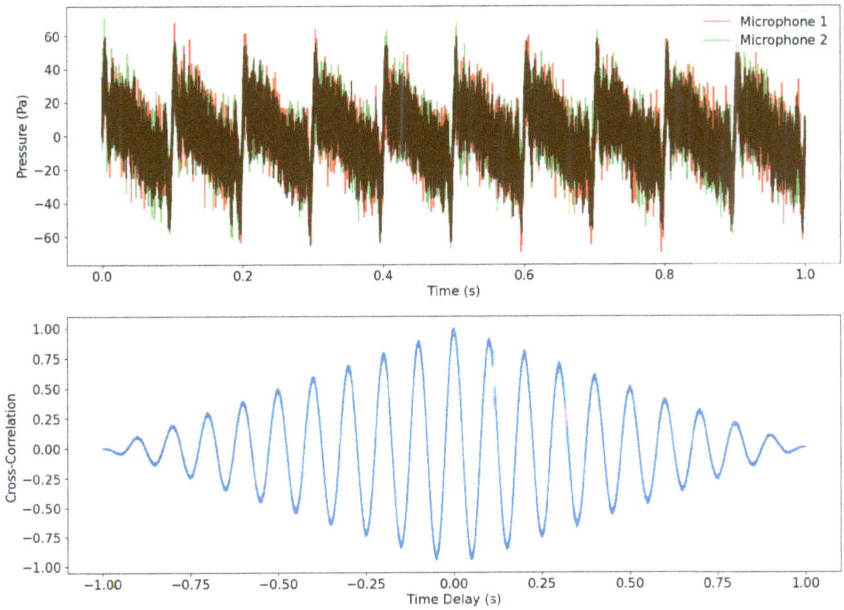

Figure 9. GCC pattern for a pair of microphone signals polluted with uncorrelated noise. The GCC feature map is symmetric about the origin. Therefore the useful correlation coefficients can be picked from either side of the origin.

3.3. *Case 3: Three-Dimensional ASL*

This case is an extension of case 2. Similar to case 2, we used the four-microphone array and the two sources (cases 3 (i) for S1 and 3 (ii) for S2) with a classification approach for this case. The ranges of the azimuth angle, θ, and the elevation angle, α, were discretized into N_1 and N_2 classes, respectively. The setup is shown in Figure 10. We placed the source (S1 and S2 in separate sub-cases) at real, random values of θ and α and fixed r (=10 m) and used the real part of the resulting CSM to train the CNN. However, instead of using a conventional CNN, we used a multi-task CNN in which the separate tasks of determining θ and α were performed simultaneously by a single model. This is made possible because both tasks rely on the same input feature (CSM for S1 and GCC for S2). Separate networks for θ and α are an option (like case 2); however, it is not very efficient as individual datasets have to be generated and each network has to be trained separately. A multi-task network improves data efficiency and reduces training time and the chances of overfitting significantly as the model has to generalize over multiple tasks. Figure 11 shows the block diagram of the multi-task CNN used. This is an example of *hard-parameter sharing*, wherein the tasks share hidden layers while having task-specific output layers [36]. For both output branches (θ and α), the activation function in the last layer was *Softmax*, and *ReLU* activation was used everywhere else. The optimizer and the loss function were *ADAM* and *cross-entropy* respectively, for both branches.

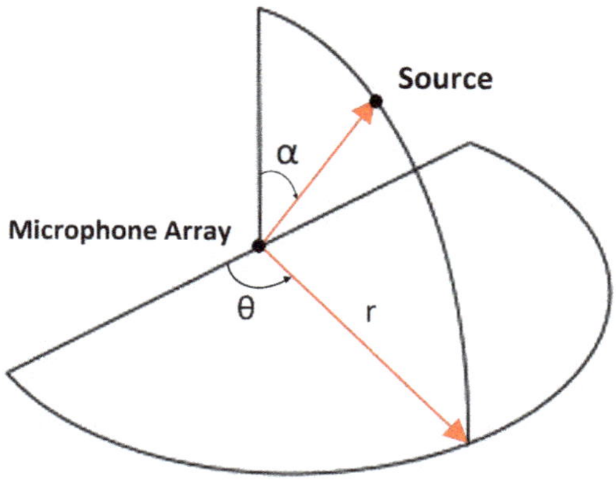

Figure 10. Case 3: Three-dimensional ASL. The four-microphone is shown as a point. The localization domain is a quarter sphere ($0° \leq \theta \leq 180°, 0° \leq \alpha \leq 90°, r = 10$). The coordinates of the source are $(r\ \sin(\alpha)\cos(\theta),\ r\ \sin(\alpha)\sin(\theta),\ r\ \cos(\alpha))$.

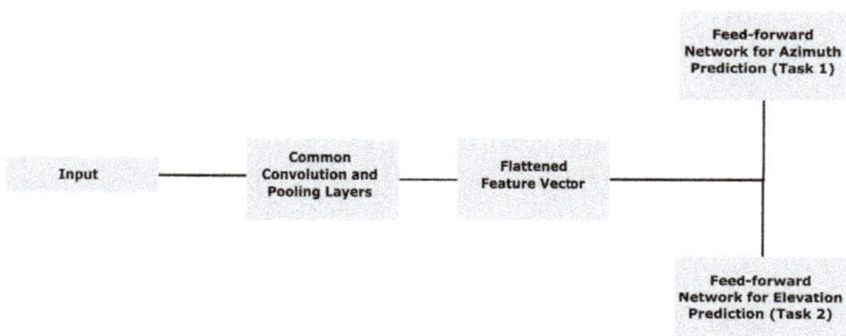

Figure 11. A multi-task CNN used for three-dimensional ASL. The main branch performed the convolution and pooling operations on the input feature. The two output branches peeled off the main branch using the flattened feature vector as the input to give separate predictions for θ and α.

All CNN models in this paper were built using the deep learning frameworks *Keras* and *Tensorflow*, the details of which are shown in Table 1. The training for all the cases was carried out on Google Colaboratory.

Table 1. Summary of the convolutional neural network architecture used in all the cases.

Cases	Conv. Layers, Dimension	Max-Pool Layers, Dimension	Dense Layers (Nodes), Output Dimension
1	3, (3 × 3), Filters: 32, 64, 64	2, (2 × 2)	4 (128), Output: 144
2 (i): S1	2, (2 × 2), Filters: 128, 64	None	1 (128), Output: N
2 (ii): S2	3, (2 × 2), Filters: 128, 64, 64	2, (2 × 2)	1 (128), Output: N
3 (i): S1	2, (2 × 2), Filters: 128, 64	None	(θ): 1 (128), N_1 (α): 1 (128), N_2
3 (ii): S2	2, (2 × 2), Filters: 128, 64, 64	2, (2 × 2)	(θ): 1 (128), N_1 (α): 1 (128), N_2

4. Results

Table 1 gives the details of the CNN models used in all three cases.

4.1. Case 1

For case 1, the model was trained to detect six monopole sources that were spread across a 12 × 12 scanning grid plane by randomly assigning coordinates. The results are presented and compared for source frequencies of 100 Hz and 300 Hz. Xu et al. [18], who also presented results for six monopole source localization using DenseNet, generated a batch of 512 training samples and 1000 validation samples for each epoch and ran the model for almost 3000 epochs. This means the training was carried out with more than 4.5 million samples. In contrast, our shallow CNN model trained for 600 epochs on 50,000 training samples. The training data are 0.00045% of the total number of possible samples $\binom{144}{6}$, which is in the order of $\approx 10^{10}$, thus exemplifying the limited nature of the data. The CNN also had a significantly smaller number of learnable parameters ($\approx$1 million) compared with DenseNet ($\approx$20 million).

The details of the CNN model are given in Table 1. The learning rate for the optimizer was fine-tuned to 0.0001. This case took approximately 100 min to train. The obtained results were post-processed to highlight the strongest sources (predicted source strengths of 0.3 and higher) and allow us to derive qualitative and quantitative trends. Figures 12 and 13 show two source configurations as predicted by the model for monopole sources at 300 Hz. Figures 14 and 15 show similar results for monopole sources at 100 Hz. The red dots represent the ground truth source configuration. These results are followed by Table 2, which gives the source detection statistics at the two source frequencies for 1000 test samples.

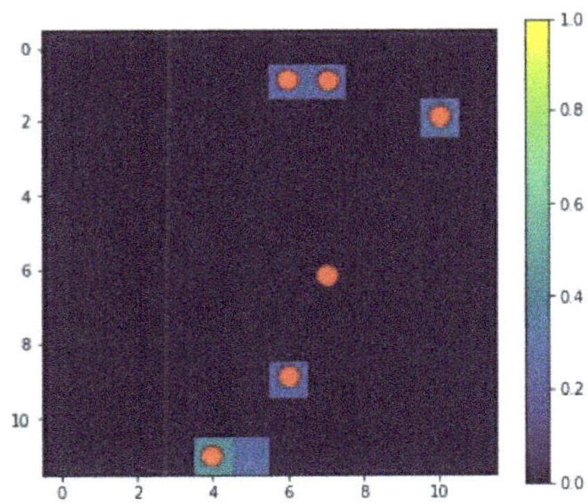

Figure 12. Source configuration 1 (300 Hz). These are representative results at this source frequency. The legend is in Pascals (Pa), representing source strength.

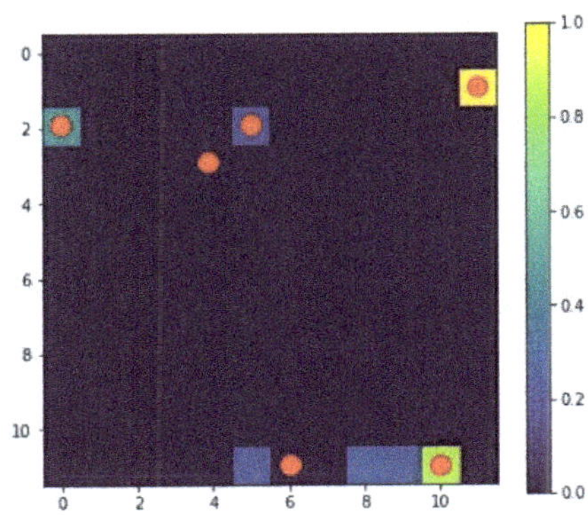

Figure 13. Source configuration 2 (300 Hz).

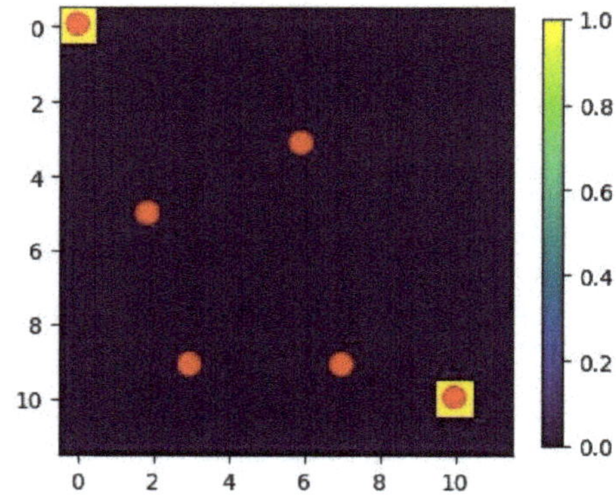

Figure 14. Sparse sources (100 Hz). The model struggles at lower frequencies when the concentration of sources is less.

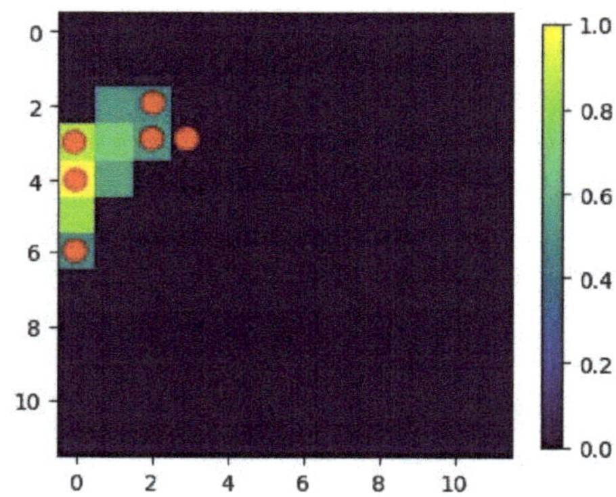

Figure 15. Clustered sources (100 Hz). The model performs relatively better when low-frequency sources are highly concentrated.

Table 2. Source detection statistics for 1000 test samples. The frequency-dependence of model performance is evident—the model was able to detect more sources when they were oscillating at a higher frequency (300 Hz).

Sources Detected	300 Hz	100 Hz
6	9	1
5	70	10
4	272	39
3	397	142
2	210	344
1	42	348
0	0	116
Total	1000	1000

Discussion

As mentioned, Xu et al. [18] used a batch of 512 training and 1000 validation samples each epoch while running the model for around 3000 epochs, the total number of samples thus amounting to ≈4.5 million. We limited our training data and epochs to 50,000 samples (≈1% of Xu et al. [18]) and 600 epochs, respectively, and sought to maximize the performance of the model under these constraints. While Xu et al. [18]'s DNN naturally showed superior performance given the vast computational resources employed, we found that, at a relatively higher source frequency of 300 Hz (Figures 12 and 13), our model was able to capture the source distribution reasonably well with a limited dataset. The model showed good resolution, less spreading, and was able to detect sparse sources. The limit of the model's performance was identified as 100 Hz since the results at 100 Hz source frequency and below (Figures 14 and 15) with the same amount of training were relatively poor. The model struggled to locate the sources when they were sparsely located (Figure 14) and tended to perform better when they were located in clusters. The increase in spreading is evident from Figure 15 but is still much less than beamforming, wherein the poor resolution renders the results unusable at low frequencies. To resolve low-frequency sources using beamforming, the size of the scanning plane and the distance between the sources would have to be much more than the size of the plane used in this case. The CNN was able to resolve low-frequency sources on the current plane, thus highlighting its superior resolution and detection capabilities. Table 2 reaffirms statistically the frequency-dependent performance of the model. For a source frequency of 300 Hz, the model was able to detect the majority of the sources (four or more) in 35.1% samples (351 out of 1000 samples), and at least half of the sources (three or more) in 74.8% samples (748 out of 1000 samples). At 100 Hz source frequency, the percentages drop to 5% for detecting the majority of the sources (50 out of 1000 samples) and 19.2% for detecting at least half of the sources (192 out of 1000 samples). To obtain better results at 100 Hz and lower frequencies, we have to go beyond the set network architecture and training limits and increase the number of layers/training data samples/epochs. The effectiveness of the shallow CNN in terms of giving promising results with very limited data compared with Xu et al. [18]'s DNN makes it an avenue worth exploring further.

4.2. Case 2

In cases 2 and 3, which are classification-type problems, the performance was measured in terms of the prediction accuracy of the correct class (and thus the DoA) given by the model. In this case, the model predicted the class of θ. The training was carried out using 50,000 training samples and 200 epochs with a fine-tuned learning rate of 0.0001. Since the source can be placed at any real value of θ between 0° and 180°, the training set of 50,000 samples is very limited as the total number of possible cases is infinite. The results for the two types of sources used in case 2 are given in Tables 3 and 4.

Table 3. Accuracy values are for a test set of 10,000 samples for the monopole source. The sharp decline in accuracy for $N = 180$ is a limitation of small-sized input.

Classes (N)	Class Size	Accuracy (θ, 100 Hz)	Accuracy (θ, 300 Hz)
20	9°	≈91%	≈95%
30	6°	≈89%	≈92%
45	4°	≈81%	≈91%
60	3°	≈69%	≈87%
90	2°	≈52%	≈77%
180	1°	≈23%	≈57%

Table 4. Accuracy values for a test set of 10,000 samples for a sinusoidal plane wave source. The accuracy (for 100 Hz and 300 Hz) is higher and the drop-off in model performance as N increases is gradual as compared with the monopole source, thus highlighting the superiority of GCC as an input feature in this case.

Classes (N)	Class Size	Accuracy (θ, 10 Hz)	Accuracy (θ, 100 Hz)	Accuracy (θ, 300 Hz)
20	9°	≈84%	≈97%	≈98%
30	6°	≈76%	≈96%	≈97%
45	4°	≈63%	≈95%	≈96%
60	3°	≈52%	≈93%	≈95%
90	2°	≈40%	≈89%	≈93%
180	1°	≈20%	≈79%	≈86%

4.2.1. Case 2 (i): Monopole (S1)

We used a monopole source at 100 Hz and 300 Hz to evaluate the model's performance under the set training constraints. The source was at a radial distance of 10 m (r = 10 m) from the center of the four-microphone array. Since the dimensions of the cross-spectral matrix (CSM) were small (4 × 4 for the four-microphone array), only two convolutional layers, without pooling layers, were used in the CNN (Table 1). The variation in accuracy of θ with the number of classes N for both source frequencies is shown in Table 3.

4.2.2. Case 2 (i): Sinusoidal Plane Wave (S2)

For this source, the drop in model performance was not as drastic as the monopole, which allowed us to test for source frequencies well into the infrasound range. Results are provided for a sinusoidal plane wave source polluted with uncorrelated noise at 10 Hz (infrasound), 100 Hz, and 300 Hz. The distance of the source from the array was 10 m (r = 10 m); however, the distance does not matter in this case as the amplitude does not undergo any decay and remains constant. The vector formed by concatenating the extracted portions from the GCC vectors of the microphone pairs (558 × 1) was reshaped into a matrix (31 × 18) and fed to the CNN. The larger size of the image allowed us to apply more convolution and pooling layers. Table 4 shows the prediction accuracy of the model and its dependence on the number of classes.

4.2.3. Discussion

For the monopole source, the prediction accuracy of the model for both source frequencies was very high when the number of classes was less (20), and decreased gradually as the number of classes increased. Between the two source frequencies, the model performed better at the higher frequency. The small size of the input image (CSM) significantly reduced the network size and the parameters to be optimized, hence the model trained very quickly. At the same time, a small input reduced the scope of learning as we were very limited in the number of convolution and pooling layers that we could apply. A consequence of this is the drop in performance as the problem becomes more complex. Fewer convolution layers means that the network cannot learn deeper and more abstract features of a complex problem, resulting in potentially overfitting and a decrease in the accuracy of prediction. This can be seen in Table 3. While the model can give good results in this case, when the number of classes N is small, the drop-off in performance is stark as N increases. This is a clear limitation of the CSM as an input feature with few microphones.

In the case of the sinusoidal plane wave source (Table 4), the GCC map allowed us to obtain an appropriately sized input feature. At the same time, selectively picking the portion of the GCC feature map containing the essential information helped keep the input size in check to save computational time and resources.

Comparing the accuracy values for source frequencies 100 Hz and 300 Hz in Table 4 with those obtained for the monopole source (Table 3), it is evident that the model displays a superior performance with the GCC input feature, which is again down to the difference in the input size. The model can thus learn much better with GCC as the input. This highlights the advantage of using a time-domain input feature (GCC) as opposed to a frequency-domain feature (CSM) for detecting very low source frequencies when the number of microphones is limited. For the infrasound source, the accuracy for smaller class sizes can be improved with more training. An accuracy value greater than 60% for 45 classes for an infrasound source in the presence of noise shows the robustness and reliability of GCC as an input feature.

4.3. Case 3

As this case is more challenging than case 2, the number of training samples was increased to 80,000, keeping the number of epochs at 200 and the learning rate at 0.0001. The learning rate was set to 0.0001. The resolution or class size was kept the same for θ and α, resulting in different numbers of classes, N_1 and N_2, respectively. The performance of the model was measured in terms of the prediction accuracy of the correct class for θ and α. For this case, we provide representative results at a single source frequency as the trends in the results will be similar to the results in case 2.

4.3.1. Case 3 (i): Monopole (S1)

Representative results are provided for a monopole source oscillating at 100 Hz. The real part of the CSM (dimensions 4×4) was used as an input to the multi-task CNN. The prediction accuracy of the model is shown in Table 5.

Table 5. Prediction accuracy for θ and α in three-dimensional ASL with a monopole source at 100 Hz for 10,000 samples. There is no negative transfer since the accuracy values for θ and α decrease at a similar rate.

Class Size	N_1 (θ)	Accuracy (θ)	N_2 (α)	Accuracy (α)
10°	18	≈93%	9	≈91%
5°	36	≈84%	18	≈79%
3°	60	≈69%	30	≈58%
2°	90	≈56%	45	≈52%
1°	180	≈29%	90	≈36%

4.3.2. Case 3 (ii): Sinusoidal Plane Wave (S2)

Representative results are provided for a sinusoidal plane wave source at 10 Hz. The GCC coefficient matrix of size (31×18) (same as case 2 (ii)) was used as an input to the multi-task CNN. The prediction accuracy of the model is shown in Table 6.

Table 6. Prediction accuracy for θ and α in three-dimensional ASL with a sinusoidal plane wave source at 10 Hz for 10,000 samples. Negative transfer is evident as the accuracy of θ prediction declines rapidly compared with α.

Class Size	N_1 (θ)	Accuracy (θ)	N_2 (α)	Accuracy (α)
10°	18	≈79%	9	≈99%
5°	36	≈58%	18	≈99%
3°	60	≈41%	30	≈97%
2°	90	≈26 %	45	≈96 %
1°	180	≈13%	90	≈91 %

4.3.3. Discussion

The multi-task CNN utilizes the same input feature for performing two related tasks—classifying the azimuth angle, θ, and the elevation angle, α. A commonly encountered problem in multi-task learning is "negative transfer", wherein one or more tasks can dominate the training/learning process and hurt the performance of other tasks. The tasks whose performance is hampered tend to perform better in a single-task model compared with a multi-task model [37]. Both tasks are learned reasonably well in the case of a monopole source (Table 5) but a clear case of negative transfer is observed for the sinusoidal plane wave source (Table 6). The prediction of α dominates the training, which is expected as it is the easier of the two tasks ($N_2 < N_1$). However, the prediction accuracy values for θ are less than what were obtained when a single-task model was used for predicting θ in case 2(ii). A suggested way to overcome negative transfer is to weigh the individual losses from the two tasks appropriately such that they are on the same scale [37].

5. Conclusions

We developed three benchmark cases for low- and very-low-frequency passive acoustic source localization using deep learning. The limitations of conventional beamforming necessitated the use of a deep learning-based approach. The cases used a shallow CNN with limited training data and sought to optimize the performance at low source frequencies under the training constraints. We obtained promising qualitative and quantitative results, and it can be concluded that the benchmark cases collectively prove the viability of deep learning-based approaches for low- and very-low-frequency ASL. At the same time, the results provide insight into the network and training parameters that can be changed to further expand the scope of these cases and obtain better results. The size of the input feature is also an aspect to be considered. Smaller input sizes would be reduced by the network to the point that learning from them would become very difficult as the problem becomes more and more complex. We would like to mention that, while obtaining good results with shallow networks and limited data is feasible, with the appropriate resources, deeper networks like ResNets and DenseNets can be trained to give better results; however, the dataset must be commensurate with the size of the network otherwise the network will tend to overfit the data and generalize poorly. Studies employing ResNet-50 used between 200–800 million training samples to prevent overfitting.

Author Contributions: Conceptualization, A.J. and J.-P.H.; methodology, A.J.; software, A.J.; validation, A.J.; formal analysis, A.J. and J.-P.H.; investigation, A.J.; data curation, A.J.; writing—original draft preparation, A.J.; writing—review and editing, A.J. and J.-P.H.; visualization, A.J.; supervision, J.-P.H.; project administration, J.-P.H.; funding acquisition, J.-P.H. All authors have read and agreed to the published version of the manuscript.

Funding: A portion of the computational resources were supported by Scinet and the Digital Research Alliance of Canada through the RAC program.

Institutional Review Board Statement: Not applicable.

Informed Consent Statement: Not applicable.

Data Availability Statement: Data and code have been uploaded to a repository: https://github.com/aljoshi/deep-learning-based-passive-ASL, accessed on 25 September 2024.

Conflicts of Interest: The authors declare no conflicts of interest.

References

1. Peyvandi, H.; Farrokhrooz, M.; Roufarshbaf, H.; Park, S.J. SONAR systems and underwater signal processing: Classic a[illegible] modern approaches. In *SONAR Systems*; IntechOpen: London, UK, 2011; pp. 173–206.
2. Carter, G. Time delay estimation for passive sonar signal processing. *IEEE Trans. Acoust. Speech Signal Process.* **1981**, *29*, 463–4[illegible] [CrossRef]
3. Fernandes, J.d.C.V.; de Moura Junior, N.N.; de Seixas, J.M. Deep learning models for passive sonar signal classification of milita[illegible] data. *Remote Sens.* **2022**, *14*, 2648. [CrossRef]

- Tosi, P.; Sbarra, P.; De Rubeis, V. Earthquake sound perception. *Geophys. Res. Lett.* **2012**, *39*, L24301. [CrossRef]
- Hill, D.P.; Fischer, F.G.; Lahr, K.M.; Coakley, J.M. Earthquake sounds generated by body-wave ground motion. *Bull. Seismol. Soc. Am.* **1976**, *66*, 1159–1172.
- Sylvander, M.; Ponsolles, C.; Benahmed, S.; Fels, J.F. Seismoacoustic recordings of small earthquakes in the Pyrenees: Experimental results. *Bull. Seismol. Soc. Am.* **2007**, *97*, 294–304. [CrossRef]
- Bocanegra, J.A.; Borelli, D.; Gaggero, T.; Rizzuto, E.; Schenone, C. A novel approach to port noise characterization using an acoustic camera. *Sci. Total Environ.* **2022**, *808*, 151903. [CrossRef]
- Booth, E.; Humphreys, W. Tracking and characterization of aircraft wakes using acoustic and lidar measurements. In Proceedings of the 11th AIAA/CEAS Aeroacoustics Conference, Monterey, CA, USA, 23–25 May 2005; p. 2964.
- Joshi, A.; Rahman, M.M.; Hickey, J.P. Recent Advances in Passive Acoustic Localization Methods via Aircraft and Wake Vortex Aeroacoustics. *Fluids* **2022**, *7*, 218. [CrossRef]

10. Schönhals, S.; Steen, M.; Hecker, P. Towards wake vortex safety and capacity increase: The integrated fusion approach and its demands on prediction models and detection sensors. *Proc. Inst. Mech. Eng. Part G J. Aerosp. Eng.* **2013**, *227*, 199–208. [CrossRef]
11. Shams, Q.A.; Zuckerwar, A.J.; Burkett, C.G.; Weistroffer, G.R.; Hugo, D.R. Experimental investigation into infrasonic emissions from atmospheric turbulence. *J. Acoust. Soc. Am.* **2013**, *133*, 1269–1280. [CrossRef]
12. Watson, L.M.; Iezzi, A.M.; Toney, L.; Maher, S.P.; Fee, D.; McKee, K.; Ortiz, H.D.; Matoza, R.S.; Gestrich, J.E.; Bishop, J.W.; et al. Volcano infrasound: Progress and future directions. *Bull. Volcanol.* **2022**, *84*, 44. [CrossRef]
13. Chiariotti, P.; Martarelli, M.; Castellini, P. Acoustic beamforming for noise source localization–Reviews, methodology and applications. *Mech. Syst. Signal Process.* **2019**, *120*, 422–448. [CrossRef]
14. de Santana, L. *Fundamentals of Acoustic Beamforming*; NATO Educ. Notes EN-AVT; NATO Science and Technology Organization: Brussels, Belgium, 2017; Volume 4.
15. Gombots, S.; Nowak, J.J.; Kaltenbacher, M. Sound source localization–state of the art and new inverse scheme. *Elektrotech. Infor. e & i* **2021**, *138*, 229–243.
16. Rayleigh, F.R.S. XXXI. Investigations in optics, with special reference to the spectroscope. *Lond. Edinb. Dublin Philos. Mag. J. Sci.* **1879**, *8*, 261–274. [CrossRef]
17. Brooks, T.F.; Humphreys, W.M. A deconvolution approach for the mapping of acoustic sources (DAMAS) determined from phased microphone arrays. *J. Sound Vib.* **2006**, *294*, 856–879. [CrossRef]
18. Xu, P.; Arcondoulis, E.J.; Liu, Y. Acoustic source imaging using densely connected convolutional networks. *Mech. Syst. Signal Process.* **2021**, *151*, 107370. [CrossRef]
19. Sarradj, E.; Herold, G. A Python framework for microphone array data processing. *Appl. Acoust.* **2017**, *116*, 50–58. [CrossRef]
20. Bianco, M.J.; Gerstoft, P.; Traer, J.; Ozanich, E.; Roch, M.A.; Gannot, S.; Deledalle, C.A. Machine learning in acoustics: Theory and applications. *J. Acoust. Soc. Am.* **2019**, *146*, 3590–3628. [CrossRef]
21. Grumiaux, P.A.; Kitić, S.; Girin, L.; Guérin, A. A survey of sound source localization with deep learning methods. *J. Acoust. Soc. Am.* **2022**, *152*, 107–151. [CrossRef]
22. Yalta, N.; Nakadai, K.; Ogata, T. Sound source localization using deep learning models. *J. Robot. Mechatronics* **2017**, *29*, 37–48. [CrossRef]
23. Vera-Diaz, J.M.; Pizarro, D.; Macias-Guarasa, J. Towards end-to-end acoustic localization using deep learning: From audio signals to source position coordinates. *Sensors* **2018**, *18*, 3418. [CrossRef]
24. O'Shea, K.; Nash, R. An introduction to convolutional neural networks. *arXiv* **2015**, arXiv:1511.08458.
25. Chakrabarty, S.; Habets, E.A. Broadband DOA estimation using convolutional neural networks trained with noise signals. In Proceedings of the 2017 IEEE Workshop on Applications of Signal Processing to Audio and Acoustics (WASPAA), New Paltz, NY, USA, 15–18 October 2017; pp. 136–140.
26. Xiao, X.; Zhao, S.; Zhong, X.; Jones, D.L.; Chng, E.S.; Li, H. A learning-based approach to direction of arrival estimation in noisy and reverberant environments. In Proceedings of the 2015 IEEE International Conference on Acoustics, Speech and Signal Processing (ICASSP), South Brisbane, QLD, Australia, 19–24 April 2015; pp. 2814–2818.
27. Ma, W.; Liu, X. Phased microphone array for sound source localization with deep learning. *Aerosp. Syst.* **2019**, *2*, 71–81. [CrossRef]
28. Huang, G.; Liu, Z.; Van Der Maaten, L.; Weinberger, K.Q. Densely connected convolutional networks. In Proceedings of the IEEE Conference on Computer Vision and Pattern Recognition, Honolulu, HI, USA, 21–26 July 2017; pp. 4700–4708.
29. Niu, H.; Gong, Z.; Ozanich, E.; Gerstoft, P.; Wang, H.; Li, Z. Deep learning for ocean acoustic source localization using one sensor. *arXiv* **2019**, arXiv:1903.12319.
30. He, K.; Zhang, X.; Ren, S.; Sun, J. Deep residual learning for image recognition. In Proceedings of the IEEE Conference on Computer Vision and Pattern Recognition, Las Vegas, NV, USA, 27–30 June 2016; pp. 770–778.
31. Prime, Z.; Doolan, C. A comparison of popular beamforming arrays. In Proceedings of the Australian Acoustical Society AAS2013 Victor Harbor, Victor Harbor, Australia, 17–20 November 2013; Volume 1, p. 5.
32. Albawi, S.; Mohammed, T.A.; Al-Zawi, S. Understanding of a convolutional neural network. In Proceedings of the 2017 International Conference on Engineering and Technology (ICET), Antalya, Turkey, 21–23 August 2017; pp. 1–6.
33. Kingma, D.P.; Ba, J. Adam: A method for stochastic optimization. *arXiv* **2014**, arXiv:1412.6980.
34. Ho, Y.; Wookey, S. The real-world-weight cross-entropy loss function: Modeling the costs of mislabeling. *IEEE Access* **2019**, *8*, 4806–4813. [CrossRef]

35. Varzandeh, R.; Adiloğlu, K.; Doclo, S.; Hohmann, V. Exploiting periodicity features for joint detection and DOA estimation o speech sources using convolutional neural networks. In Proceedings of the ICASSP 2020—2020 IEEE International Conference o Acoustics, Speech and Signal Processing (ICASSP), Barcelona, Spain, 4–8 May 2020; pp. 566–570.
36. Amyar, A.; Modzelewski, R.; Li, H.; Ruan, S. Multi-task deep learning based CT imaging analysis for COVID-19 pneumoni Classification and segmentation. *Comput. Biol. Med.* **2020**, *126*, 104037. [CrossRef]
37. Lakkapragada, A.; Sleiman, E.; Surabhi, S.; Wall, D.P. Mitigating negative transfer in multi-task learning with exponentia moving average loss weighting strategies (student abstract). In Proceedings of the AAAI Conference on Artificial Intelligenc Washington, DC, USA, 7–14 February 2023; Volume 37, pp. 16246–16247.

applied sciences

MDPI

ticle

n Interactive Transient Model Correction Active Sonar Target racking Method

ao Liu and Shiliang Fang *

College of Information Science and Engineering, Southeast University, Nanjing 210018, China; 230198986@seu.edu.cn
* Correspondence: slfang@seu.edu.cn

Abstract: Active sonar can usually only directly measure the distance and bearing information of underwater targets, and cannot directly obtain target velocity, acceleration and other information. Therefore, the amount of information is relatively small, making it difficult to support the construction of complex motion models. At the same time, the motion state of underwater maneuvering targets is changeable. In response to the problem of detecting and tracking underwater moving targets by active sonar, this paper proposes a target transient model correction (TMC) filtering tracking method. Based on the conventional Kalman filter (KF) estimation, residual covariance is used as a signal quantity. When there is a large change in it, a transient filter with constant gain is adopted to filter the measurement value. The filtered output is used to correct the KF gain matrix and the target motion state model, to avoid the problem of increasing or even diverging KF estimation errors caused by changes in process noise. Using this method can solve the problem of maintaining stability and filtering estimation accuracy of active sonar tracking of underwater maneuvering targets with less computational and engineering costs.

Keywords: active sonar; target tracking; transient model correction; Kalman filtering

1. Introduction

Active sonar target tracking is based on the discrete point tracks of underwater moving targets detected by sonar. Through track correlation, state estimation and other filtering processing, random errors in the measurement process are suppressed, and the accuracy of target measurements is improved. This makes the target track smoother and allows more state information about the target to be obtained, such as course, speed, acceleration and other parameters. Active sonar target tracking belongs to the category of maneuvering target tracking. For maneuvering target tracking, researchers at home and abroad have mainly conducted a large amount of research work from three directions: maneuvering target motion model, filtering algorithm, and track management. Among them, the motion model and filtering algorithm are the core and key.

In the 1970s, Friedland et al. [1] proposed the constant velocity (CV) model, and Hampton et al. [2] proposed the constant acceleration (CA) model. These two models belong to the most basic linear mathematical models and are mainly suitable for weakly maneuvering targets. In the context of nonlinear motion models, Singer proposed a first-order time-correlated stochastic model with a zero mean of target maneuvering acceleration, known as the Singer model [3], which is suitable for target motion patterns that fall between CV and CA movements. Moose et al. proposed a correlated Gaussian noise model with a random switch mean, known as the semi-Markov model [4,5]. The main difference between the semi-Markov model and the Singer model is that the semi-Markov model introduces non-zero acceleration. In the early 1930s, Zhou proposed the "current" statistical model for maneuvering targets [6,7], which used a more realistic non-zero mean and a modified Rayleigh distribution to characterize the maneuvering acceleration characteristics of targets. To describe the acceleration distribution of maneuvering targets more accurately, Mehrotra et al. extended the derivative of acceleration to a state variable based on the Singer model, and proposed the Jerk model [8,9]. Since the Jerk model adds the derivative of acceleration as a state variable, the description of acceleration is more accurate, which also improves tracking accuracy. The motion form of maneuvering targets is usually complex and variable [10]. When the target's motion state undergoes significant changes, the preset single model mismatches with the actual motion state, leading to reduced filtering precision, filter divergence, unstable target tracking, and target loss [11]. To address this issue, Blom et al. proposed the interacting multiple model (IMM) algorithm based on generalized pseudo-Bayesian theory [12]. This algorithm has received extensive research and applications in the tracking of maneuvering targets in the air, ground, and water in recent years. The standard IMM algorithm is a recursive algorithm that assumes the motion state of the tracked target can be described by a finite set of models. Multiple models work simultaneously, and the posterior probabilities of each model are used to weight the filtering inputs and outputs. The transition between models is described by a Markov chain process. The IMM algorithm allows the online model to closely approximate the actual motion state of the target and ensures that the inputs of all filters in the system at each discrete sampling time match the actual system state, avoiding filter divergence. These studies can improve the suitability of the model and the real motion of the target, thereby enhancing tracking accuracy.

In terms of tracking filtering algorithms, linear systems often employ two-point extrapolation filtering, Wiener filtering, least squares filtering, α-β [13], α-β-γ [14], and the KF [15] method. For nonlinear systems, the main filtering methods include the classical extended Kalman filtering (EKF) based on nonlinear approximation [16,17], unscented Kalman filtering (UKF) [18], cubature Kalman filtering (CKF) [19], and particle filtering (PF) proposed by Gordon et al. [20]. Many researchers have also optimized and improved these filtering methods. Subsequently, the emergence of improved algorithms such as the error-minimizing squared sum filter, the kernel correlation filter [21], and convolutional neural networks have made significant contributions to more precise target tracking. For specific tracking applications, the choice of filtering algorithm should be based on the availability of prior knowledge about system dynamic noise, sensor measurement error statistics, as well as constraints such as tracking accuracy and computational requirements. A comprehensive trade-off selection should be made.

At the beginning of each scanning period, the active sonar sends a pulse signal and then receives the target echo. By processing and analyzing the echo, the target information is obtained. By measuring and analyzing the time difference between pulse signal transmitting time and echo receiving time, combined with underwater sound propagation speed, the distance value of the target can be obtained directly. By using spatial directivity and multi-beam direction finding processing of the receiving transducer array, the azimuth of the echo can be determined, and the azimuth information of the target can be obtained. When the transmitting pulse signal is a CW signal, if there is relative motion between the target and the sonar, there will be a frequency offset between the transmitted CW signal and the received echo signal. Through spectrum analysis of the echo signal, the radial velocity of the target relative to the sonar can be calculated. Of course, other pulse signals will also have Doppler shifts, but because they are complex wideband signals, extracting accurate Doppler shifts requires more complex algorithms. The "velocity" obtained at this time is only the radial velocity of the target relative to the sonar and not the true speed of the target in the Earth coordinate system. At present, no active sonar can directly measure the acceleration of target motion.

Therefore, the tracking of underwater targets by active sonar has the following characteristics: Firstly, it typically adopts the track while scan (TWS) approach, which involves simultaneously searching, measuring, and tracking target information in a periodic manner. This requires high real-time tracking performance. Secondly, the target measurement information has low dimensionality and a slow update rate. Typically, only azimuth and range information in a two-dimensional plane are available, and direct measurements of target depth, velocity, and other information are generally not possible. Additionally, due to the slow propagation speed of sound waves in water compared to electromagnetic waves, the update rate of measurement information is slow, typically taking tens to hundreds of seconds to obtain the next batch of measurements. Thirdly, the target's motion state is highly variable and subject to high process noise. Fourthly, the target may easily "lose" due to the influence of the ocean environment and countermeasures, resulting in the inability to acquire target measurement information continuously and stably over multiple scanning cycles. This leads to an increase in tracking output errors, instability, or even filter divergence.

Due to the unique application scenarios, there are relatively few reports in the research of active sonar for tracking underwater maneuvering targets. The Ocean Systems Laboratory in the UK has studied the technology of forward-looking sonar for tracking and localizing underwater targets based on particle filtering [22]; The Florida Atlantic University in the United States has applied the KF algorithm to the forward-looking sonar target tracking processing of remotely operated vehicles (ROVs) [23]. Canada's El-Hawary has derived a robust EKF algorithm and applied it to underwater moving target tracking [24]. Yang and others have proposed a novel particle filtering algorithm for underwater moving target tracking [25]. References [26,27] proposed a composite filtering method that combines the robustness of particle filtering with the real-time performance of KF, effectively reducing tracking errors. Reference [28] studied the target localization and tracking method based on azimuth Doppler frequency deviation two-dimensional measurement information, which can achieve faster convergence and higher tracking accuracy compared with one-dimensional azimuth measurement information. Liu et al. [29] discussed the application of the CKF algorithm based on the variance square root in torpedo target tracking, aiming at the problem that the covariance can become non-positive definite and cause filter instability or even divergence in high-dimensional systems using the UKF algorithm. Gao et al. [30] studied underwater maneuvering target tracking based on the interactive multiple model (IMM). Zhang et al. [31] addressed the issue that the single--model KF cannot fully adapt to all motion states of underwater targets. They used the interactive multiple model KF method to process the ultra-short baseline tracking data of autonomous underwater vehicles (AUVs). The motion models enhance motion state adaptability through probability matrix transitions. The experimental results demonstrated that this algorithm has better state adaptability than the single--model KF algorithm when the multi-model set is reasonably constructed. Zhao et al. [32] combined EKF and UKF with the IMM algorithm for underwater target tracking. Their research suggests that under high measurement error conditions, the IMM-UKF algorithm has higher tracking accuracy than the IMM-EKF algorithm. In recent years, the algorithm based on depth learning and neural networks has been applied to underwater target tracking to solve model mismatches and other problems and improve tracking stability [33–35].

Due to the special nature of underwater target detection, such as submarines, there is a scarcity of statistical characteristics from known target data samples. As a result, solving the probability transition matrix poses one of the significant challenges, given that the Markov chain transition probability in the interactive multiple model tracking method relies on statistical analysis of these data. The selection of the set of maneuvering target motion models is another challenge: if the goal is to cover as many target motion modes as possible, the model set can become very large, and the model space approaches continuity, making the model set countably infinite, leading to a drastic increase in computational complexity and potential model competition, which can even worsen tracking performance. On the other hand, if there are fewer motion models in the model set, it can be difficult to cover all possible target motion modes, leading to insufficient tracking accuracy or even tracking divergence. Therefore, using a multi-model set to describe the motion of the target can, to some extent, overcome the limitations of the single model. However, the computational complexity of the multi-model approach is high, requiring a high level of prior information about the target, which leads to an increase in computational resources. This may not be suitable for some engineering applications. Additionally, when active sonar is used to detect underwater submarines that maneuver evasively, changes in target reflectivity and dynamics can cause periodic measurement values to be lost (i.e., periodic measurement information is not continuous), lead to a decrease in tracking performance and even loss of target tracking.

To address the problem of active sonar tracking of underwater submarine targets, this study proposes a novel underwater maneuvering target tracking method based on transient correction using random mixing models. This approach assumes that, although the motion state of maneuvering targets is complex and varies over time, within a certain time period, underwater targets only have one maneuvering mode that can be described by only one motion model. Therefore, the focus of this approach is how to determine whether the target's maneuvering mode has changed, and once such a change occurs, how to correct and adjust the motion model parameters to make the corrected motion model closer to the true motion state of the target.

2. Description of the TMC Tracking Method

Based on the following two points of analysis, the overall design approach of the algorithm and the overall schematic diagram as shown in Figure 1 are presented:

1. Due to the characteristics of submarine targets and water media, when a submarine target is moving underwater, sudden changes in maneuvering state generally do not occur. In combination with the long measurement acquisition period of active sonar for underwater submarine targets, it can be assumed that within two sampling intervals, the change in target motion state is uniform, and the motion state changes that occur within a number of consecutive sampling periods can be considered a transient process. By correcting this transient process, the tracking instability or decreased accuracy caused by changes in motion mode can be solved.
2. In general, after given design requirements, the precision of active sonar target measurement data is stable. Therefore, the deviation between target measurement values and state estimation values can be considered to be caused by changes in their motion state. According to the changes in the variance of measurement values or state estimation values, it can be judged whether the target's motion state has changed, and the motion state parameters can be corrected to make the motion model closer to the true motion state of the target.

As shown in Figure 1, the system state model is first established, including the displacements (r_x, r_y) and velocity components (v_x, v_y) on the X-axis and Y-axis. Then, the state model is initialized and assigned values. Subsequently, KF processing is performed according to the flow of one-step advance prediction, filtering gain matrix calculation, and filtering estimation update. Additionally, the residual covariance $\mathbf{S}(k)$ of the current cycle is calculated and analyzed. When $\mathbf{S}(k)$ is less than the preset decision threshold, the KF result is used as the tracking filter output. When it is greater than the preset decision threshold, it is judged that there is a significant deviation between the current state model and the actual motion of the target, and thus correction is necessary. Using the constant gain filtering method, the current measurement value is filtered, and the KF gain matrix is adjusted based on the filtering result. Additionally, the motion velocity, position, and process noise of the state model are corrected. With the corrected state model parameters and filter gain matrix, the KF process is re-performed. Under normal circumstances, the active sonar receives the echo signals reflected by the target and processes the echo signals to obtain direct measurement information such as radial distance and azimuth information. For the KF algorithm that models and processes tracking in a Cartesian coordinate system, it is necessary to perform coordinate system transformation and deflection removal processing on the measurement data to obtain the displacement information ($d_x(k)$, $d_y(k)$) of the target on the X-axis and Y-axis in the Cartesian coordinate system, which is used as the measurement update for tracking filtering.

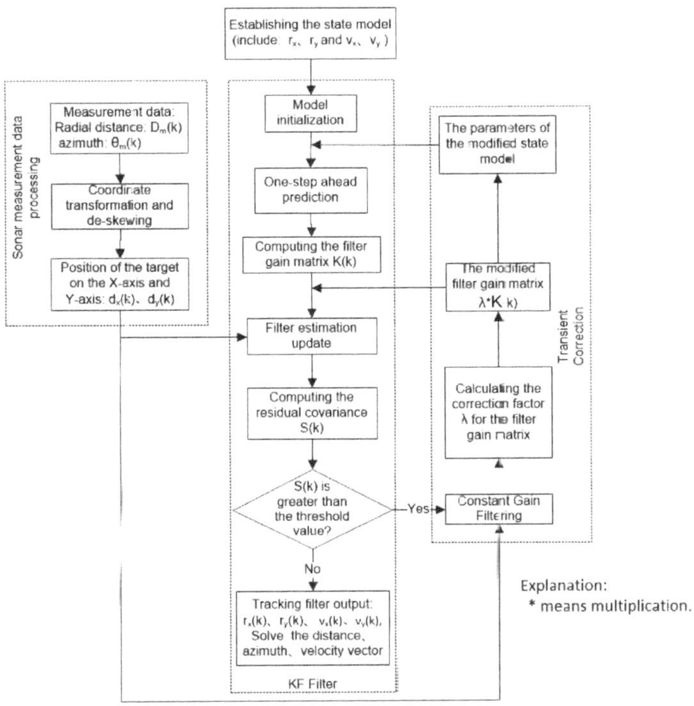

Figure 1. Schematic diagram of the general idea of the TMC tracking method.

2.1. System Model

In general, within a single measurement period of active sonar, only the radial distance $R(t)$ and azimuth $\theta(t)$ of underwater targets can be obtained. With sonar as the observation origin O, a two-dimensional coordinate system is establish ed, as shown in Figure 2 (for convenience of expression, let the Y-axis point to the north). The following Equations (1) and (2) are proposed to describe the target motion model shown in Figure 2: at time t, the target is located at Pt point, with a distance of D(t) and an azimuth of $\theta(t)$; at time $(t+\mathrm{T})$ (T is the observation period of active sonar), the target is located at $P_{t+\mathrm{T}}$ point with a distance of $D(t+\mathrm{T})$ and an azimuth of $\theta(t+T)$. The displacement of the target on the X-axis and Y-axis from time t to time $(t+\mathrm{T})$ is:

$$\begin{cases} r_x = d_x(t+\mathrm{T}) - d_x(t), \\ r_y = d_y(t+\mathrm{T}) - d_y(t). \end{cases} \tag{1}$$

in which $d_x(t)$ and $d_y(t)$ are the projections of the radial distance $D(t)$ of the target at time t on the X- and Y-axis, respectively, $d_x(t+\mathrm{T})$ and $d_y(t+\mathrm{T})$ are the projections of the radial distance $D(t+\mathrm{T})$ of the target at time $(t+\mathrm{T})$ on the X- and Y-axis, respectively.

$$\begin{cases} d_x(t+\mathrm{T}) = D(t+\mathrm{T})\cdot\sin(\theta(t+\mathrm{T})), \\ d_x(t) = D(t)\cdot\sin(\theta(t)), \\ d_y(t+\mathrm{T}) = D(t+T)\cdot\cos(\theta(t+\mathrm{T})), \\ d_y(t) = D(t)\cdot\cos(\theta(t)). \end{cases} \tag{2}$$

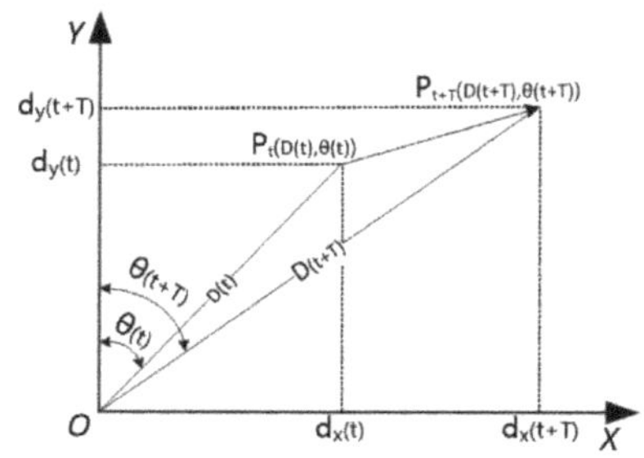

Figure 2. Schematic diagram of target movement situation.

2.1.1. State Equation

When a slowly varying target like a submarine is moving underwater, most of the time, the speed changes are weak. Therefore, it can be assumed that most of the time, it is in a uniform motion state, and the acceleration can be regarded as a random disturbance with Gaussian white noise characteristics, usually with a zero mean and a variance of q. Therefore, the continuous-time state equation of the target can be established as:

$$\dot{\mathbf{X}}(t) = \mathbf{A}\mathbf{X}(t) + \mathbf{F}w(t). \tag{3}$$

In the formula, $\mathbf{X}(t)$ represents the system state vector, and $\mathbf{X}(t) = \left[x(t)\ \dot{x}(t)\ y(t)\ \dot{y}(t)\right]^T$. $x(t)$ and $y(t)$ represent the target's displacement on the X- and Y-axis, respectively, while $\dot{x}(t)$ and $\dot{y}(t)$ represent the target's velocity on the X- and Y-axis, respectively. $\dot{\mathbf{X}}(t) = \left[\dot{x}(t)\ \ddot{x}(t)\ \dot{y}(t)\ \ddot{y}(t)\right]^T$, $\ddot{x}(t)$ and $\ddot{y}(t)$ represent the accelerations expressed in terms of random noise $w(t)$, with mean and variance given by:

$$E[w(t)] = 0, \tag{4}$$

$$E\left[w(t)w^T(\tau)\right] = q\delta(t-\tau) \tag{5}$$

$\mathbf{A}$ is the state transition matrix.

$$\mathbf{A} = \begin{bmatrix} 0 & 1\,0 & 0 \\ 0 & 0\,0 & 0 \\ 0 & 0\,0 & 1 \\ 0 & 0\,0 & 0 \end{bmatrix} \tag{6}$$

$\mathbf{F}$ is the process noise input matrix: $\mathbf{F} = [0\,1\,0\,1]^T$.

The discrete-time state equation for a constant system is:

$$\mathbf{X}(k+1) = \mathbf{\Phi}\mathbf{X}(k) + \mathbf{\Gamma}w(k) \tag{7}$$

In the formula, $\mathbf{X}(k)$ represents the discrete state vector, and $\mathbf{X}(k) = \left[r_x\ v_x\ r_y\ v_y\right]^T$, r_x and r_y represent the target's displacement on the X- and Y-axis, respectively, while v_x and v_y represent the target's velocity on the X- and Y-axis, respectively. The state transition matrix $\mathbf{\Phi}$ is defined as:

$$\mathbf{\Phi} = e^{\mathrm{AT}} = \begin{bmatrix} 1 & T\,0 & 0 \\ 0 & 1\,0 & 0 \\ 0 & 0\,1 & \mathrm{T} \\ 0 & 0\,0 & 1 \end{bmatrix} \tag{8}$$

The process noise input matrix $\mathbf{\Gamma}$ is:

$$\mathbf{\Gamma} = \int_0^{\mathrm{T}} e^{\mathbf{A}(\mathrm{T}-\tau)}\mathbf{F}d\tau = \int_0^{\mathrm{T}} \begin{bmatrix} 1 & \mathrm{T}-\tau & 0 & 0 \\ 0 & 1 & 0 & 0 \\ 0 & 0 & 1 & \mathrm{T}-\tau \\ 0 & 0 & 0 & 1 \end{bmatrix} \begin{bmatrix} 0 \\ 1 \\ 0 \\ 1 \end{bmatrix} d\tau = \int_0^{\mathrm{T}} \begin{bmatrix} T-\tau \\ 1 \\ T-\tau \\ 1 \end{bmatrix} d\tau = \begin{bmatrix} \mathrm{T}^2/2 \\ T \\ \mathrm{T}^2/2 \\ T \end{bmatrix} \tag{9}$$

The process noise matrix $\mathbf{W}(k)$ is defined as:

$$\mathbf{W}(k) = \int_0^{\mathrm{T}} e^{\mathbf{A}(\mathrm{T}-\tau)}\mathbf{F}w(k\mathrm{T}+\tau)d\tau = \int_0^{\mathrm{T}} \begin{bmatrix} T-\tau \\ 1 \\ T-\tau \\ 1 \end{bmatrix} w(k\mathrm{T}+\tau)d\tau \tag{10}$$

The covariance matrix $\mathbf{Q}(k)$ of the process noise $w(k)$ is defined as:

$$\begin{aligned} \mathbf{Q}(k) = \boldsymbol{E}\left[\mathbf{W}(k)\mathbf{W}^T(k)\right] &= \int_0^{\mathrm{T}} \begin{bmatrix} T-\tau \\ 1 \\ T-\tau \\ 1 \end{bmatrix} [\mathrm{T}-\tau \; 1 \; \mathrm{T}-\tau \; 1] q d\tau \\ &= \begin{bmatrix} \mathrm{T}^3/3 & \mathrm{T}^2/2 & \mathrm{T}^3/3 & \mathrm{T}^2/2 \\ \mathrm{T}^2/2 & T & \mathrm{T}^2/2 & T \\ \mathrm{T}^3/3 & \mathrm{T}^2/2 & \mathrm{T}^3/3 & \mathrm{T}^2/2 \\ \mathrm{T}^2/2 & T & \mathrm{T}^2/2 & T \end{bmatrix} q \end{aligned} \tag{11}$$

2.1.2. Measurement Equation

In the rectangular coordinate system, the measurement equation is:

$$\mathbf{Z}(k) = \mathbf{H}\mathbf{X}(k) + \mathbf{V}(k) \tag{12}$$

In the formula, $\mathbf{Z}(k)$ represents the measurement vector, where $\mathbf{Z}(k) = \left[r_x \; r_y\right]^T$. $\mathbf{H}$ is the measurement matrix:

$$\mathbf{H} = \begin{bmatrix} 1 & 0 & 0 & 0 \\ 0 & 0 & 1 & 0 \end{bmatrix} \tag{13}$$

$\mathbf{V}(k)$ is the measurement noise matrix, and the measurement noise is Gaussian white noise with a mean of zero, variance of r, and a normal distribution. Its covariance matrix $\mathbf{R}(k)$ is defined as:

$$\mathbf{R}(k) = \boldsymbol{E}\left[\mathbf{V}(k)\mathbf{V}^T(k)\right] = \int_0^{\mathrm{T}} \begin{bmatrix} 1 \\ 1 \end{bmatrix} [1 \; 1] r d\tau = \begin{bmatrix} \mathrm{T} & \mathrm{T} \\ \mathrm{T} & \mathrm{T} \end{bmatrix} r \tag{14}$$

2.1.3. Measurement Debiasing

In the system model described in Figure 2, when the sonar acquires the radial distance and azimuth measurement values of underwater targets, $D_m(k)$ and $\theta_m(k)$, the measurement vector $\mathbf{Z}(k)$ needs to be solved according to Formula (1). Due to the nonlinear transformation included in Formula (1), the measured vector in the Cartesian coordinate system is biased, and it needs to be debiased through compensation.

It is assumed that the measurement errors of the radial distance $D_m(k)$ and azimuth $\theta_m(k)$ are uncorrelated and follow a zero-mean Gaussian distribution, with variances of σ_D^2 and σ_θ^2, respectively. The projected targets' radial distances $d_x(k)$ and $d_y(k)$ on the X- and Y-axis after debiasing compensation are:

$$\begin{cases} d_x(k) = D_m(k) \cdot \sin(\theta_m(k))/\lambda_\theta, \\ d_y(k) = D_m(k) \cdot \cos(\theta_m(k))/\lambda_\theta. \end{cases} \tag{15}$$

In the formula, the value of λ_θ is:

$$\lambda_\theta = e^{-\sigma_\theta^2/2} \tag{16}$$

The noise covariance matrix of the compensated position measurement is:

$$\mathbf{R}(k) = \begin{bmatrix} \sigma_x^2 & \sigma_{xy} \\ \sigma_{xy} & \sigma_y^2 \end{bmatrix}. \tag{17}$$

in which:

$$\begin{cases} \sigma_x^2 = \dfrac{(D_m^2(k) + \sigma_D^2)(1 - \lambda'_\theta cos(2\theta_m(k)))}{2} + \left(\lambda_\theta^{-2} - 2\right) D_m^2(k) sin^2(\theta_m(k)), \\ \sigma_y^2 = \dfrac{(D_m^2(k) + \sigma_D^2)(1 + \lambda'_\theta cos(2\theta_m(k)))}{2} + \left(\lambda_\theta^{-2} - 2\right) D_m^2(k) cos^2(\theta_m(k)), \\ \sigma_{xy} = \dfrac{(D_m^2(k) + \sigma_D^2)\lambda'_\theta sin(2\theta_m(k))}{2} + \left(\lambda_\theta^{-2} - 2\right) D_m^2(k) sin(\theta_m(k)) sin(\theta_m(k)). \end{cases} \tag{18}$$

in which:

$$\lambda'_\theta = e^{-2\sigma_\theta^2}. \tag{19}$$

2.2. Tracking Filtering Method

When the target is moving at a constant velocity, the KF algorithm is equivalent to the filtering method designed using the minimum mean squared error estimation criterion in steady state. However, during the transient process or when the target undergoes random maneuvering, the performance of KF is superior to other methods. Additionally, KF is a recursive algorithm that only requires the current time's prediction and measurement values to obtain the current time's state filtering estimate, without the need to transmit all historical data. Therefore, it has advantages such as small computational complexity, strong real-time performance, and easy engineering implementation. Based on the above considerations, KF is adopted as the tracking filtering method.

In target tracking, the KF algorithm mainly implements the functions of prediction and filtering estimation. The filtering equation is:

$$\hat{\mathbf{X}}(k|k) = \hat{\mathbf{X}}(k|k-1) + \mathbf{K}(k)\mathbf{d}(k). \tag{20}$$

In the formula, $\hat{\mathbf{X}}(k|k)$ represents the filtered estimate at time k; $\hat{\mathbf{X}}(k|k-1)$ is the priori filtered estimate (one-step advance prediction) of $\hat{\mathbf{X}}(k-1|k-1)$ obtained by the measurement value $\mathbf{Z}(k-1)$ at time $(k-1)$:

$$\hat{\mathbf{X}}(k|k-1) = \mathbf{\Phi}\hat{\mathbf{X}}(k-1|k-1), \tag{21}$$

$\mathbf{K}(k)$ represents the filtering gain matrix:

$$\mathbf{K}(k) = \mathbf{P}(k|k-1)\mathbf{H}^T\left[\mathbf{H}\mathbf{P}(k|k-1)\mathbf{H}^T + \mathbf{R}(k)\right]^{-1} \tag{22}$$

$\mathbf{P}(k|k-1)$ is the covariance matrix of one-step advance prediction error:

$$\mathbf{P}(k|k-1) = \mathbf{\Phi}\mathbf{P}(k-1|k-1)\mathbf{\Phi}^T + \mathbf{\Gamma}\mathbf{Q}(k-1)\mathbf{\Gamma}^T, \tag{23}$$

$\mathbf{P}(k-1|k-1)$ is the covariance matrix of filtered estimation error:

$$\mathbf{P}(k-1|k-1) = [\mathbf{I} - \mathbf{K}(k-1)\mathbf{H}]\mathbf{P}(k-1|k-2) \tag{24}$$

$\mathbf{d}(k)$ is the residual (innovation) vector:

$$\mathbf{d}(k) = \mathbf{Z}(k) - \hat{\mathbf{Z}}(k|k-1), \tag{25}$$

$\hat{\mathbf{Z}}(k|k-1)$ is the predicted measurement value:

$$\hat{\mathbf{Z}}(k|k-1) = \mathbf{H}\hat{\mathbf{X}}(k|k-1) \quad (26)$$

The covariance matrix of the residual vector $\mathbf{d}(k)$ is:

$$\mathbf{S}(k) = \mathbf{H}\mathbf{P}(k|k-1)\mathbf{H}^T + \mathbf{R}(k). \quad (27)$$

The system state vector $\mathbf{X}(t)$ contains the displacement and motion velocity of the target on the X- and Y-axis. Through the filter processing of Equation (20), the displacement and motion velocity of the target on the X- and Y-axis are constantly updated. After filtering, the distance and azimuth accuracy of the target is improved. The velocity component of the target movement is synthesized by the velocity component of the two directions. Further, if the measurement vector $\mathbf{Z}(k)$ includes the speed measurement of the target, you can establish the state vector that contains the acceleration (the acceleration is no longer considered a random interference noise), and after filtering, you can obtain the motion acceleration components on the X- and Y-axis, and you can obtain the acceleration vector on the two-dimensional plane by the synthesis of the two acceleration components.

2.3. Transient Correction

When the system state equation deviates from the actual situation, the system uncertainty increases, the estimation error of the KF filter becomes larger, and the reliability of the one-step prediction estimation $\hat{\mathbf{X}}(k|k-1)$ decreases. At this time, KF adjusts the estimation by changing the filtering gain $\mathbf{K}(k)$ to ensure that the filtered estimation $\hat{\mathbf{X}}(k|k)$ is as close as possible to the actual state $\mathbf{X}(k)$. When the motion state of the underwater target changes, it causes an increase in the system process noise described in Section 3.1.1. As a result, the covariance matrix $\mathbf{P}(k|k-1)$ of the one-step advance prediction error becomes larger, and subsequently, the filtering gain $\mathbf{K}(k)$ also increases. Considering an extreme case where $\mathbf{P}(k|k-1)$ approaches infinity, we take the limit of Equation (22) as follows:

$$\lim_{\mathbf{P}^-\to\infty} \mathbf{K}(k) = \lim_{\mathbf{P}^-\to\infty} \frac{\mathbf{P}(k|k-1)\mathbf{H}^T}{\mathbf{H}\mathbf{P}(k|k-1)\mathbf{H}^T + \mathbf{R}(k)} = \mathbf{H}^{-1}, \ \{\mathbf{P}^- \ \mathrm{Rep}\mathbf{P}(k|k-1)\}. \quad (28)$$

By combining Formulas (25), (26) and (28), we can rewrite Formula (20) as $\hat{\mathbf{X}}(k|k) = \mathbf{Z}(k)\mathbf{H}^{-1}$. This indicates that when the system error reaches its limit, the KF system adjusts the reliability of the one-step prediction estimate to the lowest level, while the weight of the measurement variables reaches its maximum.

Therefore, the residual covariance $\mathbf{S}(k)$ of the variable gain KF filter can be used as a signal indicator, and the residuals of the constant gain filter can be used as a reference to correct the KF filter gain matrix and reset the state model. This process can be iterated.

The comparison judgment threshold of the residual covariance $\mathbf{S}(k)$ in Figure 1 can be obtained through error analysis of the target measurement history data of the sonar system. Normally, after the design of the sonar is completed, its measurement error is known. Therefore, the comparison threshold for $\mathbf{S}(k)$ can be determined beforehand.

The constant gain filter selects the xhe filtering method. The αil filter is a constant residual filter that has good convergence properties and can rapidly track maneuvering targets over a wide range. The α-β filtering equation is as follows:

$$\begin{cases} \hat{\mathbf{X}}_{\alpha\beta}(k) = (1-\alpha)\left[\hat{\mathbf{X}}_{\alpha\beta}(k-1) + \mathrm{T}\hat{v}_{\alpha\beta}(k-1)\right] + \alpha Z(k), \\ \hat{v}_{\alpha\beta}(k) = (1-\beta)\hat{v}_{\alpha\beta}(k-1) + \beta\left[Z(k) - \hat{\mathbf{X}}_{\alpha\beta}(k-1)\right]/T. \end{cases} \quad (29)$$

In the equation, $\hat{\mathbf{X}}_{\alpha\beta}(k)$ and $\hat{\mathbf{X}}_{\alpha\beta}(k-1)$ represent the current and previous moment's target position filtered estimation values, respectively. α and β are the filtering coefficients, while $\hat{v}_{\alpha\beta}(k)$ and $\hat{v}_{\alpha\beta}(k-1)$ represent the current and previous moment's target velocity filtered estimation values, respectively. $\mathbf{Z}(k)$ is the current moment's target position measurement value, and T is the measurement update period. The αs filter gain is a constant $\mathbf{K}_{\alpha\beta} = [\alpha\ \beta/\mathrm{T}]^T$, and the residual $\mathbf{d}_{\alpha\beta}(k)$ is defined as:

$$\mathbf{d}_{\alpha\beta}(k) = \mathbf{Z}(k) - \left[\hat{\mathbf{X}}_{\alpha\beta}(k-1) + \mathrm{T}\hat{v}_{\alpha\beta}(k-1)\right] \quad (30)$$

When the residual covariance $\mathbf{S}(k)$ of the KF exceeds the comparison judgment threshold, we select the N residual values before time k to perform mean processing on $\mathbf{d}(k-1) \sim \mathbf{d}(k-N)$. The result is then divided by the residual $\mathbf{d}_{\alpha\beta}(k)$ of the α-β filter to obtain the correction factor λ for the KF filter gain matrix:

$$\lambda = \sum_{i=k-N}^{i=k-1} \mathbf{d}(i)/\mathbf{d}_{\alpha\beta}(k). \quad (31)$$

3. Simulation Verification and Offshore Testing

In order to verify the effectiveness of the above method, we simulate the underwater trajectory of the submarine target and the measurement information (azimuth and distance) of the submarine target during each scanning period of the active sonar. At the same time, we also carried out a sea test of sonar detection and tracking of submarine targets to further verify the feasibility of the TMC method.

3.1. Simulation Verification

The conventional KF tracking processing and the proposed TMC tracking processing are applied to the simulation data, and the tracking output results are compared.

3.1.1. Simulation Conditions

The underwater target trajectory is composed of five segments, and the motion parameters for each segment are shown in Table 1 [36]. The initial speed of the target is 2.06 m/s, the heading is 90°, and the total duration of motion is 1140 s. At the end of the trajectory, the target speed is 13.35 m/s, and the heading is 47.6°.

Table 1. Simulation parameters for underwater target motion.

Motion Parameters	Initial Speed (m/s)		Initial Heading (°)	Acceleration (m/s^2)		Motion Duration (s)	Motion Type
	v_x	v_y		a_x	a_y		
Trajectory 1	2.06	0.00	90.00	0.0500	0.1000	120	CV
Trajectory 2	2.06	0.00	90.00	0.0500	0.100	120	CA
Trajectory 3	8.06	12.00	33.88	0.0025	−0.0750	240	CA
Trajectory 4	8.66	−6.00	117.60	0.0025	−0.0250	120	CA
Trajectory 5	8.96	−9.00	135.13	0.0025	0.0500	360	CA

Assuming an active sonar detection scan period of 20 s, the root mean square error (RMSE) of the target's radial distance measurement is 100 m, and the RMSE of the azimuth measurement is 0.5°. The true trajectory of the target's motion and the sonar measurements are shown in Figure 3. Specifically, in Figure 3a, when converting the target's radial distance and azimuth measurements into X- and Y-axis distance measurements in a Cartesian coordinate system, the debiasing process described in Section 2.1.3 was applied.

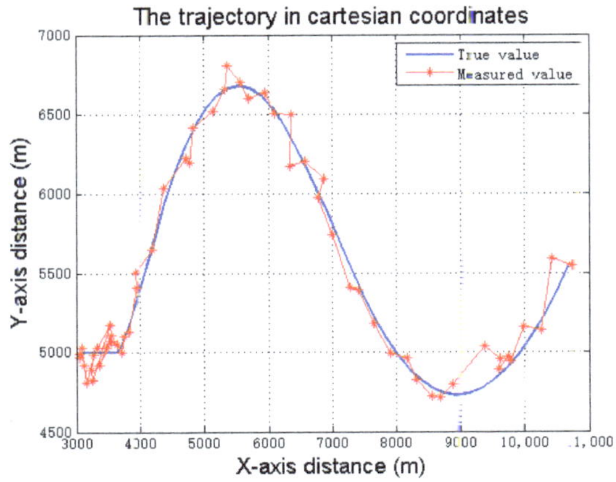

(a)

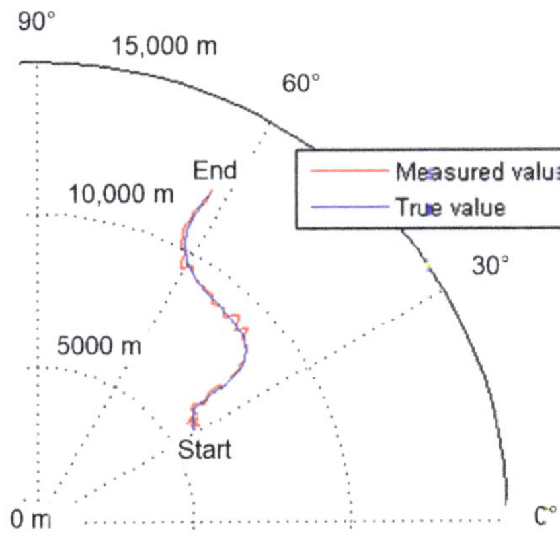

(b)

Figure 3. True trajectory and sonar measured values of the underwater simulated target. (**a**) The trajectory in cartesian coordinates, (**b**) The trajectory in polar coordinates.

3.1.2. Simulation Results and Analysis

Figure 4 compares the processing results of the simulation data using the conventional KF tracking method and the TMC tracking method. In Figure 4a, when the target transitions from uniform to accelerated motion, the tracking trajectory starts to deviate from the true target trajectory, and the tracking error gradually increases. In Figure 4b, when using the TMC tracking method, the target tracking trajectory deviates less from the true trajectory. Figure 4c further compares the tracking results of the conventional KF method with those of the TMC method. It is evident that the tracking performance of the TMC method is superior to that of the conventional KF method. In Figure 4d, the residual covariance of the two tracking methods is compared after normalization. During the first 15 scan cycles (when the target is in uniform motion), the residual covariance of the KF tracking is relatively small. As the target transitions into accelerated motion after three cycles (after the 18th scan cycle), the residual covariance of the KF tracking gradually increases. The residual covariance of the TMC tracking method is comparable to that of the KF tracking during the uniform motion stage and the initial period of accelerated motion. In the latter half of the trajectory, as the residual covariance of the KF tracking gradually increases, the residual covariance of the TMC tracking method remains at a relatively low level comparable to that during the uniform motion stage.

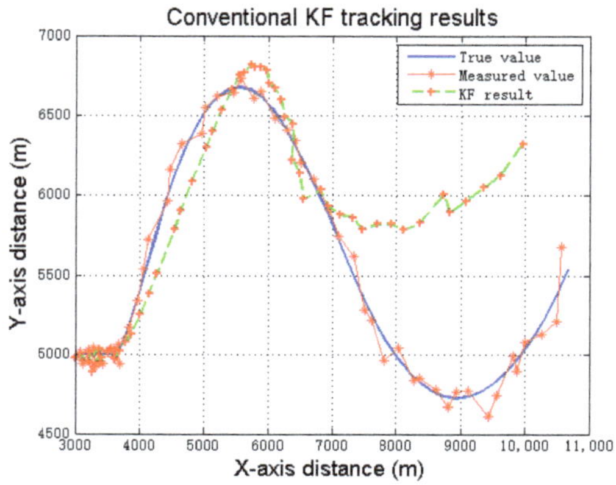

(a)

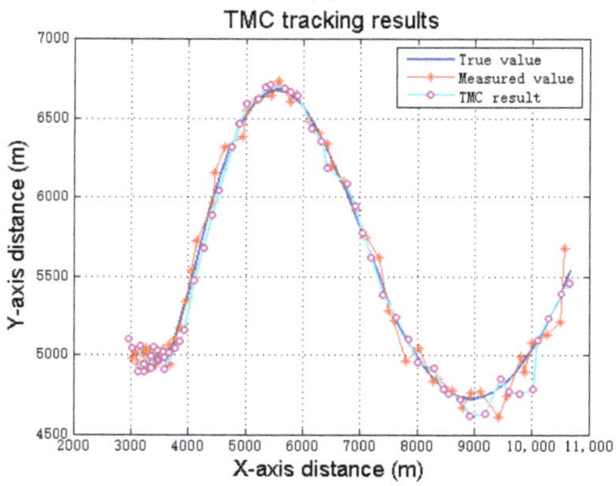

(b)

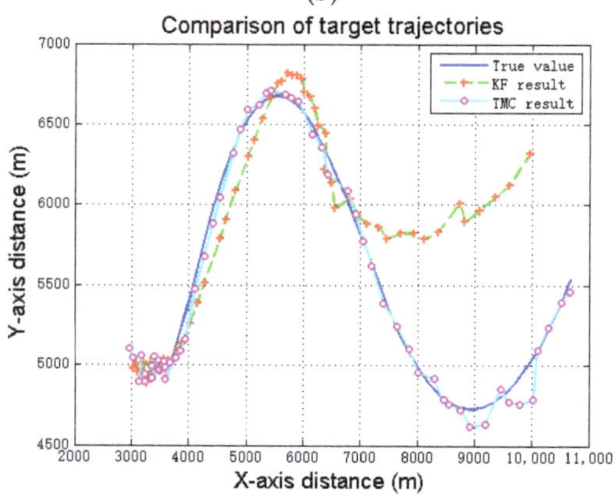

(c)

Figure 4. *Cont.*

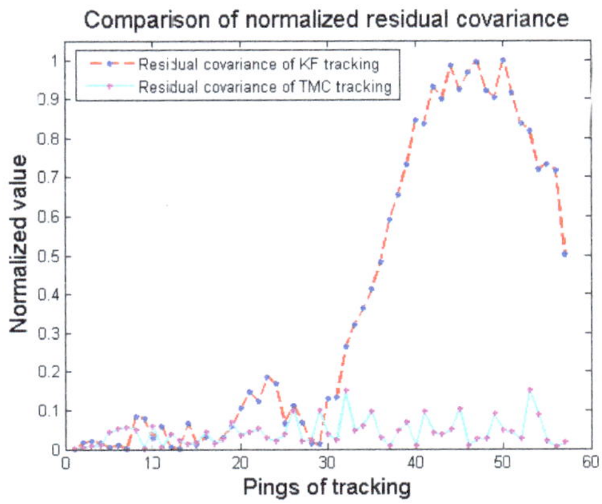

(d)

Figure 4. Comparisons of tracking results between the conventional KF method and the TMC method. (**a**) Conventional KF tracking results, (**b**) TMC tracking results, (**c**) Comparison of target trajectories, (**d**) Comparison of normalized residual covariance.

The target's distances on the X- and Y-axis obtained from both KF tracking and TMC tracking are converted to the target's radial distance and azimuth for comparison with the true value and measurement value, as shown in Figure 5. To illustrate the deviation of the measurement or tracking estimation points from the true target position, the position distance error is defined as the straight-line distance between the true target position and either the measurement point position or the filtered output position of the target tracking. The RMSE of the position distance and azimuth for KF tracking are 237.5 m and 5.17°, respectively, while those for TMC tracking are 57.33 m and 0.49°, respectively. The TMC tracking method improves the accuracy of both the target's radial distance and azimuth tracking.

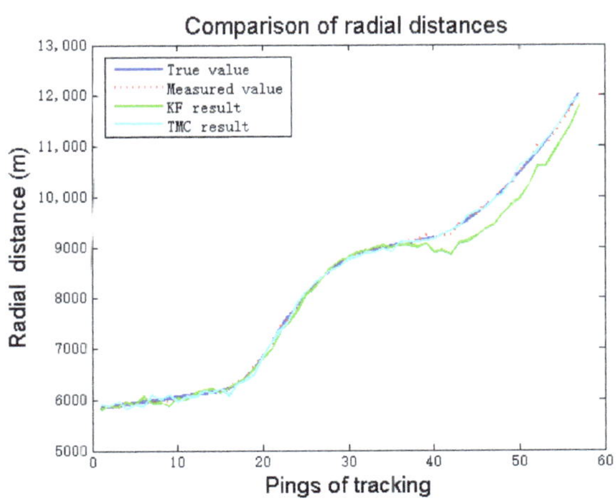

(a)

Figure 5. *Cont.*

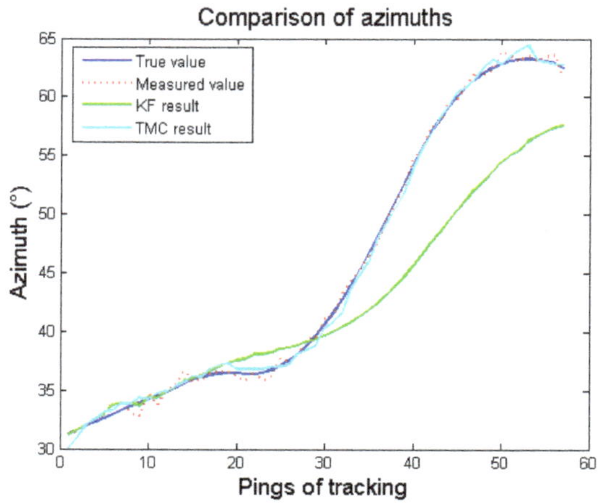

(b)

Figure 5. Comparisons of radial distances and azimuths. (**a**) Comparison of radial distances, (**b**) Comparison of azimuths.

Mean-square error (MSE) analysis of the simulation test results was carried out, as can be seen in Table 2. Due to model mismatch, the KF tracking MSE significantly increased. However, after the TMC method is processed, the tracking error can be reduced.

Table 2. MSE of simulation test.

	Measured Values	KF Results	TMC Results
MSE of Radial Distance	1918.5	56,408.0	3286.9
MSE of Azimuth	0.22	26.73	0.24

3.2. *Offshore Testing*

The experimental site is located in the South China Sea and uses active hull sonar mounted on surface ships to search for and track real underwater submarine targets.

3.2.1. Offshore Testing Description

The tracking duration is approximately 4114 s, with a sonar scan period of approximately 17.1 s, resulting in a total of approximately 240 scan cycles. Due to changes in the relative motion of the target and the sonar, resulting in fluctuations in the amplitude of the echo signal, as well as target shift, steering maneuver, etc the measurement data are not continuously sampled. In practice, a total of 155 cycles of underwater target radial distance and azimuth measurements were collected. Figure 6 shows the true target track derived from the underwater target navigation equipment data, as well as the position measurements obtained by converting the target's radial distance and azimuth detected by active sonar into Cartesian coordinates.

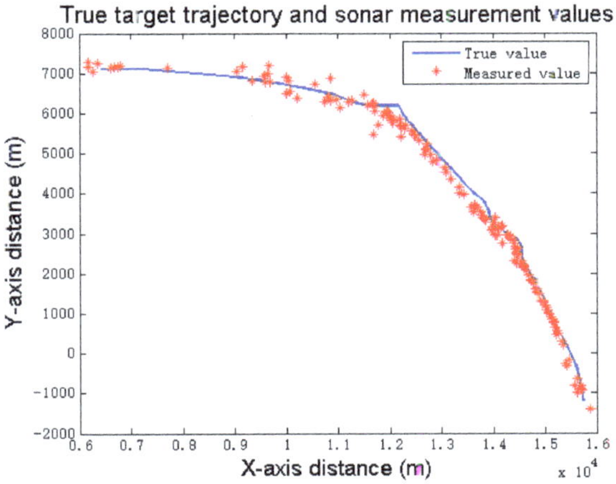

Figure 6. True target trajectory and sonar measurement values.

3.2.2. Results and Analysis

Assuming an RMSE of 100 m for the target's radial distance measurements and an RMSE of 1.0° for the azimuth measurements, both the conventional KF tracking method and the TMC tracking method were used to track the underwater target. A comparative analysis was conducted on the target's X-axis distance, Y-axis distance, radial distance, and azimuth obtained from the true values, measurements, KF tracking results, and TMC tracking results. The results are shown in Figure 7.

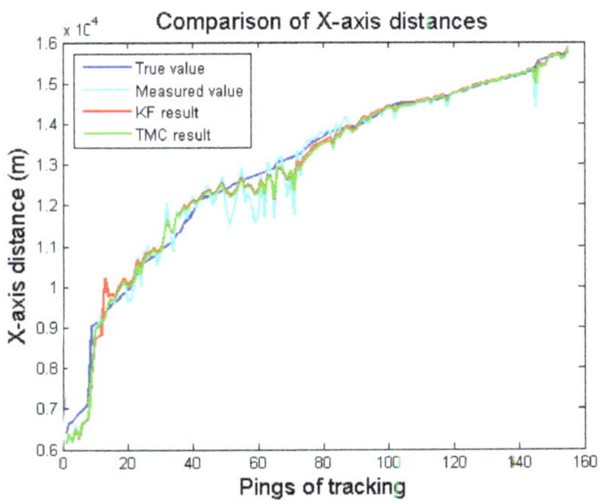

(a)

Figure 7. *Cont.*

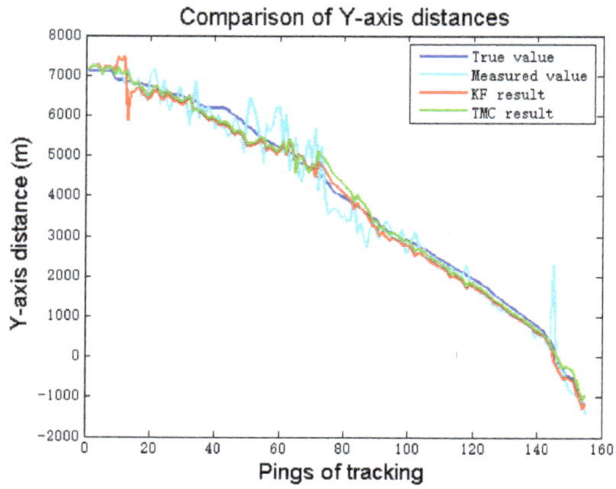

(**b**)

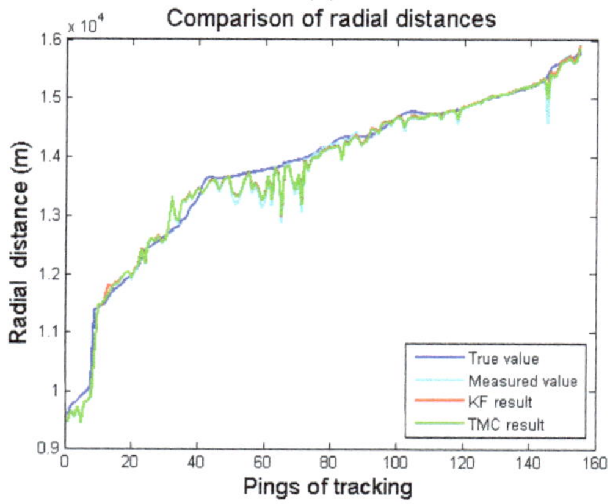

(**c**)

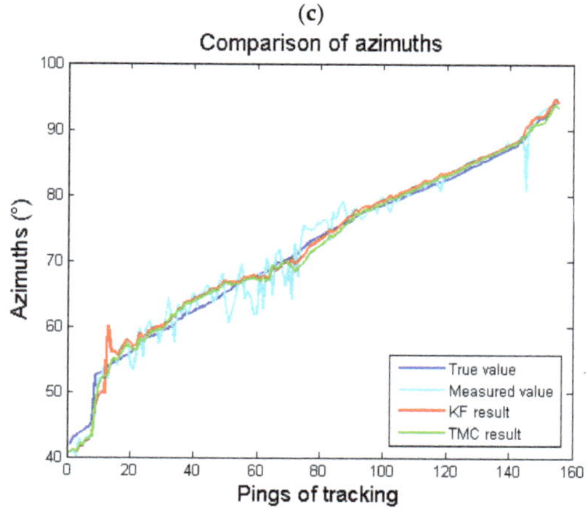

(**d**)

Figure 7. Comparison of Target's X-axis, Y-axis, Radial Distances, and Azimuths. (**a**) Comparison of X-axis distances, (**b**) Comparison of Y-axis distances, (**c**) Comparison of radial distances, (**d**) Comparison of azimuths.

Furthermore, using the true target position as a reference, the absolute errors between the measurement values, KF tracking results. and TMC tracking results and the true values were calculated. The results are shown in Figure 8. The root mean square values of the errors were then calculated and are presented in Table 2 and Figure 9.

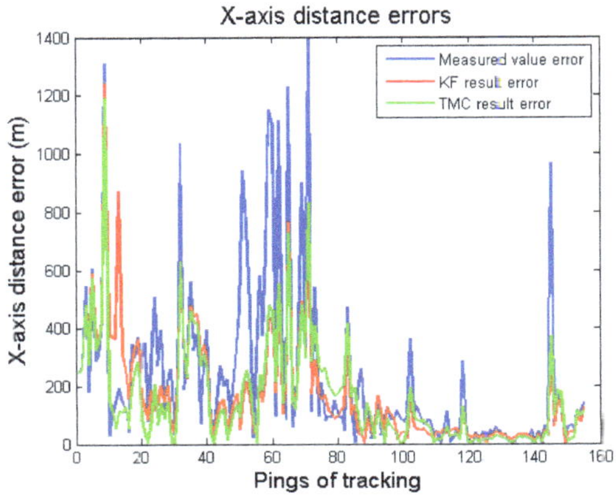

(a)

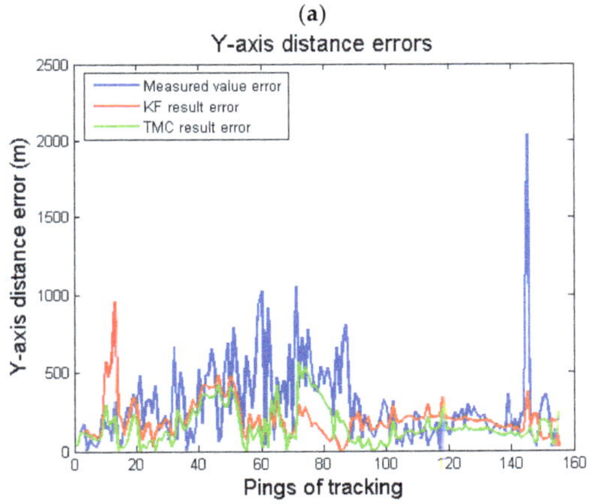

(b)

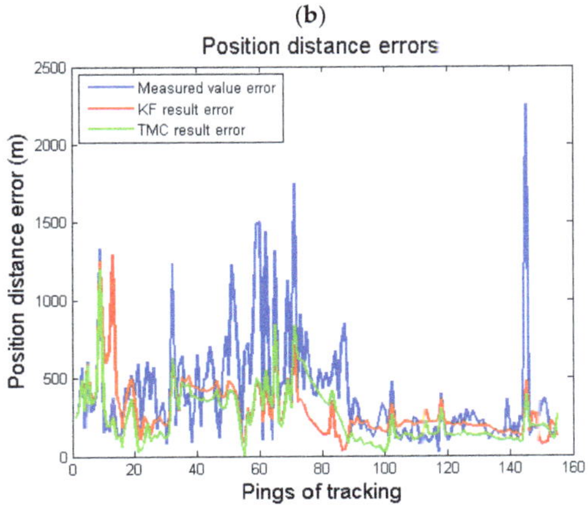

(c)

Figure 8. *Cont.*

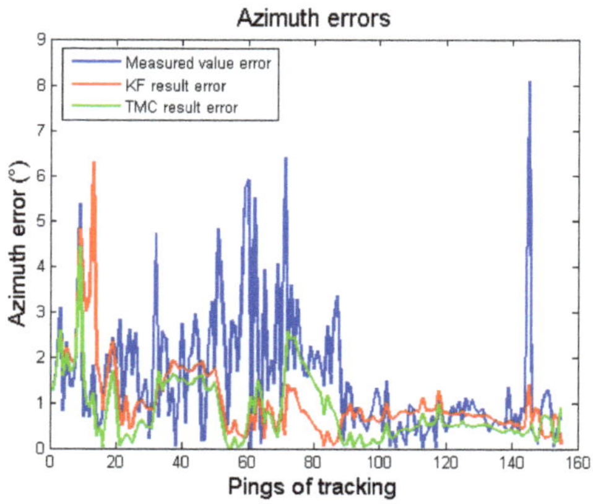

(d)

Figure 8. Comparisons of distance and azimuth errors. (**a**) X-axis distance errors, (**b**) Y-axis distance errors, (**c**) Position distance errors, (**d**) Azimuth errors.

As can be seen from Table 3, after using KF tracking processing, the RMSE of the target's position distance and azimuth were reduced by 186.07 m and 0.73°, respectively, compared with the RMSE of the sonar measurements. Furthermore, when the TMC tracking method was applied, the RMSE of the target's position distance and azimuth were further reduced: compared with the KF tracking method, the RMSE of the target's position distance was reduced by 36.08 m, and the RMSE of the azimuth was reduced by 0.25°.

Table 3. RMSE of offshore testing.

	Measured Values	KF Results	TMC Results
RMSE of X-axis Distance (m)	361.48	248.38	236.00
RMSE of Y-axis Distance (m)	386.10	236.25	195.91
RMSE of Position Distance (m)	528.87	342.80	306.71
RMSE of Azimuth (°)	2.04	1.31	1.06

MSE analysis of the offshore testing results was carried out, and as can be seen from Table 4, the TMC tracking method reduced tracking error, and performance was due to the KF tracking method.

Table 4. MSE of offshore testing.

	Measured Values	KF Results	TMC Results
MSE of Radial Distance	50,354.2	38,001.1	36,578.9
MSE of Azimuth	4.15	1.71	1.12

Through analysis of the offshore testing data, it can be seen that the TMC tracking method can modify the target motion state equation in real time, so as to make it as close to the real target motion state as possible, rather than tracking according to the established target motion state equation as the KF method. Therefore, the TMC method can improve target tracking accuracy. When analyzing the offshore test data, if the measurement error of sonar on underwater target changes greatly, the performance of the TMC method may be affected. This is because, in a test, if the measurement error of sonar on an underwater target position changes greatly due to various factors (obviously beyond the normal measurement error range of sonar), the TMC method cannot accurately determine whether this change is caused by a change in the submarine target motion state or an increase in measurement error.

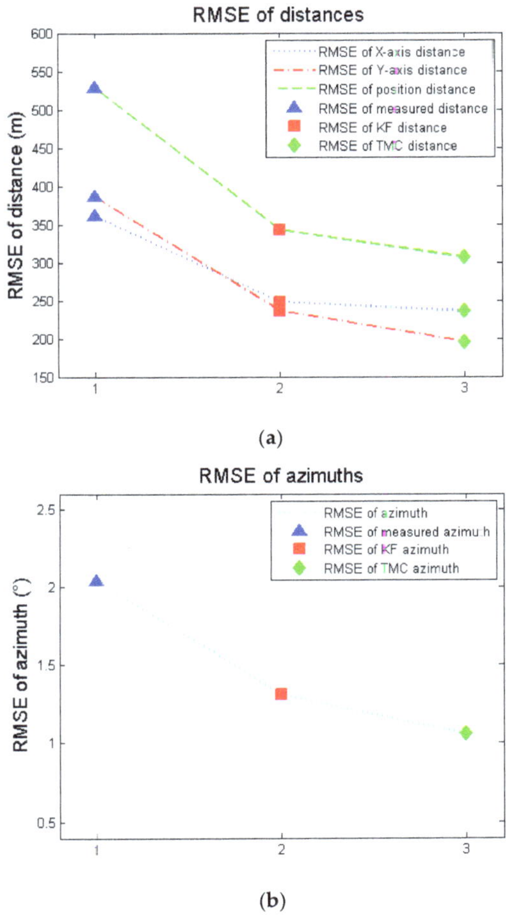

Figure 9. RMSE of distances and azimuths. (**a**) RMSE of position distances, (**b**) RMSE of azimuths.

4. Conclusions

In order to solve problems such as state model mismatch and tracking accuracy decline caused by changes underwater target motion states, this study investigated and proposeed the TMC tracking method, which innovatively adopts the idea of real-time model correction. Firstly, a KF filter is applied to track the target detected by sonar. The proportion of newly entered measurement information in the forecast output will be smaller and smaller, so that the KF filter cannot keep up with the change in the target state in time. At this time, by comparing the residual covariance of the KF filter with the threshold generated by sonar measurement error, the change in the target motion state can be judged in real time. Then, a constant gain filter is used to modify the target motion model so that it is closer to the real motion state of the target so as to achieve the purpose of transient correction of the KF filter and to improve the precision of the target tracking output. Simulation verification and offshore testing showed that the TMC tracking method could improve the tracking accuracy of active sonar on underwater targets compared with the conventional KF method.

In this research, it was found that variation in the position measurement error of an active sonar on an underwater target will affect the performance of the TMC tracking method. In addition, based on the fact that active sonar can only measure the radial distance and azimuth of a target in real time, this study only established a two-dimensional motion model of a target. If active sonar can measure the target information of more dimensions in real time, such as velocity information, then the algorithm model can be extended to a higher dimension, the corresponding constant gain filter used for transient model correction will also adopt a higher dimension filter (such as α-β-γ filter, etc.), and the algorithm processing effect will be better. Both are worth continuing.

Author Contributions: Conceptualization, C.L. and S.F.; methodology, S.F. and C.L.; software, C.L.; validation, C.L. and S.F.; formal analysis, C.L.; investigation, C.L. and S.F.; resources, S.F.; data curation, C.L. and S.F.; writing—original draft preparation, C.L; writing—review and editing, C.L. and S.F.; visualization, C.L.; supervision, S.F.; project administration, S.F.; funding acquisition, S.F. All authors have read and agreed to the published version of the manuscript.

Funding: This research received no external funding.

Institutional Review Board Statement: Not applicable.

Informed Consent Statement: Not applicable.

Data Availability Statement: The data that support the findings of this study are available from the corresponding author upon reasonable request.

Acknowledgments: Yujuan Li has conducted a lot of work in the collection, analysis and processing of offshore testing data, and put forward useful suggestions for the experimental verification of the TMC method. Xiaoyuan Chen and Qiao Xu provided specific assistance in the language, text and structure of the article. I would like to express my sincere thanks to them for their hard work and helpful help.

Conflicts of Interest: The authors declare no conflict of interest.

References

1. Friedland, B. Optimum steady-state position and velocity estimation using noisy sampled position data. *IEEE Trans. Aerosp. Electron. Syst.* **1973**, *9*, 906–911. [CrossRef]
2. Hampton, R.L.T.; Cooke, J.R. Unsupervised tracking of maneuvering vehicles. *IEEE Trans. Aerosp. Electron. Syst.* **1973**, *9*, 197–207. [CrossRef]
3. Singer, R.A. Estimating optimal tracking filter performance for manned maneuvering target. *IEEE Trans. Aerosp. Electron. Syst.* **1970**, *6*, 473–483. [CrossRef]
4. Moose, R.L. An adaptive state estimation solution to The maneuvering targets problem. *IEEE Trans. Aerosp. Electron. Syst.* **1975**, *20*, 359–362. [CrossRef]
5. Gholson, N.H.; Moose, R.L. Maneuvering target tracking using adaptive state estimation. *IEEE Trans. Aerosp. Electron. Syst.* **1977**, *13*, 310–316. [CrossRef]
6. Zhou, H.R. "Current" statistical model and adaptive tracking algorithm for maneuvering targets. *Acta Aeronaut. Astronaut. Sin.* **1983**, *4*, 73–86.
7. Kumar, K.S.P.; Zhou, H.; Kumar, K.S.P. A 'current' statistical model and adaptive algorithm for estimating maneuvering targets. *J. Guid. Control Dyn.* **1984**, *7*, 596–602.
8. Mehrotra, K.; Mahapatra, P.R. A Jerk Model Track. Highly Maneuvering Targets. *IEEE Trans. Aerosp. Electron. Syst.* **1997**, *33*, 1094–1105. [CrossRef]
9. Koteswara, R.S. Comments on "a jerk model for highly maneuvering targets". *IEEE Trans. Aerosp. Electron. Syst.* **1998**, *34*, 982–983.
10. Li, X.R.; Zhang, Y.M. Multiple-model estimation with variable structure part V: Likely-model set algorithm. *IEEE Trans. Aerosp. Electron. Syst.* **2000**, *36*, 448–466.
11. Jia, B.; Blasch, E.; Pham, K.D.; Shen, D.; Wang, Z.; Tian, X.; Chen, G. Space object tracking and maneuver detection via interacting multiple model cubature Kalman filters. In Proceedings of the 2015 IEEE Aerospace Conference, Big Sky, MT, USA, 7–14 March 2015.
12. Blom, H.A.P.; Bar-Shalom, Y. The interacting multiple model algorithm for systems with Markovian switching coefficients. *IEEE Trans. Autom. Control* **1988**, *33*, 780–783. [CrossRef]
13. Kalata, P.R. The tracking index: A generalized parameter forα-β andα-β-γtarget trackers. *IEEE Trans. Signal Process.* **1984**, *20*, 174–182.

John, J.S. The α-β-γ tracking filter with a noisy jerk as the maneuver model. *IEEE Trans. Signal Process.* **1993**, *29*, 578–580.
Kalman, R.E. A new approach to linear filtering and prediction problems. *J. Basic Eng.* **1960**, *82*, 35. [CrossRef]
Bucy, R.S.; Senne, K.D. Digital synthesis of non-linear filters. *Automatica* **1971**, *7*, 287–298. [CrossRef]
Sunahara, Y.; Yamashita, K. An approximate method of state estimation for non-linear dynamical systems with state-dependent noise. *Int. J. Control* **1970**, *11*, 957–972. [CrossRef]
Julier, S J.; Uhlmann, J.K.; Durrant-Whyte, H.F. A new approach for filtering nonlinear system. In Proceedings of the American Control Conference, Seattle, WA, USA, 21–23 June 1995; pp. 1628–1632.
Jia, B.; Xin, M.; Cheng, Y. High-degree cubature Kalman filter. *Automatica* **2013**, *49*, 510–518. [CrossRef]
Gordon, N.J.; Salmond, D.J.; Smith, A.F.M. Novel approach to nonlinear/non—Gaussian bayesian state estimation. *Radar Signal Process. IEE Proc. F* **1993**, *140*, 107–113. [CrossRef]
Joao, F.H. High-speed tracking with kernelized correlation filters. *IEEE Trans. Pattern Anal. Mach. Intell.* **2015**, *37*, 583–596.
Li, F.; Zhang, X.Y. Underwater target tracking based on particle filter. In Proceedings of the 7th International Conference on Computer Science & Education, Melbourne, VIC, Australia, 14–17 July 2012; pp. 36–40.
Shi, J.J. Research on Target Tracking Control Method of Small Autonomous Underwater Vehicles. Master's Thesis, Harbin Engineering University, Harbin, China, 2012.
El-Hawary, F.; Yang, J. Robust regression-based EKF for tracking underwater targets. *Eng. Prof.* **1995**, *20*, 31–41. [CrossRef]
Yang, Y.B.; Wang, H.G. Application of a novel particle filter theory to underwater system target tracking. *Underw. Acoust. Eng.* **2011**, *35*, 47–54.
Xu, Y.B. Research on particle filter tracking method based on Kalman filter. In Proceedings of the 2018 2nd IEEE Advanced Information Management, Communicates, Electronic and Automation Control Conference (IMCEC), Xi'an, China, 25–27 May 2018; pp. 1564–1568.
Ma, S.; Wang, H.; Shen, X.; Sun, Z.; Sun, N. Research on Area of Uncertainty of Underwater Moving Target Based on Stochastic Maneuvering Motion Model. *Sensors* **2022**, *22*, 8837. [CrossRef] [PubMed]
Ho, K.C.; Chan, Y.T. An asymptotically unbiased estimator for bearings-only and Doppler-bearing target motion analysis. *IEEE Trans. Signal Process.* **2006**, *54*, 809–822. [CrossRef]
Liu, Q.H.; Gao, J.; Deng, N.M. Application of squared root variance CKF algorithm in torpedo tracking. *Torpedo Technol.* **2015**, *23*, 428–432.
Gao, W.J.; Li, Y.A.; Chen, X.; Chen, Z.G. Application of IMM to underwater maneuver target tracking. *Torpedo Technol.* **2015**, *23*, 196–201.
Zhang, X.F.; Xin, M.Z.; Sui, H.C.; Lei, P.; Liu, Y.C.; Yang, F.L. AUV ultra-Short baseline tracking algorithm based on interactive multiple model kalman filter. *J. Underw. Unmanned Syst.* **2022**, *30*, 29–36.
Zhao, Z.Y.; Li, Y.A.; Chen, X.; Su, J. Passive track-ing of underwater maneuvering target based on double observation station. *J. Unmanned Undersea Syst.* **2018**, *26*, 40–45.
Tian, W.; Fang, L.; Li, W.; Ni, N.; Wang, R.; Hu, C.; Liu, H.; Luo, W. Deep-Learning-Based Multiple Model Tracking Method for Targets with Complex Maneuvering Motion. *Remote Sens.* **2022**, *14*, 3276. [CrossRef]
Wang, Y.; Wang, H.; Li, Q.; Xiao, Y.; Ban, X. Passive Sonar Target Tracking Based on Deep Learning. *J. Mar. Sci. Eng.* **2022**, *10*, 181. [CrossRef]
Wang, M.; Xu, C.; Zhou, C.; Gong, Y.; Qiu, B. Study on underwater target tracking technology based on an LSTM–Kalman filtering method. *Appl. Sci.* **2022**, *12*, 5233. [CrossRef]
Jin, H.M.; Li, J.X. Submarine Searching Strategies for Dipping Sonar on Antisubmarine Helicopter. *Electron. Opt. Control* **2011**, *18*, 26–28, 39.

applied sciences

MDPI

Article

Flywheel Vibration Isolation of Satellite Structure by Applying Structural Plates with Elastic Boundary Instead of Restrained Boundary

Xiangsen Kong [1], Hao Li [2], Xubin Zhou [2,*], Xiujuan Xiang [2] and Xing Shen [1]

1 State Key Laboratory of Mechanics and Control for Aerospace Structures, Nanjing University of Aeronautics and Astronautics, Nanjing 210016, China; shenx@nuaa.edu.cn (X.S.)

2 Shanghai Institute of Satellite Engineering, Shanghai 201109, China; xiangxiujuan2@163.com (X.X.)

* Correspondence: zhouxb_sise@126.com

Abstract: Flywheels play a critical role as core components in satellite attitude control systems. However, their high-speed rotation inevitably generates vibrations that have a detrimental impact on the in-orbit imaging capabilities of high-precision remote sensing payloads. This study focuses on the passive vibration isolation design of satellite flywheels. The flywheel-mounted structural plate and flywheel vibration isolation platform are considered as a whole system (termed a plate-isolator system). In this system, the structural plate is treated as an elastomer. By simplifying the plate-isolator system as a 2-degree-of-freedom vibration system, it becomes evident that obtaining an ideal vibration isolation effect through the optimization of the flywheel vibration isolation platform (FVIP) alone is difficult. In order to enhance the passive vibration isolation effect for satellite flywheels, this study introduces the concept of an elastic boundary applied to the flywheel-mounted structural plate, thus treating the elastic boundary as a design factor. Consequently, the plate-isolator system can be simplified as a 3-stage vibration isolation system. The optimization of the elastic boundary condition of the structural plate is performed using the kinetic model of the simplified 3-stage system. The vibration isolation effect of the plate-isolator system with an elastic boundary is further confirmed through finite element simulation. The calculation results demonstrate that, after establishing a reasonable elastic boundary for the satellite structural plate, the overall vibration/force transmission rate of the plate-isolator system becomes similar to that of a single-degree-of-freedom dynamic system. Finally, the proposed concept is validated through kinetic response analysis of a cube satellite. The results reveal that the vibration amplitude of the satellite's top and side structural plates can be effectively lowered if the elastic boundary condition is set for the flywheel-mounted bottom structural plate.

Keywords: elastic boundary; flywheel; structural plate; vibration isolation

1. Introduction

As the observation resolution of space payloads continues to increase, high stability and pointing accuracy of satellite platforms are required simultaneously. For example, the collaborative development of the "Solar-B" satellite involved Japan, the United States, and the United Kingdom in 2006, with a short-period pointing stability of 0.09 arcseconds (3 σ)/10 s [1,2]. Similarly, the United States developed the "Space Interferometry Mission" space telescope, which had a pointing stability of 1.6 mas (1 σ)/0.01 s [3]. Flywheels serve as commonly used attitude control actuators in spacecraft [4–6]. Nevertheless, due to the high angular velocity at which flywheels typically operate (1000~8000 rpm), various factors like rotor static and dynamic imbalance, non-ideal bearings, drive motor disturbances, and resonance in flexible structures can generate sustained vibrations characterized by harmonic and wide frequency bands. Park et al. reported that the disturbances consist of discrete harmonics of the wheel speed with amplitudes proportional to the square of the wheel speed. Some disturbances include interactions between the harmonics and the structural modes of the wheel which result in large disturbance amplifications at some wheel speeds [7]. These vibrations constitute the primary source of interference that significantly impacts the design performance of payloads [8–11]. In particular, for optical payloads, the impact of flywheel disturbance cannot be ignored and is difficult to eliminate.

For satellites that require high attitude stability and accuracy, the suppression of flywheel vibration is crucial. Since the disturbance of the flywheel system is generally multi-directional, most isolation devices for flywheels employ multiple independent isolation rod units. They form a multi-degree-of-freedom isolation platform with a certain topology configuration to suspend and isolate the flywheel system. This isolation method has greater flexibility, better omnidirectional isolation performance, and higher reliability. For example, China's FY-4 satellite [12] utilized a 6-DOF (six-degree-of-freedom) passive isolation platform to isolate the flywheel's vibration. The GOES-R satellite launched by the United States in 2016 applied viscoelastic isolators to reduce the impact of the disturbance from its six flywheels and achieved significant attenuation of vibration above 50 Hz [13]. A double-layer passive isolation system based on viscoelastic material is used in China's Gaofen-3 optical satellite for flywheel disturbance suppression [5]. D. Kamesh from India [14,15] proposed a flexible isolation platform based on a folding beam structure, which can reduce the installation stiffness of the flywheel and effectively suppress the vibration disturbance. The WorldView-I and WorldView-II Earth observation satellites [16] launched by DigitalGlobe integrated eight isolation rod units with the CMG group. Lin et al. [17] studied the influence of flywheel vibration on optical cameras. Results showed that a flywheel isolation platform with four metal rubber isolation components can reduce the optical axis angular displacement of the optical payload by over 50%. Wei et al. [18] proposed a passive isolation platform composed of multiple folding beams and established an equivalent kinetic model of the flywheel and platform system. The model was validated through eigenvalue and frequency response analysis, demonstrating that it can effectively reduce the disturbance of the flywheel.

Passive isolation devices reduce micro-vibration by lowering the system frequency and increasing structural damping, and their reliability has led to widespread use in engineering. However, recent research has focused on semi-active and active isolation platforms based on passive ones. For example, Oh et al. [19–21] from JAXA developed a variable damping isolation device to reduce the radial disturbance force caused by rotor static unbalance. Zhao et al. [22] invented an active–passive integrated 3-DOF isolation platform capable of two translational degrees of freedom in the installation plane and one perpendicular to it. Kim et al. [23,24] created an active 3-DOF isolation micro-platform using fully active piezoelectric actuators designed with the lever principle. Lee et al. [7,25,26] proposed a hybrid isolation platform with a positive Stewart configuration, utilizing voice coil motors and viscous dampers for support legs to suppress flywheel vibration. Wu et al. [27] studied the dynamic parameters of the satellite active isolation platform based on genetic and differential evolution algorithms considering load and structural weight. Zhang et al. [28,29] created the kinetic model for the satellite with a 6-DOF vibration isolation system. An adaptive controller was designed to handle the uncertainty of the payload's inertia, and the impact of the vibration isolation system on the satellite's attitude and stability was evaluated. They further proposed a 6-DOF isolation platform based on magnetic levitation actuators and investigated the electromagnetic coupling effect of the magnetic platform. They numerically verified the effectiveness of the platform for vibration isolation of the payload. It is also reported that the Stewart platforms have achieved active vibration isolation on the Worldview-II and Chandra X-ray observers [30]. Active isolation platforms typically have controllers and actuators, making them more complex than passive ones. As a result, they are typically only used to isolate effective payloads [31,32]. For instance, the Tacsat2 satellite launched by the United States in 2006 featured an active and passive combined isolation device installed on its camera [33]. On the other hand, passive isolation platforms are typically employed for flywheel vibration isolation [18].

In the aforementioned research on flywheel vibration isolation, researchers committed to improving the vibration isolation efficiency of the vibration isolation platform itself. However, their investigations have been limited to the premise that the flywheel platform is mounted on a rigid foundation. In practical engineering applications, the flywheels and isolation platforms are typically installed on an elastic foundation, such as a honeycomb structural plate with limited stiffness in the case of satellite structures. Unfortunately, there is a lack of research on whether a flywheel vibration isolation platform designed with a rigid foundation can achieve an equivalent isolation effect when installed on a flexible foundation. Therefore, in this study, the structural plate and the flywheel vibration isolation platform are treated as a plate-isolator system, and the influence of the structural plate's elasticity is investigated. It is reported that linear boundary damping can reduce the vibration energy of stiffened plates in the specific frequency band [34]. Thus, in this study, to further suppress the disturbance of flywheels, an elastic boundary is designed for the plate-isolator system, and the plate-isolator system with an elastic boundary is verified by a simplified analytical model and numerical simulation. The rest of this paper is organized as follows: Section 2 presents a finite element simulation that demonstrates that the high-frequency vibration isolation performance of the flywheel vibration isolation platform can be affected by the elasticity of its mounting surface. In Section 3, a simplified 2-DOF theoretical model is analyzed to examine the influence of the structural plate stiffness on the overall isolation efficiency of the plate-isolator system. In Section 4, a simplified 3-DOF model is used to verify that applying an elastic boundary to the structural plate can effectively improve the overall isolation efficiency of the plate-isolator system, and the stiffness of the elastic boundary is optimized. Section 5 verifies the theoretical optimization results through finite element simulation, which shows that the overall isolation efficiency of the plate-isolator system will be significantly improved due to the plate's elastic boundary. Finally, in Section 6, the research conclusions are further verified using a cubic satellite structure, and the finite element simulation results show that setting an elastic interface between the plates on which the flywheels are installed and other plates can significantly reduce the vibration response at various positions of the cubic satellite.

2. Problem Illustration

Flywheels are widely utilized in satellites as the attitude controlling device, and the high-frequency vibration of flywheels usually poses significant challenges in achieving stable mounting interfaces for high-precision payloads. Figure 1 illustrates a typical three-axis stabilized satellite with a high-precision optical payload. To attenuate the flywheel-induced vibration, the flywheels are installed on 6-DOF vibration isolation platforms. A 6-DOF vibration isolation platform can be designed to exhibit quite low vibration transmissibility. Thus, theoretically, a well-designed vibration isolator should solve the issue of vibration on a satellite very well. For instance, the 6-DOF vibration isolation platform presented in Figure 1 applies six linear springs with a stiffness K_{spring} = 50,000 N/m and the equivalent damping C_{spring} = 100 Nm/s. The overall mass of the platform is less than 2 kg, the fundamental frequency of which is about 14 Hz. However, in practice, the isolation platforms are installed on the elastic structural plate of the satellite, which possesses limited stiffness. The elastic structural plate and the isolation platform form an elastic system (plate-isolator system) in essence. Therefore, to effectively suppress the influence of flywheel vibrations, this study will demonstrate that the key is the dynamics of this plate-isolator system rather than merely the dynamics of the isolation platform.

To illustrate the influence of the elastic structural plate on the isolation of flywheel vibrations, the dynamics of a plate-isolator (structural plate and isolation platform) system are analyzed. Figure 2 illustrates the plate-isolator system and its finite element model. The flywheel has a mass of 8 kg, while the structural plate is a honeycomb sandwich structure with dimensions of 1500 mm × 1500 mm × 30 mm. It consists of a carbon fiber skin and an aluminum honeycomb core. Table 1 lists the layering and material properties of the structural plate. The dynamic response of the plate-isolator system is evaluated using the commercial finite element software ABAQUS 6.14. Shell elements (S4R) are employed to model both the flywheel and the structural plate. In addition, the vibration isolation platform is modeled using both spring and dashpot elements, as well as shell elements (S4R). The stiffness and damping coefficient of the spring and damping elements are K = 50,000 N/m and C = 100 Nm/s, respectively. The shell element size of the structural plate is 25 mm; it is 5 mm for the platform.

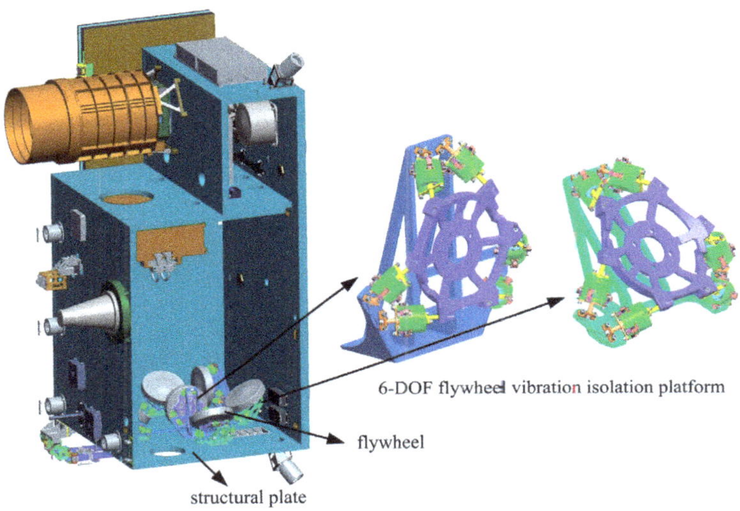

Figure 1. Satellite structure with flywheels and flywheel vibration isolators.

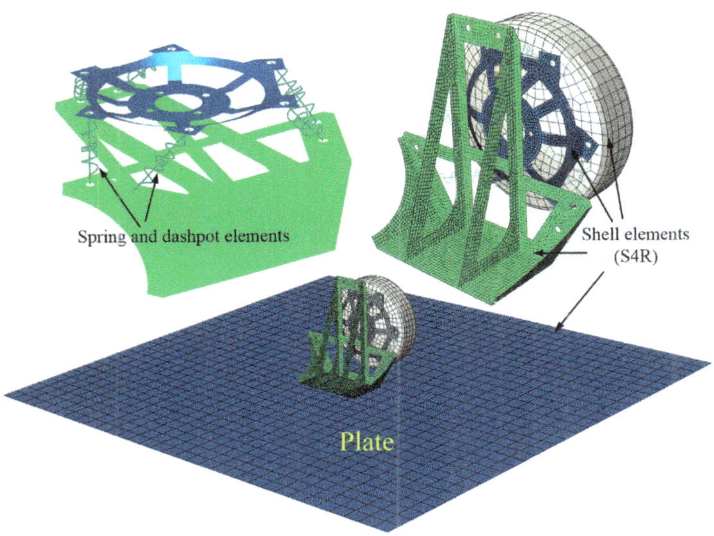

Figure 2. Finite element model of the plate-isolator (structural plate, isolation platform, and flywheel) system.

Table 1. The layering and material parameters of the honeycomb sandwich structure.

Material Name	Parameters
Layup	$[0/45/-45/90/\text{core}_{t=28.8\text{ mm}}/90/-45/45/0]$ CFRP ply thickness = 0.15 mm
CFRP skin	$E_1 = 160$ GPa, $E_2 = 9.0$ GPa, $G_{12} = 8$ GPa, $G_{13} = 4.8$ GPa, $G_{23} = 4.8$ GPa, $\mu_{12} = 0.36$, $\rho = 1600$ kg/m^3 Damping parameter: $\alpha = 200$, $\beta = 0.005$
Honeycomb sandwich	$E_1 = 1.57 \times 10^{-4}$ GPa, $E_2 = 1.57 \times 10^{-4}$ GPa, $G_{12} = 2.954 \times 10^{-5}$ GPa, $G_{13} = 0.0738$ GPa, $G_{23} = 0.1107$ GPa, $\mu_{12} = 0.33$, $\rho = 42$ kg/m^3

To analyze the force transmissibility of the vibration isolation platform itself and the plate-isolator system, frequency response analyses are conducted using the "Steady-state Dynamics, Direct" analysis step in ABAQUS. Sinusoidal excitations are applied in the X, Y, and Z directions at the mass center of the flywheel. For the isolation platform, fixed constraints are applied to its bottom, and the force transmissibility is calculated by extracting the total reaction force at the bottom of the platform. For the plate-isolator system, fixed constraints are applied to the four edges of the structural plate, and force transmissibility is calculated by extracting the total reaction force from the four edges of the structural plate. Figure 3 compares the force transmissibility curves of the isolation platform and the plate-isolator system in the frequency range of 0~200 Hz, in which obvious differences can be observed. Note that the force transmissibility is defined as 20 × Log ($F_{\text{reaction}}/F_{\text{input}}$). The force transmissibility of the plate-isolator system, especially in the Y direction, is considerably worse compared to that of the vibration isolation platform. While the force transmissibility curves of the vibration isolation platform exhibit only one peak in the X, Y, and Z directions, the force transmissibility curves of the plate-isolator system show multiple peaks. Based on the mode analysis results presented in Figure 3, it is evident that the extra peaks are the results of the local modes of the elastic structural plate. The results in Figure 3 suggest that to suppress the influence of flywheel vibration on the satellite, a systematic design is needed, considering both the vibration isolation platform and the structural plate as a multi-stage vibration isolation system.

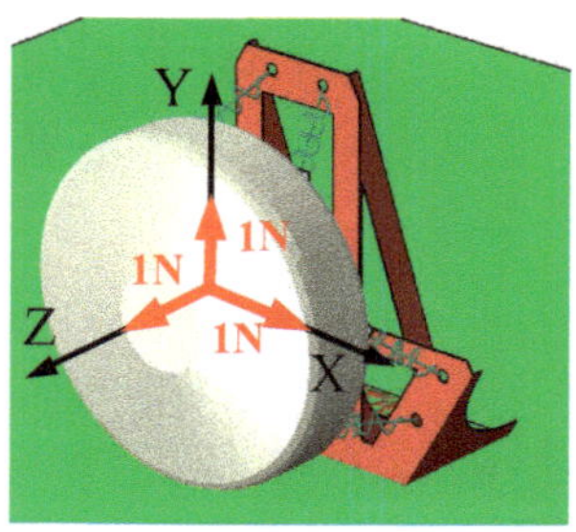

(a)

Figure 3. *Cont.*

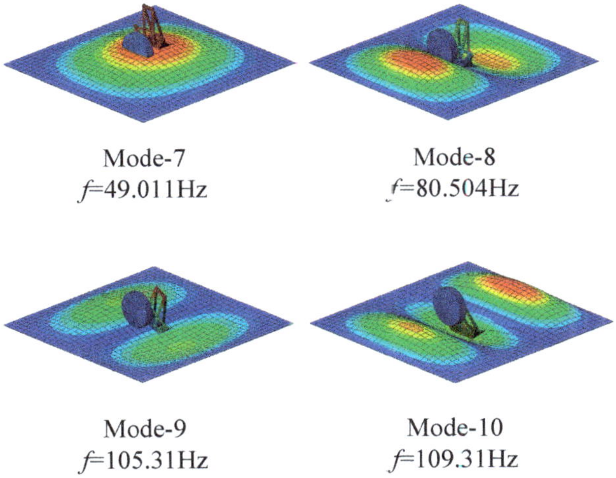

(b)

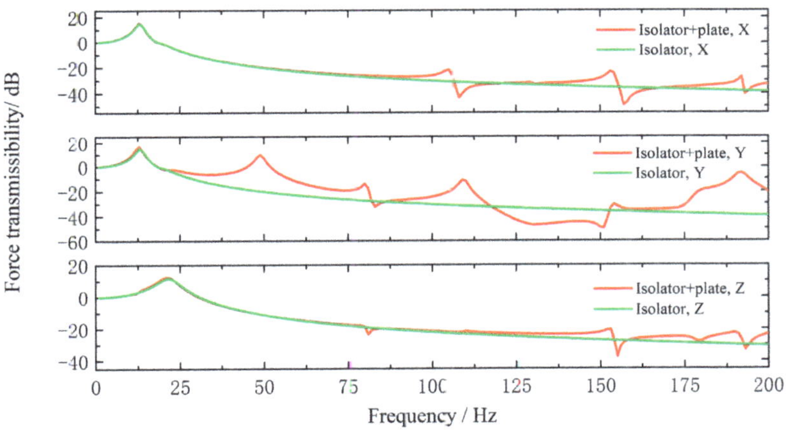

(c)

Figure 3. Comparison of force transmissibility between the signal vibration isolation platform and the plate-isolator system: (**a**) force loading mode; (**b**) load modes of structural plate; (**c**) force transmissibility.

3. Illustration of a Plate-Isolator System as a 2-Stage Vibration Isolation System

To gain insight into the basic dynamic characteristics of the plate-isolator system, the plate-isolator system is simplified into a 2-stage isolation system, as illustrated in Figure 4. In the simplified 2-stage isolation system, the structural plate is represented as a linear spring with a mass node on its upper end. The node mass m_{plate} equals the first-order modal mass of the plate. The spring stiffness K_{plate} is calculated according to the fundamental modal frequency and the corresponding modal mass of the plate. The vibration isolation platform is also represented as a linear spring, and the flywheel is modeled as a mass node. The spring stiffness $K_{isolator}$ is calculated according to the fundamental modal frequency of the vibration isolation platform and the mass of the flywheel. The coefficients C_{plate} and

C_{isolator} denote the equivalent damping coefficient of the structural plate and the vibration isolation platform.

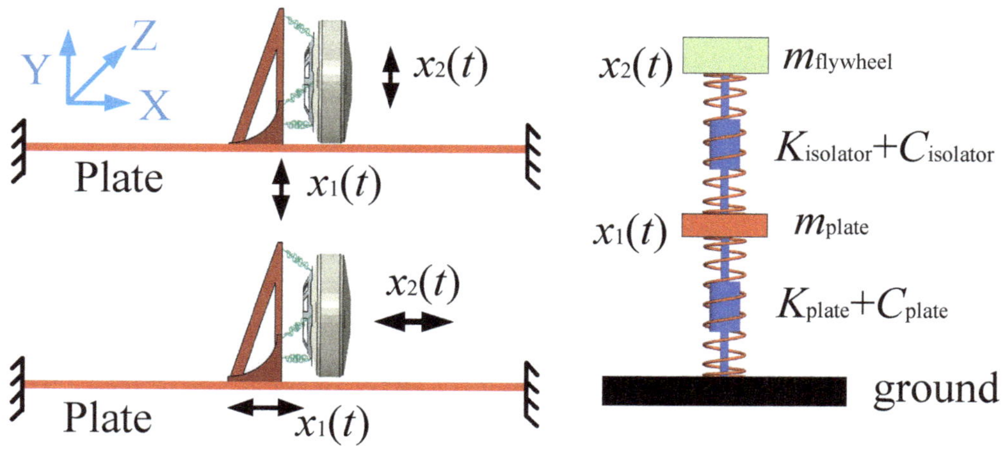

Figure 4. Plate-isolator system and its 2-stage simplified model.

Assuming a harmonic excitation $F[t] = F\mathrm{Sin}[\omega t]$ is applied on the flywheel, the kinetic equations of the 2-stage system can be derived:

$$\begin{cases} K_1x_1(t) + K_2x_1(t) - K_2x_2(t) + C_1x_1'(t) + C_2x_1'(t) - C_2x_2'(t) + M_1x_1''(t) = 0 \\ -F(t) - K_2x_1(t) + K_2x_2(t) - C_2x_1'(t) + C_2x'_2(t) + M_2x_2''(t) = 0 \end{cases} \tag{1}$$

where $m_{plate} = M_1$, $m_{flywheel} = M_2$, $K_{plate} = K_1$, $C_{plate} = C_1$, $K_{isolator} = K_2$, $C_{isolator} = C_2$, and $x_1(t)$ and $x_2(t)$ denote the displacement of mass nodes m_{plate} and m_{flywheel}, respectively. Note that these stiffness and damping parameters are different for the vertical and horizontal directions. Respectively assume:

$$x_1(t) = A_1\sin(\omega t) + A_2\cos(\omega t) \tag{2}$$

$$x_2(t) = B_1\sin(\omega t) + B_2\cos(\omega t) \tag{3}$$

Substituting Equations (2) and (3) into Equation (1), we can derive the following:

$$\begin{cases} K_1(A_1\sin(\omega t) + A_2\cos(\omega t)) + K_2(A_1\sin(\omega t) + A_2\cos(\omega t)) - K_2(B_1\sin(\omega t) + B_2\cos(\omega t)) \\ +C_1(A_1\omega\cos(\omega t) - A_2\omega\sin(\omega t)) + C_2(A_1\omega\cos(\omega t) - A_2\omega\sin(\omega t)) \\ -C_2(B_1\omega\cos(\omega t) - B_2\omega\sin(\omega t)) + M_1(-A_1\omega^2\sin(\omega t) - A_2\omega^2\cos(\omega t)) = 0 \\ -F(t) - K_2(A_1\sin(\omega t) + A_2\cos(\omega t)) + K_2(B_1\sin(\omega t) + B_2\cos(\omega t)) \\ -C_2(A_1\omega\cos(\omega t) - A_2\omega\sin(\omega t)) + C_2(B_1\omega\cos(\omega t) - B_2\omega\sin(\omega t)) \\ +M_2(-B_1\omega^2\sin(\omega t) - B_2\omega^2\cos(\omega t)) = 0 \end{cases} \tag{4}$$

By equaling the coefficients of $\mathrm{Sin}[\omega t]$ and $\mathrm{Cos}[\omega t]$ of the two kinetic equations in Equation (4) to 0 respectively, four linear equations of A_1, A_2, B_1, and B_2 can be obtained. By solving the linear equations, the vibration amplitudes $\left(A_1^2 + A_2^2\right)^{\frac{1}{2}}$ and $\left(B_1^2 + B_2^2\right)^{\frac{1}{2}}$ take the form:

$$\left(A_1^2 + A_2^2\right)^{\frac{1}{2}} = \frac{\sqrt{F^2(K_2^2 + C_2^2\omega^2)}}{\sqrt{\begin{array}{l}(K_1(K_2 - M_2\omega^2) + \omega^2(-K_2(M_1 + M_2) + M_1M_2\omega^2))^2 \\ +\omega^2(2C_1C_2M_2\omega^4 + C_1^2(K_2 - M_2\omega^2)^2 + C_2^2(K_1^2 - 2K_1(M_1 + M_2)\omega^2 + \omega^2(C_1^2 + (M_1 + M_2)^2\omega^2)))\end{array}}} \tag{5}$$

$$\left(B_1^2+B_2^2\right)^{\frac{1}{2}}=\frac{\sqrt{F^2(K_1^2+K_2^2-2K_2M_1\omega^2+2K_1(K_2-M_1\omega^2)+\omega^2(C_1^2+2C_1C_2+C_2^2+M_1\omega^2)}}{\sqrt{\begin{array}{l}(K_1(K_2-M_2\omega^2)+\omega^2(-K_2(M_1+M_2)+M_1M_2\omega^2))^2\\+\omega^2(2C_1C_2M_2\omega^4+C_1^2(K_2-M_2\omega^2)^2+C_2^2(K_1^2-2K_1(M_1+M_2)\omega^2+\omega^2(C_1^2+(M_1+M_2)^2\omega^2)))\end{array}}} \quad (6)$$

Based on the amplitude value $\left(A_1^2+A_2^2\right)^{\frac{1}{2}}$, the resultant disturbance force at the edges of the structural plate (namely the reaction force at the fixed end of the plate spring in Figure 4) can be expressed as:

$$F_{out}=\left(K_{plate}^2K_{plate}+(C_{plate}\omega)^2\right)^{\frac{1}{2}}\left(A_1^2+A_2^2\right)^{\frac{1}{2}} \quad (7)$$

3.1. Vertical (Y Direction)

When the flywheel vibrates vertically, as illustrated in Figure 4, the fundamental frequency of the edge fixed structural plate (1000 mm × 1000 mm × 30 mm, the total mass is 50 kg) is calculated to be f = 51.956 Hz via FEA. The corresponding fundamental modal mass is 31.7 kg. In the 2-stage system, the equivalent mass of the plate equals the fundamental modal mass of the plate, i.e., m_{plate} = 31.7 kg. The equivalent stiffness of the plate is K_{plate} = 3,378,239 N/m and is calculated based on the fundamental frequency and modal mass. The mass of the flywheel is 8 kg and the fundamental frequency of the vibration isolation platform is f = 13.354 Hz; thus, the equivalent stiffness of the vibration isolation platform is K_{isolator} = 56,321 N/m.

Based on the disturbance force expression of Equation (7), the force transmissibility of the simplified 2-stage vibration isolation system under harmonic excitation is studied (Figures 5 and 6). The response curves exhibit two peaks: the first peak corresponds to the isolator mode, while the second peak corresponds to the structural plate mode. The analytical solutions indicate that the increased stage (i.e., the structural plate) introduces an additional peak on each frequency response curve, resulting in a higher isolation starting frequency. To optimize a vibration isolation system, it is common to optimize the damping and stiffness of the system. However, the parameter analysis results presented in Figures 5 and 6 demonstrate that optimizing the damping or stiffness is ineffective for this two-stage plate-isolator system.

The effects of plate damping C_{plate} and isolator damping C_{isolator} on the force transmissibility are shown in Figure 5. Figure 5a demonstrates that a large damping coefficient of C_{plate} = 10,000 Ns/m is required to effectively suppress the second peak caused by the plate elasticity. If the damping of the structural plate is further increased, the response of the system approaches that of the vibration isolation platform itself. Similarly, Figure 5b illustrates that increasing the damping of the vibration isolation platform (C_{isolator} = 10,000 Ns/m) effectively reduces the peak value of the system response. If the damping of the vibration isolation platform is further increased, the overall response of the system approaches that of the structural plate itself. Therefore, the results in Figure 5 indicate that the force transmissibility of the plate-isolator system cannot be significantly improved by increasing the damping of the structural plate or the vibration isolator. Infinitely increasing the structural plate damping can eliminate the influence of the structural plate elasticity and ensure the vibration isolation effect of the isolator. However, infinite or quite large damping is usually difficult to achieve in practice for a structural plate.

The influences of the vibration isolator stiffness K_{isolator} and the structural plate stiffness K_{plate} are presented in Figure 6. The analysis results in Figure 6a indicate reducing the isolator stiffness K_{isolator} has little effect on the second peak and high-frequency response. Therefore, optimizing the stiffness of the vibration isolator alone cannot significantly improve the vibration isolation effect of the plate-isolator system. On the other hand, Figure 6b suggests that by reducing the stiffness of the structural plate, the frequency corresponding to the second peak of the force transmissibility shifts forward. Meanwhile, the force transmissibility at high frequency decreases. When the stiffness of the structural plate is reduced to 1/10 of the original value, the force transmissibility of the plate-isolator system exhibits one obvious peak. The overall response is similar to that of a soft 1-DOF vibration isolation system. Compared to optimizing the damping, reducing the stiffness of the structural plate proves to be a more effective method for improving the vibration isolation efficiency of the plate-isolator system. Nevertheless, since the structural plate serves as the mounting surface of various equipment and functions as a load-bearing structure, reducing its stiffness could lead to risks of strength issues and excessive elastic deformation. Moreover, as shown in Figure 6b, reducing the stiffness of the structural plate may also result in a large peak response, thereby increasing the risk of excessive dynamic response.

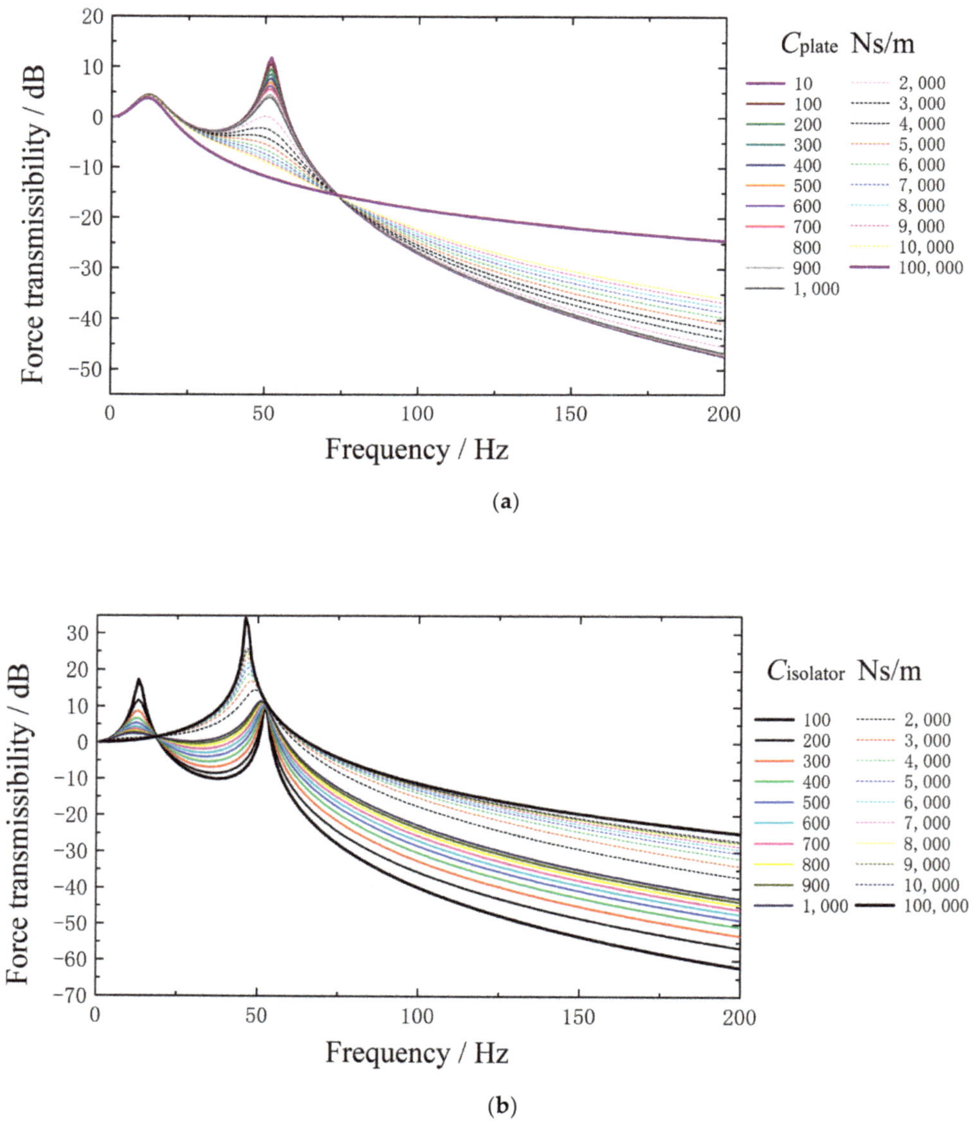

Figure 5. Influence of damping on the force transmissibility of the simplified 2-stage plate-isolator System: (**a**) variation with C_{plate}, $C_{isolator}$ = 600 Ns/m; (**b**) variation with $C_{isolator}$, C_{plate} = 60 Ns/m.

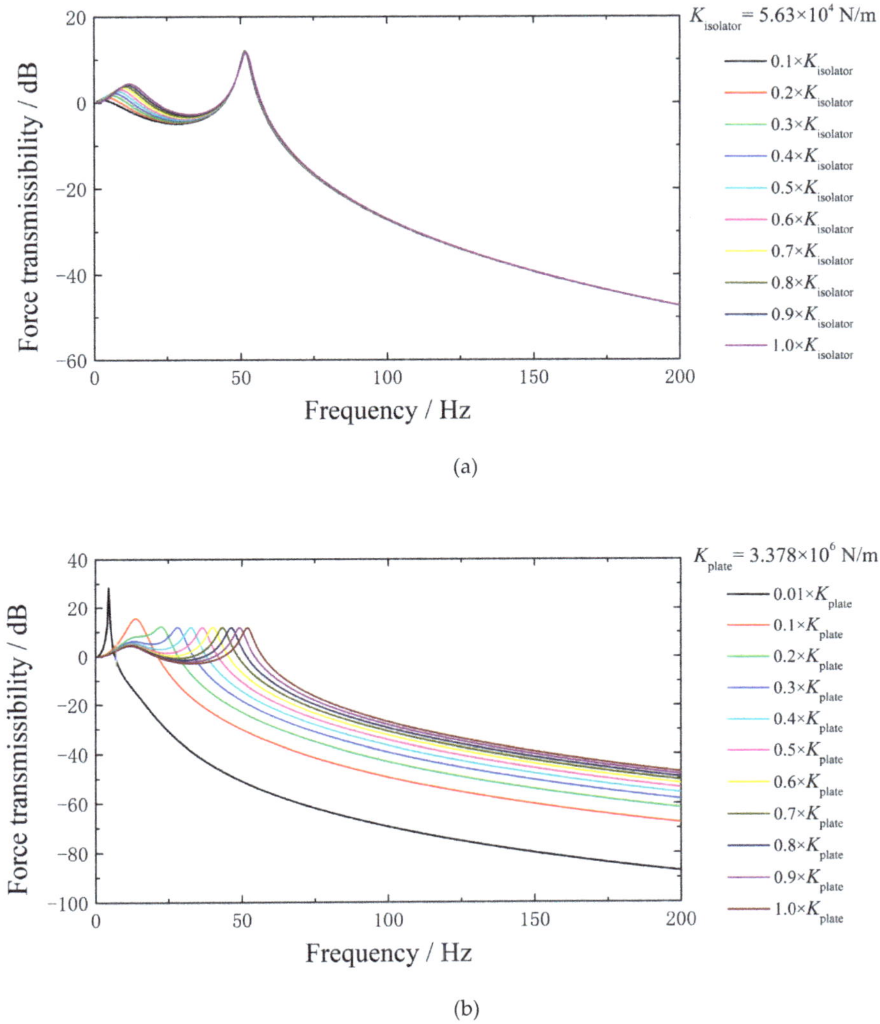

Figure 6. Influence of stiffness on the force transmissibility of the simplified 2-stage plate-isolator system: (**a**) variation with $K_{isolator}$, K_{plate} = 3,378,239 N/m, C_{plate} = 10 Ns/m, $C_{isolator}$ = 600 Ns/m; (**b**) variation with K_{plate}, $K_{isolator}$ = 56,321 N/m, C_{plate} = 10 Ns/m, $C_{isolator}$ = 600 Ns/m.

To ensure the vibration isolation effect of the plate-isolator system and the reliability of the structure, the next section will adopt the structural plate with elastic boundary conditions to achieve high vibration isolation efficiency.

3.2. Horizontal (X and Z)

For the excitation of the flywheel in the X and Z directions, the flywheel and structural plate can also be simplified into a 2-stage system ignoring the higher-order mode of the structural plate, as shown in Figure 4. The analytical solution of the force transmissibility is the same as Equation (7). However, due to the much higher in-plane stiffness of the structural plate compared with the out-of-plane stiffness, the response of the plate-isolator system in the X and Y directions within the frequency range of 0–100 Hz is similar to that of the isolator fixed at its bottom. It can be predicted from Figure 6b that reducing the in-plane stiffness of the structural plate to a relatively low value could improve the overall vibration isolation efficiency of the 2-stage system. However, achieving low in-plane stiffness for a honeycomb structural plate through mechanical optimization is difficult. Therefore, the next section will discuss how to enhance the lateral vibration isolation efficiency of the plate-isolator system by adopting the lateral elastic boundary on the structural plate.

4. Illustration of a Plate-Isolator System with Elastic Boundary as a 3-Stage Vibration Isolation System

Section 2 presents the findings of the simplified 2-stage model, which indicate that improving the performance of the plate-isolator system is challenging without reducing the stiffness of the structural plate to a relatively low value. Instead of optimizing the mechanical design of the structural plate, this section explores an alternative method of applying an elastic plate boundary.

Figure 7 shows the plate-isolator system with the elastic boundary. The rigid constraint boundary of the structural plate is replaced with a spring constraint boundary, thereby simplifying the system into an elastic 3-stage system. The first stage is the elastic boundary of the structural plate, the second stage is the structural plate, and the third stage is the vibration isolation platform.

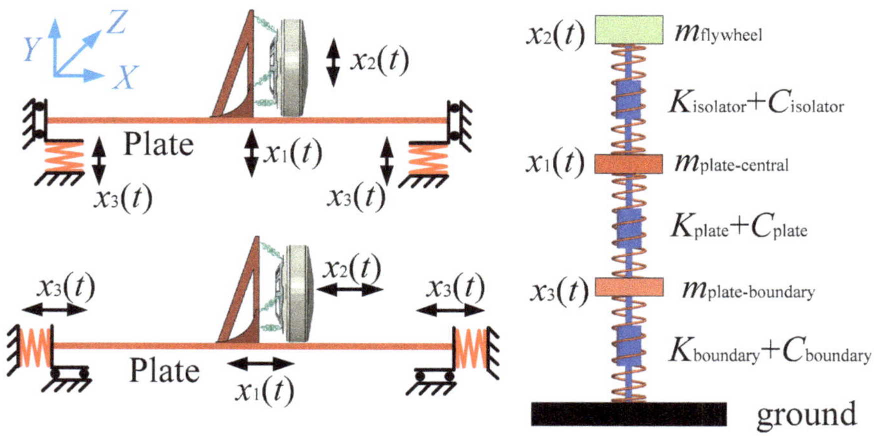

Figure 7. Plate-isolator system with elastic boundary and its 3-stage simplified model.

The kinetic equations of the 3-stage system are derived:

$$\begin{cases} K_1x_1(t) + K_2x_1(t) - K_2x_2(t) - K_1x_1(t) + C_1x_1'(t) + C_2x_1'(t) - C_2x_2'(t) - C_1x_3'(t) + M_1x_1''(t) = 0 \\ -F(t) - K_2x_1(t) + K_2x_2(t) - C_2x_1'(t) + C_2x_2'(t) + M_2x_2''(t) = 0 \\ -K_1x_1(t) + K_1x_3(t) + K_3x_3(t) - C_1x_1'(t) + C_1x_3'(t) + C_3x_3'(t) + M_3x_3''(t) = 0 \end{cases} \quad (8)$$

where $K_1 = K_{\text{plate}}$, $M_1 = m_{\text{plate-central}}$, $C_1 = C_{\text{plate}}$, $K_2 = K_{\text{isolator}}$, $M_2 = m_{\text{flywheel}}$, $C_2 = C_{\text{isolator}}$, $K_3 = K_{\text{boundary}}$, $M_3 = m_{\text{plate-boundary}}$, $C_3 = C_{\text{boundary}}$, and $x_1(t)$, $x_2(t)$ and $x_3(t)$ denote the displacement of mass node $m_{\text{plate-central}}$, m_{flywheel} and $m_{\text{plate-boundary}}$, respectively. To derive the force transmissibility of the 3-stage system, similar to Equations (2) and (3), assume that the displacement response of the structural plate boundary is:

$$x_3(t) = G_1 \sin(\omega t) + G_2 \cos(\omega t) \quad (9)$$

Substitute Equations (2), (3) and (9) into Equation (8), and equal the coefficients of $\sin(\omega t)$ and $\cos(\omega t)$ to 0 respectively. Finally, the kinetic equations of A_1, A_2, B_1, B_2, G_1 and G_2 can be obtained:

$$\begin{cases} A_1K_1 - G_1K_1 + A_1K_2 - B_1K_2 - A_2C_1\omega - A_2C_2\omega - B_2C_2\omega + C_1G_2\omega - A_1M_1\omega^2 = 0 \\ A_2K_1 - G_2K_1 + A_2K_2 - B_2K_2 - A_1C_1\omega - A_1C_2\omega - B_1C_2\omega - C_1G_1\omega - A_2M_1\omega^2 = 0 \\ -F - A_1K_2 + B_1K_2 + A_2C_2\omega - B_2C_2\omega - B_1M_2\omega^2 = 0 \\ -A_2K_2 + B_2K_2 - A_1C_2\omega + B_1C_2\omega - B_2M_2\omega^2 = 0 \\ -A_1K_1 + G_1K_1 + G_1K_3 + A_2C_1\omega - C_1G_2\omega - C_3G_2\omega - G_1M_3\omega^2 = 0 \\ -A_2K_1 + G_2K_1 + G_2K_3 + A_1C_1\omega - C_1G_2\omega - C_3G_1\omega - G_2M_3\omega^2 = 0 \end{cases} \tag{10}$$

By solving the equation above, the amplitude $\left(G_1{}^2 + G_2{}^2\right)^{\frac{1}{2}}$ of the elastic boundary response of the structural plate can be obtained, as shown in the Appendix A. Based on the amplitude value $\left(G_1{}^2 + G_2{}^2\right)^{\frac{1}{2}}$, the output force of the 3-stage system can be expressed as:

$$F_{3out} = \left(K_{boundary}^2 + (C_{boundary}\omega)^2\right)^{\frac{1}{2}} \left(G_1^2 + G_2^2\right)^{\frac{1}{2}} \tag{11}$$

4.1. Vertical (Y Direction)

When the flywheel vibrates vertically as illustrated in Figure 7, $m_{\text{plate-central}}$ = 31.7 kg, which equals the fundamental model mass of the boundary fixed plate. As the total mass of the structural plate is 50 kg, then $m_{\text{plate-boundary}}$ = (50−31.7) kg = 18.3 kg. K_{plate} = 3,378,239 N/m and is calculated according to the fundamental frequency and the modal mass of the boundary fixed structural plate. The m_{flywheel} = 8 kg and K_{isolator} = 56,321 N/m.

In this section, the influence of the stiffness and damping of the elastic boundary on the force transmissibility of the system is analyzed using the equation presented above. The results are presented in Figure 8. A sinusoidal force $F{\cdot}\text{Sin(t)}$ is applied vertically on the node flywheel, and the output force disturbance amplitude of the plate-isolator system is calculated via Equation (11). The force transmissibility is calculated by comparing Equation (11) with the excitation amplitude F.

Figure 8a illustrates the influence of the boundary stiffness on the force transmissibility of the plate-isolator system. As the system possesses three degrees of freedom, the force transmissibility curve exhibits three distinct peaks. When the boundary stiffness of the structural plate is reduced to 0.1 times that of the structural plate, the first two peaks of the force transmissibility curve overlap. As a result, the force transmissibility curve only has two obvious peaks. If the boundary stiffness is much larger than the structural plate stiffness, the frequency corresponding to the third peak will be greater than 200 Hz, and the response of the system in the frequency range of 0–200 Hz is similar to that of the 2-stage system in Section 3. Generally, smaller boundary stiffness leads to smaller force transmissibility. Therefore, the structural plate boundary stiffness is initially selected as K_{boundry} = 0.1 K_{plate} for further study.

Figure 8b illustrates the influence of structural plate boundary damping C_{boundary} on the system response. When C_{boundary} = 10^5 Ns/m, the force transmissibility of the system is similar to the scenario when the boundary of the structural plate is rigidly constrained. When C_{boundary} = 100 Ns/m, the force transmissibility curve of the system exhibits two relatively high peaks. However, when C_{boundary} is increased to 1000 Ns/m–10,000 Ns/m, the force transmissibility of the system is improved compared to the 2-stage plate-isolator system.

Based on the analysis results presented in Figure 8, the boundary stiffness of the structural plate is set to K_{boundry} = 0.1 K_{plate} = 337,800 N/m and the boundary damping coefficient is set to C_{boundary} = 2000 Ns/m. These settings enable the system to have a wider range of vibration isolation frequency and lower force transmissibility.

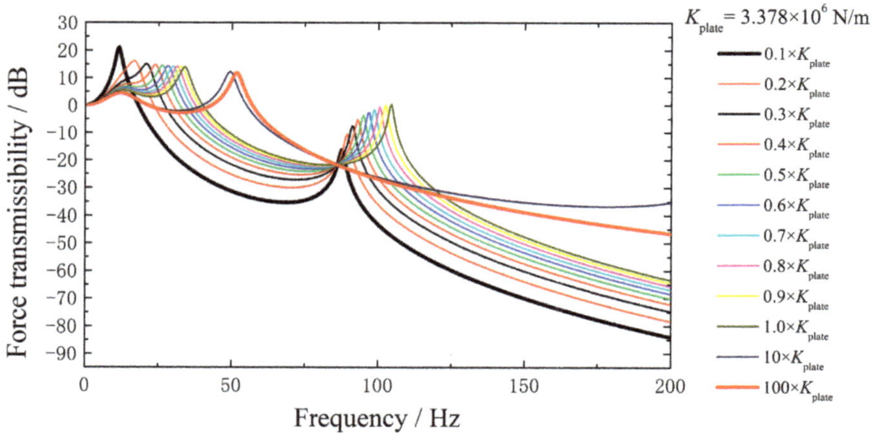

(**a**)

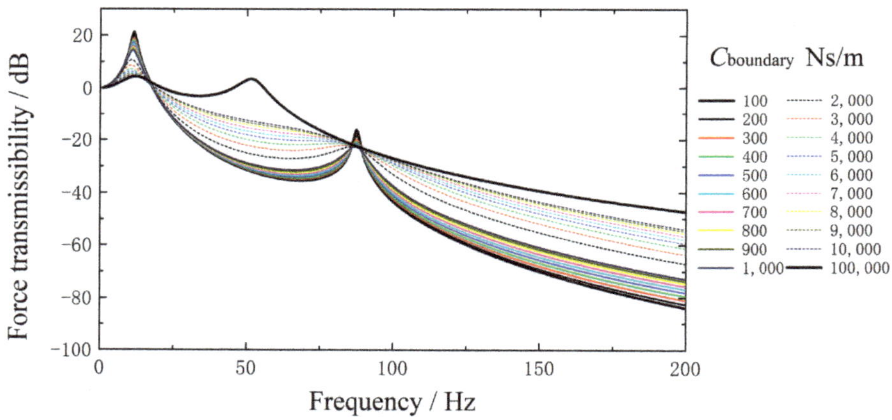

(**b**)

Figure 8. Effect of the boundary elasticity and damping on force transmissibility of the 3-stage plate-isolator system in the Y direction: (**a**) variation with $K_{boundary}$ (C_{plate} = 10 Ns/m, $C_{isolator}$ = 600 Ns/m, $C_{boundary}$ = 100 Ns/m); (**b**) variation with $C_{boundary}$ (C_{plate} = 10 Ns/m, $C_{isolator}$ = 600 Ns/m, $K_{boundary}$ = 0.1 K_{plate}).

4.2. Horizontal (X and Z)

For the horizontal (X and Z) directions, the stiffness K_{plate} can be considered to be infinitely large. As a result, the node mass $m_{plate\text{-}central}$ = 0, and $m_{plate\text{-}boundary}$ = 50 kg. The finite element analysis results indicate that the fundamental frequencies of the flywheel vibration isolation platform in the X and Z directions are 13.354 Hz and 21.976 Hz, respectively. The mass of the flywheel is 8 kg and the equivalent stiffness of the isolator in the X and Z directions are $K_{isolator\text{-}x}$ = 56,321 N/m and $K_{isolator\text{-}z}$ =152,527 N/m. The influence of the lateral boundary stiffness of the structural plate on the force transmissibility of the plate-isolator is investigated using Equation (11), with the prediction results presented in Figure 9. When the lateral boundary stiffness of the structural plate is relatively small (specifically below 500,000 N/m in the X direction and 1,000,000 N/m in the

Z direction), the force transmissibility of the system has only one peak in 0–100 Hz. If the lateral boundary stiffness of the structural plate increases, the second peak will occur. The peak moves towards a higher frequency as the lateral boundary stiffness increases. Generally, the addition of a lateral elastic boundary to the structural plate can significantly enhance the vibration isolation efficiency of the system, particularly at higher frequencies. Lower lateral boundary stiffness values yield better overall vibration isolation efficiency. In the X and Z directions, if $K_{boundary\text{-}x}$ = 563,210 N/m and $K_{boundary\text{-}z}$ = 610,108 N/m, the force transmissibility curves of the plate-isolator system exhibit a single peak at 13.5 Hz, which is in proximity to the fundamental frequency of the vibration isolation platform (13.354 Hz). For simplicity, a lateral boundary stiffness of $K_{boundary}$ = 600,000 N/m is used for the structural plate in both X and Z directions in this study.

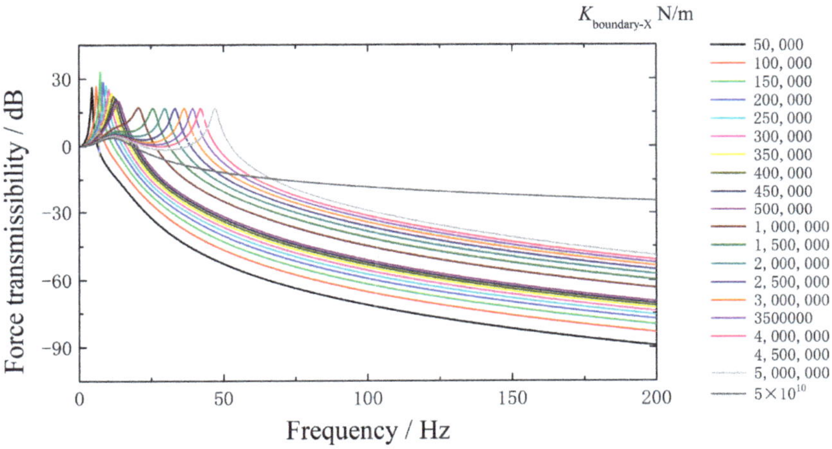

(a)

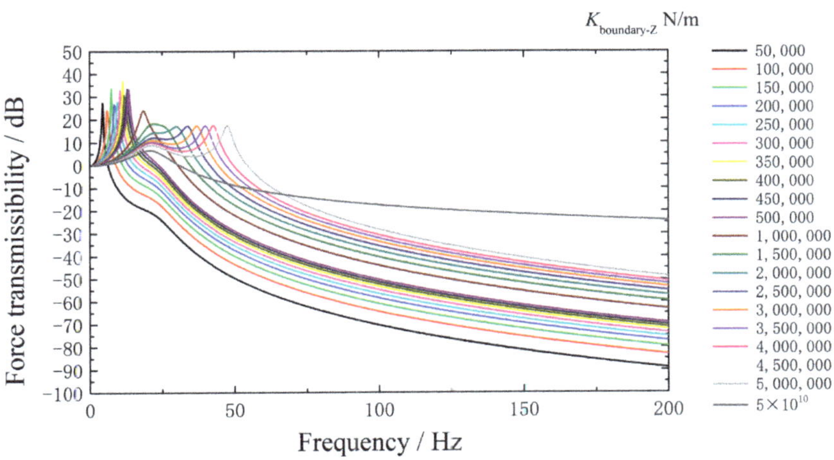

(b)

Figure 9. Effect of the horizontal boundary elasticity on force transmissibility of the 3-stage plate-isolator system: (**a**) in the X direction ($C_{boundary}$ = 10 Ns/m, $K_{isolator\text{-}x}$ = 56,321 N/m, $C_{isolator}$ = 600 Ns/m); (**b**) in the Z direction ($C_{boundary}$ = 10 Ns/m, $K_{isolator\text{-}z}$ = 152,527 N/m, $C_{isolator}$ = 600 Ns/m).

The effect of lateral boundary damping on the force transmissibility of the plate-isolator system is analyzed in Figure 10. The results show that a large value of the lateral boundary damping leads to lower peak of the system response. However, to ensure the vibration isolation effect at high frequencies, a compromise value of lateral boundary damping coefficient $C_{boundary}$ = 2000 Ns/m is selected.

Based on the simplified 3-stage plate-isolator system, a group of boundary stiffness and damping coefficients are selected. In the vertical direction (Y), $K_{boundary}$ = 340,000 N/m, $C_{boundary}$ = 2000 Ns/m. In the horizontal direction (X and Z), $K_{boundary}$ = 600,000 N/m, $C_{boundary}$ = 2000 Ns/m. In the next section, finite element simulation will be used to further verify the influence of elastic plate boundaries on the kinetic response of the structural plate.

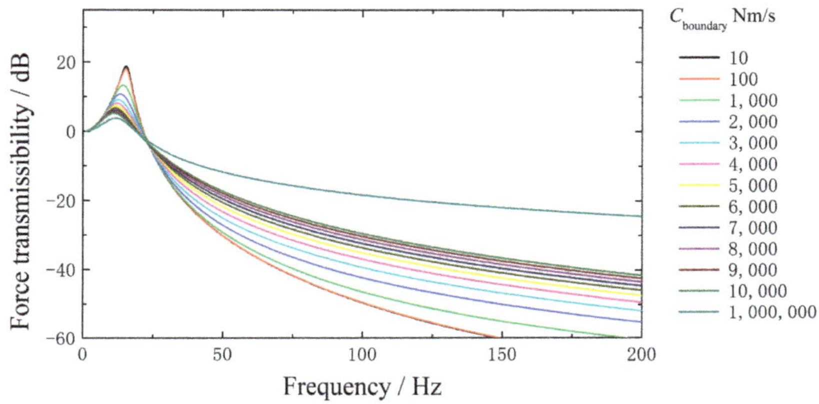

(a)

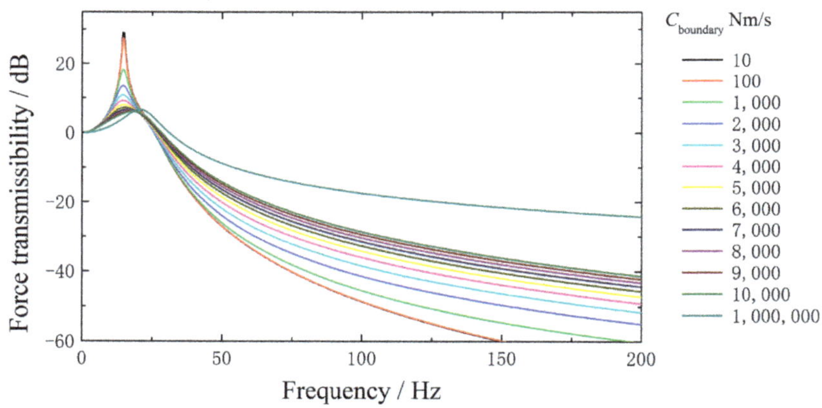

(b)

Figure 10. Force transmissibility curve of the 3-stage plate-isolator system with different lateral damping of the structural plate boundary: (**a**) in the X direction ($K_{boundary}$ = 600,000 N/s, $C_{isolator}$ = 600 Ns/m, $K_{isolator\text{-}x}$ = 56321 N/m); (**b**) in the Z direction ($K_{boundary}$ = 600,000 N/s, $C_{isolator}$ = 600 Ns/m, $K_{isolator\text{-}z}$ = 152,527 N/m).

5. A Plate with Elastic Boundaries and its Dynamic Responses

In this section, the conclusion of the simplified 3-stage model is verified via the multi-DOF finite element model. Figure 11 shows the finite element model of the plate-isolator with the elastic boundary. The modeling methods of the flywheel, 6-DOF vibration isolator, and structural plate are the same as mentioned in Section 2. In the finite element model, the X\Y\Z translation freedoms of the four edges of the structural plate are released. The four edges of the structural plate are connected to the ground with 60 vertical spring–dashpot elements and 64 transverse spring–dashpot elements, respectively. Moreover, in practice, the rotational freedoms of the edges are released due to the challenges of applying rotational constraints on the edges of elastically supported structural plates.

In the finite element model, each vertical boundary spring stiffness is set to $K = \frac{1}{60}340,000$ N/m, and each vertical damping coefficient is set to $C = \frac{1}{60}2000$ Ns/m. In the transverse direction, the spring stiffness and the damping coefficient are $K = \frac{1}{32}600,000$ N/m and $C = \frac{1}{32}2000$ Ns/m at each supporting point. Harmonic excitations are applied on the mass center of the flywheel. The predicted force transmissibility of the plate-isolator system with elastic boundaries is shown in Figure 12. In Figure 12a, FEA results of the plate-isolator system with elastic boundaries are compared with the 3-stage simplified model. The results of the lumped parameter theoretical model are qualitatively similar to the FEA results. In the vertical direction (y), the results of the multi-DOF finite element model and the lumped parameter theoretical model are a little different after 50 Hz; the main reason is that the lumped parameter theoretical model is not precise enough to illustrate the complicated mode shape of the structural plate. Nevertheless, in this study, the 3-stage simplified lumped parameter model is applied as a guide to choosing the appropriate stiffness and damping for the plate boundary. In Figure 12b, the force transmissibilities of the plate-isolator system with and without elastic boundary are compared. The predictions show that the vibration isolation effect of the plate-isolator system is obviously improved by the elastic plate boundary. In Figure 12b, it is demonstrated that the 3-stage simplified model is an effective tool to determine the boundary stiffness and damping for the plate-isolator system.

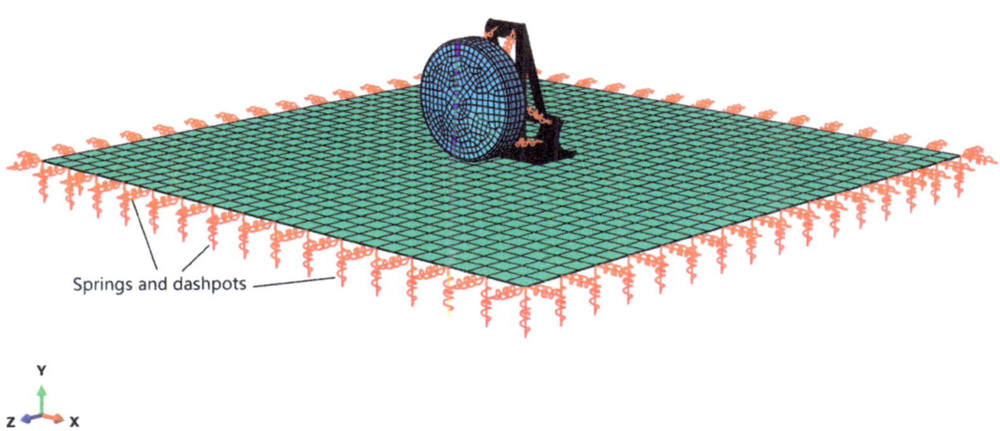

Figure 11. The finite element model of the plate-isolator system with elastic boundary.

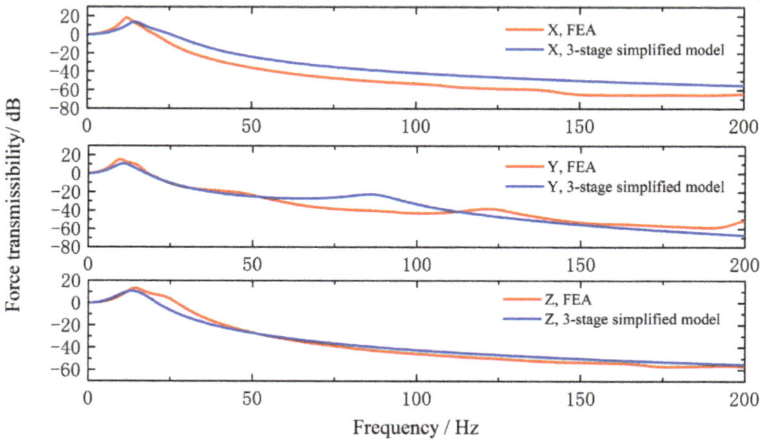

(a)

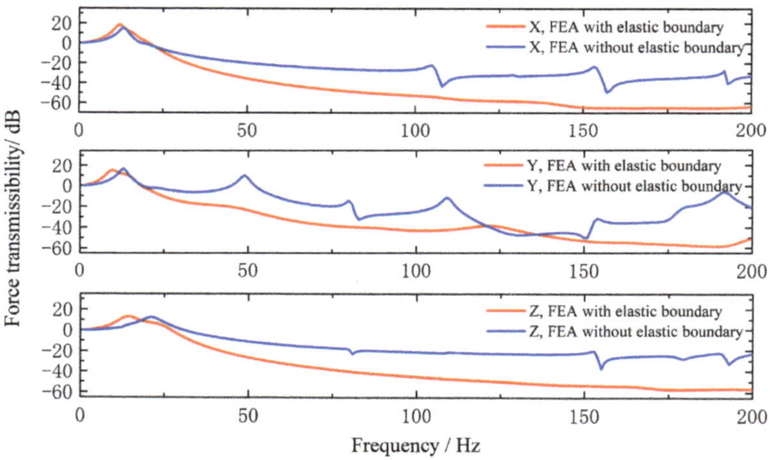

(b)

Figure 12. The force transmissibility curves of the plate-isolator system with elastic boundary: (**a**) compared with the 3-stage simplified theoretical model; (**b**) compared with the plate-isolator system without elastic boundary.

6. A Cube Satellite with Elastic Plate Boundaries and its Dynamic Responses

In this section, the idea of the elastic boundary is further verified by a 1.5 m^3 cube satellite with elastically supported bottom plate. The settlement of the cube satellite is illustrated in Figure 13. The structural plates are honeycomb sandwich plates, as mentioned above. A uniform mass of 50 kg is applied to each structural plate. The flywheel is mounted on the bottom plate of the satellite. In the finite element model, if the bottom plate is elastically supported, the edges of the bottom plate are connected to the side plates via 60 vertical spring–dashpot elements and 64 transverse spring–dashpot elements, similar to those in Figure 11. The stiffness and damping coefficient of the boundary spring and dashpot are consistent with the previous section. In addition, the responses of the satellite are also predicted for comparison when the bottom plate is rigidly connected to the side plates at its four edges.

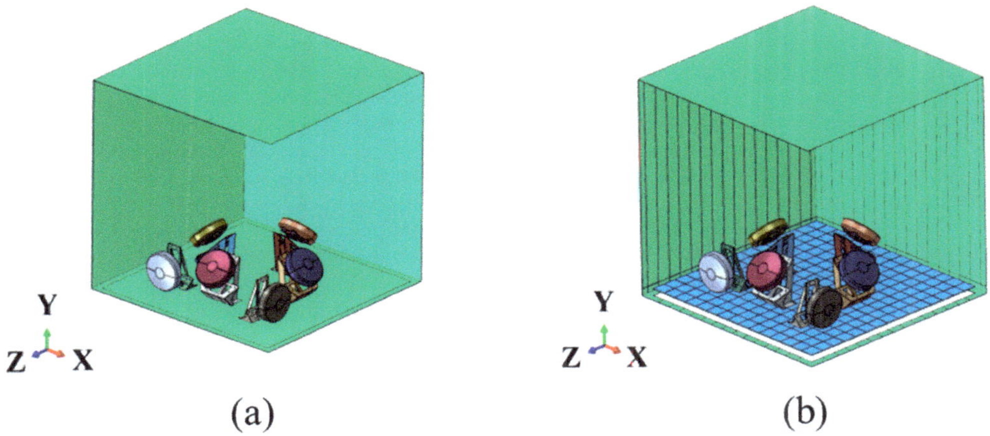

Figure 13. Schematic diagram of CubeSat and flywheel installation: (**a**) with no elastic boundary; (**b**) with elastic boundary.

In practical applications, multiple flywheels with different mounting angles are often used in a satellite to realize backup and flywheel collaborative speed control. In this paper, the cube satellite with six flywheels is studied: two flywheels mounted at 90 degrees and four flywheels mounted at 45 degrees. The flywheels are mounted on the satellite's bottom plate, and sinusoidal excitations of 1 N are applied simultaneously in the X, Y, and Z directions to the mass centers of each flywheel. The acceleration frequency response curves of the central points of the satellite top plate and side plate are presented in Figure 14.

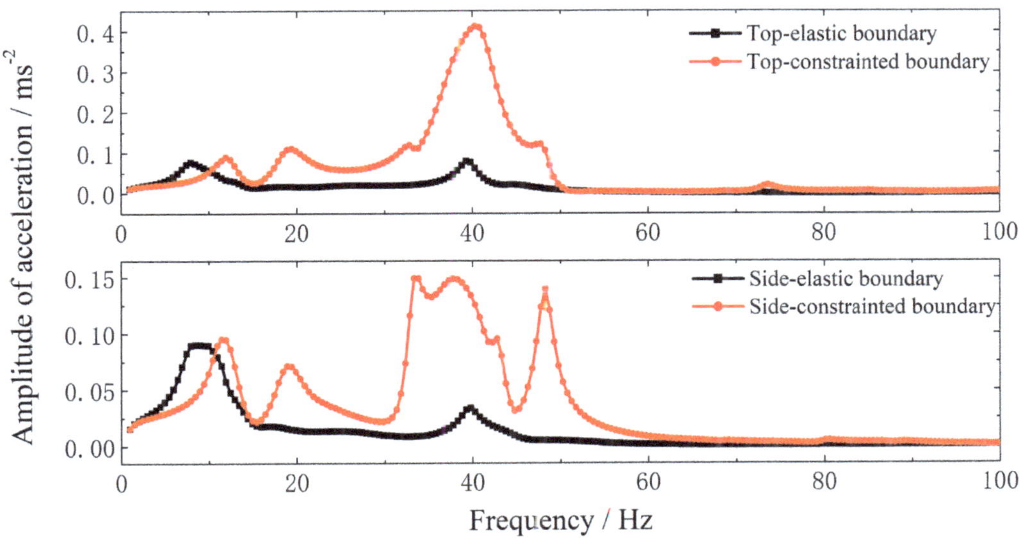

Figure 14. Frequency response curve of the acceleration amplitude at the central points of the satellite's top and side plates.

It can be seen from Figure 14 that although the flywheels are isolated on the 6-DOF isolators, the responses of the top or the side plates are not as expected when the satellite bottom plate is rigidly connected to the side plates. The acceleration responses at the central points of the top and side plates exhibit multiple peaks due to the local modes. The first peak corresponds to the local mode of the satellite's bottom plate, while the subsequent peaks correspond to the local modes of the side plates and the top plate. In contrast, when the bottom plate is elastically connected to the side plates, although the amplitudes of the first peaks are not obviously affected, the responses of the central points of the satellite's top and side plates are effectively suppressed between 20 Hz and 100 Hz. The average amplitude of acceleration from approximately 1 to 100 Hz has a decrease of 75.4% at the center of the top plate and a decrease of 64.1% at the center of the side plate. In Figure 12, it is seen that with the elastic boundary condition, as the responses corresponding to the local modes of the bottom plate are suppressed, the disturbance of the flywheels is effectively isolated. Thus, the bottom plate-isolator system with elastic plate boundary cannot output enough excitation energy at the frequencies corresponding to the modes of side or top plates, and the response of the cube satellite naturally decreases at the side of the top plates. Note that in this section, the boundary stiffness and damping are determined based on the parameter studies conducted by the simplified 3-stage analytical model in Section 4. Although in the analytical model, the bottom plate is simplified into a spring with one degree of freedom, the obtained optimal boundary stiffness and damping are effective when the bottom plate's multiple degrees of freedom are fully taken into consideration in the finite element model. Thus, the results presented in this section indicate that the simplified 3-stage model established in Section 4 is valid in determining the boundary stiffness and damping parameters of the structural plate.

In this section, the effect of the elastic plate boundary is verified using a relatively simple cube satellite. FEA results demonstrate that the adoption of an elastic boundary for the structural plate with flywheels (vibration source) can significantly reduce the in-orbit micro-vibration response of the satellite structure. For a satellite with a more complex structure and layout, the elastic boundary of the structural plate should be further designed in detail according to the flywheel (vibration source) layout and the shape of the structural plate. Furthermore, as the primary objective of this paper is to introduce the basic principle and verify its feasibility, the implementation of the elastic plate boundary is not considered in this paper. It is certain that the elastic plate boundary will introduce extra weight, and it will be a challenge to design a boundary spring–dashpot component with low weight and limited size. Nevertheless, an elastic spring with limited size can be achieved such as by using sheets [35], and the piezoelectric materials can be utilized as the damper to harvest or dissipate energy [36].

7. Summary

In this paper, a holistic approach is taken to isolate flywheel vibrations by considering the flywheel mounting plate and flywheel isolator as a system. Through finite element simulations and a 2-stage simplified model, it is demonstrated that achieving ideal flywheel vibration isolation is challenging when relying solely on the flywheel isolator due to the influence of the structural plate's elasticity. To address this issue, the elastic boundary is applied for the flywheel-mounted structural plate instead of a common rigidly fixed boundary. The stiffness and damping of the plate boundary are optimized using a simplified 3-stage model, and the optimized results are verified through finite element simulations of the plate-isolator system. The simulation results indicate that the influence of high-order modes of the plate is effectively suppressed, and the overall force transmissibility of the plate-isolator system is comparable to that of a 1-DOF isolator. Finally, the idea of an elastic plate boundary is further verified by the finite element simulation of a simple 1.5 m^3 cube satellite. The flywheels are mounted on the bottom plate of the satellite, and the kinetic responses of the satellite structure are predicted when the bottom plate is elastically or rigidly connected to the satellite's side plates. The dynamic responses of the cube satellite confirm the effectiveness of the elastic boundary of the flywheel-mounted plate in suppressing the vibration of the satellite's structural plates away from the flywheel.

Author Contributions: Conceptualization, X.Z.; Methodology, X.K.; Software, H.L.; Validation, H.L.; Formal analysis, X.K.; Investigation, X.K. and H.L.; Data curation, X.X.; Writing—original draft, X.K. and X.S.; Writing—review & editing, X.Z. and X.S.; Supervision, X.Z. All authors have read and agreed to the published version of the manuscript.

Funding: This research received no external funding.

Institutional Review Board Statement: Not applicable.

Informed Consent Statement: Not applicable.

Data Availability Statement: The data presented in this study are available on request from the corresponding author. The data are not publicly available due to privacy.

Conflicts of Interest: The authors declare no conflict of interest.

Appendix A

$$
\begin{aligned}
&(G_1{}^2 + G_2{}^2)^{\frac{1}{2}} = (F^2(K_1{}^2 + C_1{}^2\omega^2)(K_2{}^2 + C_2{}^2\omega^2))/(K_1{}^2(2C_2C_3M_2{}^2\omega^6 + M_2{}^2\omega^4(K_3{}^2 - 2K_3(M_1 + M_3)\omega^2 \\
&+\omega^2(C_3{}^2 + (M_1 + M_3)^2\omega^2)) - 2K_2M_2\omega^2(K_3{}^2 - K_3(2M_1 + M_2 + 2M_3)\omega^2 \\
&+\omega^2(C_3{}^2 + (M_1 + M_3)(M_1 + M_2 + M_3)\omega^2)) + K_2{}^2(K_3{}^2 - 2K_3(M_1 + M_2 + M_3)\omega^2 \\
&+\omega^2(C_3{}^2 + (M_1 + M_2 + M_3)^2\omega^2)) + C_2{}^2\omega^2(K_3{}^2 - 2K_3(M_1 + M_2 + M_3)\omega^2 \\
&+\omega^2(C_3{}^2 + (M_1 + M_2 + M_3)^2\omega^2))) - 2K_1\omega^2(K_2{}^2(M_1 + M_2)(K_3{}^2 - K_3(M_1 + M_2 + 2M_3)\omega^2 \\
&+\omega^2(C_3{}^2 + M_3(M_1 + M_2 + M_3)\omega^2)) - K_2M_2\omega^2(K_3{}^2(2M_1 - M_2) \\
&-2K_3(M_1{}^2 + M_2M_3 + M_1(M_2 + 2M_3))\omega^2 + \omega^2(C_3{}^2(2M_1 + M_2) \\
&+M_3(2M_1{}^2 + M_2M_3 + 2M_1(M_2 + M_3))\omega^2)) + \omega(M_1M_2{}^2\omega^2(K_3{}^2 - K_3(M_1 + 2M_3)\omega^2 \\
&+\omega^2(C_3{}^2 + M_3(M_1 + M_3)\omega^2)) + C_2{}^2(M_1 + M_2)(K_3{}^2 - K_3(M_1 + M_2 + 2M_3)\omega^2 \\
&+\omega^2(C_3{}^2 + M_3(M_1 + M_2 + M_3)\omega^2)))) + \omega^2(\omega^2(K_3{}^2 + C_3{}^2\omega^2 - 2K_3M_3\omega^2 + M_3{}^2\omega^4)(K_2{}^2(M_1 + M_2)^2 \\
&-2K_2M_1M_2(M_1 + M_2)\omega^2 + \omega^2(C_2{}^2(M_1 + M_2)^2 + M_1{}^2M_2{}^2\omega^2)) \\
&+2C_1\omega^4(C_2C_3{}^2M_2{}^2\omega^2 + C_2M_2{}^2(K_3 - M_3\omega^2)^2 + C_3(K_2{}^2(M_1 + M_2)^2 - 2K_2M_1M_2(M_1 + M_2)\omega^2 \\
&+\omega^2(C_2{}^2(M_1 + M_2)^2 + M_1{}^2M_2{}^2\omega^2))) + C_1{}^2(2C_2C_3M_2{}^2\omega^6 + M_2{}^2\omega^4(K_3{}^2 - 2K_3(M_1 + M_3)\omega^2 \\
&+\omega^2(C_3{}^2 + (M_1 + M_3)^2\omega^2)) - 2K_2M_2\omega^2(K_3{}^2 - K_3(2M_1 + M_2 + 2M_3)\omega^2 \\
&+\omega^2(C_3{}^2 + (M_1 + M_3)(M_1 + M_2 + M_3)\omega^2)) + K_2{}^2(K_3{}^2 - 2K_3(M_1 + M_2 + M_3)\omega^2 \\
&+\omega^2(C_3{}^2 + (M_1 + M_2 + M_3)^2\omega^2)) + C2^2\omega^2(K_3{}^2 - 2K_3(M_1 + M_2 + M_3)\omega^2 \\
&+\omega^2(C_3{}^2 + (M_1 + M_2 + M_3)^2\omega^2)))))
\end{aligned}
$$

References

Yoshida, N.; Takahara, O.; Kosugi, T.; Ninomiya, K.; Hashimoto, T.; Minesugi, K.; Tsuneta, S.; Ichimoto, K.; Shimada, S. A systematic approach to achieve the fine pointing requirement of SCLAR-B. *IFAC Proc. Vol.* **2004**, *37*, 101–106. [CrossRef]

Takahara, O.; Yoshida, N.; Minesugi, K.; Hashimoto, T.; Nagata, S.; Koike, M.; Shimada, S.; Nakaoji, T. Microvibration Transmissibility Test of Solar-B. In Proceedings of the 24th ISTS (International Symposition on Space Technology and Science), Miyazaki, Japan, 30 May–6 June 2004.

Lee, A.Y.; Yu, J.W.; Kahn, P.B.; Stoller, R.L. Space interferometry mission spacecraft pointing error budgets. *IEEE Trans. Aerosp. Electron. Syst.* **2002**, *38*, 502–514. [CrossRef]

Peng, C.; Zhou, X.; Wei, T.; Ren, Y. High precision synchronous vibration suppression for a MSFW subject to phase lag influence. *Mech. Syst. Signal Process.* **2019**, *120*, 408–421. [CrossRef]

Chen, S.; Xuan, M.; Xin, J.; Liu, Y.; Gu, S.; Li, J.; Zhang, L. Design and experiment of dual micro-vibration isolation system for optical satellite flywheel. *Int. J. Mech. Sci.* **2020**, *179*, 105592. [CrossRef]

Firth, J.; Black, J. Vibration interaction in a multiple flywheel system. *J. Sound Vib.* **2012**, *331*, 1701–1714. [CrossRef]

Park, G.; Lee, D.-O.; Han, J.-H. Development of multi-degree-of-freedom microvibration emulator for efficient jitter test of spacecraft. *J. Intell. Mater. Syst. Struct.* **2014**, *25*, 1069–1081. [CrossRef]

Safarabadi, M.; Haghshenas, H.; Kelardeh, H. Design of micro-vibration isolation system for a remote-sensing satellite payload using viscoelastic Materials. *Eng. Solid Mech.* **2020**, *8*, 69–76. [CrossRef]

Dai, H.; Jing, X.; Wang, Y.; Yue, X.; Yuan, J. Post-capture vibration suppression of spacecraft via a bio-inspired isolation system. *Mech. Syst. Signal Process.* **2018**, *105*, 214–240. [CrossRef]

Zhang, Y.; Guo, Z.; He, H.; Zhang, J.; Liu, M.; Zhou, Z. A novel vibration isolation system for reaction wheel on space telescopes. *Acta Astronaut.* **2014**, *102*, 1–13. [CrossRef]

11. Zhang, Y.; Zhang, J.; Zhai, G. Vibration isolation platform with multiple tuned mass dampers for reaction wheel on satelli *Math. Probl. Eng.* **2013**, *2013*, 574072. [CrossRef]
12. Dong, Y.H.; Zhou, X.B.; Shen, J.F.; Liu, X.T.; Yu, Z.-F. Study on micro-vibration suppression technology of fy-4 satellite. *Aerc Shanghai* **2017**.
13. Freesland, D.; Carter, D.; Chapel, J.; Clapp, B.; Howat, J.; Krimchansky, A. GOES-R dual isolation. In Proceedings of the Ann AAS Guidance & Control Conference (No. GSFC-E-DAA-TN20462), Breckenridge, CO, USA, 31 January–5 February 2015.
14. Kamesh, D.; Pandiyan, R.; Ghosal, A. Passive vibration isolation of reaction wheel disturbances using a low frequency flexi space platform. *J. Sound Vib.* **2012**, *331*, 1310–1330. [CrossRef]
15. Kamesh, D.; Pandiyan, R.; Ghosal, A. Modeling, design and analysis of low frequency platform for attenuating micro-vibration spacecraft. *J. Sound Vib.* **2010**, *329*, 3431–3450. [CrossRef]
16. Zhang, Y.; Zang, Y.; Li, M.; Wang, Y.; Li, W. Active-passive integrated vibration control for control moment gyros and application to satellites. *J. Sound Vib.* **2017**, *394*, 1–14. [CrossRef]
17. Li, L.; Tan, L.; Kong, L.; Wang, D.; Yang, H. The influence of flywheel micro vibration on space camera and vibration suppressi *Mech. Syst. Signal Process.* **2018**, *100*, 360–370. [CrossRef]
18. Wei, Z.; Li, D.; Luo, Q.; Jiang, J. Modeling and analysis of a flywheel microvibration isolation system for spacecrafts. *Adv. Sp Res.* **2015**, *55*, 761–777. [CrossRef]
19. Oh, H.U.; Taniwaki, S.; Kinjyo, N.; Izawa, K. Flywheel vibration isolation test using a variable-damping isolator. *Smart Ma Struct.* **2006**, *15*, 365. [CrossRef]
20. Oh, H.U.; Izawa, K.; Taniwaki, S. Development of variable-damping isolator using bio-metal fiber for reaction wheel vibrati isolation. *Smart Mater. Struct.* **2005**, *14*, 928. [CrossRef]
21. Kwon, S.C.; Jo, M.S.; Oh, H.U. Experimental validation of fly-wheel passive launch and on-orbit vibration isolation system using a superelastic SMA mesh washer isolator. *Int. J. Aerosp. Eng.* **2017**, *2017*, 5496053. [CrossRef]
22. Zhao, W.; Li, B.; Liu, P.; Liu, K. Semi-active control for a multi-dimensional vibration isolator with parallel mechanism. *J. V Control.* **2013**, *19*, 879–888. [CrossRef]
23. Kim, H.S.; Cho, Y.M.; Moon, J.H. Active vibration control using a novel three-DOF precision micro-stage. *Smart Mater. Stru* **2010**, *19*, 055001. [CrossRef]
24. Kim, H.S.; Cho, Y.M. Design and modeling of a novel 3-DOF precision micro-stage. *Mechatronics* **2009**, *19*, 598–608. [CrossRef
25. Lee, D.O.; Park, G.; Han, J.H. Experimental study on on-orbit and launch environment vibration isolation performance o vibration isolator using bellows and viscous fluid. *Aerosp. Sci. Technol.* **2015**, *45*, 1–9. [CrossRef]
26. Lee, D.O.; Park, G.; Han, J.H. Hybrid isolation of micro vibrations induced by reaction wheels. *J. Sound Vib.* **2016**, *363*, 1– [CrossRef]
27. Wu, Y.; Yu, K.; Jiao, J.; Cao, D.; Chi, W.; Tang, J. Dynamic isotropy design and analysis of a six-DOF active micro-vibrati isolation manipulator on satellites. *Robot. Comput.-Integr. Manuf.* **2018**, *49*, 408–425. [CrossRef]
28. Guo, Z.; Zhang, Y.; Hu, Q. Integrated vibration isolation and attitude control for spacecraft with uncertain or unknown paylo inertia parameters. *Acta Astronaut.* **2018**, *151*, 107–119. [CrossRef]
29. Zhang, Y.; Sheng, C.; Hu, Q.; Li, M.; Guo, Z.; Qi, R. Dynamic analysis and control application of vibration isolation system wi magnetic suspension on satellites. *Aerosp. Sci. Technol.* **2018**, *75*, 99–114. [CrossRef]
30. Bronowicki, A. Forensic investigation of reaction wheel nutation on isolator. In Proceedings of the 49th AIAA/ASME/ASCE/AHS/A Structures, Structural Dynamics, and Materials Conference, 16th AIAA/ASME/AHS Adaptive Structures Conference, 10 AIAA Non-Deterministic Approaches Conference, 9th AIAA Gossamer Spacecraft Forum, 4th AIAA Multidisciplinary Desi Optimization Specialists Conference, Schaumburg, IL, USA, 7–10 April 2008; p. 1953.
31. De Marneffe, B.; Avraam, M.; Deraemaeker, A.; Horodinca, M.; Preumont, A. Vibration isolation of precision payloads: A six-a electromagnetic relaxation isolator. *J. Guid. Control. Dyn.* **2009**, *32*, 395–401. [CrossRef]
32. Li, W.; Huang, H.; Zhou, X.; Zheng, X.; Bai, Y. Design and experiments of an active isolator for satellite micro-vibration. *Chin. Aeronaut.* **2014**, *27*, 1461–1468. [CrossRef]
33. McMickell, M.B.; Kreider, T.; Hansen, E.; Davis, T.; Gonzalez, M. Optical payload isolation using the miniature vibration isolati system (MVIS-II). In *Industrial and Commercial Applications of Smart Structures Technologies 2007*; SPIE: St Bellingham, WA, US 2007; Volume 6527, pp. 14–26.
34. Zhang, A.; Sheng, M.; Xiao, H. The Damping Forced Vibration of Rectangular Stiffened Plates with Elastic Boundary Edg Including Boundary Damping. *Appl. Mech. Mater.* **2014**, *577*, 205–208. [CrossRef]
35. Wu, Z.; Li, H.; Kong, X.; Deng, Z. A novel design of vibration isolator with high and frequency dependent damping characteristi based on large negative poisson's ratio (LNPR) structure. *Mech. Syst. Signal Process.* **2023**, *168*, 1–18. [CrossRef]
36. Shaukat, H.; Ali, A.; Bibi, S.; Altabey, W.; Noori, M.; Kouritem, S. A Review of the recent advances in piezoelectric materia energy harvester structures, and their applications in analytical chemistry. *Appl. Sci.* **2023**, *13*, 1300. [CrossRef]

applied sciences

MDPI

Article

The Modular Gait Design of a Soft, Earthworm-like Locomotion Robot Driven by Ultra-Low Frequency Excitation

Zhifeng Qi and Xiuting Sun *

School of Aerospace Engineering and Applied Mechanics, Tongji University, No. 100, ZhangWu Rd, Shanghai 200092, China
* Correspondence: 05mech_sunxiuting@tongji.edu.cn

Abstract: In complex and extreme environments, such as pipelines and polluted waters, gait programming has great significance for multibody segment locomotion robots. The earthworm-like locomotion robot is a representative multibody bionic robot, which has the characteristics of low weight, multibody segments, and excellent movement performance under the designed gait. The body segment cell can realize large deformation under ultra-low frequency excitation. The multibody segment robot can locomote under ultra-low frequency excitation with appropriate shifts. In this paper, a modular gait design principle for a soft, earthworm-like locomotion robot is proposed. The driven modules defined by modular gait generation correspond to the peristaltic wave transmissions of the excitation in the robot for different modular gait modes. A locomotion algorithm is presented to simulate the locomotion of the earthworm-like robot under different locomotion gaits. Moreover, the locomotion speeds are obtained for different modular gait modes. The results show that locomotion speed is related to the original state of the body segments and modular gaits. As the initial actuated segments and driven modules (which correspond to the excitation frequency and shift) increase, faster movement speeds can be realized, which resolves the speed saturation of the earthworm-like robot. The proposed modular gait design method gives a new gait generation principle for the improvement of the locomotion performance of soft, earthworm-like robots.

Keywords: earthworm-like robot; modular gait; driven module; gait generation principle

1. Introduction

Wheeling, crawling, and legging are the most common movement modes for land-based locomotion robots [1–3]. In a water environment, wheeling and legging movements always fail. However, crawling can move forward effectively. In environments such as danger searching, industrial inspection, and internal medical treatment, biomimetic crawling locomotion robots have been successfully applied due to their strong adaptability and controllability [4,5]. The earthworm-like robot, which is servomotor driven, is designed to achieve horizontal and vertical in-pipe locomotion [6–9]. The earthworm-like robot, with two servomotors driven per segment, can realize planar locomotion [10]. Further, when utilizing a Kirigami design to enhance anchoring, the earthworm-like robot achieves movement in multiple environments [11]. In order to increase the environmental adaptability of the bionic earthworm robot, a compliant, modular mesh worm robot with steering is made, increasing the possible degree of freedom and realizing turning movement [12,13]. The most important ability of a locomotion robot with multi-segment is movement ability, including speed, depending on the designed gait [14]. Therefore, the investigation and design method for locomotion gaits of a locomotion robot can significantly improve movement performance.

The receding peristaltic wave is an important feature of earthworm movement, while the gait is the manifestation of peristaltic waves for the earthworm-like robot. It discovers that the average speed and anchor effectiveness can be improved by adjusting the gait parameters [15] based on a dynamic model [16]. In the proposed gait, as reference [15], the earthworm-like locomotion robot is composed of three body segment states: anchoring, driving, and relaxing. The phase difference gait is the optimal gait of the locomotion robot through theoretical analysis [17,18]. With the identical phase-difference-driven mode, the maximum average speed of the robot can be obtained [15]. Via the relevant experiments, the relationship between the average speed and the phase difference of each segment of a gait can be verified [18]. However, with an increase in the number of body segments, the maximum average speed displays a saturation phenomenon.

The gait design is related to the programming and driving performance of the robot actuators. According to the observation of earthworm movement experiments in [19,20], earthworms can stretch multiple body segments simultaneously via their muscles as they move [21]. In order to simulate the actuation and deformation of the muscles, variable soft actuators [22–24], such as pneumatically-driven [5,25,26] and dielectric elastomer actuators [27], have been proposed and manufactured for earthworm-like locomotion robots. In reference [28], a pneumatically driven earthworm-like soft robot is proposed, mimicking the deformation and movement of an earthworm. In nonhomogeneous environments, the robot can deform for lateral bending and buckling by utilizing pneumatically driven actuators [29]. In addition, when considering that the necessary anchoring section can improve movement performance, the pneumatic actuator is used to induce friction by adjusting the contact between the robot and the environment [30]. Because the pneumatic actuator is powered by pumping/compressing air, the response time of the actuator is usually longer than an electric actuator [31]. In order to obtain a faster response for the programming of the body segment, dielectric elastomers [32] have been widely utilized as actuators in robots [27,33,34]. According to the actuation principle of the dielectric elastomer described in references [35–37], a dielectric elastomer actuator is proposed for application in a micro, earthworm-like robot [38]. According to the different designs of dielectric elastomer actuators, dielectric elastomer actuators can realize different deformations for the robot segments [33]. For instance, in reference [39], the dielectric elastomer actuator is embedded into the continuous cylindrical robot body, and silicone fiber is laid to avoid compression, and with this design method, the movement speed reaches 28 mm/min; in reference [40], reciprocating locomotion using different amplitudes and frequencies (of tilted bristles) induced by the dielectric elastomer actuators is generated to improve the forward speed. In order to supply a larger actuation force, dielectric elastomer films are stacked in layers [41]. Moreover, it is discovered that by attaching a prestretched dielectric elastomer to a polyethylene terephthalate frame, the dielectric elastomer with a polyethylene terephthalate frame can be considered as the body segment in a soft robot, which represents the structure-actuation integrated design [42]. Gu et al. connect three dielectric elastomer actuators within a soft, locomotion robot with three body segments. For the structure-actuation integrated design, the average speed is 5.3 mm/s [43]. Lu et al. improve the minimum energy structure with the dielectric elastomer actuator and increase the actuator body segments, which increases the movement speed to 11.5 mm/s [44]. The above researches mainly focus on the movement realization of earthworm-like locomotion robots with soft actuators without investigating the relationship between locomotion performance and gait.

In reference [15], a gait theory for a bionic earthworm-like robot is proposed. It is discovered that, for an increase in the driven segments, the saturation phenomenon for the maximum average speed occurs. The soft actuator has the advantages of large deformation and low weight, which can greatly reduce the weight of the robot and improve the movement speed. Fortunately, since the dielectric elastomer actuator has the characteristics of low weight and fast actuation, the synchronous driven of multiple segments can be achieved. Thus, the dielectric elastomer is selected as the soft actuator in this work. Periodic electrical signals are applied to the soft segments to realize the reciprocating expansion of the segments. A segment cell is a vibration-driven system. The vibration-driven is used in the capsule robot, and the effective movement of the system is realized [45]. Based on the vibration-driven, the dielectric elastomer robot realizes bidirectional movement [46]. The cell phone vibrators are employed for the vibration-driven small robot Rizeh to reduce the cost of the robot [47]. A vibration-driven robot with a time-varying stiffness structure is proposed to reveal the nonlinear driven mechanism of a vibration-driven system [48]. The vibration-driven can also be applied to multisegment earthworm-like locomotion robots. The earthworm-like robot can move forward under vibration excitation [49]. The driven mode determines the movement of the robot. Gait design can provide different movement modes. In order to improve the movement speed of the earthworm-like robot, it is very critical to investigate the gait of the earthworm-like robot under vibration-driven movement.

By designing the gait, the robot can move effectively under ultra-low frequency excitation. Therefore, by combining the deformation characteristics of a soft actuator, a gait design for a soft, earthworm-like robot is proposed in this paper. The driven module modes in this study are bio-inspired by earthworms. In the driven module, a gait generation principle is proposed for different driven wave transmission modes. The modular gait methods improve the locomotion speed of the robot under ultra-low frequency excitation. This reveals that only the driven wave frequency and amplitude affect locomotion speed. Moreover, as the failure of an individual segment in a driven module occurs, locomotion can still be guaranteed due to the driven module design. Numerical simulations for different cases of generated gaits for different driven modules can be used to verify the modular driven design that can break through the saturation phenomenon of locomotion speed. For the proposed driven module design principle, the average locomotion speed is proportional to the number of actuated body segments for the gait of a driven module. The modular gait design method proposed in this paper provides a new idea for the movement strategy of multisegment robots. More importantly, it provides an effective gait design method for special robots, such as carrier robots or robots with partially driven segment failure.

The rest of the paper is structured as follows: in Section 2, the deformation of the actuator is derived, and a description of the driven module is presented. Gait generation algorithms and cases are demonstrated in Section 3. The locomotion of the soft, earthworm-like robot based on the soft actuators is simulated and analyzed in Section 4. The conclusion is given in Section 5.

2. Deformation and State Description of a Segment

2.1. Segment Deformation

The dielectric elastomer actuator can deform the body segment under the action of periodic excitation voltage [43]. Figure 1 shows the model schematic diagram for the deformed body segment driven by the dielectric elastomer actuators. When the tail of the body segment is fixed, the displacement of the body segment head is assumed as $x(t)$, as shown in Figure 1a. The simplification model of the body segment is obtained, as shown in Figure 1b. $F_{driven}(t)$ is the ultra-low frequency excitation. The body segment can realize reciprocating deformation under ultra-low frequency excitation. We refer to the results in reference [50], where four viscoelastic-spring components accurately describe the dynamic characteristics of the dielectric elastomer actuators.

In the simplified model of one body segment with a dielectric elastomer actuator, as Figure 1b, $F_{driven}(t)$ is the ultra-low frequency excitation. The mass of the body segment is assumed to be equivalent to the lumped mass m; the equivalent stiffness of the dielectric elastomer actuator is given as k_i; and the equivalent viscous coefficient is given as c_i (i = 1,2,3,4).

The frictional resistance is defined as F_{fr}, depending on the viscous forces. The ultra-low frequency excitation $F_{driven}(t)$ drives the dielectric elastomer actuator. The dynamic model of the body segment is expressed as

$$\begin{gathered}\ddot{x} = -\frac{1}{m}\left(kx + \sum_{i=1}^{4} k_i x_i + F_{fr}\right) + \frac{1}{m} F_{driven}(t), \\ k_i x_i = c_i(\dot{x} - \dot{x}_i),\ i = 1,2,3,4, \\ F_{fr} = \zeta sign(\dot{x}), \\ F_{driven}(t) = V(t)^2(ax + b).\end{gathered} \tag{1}$$

Fixing the parameters is the same as the values in reference [46]; for the excitation voltage *V(t)*, the deformation of the body segment *x* can be calculated from Equation (1). As the excitation voltage is $V(t) = 2(\sin(2\pi t - \pi/2) + 1)$, the deformation of the body segment is shown in Figure 1c. In Figure 1c, the deformation of the body segment stays in periodic deformation under periodic excitation voltage. For the periodic deformation of the body segment, the locomotion of the earthworm-like robot can be realized.

According to the deformation of each segment *x*(*t*), the body length *l*(*t*) after deformation can be expressed as

$$l(t) = l_0 + x(t) \tag{2}$$

where l_0 is the original length of each body segment.

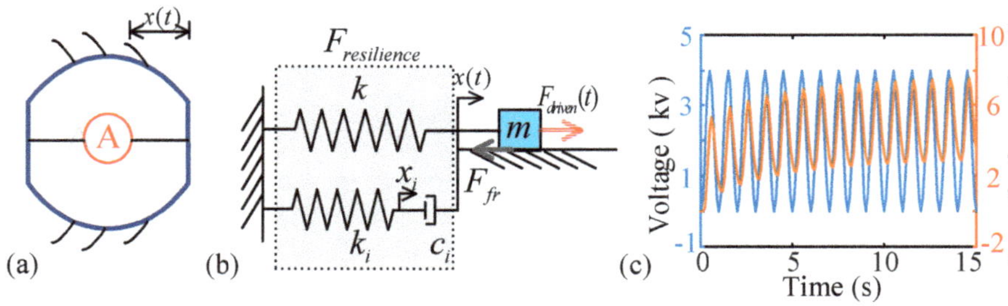

Figure 1. A model schematic diagram and the deformation response of a body segment from the earthworm-like robot driven by a dielectric elastomer actuator. (**a**) A diagram of the body segment deformation. $F_{driven}(t)$ is the ultra-low frequency excitation. Gray represents the initial state of the segment, and blue represents the actuation state of the segment. "A" indicates the actuator; gray indicates the inactive state, and red indicates the active state. (**b**) A dynamic model of the body segment. (**c**) The response of the body segment under excitation by sinusoidal excitation voltage. The yellow line represents the simulated body segment length deformation, and the blue line represents the excitation voltage.

2.2. The State Definition of a Segment

The driven muscle groups for earthworms are composed of longitudinal muscles and circumferential muscles. For each segment, a schematic diagram of muscle distribution is shown in Figure 2a,c. The red dotted lines represent the longitudinal muscles, which are distributed along the parallel direction of the segment. The solid yellow lines represent the circumferential muscles, which are distributed along the circumference of the segment. When a segment of the earthworm is in a contracted state, the circumferential muscles elongate and the longitudinal muscles contract, as shown in Figure 2a; this is defined as the initial state. The original length of the body is defined as l_{IL}, as shown in Figure 2b, and the state of the nonactuated segment is defined as "0". When a body segment of the earthworms is in the elongated state, the longitudinal muscles elongate and the circumferential muscles contract, as shown in Figure 2c. The elongation state of the body segment is defined as the actuated state, defined as "1". After the segment is driven, its length reaches the maximum value: l_{FL}, as shown in Figure 2d.

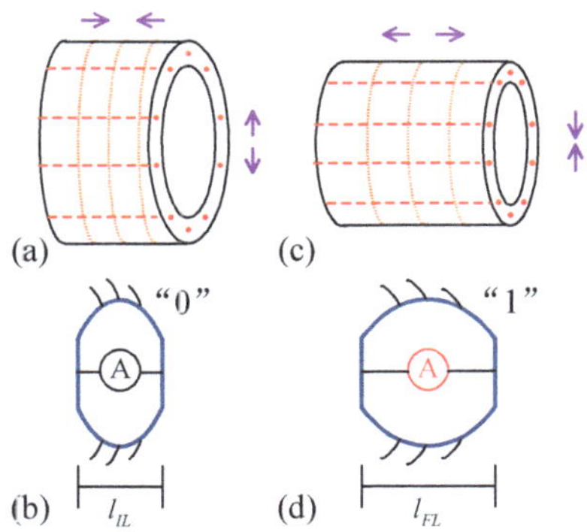

Figure 2. The kinematic state definition of the body segment of the earthworm and the earthworm-like robot. A schematic diagram of the earthworm muscles contracting the segment (**a**). The initial state of the bionic segment represents "0" in (**b**). A schematic diagram of the earthworm muscle elongating segment is shown in (**c**). The final state "1" of the bionic segment with actuation, is shown in (**d**).

2.3. The Definition of Driven Module

The alternate contraction of muscles realizes the expansion and contraction of the body segment for locomotion. Due to the advantages of the dielectric elastomer actuator, such as low weight and fast actuation, several adjacent body segments can elongate at the same time. When considering the requirements for locomotion speed, the segments are assumed to be actuated simultaneously. The simultaneously actuated segments are regarded as a module. We call the transmission mode of the simultaneously actuated segments as modularization design. The modularization driven could improve robot locomotion speed, which breaks the speed saturation phenomenon, as reference [15]. In this study, two cases of the driven module are proposed to investigate the locomotion performance of the soft, earthworm-like robots. In one case, multiple actuated body segments are continuously distributed and transmitted backward as one driven module, which we define as an unbroken driven module (U-DM). In the second case, there are nonactuated segments in one driven module, which we define as a broken driven module (B-DM), because of the easily broken characteristic of the soft actuator.

2.3.1. Unbroken Driven Module

For the U-DM, several adjacent segments are synchronously actuated. The receding peristaltic wave is transmitted as a combination of several actuated segments. In a multiple-segment robot with *TN* segments, the number of actuated body segments is n_{td} for one U-DM. Thus, for this case, there are two adjustable driven parameters, which are the number of the driven modules, k, and the number of actuated body segments in one driven module, n_{td}. The gait parameters in the earthworm-like robot with the U-DM satisfy the following conditions:

$$\begin{gathered} TN \geq (k+1)\, n_{td}, \\ n_{td} \geq 1,\ k \geq 1. \end{gathered} \tag{3}$$

Figure 3 shows two examples of the initial gait distribution of the U-DM for a 12-segment earthworm-like robot. In Figure 3a, the number of actuated segments is $n_{td} = 3$, and in Figure 3b, the number of actuated segments is $n_{td} = 4$. For the U-DM, the segments are actuated together in one driven module. Therefore, there is only one initial modular gait distribution.

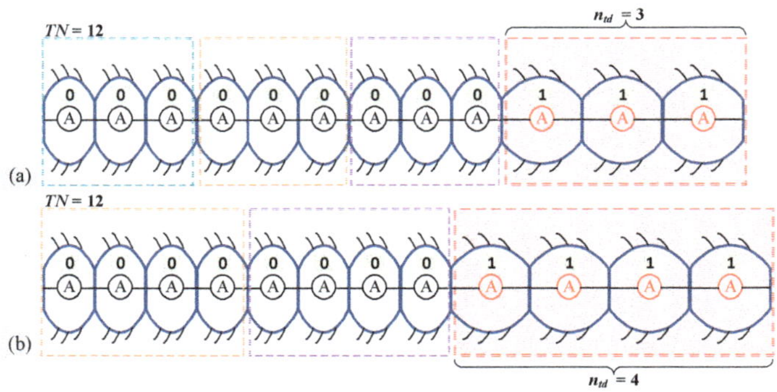

Figure 3. The initial distribution of the U-DM for a 12-segment earthworm-like locomotion robot. (**a**) The initial distribution of the U-DM with three actuated segments. (**b**) The initial distribution of the U-DM with four actuated segments.

2.3.2. Broken Driven Module

As there can exist failed body segments in one driven module, the failed segments cannot deform. This case is defined as the B-DM. In a B-DM, the number of body segments is n_p, including the actuated segments, n_{pa}, and nonactuated segments, n_{pu}. Thus, this has the condition of $n_p = n_{pa} + n_{pu}$. For the earthworm-like robot with the TN body segments, there are three independent adjustable parameters as the number of driven modules, k, actuated segments, n_{pa}, and nonactuated segments, n_{pu}. In the B-DM, all the gait parameters satisfy the following conditions:

$$\begin{gathered} TN \geq k\, n_p,\ n_p = n_{pa} + n_{pu}, \\ n_{pa} \geq 1,\ n_{pu} \geq 1, k \geq 1. \end{gathered} \tag{4}$$

For a driven module with n_p segments, the number of initial modular gait distributions with the B-DM is $2^n - 2$. For example, for a B-DM with four segments, there are 14 initial modular gait distributions that satisfy the conditions (4). Figure 4 shows two examples of initial gait distributions for the B-DM in a 12-segment earthworm-like robot. Figure 4a,b show two different initial gait distributions. In Figure 4a, we assume that a broken body segment ("0") in one of the driven modules is not at the boundary of the driven module. The broken body segment "0" is at the boundary of the driven module, as shown in Figure 4b. In practical application, the distribution of the nonactuated body segment "0" of one driven module can be designed according to the required operating conditions.

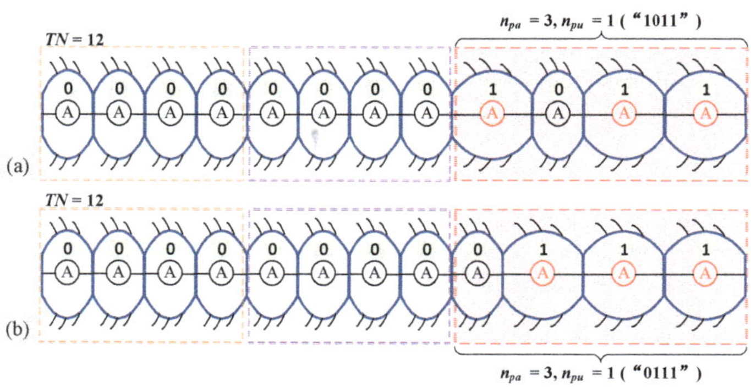

Figure 4. The initial distribution of the B-DM with four segments for a 12-segment earthworm-like locomotion robot. (**a**) A broken, nonactuated body segment exists in the driven module ("1011"). (**b**) The nonactuated body segment is located at the boundary of the driven module ("0111").

The numbers of the actuated segments in Figures 3a and 4b are the same, and the actuated segments are distributed continuously. However, the gait transmission is integrally transmitted in the form of the driven modules for the modular gait. The transmission mode of the driven module affects the locomotion performance of the earthworm-like robot.

3. Modular Gait Generation Principle

For the earthworm-like robot, the initial state of the gait is set to satisfy the transmission principle with a receding peristaltic wave. In the initial state of the earthworm-like robot, the head module is assumed to always be in the actuated state. For locomotion, the driven module may transmit in two modes for the nonfolded or folded waves. Here, we will give the transmission modes of the receding peristaltic wave on the driven module. One mode is the driven module waves without overlapping in the process of transmission. For the modular gait without any overlapping, the transmission mode is defined as the modular gait I (MG-I). The other mode is a driven module waves with overlapping in the transmission process. For the modular gait with overlapping, the relevant gait for locomotion is defined as modular gait II (MG-II).

3.1. Driven Module Waves without Overlapping

3.1.1. Generation Algorithm for MG-I

In the transmission mode of driven module waves without overlapping, the number of transmission segments n_T satisfies

$$n_T = n_{td}, \; or \; n_T = n_p \tag{5}$$

where n_{td} equals the number of actuated body segments in the U-DM, and n_p equals the sum of the actuated segments n_{pa} and nonactuated segments n_{pu} in the B-DM, defined as Equation (4).

The state of the ith segment at the t moment is defined as $s_i{}^t$, in which "0" represents the nonactuated state and "1" represents the actuated state. The states of all the segments can be composed as a state vector at a time point t, denoted by z^t. So, for the earthworm-like robot with TN body segments, there is

$$\begin{aligned} s_i{}^t &\in \{0,1\}, \\ z^t &= (s_1{}^t, s_2{}^t, s_3{}^t, \cdots, s_{TN}{}^t). \end{aligned} \tag{6}$$

The state vector at each time moment can be determined according to the receding peristaltic wave locomotion characteristic of the earthworm. The locomotion gait $(z^{t_0}, z^{t_1}, z^{t_2}, \cdots z^{t_n})$ can be successively obtained over a period of time. For the transmission of the driven module waves without overlapping, the period of the locomotion can be acquired as

$$T = \mu(TN/n_T)\Delta t \tag{7}$$

where Δt is the interval between each state transmission, and μ is a smallest positive integer, rendering the value $\mu(TN/n_T)$ to be an integer. Then, in the locomotion of an earthworm-like robot, the condition for a state switch is given as

$$s_i^{t_j} = s^{t_0}_{Mod\, i-1+(j+1)\cdot n_T, TN]+1} \tag{8}$$

where Mod[·] expresses the modulo operation. According to the locomotion characteristics of a receding peristaltic wave and the state transmission rule, a gait generation algorithm for the driven module waves without overlapping is developed to generate the locomotion gait. The routine of the algorithm is shown in Figure 5. First, the parameters, $\{k, n_T, TN\}$, are fixed. Then, the verdict of the constraint conditions for Equation (3) or (4) is confirmed. Next, the initialization gait is given. Finally, the transmission for the segments can be acquired as per Equations (6) and (8) for MG-I. According to the algorithm routine in Figure 5, arbitrary gaits can be generated.

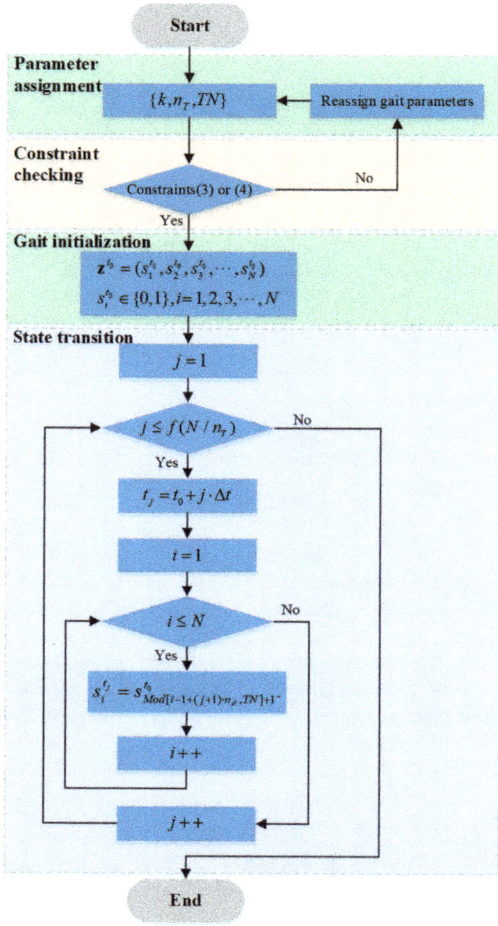

Figure 5. Routine of the generation algorithm for MG-I.

3.1.2. Illustrations for MG-I

This section gives demonstrations for the different driven modules under the MG-I. mode. In the illustration in this case, an earthworm-like robot with 12-body segments, i.e., TN = 12, is selected as an example.

With the proposed gait generation algorithm (proposed in Figure 5) for a 12-segment earthworm-like robot, the gait transmission is shown in Figure 6. Assuming that each driven module consists of four body segments, the driven module passes to the fifth body segment and to the eighth body segment at the second moment, and so on, in a similar fashion. The gait generation demonstrates a 12-segment robot under the U-DM, as shown in Figure 6a. The earthworm-like locomotion robot advances 4 Δl with each transmission of the U-DM. Figure 6b shows a gait generation demonstration for a 12-segment robot under the B-DM. The body state of the B-DM is indicated as "0111". With each state transmission of the B-DM, the earthworm-like locomotion robot advances 3 Δl. It is noticed that the fourth, eighth, and twelfth body segments of the robot are always in the nonactuated state during the whole cycle of the receding peristaltic wave transmission. Although this transmission mode is not the fastest, it is a necessary solution in some specific environments. For example, an earthworm-like locomotion robot has a carrier segment or a segment where the actuator fails.

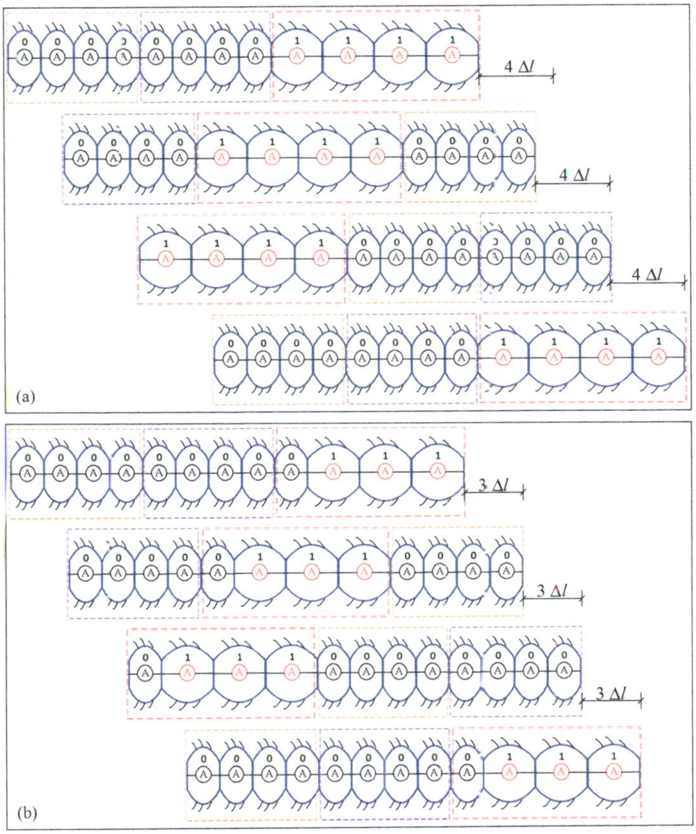

Figure 6. A gait generation demonstration for a 12-segment earthworm-like robot with two different drive modules for MG-I. A gait generation demonstration for a 12-segment robot with U-DM is shown in (**a**). The frequency of receding peristaltic wave is 1/3. The amplitude of the receding peristaltic wave is 4. A gait generation demonstration for a 12-segment robot under B-DM ("0111") is shown in (**b**). The frequency of receding peristaltic wave is 1/3. The amplitude of the receding peristaltic wave is 3.

3.2. *Driven Module Waves with Overlapping*

3.2.1. Generation Algorithm for MG-II

As the results in references [17,18] for the peristaltic waves, as the actuated segments transmit from head to tail in the locomotion robot, the optimal gait is obtained, which is called the phase difference gait. For driven module gait generation in this study, the phase difference is considered the modular gait. In this modular gait, the number of transmission segments, n_T, is less than the sum of the number of body segments in the driven module (n_{td} or n_p). For MG-II, the number of transmission actuated segments, n_T, satisfies

$$1 \leq n_T < n_{td}, \; or \; 1 \leq n_T < n_p \tag{9}$$

In contrast to MG-I, the parameters for MG-II, $\{k, n_p, n_T, TN\}$ or $\{k, n_{td}, n_T, TN\}$, are given initially. The state switch in the process of peristaltic waves transmission is defined as

$$s_i^{t_j} = s_{Mod[i-1+j\cdot n_T, TN]+1}^{t_0} \quad (10)$$

A generation algorithm for MG-II is proposed to obtain the locomotion gait, according to the receding peristaltic wave and the state transmission rule, given as Equation (10). The routine of the algorithm is shown in Figure 7, which can generate all the permissible locomotion gaits.

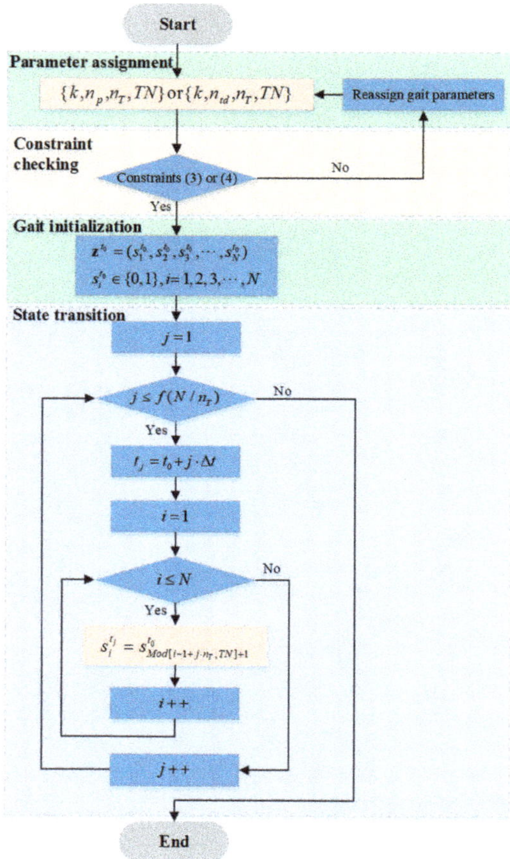

Figure 7. Routine of the generation algorithm for MG-II.

3.2.2. Illustrations for MG-II

With the proposed gait generation algorithm in Figure 7, Figure 8 demonstrates the locomotion gait transmissions of the 12-segment robot with MG-II under two cases: total or partial actuated segments. Figure 8a shows a gait generation demonstration for a 12-segment robot under U-DM, while Figure 8b shows a gait generation demonstration for a 12-segment robot under B-DM. Assuming that each driven module contains four segments, the number of transmission segments is less than the number of segments in one driven module (for the driven mode with MG-II). Then, overlapped segments can occur in the transmission of the driven module. The overlapped segments keep the state of the previous movement, which are called "K" segments, as shown in Figure 8.

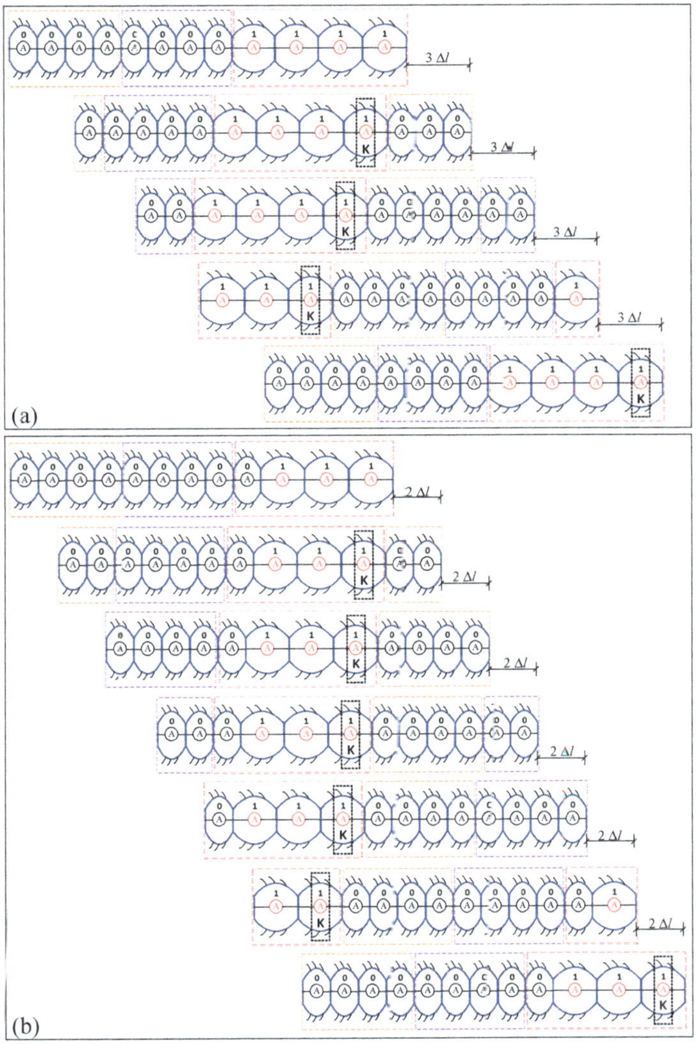

Figure 8. The gait generation demonstrations for a 12-segment robot with two different driven modules with MG-II. The "K" indicates keeping the previous state segments. A gait generation demonstration for a 12-segment robot under U-DM is shown in (**a**). The frequency of the receding peristaltic wave is 1/4. The amplitude of the receding peristaltic wave is 3. A gait generation demonstration for a 12-segment robot under B-DM ("0111") is shown in (**b**). The frequency of the receding peristaltic wave is 1/6. The amplitude of the receding peristaltic wave is 2.

Regarding the gait generation in Figure 8a for a 12-segment robot under U-DM with four actuated segments, there is a "K" segment when transmitting the three segments every time. The number of transmission segments is equal to three-quarters of the module phase difference. The number of body segments in the U-DM equals the sum of the number of transmission segments and the number of "K" segments. The earthworm-like locomotion robot advances 3 Δl with each transmission of the U-DM. In this gait module mode, locomotion speed depends only on the number of transmission segments.

For the B-DM with gait generation, as per Figure 8b, the body state of the B-DM indicates "0111". The earthworm-like robot advances 2 Δl with each transmission of the B-DM. The locomotion speed is related to the number of actuated segments and the number of transmission segments. There is only one "K" segment when transmitting two segments in every transmission, as shown in Figure 8b, since there is a nonactuated segment at the tail end of the driven module (looking from right to left). The number of "K" segments is related to the arrangement of the actuated segments and the nonactuated segments in the driven module.

4. Locomotion Simulation

In Sections 2 and 3, the driven module, the modular gait generation algorithm, and the illustrations for locomotion are given. A simulation of the locomotion of an earthworm-like robot based on a dielectric elastomer actuator is analyzed in this section. It is stated that the earthworm-like locomotion robot can realize crawling locomotion via the combination of anchoring constraint and gait.

4.1. The Locomotion Simulation of an Earthworm-like Robot

In order to simulate the locomotion of the earthworm-like robot, a flow chart of the calculations, which consists of three parts, is shown in Figure 9. It is assumed that each movement of the peristaltic wave adopts complete anchorage without slip. First, the parameters, including the geometric parameters (initial body length l_0; the number of body segments TN) and material parameters (the linear spring with stiffness k, spring stiffness k_i, the viscous coefficient c_i, and the equivalent mass m) are assigned. Then, after the input excitation voltage, the x_i is calculated by Equation (1). The minimum and maximum points of x_i are stored with $LMin[i]$ and $LMax[i]$, respectively. The body length l_i (t) of the actuated segment can be calculated by Equation (2). Finally, taking the position of the last body segment, p_{last}, as a reference point, the peristalsis locomotion p_i path of the earthworm-like robot is obtained by updating the coordinates of the body segment, according to

$$p_i = p_{last} + \sum_{m=i}^{TN} l_{TN-m+i} \tag{11}$$

According to the routine of the earthworm-like robot locomotion simulation shown in Figure 9, a 12-segment earthworm-like locomotion robot is used for numerical illustration. The results of the modular gait transmission and displacement are shown for the unbroken/broken driven module under driven module waves with/without overlapping. Figure 10 shows the gait generation and locomotion for U-DM with three/four actuated segments under MG-I. For the earthworm-like robot with only one driven module, the number of actuated segments within the driven module determines the frequency and amplitude of the receding peristaltic wave. The characteristics of the wave determine the robot locomotion performance. In Figure 10a, the frequency of the receding peristaltic wave is 1/4, and the amplitude of the receding peristaltic wave is 3. In Figure 10b, the frequency of the receding peristaltic wave is 1/3, and the amplitude of the receding peristaltic wave is 4. Locomotion performance is positively correlated with the amplitude of the receding peristaltic wave. As shown in Figure 10, the earthworm-like robot with the driven module of four actuated segments has better locomotion performance than an earthworm-like robot with three actuated segments as the driven module.

Figure 11 shows the gait generation and locomotion for one U-DM with four actuated segments. The locomotion displacements of the 12-segment robot under MG-II are shown in Figure 11. For the case in Figure 11a, two segments overlap in the driven module. The frequency of the receding peristaltic wave is 1/6, and the amplitude of the receding peristaltic wave is 2. The earthworm-like robot stretches two segments every time it updates, generating a displacement of 2 Δl. For the case in Figure 11b, when the number of transmission segments is three, it assumes that one segment overlaps. The frequency of the receding peristaltic wave is 1/4, and the amplitude of the receding peristaltic wave is 3. The earthworm-like robot stretches three segments every time it updates, generating a displacement of 3 Δl. Therefore, the locomotion speed of the earthworm-like robot is positively correlated with the amplitude of the receding peristaltic wave.

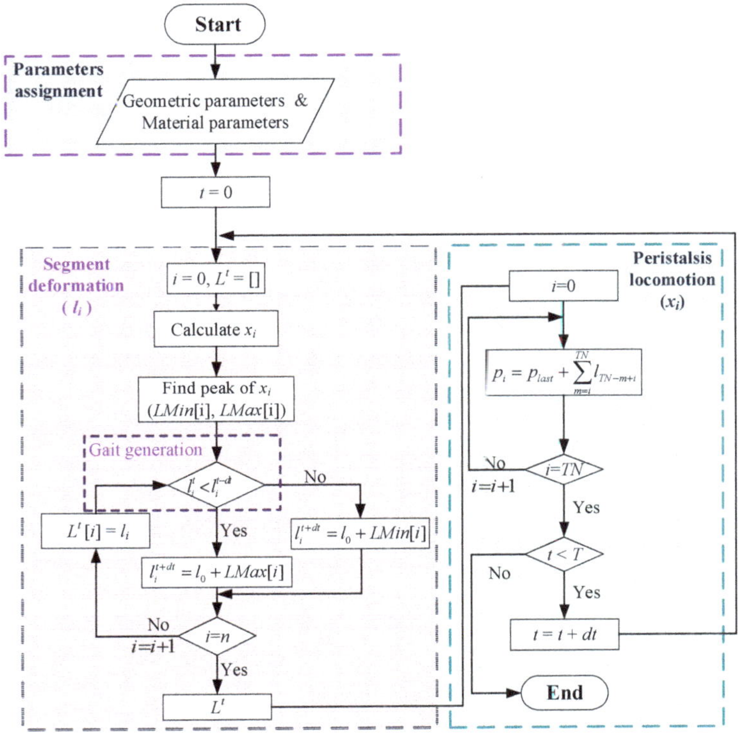

Figure 9. Routine of locomotion simulation of the earthworm-like robot driven by ultra-low frequency excitation.

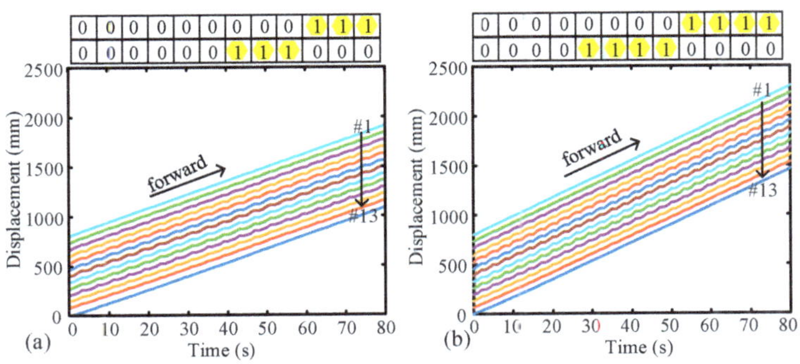

Figure 10. Locomotion simulations of a 12-segment earthworm-like robot based on U-DM under MG-I. The line located in the number is the locomotion tracks of the body segments. (**a**) The U-DM contains three actuated segments. (**b**) The U-DM consists of four actuated segments.

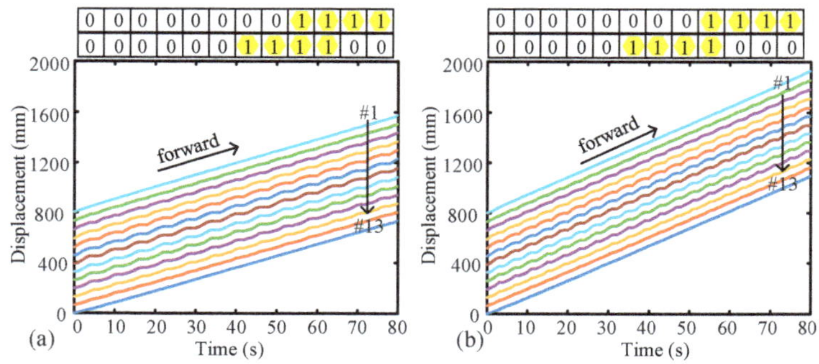

Figure 11. Locomotion simulations of a 12-segment earthworm-like robot based on U-DM with MG-II. The line located in the number is the locomotion tracks of the body segments. The driven module consists of four actuated segments. (**a**) The transmission segments contain two segments. (**b**) The transmission segments contain three segments.

Figure 12 shows the locomotion for B-DM under MG-I. For the two cases compared in Figure 12, the driven modules both consist of four segments. In Figure 12a, two segments are assumed to be broken, while in Figure 12b, only one segment is broken. In Figure 12a, the frequency of the receding peristaltic wave is 1/3, and the amplitude of the receding peristaltic wave is 2. In Figure 12b, the frequency of the receding peristaltic wave is 1/3, and the amplitude of the receding peristaltic wave is 3. In the B-DM mode under MG-I, the fewer the broken segments, the greater the amplitude of the receding peristaltic wave, and a faster speed can be obtained. That is, compared to the locomotion speeds between the two cases, this reveals that the more segments that are kept actuated, the faster the movement of the robot.

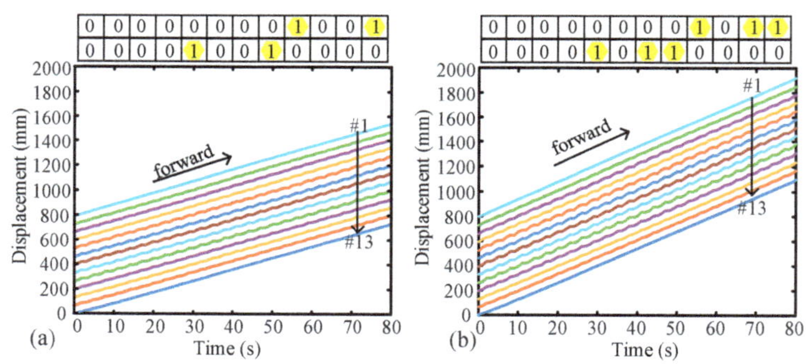

Figure 12. Locomotion simulations of a 12-segment earthworm-like robot based on B-DM with MG-I. The line located in the number is the locomotion tracks of the body segments. (**a**) The B-DM for four body segments has two actuated segments ("1001"). (**b**) The B-DM for four body segments has three actuated segments ("1011").

Figure 13 shows the locomotion for B-DM under MG-II. The B-DM consists of three actuated segments and one nonactuated segment ("1011"). As two segments are transmitted at a time, there are two segments that are overlapping waves, as shown in Figure 13a. The frequency of the receding peristaltic wave is 1/6, and the amplitude of the receding peristaltic wave is 2. When the number of transmission segments is three, there is one segment that is an overlapping wave, as shown in Figure 13b. The frequency of the receding peristaltic wave is 1/4, and the amplitude of the receding peristaltic wave is 2. Therefore, a faster frequency can also obtain greater speed. When more actuated segments are transmitted at a time, the earthworm-like robot can obtain a faster speed.

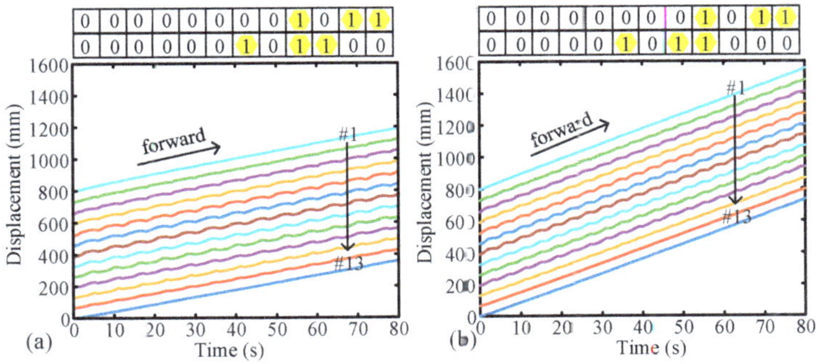

Figure 13. Locomotion simulations of a 12-segment earthworm-like robot based on B-DM with MG-II. The line located in the number is the locomotion tracks of body segments. Three actuated segments in the B-DM of four body segments ("1011"). (**a**) The transmission segments consist of two segments. (**b**) The transmission segments consist of three segments.

4.2. Gait Analysis and Discussions

Through the gait generation analysis for kinematics, the average speeds of the earthworm-like locomotion robot in different modes are obtained, as shown in Table 1. Based on the driven characteristics of a dielectric elastomer actuator, the deformations of the dielectric elastomer actuator gradually reach a stable value with an increase in actuator time. Δl is selected as the baseline to unify a comparison of the average speeds. Δl is the maximum value of Δl_{ij}. The average speed of one segment is $\overline{V} = \Delta l/\Delta t$. This shows that the value of the average speed is dependent on the parameters of the driven modes rather than the number of total body segments *TN*. Thus, an improvement in locomotion performance can be realized by the optimization of the driven modes.

Table 1. The average speeds of the different locomotion modes of the earthworm-like robot.

Modes	Constraint Conditions	The Average Speeds
The U-DM with MG-I	$k \geq 1, n_{td} \geq 1$, $TN \geq (k+1)n_{td}$; $n_T = n_{td}$.	$V = \frac{1}{\Delta t}\sum_{j=1}^{k}\sum_{i=1}^{n_{td}} \Delta l_{ij} \leq k n_{td}\overline{V}$.
The U-DM with MG-II	$k \geq 1, n_{td} \geq 1$, $TN \geq (k+1)n_{td}$; $1 \leq n_T < n_{td}$.	$V = \frac{1}{\Delta t}\sum_{j=1}^{k}\sum_{i=1}^{n_T} \Delta l_{ij} \leq k n_T\overline{V}$.
The B-DM with MG-I	$k \geq 1, n_{pa} \geq 1, n_{pr} \geq 1$, $n_p = n_{pa} + n_{pr}$, $TN \geq k n_p$; $n_T = n_p$.	$V = \frac{1}{\Delta t}\sum_{j=1}^{k}\sum_{i=1}^{n_{pa}} \Delta l_{ij} \leq k n_{pa}\overline{V}$.
The B-DM with MG-II	$k \geq 1, n_{pa} \geq 1, n_{pr} \geq 1$, $n_p = n_{pa} + n_{pr}$, $TN \geq k n_p$; $1 \leq n_T < n_p$.	$V = \frac{1}{\Delta t}\sum_{j=1}^{k}\sum_{i=1}^{n_T} \Delta l_{ij} \leq k n_T\overline{V}, (if: 1 \leq n_T < n_{pa})$; $V = \frac{1}{\Delta t}\sum_{j=1}^{k}\sum_{i=1}^{n_{pa}} \Delta l_{ij} \leq k n_{pa}\overline{V}, (if: n_{pa} \leq n_T < n_p)$.

Table 2 analyzes the upper limit of the average speeds with different locomotion modes when the earthworm-like robot has one driven module. For the driven module with three segments, the maximum locomotion speed is $3\overline{V}$. For the driven module with four segments, there are four locomotion modes. When all segments in the driven module are actuated, the average speed is the fastest (up to $4\overline{V}$) under the driven module with MG-I. As the driven module has a broken segment in it, the average speed can reach $3\overline{V}$, which is 75% of the maximum locomotion speed of the U-DM. The average speed ($3\overline{V}$) is the same as the maximum locomotion speed of the three-segment driven module, and this is better than the average speed of the four-segment driven module with MG-II. According to the analysis, the desired locomotion speed of the earthworm-like robot can be obtained by choosing the appropriate locomotion mode when there are broken or overloaded segments in the earthworm-like robot.

Table 2. The average speeds when $k = 1$.

The Number of Body Segments in a Driven Module (n)	Driven Modules	Wave Transmission Modes	Average Speeds
n=3	U-DM	MG-I	$V = 3\,\overline{V}.$
		MG-II	$n_T = 1 : V_1 = \overline{V};$ $n_T = 2 : V_2 = 2\,\overline{V}.$
n=4	U-DM	MG-I	$V = 4\,\overline{V}.$
		MG-II	$n_T = 1 : V_1 = \overline{V};$ $n_T = 2 : V_2 = 2\,\overline{V};$ $n_T = 3 : V_3 = 3\,\overline{V}.$
	B-DM ($n_{pa} = 3$, $n_{pr} = 1$)	MG-I	$V = 3\,\overline{V}.$
		MG-II	$n_T = 1 : V_1 = \overline{V};$ $n_T = 2 : V_2 = 2\,\overline{V};$ $n_T = 3 : V_3 = 3\,\overline{V}.$

For the same number of body segments, *TN*, the average speed is positively correlated with the number of driven modules, the number of actuated body segments, and the number of transmission segments. The average speed does not depend on the number of segments of the earthworm-like robot, *TN*. The optimal phase difference gait control makes the earthworm-like robot obtain an effective average speed in related work [15]. However, with an increase in robot body segments, its weight also increases, resulting in the locomotion speed saturation phenomenon. When compared with the optimal phase-difference gait control of the servo-driven rigid-body robot, the modular gait control shows better performance on the light flexibility robot. There is no saturation phenomenon regarding the average speed with an increase in the number of body segments. When the proportion of the actuated segments is larger, the robot has a greater speed. More importantly, different modular gait control designs can compensate for the lost mobility of the robot due to the inoperable parts of its body segments.

Because the mass of the body segments of the rigid-body earthworm-like robot is large, a large number of body segments leads to a heavy load. Lumping resistance will lead to a decrease in the locomotion efficiency of the earthworm-like robot. For the robots with dielectric elastomer actuators and multiple body segments, it will not be difficult to move forward because of the light weight of the earthworm-like robot. Therefore, this is an important reason for the use of soft, lightweight actuators in earthworm-like locomotion robots.

5. Conclusions

In this paper, driven modules and modular gaits that are realized by using soft actuators due to their low weight and flexibility are proposed. Two driven modules and two locomotion transmission modes are analyzed. For the different driven modules, we give the gait generation algorithms. When compared to rigid-body earthworm-like robots, the soft, earthworm-like robots with a modular driven mode has great advantages in locomotion performance. The soft, earthworm-like robots can locomote under ultra-low frequency excitation with appropriate shifts. Based on the gait analysis and simulation results, the main contributions of this study are summarized as follows:

1. A locomotion algorithm is proposed to simulate the locomotion of the soft, earthworm-like robot. The locomotion of a 12-segment earthworm-like robot is numerically

simulated based on different modes. The locomotion speed of the earthworm-like robot is positively correlated with the frequency and amplitude of the receding peristaltic wave. The robot can obtain higher speeds when the proportion of the actuated segments increases. For the driven module containing n segments, the maximum speed is $kn\overline{V}$;

2. The average speeds for different locomotion modes are obtained. For the dielectric-elastomer-driven robot, the proportion of the number of actuated segments strongly affects the average speed. As the proportion of the number of actuated segments increases, the average speed increases;
3. When there are failed segments in the robot, a modular gait mode can be designed to improve the locomotion speed of the robot. For the driven module, $n_{pa} = 3$ and $n_{pr} = 1$, there are three different speeds: $\overline{V}$, $2\overline{V}$, and $3\overline{V}$.

Based on the results of the modular gait generation method and the corresponding average speed, the modular driven mode has excellent locomotion performance. The theoretical analysis and simulation results of this paper provide the necessary theoretical support for the flexibility and low weight of earthworm-like locomotion robots.

Author Contributions: Conceptualization, X.S. and Z.Q.; methodology, Z.Q.; software, Z.Q.; validation, X.S. and Z.Q.; formal analysis, Z.Q.; investigation, Z.Q.; resources, Z.Q.; data curation, Z.Q.; writing—original draft preparation, Z.Q.; writing—review and editing, X.S.; visualization, X.S. and Z.Q.; supervision, X.S.; project administration, X.S.; funding acquisition, X.S. All authors have read and agreed to the published version of the manuscript.

Funding: This research was funded by National Natural Science Foundation of China grant number 12122208, 11972254, and 11932015 and the Fundamental Research Funds for Central Universities.

Institutional Review Board Statement: Not applicable.

Informed Consent Statement: Not applicable.

Data Availability Statement: All data generated or analyzed during this study are included in this published article.

Acknowledgments: The authors would like to thank the reviewers and editors for improving this manuscript.

Conflicts of Interest: The authors declare that they have no conflict of interest.

References

1. Lin, H.T.; Leisk, G.G.; Trimmer, B. GoQBot: A caterpillar-inspired soft-bodied rolling robot. *Bioinspir. Biomim.* **2011**, *6*, 026007. [CrossRef] [PubMed]
2. Li, W.-B.; Zhang, W.-M.; Zou, H.-X.; Peng, Z.-K.; Meng, G. A Fast Rolling Soft Robot Driven by Dielectric Elastomer. *IEEE/ASME Trans. Mechatron.* **2018**, *23*, 1630–1640. [CrossRef]
3. Zhong, B.; Zhang, S.; Xu, M.; Zhou, Y.; Fang, T.; Li, W. On a cpg-based hexapod robot: Amphihex-ii with variable stiffness legs. *IEEE/ASME Trans. Mechatron.* **2018**, *23*, 542–551. [CrossRef]
4. Chen, S.; Cao, Y.; Sarparast, M.; Yuan, H.; Dong, L.; Tan, X.; Cao, C. Soft Crawling Robots: Design, Actuation, and Locomotion. *Adv. Mater. Technol.* **2020**, *5*, 1900837. [CrossRef]
5. Shepherd, R.F.; Ilievski, F.; Choi, W.; Morin, S.A.; Stokes, A.A.; Mazzeo, A.D.; Chen, X.; Wang, M.; Whitesides, G.M. Multigait soft robot. *Proc. Natl. Acad. Sci. USA* **2011**, *108*, 20400–20403. [CrossRef]
6. Fang, H.; Wang, C.; Li, S.; Xu, J.; Wang, K.W. Design and experimental gait analysis of a multi-segment in-pipe robot inspired by earthworm's peristaltic locomotion. In *Bioinspiration, Biomimetics, and Bioreplication 2014*; SPIE: Bellingham, WA, USA, 2014; Volume 9055.
7. Du, Z.; Fang, H.; Xu, J. Snake-worm: A Bi-modal Locomotion Robot. *J. Bionic Eng.* **2022**, *19*, 1272–1287. [CrossRef]
8. Luo, Y.; Zhao, N.; Shen, Y.; Li, P. A Rigid Morphing Mechanism Enabled Earthworm-Like Crawling Robot. *ASME J. Mech. Robotics.* **2023**, *15*, 011008. [CrossRef]
9. Zhan, X.; Xu, J.; Fang, H. In-plane gait planning for earthworm-like metameric robots using genetic algorithm. *Bioinspir. Biomim.* **2020**, *15*, 056012. [CrossRef]
10. Zhan, X.; Fang, H.; Xu, J.; Wang, K.-W. Planar locomotion of earthworm-like metameric robots. *Int. J. Robot. Res.* **2019**, *38*, 1751–1774. [CrossRef]

11. Rafsanjani, A.; Zhang, Y.; Liu, B.; Rubinstein, S.M.; Bertoldi, K. Kirigami skins make a simple soft actuator crawl. *Sci. Robot.* **201** *3*, eaar7555. [CrossRef]
12. Kandhari, A.; Huang, Y.; Daltorio, K.A.; Chiel, H.J.; Quinn, R.D. Body stiffness in orthogonal directions oppositely affect worm-like robot turning and straight-line locomotion. *Bioinspir. Biomim.* **2018**, *13*, 026003. [CrossRef] [PubMed]
13. Kandhari, A.; Mehringer, A.; Chiel, H.J.; Quinn, R.D.; Daltorio, K.A. Design and Actuation of a Fabric-Based Worm-Like Robo *Biomimetics* **2019**, *4*, 13. [CrossRef] [PubMed]
14. Schwebke, S.; Behn, C. Worm-like robotic systems: Generation, analysis and shift of gaits using adaptive control. *Artif. Intell. Re* **2012**, *1*, p12. [CrossRef]
15. Fang, H.; Wang, C.; Li, S.; Wang, K.W.; Xu, J. A comprehensive study on the locomotion characteristics of a metameric earthworm like robot Part B: Gait analysis and experiments. *Multibody Syst. Dyn.* **2015**, *35*, 153–177. [CrossRef]
16. Santhosh, S.; Serra, M. Optimal locomotion for limbless crawlers. *Phys. Rev. E* **2022**, *106*, 024610. [CrossRef]
17. Agostinelli, D.; Alouges, F.; DeSimone, A. Peristaltic Waves as Optimal Gaits in Metameric Bio-Inspired Robots. *Front. Robot. A* **2018**, *5*, 99. [CrossRef]
18. Fang, H.; Li, S.; Wang, K.W.; Xu, J. Phase coordination and phase–velocity relationship in metameric robot locomotion. *Bioinspi Biomim.* **2015**, *10*, 066006. [CrossRef]
19. Chapman, G. Of the Movement of Worms. *J. Exp. Biol.* **1950**, *27*, 29–39. [CrossRef]
20. Quillin, K.J. Kinematic scaling of locomotion by hydrostatic animals: Ontogeny of peristaltic crawling by the earthworm lumbricus terrestris. *J. Exp. Biol.* **1999**, *202*, 661. [CrossRef]
21. Kurth, J.A.; Kier, W.M. Differences in scaling and morphology between lumbricid earthworm ecotypes. *J. Exp. Biol.* **201** *218*, 2970–2978. [CrossRef]
22. Ilami, M.; Bagheri, H.; Ahmed, R.; Skowronek, E.O.; Marvi, H. Materials, Actuators, and Sensors for Soft Bioinspired Robots. *Ad Mater.* **2021**, *33*, e2003139. [CrossRef]
23. Cianchetti, M.; Laschi, C.; Menciassi, A.; Dario, P. Biomedical applications of soft robotics. *Nat. Rev. Mater.* **2018**, *3*, 143–15 [CrossRef]
24. Hines, L.; Petersen, K.H.; Lum, G.Z.; Sitti, M. Soft Actuators for Small-Scale Robotics. *Adv. Mater.* **2017**, *29*, 1603483. [CrossRef]
25. Mosadegh, B.; Polygerinos, P.; Keplinger, C.; Wennstedt, S.; Shepherd, R.; Gupta, U.; Shim, J.; Bertoldi, K.; Walsh, C.J Whitesides, G.M. Pneumatic Networks for Soft Robotics that Actuate Rapidly. *Adv. Funct. Mater.* **2014**, *24*, 2163–2170. [CrossRef
26. Kim, W.; Seo, B.; Yu, S.Y.; Cho, K.J. Deployable soft pneumatic networks (d-pneunets) actuator with dual-morphing origam chambers for high-compactness. *IEEE Robot. Autom. Lett.* **2022**, *7*, 1262–1269. [CrossRef]
27. Guo, Y.; Liu, L.; Liu, Y.; Leng, J. Review of Dielectric Elastomer Actuators and Their Applications in Soft Robots. *Adv. Intell. Sys* **2021**, *3*. [CrossRef]
28. Calderón, A.A.; Ugalde, J.C.; Chang, L.; Zagal, J.C.; Pérez-Arancibia, N.O. An earthworm-inspired soft robot with perceptive artificial skin. *Bioinspir. Biomim.* **2019**, *14*, 056012. [CrossRef]
29. Ozkan-Aydin, Y.; Liu, B.; Ferrero, A.C.; Seidel, M.; Hammond, F.L.; Goldman, D.I. Lateral bending and buckling aids biologica and robotic earthworm anchoring and locomotion. *Bioinspir. Biomim.* **2021**, *17*, 016001. [CrossRef] [PubMed]
30. Ge, J.Z.; Calderon, A.A.; Perez-Arancibia, N.O. An earthworm-inspired soft crawling robot controlled by friction. In Proceedings of the IEEE International Conference on Robotics and Biomimetics (ROBIO), Macau, Macao, 5–8 December 2017; pp. 834–841.
31. Liang, W.; Liu, H.; Wang, K.; Qian, Z.; Ren, L.; Ren, L. Comparative study of robotic artificial actuators and biological muscle *Adv. Mech. Eng.* **2020**, *12*, 2072262428. [CrossRef]
32. Pelrine, R.; Kornbluh, R.; Pei, Q.; Joseph, J. High-Speed Electrically Actuated Elastomers with Strain Greater Than 100%. *Science* **2000**, *287*, 836–839. [CrossRef] [PubMed]
33. Gupta, U.; Qin, L.; Wang, Y.; Godaba, H.; Zhu, J. Soft robots based on dielectric elastomer actuators: A review. *Smart Mater. Struct* **2019**, *28*, 103002. [CrossRef]
34. Li, W.B.; Zhang, W.M.; Zou, H.X.; Peng, Z.K.; Meng, G. Multisegment annular dielectric elastomer actuators for soft robots. *Smar Mater. Struct.* **2018**, *27*, 115024. [CrossRef]
35. Li, B.; Chen, H.; Qiang, J.; Hu, S.; Zhu, Z.; Wang, Y. Effect of mechanical pre-stretch on the stabilization of dielectric elastomer actuation. *J. Phys. D Appl. Phys.* **2011**, *44*. [CrossRef]
36. Zhang, J.; Chen, H.; Li, D. Leakage current and induced electrical energy dissipation in nonlinear oscillation of dielectric elastomer actuators. *J. Phys. D Appl. Phys.* **2017**, *50*, 365602. [CrossRef]
37. Jiang, L.; Betts, A.; Kennedy, D.; Jerrams, S. Eliminating electromechanical instability in dielectric elastomers by employing pre-stretch. *J. Phys. D Appl. Phys.* **2016**, *49*, 265401. [CrossRef]
38. Choi, H.R.; Ryew, S.; Jung, K.M.; Kim, H.M.; Jeon, J.W.; Nam, J.D.; Maeda, R.; Tanie, K. Microrobot actuated by soft actuators based on dielectric elastomer. In Proceedings of the IEEE/RSJ International Conference on Intelligent Robots & Systems, Lausanne Switzerland, 30 September–4 October 2002.
39. Pfeil, S.; Henke, M.; Katzer, K.; Zimmermann, M.; Gerlach, G. A Worm-Like Biomimetic Crawling Robot Based on Cylindrical Dielectric Elastomer Actuators. *Front. Robot. AI* **2020**, *7*, 9. [CrossRef]
40. Du, Y.; Cao, C.; Wu, X.; Xue, J.; Wang, L.; Gao, X. A low-profile vibration crawling robot driven by a planar dielectric elastomer actuator. In Proceedings of the 2022 IEEE International Conference on Real-time Computing and Robotics (RCAR), Guiyang China, 17–22 July 2022; pp. 413–418.

Mihai, D.; David, R.C.; Robert, J.W. A high speed soft robot based on dielectric elastomer actuators. *IEEE Int. Conf. Robot. Autom. (ICRA)* **2017**, *5*, 466–474.
Zhao, W.; Zhang, Y.; Wang, N. Soft robotics: Research, challenges, and prospects. *J. Robot. Mechatron.* **2021**, *33*, 45–68. [CrossRef]
Xu, L.; Chen, H.-Q.; Zou, J.; Dong, W.-T.; Gu, G.-Y.; Zhu, L.-M.; Zhu, X.-Y. Bio-inspired annelid robot: A dielectric elastomer actuated soft robot. *Bioinspir. Biomim.* **2017**, *12*, 025003. [CrossRef]
Lu, X.; Wang, K.; Hu, T. Development of an annelid-like peristaltic crawling soft robot using dielectric elastomer actuators. *Bioinspir. Biomim.* **2020**, *15*, 046012. [CrossRef]
Nguyen, V.D.; La, N.T. An improvement of vibration-driven locomotion module for capsule robots. *Mech. Based Des. Struct. Mach.* **2020**, *50*, 1658–1672. [CrossRef]
Wu, C.; Yan, H.; Cai, A.; Cao, C. A Dielectric Elastomer Actuator-Driven Vibro-Impact Crawling Robot. *Micromachines* **2022**, *13*, 1660. [CrossRef] [PubMed]
Akbarimajd, A.; Sotoudeh, N. Design and motion analysis of vibration-driven small robot Rizeh. *Adv. Robot.* **2014**, *28*, 105–117. [CrossRef]
Wang, X.J.; Meng, L.L.; Yao, Y.H.; Li, H.G. A vibration-driven locomotion robot excited by time-varying stiffness. *Int. J. Mech. Sci.* **2023**, *243*, 108009. [CrossRef]
Diao, B.; Zhang, X.; Fang, H.; Xu, J. Bi-objective optimization for improving the locomotion performance of the vibration-driven robot. *Arch. Appl. Mech.* **2021**, *91*, 2073–2088. [CrossRef]
Gu, G.-Y.; Gupta, U.; Zhu, J.; Zhu, L.-M.; Zhu, X. Modeling of Viscoelastic Electromechanical Behavior in a Soft Dielectric Elastomer Actuator. *IEEE Trans. Robot.* **2017**, *33*, 1263–1271. [CrossRef]

applied sciences

MDPI

Article

A New Vibration Controller Design Method Using Reinforcement Learning and FIR Filters: A Numerical and Experimental Study

Xingxing Feng [1,2], Hong Chen [1,*], Gang Wu [1], Anfu Zhang [1] and Zhigao Zhao [1]

1 Wuhan 2nd Ship Design and Research Institute, Wuhan 430205, China
2 School of Naval Architecture and Ocean Engineering, Huazhong University of Science and Technology, Wuhan 430074, China
* Correspondence: chen_hong0628@163.com

Abstract: High-dimensional high-frequency continuous-vibration control problems often have very complex dynamic behaviors. It is difficult for the conventional control methods to obtain appropriate control laws from such complex systems to suppress the vibration. This paper proposes a new vibration controller by using reinforcement learning (RL) and a finite-impulse-response (FIR) filter. First, a simulator with enough physical fidelity was built for the vibration system. Then, the deep deterministic policy gradient (DDPG) algorithm interacted with the simulator to find a near-optimal control policy to meet the specified goals. Finally, the control policy, represented as a neural network, was run directly on a controller in real-world experiments with high-dimensional and high-frequency dynamics. The simulation results show that the maximum peak values of the power-spectrum-density (PSD) curves at specific frequencies can be reduced by over 63%. The experimental results show that the peak values of the PSD curves at specific frequencies were reduced by more than 47% (maximum over 52%). The numerical and experimental results indicate that the proposed controller can significantly attenuate various vibrations within the range from 50 Hz to 60 Hz.

Keywords: active vibration control; reinforcement learning; deep deterministic policy gradient (DDPG); neural network; finite-impulse-response filter; experiment

1. Introduction

Active vibration control is a challenging problem with high-dimensional, high-frequency and complex dynamics. Many conventional vibration controllers have been presented to solve this problem. For instance, PID controllers [1–4], which are not very suitable for high-dimensional vibration-control problems, and the determination of the controller parameters requires substantial design effort; LQR controllers [5–7], which are suitable for the systems that can be formulated by state-space equations; FxLMS controllers [8–10], which require the construction of a reference signal and the identification of a secondary path. It was found that, although these conventional controllers are usually effective, they require substantial engineering effort, design effort and expertise.

A new simple method for vibration-controller design is made possible by using RL. The parameters of the controller are automatically obtained by reinforcement-learning algorithms. Moreover, the new method is a data-driven method, which means that it does not require the physical information of the system, such as the mass matrix, stiffness matrix or damping matrix. Therefore, the new method requires less engineering effort and design effort in comparison with the conventional controller design methods.

Actually, RL has been widely used for building agents to learn complex control in complex environments, and it has achieved some successes in a variety of domains [11–15]. Moreover, its applicability has been extended to the vibration-control domain, such as the vibration control of the suspension [16–19], manipulator [20–22], magneto rheological damper [23,24], flexible beam/plate [25–27], etc.

In suspension vibration-control problems [16–19], the controllers are trained to suppress the vibration caused by road profiles, and they are only validated by numerical simulations. Bucak et al. [16] used a stochastic actor–critic reinforcement-learning control algorithm to provide control forces to a nonlinear quarter-car active-suspension model subjected to a sinusoidal road profile. The simulation results showed that the new algorithm stabilized the suspension very quickly. Kim et al. [17] applied the DDPG (deep deterministic policy gradient) algorithm to the vibration-control simulation of a quarter-vehicle active-suspension model. The quarter-vehicle model with a trained agent (controller) was tested at the low-frequency cosine road and step road, which confirmed the effectiveness of the DDPG algorithm. Liu et al. [18] presented an improved DDPG algorithm using empirical samples, and they applied it to a quarter-vehicle semiactive-suspension vibration-control simulation. The simulation results showed that, compared with the passive suspension, the semiactive suspension with the improved DDPG algorithm could better adapt to various road levels and vehicle speeds. Han et al. [19] presented a PPO-based vibration-control strategy for a vehicle semiactive-suspension system, in which the designed reward function realizes the dynamic adjustment according to the road-condition changes. The simulation results showed that the body acceleration was reduced by 46.93% under the continuously changing road. These suspension vibration-control studies mainly considered single-input control problems.

In flexible-manipulator control problems [20–22], the controllers are trained to suppress the transient vibration, as well as to follow the given trajectories. Ouyang et al. [20] applied the actor–critic algorithm for a single-link flexible manipulator in an attempt to suppress the vibration due to its flexibility and lightweight structure. In the experiment, when the single link was given a desired position, the reinforcement-learning control could obtain a satisfactory tracking and vibration-suppression performance. He et al. [21] investigated the actor–critic reinforcement-learning control of a flexible two-link manipulator by a numerical and experimental study. In the simulation and experiment, when the links were given desired trajectories, the reinforcement-learning control had feasibility and stability in suppressing the vibration. Long et al. [22] presented a combined-vibration-control method for a hybrid-structured flexible manipulator based on sliding-mode control and reinforcement learning. The experimental results showed that the combined control method had good robustness to the tip trajectory and tip-load mass under the condition that the learning parameters of the controller remained unchanged.

In terms of the vibration-control problems of magneto rheological dampers [23,24], as the controller was designed based on Q-learning [28], they are theoretically not suitable for high-dimensional continuous-action spaces. Park et al. [23] proposed a novel reinforcement-learning method based on Q-learning for the vibration control of a magneto rheological elastomer. The experimental results showed that the proposed method could minimize the vibration level with respect to the tonal disturbance or sine-sweep disturbance. Yuan et al. [24] proposed a semiactive control strategy of a magneto rheological damper based on the Q-learning algorithm, and the simulation results showed that it was better than simple bang-bang control.

In the vibration-control problems of flexible beams or plates [25–27], accurate finite element models are constructed as the simulation environment, and then reinforcement-learning algorithms, such as the soft actor–critic algorithm, DDPG algorithm and multiagent twin delayed DDPG algorithm, are applied to train the vibration controllers. Finally, the well-trained controllers are validated in experiments. The simulation and experimental results demonstrate that the controllers trained by the proposed RL algorithms have better control effects compared with PD control. However, an accurate finite element model is difficult to build for complex vibrating systems, and the proper PD parameters are difficult to estimate.

Although RL algorithms were applied in the above vibration-control research, they mainly considered vibration-control problems of low dimension (for instance, the single-input suspension control problem) and simple dynamics, such as link, beam, plate, quarter-car, etc., simulation models. However, this paper solved the multi-input/multi-output real-world vibration-control problem within a frequency range by using RL and an FIR filter, which was inspired by the least-mean-square (LMS) adaptive algorithm. To the best of the authors' knowledge, this is the first time that the high-dimensional high-frequency vibration-control problem has been solved by using reinforcement learning.

In this paper, the FIR filter was used to establish the transfer-function channels (i.e., the simulator) from the exciter and actuators to the sensors. Then, a reinforcement-learning algorithm interacted with the simulator to find a near-optimal control policy to meet the specified goals. Furthermore, the RL-based controller was verified in high-dimensional high-frequency vibration-control experiments.

The rest of this paper is organized as follow. First, the vibration-control problem is formulated. Second, a new method for a vibration-controller design through RL is presented. Third, the RL-designed vibration controller is experimentally verified. Finally, the conclusions are drawn.

2. Problem Formulation

Figure 1 shows the schematic diagram of the vibration-control system. The well-trained neural network is compiled into binary code, and it is then run on the controller hardware. The controller receives four acceleration signals from the sensors, and it outputs four control signals according to the control policy. Then, the control signals are sent to the four electromagnetic actuators to generate four control forces, which are expected to reduce the vibration in real time.

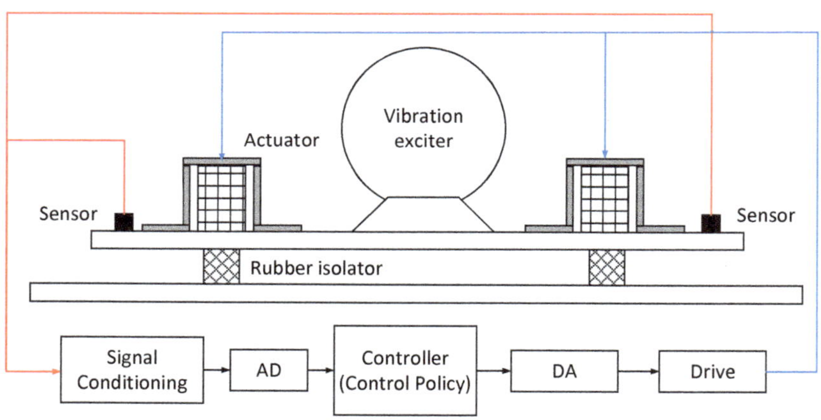

Figure 1. Schematic diagram of vibration-control system.

This is a high-dimensional high-frequency vibration-control problem. Our goal was to design an effective controller through reinforcement learning that can reduce vibrations under different vibration excitations.

3. Method

3.1. Method Overview

First, as shown in Figure 2, a simulator was built for the vibration system with an FIR filter. The vibration system has 5 inputs and 4 outputs. The 5 inputs refer to the forces of the vibration exciter and 4 electromagnetic actuators. The 4 outputs refer to the 4 acceleration signals. In detail, we used experimental data to identify an FIR filter, which acted as the simulator. We gave specified force signals to the vibration exciter and electromagnetic actuators, which applied forces to the vibration system. Both the force signals and corresponding acceleration signals were recorded and used to identify the FIR filter.

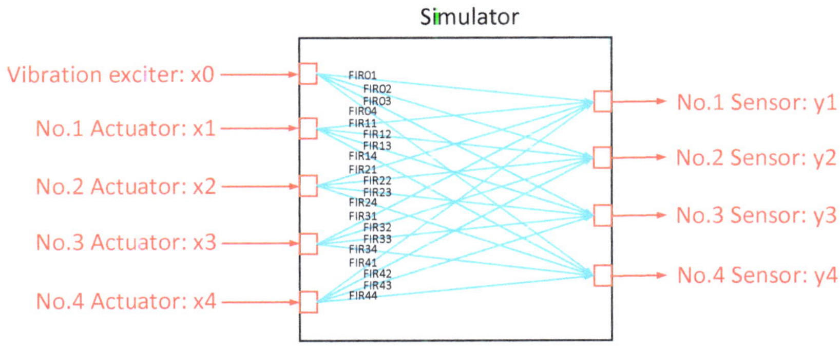

Figure 2. Depiction of the simulator for the vibration system. The simulator, which has enough physical fidelity, receives force signals and outputs acceleration signals.

Then, an RL algorithm collected data and found a control policy through the interaction with an environment, as shown in Figure 3. The simulator, which had enough physical fidelity, was used to describe the evolution of the acceleration signals. The RL algorithm used the collected simulator data to find a near-optimal policy with respect to the specified reward function.

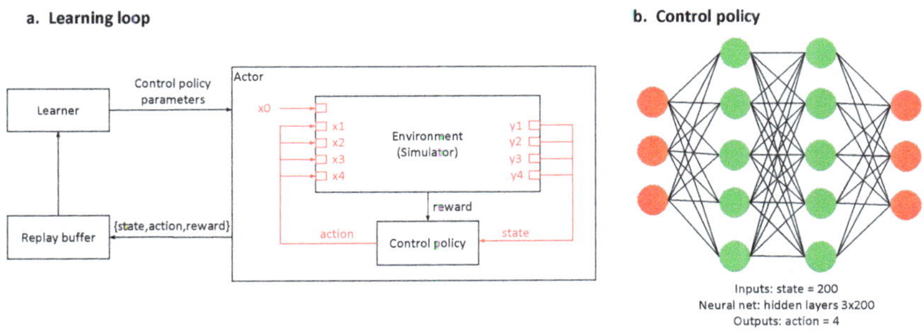

Figure 3. The RL algorithm and control policy. (**a**) Depiction of the learning loop. The controller sends force commands on the basis of the acceleration state and control targets. (**b**) The control policy is a feed-forward neural network, with three hidden layers, which takes measurements and outputs force commands.

Many RL algorithms have been presented to solve the optimal solution, including value-based algorithms, such as the DQN [29], DDQN [30], prioritized DDQN [31], dueling DDQN [32], distributional DQN [33], noisy DQN [34] and Rainbow [35] algorithms. These value-based algorithms are suitable for problems with discrete and low-dimensional action spaces, such as electronic games, and therefore they were not used in this work. The DDPG [36] algorithm was chosen for the vibration control in this work, as it is suitable for high-dimensional continuous-action spaces. The DDPG is a model-free off-policy actor–critic algorithm that uses deep networks and that can learn the control policy. The representation of the control policy of the actor is restricted, as it must run on hardware with real-time guarantees. Therefore, we used a fast five-layer feed-forward neural network in the actor. The actor was trained by the PyTorch software package.

Finally, the control policy was bundled with the associated experiment control targets into an executable using a compiler tailored towards real-time control at 1 kHz. The deterministic nature of the DDPG gives a deterministic policy to execute on the plant. Although the actor is trained by the PyTorch software package, the well-trained actor is rewritten by the Simulink and NI/Veristand software packages, where the NI/Veristand acts as a plug-in of Simulink. The actor written in Simulink is then compiled into binary code. Finally, the binary code is run on the NI controller hardware.

3.2. Vibration-System Simulator

3.2.1. FIR Filter

An adaptive FIR filter was used for building the simulator. As shown in Figure 4, in order to implement an FIR filter, the input signal ($\mathbf{x}(n)$) and desired output signal ($\mathbf{d}(n)$) should be given. Note that the $\mathbf{x}(n)$ and $\mathbf{d}(n)$ are both vectors:

$$\mathbf{x}(n) = [x(n)\ \ x(n-1)\ \ \cdots\ \ x(x-N+1)]^T \tag{1}$$

$$\mathbf{d}(n) = [d(n)\ \ d(n-1)\ \ \cdots\ \ d(x-N+1)]^T \tag{2}$$

where N is the length of the filter. The given input signal ($\mathbf{x}(n)$) of the filter is known, and the filter output signal ($\mathrm{y}(n)$) is formulated as:

$$\mathrm{y}(n) = \boldsymbol{\omega}^T(n)\mathbf{x}(\mathrm{n}) \tag{3}$$

where n indicates the time sequence, and $\boldsymbol{\omega}(n)$ is the vector of the filter weights.

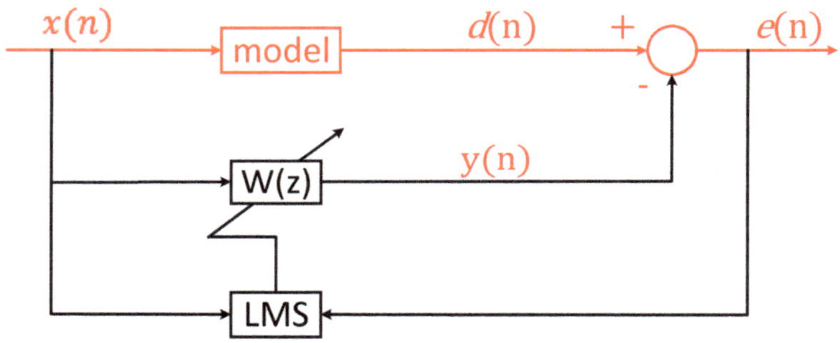

Figure 4. Schematic diagram of FIR filter.

The output signal ($\mathrm{y}(n)$) is the estimate of the desired signal ($d(n)$). The error ($e(n)$) between the output signal ($\mathrm{y}(n)$) and desired output signal ($d(n)$) is defined as:

$$e(n) = d(n) - y(n) \tag{4}$$

We estimate the filter weights ($\boldsymbol{\omega}(n)$) to minimize the error ($e(n)$) by using the least-mean-square (LMS) algorithm [37]:

$$\boldsymbol{\omega}(n+1) = \boldsymbol{\omega}(n) + 2\mu e(n)\mathbf{x}(n) \tag{5}$$

where μ is the step size.

The filter weights ($\boldsymbol{\omega}(n)$) can be easily well estimated if the appropriate input signal ($\mathbf{x}(n)$) and desired output signal ($\mathbf{d}(n)$) are given. In this work, the input signal and desired output signal are the experimental data.

3.2.2. Simulator Established with FIR Filter

The simulator can be considered as a 5-input/4-output filter. The input signals are denoted as $\mathbf{x}_0(n)$, $\mathbf{x}_1(n)$, $\mathbf{x}_2(n)$, $\mathbf{x}_3(n)$ and $\mathbf{x}_4(n)$, where $\mathbf{x}_0(n)$ stands for the force signal of the vibration exciter, and $\mathbf{x}_1(n)$, $\mathbf{x}_2(n)$, $\mathbf{x}_3(n)$, $\mathbf{x}_4(n)$ stand for the force signals of the 4 electromagnetic actuators. The desired-output signals are denoted as $\mathbf{d}_1(n)$, $\mathbf{d}_2(n)$, $\mathbf{d}_3(n)$, $\mathbf{d}_4(n)$, which stand for the acceleration signals. Moreover, $\mathbf{y}_j(n)$ is the estimate of the desired output ($\mathbf{d}_j(n), j = 1,2,3,4$).

Obviously, there are $5 \times 4 = 20$ channels between the inputs and desired outputs. Each channel can be expressed by an FIR filter. It is assumed that the symbol C_{ij} stands for the filter between $\mathbf{x}_i(n)$ and $\mathbf{d}_j(n)$, where $i = 0,1,2,3,4$ and $j = 1,2,3,4$.

Note that $\mathbf{d}_1(n)$ is the open-loop response under excitations of $\mathbf{x}_0(n), \mathbf{x}_1(n), \mathbf{x}_2(n), \mathbf{x}_3(n), \mathbf{x}_4(n)$. Thus, the estimate of $d_1(n)$ can be formulated as follows:

$$\begin{aligned} y_1(n) = \boldsymbol{\omega}_{01}^T(n)\mathbf{x}_0(n) + \boldsymbol{\omega}_{11}^T(n)\mathbf{x}_1(n) + \boldsymbol{\omega}_{21}^T(n)\mathbf{x}_2(n) + \\ \boldsymbol{\omega}_{31}^T(n)\mathbf{x}_3(n) + \boldsymbol{\omega}_{41}^T(n)\mathbf{x}_4(n) \end{aligned} \tag{6}$$

where $y_1(n)$ is the estimate of $d_1(n)$, and $\boldsymbol{\omega}_{i1}(n)$ are the filter weights of filter C_{i1}. It can be found that $y_1(n)$ is the superposition of the outputs of 5 FIR filters. Similarly, the estimates of $d_2(n), d_3(n), d_4(n)$ are formulated as:

$$\begin{aligned} y_2(n) = \boldsymbol{\omega}_{02}^T(n)\mathbf{x}_0(n) + \boldsymbol{\omega}_{12}^T(n)\mathbf{x}_1(n) + \boldsymbol{\omega}_{22}^T(n)\mathbf{x}_2(n) + \\ \boldsymbol{\omega}_{32}^T(n)\mathbf{x}_3(n) + \boldsymbol{\omega}_{42}^T(n)\mathbf{x}_4(n) \end{aligned} \tag{7}$$

$$\begin{aligned} y_3(n) = \boldsymbol{\omega}_{03}^T(n)\mathbf{x}_0(n) + \boldsymbol{\omega}_{13}^T(n)\mathbf{x}_1(n) + \boldsymbol{\omega}_{23}^T(n)\mathbf{x}_2(n) + \\ \boldsymbol{\omega}_{33}^T(n)\mathbf{x}_3(n) + \boldsymbol{\omega}_{43}^T(n)\mathbf{x}_4(n) \end{aligned} \tag{8}$$

$$\begin{aligned} y_4(n) = \boldsymbol{\omega}_{04}^T(n)\mathbf{x}_0(n) + \boldsymbol{\omega}_{14}^T(n)\mathbf{x}_1(n) + \boldsymbol{\omega}_{24}^T(n)\mathbf{x}_2(n) + \\ \boldsymbol{\omega}_{34}^T(n)\mathbf{x}_3(n) + \boldsymbol{\omega}_{44}^T(n)\mathbf{x}_4(n) \end{aligned} \tag{9}$$

Equations (6)–(9) can be written in the compact form of Equation (10), which is the simulator of the vibration system:

$$\mathbf{y}(n) = \mathbf{W}(n)\mathbf{X}(n) \tag{10}$$

where

$$\mathbf{y}(n) = \begin{bmatrix} y_1(n) & y_2(n) & y_3(n) & y_4(n) \end{bmatrix}^T$$
$$\mathbf{X}(n) = \begin{bmatrix} \mathbf{x}_0^T(n) & \mathbf{x}_1^T(n) & \mathbf{x}_2^T(n) & \mathbf{x}_3^T(n) & \mathbf{x}_4^T(n) \end{bmatrix}^T$$
$$\mathbf{W}(n) = \begin{bmatrix} \boldsymbol{\omega}_{01}^T(n) & \boldsymbol{\omega}_{11}^T(n) & \cdots & \boldsymbol{\omega}_{41}^T(n) \\ \boldsymbol{\omega}_{02}^T(n) & \boldsymbol{\omega}_{13}^T(n) & \cdots & \boldsymbol{\omega}_{42}^T(n) \\ \cdots & \cdots & \cdots & \cdots \\ \boldsymbol{\omega}_{04}^T(n) & \boldsymbol{\omega}_{14}^T(n) & \cdots & \boldsymbol{\omega}_{44}^T(n) \end{bmatrix}$$

The simulator is composed of 20 single-input/single-output filters. The matrix ($\mathbf{W}(n)$) contains the filter weights of the 20 filters, where $\boldsymbol{\omega}_{ij}(n)$ is the vector of the weights of filter C_{ij}: $i = 0,1,2,3,4$ and $j = 1,2,3,4$.

3.2.3. Estimate of Simulator Weights

The simulator can be considered as a 5-input/4-output filter. We estimated the simulator weights and validated the physical fidelity of the simulator. Because the simulator is composed of 20 single-input/single-output filters, the weights of the 20 filters can be estimated independently. Without losing generality, we take filters C_{4j}, $j = 1,2,3,4$ as examples to show how to estimate the filter weights and validate the filters.

We turned on the No. 4 actuator and left the other actuators and the vibration exciter off. A narrow-band random white-noise signal, shown in Figure 5, was used as the input signal $\mathbf{x}_4$(n), and then the signals of the acceleration sensors were collected ($\mathbf{d}_1(n)$, $\mathbf{d}_2(n)$, $\mathbf{d}_3(n)$, $\mathbf{d}_4(n)$). Because only the No. 4 actuator was turned on, $\mathbf{x}_0(n)$, $\mathbf{x}_1(n)$, $\mathbf{x}_2(n)$, $\mathbf{x}_3(n)$ were zeros, and so Equations (6)–(9) were simplified as follows:

$$y_1(n) = \boldsymbol{\omega}_{41}^T(n)\mathbf{x}_4(n) \tag{11}$$

$$y_2(n) = \boldsymbol{\omega}_{42}^T(n)\mathbf{x}_4(\mathrm{n}) \tag{12}$$

$$y_3(n) = \boldsymbol{\omega}_{43}^T(n)\mathbf{x}_4(n) \tag{13}$$

$$y_4(n) = \boldsymbol{\omega}_{44}^T(n)\mathbf{x}_4(n) \tag{14}$$

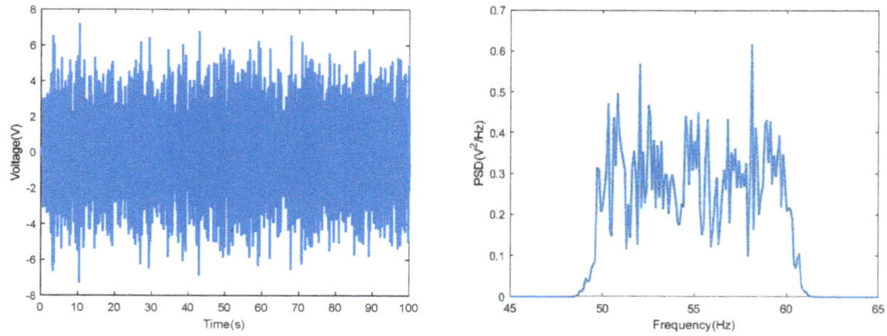

(a) (b)

Figure 5. The narrow-band random white-noise signal. (**a**) Time-series signal. It is used as the input voltage signal of the actuator that applies force on the vibration system, where 1 V represents 12.3 N. (**b**) Power-spectrum density (PSD).

According to Equation (5), the filter weights ($\omega_{41}(n)$, $\omega_{42}(n)$, $\omega_{43}(n)$, $\omega_{44}(n)$) can be obtained.

It is known that $\mathbf{y}_j(n)$ is the estimate of the desired output ($\mathbf{d}_j(n)$, $j = 1,2,3,4$). The desired outputs and their estimates by FIR filters are compared in Figure 6. The normalized mean square error (NMSE) [38] was used to evaluate the estimate precision. The NMSEs were all smaller than 20%, which shows that the desired outputs were well estimated, and the filters were validated. It also means that the simulator shown in Equation (10) had enough physical fidelity to describe the vibration system.

The definition of the NMSE is formulated by:

$$\text{NMSE} = \frac{\|\mathbf{d}_j(n) - \mathbf{y}_j(n)\|^2}{\|\mathbf{d}_j(n) - mean(\mathbf{d}_j(n))\|^2} \tag{15}$$

where $\|\cdot\|$ indicates the 2-norm of a vector.

Next, the other filters can be estimated and validated in a similar way. For instance, we turned on the vibration exciter and left the actuators off, and we gave the same signal shown in Figure 5 to the vibration exciter. The filter weights ($\omega_{01}(n)$, $\omega_{02}(n)$, $\omega_{03}(n)$, $\omega_{04}(n)$) could be obtained. It should be noted that the simulator can only well estimate the outputs of the vibration system when the input forces are from 50 Hz to 60 Hz.

3.3. Control Policy by Reinforcement Learning

3.3.1. Learning Loop

The control policy is learned through reinforcement learning. The RL algorithm collects simulator data and finds a control policy through the interaction with an environment. The episode-training approach is used, in which data are collected by running the simulator with a control policy in the loop, as shown in Figure 3. The data from these interactions are collected in a finite-capacity first-in/first-out buffer. The interaction trajectories are sampled from the buffer by a 'learner', which executes the DDPG algorithm to update the control-policy parameters. The details of the training loop are introduced in the following sections.

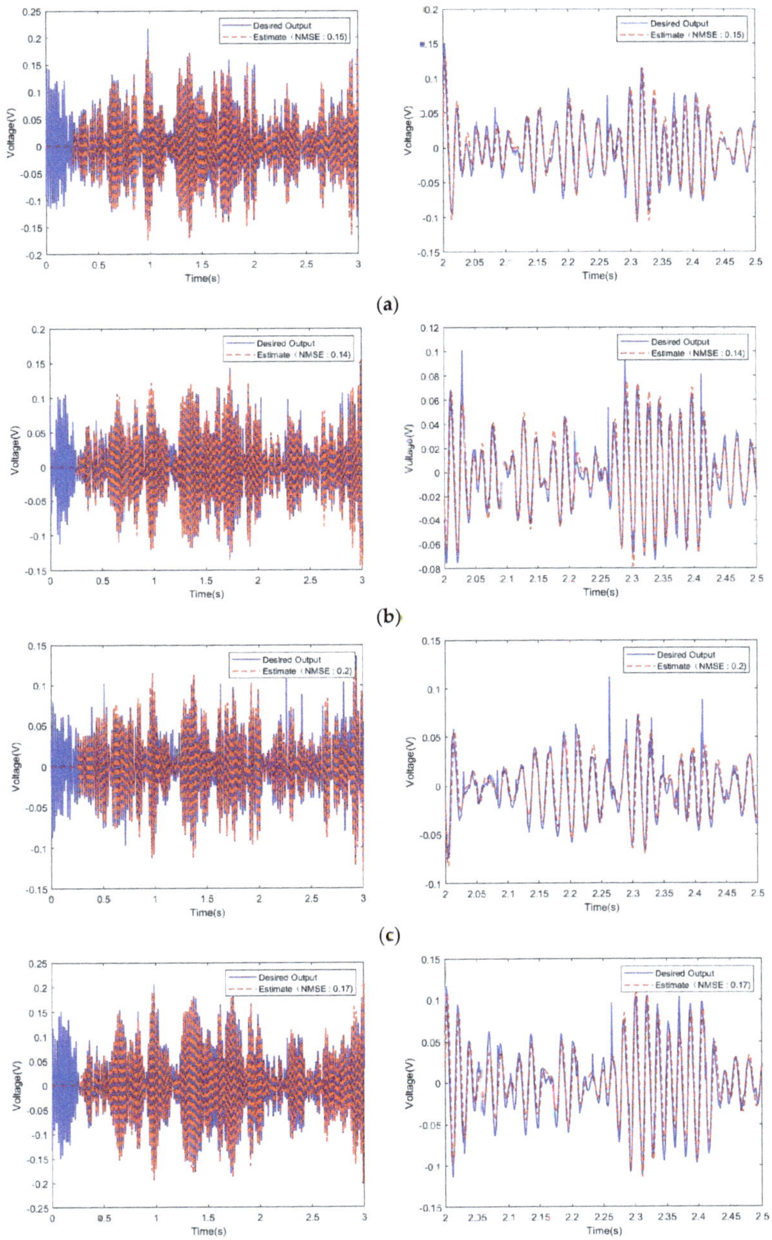

Figure 6. Comparisons of desired outputs and their estimates. Turn on the No. 4 actuator only. Desired outputs are voltage signals, where 1 mV represents 0.1 m/s^2: (**a**) comparison of $\mathbf{y}_1(n)$ and $\mathbf{d}_1(n)$; (**b**) comparison of $\mathbf{y}_2(n)$ and $\mathbf{d}_2(n)$; (**c**) comparison of $\mathbf{y}_3(n)$ and $\mathbf{d}_3(n)$; (**d**) comparison of $\mathbf{y}_4(n)$ and $\mathbf{d}_4(n)$..

3.3.2. State Space and Action Space

In Figure 3, the state space is composed of the acceleration signals. The state space is formulated by:

$$\mathbf{s} = \begin{bmatrix} \mathbf{y}_1^T(n) & \mathbf{y}_2^T(n) & \mathbf{y}_3^T(n) & \mathbf{y}_4^T(n) \end{bmatrix}^T \quad (16)$$

where n indicates the time sequence, and $\mathbf{y}_1^T(n), \mathbf{y}_2^T(n), \mathbf{y}_3^T(n), \mathbf{y}_4^T(n)$ are the outputs of the simulator. It is known that:

$$\mathbf{y}_j(\mathrm{n}) = \begin{bmatrix} y_j(n) & y_j(n-1) & \cdots & y_j(x-\mathrm{N}+1) \end{bmatrix}^T \quad (17)$$

where $j = 1,2,3,4$, and N is the length of the filter. In this work, N=50, and so the space state is the vector that contains 200 elements.

The action space is composed of the force signals of the actuators. The action space is formulated by:

$$\mathbf{a} = \begin{bmatrix} x_1(n) & x_2(n) & x_3(n) & x_4(n) \end{bmatrix}^T \quad (18)$$

where $x_1(n), x_1(n), x_1(n), x_1(n)$ are the inputs of the simulator. The space state is the vector that contains 4 elements.

3.3.3. Reward

On the one hand, in reinforcement learning, the goal of the control policy is to interact with the simulator by selecting actions in a way that maximizes future rewards. On the other hand, the goal of vibration control is to minimize the accelerations. Therefore, for each time step, the reward is defined by:

$$r(n) = -\left(y_1^2(n) + y_2^2(n) + y_3^2(n) + y_4^2(n)\right) \quad (19)$$

where n indicates the time sequence, and $y_1(n), y_2(n), y_3(n), y_4(n)$ are the output acceleration signals of the simulator.

In general, we seek to maximize the expected return, where the return is defined as the sum of the discounted rewards [39]:

$$\mathrm{G}(n) = r(n) + \gamma\, r(n+1) + \gamma^2\, r(n+2) + \cdots + \gamma^T\, r(n+T) \quad (20)$$

where T is the final time step, and γ is the parameter $0 \leq \gamma \leq 1$, which is called the discount rate. In this work, $\gamma = 1$.

3.3.4. Neural-Network Architecture

DDPG uses two neural-network architectures to design and optimize the policy: the critic network and policy network. Both networks are updated during training, but only the policy network is deployed on the plant.

The critic network is a five-layer feed-forward neural network that contains three hidden layers with 200 neurons each. The state space and action space are the input data to be fed into the input layer. For each hidden layer, the activation function, the hyperbolic-tangent function, is used. A last linear layer is used to output the Q-value.

The policy network is also a five-layer feed-forward neural network. It deterministically maps states to specific actions. The input layer represents the space state, and the output layer represents the action space. Each of the three hidden layers has 200 neurons and is activated by the hyperbolic-tangent function.

3.3.5. Learning Curve

The training loop has been defined in detail. The vibration-exciter input should be given to the simulator before starting training. The narrow-band random white-noise signal from 50 Hz to 60 Hz, shown in Figure 5, is used as the vibration-exciter input. The controller controls the actuators to reduce the vibration caused by the exciter. The learning curve, shown in Figure 7, shows the return of each training episode. Each episode has the same length of 1×10^5 time steps, and the simulation time step is 0.001 s. The return is defined by Equation (19). At the end of each episode, the control policy is updated. The learning curve shows that the control policy converges to a near-optimal point after about 60 training episodes.

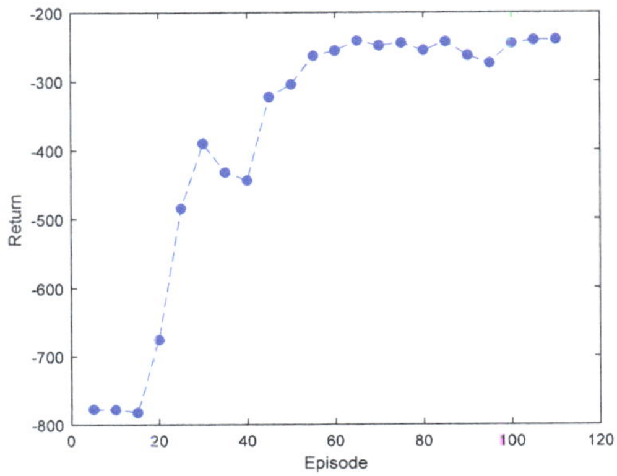

Figure 7. Learning curve of DDPG algorithm on vibration-control task.

3.4. Simulation of the Control Performance

After the control policy was well trained, we tested the control policy by vibration-control simulations. Figure 8 shows the vibration-control-simulation architecture. The control policy, the parameters of which are fixed, and the simulator are used together for the vibration-control simulations.

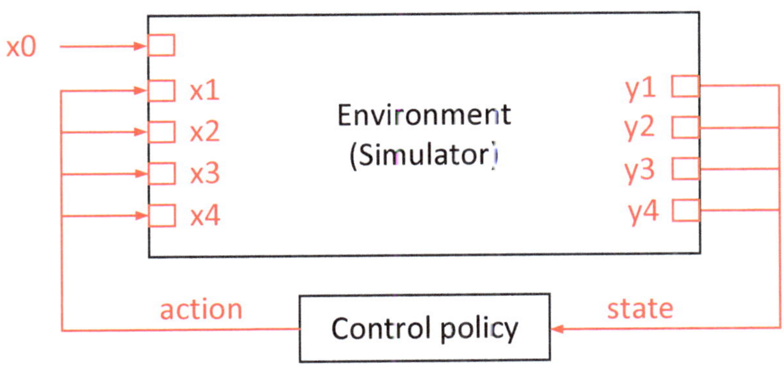

Figure 8. Vibration-control-simulation architecture.

We carried out many simulations with different excitation signals. The simulation results show that the control policy can effectively reduce vibrations from 50 Hz to 60 Hz. For clarity, one simulation case was chosen to be shown.

Simulation #1

A superposition signal of 52 Hz, 55 Hz and 58 Hz sinuous signals was given to the vibration exciter. The control policy controls the actuators to reduce the vibration caused by the exciter. We simulated and compared the simulator sensor responses with or without control. The simulation time was as long as 30 s. For clarity, a short time span of 0.5 s is shown.

Figure 9 shows the sensor signals in the time domain. The root-mean-square (RMS) value was used to evaluate the sensor signals. A smaller RMS value generally means a weaker vibration. Table 1 shows the RMS values of the uncontrolled and controlled sensor signals. It was found that the RMS values were all reduced by more than 45%.

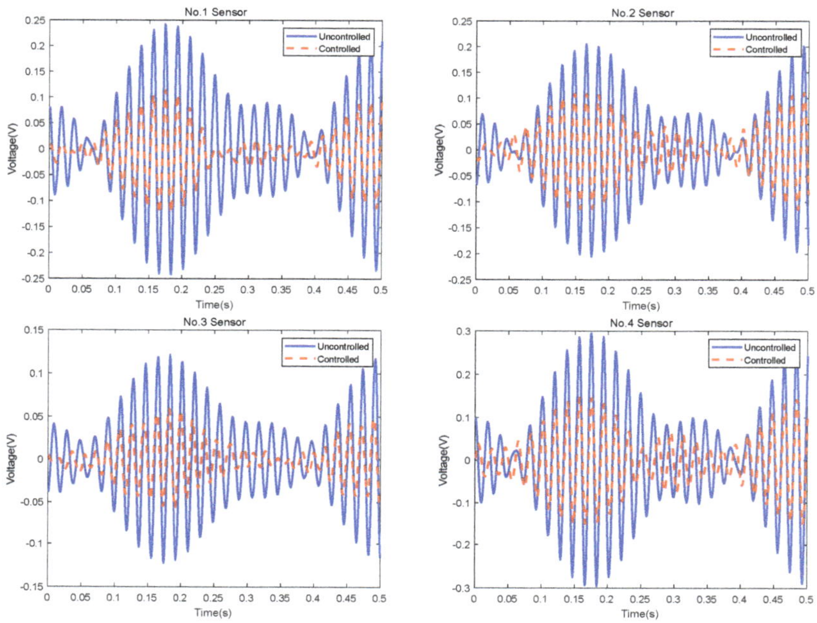

Figure 9. Sensor signals obtained by simulations (1 mV represents 0.1 m/s^2).

Table 1. RMS values of sensor signals: Simulation #1.

	Uncontrolled (V)	Controlled (V)	Reduction (%)
No. 1 Sensor	0.1060	0.0449	57.65%
No. 2 Sensor	0.0880	0.0482	45.21%
No. 3 Sensor	0.0541	0.0231	57.36%
No. 4 Sensor	0.1269	0.0646	49.10%

The vibration reduction can also be seen from the PSD curves of the sensor signals, as shown in Figure 10. Table 2 shows the peak values of the PSD curves of the sensor signals. It can be seen that the peak values of the PSD curves at specific frequencies were all reduced by more than 63%. Moreover, Figure 11 shows that the neural-network outputs were bounded from −2 V to 2 V.

Table 2. Peak values of PSD curves of sensor signals: Simulation #1.

		Uncontrolled (V^2/Hz)	Controlled (V^2/Hz)	Reduction (%)
No. 1 Sensor	@52 Hz	0.0297	0.0035	88.24%
	@55 Hz	0.0190	0.0034	82.13%
	@58 Hz	0.0063	0.0023	63.95%
No. 2 Sensor	@52 Hz	0.0187	0.0051	72.77%
	@55 Hz	0.0137	0.0037	73.18%
	@58 Hz	0.0055	0.0021	62.24%
No. 3 Sensor	@52 Hz	0.0089	0.0006	93.71%
	@55 Hz	0.0044	0.0016	63.97%
	@58 Hz	0.0010	0.0003	74.42%
No. 4 Sensor	@52 Hz	0.0409	0.0098	75.95%
	@55 Hz	0.0272	0.0055	79.64%
	@58 Hz	0.0106	0.0038	64.15%

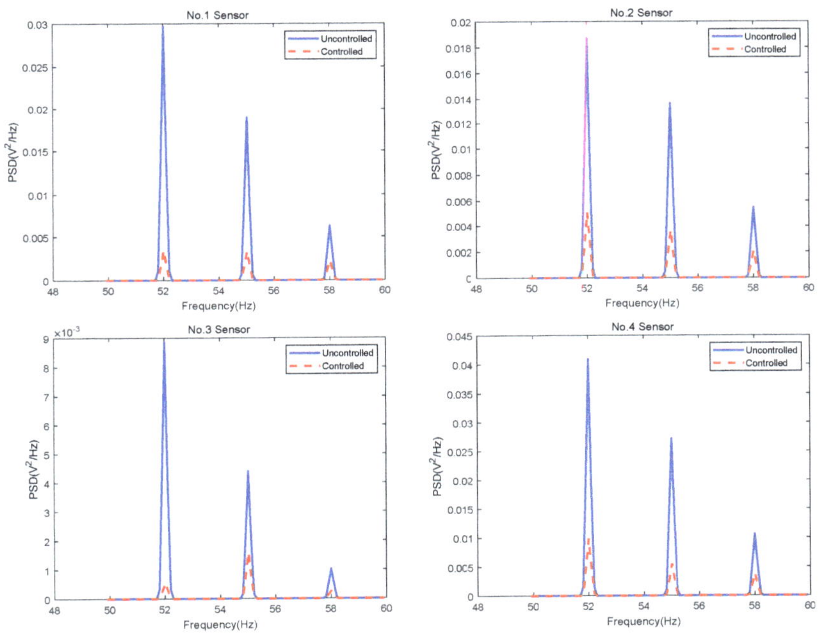

Figure 10. PSDs of sensor signals obtained by simulations.

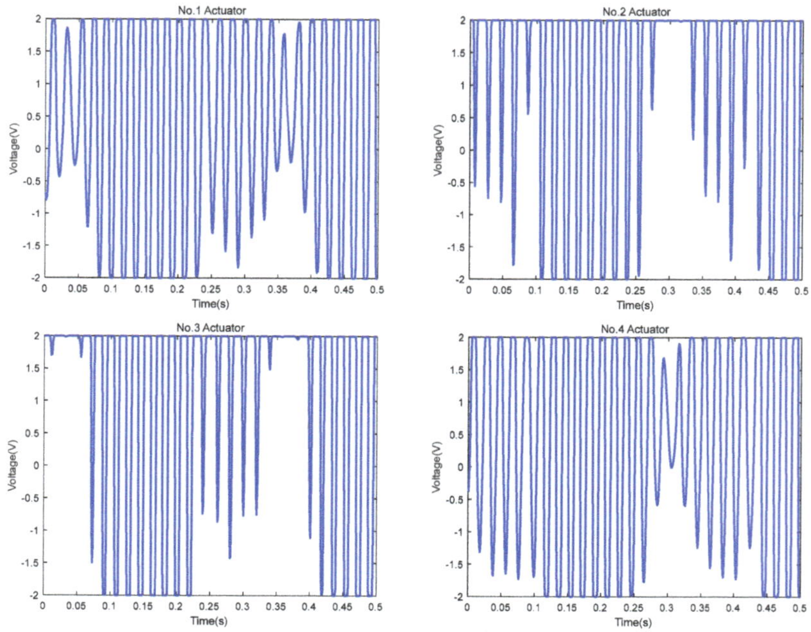

Figure 11. Actuator control signals obtained by simulations (1 V represents 12.3 N).

4. Experiment

4.1. Experimental Setup and Procedure

As shown in Figure 12, the vibration system was supported on the ground by rubber isolators. A vibration exciter was installed on the vibration system to generate the vibration-excitation force. The control system includes the acceleration sensors, signal-conditioning module, AD module, controller, DA module, drive module and electromagnetic actuators. The acceleration sensors measure the system vibration. The well-trained neural network is compiled into binary code, and it is then run on the controller hardware. The controller controls the electromagnetic actuators to reduce the vibration caused by the exciter.

We carried out many different experiments by giving different signals to the vibration exciter. For clarity, three experiments were chosen to be shown.

In Experiment #1, the signal given to the exciter is the superposition of the 52 Hz, 55 Hz and 58 Hz sine signals, and it is the same as that in Simulation #1.

In Experiment #2, the signal given to the exciter is the superposition of the 53 Hz, 56 Hz and 59 Hz sine signals.

In Experiment #3, the signal given to the exciter is the superposition of the 53 Hz, 56 Hz, and 59 Hz sine signals, but its amplitude is completely different from that in Experiment #2.

The parameters of the well-trained neural network were fixed in all the experiments. The controller controls the actuators to reduce the vibration caused by the exciter. In each experiment, the sensor signals were recorded when the controller was turned on or off. Some of the experimental results were chosen to be shown in the following sections.

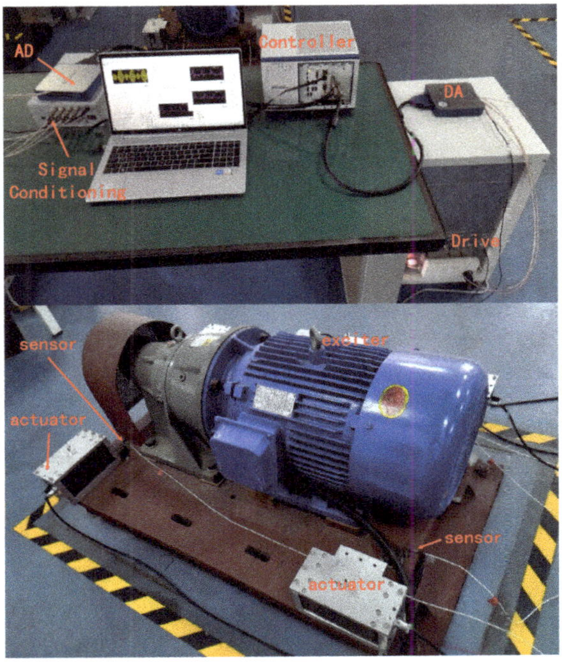

Figure 12. Vibration system and control system.

4.2. Experimental Results and Discussions

4.2.1. Experiment #1

Figure 13 shows the sensor signals in the time domain. The controlled signals were recorded when the controller was on, and the uncontrolled signals were recorded when the controller was off. Although the controlled signals and uncontrolled signals are shown in the same figure, they were not sampled at the same time. The sampling frequency was 1 kHz. The amount of the total sampled data was more than 30 s. For clarity, a small amount of data is shown in the figures.

Table 3 shows the RMS values of the uncontrolled and controlled sensor signals. The RMS values were calculated based on the total sampled data. It was found that the RMS values were reduced by more than 39%. The vibration reduction can also be seen from the PSD curves of the sensor signals, as shown in Figure 14. Table 4 shows the peak values of the PSD curves of the sensor signals. It can be seen that the peak values of the PSD curves at specific frequencies were reduced by more than 47%. Moreover, Figure 15 shows that the controller outputs were bounded from −2 V to 2 V.

Table 3. RMS values of sensor signals: Experiment #1.

	Uncontrolled (V)	Controlled (V)	Reduction (%)
No. 1 Sensor	0.1303	0.0439	66.26%
No. 2 Sensor	0.1060	0.0644	39.23%
No. 3 Sensor	0.0655	0.0237	63.78%
No. 4 Sensor	0.1625	0.0885	45.52%

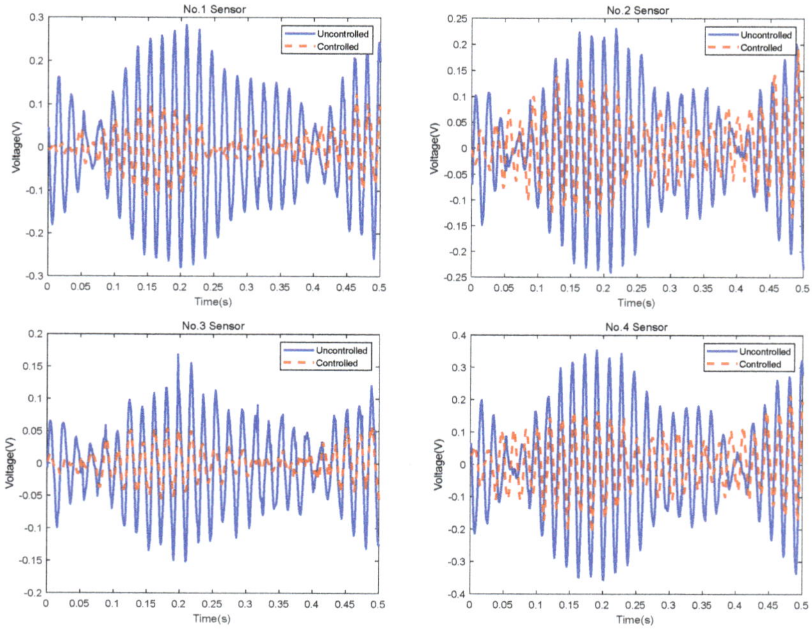

Figure 13. Sensor signals obtained by experiments (1 mV represents 0.1 m/s^2).

Table 4. Peak values of PSD curves of sensor signals: Experiment #1.

		Uncontrolled (V^2/Hz)	Controlled (V^2/Hz)	Reduction (%)
No. 1 Sensor	@52 Hz	0.0520	0.0031	94.04%
	@55 Hz	0.0209	0.0030	85.75%
	@58 Hz	0.0067	0.0020	66.93%
No. 2 Sensor	@52 Hz	0.0302	0.0088	70.83%
	@55 Hz	0.0156	0.0047	69.82%
	@58 Hz	0.0060	0.0032	47.49%
No. 3 Sensor	@52 Hz	0.0142	0.0008	94.53%
	@55 Hz	0.0040	0.0013	68.00%
	@58 Hz	0.0009	0.0002	72.66%
No. 4 Sensor	@52 Hz	0.0747	0.0169	77.36%
	@55 Hz	0.0372	0.0092	75.24%
	@58 Hz	0.0133	0.0062	53.19%

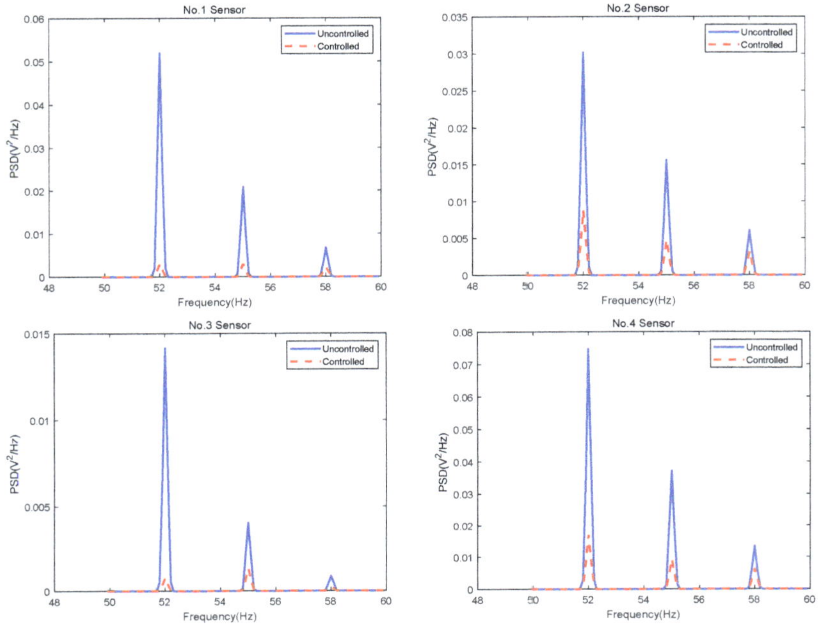

Figure 14. PSDs of sensor signals obtained by experiments.

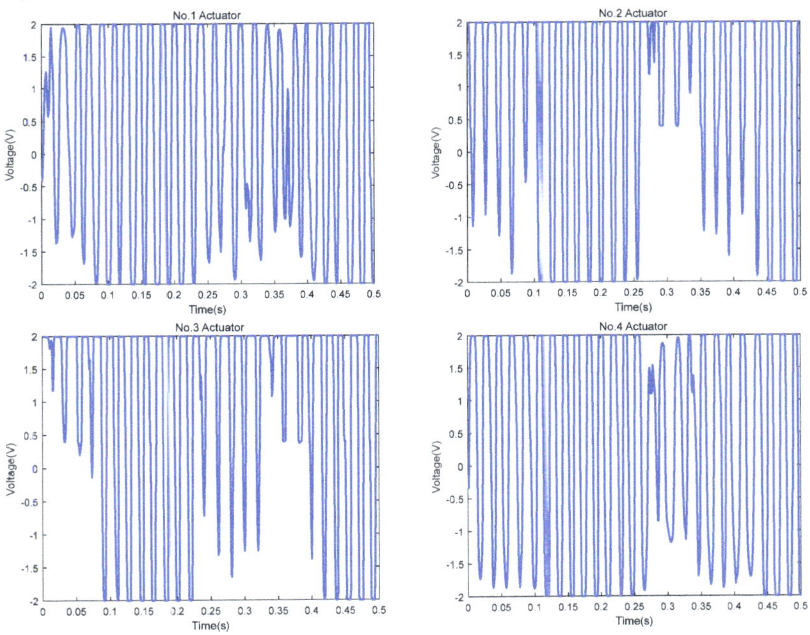

Figure 15. Actuator control signals obtained by experiments (1 V represents 12.3 N).

4.2.2. Experiment #2

Figure 16 shows the sensor signals in the time domain. Table 5 shows the RMS values of the uncontrolled and controlled sensor signals. It was found that the RMS values were all reduced by more than 40%. The vibration reduction can also be seen from the PSD curves of the sensor signals, as shown in Figure 17. Table 6 shows the peak values of the PSD curves of the sensor signals. It can be seen that the peak values of the PSD curves at specific frequencies were nearly all reduced by more than 50%.

Table 5. RMS values of sensor signals: Experiment #2.

	Uncontrolled (V)	Controlled (V)	Reduction (%)
No. 1 Sensor	0.1290	0.0392	69.60%
No. 2 Sensor	0.1070	0.0632	40.94%
No. 3 Sensor	0.0616	0.0220	64.35%
No. 4 Sensor	0.1641	0.0799	51.32%

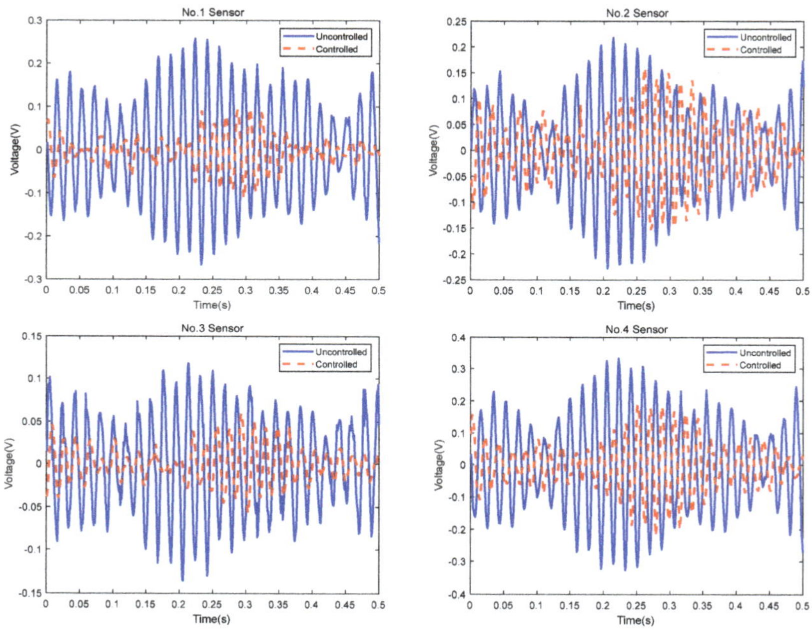

Figure 16. Sensor signals obtained by experiments (1 mV represents 0.1 m/s^2).

Table 6. Peak values of PSD curves of sensor signals: Experiment #2.

		Uncontrolled (V^2/Hz)	Controlled (V^2/Hz)	Reduction (%)
No. 1 Sensor	@53 Hz	0.0605	0.0027	95.47%
	@56 Hz	0.0127	0.0021	83.41%
	@59 Hz	0.0050	0.0017	65.36%
No. 2 Sensor	@53 Hz	0.0385	0.0096	74.96%
	@56 Hz	0.0100	0.0046	54.58%
	@59 Hz	0.0046	0.0034	24.59%
No. 3 Sensor	@53 Hz	0.0141	0.0010	92.88%
	@56 Hz	0.0021	0.0009	59.92%
	@59 Hz	0.0006	0.0002	68.66%
No. 4 Sensor	@53 Hz	0.0942	0.0154	83.61%
	@56 Hz	0.0235	0.0089	62.31%
	@59 Hz	0.0101	0.0050	50.38%

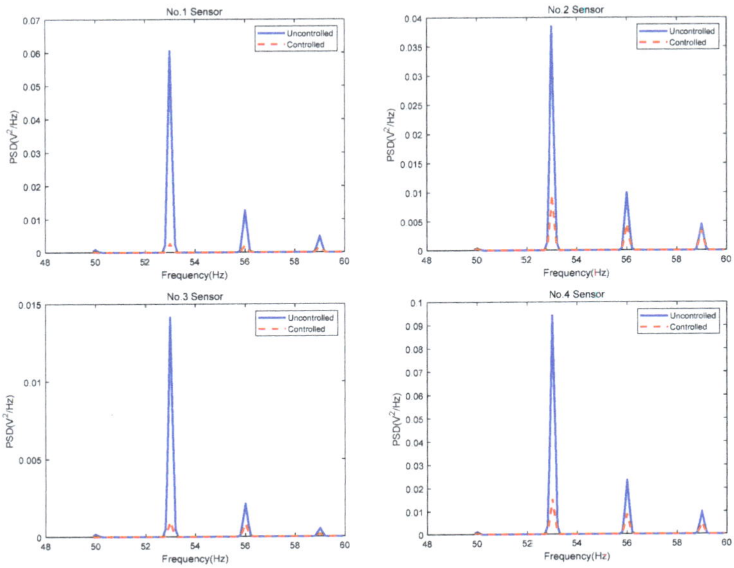

Figure 17. PSDs of sensor signals obtained by experiments.

4.2.3. Experiment #3

Figure 18 shows the sensor signals in the time domain. Table 7 shows the RMS values of the uncontrolled and controlled sensor signals. It was found that the RMS values were all reduced by more than 32%. The vibration reduction can also be seen from the PSD curves of the sensor signals, as shown in Figure 19. Table 8 shows the peak values of the PSD curves of the sensor signals. It can be seen that the peak values of the PSD curves at specific frequencies were all reduced by more than 52%.

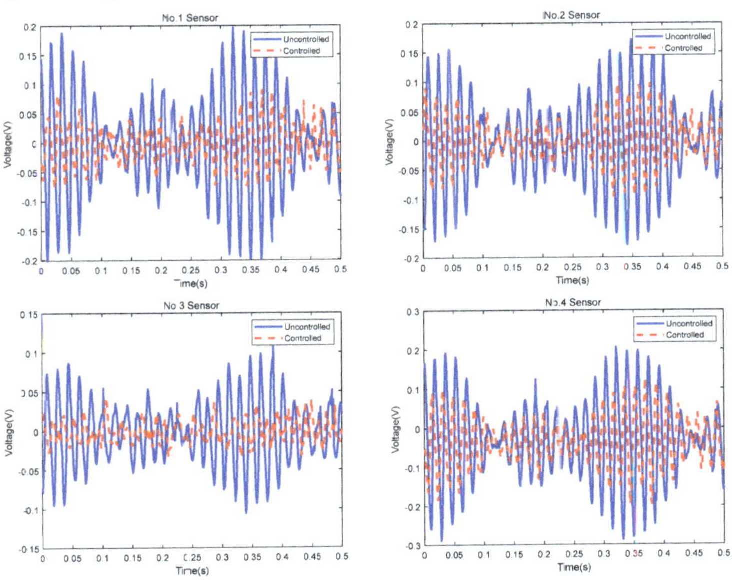

Figure 18. Sensor signals obtained by experiments (1 mV represents 0.1 m/s^2).

Table 7. RMS values of PSD curves of sensor signals: Experiment #3.

	Uncontrolled (V)	Controlled (V)	Reduction (%)
No. 1 Sensor	0.0875	0.0394	55.02%
No. 2 Sensor	0.0767	0.0422	44.98%
No. 3 Sensor	0.0425	0.0203	52.28%
No. 4 Sensor	0.1139	0.0773	32.10%

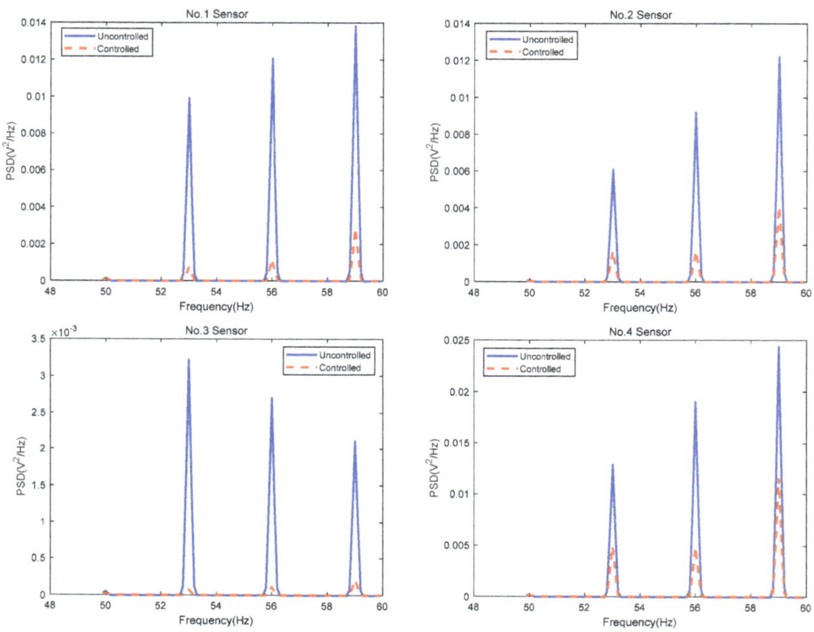

Figure 19. PSDs of sensor signals obtained by experiments.

Table 8. Peak values of PSD curves of sensor signals: Experiment #3.

		Uncontrolled (V^2/Hz)	Controlled (V^2/Hz)	Reduction (%)
No. 1 Sensor	@53 Hz	0.0099	0.0007	92.65%
	@56 Hz	0.0121	0.0012	90.39%
	@59 Hz	0.0138	0.0029	79.31%
No. 2 Sensor	@53 Hz	0.0061	0.0017	72.52%
	@56 Hz	0.0092	0.0017	81.76%
	@59 Hz	0.0122	0.0041	66.49%
No. 3 Sensor	@53 Hz	00032	0.00008	97.55%
	@56 Hz	0.0027	0.0001	95.78%
	@59 Hz	0.0021	0.0002	90.00%
No. 4 Sensor	@53 Hz	0.0129	0.0049	61.80%
	@56 Hz	0.0191	0.0049	74.47%
	@59 Hz	0.0244	0.0116	52.53%

4.3. Comparison of Experimental and Simulation Results

The results of Simulation #1 and Experiment #1 were compared. The physical fidelity of the simulation model, including the simulator and control policy, was validated.

Figure 20 shows the sensor signals obtained by the simulation and experiment. The NMSEs between the experimental and simulation signals from the No. 1 to No. 4 sensors are 14%, 17%, 15% and 19%, respectively. Figure 21 shows the actuator signals obtained by the simulation and experiment. The NMSEs between the experimental and simulation signals from the No. 1 to No. 4 actuators are 17%, 11%, 13% and 15%, respectively.

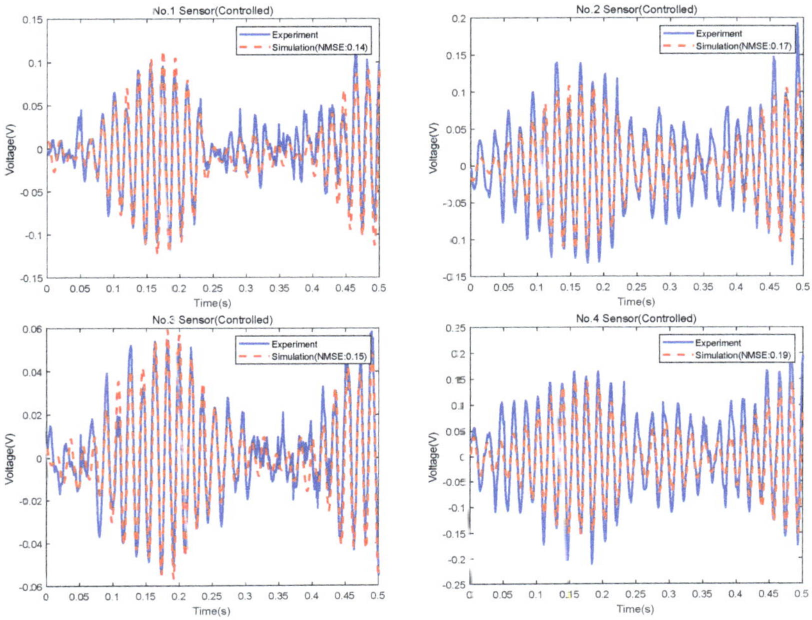

Figure 20. Comparison of sensor signals in time domain. Comparison of Experiment #1 and Simulation #1.

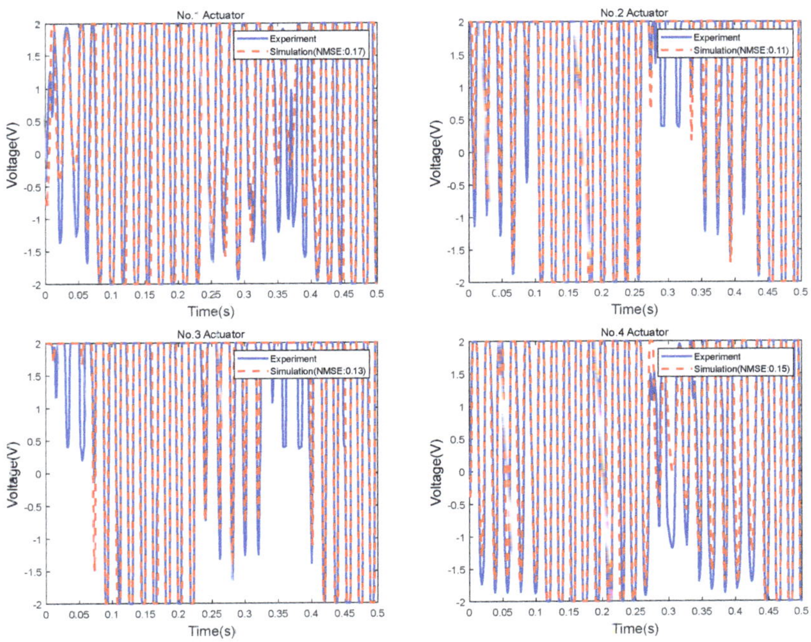

Figure 21. Comparison of actuator signals in time domain. Comparison of Experiment #1 and Simulation #1.

The errors mainly come from the errors between the real-world vibration system and the simulator, the time delay and signal interference of the electronic components, external disturbances, and so on. However, the errors can be accepted. On the one hand, the errors are smaller than 20%, which can be accepted in most engineering problems. On the other hand, the experiment results also show that the simulation model has enough physical fidelity, and the proposed method for designing the vibration controller is effective and useful.

5. Control-Performance Verification

In order to further verify the effectiveness of the simulator established with the FIR filter, we carried out experiments based on another simulator that was established with dynamics equations. We set up the dynamics equations in the simulation software and trained the proposed RL-based controller, which interacted with the dynamics equations to find the optimal control policy, which was then used in the experiments.

The vibration system shown in Figure 22 is simplified as a spring–mass–damper system, which can be formulated by ordinary differential equations. The spring–mass–damper system has three degrees of freedom, including vertical motion along the Z-axis, rotation motion along the X-axis, and rotation motion along the Y-axis. The symbol $F_{ci}(i = 1, 2, 34)$ stands for the control force of the actuator, and $F_{bi}(i = 1, 2, 34)$ stands for the force of the rubber isolator. The symbol F denotes the force of the exciter, and its location is determined by the coordinates (x, y). The dynamics equations are obtained at the equilibrium position:

$$M\ddot{z} = F + \sum_{i=1}^{4}(F_{ci} + F_{bi}) \tag{21}$$

$$I_{xx}\ddot{\theta} = (F_{c2} + F_{c3})L_1 - (F_{c1} + F_{c4})L_2 + F \cdot y \tag{22}$$

$$I_{yy}\ddot{\gamma} = (F_{c1} + F_{c2})L_3 - (F_{c3} + F_{c4})L_4 - F \cdot x \tag{23}$$

where z denotes the vertical displacement of the mass center; θ denotes the rotation angle along the X-axis; γ denotes the rotation angle along the Y-axis; M denotes the mass; I_{xx} and I_{yy} denote the inertias.

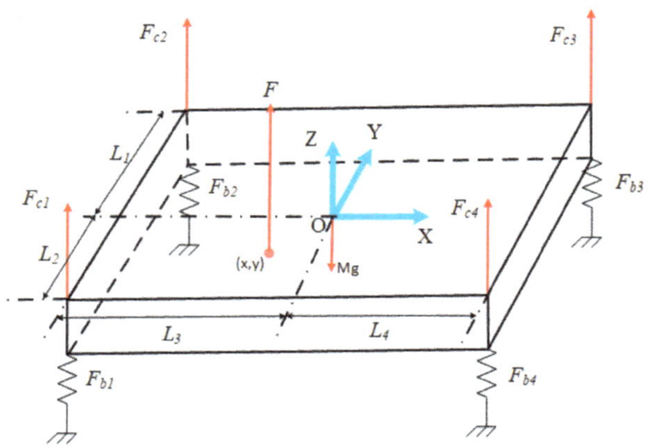

Figure 22. Dynamic model.

Next, the proposed RL-based controller that interacts with the dynamics equations was trained to find the optimal control policy. Then, the control policy was compiled into binary code and run on the controller hardware in the experiment. We performed the experiments by giving different signals to the vibration exciter. The controlled sensor signals were recorded when the controller was on, and the uncontrolled sensor signals were recorded when the controller was off.

Figure 23 shows the sensor signals when a simple 55 Hz sine signal was given to the exciter. The sampling frequency was 1 kHz. The amount of the total sampled data was more than 30 s. For clarity, a small amount of data is shown. Table 9 shows the RMS values of the uncontrolled and controlled sensor signals. It was found that the RMS values were increased by more than 53%. The vibration enhancement can also be seen from the PSD curves of the sensor signals, as shown in Figure 24. Table 10 shows the peak values of the PSD curves of the sensor signals. It can be seen that the peak values of the PSD curves at specific frequencies were increased by more than 140%.

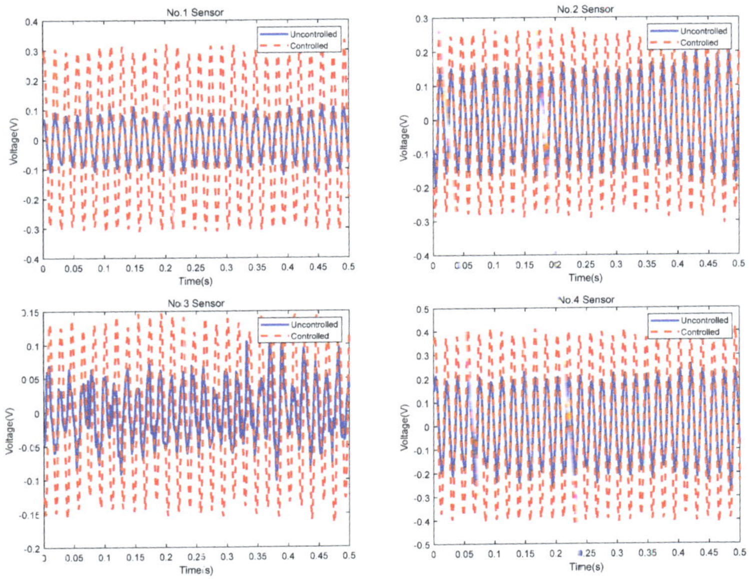

Figure 23. Sensor signals obtained by experiments (1 mV represents 0.1 m/s^2).

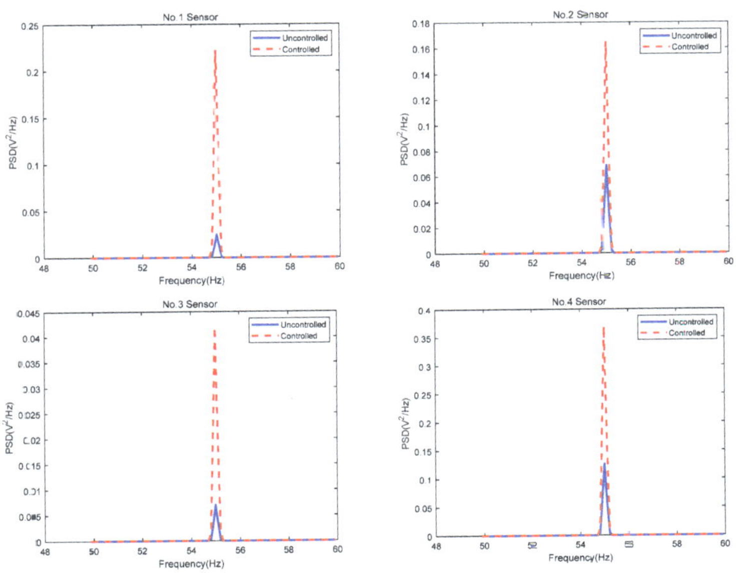

Figure 24. PSDs of sensor signals obtained by experiments.

Table 9. RMS values of sensor signals.

	Uncontrolled (V)	Controlled (V)	Reduction (%)
No. 1 Sensor	0.0732	0.2140	−192.29%
No. 2 Sensor	0.1206	0.1852	−53.56%
No. 3 Sensor	0.0420	0.0948	−125.43%
No. 4 Sensor	0.1624	0.2753	−69.47%

Table 10. Peak values of PSD curves of sensor signals.

		Uncontrolled (V^2/Hz)	Controlled (V^2/Hz)	Reduction (%)
No. 1 Sensor	@55 Hz	0.0248	0.2225	−797.05%
No. 2 Sensor	@55 Hz	0.0687	0.1650	−140.21%
No. 3 Sensor	@55 Hz	0.007	0.0419	−499.75%
No. 4 Sensor	@55 Hz	0.1264	0.3692	−192.00%

It was found that the control policy obtained by using the dynamics equations led to the vibration enhancement. In comparison with the control policy obtained by using the FIR filter, which effectively reduces the vibration, the effectiveness of the FIR filter could be verified.

The main reason for the vibration enhancement may be that the dynamics equations can only be used to effectively solve vibration-control problems of low dimension and simple dynamics. The parameters of the dynamic model were carefully verified, such as the mass, stiffness, damping, size, and so on, but it is still much less accurate than the FIR filter. Thus, it is difficult for the RL-based controller to successfully learn an effective control policy from the dynamics equations. To solve this problem, we present an RL-based controller that interacts with the accurate parametric model (FIR filter) instead of dynamics equations. Therefore, the RL-based controller converges more easily, and the vibration can be effectively reduced.

6. Conclusions

This paper presents an effective control method for solving high-dimensional high-frequency vibration-control problems based on reinforcement learning (RL) and a finite-impulse-response (FIR) filter. First, the FIR filter was used to build a simulator for the vibration system with five inputs (the forces of the vibration exciter and the four electromagnetic actuators) and four outputs (the four acceleration signals). Then, a reinforcement-learning algorithm interacted with the simulator to find a near-optimal control policy to meet the specified goals. Finally, the controller was validated by numerical simulations and experiments. The numerical results show that the peak values of the PSD curves at specific frequencies were maximumly reduced by more than 63%. The experimental results show that the controller can effectively reduce various vibrations (the peak values of the PSD curves maximumly reduced by more than 52%) within a frequency range from 50 Hz to 60 Hz. This means that we can provide an effective method to solve high-dimensional high-frequency vibrational-control problems.

In this work, the controller was designed and validated within a frequency range from 50 Hz to 60 Hz. In fact, the controller can be designed within a wider frequency range, such as a range from 10 Hz to 100 Hz. Generally, a larger neural network is needed for vibration control in a wider frequency range. Moreover, it will be much more difficult to train. Meanwhile, the controller hardware should be improved to guarantee the computation speed, as a larger network costs more computation resources. Our further work focuses on designing and training a complex neural-network architecture for a vibration controller in a wider frequency range. Meanwhile, we also have to update the hardware to achieve a faster computation speed.

Author Contributions: Conceptualization, H.C. and X.F.; methodology, X.F.; software, A.Z.; validation, G.W.; formal analysis, Z.Z.; investigation, G.W.; resources, Z.Z.; data curation, G.W.; writing—original draft preparation, X.F.; writing—review and editing, H.C.; visualization, A.Z.; supervision, H.C.; project administration, H.C.; funding acquisition, H.C. All authors have read and agreed to the published version of the manuscript.

Funding: This research was funded by National Natural Science Foundation of China (11991034). And The APC was funded by National Natural Science Foundation of China (11991034).

Acknowledgments: The authors are thankful for the support of the Postdoctoral Research Station of Huazhong University of Science and Technology. The research was also supported by the National Natural Science Foundation of China (11991034). This financial support is gratefully acknowledged.

Conflicts of Interest: The authors declare no potential conflict of interest with respect to the research, authorship and/or publication of this article.

References

1. Ab Talib, M.H.; Mat Darus, I.Z.; Mohd Samin, P.; Mohd Yatim, H.; Ardani, M.I.; Shaharuddin, N.M.R.; Hadi, M.S. Vibration control of semi-active suspension system using PID controller with advanced firefly algorithm and particle swarm optimization. *J. Ambient. Intell. Hum. Comput.* **2021**, *12*, 1119–1137. [CrossRef]
2. Li, W.; Yang, Z.; Li, K.; Wang, W. Hybrid feedback PID-FxLMS algorithm for active vibration control of cantilever beam with piezoelectric stack actuator. *J. Sound Vib.* **2021**, *509*, 116243. [CrossRef]
3. Wang, L.; Liu, J.; Yang, C.; Wu, D. A novel interval dynamic reliability computation approach for the risk evaluation of vibration active control systems based on PID controllers. *Appl. Math. Model.* **2021**, *92*, 422–446. [CrossRef]
4. Zhang, Q.; Yang, Z.; Wang, C.; Yang, Y.; Zhang, R. Intelligent control of active shock absorber for high-speed elevator car. *Proc. Inst. Mech. Eng. Part C J. Mech. Eng. Sci.* **2019**, *233*, 3804–3815. [CrossRef]
5. Tian, J.; Guo, Q.; Shi, G. Laminated piezoelectric beam element for dynamic analysis of piezolaminated smart beams and GA-based LQR active vibration control. *Compos. Struct.* **2020**, *252*, 112480. [CrossRef]
6. Takeshita, A.; Yamashita, T.; Kawaguchi, N.; Kuroda, M. Fractional-order LQR and state observer for a fractional-order vibratory system. *Appl. Sci.* **2021**, *11*, 3252. [CrossRef]
7. Lu, X.; Liao, W.; Huang, W.; Xu, Y.; Chen, X. An improved linear quadratic regulator control method through convolutional neural network–based vibration identification. *J. Vib. Control* **2021**, *27*, 839–853. [CrossRef]
8. Niu, W.; Zou, C.; Li, B.; Wang, W. Adaptive vibration suppression of time-varying structures with enhanced FxLMS algorithm. *Mech. Syst. Signal Process.* **2019**, *118*, 93–107. [CrossRef]
9. Puri, A.; Modak, S.V.; Gupta, K. Modal filtered-x LMS algorithm for global active noise control in a vibro-acoustic cavity. *Mech. Syst. Signal Process.* **2018**, *110*, 540–555. [CrossRef]
10. Seba, B.; Nedeljkovic, N.; Paschedag, J.; Lohmann, B. H∞ Feedback control and Fx-LMS feedforward control for car engine vibration attenuation. *Appl. Acoust.* **2005**, *66*, 277–296. [CrossRef]
11. Carlucho, I.; de Paula, M.; Wang, S.; Petillot, Y.; Acosta, G.G. Adaptive low-level control of autonomous underwater vehicles using deep reinforcement learning. *Robot. Auton. Syst.* **2018**, *107*, 71–86. [CrossRef]
12. Pane, Y.P.; Nageshrao, S.P.; Kober, J.; Babuška, R. Reinforcement learning based compensation methods for robot manipulators. *Eng. Appl. Artif. Intell.* **2019**, *78*, 236–247. [CrossRef]
13. Silver, D.; Hubert, T.; Schrittwieser, J.; Antonoglou, I.; Lai, M.; Guez, A.; Lanctot, M.; Sifre, L.; Kumaran, D.; Graepel, T.; et al. A general reinforcement learning algorithm that masters chess, shogi, and Go through self-play. *Science* **2018**, *362*, 1140–1144. [CrossRef] [PubMed]
14. Ye, D.; Liu, Z.; Sun, M.; Shi, B.; Zhao, P.; Wu, H.; Yu, H.; Yang, S.; Wu, X.; Guo, Q.; et al. Mastering complex control in MOBA games with deep reinforcement learning. *arXiv* **2020**, arXiv:1912.09729. [CrossRef]
15. Degrave, J.; Felici, F.; Buchli, J.; Neunert, M.; Tracey, B.; Carpanese, F.; Ewalds, T.; Hafner, R.; Abdolmaleki, A.; de las Casas, D.; et al. Magnetic control of tokamak plasmas through deep reinforcement learning. *Nature* **2022**, *602*, 414–419. [CrossRef] [PubMed]
16. Bucak, İ.Ö.; Öz, H.R. Vibration control of a nonlinear quarter-car active suspension system by reinforcement learning. *Int. J. Syst. Sci.* **2012**, *43*, 1177–1190. [CrossRef]
17. Kim, S.-J.; Kim, H.-S.; Kang, D.-J. Vibration control of a vehicle active suspension system using a DDPG algorithm. In Proceedings of the 18th International Conference on Control, Automation and Systems, PyeongChang, Korea, 17–20 October 2018; pp. 1654–1656.
18. Liu, M.; Li, Y.; Rong, X.; Zhang, S.; Yin, Y. Semi-active suspension control based on deep reinforcement learning. *IEEE Access* **2020**, *8*, 9978–9986.
19. Han, S.-Y.; Liang, T. Reinforcement-learning-based vibration control for a vehicle semi-active suspension system via the PPO approach. *Appl. Sci.* **2022**, *12*, 3078. [CrossRef]
20. Ouyang, Y.; He, W.; Li, X. Reinforcement learning control of a single-link flexible robotic manipulator. *IET Control. Theory Appl.* **2017**, *11*, 1426–1433. [CrossRef]

21. He, W.; Gao, H.; Zhou, C.; Yang, C.; Li, Z. Reinforcement learning control of a flexible two-link manipulator an experiment investigation. *IEEE Trans. Syst. Man Cybern. Syst.* **2020**, *51*, 7326–7336. [CrossRef]
22. Long, T.; Li, E.; Hu, Y.; Yang, L.; Fan, J.; Liang, Z.; Guo, R. A vibration control method for hybrid-structured flexible manipulat based on sliding mode control and reinforcement learning. *IEEE Trans. Neural Netw. Learn. Syst.* **2020**, *32*, 841–852. [CrossRe [PubMed]
23. Park, J.-E.; Lee, J.; Kim, Y.-K. Design of model-free reinforcement learning control for tunable vibration absorber system based c magnetorheological elastomer. *Smart Mater. Struct.* **2021**, *30*, 055016. [CrossRef]
24. Yuan, R.; Yang, Y.; Su, C.; Hu, S.; Zhang, H.; Cao, E. Research on vibration reduction control based on reinforcement learnin *Adv. Civ. Eng.* **2021**, *2021*, 7619214. [CrossRef]
25. Qiu, Z.; Yang, Y.; Zhang, X. Reinforcement learning vibration control of a multi-flexible beam coupling system. *Aerosp. S Technol.* **2022**, *129*, 107801. [CrossRef]
26. Qiu, Z.; Chen, G.; Zhang, X. Trajectory planning and vibration control of translation flexible hinged plate based on optimizatic and reinforcement learning algorithm. *Mech. Syst. Signal Process.* **2022**, *179*, 109362. [CrossRef]
27. Qiu, Z.; Chen, G.; Zhang, X. Reinforcement learning vibration control for a flexible hinged plate. *Aerosp. Sci. Technol.* **202** *118*, 107056. [CrossRef]
28. Watkins, C.J.C.H. Learning from Delayed Rewards. Ph.D. Thesis, University of Cambridge, Cambridge, UK, 1989.
29. Mnih, V.; Kavukcuoglu, K.; Silver, D.; Rusu, A.A.; Veness, J.; Bellemare, M.G.; Graves, A.; Riedmiller, M.; Fidjeland, A.F Ostrovski, G.; et al. Human-level control through deep reinforcement learning. *Nature* **2015**, *518*, 529–533. [CrossRef]
30. Van Hasselt, H.; Guez, A.; Silver, D. Deep reinforcement learning with double Q-learning. In Proceedings of the Thirtieth AA Conference on Artificial Intelligence, Phoenix, AZ, USA, 12–17 February 2016; pp. 2094–2100.
31. Schaul, T.; Quan, J.; Antonoglou, I.; Silver, D. Prioritized experience replay. *arXiv* **2016**, arXiv:1511.05952.
32. Wang, Z.; Schaul, T.; Hessel, M.; van Hasselt, H.; Lanctot, M.; de Freitas, N. Dueling network architectures for deep reinforceme learning. *arXiv* **2016**, arXiv:1511.06581.
33. Bellemare, M.G.; Dabney, W.; Munos, R. A distributional perspective on reinforcement learning. In Proceedings of the 34 International Conference on Machine Learning, Sydney, Australia, 6–11 August 2017.
34. Fortunato, M.; Azar, M.G.; Piot, B.; Menick, J.; Osband, I.; Graves, A.; Mnih, V.; Munos, R.; Hassabis, D.; Pietquin, O.; et al. Nois networks for exploration. *arXiv* **2019**, arXiv:1706.10295.
35. Hessel, M.; Modayil, J. Rainbow: Combining improvements in deep reinforcement learning. In Proceedings of the Thirty-Secor AAAI Conference on Artificial Intelligence, New Orleans, LA, USA, 2–7 February 2018; pp. 3215–3222.
36. Lillicrap, T.P.; Hunt, J.J.; Pritzel, A.; Heess, N.; Erez, T.; Tassa, Y.; Silver, D.; Wierstra, D. Continuous control with dee reinforcement learning. *arXiv* **2019**, arXiv:1509.02971.
37. Hayes, M.H. *Statistical Digital Signal Processing and Modelling*; John Wiley & Sons: Hoboken, NJ, USA, 1996.
38. Poli, A.A.; Cirillo, M.C. On the use of the normalized mean square error in evaluating dispersion model performance. *Atm Environ. Part A Gen. Top.* **1993**, *27*, 2427–2434. [CrossRef]
39. Sutton, R.S.; Barto, A.G. *Reinforcement Learning: An Introduction*; The MIT Press: Cambridge, MA, USA, 1998.

MDPI AG
Grosspeteranlage 5
4052 Basel
Switzerland
Tel.: +41 61 683 77 34

Applied Sciences Editorial Office
E-mail: applsci@mdpi.com
www.mdpi.com/journal/applsci

www.ingramcontent.com/pod-product-compliance
Lightning Source LLC
Chambersburg PA
CBHW061605220926
51850CB00005B/430
* 9 7 8 3 7 2 5 8 7 0 9 4 3 *